Finding the Middle Way

Finding the Middle Way
The Utraquists' Liberal Challenge
to Rome and Luther

ZDENĚK V. DAVID

WOODROW WILSON CENTER PRESS
Washington, D.C.

THE JOHNS HOPKINS UNIVERSITY PRESS
Baltimore and London

EDITORIAL OFFICES:

Woodrow Wilson Center Press
Woodrow Wilson International Center for Scholars
One Woodrow Wilson Plaza
1300 Pennsylvania Avenue, N.W.
Washington, D.C. 20004
Telephone 202-691-4029
www.wilsoncenter.org

Order from:

The Johns Hopkins University Press
P.O. Box 50370
Baltimore, Maryland 21211
Telephone 1-800-537-5487
www.press.jhu.edu

© 2003 by the Woodrow Wilson International Center for Scholars
All rights reserved
Printed in the United States of America on acid–free paper

2 4 6 8 9 7 5 3 1

Library of Congress Cataloging–in–Publication Data

David, Zdeněk V.
Finding the middle way : the Utraquists' liberal challenge to Rome and
Luther / Zdeněk V. David.
p. cm.
Includes bibliographical references (p.   ) and index.
ISBN 0-8018-7382-7
1. Utraquists.   2. Bohemia (Czech Republic)—Church history.   I.
Title.
BX4915.3.D38 2003
284'.3—dc21   2003003821

THE WOODROW WILSON
INTERNATIONAL CENTER FOR SCHOLARS
Lee H. Hamilton, President and Director

BOARD OF TRUSTEES

Joseph B. Gildenhorn, Chair; David A. Metzner, Vice Chair. Public Members: James H. Billington, Librarian of Congress; John W. Carlin, Archivist of the United States; Bruce Cole, Chair, National Endowment for the Humanities; Colin L. Powell, Secretary of State; Lawrence M. Small, Secretary of the Smithsonian Institution; Roderick R. Paige, Secretary of Education; Tommy G. Thompson, Secretary of Health and Human Services. Private Citizen Members: Joseph A. Cari, Jr., Carol Cartwright, Donald E. Garcia, Bruce E. Gelb, Daniel L. Lamaute, Tami Longaberger, Thomas R. Reedy

WILSON COUNCIL

Bruce S. Gelb, President. Diane Aboulafia-D'Jaen, Elias F. Aburdene, Charles S. Ackerman, B. B. Andersen, Cyrus A. Ansary, Lawrence E. Bathgate II, John Beinecke, Joseph C. Bell, Steven Alan Bennett, Rudy Boschwitz, A. Oakley Brooks, Melva Bucksbaum, Charles W. Burson, Conrad Cafritz, Nicola L. Caiola, Raoul L. Carroll, Scott Carter, Albert V. Casey, Mark Chandler, Peter B. Clark, Melvin Cohen, Willian T. Coleman, Jr., Michael D. DiGiacomo, F. Sheldon Drobny, Samuel Eberts III, J. David Eller, Mark Epstein, Melvyn Estrin, Sim Farar, Susan R. Farber, Joseph H. Flom, John H. Foster, Charles Fox, Barbara Hackman Franklin, Norman Friedkin, Morton Funger, Gregory M. Gallo, Chris G. Gardiner, Eric Garfinkel, Gordon D. Giffin, Steven J. Gilbert, Alma Gildenhorn, David F. Girard-diCarlo, Michael B. Goldberg, Gretchen M. Gorog, William E. Grayson, Ronald Greenberg, Raymond A. Guenter, Gerald T. Halpin, Edward L. Hardin, Jean L. Hennessey, Eric Hotung, John L. Howard, Darrell E. Issa, Jerry Jasinowski, Brenda LaGrange Johnson, Shelly Kamins, Edward W. Kelley, Jr., Anastasia D. Kelly, Christopher J. Kennan, Steven Kotler, Michael V. Kostiw, Paul Kranhold, William H. Kremer, Raymond Learsy, Abbe Lane Leff, Perry Leff, Francine Gordon Levinson, Dennis LeVett, Harold O. Levy, David Link, Frederic V. Malek, David S. Mandel, John P. Manning, Jeffrey A. Marcus, Edwin S. Marks, Jay Mazur, Robert McCarthy, Linda MaCausland, Stephen G. McConahey, Donald F. McLellan, J. Kenneth Menges, Jr., Philip Merrill, Kathryn Mosbacher, Jeremiah L. Murphy, Martha T. Muse, Della M. Newman, John E. Osborn, Paul Hae Park, Gerald L. Parsky, Michael

J. Polenske, Donald Robert Quartel, Jr., John L. Richardson, Margaret Milner Richardson, Larry D. Richman, Carlyn Ring, Edwin Robbins, Robert Rogers, Otto Ruesch, B. Francis Saul III, Alan M. Schwartz, Timothy R. Scully, J. Michael Shepherd, George P. Shultz, Raja W. Sidawi, Deborah Siebert, Thomas L. Siebert, Kenneth Siegel, Ron Silver, William A. Slaughter, James Small, Thomas F. Stephenson, Norma Kline Tiefel, Mark C. Treanor, Anthony G. Viscogliosi, Christine M. Warnke, Ruth Westheimer, Pete Wilson, Deborah Wince-Smith, Herbert S. Winokur, Jr., Paul Martin Wolff, Joseph Zappala, Richard Zimon, Nancy Zirkin

ABOUT THE CENTER

The Center is the living memorial of the United States of America to the nation's twenty-eighth president, Woodrow Wilson. Congress established the Woodrow Wilson Center in 1968 as an international institute for advanced study, "symbolizing and strengthening the fruitful relationship between the world of learning and the world of public affairs." The Center opened in 1970 under its own board of trustees.

In all its activities the Woodrow Wilson Center is a nonprofit, nonpartisan organization, supported financially by annual appropriations from the Congress, and by the contributions of foundations, corporations, and individuals. Conclusions or opinions expressed in Center publications and programs are those of the authors and speakers and do not necessarily reflect the views of the Center staff, fellows, trustees, advisory groups, or any individuals or organizations that provide financial support to the Center.

To
*Stephen, Michael, Meg, Katja,
Angel, Ann, and Julie*

Contents

Preface		xi
Acknowledgments		xix
1.	The Travails of the *Via Media:* Historiography	1
2.	A Prolegomenon: The First Century of Utraquism, 1415–1517	18
3.	Utraquism's Curious Encounter with Luther	45
4.	Bohuslav Bílejovský and the Geography of Utraquist Ecclesiology	80
5.	Pavel Bydžovský and Utraquism's Second Confrontation with Luther	111
6.	The Utraquist Consistory, the Archbishop of Prague, and a Brief Honeymoon	143
7.	The Plebeianization of Utraquism: The Controversy over the Bohemian Confession of 1575	168
8.	Orthodoxy and Toleration: The Utraquists and the Lutherans, 1575–1609	198
9.	The Utraquists versus the Curia: Liberal or Authoritarian Church, 1575–1609	240
10.	The Curia Tightens the Noose: The Advance of Confessionalization, 1575–1609	278

11.	A Cohabitation of Convenience: The Utraquists and the Lutherans under the Letter of Majesty, 1609–1620	302
12.	White Mountain, 1620: The Transfiguration and the Protean Legacy of Utraquism	349

Epilog: The Meaning of the Bohemian Reformation	378
Appendix	383
Notes	387
Bibliography	535
Index	553

Preface

The Enigma of the Bohemian Reformation

The sixteenth-century Czech Utraquist Church, which tried to steer a middle course between Lutheranism and the Roman Church, is the subject of a new interpretation in this book. As I argue, the Utraquists were the Anglicans of Central Europe and a forerunner of liberal Catholicism today. The central theme of this study is how the Utraquist Church developed in the century after the onset of the Protestant Reformation. It offers a view of Czech sixteenth- and early seventeenth-century church history from the standpoint of mainline Utraquism: its theologians, confessional writings, and other documents, as well as polemics with the Roman Church, the Lutherans, and the Unity of Brethren. This study highlights Utraquism's notable contribution to the ecclesiastical and intellectual history of Europe, namely, its relative intellectual freedom and tolerance, engendered in part by its *via media*. With its emphasis on dialog in theoretical questions and its consensual approach to ecclesiastical administration, it also perpetuated the liberal spirit that the Bohemian Reformation had displayed on the European stage through Jan Hus and the witness of its lesser martyrs, such as Jerome of Prague. This theme raises four major issues: relevance to the currents of contemporary historical literature, the character of the Utraquist church, liberal features, and the state of Utraquist studies.

Relevance

This study's theme has its place in a broader setting among the currents of contemporary historiography. Recent researchers in the social history of religion have reminded us that the ideas of political liberty and human rights could emerge in harmony with a religious milieu, not necessarily in opposition to it through a secularist revolt. As Alexandra Walsham points out, these recent approaches also imply that "the demise of religious intolerance is not neatly related to the process of secularization."[1] This could be the case even if eventually the liberal political culture separated itself from the religious context by which it had been originally nurtured. One of these trends is the search for the historical role played in that regard by the *via media* of the Church of England; another is the interest in the role of liberal Catholicism in engendering the Enlightenment.[2] The Anglican historiographical problem, moreover, is analogous to the Utraquist one, which is treated in this study: to unearth the real character, or the very existence, of the religious *via media,* historically obscured by its depiction through the eyes of more radical Protestantism.[3] The analogy with the Church of England also dovetails with the thesis that a religion need not be radical or innovative to foster a liberal political culture, but can be moderate and conservative.[4]

More broadly the subject of this book shares in the general revival of the history of religion, which has occurred in the last few decades. A part of the reason for this phenomenon has been the role of religion in the conflicts of the postcommunist world, but probably more significant for the revival was the change in the paradigms of historical writing. As Tony Claydon and Ian McBride point out, with the decline of teleological approaches, religion need no longer be regarded as necessarily irrelevant or detrimental, but could be assigned a new explanatory role in historical explorations. Political, social, cultural, and intellectual historians could begin to draw on church history in efforts to interpret developments and motivations.[5]

The Utraquist Church's Character

Building directly on the Bohemian Reform movement, which had gathered momentum since the mid-fourteenth century, the Utraquists developed an organizational structure that was largely independent of the Roman Church, intellectually nourished by the University of Prague, and articulated by the early Utraquist synods by the end of the Bohemian wars of religion in the mid-1430s.[6] The formal name of the Utraquist (*pod obojí*) Church, which of course did not exhaust its specificity, was derived from the Latin phrase *sub utraque specie* (under each of two kinds) referring to its belief, contrary to the then-current rules of the Church of Rome, in the theological necessity of communion for the laity under both kinds—that is, both bread and wine—not only for adults and older children, but also for infants and young children. Except for several islands of loyalty, the defection from the Roman Church encompassed virtually the entire population of Bohemia.

During the Bohemian wars of religion, the center stage was occupied by religious radicals, the Taborites and the Orebites, whose enthusiasm and fighting spirit were probably indispensable to save the Bohemian Reformation from the onslaught of five imperial and papal crusades between 1420 and 1431. The ecclesiastical leadership of the Utraquist Church never endorsed, and ultimately (after the war emergency) rejected, these "heretics" who questioned a substantial part of medieval beliefs and rituals. The Utraquists might be classified instead as "schismatics" who rejected Roman ecclesiastical authoritarianism, but retained all the instrumentalities of traditional Christianity, including the historical apostolic succession, the real presence, the seven sacraments, the word of God, the law of God, saints, images, good works, and liturgical books and vestments. Of course, their schism existed only in the eyes of the Roman Church. From their own viewpoint, it was Rome that was separated from the true church, as long as it did not adopt the biblical Eucharistic teaching and maintained its apparatus of enforcement and coercion.

A relatively small sect, the Unity of Brethren (Jednota Bratrská) separated in 1457 from the Utraquist Church, and—while rejecting the idea of holy warfare—revived in other respects the theological radicalism of the Taborites and the Orebites. The Unity of Bohemian (or Moravian) Brethren remained separate from, and opposed to, mainline Utraquism throughout the sixteenth into the seventeenth century.[7] While the Unity, like the Taborites and the Orebites before them, prefigured the character of the post–1517 Protestant Reformation, the mainline Utraquist Church was to persist essentially unchanged in the tradition of the fourteenth-century reformism, much of the time under the Consistory and a succession of "administrators," for almost two hundred years.[8] After 1517 it came to occupy a middle position between post–Tridentine Catholicism and the Protestant churches. Albeit in a muted form it also perpetuated the chiliasm and the egalitarianism of the initial Bohemian Reformation, the former in its conviction of exemplifying true Eucharistic practice and ecclesiology, and the latter as a nonaristocratic institution serving the urban and rural commoners.

In this study, the terms Utraquist Church and Utraquism are normally used rather than the conventional terms "Hussite Church" and "Hussitism." The

Utraquist Church did venerate Hus among the Bohemian saints as both a symbol and an eminent example of its liberal stance in ecclesiology. But Jan Hus was in one respect much more than the Bohemian church, and in another respect much less. As the champion of human rights on a world stage, he belongs to all ages and all humankind. As a participant in the Bohemian reform movement, he did not aspire to found a new religion, but rather shared with his fellow reformers a search for no more (and no less) than the standard church of the West cleansed from the (for them) unacceptable overlay of papal monarchism. The term "Hussite" was never adopted by the Utraquists themselves, but was pejoratively applied to them by their enemies.[9] The Utraquists were, in fact, offended by this designation. The term "Hussite" was not used for self-identification even by the more radical Bohemian dissidents, be they the Taborites, the Orebites, or the subsequent Unity of Brethren.[10] For historians to apply the term to the Utraquists would be like calling the Church of England the "Cranmerian Church" and its adherents "Cranmerians."

Approaching the issue of nomenclature from the opposite side, in contrast to Hus, Luther could rightfully impose a personal stamp on his followers in the German Reformation, as one who had achieved a basic reorientation of religious doctrine and practice, or a redefinition of the central meaning of Christian life. Hus's personal standing within Utraquism was not comparable to the intensity of Luther's personal imprint on the German Reformation. Hus may have been a charismatic personage, but he was not a "paradigm-changing figure" like Luther.[11]

Liberal Features

The Utraquists' disavowal of Roman authoritarianism and exclusivity, and their replacement by more permissive instrumentalities, such as dialog, search for consensus, and toleration, can be illustrated in several areas. The injunction to preach the Word of God freely, originally raised by Hus among others, passed into the mainstream of Utraquism through its incorporation into basic Utraquist creeds.[12] It was reinforced by the Test or so-called Judge of Cheb (*iudex in Egra compactatus, soudce chebský*) of 1432, which had adopted discussion based on Scripture rather than administrative fiat, as a way of resolving theological disputes. Subsequently, in the sixteenth and early seventeenth centuries the Utraquists fostered discussion and preserved a nonconfrontational, even cordial tone toward their counterparts, especially the Brethren and the Lutherans.

In ecclesiastical government the Utraquist Church renounced interdicts, anathemas, excommunications, and other dreaded spiritual weapons employed conspicuously by the Roman Church in the late medieval and early modern times.[13] While, as firm adherents to the historical apostolic succession for valid ordination of priests, the Utraquists remained episcopalians and even papalists; from the viewpoint of church governance they feared the heavy hand not only of the pope, but also of the monarchic bishops, and preferred to rely on a collegium of priests, the Consistory, so that their system of ecclesiastical administration could be called presbyterial (though of course not Presbyterian). In this one regard, they differed markedly from their counterpart on the *via media,* the Church of England, which had retained an administrative episcopacy as one of its cornerstones. The Utraquists also afforded freedom from the oppressive feature of the luxuriant fiscalism of the Roman Church. Although they maintained the belief in the soteriological value of good works and did not deny the existence of purgatory, the practice of good deeds was not to be an occasion for fleecing the faithful for the purposes of architectural splendor or military campaigns.[14] One can see this going back to Hus's controversy with the Curia over the marketing of indulgences in 1412. Furthermore, the stress on assent rather than submission within Utraquism's administrative system was also reflected in the appointments or transfers of priests, particularly urban parishes, which were not dictated, but rather negotiated between the Consistory and the local authorities.[15] Ironically, modern Central European historians accustomed to the automatic obedience claimed by the typically overbureaucratized state of their region, viewed this practice with disapproval as a descent into administrative chaos. Another liberalizing feature was the deemphasis of auricular confession as a prerequisite for communion or as an annual obligation. This was so particularly in view of the Roman Church's use of confession as a means of disciplinary enforcement.[16]

Moving on to other characteristics, the Utraquists' sense of preserving an integrity of doctrinal fundamentals, compared with the more radical dissidents, probably freed them, at least in part, from the compulsion of a militant assertion of orthodoxy. One may recall in those regards the harsh self-righteous stance of the Lutherans toward the Calvinists and the Zwinglians, and that of the Calvinists vis-à-vis the Unitarians.[17] Their relative serenity led the Utraquists to acquire the aura of flexibility and tolerance, verging on a gentle bemusement and bonhomie, with respect to what they regarded as the foibles of others.

Another way of looking at this exceptional characteristic of the Utraquists is to say that they escaped the need of confessionalization in the late sixteenth and early seventeenth centuries.[18] They avoided the process by which the Protestant groups had to define themselves against each other and against the Church of Rome, and by which the latter had to adopt its own demarcations against the churches of the Reformation. The Utraquists were already secure in their own delimitation both vis-à-vis Roman authoritarianism (since the period of Hus and the Compactata), and vis-à-vis the Protestant biblical reductionism through the fifteenth-century encounters with the Taborites and the Brethren. Accordingly, in the sixteenth and early seventeenth centuries, they were spared the process of differentiation, sometimes called "confessionalization," which often led others to cast anathemas against one another, and which in general militated against the adoption of tolerant attitudes.

Finally, the Utraquists had become accustomed to a considerable degree of tolerance by their earlier legal coexistence with the remnants of the Roman Church, explicitly codified by the Peace of Kutná Hora of 1485, and informally observed since the adoption of the Compactata of Basel in 1436, which proscribed accusations of heresy and mutual vilification.[19] These pacific inclinations were in turn conditioned and enhanced by the memory of the destructiveness of the internal and external conflicts of the Bohemian Reformation.

State of Utraquist Studies

The substantial accomplishments of the Bohemian Reformation, which became reflected in the Utraquist Church, have remained largely unnoticed and uncredited not only abroad but also in Czech historiography.[20] This occurred despite the otherwise sizable literature on Bohemia's sixteenth- and early seventeenth-century religious history, references to which appear in the footnotes and in the bibliography of this study, particularly by Václav V. Tomek, Anton Gindely, Klement Borový, and Antonín Podlaha in the nineteenth century, and Julius Glücklich, Ferdinand Hrejsa, František Hrubý, Kamil Krofta, Josef Matoušek, Karel Stloukal, and František Tischer, as well as Rudolf Říčan, Jarold K. Zeman, František Kavka, Anna Skýbová, and Frederick G. Heymann in the twentieth century. This literature has tended to emphasize the Unity of Brethren, the halting inroads of the Lutheran Reformation, and the incipient advances of the Counter-Reformation. There was a tendency to minimize, trivialize, or even deny the existence of Utraquism in the sixteenth and the seventeenth centuries, usually with the claim of its fusion with Lutheranism in a form for which modern historians coined the term "Neo-Utraquism." One may speculate that standard Utraquism had proven uncongenial to the Catholics who preferred an outright heresy in order to justify its suppression (in 1621–1622); to the Protestants who deplored its unwillingness to embrace the Reformation; and to the teleologically oriented Hegelians, Comteans, and Marxists, for whom it violated the proper trajectory of progress from medieval piety through the Reformation to modern secularism.

One of the principal directions of my study is to question the established concept of a syncretic Neo-Utraquism. Delving into the topic convinced me that no one has yet unearthed a Neo-Utraquist theological text, or even made a suggestion along which lines a genuine dogmatic or liturgical synthesis of Utraquism and Lutheranism could proceed. For the late sixteenth and early seventeenth centuries one can name Utraquist theologians, and one can name Bohemian Lutheran theologians, but no one has named an authentic Neo-Utraquist theologian who has meaningfully combined elements of Utraquism and Lutheranism. The Bohemian Confession of 1575 has been cited at times as a prime example of a Neo-Utraquist text, but in fact it is virtually identical with the Augsburg Confession. Its modest tilt is not toward Utraquism, but toward the Unity of Brethren.[21]

In recent years, historians have voiced concerns about what may be called "blank spots" in Bohemian Reformation studies. Thus, Frederick G. Heymann has commented that while for the Brethren there was a substantial literature in German and to a lesser extent in English, "the history of Utraquism in this period (i.e., the sixteenth century) has been treated hardly at all in any western language and only in a rather perfunctory way (except by Hrejsa) in Czech . . ."[22] Winfried Eberhard, according to Malcolm Lambert, had discontinued his planned project on the theme of Luther in Bohemia in the 1520–1620 period on discovering "that (a) basic groundwork had not been undertaken; [and] (b) it was not easy to avoid analysing one-sidedly, in terms of the one-way influence of the German Reformation on Bohemian neighbours."[23] Robert Evans has called attention to the possible skewing of the image of Utraquism in the literature on the Bohemian Reformation.[24]

This study aims at reconstructing the characteristic features of mainline

Utraquism, and exploring its witness to the issues of human rights and dignity in the sixteenth and early seventeenth centuries. Utraquism can be viewed variously as a revival of patristic Christianity of the first millennium in its rejection of papal jurisdictional authoritarianism; as a middle ground between Rome and the Protestant Reformation; and as a prototype of liberal Catholicism, in its combination of traditional orthodoxy with a liberal view of the church community and with tolerance.

This study deals with Utraquism almost exclusively in Bohemia proper. The treatment of the sixteenth and early seventeenth-century course of the Reformation in Bohemia's adjacent sister realm of Moravia, which enjoyed an autonomous governance and distinct political culture, has over the last two hundred years become a veritable Augean stable of multilayered historiographic interpretations, inspired by a profusion of conflicting viewpoints and special pleadings for and against Lutheranism, the Roman Church, and Calvinism, as well as in opposition to Utraquism.[25] The task of clean-up needs to engage the energies of a future historical Hercules, or the excavatory skills of a Foucaultian archeologist of knowledge. In the meantime, the essential message of the *via media* with its intellectual gentleness and spirit of tolerance is sufficiently conveyed by an examination and assessment of the Utraquist Church of Bohemia proper.

Acknowledgments

My early research interest in religious history, stemming from my doctoral dissertation at Harvard, was sustained by my advisers, James H. Billington and Georges Florovsky. The thesis focused on Russia, particularly the influence of Jacob Boehme and other German mystics on Russian theology and philosophy. The ecclesiastical history of Bohemia attracted my attention as I researched and wrote *The Peoples of the Eastern Habsburg Lands, 1526–1918* (Seattle: University of Washington Press, 1984), co-authored with the late Robert H. Kann. The structure of the present book emerged over the course of the 1990s, when I joined David R. Holeton, Thomas Fudge, Vilém Herold, and František Šmahel in organizing several international symposia on "The Bohemian Reformation and Religious Practice."

Two colleagues made major contributions to the development of my basic ideas on the Bohemian Reformation. Robert J. W. Evans, Regius Professor of Modern History at Oxford, provided a general encouragement to take a fresh look at the Utraquists, and to approach the task, in part, through a comparison with the *via media* of the Church of England. The other spiritus movens was David R. Holeton, currently professor of liturgics at the University of Prague, and a canon of the Anglican Church of Canada. Through his pioneering research in Utraquist history, especially its liturgical aspects, David provided a raison d'être for pursuing the study of Utraquism, beyond righting a historiographical wrong, and highlighting the Utraquist contribution to the spirit of human freedom. His personal interest and advice, both specialized theological, and general scholarly, were indispensable.

Two former fellows of the Woodrow Wilson Center, Professor Carole Fink of the history department at Ohio State University and Professor Patricia M. Springborg of the government department, University of Sydney, Australia, gave encouragement and advice at important junctures of the work. In addition, John W. Brennan, chairman of the history department, Long Island University in New York City, read most of the chapters for coherence and style, and made a number of helpful suggestions. Six authors, whom I did not know personally, Brendan Bradshaw, Wilfried Eberhard, Carter Lindberg, Diarmaid MacCulloch, John S. Marshall, and Alexandra Walsham, opened new perspectives on the era of the Reformation.

Although I argue persistently against the intellectual construct of "Neo-Utraquism," standing for an amalgam of Utraquism with Lutheranism, over the years I have developed a respect and admiration for its principal promoters, Ferdinand Hrejsa (1867–1953) and Kamil Krofta (1876–1945). One cannot help but appreciate the conscientious scholarship, essential honesty, and inquisitive zeal of these two veritable titans of Central European historiography. In the same context, the immersion into his early treatises led me to develop a similar appreciation for Martin Luther for his courage, ingenuity, and compassion. At the other side of the ledger, the intention was not to universalize the harsh judgments about the Society of Jesus, which apply to its less than fortunate role in the Bohemian Counter-Reformation.

My senior colleagues in the Woodrow Wilson Center, James H. Billington, Charles Blitzer, Lee Hamilton, Prosser Gifford, Dean Anderson, and Michael Van Dusen created an environment conducive to scholarship in the spirit of Woodrow Wilson's principles informed by universal human values, stressing, like the subjects of this book—the Utraquists—the worth of disputation and dialectical modes of thought. I trust that the conception of my work reflects some of this spirit. Jim, in particular, was a most cherished mentor and friend since, as noted, he supervised my doctoral dissertation. The active interest in, and generous advice on, the project by Dean, as well as by Robert Landers, article editor of the *Wilson Quarterly,* were particularly helpful and stimulating. On the other side of the Atlantic, mainly in my native Bohemia, I was assisted by František Šmahel, Vilém Herold, Jaroslav Pánek, Eva Hahn, Noemi Rejchrtová, and Martin Wernisch, who published my articles in historical journals. Perhaps as a sign of globalization and the worldwide interest in the Bohemian Reformation and its originality, my scholarly contacts with Thomas A. Fudge ranged over North America, Central Europe, and New Zealand. I have benefitted from the interest and enthusiasm of my junior fellow laborers in the fields and groves of the Bohemian Reformation: Howard Louthan and James R. Palmitessa, as well as Peter Morée, Petr Hlaváček, Joel Seltzer, David Mengel, and Daniel Neval.

Several institutions and organizations were particularly helpful. I wish to thank the Czechoslovak Society of Arts and Sciences for sponsoring the first three symposia on "The Bohemian Reformation and Religious Practice" (Prague 1994, Brno 1996, Bratislava 1998), and the Philosophy Institute of the Czech Academy of Sciences, as well as its Center for Medieval Studies, for patronage over the latest two (Prague 2000 and 2002). I am indebted for their services and advice to the librarians and archivists of several depositories, particularly in the National Library, the National Museum, the Historical Institute of the Czech Academy of Sciences, the Jewish Museum, the Strahov Monastery, and the Central National Archive in Prague, as well as in the Library of Congress and the Folger Shakespeare Library in Washington, D.C. The State Research Library in Olomouc, the National Library in Vienna, and the Royal Library in Stockholm provided microfilms of relevant documents. The State Regional Archive in Tábor, Czech Republic, granted permission for the reproduction of a woodcut. My coworkers in the Woodrow Wilson Center library, Linda Warden, Janet Spikes, George Wagner, Dagne Gizaw, and Michelle Kutler helped and encouraged me in my work. I am grateful to Joseph Brinley and Yamile Kahn of Woodrow Wilson Center Press for seeing the book through to publication.

Some material in the book is adapted from my articles: "The Strange Fate of Czech Utraquism: The Second Century, 1517–1621," *Journal of Ecclesiastical History,* 46 (1995), 641–668; "Pavel Bydžovský and Czech Utraquism's Encounter with Luther," *Communio Viatorum,* 38 (1996), 36–63; "Central Europe's Gentle Voice of Reason: Bílejovský and the Ecclesiology of Utraquism," *Austrian History Yearbook* 28 (1997), 29–58; "A Brief Honeymoon in 1564–1566: The Utraquist Consistory and the Archbishop of Prague," *Bohemia: A Journal of History and Civilization in East Central Europe,* 39 (1998), 265–284; "The Plebeianization of Utraquism: The Controversy over the Bohemain Confession of 1575," *BRRP: The Bohemian Reformation and Religious Practice,* 2 (1998), 127–158; "Utraquists, Lutherans, and the Bohemian Confession of 1575," *Church History,* 68 (1999), 294–336; "A Cohabitation of Convenience: The Utraquists and the Lutherans under the Letter of Majesty, 1609–1620," *BRRP* 3 (2000), 173–214; "Utraquism's Curious Welcome to Luther and the Candlemas Day Articles of 1524," *Slavonic and East European Review,* 79 (2001), 51–89; and "The Utraquists and the Roman Curia, 1575–1609: Institutional Aspects," *BRRP* 4 (2002), 225–260.

Above all, Eleanor Miller David, my wife, with her authentic and deep intellectual interests, both encouraged me and provided a balance during the ten-year engagement with Utraquism. Moreover, she shared certain insights from the African American experience that helped to free my imagination from accepted paradigms and stimulate exploration of new connections and contexts in history. My daughters and sons, to whom this book is dedicated, each contributed, directly or indirectly, to bring it to fruition.

Needless to say, not those mentioned above, but I myself bear the responsibility for the interpretations and other contents of this book.

Washington, D.C.
November 17, 2002

Finding the Middle Way

1

The Travails of the *Via Media:* Historiography

In this study, I seek a balanced view of the Bohemian Utraquist Church during the second century of its existence, 1517 to 1621. In assessing the prevalent unfavorable historical judgments, I intend to outline the special problems that Bohemian Utraquism faced as a religious *via media,* partly viewed from a comparative perspective of the kindred phenomenon of the post-Reformation Church of England.

Central to this study's thesis is the proposition that the church's negative imaging in historical literature primarily stemmed from its distinctive religious orientation. The *via media* ran initially against the ingrained principles of the chief protagonists emerging from the Reformation era (post-Tridentine Catholicism and fully reformed Protestantism), and then, more importantly, against the later ingrained conventions of nineteenth- and twentieth-century secular historiography. Nevertheless, the Utraquist Church made a fundamental theological contribution in the field of ecclesiology, akin to that of the Church of England. Like the *Ecclesia Anglicana,* Utraquism stood out as a model of a national church, emerging in the milieu of distinctly Western Christianity, and with a traditionalist emphasis on the antiquity and historical continuity of their doctrine and institutions. While seeking to preserve much of traditional religious orthodoxy, both aimed at eluding the ultrabureaucratic and imperious style of ecclesiastical governance exemplified by the early modern papacy. At the other end of the ecclesiastical spectrum, against Luther's or Calvin's biblical reductionism, the Utraquist Church, like the *Ecclesia Anglicana,* defended the historical tripod of Western Christendom, namely the Bible, Aristotelian rationalism (in its scholastic and/or patristic incarnation), and the extrabiblical ecclesiastical tradition.[1] Like the Church of England, Utraquism would oppose the reason and reasoning to the unquestioning discipline of ecclesiastical autocrats, as well as to the unreflective impetuosity and rigorism of the chiliasts and other sectarians.[2] Like Anglicanism, Utraquism would be excoriated as representing an incomplete Reformation.[3]

Instead of earning respect, or admiration, for its steadfastness, moderation, and patriotism, the sixteenth-century Utraquist Church in later historical tradition has become an object of abuse and derision, above all (ironically) in Czech historiography, for which it might have provided a unique example of national achievement.[4] Judged by historians from either narrowly Protestant or Catholic partisan viewpoints, it could not be forgiven its indomitably independent stance during the sixteenth and early seventeenth centuries. Subsequently, similar attitudes persisted in secular historiography. Parallels to these opinions tended to emerge also in Western European historical writing, although it was the British historian Robert Evans who recently raised a voice of mild dissent against the historical chorus of anathema aimed at the Utraquist Church.[5]

A classic example of the modern critique of Utraquism can be found in Ferdinand Hrejsa's *magnum opus* of 1912. After discussing the emergence of the Lutheran Reformation, he writes:

> The more progressive among the Utraquists . . . seeing in the Bohemian Church nothing but moral and intellectual stagnation . . . acquired new strength from Wittenberg . . . They became more decisive, seeking to realize their principles in the direction of separation from the Catholic Church in the synods and the diets, as well as in the entire church. The more conservative and reactionary Utraquists, to the contrary, closed themselves to Luther's influence and clung even more tenaciously to the Catholic Church . . . [S]o two trends were constantly affirmed: a reactionary one, seeing in the Compactata the peak of its religious yearnings and only heresy beyond them, and a progressive trend . . . advancing further, strengthened by the influence of Luther and Melanchton.[6]

The condemnation grew even stronger in a Marxian analysis in 1963:

> We have used the expression "vegetated," and truly one cannot characterize otherwise the condition of the Utraquist Church in the mid-sixteenth century. This Church, a faithful servant of the feudal lords, had become an ideological buttress of Ferdinand [I]. However harsh this assessment might appear, it is nevertheless true. The Utraquists were assisting Fer-

dinand in stemming the tide of the Reformation, which was reaching Bohemia from neighboring Germany. The toothless ideology of the Utraquists was now in no way dangerous to the Habsburgs, because the world conditions had changed thoroughly. What fifty years previously could still appear daringly reformational, had become merely a feeble compromising and a cowardly lip service to the ruling regime.[7]

Part of the explanation for the jaundiced view of Utraquism in modern Czech historiography lies in the manner by which religious toleration was established in Bohemia and Moravia under Habsburg rule in 1781 after a complete proscription of any religion other than Roman Catholicism for over a century and a half. The Toleration Patent of Emperor Joseph II permitted the creation of non-Catholic churches only on the basis of the formal Lutheran or Reformed creeds. Thus there was no question of recreating either the authentic Utraquist Church or, for that matter, the congregations of the Unity of Brethren.[8] The critical interpretation of the heritage of the Bohemian Reformation thus fell into the hands of Lutherans and Calvinists—whether clerics or academics—who would naturally frown on the quasi-Roman and conservative character of the sixteenth-century Utraquist Church, and would applaud any tendency to replace Utraquism with fully reformed churches.

The leading nineteenth-century Czech historian František Palacký, whose expertise focused on Bohemian Reformation and the Hussite Revolution, was the son of a freshly emancipated dissenter. Even in his case it is likely that the aversion to sixteenth-century Utraquism, which he displayed in the last volume of his monumental *History of the Czech Nation,* stemmed partly from his education in the Lutheran schools of Moravia and Slovakia at the dawn of the nineteenth century.[9] In his view of history, Christian religious development, reflecting a Providential design, depended on the antithetical interactions between biblicist Protestantism and unreformed Catholicism, each embodying one of the essential poles of the Christian faith: reason and authority.[10] Inasmuch as Palacký's historical paradigm did not allow for a synthesizing *via media,* which would adopt the positive and reject the negative emanations of each pole, the famous historian viewed Utraquist centrism as irrelevant, if not perverse.

Certain misconceptions outside Bohemia and Moravia helped to skew the historical view of both Jan Hus and Utraquism. As Enrico Molnar points out in a seminal article, it was Luther himself who began the myth of an illusory Lutheranization or Calvinization of the essentially "High" Utraquist

Church when in 1520 the great reformer implied that Bohemian Utraquism was a mere prelude to the German Reformation.[11]

For its part, the Roman Church was no less instrumental in promoting an illusory connection between Hus and Luther, first by pinning on the latter the label of "Hussitism," partly in order to discredit Luther and his movement in German eyes by linking him and the Reformation with an alien Czech phenomenon.[12] Subsequently, however, the Roman Church continued to equate Hus's religious outlook with those of Luther and Calvin.[13] Paradoxically, therefore, Lutheran and Catholic views of Hus as a proto-Lutheran tended to reinforce one another, allowing the former to claim a historical pedigree extending to the fifteenth century, and tending to validate for the latter the death sentence imposed on Hus as a "heretic." To accept the real Hus would have meant for the Catholics that an injustice was committed, and for the reformers of the Lutheran and Calvinist type that Hus would have condemned the departure from the High Church tradition to a strict biblicism. Parenthetically, it may be noted that Erasmus was subject to similar praises (from the Reformed side) and accusations (from the Roman side) of being Luther's precursor.[14]

There were other factors that tended to conceal the conservative nature of mainstream Utraquism from religious writers abroad. The more radical confessional statements were more frequently translated and circulated outside Bohemia. While a Utraquist statement of faith appeared in one Latin translation in 1539,[15] the quasi-Lutheran Bohemian Confession of 1575 enjoyed three German (1584, 1609, and 1610) translations and two Latin ones (1614 and 1619).[16] Outside observers probably viewed the latter document as a reflection of the real religious situation in Bohemia rather than as a flawed attempt at an ex post facto Lutheranization of an essentially High Church Utraquism. Confessional statements by the Unity of Brethren, published in Latin in 1511, 1538, and 1573, attracted even more attention.[17] This is attested by, among other things, the inclusion of the 1573 Confession into the prestigious international compendium, *Harmonia confessionum fidei, Orthodoxarum, et Reformatorum Ecclesiarum* (Geneva, 1581). Ironically, Richard Hooker himself, about whom more will be said later, can be used as an illustration. Instead of recognizing the Utraquists as kindred theological champions of the *via media,* in his one reference to the "Bohemians" in the *Laws of Ecclesiastical Polity,* he lumps them together with the Lutherans, particularly the Saxons, citing from the Brethren's Bohemian Confession on the rites of repentance.[18] The famous Jacques B. Bossuet, Catholic bishop of Meaux, also seems to have considered it authoritative.[19]

In addition, the enthusiastic embrace of Hus and the Bohemian martyrs by the Puritan John Foxe might have contributed to an unwarranted radicalization of Bohemian Utraquism's image.[20] Alexandra Walsham points out that a similar fate met the moderate John Frith, who has been characterized as "the forerunner of the liberal element in later Anglican thought," yet under Foxe's influence was transformed into "a confessional mascot" of radical Puritans.[21] Interestingly enough, Foxe's view of Hus was validated at the opposite side of the religious spectrum by Thomas More's earlier portrait of Hus as a faithful disciple of Wyclif and a full-fledged member of the heretical group, including Luther and Zwingli.[22] Similarly, the leaders of the English anti-Protestant movement, the Pilgrimage of Grace, in late 1536 included Hus among the heretics whose errors had to be extirpated.[23] Like Foxe, Jean Crespin, the French Calvinist and associate of Theodor Béza in Geneva, featured Jan Hus at the beginning of his famous and influential martyrology, *Le livre des Martyrs . . . depuis Jean Hus iusques à cette anneé présente* (Geneva, 1554).[24] Later, the post-White Mountain Czech religious exiles, other than the Bohemian Brethren, were rapidly cajoled or pressured into full conformity with official Lutheranism in their north German places of refuge, particularly in Saxony.[25] In the English-speaking world there was a tendency to consider the Brethren as typical representatives of the Bohemian Reformation. Thus, in the post–White Mountain period, the Unity was asked to supply additional material for a new edition of Foxe's martyrology. When the deadline was missed in 1632, the Brethren's intended contribution was published separately in London in 1650 as *The History of the Bohemian Persecution.*[26]

In a paradoxically similar vein, Roman propagandists tended to denounce the relatively moderate Hus more severely than the later authentic Protestant reformers. Thus Luther's opponent, Johannes Cochlaeus, would refer to Hus in 1549 as worse than the pagans, the Turks, the Tartars, or the Jews. Hus has been called the king of hell's general with Luther and Calvin as his officers. Indeed, it appears that the Roman Curia in the late sixteenth century viewed Bohemia as the fountainhead of the entire Protestant Reformation.[27] This odium carried over to Hus's followers so that the Czechs were considered a "nation of heretics" par excellence, while no similar stigmatization seemed to be collectively inflicted on any nation producing or following the teachings of Luther, Zwingli, or Calvin. The continuous presence of a significant, often zealous, minority of Roman Curia loyalists among the Czechs from 1415 to 1620 does not seem to have redeemed the nation's reputation in the eyes of the Holy See and its allies (contrary to Genesis 18, 22–32).[28]

There were, however, modest exceptions to the routine damning of Jan Hus on the Roman side in Bohemia during the sixteenth century. One was Johann Faber's pamphlet of 1537, which will be discussed later.[29] In the second instance, after their expulsion from Prague in June 1618 following the Second Defenestration, Bohemian Jesuits praised Hus and the Utraquists for their belief in the invocation of the saints, relics, priestly celibacy, the seven sacraments, the sacrifice of the mass, transubstantiation, and purgatory in an *Apology,* published in Vienna. This document, significant for its seeming exculpation of Hus himself, is a tribute to the Jesuits' tactical flexibility, and is possibly linked with Ferdinand II's short-lived intent of mid-1620 to tolerate Utraquism after the anticipated end of the Bohemian revolt.[30] These modest internal overtures, however, ended with the victory of the Counter-Reformation in Bohemia in 1621, and Roman frigidity toward Hus and Utraquism was destined to persist for over the next three centuries, with a brief intermezzo during Joseph II's Catholic Enlightenment of the late eighteenth century.[31] Outside Bohemia, however, as another exception, Bossuet expressed his admiration for Hus's character. In his *Histoire des Variations des Églises Protestantes* (1688), the French prelate claims that Hus's deviations from the Roman Church were insubstantial, and thus he did not deserve the status of a precursor of the Protestant Reformation.[32]

Apparently, only the thaw of the *aggiornamento* has elicited a more generous attitude, marked by Paul de Vooght's virtual vindication of Hus. Similarly, Francis Oakley has spoken of Hus's religious commitment "that was certainly not Wycliffite, that was traditionally orthodox in intent, and that was within a hair's breadth of being orthodox in fact."[33] Daniel DiDomizio has suggested that Hus's treatise, *De ecclesia,* for which he was chiefly condemned at Constance, may be viewed as a model of Church reforms at Vatican II, reflected especially in the statement "Lumen gentium."[34] More recently at the behest of the Vatican, the Conference of Czech Catholic Bishops established a Commission in 1993 to examine the person, life, and work of Hus.[35] At the International Symposium on Master Jan Hus (Convegno Internazionale su Johannes Hus), which was held at the Papal Lateran University in Rome and in the Vatican in December 1999, Pope John Paul II spoke of Hus as one of the reformers of the Church, thus apparently lifting from him authoritatively, although informally, the stigma of heresy.[36]

While the stern treatment of Utraquism by modern religious historians might be ascribed to denominational bias, other explanations must be sought for the negative attitudes of Czech liberal/positivist (and later Marxist) historians, agnostic or atheist in their orientation. One explanation may well be a Central European version of the English phenomenon of the Whig interpretation of history.[37] In English historiography the skewing of the record in favor of religious radicalism has been recently attributed by Alexandra Walsham to "the resilience of sectarian paradigms."[38] Czech liberal and positivist historians (as well as later Marxist ones)—inspired, as they were, by the ideals of nineteenth-century progressivism—tended to view a fully fledged religious Reformation (of the Lutheran or Calvinist type) as a generally legitimate and necessary stage in the intellectual development of Europe. This Weltanschauung would predispose the historian to regard any continuing actual or potential ties with the Roman Church as defects or imperfections in the supposedly correct developmental trajectory of Czech Utraquism. Hence the powerful temptation to consign the Utraquists to the realm of historical aberrations for violating the laws of history postulated by Hegel, or Comte, or Marx.[39] The pattern for this thinking was set outside of Bohemia already by Louis Blanc in *Histoire de la Révolution française* (1847), where he assigned the role of Thermidorians to the mainline Utraquists following the revolution precipitated by the Bohemian Reformation.[40]

Conversely, within the same mind-set, linking the Czech religious movement with the Lutheran Reformation would enhance the historical stature of the Bohemian Reformation by making it the prototype of a world-class historical phenomenon, instead of a merely limited local defection, no matter how dramatic and ominous in its implications. In a somewhat paradoxical way, this stand appeared to associate Czech national pride with a primarily German occurrence.[41] The efforts to deal with this problem strengthened two questionable historiographical tendencies. One, already touched upon, was to amplify the link between Hus and Luther. The other involved the model of Neo-Utraquism. According to this notion, the outcome of Reformation in Bohemia was a type of Lutheranism that also synthesized salient features of the antecedent Czech reformism. One of the major concerns of this book is to deal with this problem.

A second explanation for the negative judgment of Utraquism, although perhaps less obvious, may be that the Czech liberal and positivist historians (as well as later Marxist ones) were under the spell of the widespread nineteenth- and twentieth-century intellectual malaise of absolute ethical perfectionism, the spirit of which emanated largely from the otherwise admirable world of German scholarship, and its sway affected much of Central and Eastern Europe. This outlook favored radical solutions rather than moderation or compromise. In a strange reversal of the golden rule, or the rules of Aristotle's *Nicomachean Ethics,* an extreme stand was considered a virtue, and a moderate one denounced as a vice. Utraquism, on the contrary, occupied a centrist position between extremes of Christian thought and practice, sharing with Hooker and subsequent Anglicanism the Aristotelian ideas about the importance of moderation and the middle way.[42] The maximalist mentality of the intellectual climate of Central Europe—which might have prepared the way for the fateful appeal of totalitarian ideologies later in the twentieth century[43]—would instinctively prefer a clear-cut reformed solution to the Utraquist *via media.* It may also account for the appeal to the historians of the Bohemian Brethren, whose uncompromising moral rigorism was consonant with the absolutist mentality.[44]

Those out of sympathy with the middle way, or the *via media,* have tended to see the Utraquist, as well as the Anglican, positions as a matter of political expediency (combined with a lack of firm intellectual foundation) rather than a matter of genuine religious conviction. In the Czech case and explicitly leaning on the interpretations of the French historian Ernst Denis, Thomas Masaryk, the Czech statesman and philosopher, viewed the Utraquist *via media* as unprincipled.[45] More recently, voices have been raised by those who view Utraquism's centrist position not as a mark of strength, but as the stance of a debilitating spirit of compromise.[46] Actually, another major concern of this book is to show that Utraquism's centrist position, eschewing the Roman dogmatism on the right, and the Lutheran and Calvinist dogmatism on the left, acquired a distinct intellectual purpose. It allowed a significant latitude and tolerance for the discussion of religious issues in the spirit of the seminal documents of the Bohemian Reformation.[47]

A third causal factor may be suggested to account for modern critics' aversion to Utraquism: its real or apparent overtures to Eastern Orthodoxy. This may be a result of the implicit presumption of an unbridgeable cultural gap between the West and the East. The leading role of Western civilization (Hegel's Romance-Germanic world) was a salient feature of European historical consciousness at least from Hegel through Comte and Marx to Arnold Toynbee, and the Czechs, like other nations at the eastern fringes of the West, were particularly susceptible to the appeal of such an elite status in world development.[48] A major irony rests in the fact that the Utraquists' sense of kinship with the Orthodox—as an analysis of Bílejovský's views will show[49]—was much more limited than their modern opponents have usually assumed.

Apart from the irritant of the *via media,* the modern historical critique of Utraquism tended to focus on the allegedly low moral and intellectual levels of the Utraquist clergy and laity, as well as the imputed duplicity and toadyism of Utraquist administrators and Consistories toward the agents of the Habsburg kings and the Roman Curia, especially on the issues of priestly ordinations, and of other relations with the Church of Rome. A predisposition to this second tendency seemed to be compatible with, and possibly reinforced by, the first set of considerations just discussed. If—in the eyes of their critics—the Utraquist leaders failed to respond to what was assumed to be the historically "inevitable" force of the Lutheran Reformation, it would be logical (or at least reassuring), if they were markedly flawed, either morally, or intellectually, or both.[50]

It is now necessary to examine these charges from a more empirical point of view. First, one may wonder whether the judgments of the modern critics of Utraquism reveal more about the unrealistic standards of nineteenth-century morality than about sensitivity to the mores of the sixteenth century. Krofta, for instance, chides Ernst Denis for such a misplaced perspective in the latter's seminal *Fin de l'indépendance bohême*.[51] Illustrations of questionable behavior on the Roman side include papal nuncios' bribes to the Utraquist leaders, their use of misleading statements, and their comments on the scandalous or cowardly behavior of Bohemia's Roman clergy.[52] The system of nepotism is known to have caused a moral decline at the papal court.[53] Within the Bohemian context, Bílejovský, for instance, cites a house in Prague in which Roman priests allegedly consorted with prostitutes. A priest of the Roman Church, Tomáš Bavorovský, in his *Postila česká* (Bohemian Homiliary) (1557), chastises the priests of his denomination who "do not let the faithful read religious books . . . so that the latter would not note the priests' ignorance and careless indifference; the clergy toady up to the nobles and minimize their sins."[54] Kavka and Skýbová refer to the shocking findings of a papal commissioner's inspection of Bohemian monasteries in 1574.[55] In 1585, Bohemian nobles adhering to Rome complained to Nuncio Filip Sega about the "immoral and scandalous" behavior of the Roman clergy, and Nuncio Camillo Caetano confirmed this state of affairs in a letter to his successor Nuncio Cesare Speciano in 1592.[56] In a similar vein, Zikmund Winter cites examples of coarse manners and moral lapses among Lutheran (Czech, as well as Bohemian German) clergy in the sixteenth and early seventeenth centuries.[57] Period memoirs attest to the violence permeating ordinary human existence with concomitant threats to life and property in the sixteenth century.[58] Comparing the Bohemian situation with another region we find that in an area of exemplary Protestant virtue, such as the Swiss canton of Zurich, there were large numbers of defaulting clerics with 35 percent to 40 percent of the ministers disciplined in the 1532–1580 period.[59]

More important is the problem of the type of sources that have been used. The Utraquists have been traditionally depicted on the basis of the Consistory's administrative and court records, revealing primarily the seamy side in the behavior of their clergy and laity. Their historical self-descriptions, like Bílejovský's work, have been almost routinely dismissed.[60] In contrast, the Bohemian Brethren have been assessed on the basis of their historical self-descriptions. In addition, the Brethren carried much of their documentation into the safety of exile, while material favorable to the Utraquists tended to perish during the Counter-Reformation in Bohemia and Moravia. Reliance on the Brethren's accounts of events has tended to skew the record not only in favor of the Brethren, but also against the Utraquists, since the Brethren, despite their many virtues, were notoriously uncharitable toward their opponents.[61] For instance, even the sympathetic Krofta demurs at the Brethren's unsubstantiated characterization of the Utraquist administrator Martin Mělnický, as "a dishonourable man, a liar, a drunkard, an obvious whoremonger . . ."[62] One is almost forced to assume that Jan Augusta, bishop of the Brethren, was exercising poetic license in 1543 in his sweeping judgment of the Utraquist clergy when he escalated his charges from relatively innocent playfulness and epicureanism—albeit offensive to sectarian gravity and asceticism—to outright criminality:

> All the Utraquist priests are dishonorable, immoral, proud, conceited, avaricious, cruel, merciless, slanderers without goodness or holy obedience, discordant, disorderly, simoniacal, ignorant, unclean, fornicators, adulterous, luxurious, banqueters, worthless, impious, clownish, jokers, lazy, vagabondish, tavern seekers, gamesters, gluttons, imbibers, drunkards, flirtatious, living with concubines, mockers, rumormongers, detractors, thieves, murderers, insubordinate to the ordinances of manorial lords and of municipalities, self-willed, unmannerly, restless, stormy, vengeful, envious, and in brief accustomed to many sins, devoid of Christ's ecclesiastical discipline, and incorrigible, etc.[63]

Similarly, the charge that the ordination of Utraquist priests involved a double apostasy (from Utraquism to Roman obedience and back) seems to have originated from Jan Blahoslav, also a bishop of the Unity.[64] In another context, the Brethren did not hesitate to slander even a staunch and upright Lutheran such as Václav Mitmánek.[65]

One is tempted to apply to the Brethren the critical characterization of the Puritans as those "who delighted in nothing so much as the contemplation of their own virtue and the condemnation of the supposed vices of others."[66] In England, the Puritans similarly attempted to undermine the reputation of their opponents by assailing the leaders of the Church of England as "worldlings, timeservers, pleasers of man not of God."[67] In 1586, the Anglican priest, Ellis of Bowers, was alleged to be "a dicer, a carder, a pot companion, a company keeper of riotous persons, living very offensively to all men."[68] William P. Haugaard points out the misleading character of this critique, which could be also applied to the Brethren's critique of the Utraquist establishment: "We need not be seduced by the polemics of sixteenth-century opponents of the establishment into judging that lukewarm devotion or sheer vocational opportunism inevitably characterized its supporters . . . The anti-establishment campaign left a large body of documentary evidence of commitment and fervor, the uncritical reading of which has sometimes led historians to take the indictment of the establishment and its adherents at face value."[69] Similarly, the Brethren's negative comments on the character and motives of the Utraquist ecclesiastics should be accepted with a sizable grain of salt. Yet, historians like Václav Tomek and Anton Gindely (and after them Ernest Denis) tended to take at face value the parodies and caricatures of the Brethren's historiography.[70]

Aside from the Brethren, the adherents of the Roman Curia had a special reason to depict Utraquist priests in an uncomplimentary way. The Utraquist Church received a steady supply of priests by conversions from Roman obedience, and in the eyes of the *sub una* adherents such converts were ipso facto tainted morally or intellectually. The blanket and unsubstantiated charges from the Roman side, which ordinarily might be dismissed as self-serving, gained in credibility when reproduced, for reasons of their own, by Protestant and secular historians.[71] Finally, some of the disparaging characterization of the Utraquists has probably stemmed from the reports of papal nuncios, such as Cesare Speciano and Giovanni Dolfin, who from the vantage point of Italian cultural refinement marveled at the crude manners and behavior of the transalpine Central Europeans.[72] This may be already sensed from the following description by Aeneas Sylvius of the proud Bohemian warriors who had defeated five genocidal crusades launched against their homeland in the 1420s and 1430s: "[P]eople of dark complexion, sunburnt and lashed by wind, ugly and terrible to behold, who hitherto have lived around campfires, people with eagle eyes, uncombed hair, long beards, large stature, hairy limbs and skin so hard that it appeared able to deflect the sword like a metal shield."[73]

As for the willingness of historians to accept at face value the slanderous assertions against the Utraquists, Kamil Krofta supplies an intriguing insight in this area. According to him, mid-nineteenth-century Czech historians, particularly Tomek and Josef Kalousek, held anti-Lutheran convictions that were not verbalized in their publications, but evident to their biographers, namely that the Lutheran principle of *sola fide* encouraged amoral attitudes and behavior,[74] and that Lutheranism tended to Germanize the Bohemian lands. They compounded these questionable propositions by the erroneous presumption that sixteenth-century Utraquism became virtually synonymous with Lutheranism. Projecting these negative attitudes into their assessments of Utraquism, these writers welcomed and drew freely on readily available denunciations in the Brethren's polemical and historical writings. From Tomek and Kalousek, the images of Utraquist immorality passed on into the prestigious work of French historian, Denis, who if anything amplified them.[75] Denis's high standing helped to reflect his uncomplimentary views about late Utraquism back into Czech historical writing. Above all, Thomas Masaryk specifically credited him with the image of Utraquist decay, contrasted with the Brethren's purity. This became one of the key themes in his highly influential work on Czech political culture, *Česká otázka* (The Bohemian Question) of 1895.[76]

Once set on its course, the largely contrived and dubious claim of the Utraquists' deficiency of moral fiber ultimately reached a bizarre level when it became used inversely for the questioning or denying of the status of "Utraquist" to an individual who obviously could not be viewed as morally flawed or delinquent. Thus, Jakubec maintains that Daniel Adam of Veleslavín (1546–1599), the notable publisher and writer, must have been a secret sympathizer, if not a secret member of the Unity of Brethren because "he sought to strengthen the noble inclinations in his compatriots, elevate moral and religious life, and enhance patriotic devotion. From this activity we recognize a partisan of the Unity of Bohemian Brethren—of course a discreet one."[77] There were similar attempts to postulate secret membership in the Unity, for instance, for Jan Kocín of Kocinét, Martin Lupáč, and Pavel Stránský.[78] The rationale for such pseudo-identifications was evidently the illusory maxim that a Utraquist could not by definition display conspicuous qualities of morality, religiosity, or patriotism, inasmuch as these virtues were incompatible with Utraquism as represented by historians. The prevalence of this preconception is reflected in the fact that even a dispassionate and fair-minded scholar, such as Josef Jireček, went along with this theory of a widespread secret membership in the Unity: "Between the beginning of the sixteenth until the mid-seventeenth century there were few significant writers who were not either overt or covert Brethren."[79]

In reality, Utraquist theology and homiletics run counter the charges of Utraquism's inherent immorality. The exhortation to good deeds in fulfillment of the "Law of God" was one of the leitmotifs of Utraquist teaching. While Luther, indeed, taught his followers not to worry—because of Christ's redemptive sacrifice—about religious laws and commandments, the Utraquists to the contrary held the observance of the Law of God among their highest priorities. Consequently, responsible Utraquist ecclesiastics looked askance at Lutheranism's denial of the soteriological value of works. This will be discussed further on in connection with the theology of Pavel Bydžovský and the declaration of the Utraquist Consistory of 1570.[80] Consequently, the charge of immorality or Epicurean-like licentiousness on the basis of solafideism, whatever validity it may have had—on a theoretical level—vis-à-vis Lutheranism, was not applicable to Utraquism at all. Far from indifference to moral values, examples of fervent exhortation to virtue and good works can be found in surviving homiliaries from each of the three centuries of Utraquist preaching.[81] Contrary to the Brethren's assertions, Utraquist priests held a particularly exalted view of their calling and duties. Thus Vavřinec Leander Rvačovský of Rvačov, in his famous *Masopust* (1580) wrote the following about the clergy's obligation: "We ourselves must strive so that our light would shine before us, so that the people seeing our faithfulness in God's Church and in our administration of the sacraments and other ecclesiastical services, and seeing also in our conduct good and honorable deeds (confirming by acts what we teach God's people by words), they [the people] would therefore praise the Lord, our God, who is in heaven."[82] Valentin Polon in 1589 cited St. Paul exhorting priests to serve as examples to the believers, St. Luke calling them blessed, and St. Peter promising them, as a reward for inspiring their flock, "a crown of glory that fadeth not away."[83] The office imposed an awesome responsibility for which God would require a stern accounting.[84] Polon summed up his view of the glory and duty of priesthood, stipulating the following for the clergy: "[T]hey should conscientiously tend to their office, remain steady in their calling, lead the people in goodness and morality, follow Christ in his footsteps and [follow] the holy Fathers in their salvific teachings, point the way to good order and Christian piety, provide examples of virtue, avoid scandal, shine like lights and radiate virtue among the faithful (Matthew 5), and resist the sins and temptations of the world . . ."[85] If despite all, the Utraquists did not quite measure up to the moral rigorism and perfectionism of the Unity of Brethren, it is relevant to recall Ernst Troeltsch's famous ecclesiastical topology, according to which a sect composed of those specially "elect" can, as a rule, establish and maintain higher moral standards for its members than a church open to those simply baptized.[86] It is paradoxical, even amusing, to see agnostic and secularist critics in modern times pick up on the theme of laxity, and hear them excoriate the Utraquists for their "low level of religiosity" or their lack of "higher religious feelings."[87]

Taking a more sympathetic view, although without fully condoning the Utraquists' occasional distasteful equivocations, procrastinations, and flattery to the emperor-kings, their questionable behavior may be viewed as a part of the customary diplomacy of the sixteenth century. Rarely, these humiliating acts may be also seen as prerequisites for survival in confrontations with the awesome power of the Habsburg monarchy, bent on assisting the Roman Curia.[88] Encounters of this kind might test the moral fiber of the most forthright and courageous of men and women. Even Jan Hus may have hurt his cause at Constance in 1415 by equivocation ("lack of clarity and candor") on certain disputed issues, especially concerning Wyclif, as Oakley points out.[89] On deception, a strict formalist might censure in particular the Utraquist ordinations by Roman bishops. The sternest charge, cited earlier, that this process involved a double apostasy on the part of the candidates for priesthood, however, seems to be based on an isolated instance. The consternation, which this one event caused in the Utraquist circles, would indicate that an absolution from a promise to administer sub una was not a routine practice, but an extraordinary occurrence.[90] Another charge was that the Utraquist Church willingly accepted any priest, no matter how unworthy, who was ready to shift allegiance from the Roman Curia. The actual record indicated that the Consistory was rather careful in examining the record of such candidates and by no means accepted just anyone who presented himself.[91] As for the recourse to the Roman bishops as such, the Utraquists always thought of themselves as an integral part, not a severed branch, of the traditional church of Western Christendom.[92] Moreover, their ordinations had been approved by the Council of Basel, the ecumenical character of which the Roman Church did not doubt. Hence, the administrator and the Consistory could have felt entitled to tap directly into the flow of apostolic power circulating through the episcopal system of the

Western Church. The image of cowering deference on the part of Utraquist ecclesiastics also needs to be qualified by the fact that, when the need and opportunity arose, the Consistory could assert its independence with firmness and dignity, for instance, by returning papal missives unopened to the Roman Archbishop of Prague, and by declining to meet emissaries of the papal Curia during the 1560s.[93] In fact, in a refreshing change from the charges of excessive submissiveness, František Kameníček accuses the Utraquists of disruptive and unnecessary displays of insolence toward the Roman clergy and laity.[94]

A subsidiary charge by the critics of Utraquism has been that the Utraquist ecclesiastics were not only immoral, but also ignorant.[95] This claim seems to reflect a major misperception, although it might also reflect the views of biased contemporary commentators, such as those of Nuncio Giovanni Dolfin in 1575.[96] Their publications show the Utraquist ecclesiastic to have been learned, theologically sophisticated, and academically minded scholars who continued to infuse Utraquism with a spirit of reasonableness and with informed discussion. Their engagement with the patristic and scholastic writers was not based on mere citations from compendia of excerpts (*fl orilegia*), but on creative intellectual engagement with their text. Thus, an examination of the Second Book of Bílejovský's *Kronyka Cýrkevní* (Ecclesiastical Chronicle), for instance, indicates a theological erudition documented by sixty-eight references to the opinions of at least twenty-four fathers and doctors of the Church, and other distinguished theologians, namely (in alphabetical order and with the number of references in parentheses): Albertus Magnus (2), Ambrose (2), Augustine (7), Bede (1), Bernard of Clairvaux (2), Eusebius (1), Gregory the Great (4), Hilary of Poitiers (1), Hugh of St. Victor (1), John Hus (2), Innocent III (1), Jerome (5), John Damascene (1), Nicholas of Lyra (6), Origen (6), Paskasius (1), Peter Payne (6), John of Příbram (1), Pseudo-Dionysius (1), Remigius of Auxerre (1), John Rokycana (1), Theodore of Tarsus (1), Thomas Aquinas (3), and John Wyclif (11).[97]

Similarly, one can cite the example of Bílejovský's colleague, Pavel Bydžovský, who directed the resistance against the Lutheran takeover of the Utraquist Consistory in 1541–1543. His knowledge was exhibited by a substantial command of patristic literature (both Greek and Latin), in which he showed familiarity with recent editions.[98] His theological erudition further covered the medieval doctors of the church, decisions of both ancient and medieval church councils, provisions of canon law (specifically the Decretum of Gratian),[99] and the classics of Utraquism, as well as Luther's and

Melanchton's doctrines. This whole gamut of learning was displayed in the discussion of every major theological proposition.[100] One may also recall the erudition of two important Utraquist ecclesiastics, Jan Hortensius Zahrádka (1501–1557) and Jindřich Dvorský z Helfenberka (1505–1582), each of whom held the office of administrator in 1541 and 1572–1581, respectively. Having studied in Padua and Venice in the early 1530s, Hortensius was not only a distinguished theologian (particularly as a specialist on St. Paul's epistles), but also the outstanding Bohemian mathematician of his times.[101] In the early 1540s, Dvorský had entered into scholarly communication concerning the classics of antiquity with no lesser a figure than the "praeceptor Germaniae," Philipp Melanchton himself.[102] During the early years of the seventeenth century, Martin Bacháček, professor of astronomy and rector of the University of Prague, was a respected colleague of such luminaries as Johannes Kepler and Tycho de Brahe.[103] Even a regular Utraquist priest, Vavřinec Leander Rvačovský of Rvačov, is praised for his "unusual linguistic, historical, and theological knowledge."[104] The tradition of learned clergy continued into the early decades of the seventeenth century. Matouš Pačuda in his *Spis v němž se obsahuje* (1616) not only cited profusely from the fathers and doctors of the Church, but also displayed a working knowledge of Latin and Greek classical authors, such as Homer, Herodotus, Euripides, Plutarch, and Plautus.[105]

Thus, it can be hardly maintained that the leaders of Utraquism did not accept the fruits of the Lutheran or Calvinist Reformation simply because they lacked a sufficient intellectual training. The scope of educated townsmen's intellectual interest reached beyond practical knowledge of law, medicine, and technology to the sphere of pure science and scholarship in philosophy, classics, theology, linguistics, and history.[106] Erasmus was familiar with the scholarly and religious life of Utraquist Bohemia, which he listed among the few countries where the humanities were valued and flourished.[107] The critics who have voiced their low opinions concerning Bohemia's intellectual scene, frequently failed to take into account the situation in other countries, especially in their disparagement of the Utraquist University of Prague.[108] To the extent that this institution suffered a decline in scholarly productivity, and perhaps standards, by the sixteenth century, the same affliction was common to universities, particularly in Central Europe of that period. During the fifteenth century, German universities had shrunk virtually to artistic faculties, and acted largely as "finishing schools" for local audiences.[109] On the brighter side, the University of Prague, in fact, scored a notable achievement in maintaining an effective network of secondary schools in the towns of Bohemia, culminating during the rectorate of Martin Bacháček. Zikmund Winter, moreover, concludes his exhaustive study of the Utraquist university with the following words: "[M]any men were educated there, who excelled in the sciences, although they did not excel in self-promotion [*chlubením*]."[110] No less a figure than Kepler expressed his admiration for the university.[111]

Inasmuch as earlier interpretive frameworks have lost much of their cogency in the postmodern world of the later twentieth century, the time seems ripe to view Bohemian Utraquism on its own merits rather than through the prism of largely outdated historiographic frameworks. Utraquism should not be shaped, as it has been so often in the past, to conform with the preconceptions of other sects or points of view—whether Catholic, Lutheran, Reformed, liberal, progressivist, positivist, or Marxist—either as a prelude to, or an incomplete form of, Lutheranism, or as an epiphenomenon of political or economic interests, but rather should be seen as a fully developed religious movement in its own right, firmly rooted both in the domestic Bohemian tradition, as well as in the apostolic, sacramental, and liturgical principles of the High Church orientation.

2

A Prolegomenon: The First Century of Utraquism, 1415–1517

Although the focus of this book is on the fate of the Bohemian Reformation after the emergence of Luther, for the sake of clarity, it is useful to review briefly the history of the Utraquist Church during the first century of its existence before the Protestant Reformation. While the characteristic features of Bohemian reformism were rooted in the late fourteenth century, the Utraquist Church attained its organizational embodiment in the first half of the fifteenth century and reached its maturity in the latter part of the same century. On the way, the Church faced two challenges to its integrity: first a transient one from the radicals, in particular the Taborites, and second, a lasting one from the Unity of Brethren.

The Gestation, 1360–1415

The principal progenitors of the Bohemian Reformation, particularly, Jan Milíč of Kroměříž, Matěj of Janov, Vojtěch Raňkův, and Tomáš of Štítné entered enthusiastically after 1360 into the mainstream of criticism of the existing church of Western Christendom accused of embracing material wealth and earthly domination.[1] Regarding another of its prominent characteristics, the Bohemian Reformation did not follow a common European trend, but originated its own peculiar departure, namely the proposition that frequent communion was central to Christian life. Jan Hus and his academic entourage completed the preparatory stage of the Bohemian Reformation. Hus not only became a saint of the Utraquist Church, but his role at the Council of Constance in defiance of mindless authority also gained him world-class status as a defender of human rights. The relative freedom engendered by the Bohemian Reformation provided space for input by sectarian outsiders who would challenge the mainstream Utraquism of the learned university men, and engendered dissident folkish radicals, as noted, first in the form of the Taborites, and eventually that of the Unity.

Moral and Administrative Reform of the Church

The very beginning of the movement in Bohemia can be traced to the Austrian preacher in Prague, Konrad Waldhauser, who focused on contemporary corruption of morals and directly inspired Milíč.[2] The early reformers characteristically targeted clerical transgressions, especially simony, nepotism, pluralism, and absenteeism. To these were added the charges of abuses, ignorance, immorality, and laziness of the priests and monastics; fiscal chicanery of the Curia; and financial exploitation of believers.[3] The harsh critique of the administrative practices and the moral condition of the Church, directed against the papacy, the hierarchy, and the clergy, was not peculiar to Bohemia, but was widespread in the second half of the fourteenth century, and drew on even earlier antecedents in mainline Western Christianity. Thus, Petrarch, St. Catherine of Siena, and St. Bridget of Sweden in their writings pilloried the Avignonese papacy as "morally corrupt, financially extravagant, [and] administratively tyrannical."[4] In her critical zeal, St. Bridget went so far as to state: "The successor of Peter is now the destroyer of souls, worse than the devil, less just than Pilate, more cruel than Judas."[5] Similarly, the warnings of the Bohemian reformers, especially Janov,[6] against the corrupting influences of ecclesiastical splendor and profusion of decrees, mandates, and rules, echoed the concerns of unimpeachably orthodox Church doctors, such as Bernard of Clairvaux. The Bohemian reformers began to play with fire when they endorsed and borrowed the rhetoric of John Wyclif in their denunciation of the abuses and worldly dominion of the clergy. The circumstances of Wyclif's influence will be discussed.[7] On the whole, while the Bohemian theologians endorsed Wyclif's criticism of clerical abuses, they by and large stopped short of embracing the doctrines that anticipated the Protestant Reformation, such as his denunciation of the priesthood's sacramental power and his radical Eucharistic departures.

There was an important implication of the rights of critical reason in the Bohemian reformers' challenge to what they considered a tyrannical exercise of administrative and magisterial authority on the part of ecclesiastical officialdom. Not rejecting the extra-biblical tradition of the Christian Church, the Bohemian Reformers sought to subject its tenets to the check of noncontradiction with the Scripture, and thus curb what they viewed as arbitrariness of the ecclesiastical bureaucracy. To gain insight into the resistance to surrendering the function of reason and argument in the face of naked magisterial authority, it is relevant to consider the professional status of the Bohemian Reformation's leaders. The latter consisted mainly of university teachers and other theological academics accustomed to the application of reason and reasoning, and to the freewheeling (*quodlibet*) disputations of the late medieval universities.[8] The system of formal *quaestiones* deliberately opposing the theological consensus served to cushion the thrust of the ecclesiastical authority vis-à-vis its subjects.[9]

The academic background of the Bohemian reformers, nurtured by the practice of quodlibet disputations at the University of Prague helps to explain their predilection for the test of reason and for displaying authentic learning. It also led them to insist on "the free preaching of God's Word," which was already true of Milíč.[10] Likewise, their academic background predisposed the reformers to skepticism about the magisterial authority of the prelates whose power was based simply on an their bureaucratic status rather than on theological learning. This helps to explain, for instance, the reformers' quarrels with Archbishop of Prague, Zbyněk of Hasenberk, who—according to rumors—learned to read only on the assumption of the archiepiscopal office.[11] Similarly, Štepán of Kolín, Hus's teacher at the University of Prague, had sharply criticized Zajíc's precursor, Archbishop Jan of Jenštejn (1379–1396), for his imperiousness and ostentation of riches.[12] The strained relationship between the University of Prague and Archbishop Zbyněk can be seen as a parallel to the contemporary resistance of Oxford University to interference by Archbishop Arundel of Canterbury.[13] More generally, the tension between the argumentative claims of academic theologians and the prelates' disciplinary claims has been recognized as a problem in the late medieval Church, an experience that the Bohemian Reformers shared with Wyclif.[14]

Liturgical Deepening: Frequent Communion

Against the established norm in the Western Church of annual lay communion, the early Bohemian reformers advanced the ideal of weekly (and preferably daily) communion, as a means of a moral renewal for both individuals and their society.[15] In a pioneering study, David Holeton identified three factors that happily conspired to promote the cause of frequent communion in Bohemia: academic learning, vernacular popularization, and hierarchical approbation. Milíč of Kroměříž and Janov elaborated the theological justification for frequent, even daily communion against the prevalent medieval insistence on Eucharistic abstemiousness. Milíč referred to Augustine, John Chrysostom, Gregory the Great, and Bernard of Clairvaux.[16] Matěj asserted a direct relationship between baptism and communion, and battled against the notion that a devotion to the Eucharist was somehow superior to its reception.[17] Other figures in this movement, providing an academic foundation, were Vojtěch Raňkův, Matthew of Cracow, and Henry of Bitterfeld.[18]

The academic teaching of these theologians was popularized by the Czech tractates of Tomáš of Štítné, especially *Knížky šestery o obecných věcech křestanských,* which in the section on the Eucharist contains "a fine theological and pastoral apology for frequent communion."[19] A final element needed to permit general introduction of frequent communion was ecclesiastical approbation, which came with an understandable reluctance. After the Prague Synod of 1388 would tolerate at most a monthly communion, the opposition was broken thanks to Archbishop Jenštejn, who attributed his recovery from a deathly illness in 1390 to the reception of the Eucharist. Henceforth, he abandoned his position against frequent communion, and a synod of 1391, under his direction, lifted any restriction on the frequency of lay communion.[20]

Rights of the Individual: Jan Hus

Hus and his Czech colleagues and disciples in the first fifteen years of the fifteenth century brought the cause of the Bohemian Reformation to the brink of its consummation.[21] Their efforts clashed with the standpoint of their foreign colleagues, who accused the Bohemians of Wyclifite heresy until their own departure from the University of Prague in 1409.[22] Hus exemplified to a high degree the first of the two main objectives of the Bohemian Reform movement. His primary concern was with the institutional reform of the Church: stripping away the administrative and magisterial authoritarianism that prohibited constructive discussion. As an advocate of rational discourse and theological openness, he maintained: "From the very beginning of my studies I have made it a principle that whenever I would hear in whatever matter a better opinion, I shall gladly and humbly forsake an earlier view, knowing that what we know is minuscule compared to what we do not know."[23] In a treatise of 1410, he defended the reading of heretical books and opposed their burning as contradictory to sound reason and to the teaching of the church fathers.[24] Even papal pronouncements were subject to examination and should not be obeyed if they were in opposition to the prescriptions of Christ. This conviction led him to condemn Pope John XXIII's declaration of indulgences in support of his war against King Ladislas of Naples in 1412.[25] The core of his liberal ecclesiology, his most conspicuous bequest to the subsequent Bohemian Reformation, was a rejection of the principle that whatever the pope and/or the Curia ordered had to be automatically accepted, even if such order reversed previous positions or practice.[26] Hus applied in religious practice what William of Ockham had taught as an academic theory that "the moral sovereignty of Christians ... could not be alienated by any coercive power."[27] The tenet of resistance to improper authority and to carrying out improper orders foreshadowed modern ideas of political theory and morality, including the respect for human rights.[28] This was his wider legacy to the civilized world.

It has been pointed out that Hus antagonized both wings of the Council of Constance by his reformism. His challenge to the worldliness and opulence of the clerical establishment inspired the majority's hostility, while his zeal for the claims of discussion vis-à-vis authoritarian edicts alienated the minority which, like him, embraced the reform of ecclesiastical morals (in its fourteenth-century context).[29] Moreover, Hus encountered the fathers of the Council in a peculiar psychological bind. First, challenging the power of the papacy with their conciliarism, they felt compelled to counterbalance their daring departure—and the likely appearance of doctrinal impropriety—by the demonstration and reaffirmation of their doctrinal strictness in other respects. Second, with the principle of authority severely shaken by the papal schism, the fathers were tempted to bolster the obedience to ecclesiastical power by an exemplary punishment of Hus for his questioning attitude.[30] According to this view, it was the defensive mentality of Pierre d'Ailly, Jean Gerson, and Francesco Zabarella to which Hus owed to a large extent his martyrdom and subsequent fame, and his judges their damaged reputations.[31] Ironically, the clash at Constance involved two poles of the assertion of rights against the authoritarianism of a monarchic ecclesiology: Gerson and his colleagues stood for the conciliar way, and Hus represented the individual way.[32]

Blinded by the dignity and the protective screen of their high offices, the Council fathers refused to debate the controversial propositions on their merit despite Hus's high intellectual standing. In their subsequent critique of Hus's trial, the humanists of Erasmus's circle indeed viewed the learning of Hus's colleague and his fellow martyr, Jerome of Prague, as of a higher order than that of any of the Council members, inasmuch as none of the latter knew Greek.[33] Martin Luther, whose judgment cannot be entirely discounted, had an even lower opinion of the Council fathers' wisdom, erudition, or moral stature.[34] Instead of rising to the monumental challenge, the Council relegated intellectual honesty—to say nothing of Christian charity—to second place, and resorted to the mindless formalism of legal process.[35] Hus's judges also embraced the outworn superstitious cliché about the obstinacy of heretics, and topped off their performance by briefly metamorphosing into a quasi-Satanist cult to commit the heretic's soul to the devil.[36] In sum, they came to symbolize the qualities that would be subsequently found abhorrent, by both believers and secularists—pharisaic pride, fear of rational discussion, contempt for human rights, and a penchant for inhumane mechanistic legalism.[37] The end result was not setting up the highest moral standards, but a demonstration of how much even an initially beneficent and charitable organization could depart from its intended mission.

Hus was not particularly vocal about the second basic concern of the Bohemian Reform movement, frequent communion, although he instituted the practice at the Bethlehem Chapel in 1403. He was virtually uninvolved in promoting the later communion under both kinds for the laity. Paradoxically, the most prominent son of the Utraquist Church was not himself directly involved in instituting "utraquism" in the narrow sense of the term, although shortly before his death he approved of lay communion *sub utraque* definitely in theory and probably also in practice.[38] Thus, while on the one hand, Hus's stature was greater than that of the Bohemian Church, on the other hand, his emphases were narrower than those of that church. As David R. Holeton points out: "Jan Hus was not a liturgical reformer in the common sense of that term. Liturgical and sacramental questions were of secondary or even tertiary interest to him; for Hus, other matters of ecclesial reform were far more pressing priorities."[39] The devotion and affection of the Czech people were bound up with his charismatic personality and his own manifest attachment to the interests and the language of his compatriots. This bond would be sealed by his martyrdom at Constance.

Radical Interlopers: Waldensians and Other Sectarians

The considerable presence of sectarians, especially German-speaking Waldensians, is evident by the lively inquisitorial activities in Bohemia since 1315 to 1414.[40] Lollard literature had made its appearance in Prague by

1410, and the German theologians who found refuge at the house of Černá růže (Black Rose) a year later, such as Peter and Nicholas of Dresden and Friedrich Eppinge, were said to be influenced by the Waldensians.[41] The Waldensians were joined in Bohemia by other heretics, called Picards, who originated in northern France and in present-day Belgium.[42] The academic background of the Czech reformers from Milíč to Hus, however, militates against the presumption of the influence of various folkish sectarians, such as Waldensians or Picards, on the mainstream of Bohemian Reformism. Thus, Jakoubek of Stříbro early rejected Waldensian doctrines propagated by the Dresdeners.[43] The dichotomy between the academic reformers and the populist sectarians, however, helps to explain the future divergence between mainline Utraquism and radical Taboritism in the Bohemian Reformation after 1419. Thus, while mainline Utraquism remained rooted in the teachings of the academic reformers, including Hus, outside sectarians—who incidentally gained relatively safe access to Bohemia in the last phase of Wenceslaus IV's reign—stimulated Taborite radicalism.[44] Evidently, the Waldensians also influenced Petr Chelčický, who provided a link with the Unity of Brethren.[45] The relationship would be thus perceived by mainline Utraquist theologians in the sixteenth century, especially Bohuslav Bílejovský and Pavel Bydžovský.[46] Regardless of claims by the Taborites, Bohemian Brethren, and Lutherans to be the followers of Hus, it was the mainline Utraquist Church that reflected the moderate and conservative views of Hus and his precursors in the early stages of the Bohemian Reformation.

Inception of Bohemian Reformation and the Taborite Challenge, 1415–1452

Building on the religious reform movement of the late fourteenth century, Bohemia's defiance of Rome was sparked by the execution of Hus by fire at the Council of Constance on July 6, 1415, followed by that of Jerome a year later. Most of the country's inhabitants and its church opposed the condemnation of Hus and Jerome.[47] Just before Hus's death in 1414, the liturgical core of the Bohemian Reformation had been deepened by confirmation of the communion in both kinds, or *sub utraque specie* by the laity and not only priests. Championed by Hus's colleague, Jakoubek, it was a logical extension of the emphasis on the paramount role of frequent communion in Christian life. Henceforth, the appellation of Utraquist would be applied to the Bohemian Church.[48] A second logical extension of the arguments for frequent communion led to the adoption of the Eucharist for small children, including infants in 1417. Endorsed by Jakoubek, Jan of Příbram, and Martin Lupáč, this practice also remained a permanent part of Utraquism.[49] Like the lay communion sub utraque, communion for infants had a long tradition in the Western church that was interrupted in the thirteenth century.[50] This Eucharistic restoration—as David Holeton notes—brought back a condition neglected in the Western Church since the patristic times.[51]

In the meantime, the Bohemian Reformation was capturing adherents among the ecclesiastical organization in Bohemia beginning with the All Souls' Day upheaval (Dušičkový převrat) of November 2, 1415. King Wenceslaus IV attempted to restore churches to the opponents of the Bohemian Reformation, who became known as communicants *sub una,* inasmuch as they continued to maintain lay communion under one kind, or *sub una specie.* The move failed in the winter of 1416–1417.[52] The basic platform of the irrepressible Utraquism, the Four Articles of Prague, was adopted in 1419. The articles defined the desiderata of the Bohemian Reformation: both kinds of communion for the laity, free preaching of the Word of God, freeing the Church from the shackles of material wealth and earthly power, and a role of secular authority in maintaining, although not instituting religious principles, was implied in the grant of power to punish serious sins. The Articles brought together ideas that had been foreshadowed by the Bohemian reform movement since Jan Milíč of Kroměříž.[53]

Also in the winter of 1416–1417, the mainstream of the Utraquist Church, based in Prague and intellectually nourished by the university, encountered the Taborite undercurrent based in the provinces and inspired by folkish sectarians.[54] Destined to gain prominence during the Bohemian religious wars in 1420 to 1431, this latter trend was inclined to question the apostolic, sacramental, and liturgical principles of traditional Western Christianity, and developed a nucleus of some fifteen priests gathered around Pavel of Olešná in 1417.[55] Subsequently, the religious radicals coalesced under the leadership of Mikuláš Biskupec of Pelhřimov (c. 1385–1460). Its tenets were defined in the Twelve Articles in August 1420, showing, among other things, the influence of Waldensian teachings. This document looked forward to an elimination of monasteries, images, precious metals, and church vestments. In a stark biblicism and religious fundamentalism, it opposed secular education and learning, and rejected in particular all Roman and other secular ("German") law as not based on Scripture.[56] Božena Kopičková points out that the Taborite aversion to oath taking and rejection of the belief in purgatory were specific reflections of Waldensian doctrines.[57]

Kaminsky tends to emphasize the influence of the Brethren of Free Spirit, also known as Berghards or Picards, and subsequently as Pikarts. According to Kaminsky, their ideas eventually became dominant among the Taborites.[58] It is possible that the Taborite doctrines, particularly Mikuláš Biskupec's *Confessio Taboritarum,* in turn, influenced the Waldensians of Italy.[59] The Taborite wing, although based largely on the countryside, briefly found allies for its military chiliasm in Prague under the priest Jan Želivský, who was somewhat affected by Waldensian teachings.[60] An attempt to resolve differences occurred at a synod known as Hádání u Zmrzlíků, which convened in Prague in December 1420, where the point of departure for the debate was the use of vestments at mass.[61]

A particularly notorious element in the radical wing of the Bohemian Reformation was a short-lived sect of the Adamites, which was to the left of the Taborites. Engaging in orgiastic practices and claiming to live in the new age of the Spirit, the sect might have been subject to influences from the Netherlands. Pierre d'Ailly had conducted in 1411 an inquisitorial investigation into a Brussels sect, Homines intelligencie, for which spiritual freedom expressed itself in sexual permissiveness.[62] Despite its limited size, marginality, and short duration, the Adamite sect gave the Bohemian Reformation a reputation for sexual licentiousness abroad. A prime mover in this prurient interest was Aeneas Sylvius Piccolomini (later Pope Pius II) in his famous *Historia Bohemica.*[63] The concern with alleged sexual excesses in Bohemia continued into the opening decades of the sixteenth century, expressed by Jacob Ziegler in his *Contra heresim Valdensium* (Leipzig, 1512), and by Thomas More in *Responsio ad Lutherum* (London, 1523).[64]

Mainline Utraquism has been occasionally called the Prague Party,[65] reflecting the fact that during the religious wars of 1420–1434 the towns of Prague stood at the pinnacle of political power and of intellectual influence in the Bohemian Reformation. Prague controlled, and spoke for, most other towns in Bohemia and became the highest estate in the Bohemian Diet.[66] In fact, the city of Prague took over the office of subchamberlain (*podkomoří*), which controlled royal towns and appointed the captains of the town militias (*hejtmané*).[67] Moreover, the original Four Articles of Prague of 1419, the fundamental creed of the Bohemian Reformation, in a version cited by Vavřinec of Březová, were proclaimed as follows: "We the mayor and the councilors and elders, as well as the entire community, of our capital city of the Kingdom of Bohemia, declare in our names and those of all the faithful in this kingdom . . ."[68] Hence, the label of Prague Party does not imply a minimization or trivialization (rather an underscoring) of the stature of mainline Utraquism during the period of the religious wars. In comparison with Prague and other towns of Bohemia, the attachment of the Bohemian nobility to the cause of the Bohemian Reformation was more ambiguous, a fact that helps to account for the massive defection of Bohemian barons and knights from Utraquism to Lutheranism later in the sixteenth century, or from the Four Articles of Prague to the so-called Bohemian Confession.

The reform movement continued to be intellectually guided by the University of Prague and articulated by the early Utraquist synods.[69] This provided a continuity with the earlier phases of the Bohemian Reformation from Hus's precursors on, as well as a bulwark against new radical ideas that had taken root among the Taborites and their equally radical offshoot, the Orebites. During the 1420s, the leading role in mainline Utraquism belonged to Jakoubek. Although the Archbishop of Prague, Konrad of Vechta, joined the Reformation in April 1421, he was restricted—in a precedent-setting arrangement—to the exercise of sacramental functions, while the management of the Church was entrusted to the administrators. After Jakoubek's death in 1429, Křišt'an of Prachatice and Jan of Příbram became the principal defenders of mainstream Utraquism against Taborites' radicalism. Mainline Utraquism manifested a clear continuity with respect to fourteenth-century religious reformism. Above all, Janov's *Regula* deeply influenced Jakoubek, Příbram, Jan Rokycana, and Martin Lupáč.[70]

The era of glory for the Taborite radicals coincided with their participation as the fiercest combatants in the wars of the Bohemian Reformation. The onset of violence dated to 1419 when the external campaigns to suppress the reformation began in earnest. King Sigismund of Hungary, brother and heir-apparent of the childless Bohemian King Wenceslaus, first threatened a complete eradication of all partisans of the Bohemian Reformation on December 4, 1418. After the death of Wenceslaus in August 1419, Sigismund was barred from the country.[71] A crusade of all Christendom against Bohemia was ordered by Pope Martin V in Florence on March 1, 1420. This was the first in a series of such campaigns up to 1431.[72] The Utraquists did not fail to learn from history. As a reminder of what happened during the Albigensian Crusades of 1209–1229, the same spiritual weapons were employed on the papal side, such as indulgences and remission of sins for violence committed by the crusaders.[73]

Their respective attitudes toward warfare helped to underline the difference between the moderation of the mainline Utraquists and the radicalism of the Taborites. In 1419, the leading theologians of Utraquism, Jakoubek and Křišt'an of Prachatice, ruled that defense of the true faith against tyrants was permitted, and even required by divine law, but only for the purposes of defense. For the Taborites, such as Jan Čapek in 1420, war was a creative vehicle of divine purpose. In an approach reminiscent in a sense of nineteenth-century Bakuninist anarchism, the Taborites viewed violent destruction as a means of clearing the way for a new creation.[74] Under the threat of their own damnation, the believers—according to the Taborites—had to kill and eradicate without pity sinners and opponents of the law of God.[75] The Utraquists proscribed, while the Taborites mandated, the clergy's active participation in military combat. The Utraquists found the Taborite stance objectionable, inasmuch as the Taborite warrior-priest represented a curious return to the clergy's wielding secular power, against which the Bohemian reformers, including Hus, had objected so vehemently.[76]

In assessing the harsh conduct of the Bohemians during the wars of the Reformation it must be pointed out that their brilliant victories tended to obscure in retrospect their initial unpromising situation. Their engagements with the crusading armies of Europe were actually conducted from a position of extreme weakness, and the probability of defeat was overwhelming. Their clear status of underdogs may help to put into perspective the later charges of atrocities against the internal (mainly German) communicants sub una that, in fact, recently led to accusations of a holocaust.[77] It could be argued that in view of their highly precarious position, the Bohemians had little choice other than to neutralize those who overtly sympathized with the crusading invaders.[78]

From the time of the religious wars, a messianic impulse also persisted in mainline Utraquism, namely a conviction that God had chosen the Czech people to be his instrument in purifying the Western Church.[79] Aimed at cleansing the historical church of its late medieval corruption, its goal was relatively modest compared to the Taborites' expectation to establish the apocalyptic Kingdom of God on earth. Nevertheless, in its own terms it was ambitious enough. The Utraquists remained convinced that their church preserved, on behalf of all Western Christianity, the true traditional Catholic and apostolic faith against the deviations of the Roman Curia that eventually would come around to the Utraquists' point of view.[80] Figuratively speaking, the Utraquist Church had to make up for the fact that the immune system of the Rome had failed temporarily to repel the corrupting infections of material wealth and earthly power.

Vilém Herold has recently called attention to the philosophical preoccupations of Hus and his entourage as an ingredient in the dynamics of the

Bohemian Reformation in addition to the critique of the contemporary condition of the Church and a call for its reform. Their well-known attachment to metaphysical realism stemmed from the teachings about universals and the ideas of Plato.[81] This metaphysics inspired a penchant for reform by conjuring up "a prototypical world of Ideas (*mundus archetypus*), a world that was luminous, beautiful, harmonious, unchangeable, and eternal, and that stood in contrast with the sensually perceptible world (*mundus sensibilis*) of the ordinary everyday experience." This trend was abhorrent to the nominalistically oriented philosophers and theologians, such as Gerson and Pierre d'Ailly, and the fathers at Constance sensed the explosive potential behind the Bohemian ideal. Gerson had emphatically warned Prague Archbishop Konrád of Vechta against "such a heresy and its authors" already in 1414.[82] Somewhat surprisingly, this Neoplatonic radical realism, derived partly from Wyclif, did not seem to play any significant role in the subsequent intellectual life of the Utraquist Church.

In 1436, the legitimacy of Utraquism was recognized, in a qualified way, on behalf of Rome by the Compactata of the Council of Basel.[83] Among other provisions, the stigma of heresy was lifted from the Utraquists, the lay communion of both kinds declared legitimate, and the issue of infant communion left unresolved. It would be wrong, however, to attribute to the Compactata a formative influence on the character of Utraquism. The Utraquists did not learn anything new from the Council or the Curia via the agreement. The Utraquists' ecclesiology and liturgy had crystallized fully prior to negotiations with the Roman authorities. The Compactata were a spin-off, not the foundation, of Utraquism. The Utraquist Church had existed before the Compactata, and could continue to exist without them, as the eventual course of historical development would show. It is, therefore, incorrect to speak of a "Compactata Utraquism" as a new phenomenon or entity beginning in 1436.

Prior to the Utraquists' accord with the Council of Basel, the Taborite faction was defeated militarily at Lipany on May 30, 1434. Two provisions, however, were made to fortify the basic character of Utraquism: the theological openness to rational argument, and repudiation of the administrative and juridical jurisdiction of the Roman Curia. These two principles became the cornerstones of Utraquism's liberal ecclesiology. First, the curb on Rome's magisterial authority was put on the record. The Utraquists reaffirmed their commitment to the authority of the Bible interpreted by rational argument before participating in the Council. Their attendance became contingent on the observance of the Judge of Cheb stipulating that the Bible and opinions in conformity with Scripture would govern the theological discussions.[84] Second, the dismantling of Rome's administrative authority was put on the record. Emperor/King Sigismund issued an imperial charter of ecclesiastical liberties, dated January 6, 1436, reaffirming a virtual jurisdictional independence of the Utraquist Church in Bohemia and Moravia from the Roman See. The document excluded nonresidents from appointments to ecclesiastical offices and dignities, and more importantly, reserved the right of making appointments to such posts to the Bohemian king and local inhabitants. The decree not only denied the papacy and the Curia the right to sell or donate ecclesiastical vacancies, but also exempted the inhabitants of Bohemia and Moravia from the jurisdiction of ecclesiastical courts located abroad.[85] This last provision renewed, in part, a decree by Wenceslaus IV of June 9, 1418, that protected inhabitants of Bohemia from summonses to ecclesiastical tribunals abroad.[86] This legislation foreshadowed the separation of the Church of England from the See of Rome, although it was not so drastic, as it recognized Rome's power to confirm appointments of episcopal rank.[87]

In addition, Sigismund authorized the Diet of Bohemia, with participation of the clergy's representatives, to elect the archbishop of Prague and two suffragan bishops. It was on this basis that Sigismund recognized the election of Rokycana as archbishop and of two other bishops in October 1435. Without a papal or conciliar confirmation, which were never granted, the electees could exercise only administrative, not sacerdotal, functions.[88] Subsequently, the Utraquists had to depend for ordination of their clergy on bishops outside Bohemia, except that three Roman bishops from the West did become temporary residents in Bohemia and served the Utraquists over the next seventy years: from 1435 to 1439, Philibbert, bishop of Coutances and apostolic administrator of the see of Prague (one of the conciliar legates in Bohemia); from 1482 to 1493, Augustine Sancturien, bishop of Mirandola (near Modena); and from 1504 to 1507, Philip of Novavilla, bishop of Sidon (but auxiliary of Modena).[89]

By the mid-fifteenth century, the second (unconsecrated and last) Utraquist archbishop, Rokycana, elected as noted in 1435, and a governing consistory, probably in existence since 1431, had confirmed and stabilized the Bohemian ecclesiastical body in a particular doctrinal orientation that was distinctly conservative.[90] The Utraquists retained the traditional Christian liturgical and sacramental teaching, including the seven sacraments, and upheld the historical principle of apostolic succession for the valid ordination of clergy.[91] Thus, the Utraquists maintained their theological centrism.

On the right, they rejected the papal authority in administrative and judicial matters, although a small, but juridically distinct and influential minority of adherents to the Roman Curia continued to exist in a separate organization under a consistory of their own. Communicating sub una, this faction received—like the Utraquists—legitimacy and protection under the Compactata. On the left, the Utraquists ratified the earlier rejection of the Taborite faction. The Taborites, having been defeated militarily at Lipany in 1434, were suppressed after the conquest of their stronghold of Tábor by King George of Poděbrady in 1452.[92]

This centrism or *via media* was also maintained in the Church's attitude toward the images and veneration of saints. Concerning church decorations and religious art, Utraquism gravitated toward a relative austerity under Jakoubek, although the Taborites' outright iconoclasm was rejected. During the negotiation for the Compactata and during Sigismund's reign in the late 1430s, the legates of the Council of Basel expressed their concern about the scarcity of crucifixes, images, and saints' relics in Bohemia's churches. Rokycana freely admitted paintings and statues on altars of Prague churches in 1436, and under his leadership, by the 1450s a middle way was found between barren altars and walls and flamboyantly adorned sanctuaries.[93] The same avoidance of extremes applied to the veneration of saints. On the one hand, Jan of Příbram sought to justify the practice in the 1430s, citing authorities such as Origines, Pseudodionysius, Augustine, Jerome, and Aquinas.[94] At the Synod of Kutná Hora in 1441, the Utraquist Church had reaffirmed the veneration of saints against the denunciations of Taborite theologians, especially Mikuláš of Pelhřimov.[95] On the other hand, the Utraquists—in a tradition going back to Janov in the late fourteenth century[96]— had called for moderation in the veneration of the saints, and had adopted a particularly reserved attitude toward the saints' relics, which Rokycana counseled to be discreetly locked away rather than publicly exhibited.[97]

The Utraquist attitude toward two types of institutions, traditionally linked with the ecclesiastical establishment, the university and the monasteries, offered a spectacle of sharp contrasts. The university naturally continued to be highly favored as the fountainhead of Reformist thought, while the monasteries as strongholds of the sub una fell into a state near abomination. The University of Prague still played a crucial role in the consolidation of the Bohemian Reform movement. Mainline Utraquism owed its judicious approach to religious doctrines, nurtured in the tradition of scholastic disputation, to the university's leadership. From among the university's faculty members emerged most of the theologians who spoke for the Utraquist

Church. Following the adoption of the Compactata, local adherents of the Roman Curia returned, and even foreigners, largely from the adjacent areas of the Holy Roman Empire, including a contingent of students and teachers from the University of Vienna in 1443.

In contrast to its benign relationship with the university, the Bohemian Reformation entertained an early aversion toward the monasteries, which even Hus's precursor Janov had wished to see dissolved.[98] This distaste, partly influenced by Wyclif's animadversions, was further reinforced by the regular clergy's hostility during the Reformation's struggle for survival.[99] Despite their general antimonasticism, the Utraquists did initially acquire, more or less by accident, a major Prague convent, the Emmaus Monastery (Na Slovanech), when Abbot Paul joined their ranks in 1419.[100] In what may be viewed as a highly incongruous situation, the monastery sheltered an archenemy of religious orders, the English Wyclifite Peter Payne, who would act as a mediator between the Utraquists and the Taborites in the 1420s and 1430s.[101] In 1446 the Utraquist administrator Jan of Příbram, who played the role of a surrogate abbot, inducted into the monastery five new monks. Subsequently, the Utraquists perpetuated and consolidated their aversion toward monasticism enshrined in the dictum that it was "more fitting to obey God than the monastic rules."[102] After the Compactata, the remaining monasteries, often—as in Prague—the only places of worship for the sub una continued to be viewed as foci of hostility and treason by the Utraquist populace.

The insecure remnant of those adhering to communion sub una and fully obedient to the Roman Curia likewise came under royal protection after 1436. Their precarious ecclesiastical government, consisting also of a consistory and an administrator, functioned in exile in the town of Zittau (Žitava) of Upper Lusatia during the wars of the Bohemian Reformation. As noted later, they withdrew from Prague again later in the century, until the conclusion of a modus vivendi in 1485 with the Utraquists in Kutná Hora. In an interesting parallel to the Utraquists, the communicants sub una in Bohemia were also served by itinerant bishops, of whom at least one, Jan Wilde, bishop of Pomerania, apparently resided in the country for an extended period of time (between 1498 and 1505).[103]

The Role of the Jews

In assessing external influences on Bohemian Utraquism, the effect of the Waldensians (albeit mainly on the Taborites) has been discussed. Judaism also exercised a marginal influence. Its effect has been seen again primarily among the Taborites and via the Waldensian input.[104] With respect to mainline Utraquism, the suggestions of kinship focused mainly on the image of a small nation facing a powerful external threat, largely embodied in a menacing empire.[105] Nevertheless, the Utraquists were accused by their opponents in the 1420s of treating the Jews with more consideration than they had displayed toward the supporters of the Roman Curia.[106]

Bohemia, and especially its capital of Prague, had the reputation of a flourishing center of Jewish cultural life during the sixteenth century. By 1512, Prague had become the first city north of the Alps where Hebrew books were printed. This cultural flowering was based on a tradition of Jewish presence in the country for probably more than half a millenium.[107] The Jews had played a generally constructive role in the economic development of the country since the High Middle Ages. More specifically, during the wars of the Bohemian Reformation, Jews tended to sympathize with the Czech reformers. Salo W. Baron, in particular, has speculated that a predisposition in that sense was traceable to Judaizing elements in the outlook of Wyclif, who clearly affected the intellectual outlook of Hus and his colleagues.[108] Ruth Kestenberg-Gladstein further points out that Hus's precursors, in particular Janov, lifted some of the animus against the Jews by disassociating them from the image of the Antichrist, into which the conventional medieval theology had encapsulated them.[109]

After the outbreak of the Bohemian religious wars, the Jews felt a measure of kinship with the Czechs, particularly the radical Taborites, for their attachment to Old Testament sources and as fighters in a just national war. There is also evidence that among the Jews of Bohemia the struggles connected with the Reformation inspired an eschatological vision that foresaw an impending conversion of the Bohemians in conjunction with the arrival of the Messiah. Such ideas were suggested by Avigdor Kara (1382–1439), a rabbi in Prague, in a Hebrew poem, beginning with the words "One, alone, unique is God," which may have been sung to the same tune as the Taborites' battle hymn, "Ye who are God's warriors." The apocalyptic expectations were apparently in part supported by the Taborites' iconoclasm and attacks on the clergy and monasteries sub una.[110] The Prague Jews were, in fact, credited with concrete acts of assistance to the Bohemian cause. Thus, in the spring of 1420 they participated in fortifying the city against the forces of the first crusade designed to stamp out the Bohemian Reformation.[111] A Jewish literary source attributed to special divine favor the defeat of the second crusade at the town of Žatec in October 1421.[112] In their turn, the (largely German) crusaders attacked the Jews, even before reaching Bohemian territory. The Dominican preachers of the crusades likewise tended to associate the Czech religious insurgents with the Jews.[113] For their part, Jews in Vienna were subjected to persecution, and all of them were expelled from Austria in 1421 for alleged collaboration with the Bohemians. The Jews of Bavaria faced similar accusations.[114] In contrast, the authorities in Utraquist Prague permitted the Jews to stay in 1420–1421, while the adherents of communion sub una were expelled.[115] Hence, the thrust of the Czechs' animosity was aimed at the supporters of the Roman Curia, while the Jews were protected during the early stages of the Bohemian religious wars.[116]

Along the same lines, the fathers of the Council of Constance had pronounced the following bizarre invective during the defrocking of Hus prior to his execution in 1415: "O, cursed Judas, because you have abandoned the counsels of peace, and have counseled with the Jews, we take away from you the cup of redemption."[117] Hus drew a parallel between the situation of the Jews under the Persian Empire and the Czechs under the Holy Roman Empire, with each nation defending its own language against alien encroachments.[118] To be sure, there had been isolated cases of violence against the Jews in Bohemia, and Ruth Kestenberg-Gladstein attributes the most scandalous one, the pogrom in Prague of 1389, to the clerical opponents of the Bohemian Reformation.[119] Until 1500, however—in any case during the thirteenth through the fifteenth century—Bohemia was free of wholesale anti-Jewish persecution, such as the summary evictions that had occurred in Western Europe and the neighboring German lands.[120]

As noted above, the influences of Judaism were, on the whole, marginal. Much more significant were influences from England, and the issue of contacts with Eastern Orthodoxy.

Influences from England

In seeking to place the Czech ecclesiastical body within the religious currents of Europe, a strong case can be made for comparing the Utraquist Church with the Church of England shaped by Elizabethan settlement, especially in their relative confessional and liturgical orthodoxy combined with nationalist tendencies in jurisdictional and language matters, as well as an aversion to heavy-handed papal directives. Aside from formal similarities, there were in fact concrete historical links between Czech and English religious thought, particularly on the issue of papal authority. Above all, the writings of Wyclif—superimposed (often awkwardly) on indigenous Bohemian ideas of religious reform—had an undeniable influence on Hus and his colleagues in the area of ecclesiastical governance (and much less, if any, on their Eucharistic concepts).[121] Even in the assessment of Wyclif, the positions of mainstream Utraquism seem to have paralleled those of the English Reformation. As Anthony Kenny notes: "In the latter part of Henry [VIII]'s reign Wyclif's anti-papalism was congenial to those in power, but his Eucharistic doctrine remained anathema.... On the same day as Edward Powell was hanged for protesting against the king's rejection of Papal authority, the Lutheran Dr Barnes was burnt for denying transubstantiation."[122] Wyclif's influence evidently also strengthened the Bohemian reformers' opposition to monasticism and ecclesiastical landholdings, as it had apparently done in England during the Peasant Rebellion of 1381.[123]

While the University of Paris had likewise played a role in shaping the ideas of the early Bohemian reformers,[124] there were special reasons for the development of the intellectual links between Bohemia and England, and primarily between the university of Oxford and that of Prague, the oldest in Central Europe, established in 1348. The outbreak of the Great Schism in 1378 diverted Czech students from Paris, obedient to the Avignonese popes, to England, which maintained loyalty to the popes in Rome, as did Wenceslaus IV, the king of Bohemia and the Holy Roman Emperor. Contacts increased with the preparations for marriage in 1382 between the English king Richard II and Anne, Wenceslaus IV's sister. A scholarship for Czech students was established at Oxford in 1388.[125] The way to Wyclif's theological influence was paved by the eager acceptance of his philosophical ultrarealism brought by students returning from England into the Czech university circles by about 1390. The appeal of Wyclif's philosophy—unlike his theology, not yet condemned at Oxford—was enhanced by the prior dissemination of moderate Thomistic realism by the Dominican college, which had fortuitously moved to Prague from Paris in 1383. Above all, the Czech professors found in Wyclif's realism an intellectually intoxicating alternative to the seemingly pedestrian nominalism of the *via moderna* embraced by most of their German university colleagues.[126]

The later reception of Wyclif's theological views, dating to the beginning of the fifteenth century, largely coincided with the return of Jerome from Oxford in 1401. The available stock of Wyclif's theological writings substantially increased thanks to the labors of two Czech scholars who spent the year 1406–1407 at Oxford, and were apparently in contact with English

Lollards. On the one hand, as noted earlier, the traditional ideas of the Czech religious movement made the reformers receptive to some aspects of Wyclif's theology, particularly the stern moralism applied to the clergy, a stress on preaching and the study of Scripture, and bringing the Christian message directly to the faithful in the vernacular. On the other hand, a marked devotion to the Eucharist with an emphasis on frequent communion imposed a definite limit on the Bohemian reformers' susceptibility to Wyclifism.[127] Wyclif's influence was combined and intertwined with that of the domestic reformers, above all, Janov.[128]

Having read Wyclif's philosophical works earlier, Hus began to study the English reformer's theological writings by 1408. As Oakley notes: "In the next half-dozen years, by his borrowings from those works, his propensity for expressing some of his own views in Wyclifite language, and his willingness even to defend in public some of the condemned Wyclifite propositions, he set his feet on the path that led to his condemnation by the Council of Constance in 1415 and his subsequent burning as a heretic."[129] A prime example of Hus's use of Wyclif's term with his own (actually opposite) meaning was his speaking of the Church as "community of the predestined" (*universitas praedestinatorum*), while his actual understanding of the Church coincided with the orthodox "community of the faithful" (*congregatio fidelium*).[130] Similarly, he spoke in a Wyclifite manner of the body of Christ (after consecration) as bread, while adhering firmly to the doctrine of transubstantiation.[131] In addition to the Eucharistic tenet of remanence (i.e., persistence of bread and wine after consecration), Hus eschewed Wyclif's other innovative doctrines that anticipated the Protestant stance, such as the rejection of episcopal rank, placing the laity on an equal footing with priests in the exercise of ministry, and rejection of the auricular confession and priestly absolution in penance. On the highly visible matter of indulgences, Hus questioned only their specific misuse by Pope John XXIII (XXII) in support of his war on King Ladislas in 1412, not their ultimate basis like Wyclif, who denied the very existence of a reservoir of excess merit in the Church at the disposal of the pope to distribute.[132]

Thus, at its core Hus's relationship to Wyclif was not particularly complex or enigmatic. He felt a deep kinship, even affection, for Wyclif as long as the evangelical doctor stayed within the orthodox fourteenth-century agenda of seeking to purify the Church. He did not follow the path that crossed the line to proto-Protestantism when the Englishman embraced an agenda that anticipated Luther and Calvin. In his cautious approach to Wyclif's theology, Hus was influenced by his favorite teacher at the University of Prague, Štepán of Kolín, whom he calls "the most fervent zealot for his homeland."[133] Among his English contacts, Hus is also known to have corresponded in 1410–1411 with two of Wyclif's disciples: Sir John Oldcastle and Richard Wyche. To the latter, he wrote: "I am thankful that Bohemia has under the power of Jesus Christ received so much good . . . from the blessed land of England."[134] Displaying his knowledge of English ecclesiastical history in his famous appeal of 1412 from the pope's judgment to that of Christ, Hus cited as a precedent Robert Grosseteste's defiance of Innocent IV in 1253 in refusing to appoint the pope's nephew to a lucrative English benefice.[135] As indicated by surviving copies of Grosseteste's works in Prague from the early fifteenth century, Czech scholars showed a significant interest in his teachings during the Bohemian Reformation.[136]

Later, Lollard influence on the Bohemian Reformation was manifest in Peter Payne's contributions to Taborite theology that—in contrast to mainstream Utraquism—was closer to Wyclif than Hus.[137] Exchange of ideas between Lollards and Bohemian reformers is likewise documented by surviving copies from fifteenth-century Bohemia of writings by English Lollards that are not currently found in England, with the manner of their transmission from Oxford to Prague remaining rather enigmatic. Incidentally, of Wyclif's two hundred known writings about one half have survived only in Bohemian copies, including a number of his most important texts. By 1415, about 170 of Wyclif's works were known in Bohemia.[138] Another major piece of evidence of contact with the Lollards is the martyrdom of a Utraquist emissary to them, Pavel Kravař, in Scotland in 1433.[139] In addition, high-level contact between the Utraquists and the Eastern Orthodox leadership was mediated at Constantinople in 1452 by a priest named Constantine Anglikos, who was probably English.[140] The Lollards had more in common with the Taborites and other radicals of the Bohemian Reformation than with mainstream Utraquism.[141]

As for the English side, John Foxe would return, in the sixteenth century, Hus's compliment to England by assigning him a stellar role in his *Actes and monuments*.[142] Aeneas Sylvius Piccolomini (Pope Pius II), writing in his *Historia Bohemica* about the confiscation of ecclesiastical estates during the Bohemian Reformation, apparently was thought to have inspired— by his reference to Bohemia's example—similar proceedings in England under Henry VIII.[143] The story of Anglo-Bohemian relations, however, would be incomplete without pointing out that there were also Englishmen on the other side of the fence. In 1411, Hus himself challenged to a debate John Stokes of Cambridge University, an opponent of Wyclif, and a member of the English embassy returning from Hungary through Prague. Later, as an English envoy, Stokes would oppose Hus at the Council of Constance, and in 1422 he would urge the estates of the Holy Roman Empire to suppress the Bohemian Reformation.[144] Most notably, Cardinal Henry of Beaufort (mis)managed the fourth crusade of the Bohemian religious wars in 1427.[145] At Basel, the English delegation attempted to arrest Payne, who participated in the Bohemian delegation defending the Four Articles of Prague before the Council.[146] Later on, I note the efforts of Edmund Campion, S.J. to do his best in Brno and Prague (c. 1573–1579) to shepherd the straying Czechs back into the bishop of Rome's fold. In sum, on historical maps depicting the religious divisions of Europe, Utraquist Bohemia would deserve a color similar to, if not identical with, sixteenth- and early seventeenth-century England, demarcating it clearly from its Lutheran neighbors to the north.

Contacts with Eastern Orthodoxy

As already indicated, the Utraquist Church had also maintained certain contacts with the Eastern Orthodox Church. Russian historians of the Slavophile school tended to exaggerate these connections and misinterpret them, viewing the Bohemian Reformation as a manifestation of the Slav/Orthodox spirit, while the Bohemian religious wars were perceived as a clash between the irreconcilable cultures of Slav Orthodoxy and Western Catholicism.[147] In fact, the Utraquists' desire for relations with the Eastern Orthodox Church did not stem from a sense of Slavic cultural heritage, but from a need to find support and justification in a kindred religious body that maintained the principle of apostolic succession and traditional sacraments, while being at odds with the papacy. It is possible that the initial impetus for contacts with the Orthodox Church came from the writings of Wyclif, who had displayed a friendly interest in Eastern Christendom. Subsequently, the Church of England would also try to reach out to the Orthodox Church as a kindred institution.[148] Some historians have speculated that it was particularly Wyclif's reference to the Orthodox practice of communion of both kinds for the laity that sparked the interest of the early Bohemian reformers in seeking support in the East for their Eucharistic views.[149] Of course, they needed neither Wyclif nor the Orthodox to convince them of the necessity of communion sub utraque, inasmuch as that decision had earlier domestic origins, probably going back to Janov in the late fourteenth century.[150] Nevertheless, in 1413 Jakoubek dispatched the zealous Jerome to visit the Orthodox churches of Poland, Lithuania, Belarus, and Russia, and to study their rules and rituals.[151]

Attitudes toward the Eastern Church were also defined as early as 1421 by the leading Utraquist theologian Příbram. The latter praised the Greek Church as an immediate product of the teaching of the original apostles, while the Church of Rome, in contrast, received the Christian message only at second hand through the mediation of its twin sister in the east. The teachings of the Greek Church enjoyed a special claim to respectful attention, yet its authority was not unique since other churches of Asia (especially in Armenia and India) could also trace their origins to the immediate initiatives of the apostles.[152] This limited ecumenicism was likewise in line with Hus's own skepticism about the absolute uniqueness of the Roman Church. His thinking specifically on the Eastern Orthodox evolved from regarding them as "heretics" in 1404 to seeing them in 1413 as a living proof that a reasonably orthodox form of Christianity could function outside papal jurisdiction.[153] Hus's thinking also reflected a genuine respect for the achievements for the Greek fathers of the Church, overshadowing that of the Latin ones, in developing the Christian theological corpus. This contribution continued to be recognized by the future generation of Utraquist theologians, such as Pavel Bydžovský, in the sixteenth century.

Accordingly, the Utraquists at Basel in 1432 had urged that the Greek Orthodox be invited to participate in the sessions of the council. Moreover, at mid-century, the Utraquist Church had sought a formal rapprochement with the East. An anti-Uniate Orthodox synod under Gregorios Scholarios (Gennadius) at Constantinople in 1452 was inclined to recognize the proximity of Hus's ideas to Orthodoxy, as well as to recant the earlier condemnations of Utraquism. The fall of Constantinople to the Turks inhibited further negotiations.[154] Among other contacts with the eastern Churches, the resort to Orthodox bishops in Poland or Moldavia for ordination of clergy evidently stemmed from the Unity of Brethren.[155] On the whole, the Utraquists' contacts with Eastern Orthodoxy were rather sporadic and slight and, as discussed later, the Utraquists did not claim a direct spiritual or historical bond with the Byzantine Church.

Maturity and the Brethren's Challenge, 1452–1517

The Utraquist ruler of Bohemia, George of Poděbrady, first as governor (*zemský správce*) since 1452 and then as king (1458–1471) protected the mature Utraquist Church and helped it to weather the abrogation of the Compactata (on questionable grounds) by Pope Pius II in 1462. Pius II's act left formal relations between Rome and the Utraquists in an unsettled state for a century and a half.[156] King George, in turn, suffered excommunication by Pope Paul II for heresy in 1466, and had to face for the rest of his reign papal-sponsored crusades implemented by Hungarian King Matthias Corvinus.

On theological grounds, the Utraquists reacted calmly to the pope's revocation of the Compactata. Their response, written by Martin Lupáč, argued that the abrogation was a loss for Rome, not for Utraquism. The Utraquist church still maintained the correct religious view, while Rome deprived itself of the cleansing benefit that it might have derived from the Four Articles of Prague. Although recognizing the papacy as a guarantor of the apostolic succession for their priesthood, the Utraquists consistently rejected papal administrative or judicial authority. On the separate issue of papal teaching authority, their position was that—in cases of conflict—the Scripture or the law of God stood above the pope's edicts.[157] The Utraquist Church, despite the revocation of the Compactata, continued to maintain its sense of belonging to the universal or catholic (*obecná*) Church, emphasizing the lawfulness of this tie, as well as persisting in its distinct ecclesiology and critical stance toward the papacy. Such was the attitude of Administrator Václav Koranda, Junior, Rokycana's successor in the leadership of Utraquism (1471–1497).[158]

A relatively small but devout and zealous sect, the Unity of Brethren, also known as the Bohemian or Moravian Brethren, separated in 1457 from the Utraquist Church. The Brethren revived in some respects the theological radicalism of the Taborites. In fact, they would openly claim an affinity to Tábor, for example, in the *Trialog* (1524) of Brother Lukáš.[159] The Brethren also maintained contact with Waldensians.[160] The Utraquists, above all Rokycana and Koranda, conducted theological polemics against the Brethren, particularly their failures to recognize canonical priesthood and to affirm explicitly the real presence in the Eucharist.[161] In 1495, the Unity temporarily split due to the secession of the conservative and rigorous Minority Party.[162] The Unity of Brethren would remain separate from, and opposed to, its parent body throughout the sixteenth and into the seventeenth century.[163]

Under George of Poděbrady, the Utraquist Church consolidated its control of the University of Prague. The assumption of government by George in 1448 discouraged attendance by students from the Holy Roman Empire.

The advocates of Taborite and kindred ideas, such as Mikuláš of Hořepník, left the university in the early 1460s. A provision was introduced in March 1462 that all degree candidates at the time of their examinations had to profess belief in the necessity of lay communion sub utraque. This requirement effectively excluded further attendance by communicants sub una.[164] Inasmuch as the university then lacked a theological faculty, candidates for Utraquist priesthood were tutored by theologians who also served as pastors of churches in Prague.[165]

After the death of King George in 1471, Vladislav II was elected to the throne of Bohemia. The new king stemmed from the Jagellon dynasty of Poland and was a communicant sub una. An oath to uphold the Compactata which, like his successors, he was required to swear after his election, helped to alleviate concerns in the Utraquist ranks about a possible increase in the influence of Rome in Bohemian affairs.[166] The Bohemian Diet in August 1478 renewed the Consistory in the customary manner, and in addition elected three deputies of the estates to watch over the interests of the Church.[167] At about this time, the structure of the Utraquist Church was strengthened through the creation of deaneries in each circuit (*kraj*). The deans would convoke synods of clergy to tighten discipline and guard against encroachments by the Roman Church and the spread of radical dissenters, especially the Brethren. Under Rokycana, the seat of the Consistory alternated between the parish house of the Church of Our Lady Before the Týn, and the city hall of the Old Town of Prague. Under his successor, Administrator Koranda, the locus shifted more to the Bethlehem Chapel.[168] Koranda's successors were Jakub of Stříbro (1497–1499), Pavel of Žatec (1500–1517), and Matěj Korambus (1517–1520).[169]

For their worship, the Utraquists remained attached to the liturgical books of the archdiocese of Prague, as they had been consolidated in the fourteenth century. The importance attached to these pre-Tridentine liturgical tomes is attested by their appearance already among the Bohemian incunabula, including the statutes of Archbishop Arnošt of Pardubice (1476), the Prague missal (1479) and the agenda of the Church of Prague (c. 1479).[170] Although these volumes might have been printed in Plzeň und thus presumably under the auspices of the Roman Church (which prevailed there), this fact per se need not have interfered with their use by the Utraquists. The same was true about their designation for use by the archdiocese of Prague, inasmuch as the Utraquist ecclesiastical establishment was viewed as a direct continuation of the Prague metropolitan see.[171] The few preserved liturgical texts, translated into Czech and hence clearly Utraquist, did not differ from the

Prague ritual of the Roman rite.[172] The printing of a Czech adaptation of Iacopo da Varagine's *Aurea legenda sanctorum seu Historia Lombardica seu Passionale sanctrum* as *Passional všech svatých* (Prague, 1495) testified to the Utraquists' attachment to the veneration of saints. This publication substituted traditional Bohemian saints for those less well known in Bohemia, and appended an exaltation of Hus and Jerome to signify their inclusion within the heavenly host.[173]

The small minority of adherents to the Roman Curia, or those sub una, continued to be served in Bohemia by an administrator and a consistory, normally resident at the Cathedral of Prague. For an extended period, however, after the excommunication of King George by the pope in 1466 and until the peace between King Vladislav II and Matthias Corvinus in 1478, the religious establishment of the sub una sought refuge in the West Bohemian town of Plzeň which, together with České Budějovice, remained strongholds of Rome's loyalists.[174] In a remarkable step for this historical era, a durable peaceful solution was found when the noble adherents to Utraquism and to the communion sub una, assembled in a Diet at Kutná Hora in 1485, granted each other legal recognition and respect for the free exercise of their respective religious practices. This unique act of tolerance, originally valid for thirty-one years, was extended indefinitely by the Bohemian Diet in 1512.[175] The outstanding feature of the peace of Kutná Hora in contrast to other religious settlements, in particular the later Peace of Augsburg of 1555, was its protection of religious freedom not just for territorial princes or manorial lords, but also for seigneurial subjects. This practice was in harmony with earlier documents of the Bohemian Reformation, especially the Compactata.[176] The Bohemian Brethren did not share in this settlement, but they remained undisturbed until the St. James Day Mandate, which threatened them with suppression and was enacted by the Bohemian Diet in 1508. The enforcement of this edict, however, remained lax, and was virtually suspended during the reign of King Louis (1515–1526), successor of Vladislav II.[177]

A Living and Vibrant Church

In summing up the genesis of Utraquism, it should be noted that there was not a straight line of progress from Jan Hus to Taboritism, followed by degeneration into mainline Utraquism, as has often been claimed. Rather, during the religious wars, extrinsic radical elements attached themselves to, and coexisted with, the reform movement stemming from Hus and the masters of the University of Prague, that is, with mainline Utraquism. The radical militants fell away, partly through exhaustion and an ideological flameout, after having performed a helpful, possibly indispensable, role in preventing a victory by the imperial and papal crusaders.[178] This permitted mainline Utraquism to reassert itself and to continue the tradition of Hus and Hus's academic precursors and associates. This was not a degeneration, but essentially a reaffirmation of Utraquism's original image and its roots in the fourteenth-century Bohemian Reformation.[179] The doused flames of the essentially extrinsic (Waldensian and Picard) radical trend or Taboritism would, however, partly rekindle in the Unity of Brethren by 1457. With King George's ascent to power and under Rokycana's guidance, the theological self-definition of mainline Utraquism was essentially completed. As I discuss in subsequent chapters, another phase of theological creativity would follow in the 1530s and 1540s when Bohuslav Bílejovský and Pavel Bydžovský would respond on behalf of Utraquism to the challenge of the German Reformation, particularly Lutheranism. Their reaffirmations of Hus's legacy would inform the Utraquists' stand vis-à-vis the two subsequent challenges, namely the Bohemian Confession of 1575 and the Letter of Majesty of 1609.

As for the future, the condition of the Utraquist Church, as it stood at the turn of the fifteenth century, has been also subjected to much critical questioning. It has been berated for its excessive dependence on the monarch, to the extent of being a passive tool in the hands of the royal government, particularly to combat religious radicalism.[180] Its attachment to the idea of belonging to a universal or catholic church has been viewed as a naive or even perverse reluctance to part with Rome.[181] Perhaps, most harshly, the Utraquist church has been described as an atrophied community no longer possessed of moral or creative vitality.[182] The story of the next hundred years presented in this book provides answers to such critical queries. While the monarch needed to replace some of the abrogated papal administrative authority, most of it devolved to the Utraquist Consistory, which exercised it independently of the royal government. The Utraquist Consistory continued to uphold the ideal of liberal ecclesiology, highlighted by Hus's sacrifice, and its stance vis-à-vis the Roman Curia was one of salutary critique not one of abject sycophancy. The church's energy and vitality would be displayed not only in its challenge to the Curia, but also in responding to the Lutheran

Reformation, which would join the Unity of Brethren as a challenger on the left. Most important, however, the Utraquists' living contribution would be reflected in their fostering of the tolerance and intellectual liberalism of the *via media*.

3

Utraquism's Curious Encounter with Luther

After the opening of the Reformation era in 1517, following almost a century of institutional existence under an administrator and a governing Consistory, the Utraquist Church of Bohemia found itself at a crossroad. On the one hand, the choice was to reaffirm its late medieval reformist tradition that preserved the traditional liturgy (including the seven sacraments), a belief in the sacramental episcopate and priesthood in a historic apostolic succession, and the belief in a soteriological efficaciousness of good works. On the other hand, the choice was to embrace the German Lutheran Reformation, which rejected all of the above.

The traditional view in Czech historiography has been that the appeal of the Protestant Reformation proved virtually irresistible for the Utraquist Church from the very beginning. In this context, the events around the convocation of January/February 1524, producing the so-called Candlemas Day Articles, are viewed as a near-transformation of Utraquism into Lutheranism. For instance, Josef Čihula has written that following the emergence of Luther "the more ardent of the Utraquists turned to Wittenberg."[1] As noted earlier, Ferdinand Hrejsa echoed this statement fifteen years later: "The more progressive among the Utraquists . . . seeing in the Bohemian Church nothing but moral and intellectual stagnation . . . acquired new strength from Wittenberg. . . . They became more decisive, seeking to realize their principles in the direction of separation from the Catholic Church . . ."[2] Eduard Winter wrote in 1938: "No country was as prepared to adopt Luther's teaching, as exactly Bohemia." He further asserted that since the mid–1520s the Utraquist Church was split into an "Evangelical" and a "Catholic" branch looking respectively toward Luther and the Roman Church.[3] Similar views have been put forth to the present. A prestigious history of Prague, published in 1997, claims that in 1523–1524 the city was dominated not just by Lutheranism, but an outright "radical" Lutheranism.[4]

My objective in this chapter is to test the proposition with respect to the initial contacts between the Bohemian and the German reformations in the 1520s. I argue that when Hrejsa or others spoke of revitalizing Utraquism after the emergence of the Lutheran Reformation in the sixteenth century, the wrong direction is attributed to this process of instauration. The Utraquists' renewal and revitalization came not from accepting Luther, but from redefining themselves in contrast to the Protestant Reformation. Reacting to its encounter with Luther, Utraquism did not sever, but reaffirmed its roots in the Bohemian reform movement. Later this rededication would be codified in the writings of Bohuslav Bílejovský and Pavel Bydžovský in the 1530s and 1540s. This chapter explores the following topics: the reasons for the Utraquists' welcome of Luther's revolt against Rome, the reasons militating against the Utraquists' adoption of Luther's doctrinal reforms, the nature of the religious Articles of February 1524, and the evidence of Utraquism's strength and integrity after 1524.

The Attractive Luther, 1517–1523

The initial impact of Luther's emergence on Bohemia is examined from four points of view: (1) its relevance to the anti-papal feelings; (2) its breaking of the circle of national isolation; (3) an assurance of the righteousness of Bohemian Reformation; and (4) Luther's seeming endorsement of Hus. Luther attracted attention in Bohemia beginning with his qualified defense of Hus in the Leipzig disputation of 1519, reported almost immediately to Bohemia, by Hieronymus Emser, among others.[5] The knowledge of Luther's teaching spread in Hus's homeland, first of all, through translation of several of his works.[6] The first of these, *O velebné svátosti svatého pravého těla Kristova* (*Ein Sermon von dem hochwürdigen Sacrament des heiligen waren Leichnams Christi*) appeared in 1520, published and probably translated by the Humanist Oldřich Velenský of Mnichov.[7] Another early translation, which appeared also in 1520, was the lengthy *Kázání . . . na desatero přikázání Božích* (*Decem praecepta Wittenbergensi praedicata populo*), and consisted of Luther's sermons delivered in 1516 and 1517. The translator, Utraquist Pavel Příbram, professor of mathematics and astronomy at Charles University, died before the publication. Another unknown Utraquist supplied the introduction.[8] Luther's teaching became known in Bohemia also because students from Prague traveled to Saxony to find out more about the new lore, especially in Wittenberg. Humanist Burián Sobek of Kornice, who became an important official in the city administration of Prague, studied at Wittenberg, received there a *doctor iuris* degree, and actually met Luther.[9] He is the probable translator of five of Luther's works, published in 1520 to 1523, including the Czech rendition of *De Libertate Christiana,* printed in 1521.[10] Among the visitors to Wittenberg who knew Luther personally, was the notable Utraquist priest Havel Cahera, about whom more will be said later.[11]

Defusion of the Roman Menace

Luther's successful revolt against Rome could not but make a deep impression on the Utraquists. After all it was the Council of Constance, an organ of the Roman Church, which was largely responsible for the death of Jan Hus, and it was Pope Martin V who had blessed the subsequent crusades during the wars of the Bohemian Reformation in 1420–1431. Then came the excommunication of the Bohemian king, George of Poděbrady, by Pope Paul II in 1466, combined with an exhortation to the neighboring monarchs for yet another crusade against Utraquism.[12] As Jaroslav Kadlec and Frederick G. Heymann pointed out, the bitter feelings against Rome among the Utraquists continued into the sixteenth century, reflected in pamphlets published around 1513.[13] Heymann also cites the attacks on the pope in popular literature, such as the tale of Pope Leo's friendly correspondence with Lucifer.[14] Against this background it was natural that the Utraquists would welcome a Czech version of *Answer to Emperor and Princes . . . before the Reichstag in Worms (Před velebností císařskou i přede všemi knížaty říše . . .* [1521]) in which Luther had justified his public burning, on December 10, 1520, of a papal bull. The Czech translator added a commentary to this pamphlet praising Luther's stand at Worms, comparing his courage to Hus's at Constance.[15]

Shortly after the Leipzig disputation, Jan Poduška, a priest of Utraquism's most important church, that of Our Lady Before the Týn in Prague, expressed his enthusiasm about Luther's stance against suppression of free discussion in the church, writing to the German reformer on July 16, 1519: "Martin, dear brother in the Lord, . . . Now many of your writings have got into our hands, from which we can get to know . . . that you are not afraid to preach freely and publically the doctrines of Christ and his apostles among the enemies of the evangelical truth. . . . Be strong in the Lord and be a robust pursuer of the pseudo-apostles. . . . Be confident, truth will liberate you."[16] In the same period after the Leipzig disputation, Hieronymus Emser likewise reported the Utraquists' delight in Luther's critique of the popes' misuse of power. This champion of Rome further complained that Luther provided the Utraquists with justification for their secession from papal jurisdiction.[17]

Although initially Luther may have had some qualms about the Bohemians' disobedience of the pope, by 1520 in his *De captivitate Babylonica ecclesiae praeludium,* he had overtly signaled his objection to the *Romana tyrannis.*[18] The Utraquists could subscribe also to Luther's sweeping admonitions that prelates, including bishops and popes, should not aspire to become lords over the faithful, but rather remain their servants. More concretely, they could agree with protests against the assumption of executive and judicial power by priests in Luther's treatise *On Christian Liberty,* which, as noted, had been available in Czech since 1521 under the title *O svobodě křesťanské.* According to Luther, the priestly despotism had reached a level that almost no other system of authority on earth could measure up to it: "[N]ow this ministry was converted in such a proud power, in such a terrible tyranny that there is none other under the heavens which could equal it, as if its subject people were not Christians . . ."[19]

The Utraquists could further agree with Luther's censure of the apparatus of the Roman Church for not only political, but also spiritual oppression as stated, for instance, in his treatise of 1521, *Ad librum eximii Magistri Nostri Magistri Ambrosii Catharini . . .,* partially translated into Czech by Oldřich Velenský in 1522 as *Výklad o Antikristu na vidění Danielovo.*[20] In particular, Luther resonated with the Utraquists' convictions in his accusation that the Roman See, which "overtly condemned the truth of the Word of God in Jan Hus at Constance, maintaining its opposition and condemnation with the same stubbornness to this day."[21] The translator highlighted Luther's charge that the popes' perverse earthly dominion had its roots in the cruelties of the Roman Empire from which it was born.[22] Moreover, in the translation of *Answer to Emperor and Princes . . . before the Reichstag in Worms* (1521), the Czechs could read that not only the popes, but also the church councils were fallible despite their pretensions and claims of spiritual power.[23]

Thus, the Utraquists could acclaim enthusiastically Luther's successful defiance of the administrative and judicial power of Rome. Although Luther was officially excommunicated and pronounced a heretic by the bulls of 1520 and 1521, he avoided a trial and execution. Before the Council of Worms in late 1520, Luther himself, in fact, had been aware of a possible parallel between his situation and Hus's at Constance.[24] The Utraquists were delighted that this (for them) menacing apparatus of the Roman Church proved powerless to harm Luther, who thus exposed its weakness. Although some residual anxiety remained about the fate of potential reformed participants at the next General Council,[25] in the light of Luther's experience it appeared unlikely that the Holy See could organize another crusade against Bohemia, or successfully prosecute Utraquist theologians. Thus in the 1520s, the Prague chronicler, Bartoš Písař, could rejoice that after Luther's success, papal excommunications and anathemas lost most of their force, particularly in Germany.[26]

End of National Isolation

What seemed, perhaps, even more astonishing to the Utraquists about Luther's revolt, and engendered enthusiasm for him, was the profound feeling of relief that the Germans, Bohemia's most powerful neighbors, after castigating the Czechs for a century for heresy, had now joined them on the other side of the fence of the bishop of Rome's fold, from which the Czechs had been expelled by Pope Pius II's abrogation of the Compactata of Basel in 1462.[27] Much of the Germans' antagonism toward the Czechs stemmed from the memories of the wars of the Bohemian Reformation.[28] Derisive views about the Bohemians and their religious deviations were voiced even by such respectable German figures as the leading humanist and poet laureate, Konrad Keltes (1459–1508).[29] The Roman Curia in a Machiavellian move, in fact, initially sought to manipulate those unfriendly sentiments of the Saxons, Brandenburgians, and Thuringians against Luther and expected to stem the tide of the Protestant Reformation, if it were shown to be a Bohemian-like phenomenon. This helped to explain Johann Eck's notable emphasis on an alleged similarity between Luther and Hus at the Leipzig disputation, following his remarks of the previous year about the "Bohemian scent" of some of Luther's ninety-five theses.[30]

Some of Luther's German critics agreed with the view that his early writings were rooted in the ideas of the Bohemian Reformation. Thus, Duke George of Saxony characterized in December 1519 Luther's pamphlet *Ein Sermon von dem hochwürdigen Sacrament des heiligen waren Leichnams Christi* (1519) as full of "Bohemian poison," and its content as "almost Prague-like" (*fast pragisch*).[31] In 1520, there were also rumors about Luther's imminent escape to Bohemia to avoid papal retribution. Although the German reformer had no such intention, his opponents urged him to do so, and his supporters pleaded with him not to seek refuge among the Czechs.[32] Henry VIII suspected that Luther curried favor with the Bohemians so that he might find refuge among them.[33] In a letter of July 5, 1522, to the Bohemian noble Sebastian Schlick, Luther pointed out that he did not contemplate a physical flight to Bohemia, but a spiritual flight whereby his writings would lift the odium of heresy from the Bohemians. He prefixed this letter to the Latin (but not to the German) version of his response to Henry VIII of 1522, and Thomas More, in turn, prefixed this missive to his *Responsio ad Lutherum* of 1523 on behalf of his sovereign.[34] Subsequently, the controversialists for the Roman Church continued the tendentious linking of Luther with Bohemia. Johannes Cochlaeus denounced in 1523 Luther's tract *Ein Sermon von dem neuen Testament, das ist von der heiligen Messe* (1520) as Hussite as well as heretical and seditious (*ketzerisch, hussitisch, bundshuhisch*).[35] Emser chimed in the same year that Luther's attack on the veneration of saints, *Wider den neuen Abgott und alten Teufel, der zu Meissen soll erhoben werden,* was extracted from old heretics, among whom he enumerated Hus together with Vigilantius of Toulouse and Wyclif.[36]

The enthusiastic accolades bestowed on Luther in Bohemia need to be assessed from the viewpoint of his (albeit largely undeserved) image as a champion of the Czech cause. Thus, in the 1520s Bartoš Písař praised Luther, who "converted the enraged Germans (*zlostné Němce*) into sympathizers with the Czechs (*příznivce Čechův*)."[37] Bartoš exalted Luther over earlier theologians, including (in this order) "Bernard of Clairvaux, Augustine, Dominic, Jerome, Bonaventure, Francis, Benedict, and Thomas Aquinas." Antonín Rezek interpreted this praise as stemming from a Bohemocentric view that placed Luther above the earlier distinguished theologians because he performed the marvel of gaining for the Czechs the Germans' favor.[38] Thus, the repercussions of Luther's public relations impact, not necessarily his theological acumen, exceeded the achievements of the enumerated patristic and scholastic luminaries.[39] The delight over the Germans' realization of the errors of their previous judgment about the Bohemian Reformation was stated explicitly by the anonymous author of the preface to the Czech translation of Luther's *Kázání . . . na desatero přikázání Božích* (1520), who maintained that in sending Luther to the Germans: "God did all this to open the blind hearts of those people who were puffed up by their vanity, who boasted about being the best and wisest in divine law, and who held others for heretics, so that they would understand and see that they were in error . . ."[40]

Luther's influence ended the religious stigma of the Czech Utraquists as unique rebels from Rome. The Utraquists were no longer surrounded by enemies who in the 1420s and again in the 1460s threatened to destroy them, with the Papacy inciting the neighboring nations to attack the Czechs. Now this menacing encirclement vanished. Luther himself pleaded for an end to the old "awful slandering, hatred and envy" between the Germans and the Czechs.[41] Taunted by Emser with heresy for his friendliness to the Czechs, Luther sarcastically replied that Emser had to be a heretic as well since he liked Bohemian gold and had a Bohemian mistress.[42] Thomas Murner scolded Luther in 1520 for seeking friendship with the uncouth folk who defenestrated pious Germans, ruined Charles University, and spoke of the Germans as "teutsche Hund" (German dogs).[43] As the author of the preface to Luther's *Výklad o Antikristu* (1522) noted, earlier "wherever the Czech turned among the neighboring nations he was among cruel enemies," and now thanks to the German reformer, "the Czechs were willingly accepted as brethren."[44] It may be added that if the Czechs had a reason to rejoice because Luther's stand had rescued them from their earlier isolation on the antipapal front, so Luther also had an incentive to praise the Czechs to keep them from making a deal with Rome that could leave the German revolt in isolation. Hence, Luther's plea addressed to the Bohemian estates on July 15, 1522, in which he reminded them of their grievances against the papacy, and warned them against negotiations with Rome.[45]

Vindication of Utraquism's Righteousness

The benefit of Luther's revolt for the status of Utraquism was not only in annihilating the external encirclement. In addition, God himself showed to the Germans and to the rest of Christendom that the Czechs had pursued the correct path in their rebuke and resistance to Rome, and had acted as God's chosen people to reveal his truth to the world.[46] Because of the Lutheran Reformation, the foreign ill-wishers of the Bohemian religious movement were forced to acknowledge their errors, retract their condemnations, and apologize for their past behavior. Explicit and firm assertions in that regard may be found in the preface to the Czech translation of Luther's *Kázání . . . na desatero přikázání Božích* (1520): the anonymous author of the preface stated concerning the meaning of the current religious movement among the

Germans, "thereby also God shows us his grace that the nation which detested, and considered heretical, our enlightenment by God and acceptance of the true faith of Christ, now recognizes because of his mercy what it detested and called heretical . . ."[47] The author of the preface to Luther's *Výklad o Antikristu* noted with satisfaction that the great German doctor had proclaimed the Czechs "faithful Christians who stand in the truth."[48]

The fact that God used Luther, in the eyes of the Utraquists, as his instrument to vindicate the Bohemian Reformation did not necessarily imply that Luther's teaching was superior to that of the Bohemians. Quite to the contrary, if God recognized the need to justify so dramatically and spectacularly the virtue of Utraquism, the implication was that the Bohemian religion was valuable per se, not that it should be abandoned for Luther's teaching. The preface, cited above, continued: "God announces to us the truth of that truth, which we have first recognized, also through another nation so that we might be more certain that we have not gone astray; he leads marvelously our enemies to recognize what they previously held as error, and thus also shows to them our election [as a chosen people] so that they might not oppose us and his will."[49] In fact, the same author further amplified the special religious status granted to the Czechs by God's action:

> When it then pleased the one, who had led us out of our mother's womb, to show us his mercy, and reveal to us his Son and his truth so that we would be *his kingdom and his chosen nation* [my emphasis], he sent to us men enlightened by him through the grace of his law, Master Hus and others whose names are inscribed in heaven . . . to illumine our minds so that we could recognize our salvation which God had prepared for us in his own dear Son, the Christ . . .[50]

Luther himself repeatedly proclaimed the righteousness of the Bohemian Reformation. As noted earlier, in the Leipzig disputation of July 1519 he declared several of Hus's articles, condemned by the Council of Constance, as evangelical and truly Christian.[51] Significantly from the viewpoint of the Utraquists, he argued that the condemnations of Hus were invalid even within the framework of traditional ecclesiology. The Utraquists could rejoice in this stand without condoning Luther's subsequent, more radical notions about the evils of the papacy. Jakub the Organist, a Utraquist eyewitness of the debate, reported Luther's vindication of Hus almost immediately to Prague.[52] After the Leipzig disputation in November 1519, the German reformer endorsed Hus further and proclaimed that he now held even more of Hus's articles as truly Christian.[53] Before the end of the same year he also approved the Utraquist practice of lay communion in both kinds as "zimlich und feyn," although he abstained from commanding the practice.[54] In *The Babylonian Captivity of the Church* (1520), he maintained that the prohibition of the lay chalice stemmed not from the Church, but from the Church's tyrants. The words of Christ were on the side of the Utraquists.[55] In his *Address to the Christian Nobility* (1520), Luther signified his general approval of the Bohemians' defiance of what he labeled as papal tyranny. For him, the Utraquists remained true Christians, even if they disregarded papal edicts and institutions. According to Luther in the *De captivitate Babylonica ecclesiae* (1520), if some had to be called schismatics from the true church, it was not the Bohemians, but the Romans.[56] In a famous pronouncement of 1520, Luther claimed that not even Saints Augustine or Paul could have found any fault with Utraquism.[57] Needless to say, his Roman critics took notice of his flirtation with the Bohemian Reformation. Eck and Emser taunted him for receiving applause from the heterodox Bohemians, particularly for his whitewash of Hus's condemned articles.[58] Even the judicious Erasmus felt in early 1521 that Luther was unduly flattering the Bohemians.[59] Again at Worms in 1521, Cochlaeus charged that by his stand Luther had joined "the barbarous sect of the Hussites." The final edict of the Diet of Worms blamed Luther for demeaning the Council of Constance, having called its members "apostles of the devil" for condemning Hus to death.[60] Nevertheless, Luther continued to court the Utraquists. In his letter of July 15, 1522, he assured the Bohemian estates of fully sharing their conviction that the executioners of Hus and Jerome of Prague had shed innocent blood.[61] Also in 1522 in another Eucharistic treatise, *Von beyder gestallt des Sacraments zu nehmen,* which was also translated into Czech, he reaffirmed his support for lay communion from the chalice even against his earlier hesitation.[62] Finally, Bishop John Fisher—in the service of Henry VIII—censured Luther for siding with the Hussites in his *Defense of the Royal Assertion,* written in 1522–1523 and published in 1525.[63] He also noted with disapproval Luther's vituperation of "the learned and virtuous delegates at the Council of Constance" for their treatment of Hus.[64] Similarly, Celio Calcagnini maintained that Luther discredited himself by embracing "the old sad stuff of Jan Hus and all the perverse nonsense of the Bohemians."[65] Thomas More castigated Luther for stating that the Bohemians "were good Christian men and all their opinions good and Catholic . . ." in his *Dialogue Concerning Heresies* (1531).[66]

Luther as a Counterpoint to Hus

Luther's revolt against Rome had potential appeal to the Utraquists also because of the German reformer's relation to the legacy of Jan Hus. The use of Hus's name in Luther's controversy with the Roman Church was a matter of a convenient symbol, having little, if any, specific relation to the substance of the dispute. Because of his clear-cut condemnation by the Council of Constance, Hus provided a ready-made, or prepackaged, weapon for the papal propagandists against Luther.[67] With the Roman build-up of Hus into a symbol of almost titanic proportions, Luther on his part could also use the Bohemian reformer as a vehicle for a dramatic gesture of defiance. As for Hus himself, the injection of his name into the highly visible dispute between Luther and the Roman Church assured that the Bohemian reformer would not be forgotten by the European public a hundred years after his death, and that his memory would be in fact perpetuated further in connection with this seminal historical event.[68]

The turning point of Luther's attitude toward Hus were the attacks launched by Eck during the Leipzig debate, of which, as pointed out earlier, the Czech Utraquists were well aware.[69] On the basis of available reports, Utraquist Master Václav Rožd'alovský, provost of Charles College in the University of Prague, and one of the preachers in the Týn Church, wrote to Luther on July 17, 1519: "What Jan Hus was once in Bohemia, thou, Martin, art now in Saxony."[70] Seven month later, in February 1520, Luther himself wrote to his friend Georg Spalatin the famous letter in which he affirmed that he and his revered teacher Johannes Staupitz had held the views of Hus all along: "In short, we all are Hussites and did not know it." Also, he wrote, Hus's writing was "the most evident evangelical truth," and for one hundred years no one was allowed to avow it.[71] Luther was apparently referring to Hus's *De ecclesia,* a copy of which he received soon after the Leipzig disputation from Rožd'alovský.[72] In his response to Eck in late 1520, Luther maintained that all of Hus's articles, condemned at Constance, were not only his, but also those of Christ, St. Paul and St. Augustine.[73] It was also the Roman Church, however, that continued to link Luther with Hus in this period. At the Diet of Worms in 1521, Rome's principal spokesman, Nuncio Girolamo Aleandro, charged Luther with endorsing all the articles for which Hus had been condemned as a heretic by the Council of Constance. Further, according to the papal official, by undermining the established authority Luther was preparing the way for disturbances and bloodshed like those that had followed Hus's challenge to the existing order. At the same assembly, Eck also repeated the charges that Luther's writings contained propositions condemned previously as those of Hus, as well as those of Wyclif, the Picards, and the Waldensians.[74]

The Utraquists continued to indicate their awareness of the (largely extrinsic) parallels between Hus and Luther. A comparative treatment of the two appeared in 1520, prefixed to the Czech version of the *Decem praecepta Wittenbergensi praedicata populo*. The introduction, supplied by an unknown Utraquist, defined Luther's role thus: "We Czechs walked in darkness . . . , until God in his mercy showed us His Son and His Truth. . . . In his grace he sent us Master Hus. . . . And what he first deigned to grant to the Czechs, this he now grants also to other nations. . . . He deigned to send them Martin Luther, so that the blind heart of the [German] nation be opened . . ."[75] Significantly enough, there were no early Czech translations of Luther's important work, *Address to the Christian Nobility* (1520), which still called Hus a heretic, and which rejected the Bohemians' view of him as a saint and a martyr.[76]

The force of Luther's allegiance to Hus was, however, blunted by his own dilution. Thus, he claimed that the similarity with Hus's teaching was unconscious or accidental, and that, as mentioned earlier, Sts. Paul and Augustine were also Hussites.[77] Even more significant was the subsequent way in which Luther distanced himself fundamentally from Hus, as well as from Wyclif. When it came to the real relation of ideas and objectives, Luther drew a crucial distinction—his own concern was with a doctrinal change, and Hus's with a moral renewal. There was a basic difference between a real reformation of the church and a call for a mere renewal in the church. Luther, indeed, stood for the former, Hus for the latter.[78] Luther explicitly highlighted the crucial distinction: "Doctrine and life are to be distinguished. Life is as bad among us as among the papists. Hence we do not fight and damn them because of their bad lives. Wyclif and Hus, who fought over the moral quality of life, failed to understand this."[79] In the Lutheran polemical writings of the 1530s, Hus would figure as an anti-Roman symbol, not as a teacher of theology. Luther himself would further amplify what he considered fundamental differences between his and Hus's teaching.[80] This is not to say that Hus was not (mis)used for the purposes of Lutheran propaganda. Apropos here is the image of Hus helping Luther distribute communion *sub utraque*, and another linking Hus with Luther and Wyclif as respectively his successor and predecessor.[81] One is reminded of a similarly unwarranted iconographic linkage of Erasmus with Luther on a woodcut in the anonymous *Die göttliche Mühle* of 1521. The difference was that, while Erasmus could object in person, Hus was no longer around to do so.[82]

In view of the above, Luther's purpose in defending Hus's ideas was not that he ultimately shared them or was particularly impressed by them. At bottom, he was actually using his defense of Hus's orthodoxy as a weapon against the magisterial authority of the existing governing apparatus of the Roman Church. His insistence on the truly Christian and evangelical character of Hus's articles was a way of undermining the credibility and legitimacy of Rome's edicts. If the Council of Constance and the Roman Curia erroneously asserted the heretical character of Hus, their judgment in matters of faith could not be authoritative. Hence, the papal bulls condemning Luther also lost their aura of authenticity and credibility. If parts of Luther's performance were useful to the Utraquists for their own ends, the German reformer in turn made tactical use of certain elements of the Bohemian Reformation. In this sense it could even be said that Hus was a catalyst for the German Reformation, inasmuch as his (mis)treatment at Constance provided in Luther's hands a basis for discrediting the magisterial authority of the Roman Curia. Thomas More noted in 1523 that Luther used the Bohemian heresies to attack Rome's authority.[83]

The Repugnant Luther, 1517–1523

While the enthusiasm for Luther's daring stand in the early 1520s was genuine among the Bohemian Utraquists, it concerned by and large its positive impact on the status of the Bohemian Reformation within the European context by breaking the hostile encirclement and ending its isolation. This rejoicing did not cover the substance of his doctrinal reforms, which contradicted the Utraquists' religious tenets.[84] After exploring what superficially attracted the Utraquists to Luther's stand, let us examine what fundamentally repelled them. What militated against a genuine rapprochement between the Utraquists and Luther was exactly the disparity that the German reformer saw between himself and Hus in their basic theological standpoints, namely the distinction between dogmatic reformism and moral activism. Luther's repudiation of a large portion of long-established Christian traditions left the Utraquists cold. Furthermore, the Utraquists were both fully aware of the nature of Luther's reductionist propositions, and also forearmed by their previous experience to meet the challenge of these drastic reforms. In this connection three main areas will be addressed: (1) the evidence for the Bohemian theologians' familiarity in the early 1520s with the radicalism of Luther's proposed restructuring of Christian institutions and way of life; (2) the ideological and historical reasons for their readiness to resist the allure of Luther's allegedly novel theological propositions; and (3) the reasons for the seemingly receptive, or even deferential, tone in the Utraquists' discussions of Luther's repugnant ideas.

Doctrinal Incompatibility

By the early 1520s, the Utraquist priests and theologians had had ample opportunities to study the fundamentals of Luther's doctrinal reforms. The several translated pamphlets by Sobek, Velenský, Příbram, and possibly others, informed them fully not only about the aspects of Luther's teaching that were congenial to them, but also about those that were unacceptable. The doctrines that were repugnant to the Utraquists were in brief, his solafideism, his principle of sola scriptura, and his rejection of sacramental priesthood in historic apostolic succession, including the papacy.

Among Luther's works perhaps, the most dissonant with Utraquism was *On the Liberty of a Christian Man* (published in Czech in 1521) that emphasized the justification by faith as against good works, a flat denial of the traditional view, upheld by the Utraquists, that the free will of man was tested by his cooperation in the process of salvation.[85] Solafideism was not a doctrine to which the Utraquists (or even the Brethren) could subscribe.[86] The principle of relying for salvation solely on Christ, and not on good works, was presented again in a general way in *Kázání o novém zákoně,* and in *Výklad o Antikristu na vidění Danielovo,* which denounced, among other things, the observation of fasts and the celebration of holy days.[87] *Kázání o novém zákoně* documented, moreover, Luther's denial that the mass was a sacrifice and a good work.[88]

The cited translations of Luther's treatises linked the rejection of the soteriological function of good deeds with another basic principle, unacceptable to the Utraquists, that of sola scriptura. According to Luther, the medieval doctors of the Church had spun many artificial mental constructs that hardly could be understood even by themselves, and their ratiocinations tended to obscure the fact that the word of God, contained in the Bible, was entirely sufficient for salvation.[89] The main culprit for Luther was Thomas Aquinas who had assigned to Aristotle an unwarranted place in Christian philosophy and, as a result, his worldly wisdom encroached on Christ's divine truth.[90] The scholastics in the Aristotelian tradition, who were by and large respected by the Utraquists, were also viewed by Luther as largely responsible for the misplaced emphasis on good deeds. The Czechs read the German reformer's unflattering assessment of scholastic philosophy: "Hence Christ, the sun of truth and justice, was obscured, when moral virtues were stressed instead of faith, and innumerable hypotheses instead of the truth."[91] In another translated treatise, Luther ultimately linked his objection to extra-biblical theology with his objection to the doctrine of good deeds in the following way: "[T]he soul needs for justification only the Word of God. Thus by faith alone and by no works it is justified. Because if it could be justified by something else, it would not need the Word of God . . ."[92]

Finally, the Czechs were informed about another of Luther's fundamental reforms of Christian doctrine, which was abhorrent to the Utraquists, namely a repudiation of the need for historical apostolic succession for the ministers of the church. This topic was already broached by Velenský in his introduction to Luther's *Výklad o Antikristu na vidění Danielovo,* and in Luther's *Kázání o novém zákoně.*[93] The subject is stressed explicitly in *O svobodě křest'anské* in which Luther maintained that Christ as the quintessential priest conferred priestly power on every Christian soul by virtue of his mystical marriage, inasmuch as what belonged to the groom had to belong also to the bride.[94] The Utraquists had no quarrel with Luther's idea that the clergy should be servants, not masters of the Christians, but they could not accept his definition of the ministerial service—for Luther it was simply the teaching or preaching of the Word of God, and for the Utraquists it was the traditional role of dispensing sanctification.[95] In other words, from the Utraquist perspective, Luther threw away the baby of wholesome Christian orders and rites together with the bath of the ecclesiastical *Befehlsstaat.* Luther's view on the clergy was most conspicuously put forth for the Bohemians in a special treatise that the German reformer addressed specifically to the city council of Prague in 1523, titled *De instituendis ministris Ecclesiae, ad clarissimum senatum Pragensem Bohemiae.* Sobek translated the pamphlet into Czech later in 1523.[96] Reminding the Bohemians once again of Rome's hostility toward their reformation, the sage of Wittenberg urged them to replace the episcopally ordained priests with a reformed ministry based on the idea of the general priesthood of all believers.[97]

As a matter related to the repudiation of sacramental priesthood, the Utraquists had ample opportunities to learn about Luther's absolute rejection of the papacy, which qualitatively surpassed their own, albeit weighty, reservations about the Holy See.[98] Among other reasons, the Utraquists had no need—as reformers elsewhere may have had—to reach for apocalyptic imagery in order to wean the faithful away from the ingrained habits of obedience to the papacy. After all, the course of the Bohemian Reformation had supplied the Czechs with more than enough normal historical grievances against the bishops of Rome. Rather than corresponding to the apocalyptic censures of Wyclif or Luther, the Utraquists' denunciations focused more on natural human failings. Although at times their censures could be ferocious, they remained in line with the fourteenth-century orthodox critics of the papacy, such as Bridget of Sweden.[99] A Roman apologist, Hieronymus Dungersheim noted already in the fall of 1519 that Luther's complete devaluation of the papacy did not reflect the view of the Utraquists, but that of the more radical Picards.[100] While the Utraquists could derive a measure of satisfaction from seeing the Roman authorities cringe in the face of Luther's onslaught, Luther's outright diabolization of the Holy See was unacceptable to them. Luther's view of the pope as the Antichrist was available to the Czechs, for instance, in the treatise *Výklad o Antikristu na vidění Danielovo*. The bishop of Rome was equated there with "that man of sin . . . the son of perdition" of Saint Paul's epistle (2 Thes 2.3; see also 1 Jn 4.3) on the intriguing ground that the pope invented many new rules and laws and thus created numerous occasions of sin and possibilities of damnation.[101]

The main difference between the two positions was that for Luther the pope was useless in consequence of his rejection of a sacramental priesthood in apostolic historical succession. Utraquism, on the contrary, accepted the pope as an irreplaceable part of the sacerdotal system of Western Christendom, no matter how much the papal exercise of executive and judicial power had been deplored and excoriated. Indeed, the attitude of taking the papacy seriously in the sacramental context was attested most concretely by the Utraquists' readiness to embark on another round of negotiations with the Roman Church. These *pourparlers* would take place in May 1525 in Buda and, as usual, fail to reach a modus vivendi.[102] In sum, in order to destroy the oppressive authority of the ecclesiastical apparatus in the Western Church, Luther found it appropriate to reject the priestly sacramental powers. The Utraquists had accomplished the ecclesial tour de force of rejecting the oppressive apparatus while preserving the concept of a sacramental hierarchical priesthood. They seemed to be in the proverbially enviable position of having one's cake and eating it too.

Immunity to Luther's Appeal

It is important to note that the Utraquist theologians did not face the substance of Luther's ideas as something unprecedented and unfamiliar that they might rush to embrace. Far from being caught like innocent babes in the woods, the Utraquists were, in fact, prepared for the encounter with the German reformer through their perennial polemics with the Taborites between the 1420s and 1440s and with the Unity of Brethren after 1457.[103] The Utraquist *via media* was sufficiently entrenched during the previous century to have produced effective antibodies against the seductiveness of Lutheran reductionism. In fact, in the 1520s and beyond the Lutherans were referred to as "Pikarts," the same term as was used for the Brethren. In other words, the Utraquists recognized in Lutheranism a religious orientation with a number of features that they had found objectionable in the Unity of Brethren.[104] Incidentally—within the wider European setting—this déjà vu quality of Lutheranism might make questionable the utility of the concept of a Second Reformation as something new and avantgarde.[105] The ideas of the Taborites and the Brethren seemed to be as trenchant and far-reaching as those of the Lutheran and Calvinist reformers.

The opposition to Luther's teaching can be viewed in large part as an extension of the earlier rejection of the proto-Protestant doctrines of the Unity of Brethren. The connection can be illustrated by the correspondence of Jan Šlechta of Všehrdy with Erasmus in 1519. Šlechta's letter itemized for the Dutch guru the Brethren's beliefs and practices of which the Utraquists disapproved. It read like a catalog of what the Utraquists would also consider Lutheranism's gravest errors—disrespect for a properly consecrated priesthood, rejection of patristic and scholastic writers and of their teachings, and discarding of traditional church vestments and ceremonies.[106] Mikuláš Konáč of Hodíškov, a notable author and printer, followed—without missing a beat—the critique of the Unity with a literary campaign against Lutheranism. In 1515, prior to Luther's epiphany, he published a treatise of Jan Stanislaides, *O klanění velebné Svátosti oltářní proti pithartským bludom* (On the Adoration of the Venerable Sacrament of the Altar Against the Pitharts' Errors) (1515), reproving the Brethren for their Eucharist doctrines. In the early 1520s, Konáč wrote in opposition to Lutheran reforms in his treatise *O Turcích* (About the Turks). In an unusual breech of Utraquist etiquette, he referred to Luther as a runaway monk and described his doctrines as *lotrovství* (villainy), playing on the similarity between the Czech word for villain—"lotr"—and Luther's name.[107]

What fundamentally rubbed against the grain of the Utraquist tradition was Luther's linking of justification by faith alone to the irrelevance of biblical laws and commandments. While the Utraquists' central preoccupation since the onset of the Bohemian Reformation was with moral purification and implementation of the "law of God," they read in *O svobodě křest'an-*

ské Luther's contrary position: "It is the Christian liberty, our faith, which acts . . . in such a way that no one needs the law or deeds for his justification and salvation," and "the Christian man needs no law for his salvation because through faith he is freed from every law."[108] In other words, Luther opposed the explicit emphasis on moral activism, which the Utraquists had always strongly embraced. One may be tempted to reverse Eduard Winter's dictum cited at the beginning of this article to state that no country was as well prepared to resist Luther's teaching as Bohemia.[109] It seems clear that the attacks conducted by the Utraquists and the Lutherans "upon the bastions of late medieval clericalism" were mounted "from mutually conflicting standpoints."[110]

Mask of Curiosity, Broad-Mindedness, and Politeness

On closer examination, the Utraquists' discussions of Luther's substantive doctrines were less signs of acceptance than marks of curiosity about a reform movement that, despite fundamental differences, also bore certain surface similarities with the Bohemian Reformation. Such uncommitted considerations and rather dispassionate examinations of diverse religious viewpoints were solidly embedded in the Utraquist tradition. In part, these attitudes can be traced to the freewheeling disputations prevalent at Charles University in the late fourteenth and early fifteenth centuries, which constituted the intellectual milieu from which Utraquism had largely emerged.[111] This open-minded approach was signaled already by Hus when in 1409 he objected to Archbishop Zajíc's plans to burn Wyclif's works, maintaining that "books should be read for the truth they may contain, not destroyed for the error they might disseminate."[112] Later, the principles of free examination and discussion were codified in the seminal documents of Utraquism, the Four Articles of Prague of 1419, and the Judge (or Test) of Cheb (*iudex in Egra compactatus*) of 1432.[113] Master Jiří Písecký, one of the intellectual luminaries of Utraquist Bohemia, as dean of the Philosophical Faculty of Charles University from 1523 to 1527, and subsequently as a member of the Utraquist Consistory, exemplifies a nuanced appreciation of Luther. While ultimately disagreeing with the German reformer, Písecký praised him for turning away from the Roman emphasis on display of splendor and toward the simplicity of the Scripture. Nevertheless, he rejected specific Lutheran doctrines, and was particularly offended by Luther's low regard for classical philosophy, the backbone of scholasticism, which—as noted earlier—the sage of Wittenberg had in turn considered the root of the pernicious emphasis on good works.[114] Even the much maligned Cahera, of whom more will be said later, maintained that he was never a convinced Lutheran even prior to 1524. When questioned about first seemingly favoring, then rejecting Luther, he explained that his purpose in visiting Luther and his entourage in Wittenberg was to get to know their principles better so that he might refute them more effectively.[115] Significantly, writing to the Prague city council in 1523, Luther himself deplored the theological laissez-faire prevalent in Utraquist Bohemia, which he found reprehensible for its intellectual untidiness.[116] Paradoxically, an analogous censure of Bohemia for its religious pluralism is found in Thomas More's *Dialogue Concerning Heresies* (1531).[117]

The broad-mindedness of Utraquist theologians and their willingness to hear diverse messages was epitomized by their readiness to admit into the circle of Charles University of Prague the religious radical Thomas Müntzer in 1521–1522 and let him preach in the chapels of Bethlehem and Corpus Christi. Nobody would claim that giving him an extended and curious hearing signified the Utraquists' readiness to embrace Müntzer's brand of utopian Christianity. In fact, once the radicalism of his ideas became evident, his Utraquist hosts turned distinctly frigid. Before his departure from Prague, the German radical composed the famous Prague Manifesto addressed first to the Bohemians, and second to all Christians, urging the abolition of the clergy and institution of direct rule by the Holy Spirit. In the pursuit of this goal, he espoused a Táborite-like chiliasm that justified the violence of the elect against the persons and institutions of their opponents.[118] It is relevant to recall in this connection the Utraquists' indulgence toward German radicals, such as Nicholas and Peter of Dresden at the time of Hus, or toward the English Wyclifite, Peter Payne, a generation later.

The Utraquists' seeming predisposition to take Luther more seriously than warranted also could stem from their temperate use of language. The restraint on perjorative language in religious discussion had been embedded in Bohemia's legal tradition, particularly of course by the Compactata of 1436 and the Peace of Kutná Hora of 1485, which had banned vituperation between the Utraquists and adherents of the Roman Church.[119] Following in these footsteps, a Utraquist assembly of clergy and lay estates in April 1523 issued an injunction against the derisive labeling of disagreeable doctrines or opinions as heretical.[120] Likewise, Erasmus, who enjoyed unusual moral authority in Bohemia, counseled prudence and moderation in combating even unacceptable religious ideas.[121] An illustrative example of a curious, calm, and civil examination of Luther's doctrines by two Utraquist priests was offered by the correspondence between Šimon of Habry and Jan of Německý Brod in 1528–1529. Characteristic of this nonconfrontational attitude was also the complaint by priest Šimon about the excesses of Luther's polemical language, particularly his insults of Henry VIII in *Contra regem Angliae* (1522).[122] This censure appeared to be in the spirit of Erasmus who likewise had objected to Luther's "savage torrent of invective."[123] To this may be added the courteous tone of Bydžovský as we shall see in his discussions of Luther's tenets in the early 1540s, despite his uncompromising rejection of the German reformer's innovations.[124] How this dispassionate treatment of religious issues could be (mis)interpreted is shown by Eduard Winter's claim that the correspondence between the priests Šimon and Jan demonstrated the seriousness of Lutheran inroads in Bohemia by the late 1520s.[125] What might have contributed to the misleading impression of the Utraquists' receptivity to the German Reformation was their praise of certain of Luther's doctrinal stands that—rather paradoxically—appeared more moderate than those of the Brethren. Already, the Czech commentator on Luther's *Kázání . . . na desatero* expressed his satisfaction about Luther's chastising of the "Pikarts." The Utraquists' polemical mildness found its counterpart later in England, where representatives of another *via media,* such as Richard Hooker, found a way to laud Calvin, while combating the influence of Puritan doctrines within the Church of England.[126]

This is not to say that some Bohemian commentators did not praise Luther despite their ignorance of his teaching, or that there were not individuals genuinely attached to Luther's tenets in a properly informed way. Bartoš Písař may serve as an example of an ill-informed stance. While dissatisfied with prevailing (and to him) lukewarm religious and moral feelings, and lauding the German reformer highly, he apparently never read any of Luther's works. Hence he could not judge Luther's theology from firsthand knowledge, and in fact he upheld no concrete doctrinal Lutheran prescriptions for a change.[127] In the second category, that of genuine converts, we can include Sobek of Kornice and the anonymous author of the introduction to *Kázání . . . na desatero přikázání Božích,* who appeared to endorse without reservation Luther's solafideism.[128] In addition, there were Brethren, or would-be Brethren, who could laud certain of Luther's doctrines in clear conscience. Among them was the abovementioned Oldřich Velenský, who seemed to accept fully Luther's identification of the pope with the Antichrist of St. Paul's epistle. Velenský had definitely joined the Brethren by 1531 or 1532, if he had not done so earlier.[129] He was identical with "Ulrichus

Velenus," who had upset John Fisher in 1521 by denying St. Peter's residence in Rome. Writing a book against the "impudent" Bohemian, the famous Bishop of Rochester granted Velenus a distinction that he otherwise bestowed on only a few foreign theologians, namely Jacques Lefèvre d'Étaples, Luther, and Johann Oecolampadius.[130]

The Illusion of a Lutheran Coup, 1524

The centerpiece for those arguing the case for a sweeping Lutheran influence in Bohemia in the early 1520s was the religious propositions adopted by a Utraquist assembly in Prague on February 2, 1524, and known as the Candlemas Day Articles. Scholars convinced of a profound impact of Luther's teaching on Bohemia, and its undermining of traditional Utraquism, focused on the ominous meaning of these articles. To them, it was an early major Lutheran initiative, aimed at assuming control of the Utraquist Consistory (with Luther's own support from afar).[131] According to the standard version, a prominent Utraquist priest Havel Cahera, having appeared in Wittenberg in the summer of 1523, persuaded Luther to send a letter to the city council of Prague against Roman ordinations, the previously mentioned missive, *De instituendis ministris Ecclesiae, ad clarissimum senatum Pragensem Bohemiae*.[132] Cahera then returned to Bohemia filled with expectations that he would incorporate his homeland into the Lutheran camp with himself as a bishop. Already in the summer of 1523, new members were introduced into the Utraquist Consistory. Then Administrator Václav Šišmánek died and was replaced by four administrators in August 1523. Cahera was elected the first among the administrators, and he also became the pastor of the all-important Týn church. These changes were allegedly facilitated by the assumption of the mayoralty in Prague by Jan Hlavsa of Liboslav, who was subsequently accused of Lutheran leanings. In March 1523, Hlavsa replaced his predecessor and political rival Jan Pašek of Vrat, who was then ousted also from the town council.[133] Cahera's main initiative was to call a comprehensive assembly including all Utraquist estates (barons, knights, and cities), which gathered early in 1524, beginning on January 29, in the Carolinum, the principal edifice of Charles University. All Utraquist clergy from Bohemia and Moravia were likewise invited. Duke Charles of Münsterberg, a grandson of King George of Poděbrady, officially represented King Louis of Bohemia (1516–1526), who habitually resided in his other realm of Hungary. Cahera presented to the assembly a list of twenty-two propositions, of which twenty were accepted on Candlemas Day, that is, February 2.[134]

Keynoting subsequent historical opinion, František Palacký saw the Candlemas Day Articles as "written entirely in the spirit of Luther."[135] Václav Tomek characterized their tendency to be "to introduce gradually innovations in ecclesiastical teaching and rites according to Luther's intentions into the entire party *sub utraque*," and added that "The final victory of the Lutheran view was . . . presupposed."[136] Anton Gindely described them as mainly, although not totally Lutheran (*nicht ganz luterisch*).[137] Kamil Krofta called the articles "revolutionary" and adopted under the influence of Luther's Reformation.[138] For Eduard Winter, the articles began "the assimilation of the Utraquist Church to Lutheranism . . ."[139] Surprisingly, Hrejsa—who normally applauded Protestant input—called the articles only partly "Neo-Utraquist," not outright Lutheran.[140] Winfried Eberhard sidestepped the issue of whether the articles were "Lutheran," but seemed to hold a position akin to Hrejsa's that they represented a departure toward a "new radical Utraquism."[141] In his last work, *Jagellonský věk v českých zemích* (The Jagellon Era in the Bohemian Lands, in volume 3 published posthumously in 1998), the notable Czech historian Josef Macek added another twist to the story. Without subjecting the Articles to concrete analysis, he claimed the presence of Protestant-like features in them, but not due to Lutheran borrowings, but to a theological convergence between mainline Utraquism and the Unity of Brethren.[142]

Let us first consider the traditional argument, still prevalent in the historical literature, that the Candlemas Day Articles were "Lutheran," or near-Lutheran. While some ambiguity exists, a plausible case may be made that they remained Utraquist, and in that sense not just non-Lutheran, but also anti-Lutheran. Recently, Frederick G. Heymann examined the Articles with the assumption that they stood in the shadow of Wittenberg; despite his best efforts, he found it difficult to identify any of Cahera's propositions of early 1524 as specifically Lutheran.[143] There were repeated references to the authority of the Bible, called the "Law of God" (Articles 2, 10, and 19), which—according to Heymann—could be related to Luther's biblicism. Stress on the authority of the Scripture, however, had been endemic in Utraquism from the pioneer days of Hus, Jakoubek of Stříbro, and Jan Rokycana, and it was on the literal acceptance of the text of the New Testament that the sub utraque lay communion was defended (Article 17). Moreover, emphasis on the "Law of God" actually could be construed as anti-Lutheran in that it militated against the concept of solafideism, which Luther had grounded in the obsolescence of biblical laws and commandments. In addition, two other points were consistent not only with Lutheranism, but also with traditional Utraquism: Article 10 states that every pious man should study the Bible and teach it to his wife and children, and Article 15 states that mass should be conducted as much as possible in the vernacular.

While either ignoring solafideism, or rejecting it implicitly by stressing obedience to the Law of God, the Candlemas Articles clashed outright with Luther's second cardinal principle, that of *sola scriptura*. It happened in Article 8, which endorsed the teachings of the Holy Doctors as long as they agreed with the Scripture, as well as the teachings in the sermons of Hus, Rokycana, and other (unspecified) Utraquist divines. Article 13 on offering communion (both kinds) to infants right after baptism was not at all Lutheran. Communion for infants had been a mark of distinction of the Bohemian Reformation since 1417, which was rescued from virtual oblivion only recently by the scholarly work of David R. Holeton. Hitherto, Czech historiography had tended to pass over this feature in silence or trivialize it as a matter that was rather embarrassing, if not distasteful or repugnant,[144] inasmuch as it was not a merely symbolic act, but a genuine consuming of the two species by the infant.[145] Article 20 declared a holiday for Jan Hus as a saint and a martyr, a type of commemoration that Luther had specifically condemned.[146] Similarly, Article 15, which commanded the observance of traditional feast days in addition to those of the Bohemian Reformation's martyrs, was in its essence not simply non-Lutheran, but in effect anti-Lutheran. The same was true of the characterization of the mass as a commemoration of Christ's sacrifice (Article 14),[147] and also of the order of the mass stipulated in Article 15. The latter provided for the Introit (with proper commemoration of the Virgin Mary, the apostles, and other saints), Kyrie Eleison, Gloria, Epistle, Alleluia with the Gradual, Gospel, Creed, Preface, Sanctus, Agnus Dei, Communion, and Collects.

Finally, the Articles dealt with organizational and disciplinary matters. Articles 7, 9, and 12 reaffirmed the customary Utraquist indulgence and courtesy in religious discourse, as long as it was conducted within the paradigms of the Scriptures. Procedures were specified for peaceful resolution of disagreements arising from such encounters. These provisions reflected the notable spirit of toleration, which, as pointed out by Winfried Eberhard among others, had characterized Utraquism from its very inception.[148] This attitude was the fruit of the Utraquists' perennial resistance to surrendering the role of reason and argument to naked magisterial authority. Exemplified by Hus at Constance in 1415 and embodied in 1432 in the abovementioned

Judge of Cheb, the liberal spirit was reinforced by the injunction to preach the word of God freely in the Four Articles of Prague and in the Compactata of 1437.[149] Concerning organizational matters, Articles 1 through 6 and 11 reemphasized the customary authority of the administrator and the Consistory over the Utraquist Church and its priesthood in Bohemia and Moravia. Regular channels of appeals were provided for both the clergy and the laypeople in ecclesiastical matters, leading from the parishes to the deaneries and from the latter to the Consistory. This assertion of an independent ecclesiastical jurisdiction clearly contradicted Luther's vesting of the spiritual power in secular authority.[150] In connection with the ecclesial articles, Krofta raised a basic issue when he argued that the principle of canonical priestly ordinations by bishops (those in historical apostolic succession) had been tacitly abandoned because the Articles did not explicitly command canonical procedures in the points concerning the clergy. He saw here an implicit admission of noncanonical ordination of ministers in the Lutheran style.[151] This conclusion, however, was mere speculation on Krofta's part, not otherwise substantiated, inasmuch as no alternate method of ordination was specified.

The one aspect of the Candlemas Articles that might be construed as Lutheran was the proposal for eventual discontinuation of exhibiting the Eucharist for adoration aside from the Lord's Supper (in Article 16). Here the issue between traditional Utraquism and Lutheranism was doctrinally complicated. While Luther insisted on the adoration of the Eucharist during the communion service (in view of the real presence), he would condemn adoration not concurrent with the Lord's Supper, which the Utraquists practiced, especially by carrying the host in a monstrance during outdoor processions. The Lutherans held that outside the context of the communion service, the Eucharistic elements reverted to ordinary bread and wine, and adoring them was idolatrous. Thus, an eventual prohibition of the adoration of the Eucharist in a monstrance by Article 16 could be viewed as yielding to a Lutheran desideratum. Parenthetically, Luther was also upset by the Brethren's refusal to adore the Eucharist even *during* the communion service, scolding the Brethren for this in a treatise of 1523 with the charming dedication to "Meinen lyben herrn und freunden den Brudern, genant Valdenser, ynn Behemen und Mehren."[152] This controversy, however, did not concern the mainline Utraquists, nor did it have a direct bearing on the provision of Article 16.

Oddly, however, another stipulation which would have seemed to support the end of adoration (extrinsic to the communion service) was among the propositions rejected by the Assembly of 1524, namely a prohibition on the preservation of the consecrated species.[153] In addition, endorsement of the feast of Corpus Christi (in Article 20) apparently implied acceptance of the processions, which involved the adoration of the Eucharist in a monstrance. The other rejected proposition, which also might have appeared Lutheran, was approval of marriage for the clergy. This would have constituted a relatively significant departure from the current practice of Roman Christianity, inasmuch as the rule of priestly celibacy had been instituted by Rome in about 1100. Nevertheless, priestly marriage could be seen, in line with the sub utraque lay communion or communion for infants, as a restoration of an ancient practice of Western Christianity, as it had evolved during the first millennium. Even such a staunch champion of the Roman Church as the Emperor Ferdinand I would favor clerical marriages at the time of the Council of Trent in 1563.[154] Rather than an innovation inspired by Luther, the change could be viewed as the reparation of a latter-day papal deformation inflicted on the standard Western Church. The rejection of even such an ambiguous reform further pointed to a doctrinally conservative character of the assembly of 1524.[155]

In general, except for the matter of exhibiting the host for adoration, it can be said that there were no clear signs of a significant convergence between Utraquism and Lutheranism in the Articles of February 1524. There was no ratification of precepts, which were specific and basic to Lutheranism, particularly sola fide, sola scriptura, or the priesthood of all believers. On the contrary; there were affirmations of principles opposed to Lutheran tenets, such as infant communion, preserving the traditional components of the mass, veneration of Jan Hus as a saint, observance of other traditional feast days, and the acceptance of patristic and scholastic extra-biblical theology. If there were a desire to transform Utraquism into Lutheranism, one is tempted to say that such a wishful thinking might have been more in the minds of later commentators than in those of participants in the Candlemas Day Assembly of 1524. It is significant that the new city council of Prague under Pašek would, as early as May 11, 1524, interpret the sensitive Candlemas Day Articles entirely in the Utraquist sense. In particular, the council's *Decretum* would clear up the one ambiguity that could be interpreted as a Lutheran input, and mandate explicitly a respect for the exhibition of the host outside the communion service as in a monstrance, when displayed on the altar or carried in an outdoor procession.[156]

Macek's assertion that the Candlemas Day Articles leaned—independently of Lutheranism or Luther's influence—toward the Brethren's theology and thus departed from the *via media* of mainline Utraquism, is even less plausible than the assertions of Luther's direct impact. The same features that have been pointed out as questionably Lutheran could be attributed—but even less convincingly—to the influence of the Brethren, namely (1) silence on the ordination of clergy, and (2) the negative view of the adoration of the Eucharist outside the communion service. The second point, moreover, which was sufficient for the Lutherans, would have been inadequate for the Brethren who (as noted, in conflict with Luther) objected to the adoration even during the Lord's Supper. At the other end of the spectrum, the same propositions that would have been unacceptable to Luther, were also contrary to the Brethren's tenets: (1) communion for infants; (2) veneration of the Virgin Mary and other saints; and (3) the magisterial authority of the classics of fifteenth-century Utraquism, above all Rokycana and his elder and younger associates such as Jakoubek and Václav Koranda. Even more important, while the Utraquists may have regarded the Brethren as their lost sheep, there was no evident desire on the Brethren's part in the 1520s to enter into negotiations with mainline Utraquism in general, or any concrete evidence of their significant impact on the Candlemas Day assembly in particular.[157] Quite to the contrary, the authoritative theologian of the Unity, Lukáš of Prague, writing precisely in 1524, once more emphatically rejected mainline Utraquism (as defined by Rokycana), and reemphasized the Unity's theological pedigree in Taboritism. While abominating mainline Utraquism, the Brethren sought an understanding in the 1520s and 1530s with Luther, despite their disagreements with him on the real presence, solafideism, and re-baptism of converts, and subsequently their search for theological kinship would shift to West European Calvinism, which diverged even further from standard Utraquism than Luther did.[158]

The Retrenchment of Utraquism, 1524–1528

In any case, soon after the Candlemas Day Assembly of 1524 a strong popular response in favor of affirming Utraquism reverberated through Prague. A determined opponent of the alleged Lutherans, Jan Pašek, was swept into office as mayor in March 1524. He replaced Jan Hlavsa, just a year after he himself had been toppled by the latter in March 1523.[159] As noted earlier, the Prague city council decreed on May 11, 1524, an orthodox Utraquist interpretation of the Candlemas Day Articles, which affirmed the exhibition of the Eucharist and the conduct of religious processions. Another set of ecclesiastical articles was confirmed by the city council on October 31, 1524, which was even more definite in stipulating Utraquist practices, such as observance of feast days and traditional fasts.[160] In an alleged contrast to his presumed earlier Lutheran sympathies, Cahera, now the sole administrator of the Utraquist Consistory, supported Pašek's return and cooperated with him for the duration of his tenure until 1528. Starting in September 1524, Pašek and his colleagues on the city council, such as Ziga Vaníčkovic, who enjoyed the full support of the city's communal assembly (*velká obec*), launched accusations of conspiracy against a number of the city's residents who were viewed as sympathizers of Lutheranism or more specifically of "Pikartism," an epithet traditionally used for the Brethren and other religious radicals. Some were exiled from Prague, among them town chancellor Burián Sobek who had supposedly introduced Cahera to Luther. Once more the anti-Lutheran campaign enjoyed a wide popular support, reflected in its endorsement by the city's communal assembly.[161]

According to the earlier belief, held for instance by Tomek and Gindely, the group suppressed by Pašek was clearly Lutheran, not composed of mere scapegoats. Gindely even spoke of "a Lutheran aggression."[162] Eduard Winter referred to Hlavsa as "friendly to the Lutherans," and to the exiles of 1525 as "Luther's friends."[163] Václav Husa characterized Hlavsa, as well as Brikcí of Licko, as "inclining toward Lutheranism" (*klonil se k luterství*).[164] František Kutnar maintained that Hlavsa and his followers formed a Lutheran party.[165] Among earlier writers, however, Karel Erben remarkably does not refer to any religious difference between Pašek and Hlavsa.[166]

More recent researchers have leaned more plausibly to the view that the leaders of the political upheaval in Prague in 1524 artificially fomented the Lutheran scare. Eager to persecute certain individuals, Pašek and his followers exploited their victims' earlier real or alleged curiosity about Lutheranism. These interests were exaggerated and used against them for political reasons. Eberhard pointed to the importance of political motives, as distinct from the seemingly religious ones.[167] Macek most recently denied that religious convictions inspired Pašek's campaign of repression, and his view does not necessarily lose its validity, even if it might in part reflect a former Marxist's skepticism about religious causation in history. According to Macek, the political cause of the conflict was that Pašek favored the townspeople's cooperation with the Bohemian nobility, while Hlavsa advocated reliance on the king. Aside from political repression, the objective of the persecution was to confiscate the property of those accused. Macek nevertheless admitted that religion served as a useful pretext, citing the heavy-handed pressure on Hlavsa's followers to incriminate their leader as a "Pikart."[168] Despite his belief in the existence of a genuine Lutheran party, Tomek also pointed out that those arrested under Pašek were ultimately convicted because of conspiracy against good order, not because of heretical beliefs. This is also clear from the statement of readmission to Prague of Brikcí of Licko in 1532. Finally, King Louis in his rare interventions in Bohemian affairs from Buda twice requested a reprieve for the exiles (in June and September 1525). It was most unlikely that this devotee of Roman Christianity would have sided with the exiles if they, in his eyes, were authentic Lutheran heretics.[169] In other words, the vague and isolated efforts to promote Lutheranism apparently served as a red herring to mask the search for political power or material enrichment by a faction of Pašek's supporters.[170]

In all of this, Cahera remains the mystery man. The question that arises is whether he was a proper Utraquist who had merely engaged in an innocent flirtation with Lutheranism. As noted earlier, Cahera himself claimed that he was not a convinced Lutheran in 1523–1524, but merely desired to learn the true nature of Luther's tenets in Wittenberg.[171] Czech historiography has tended to depict the administrator as a spineless opportunist.[172] Janáček still echoed the view that Cahera had been Luther's disciple, but "became almost overnight from an enthusiastic Lutheran an even more enthusiastic Utraquist and supporter of Pašek."[173] On the Roman side, Jaroslav Kadlec maintained that Cahera had a change of mind due to the popular hostility to the feared Lutheran influences.[174] According to Heymann, Cahera simply abandoned his advocacy of Lutheran ideas when he formed an alliance with Pašek in 1524, and henceforth started denouncing religious innovators and Luther himself.[175]

The tangible evidence of Cahera's perfidy consists of two letters by Luther, dated after the onset of Pašek's repressive campaign in 1524—a letter of sympathy to Sobek, and an angry letter of warning to Cahera. Heymann's assumption that Cahera probably discussed in detail with Luther the contents of his religious propositions of early 1524 becomes largely irrelevant, if the Candlemas Day Articles in fact revealed no specifically Lutheran characteristics.[176] As for the two crucial letters, their authenticity is not beyond doubt. Bartoš Písař, their only source, is not considered a trustworthy witness even by those who are in sympathy with his seemingly Lutheran viewpoint.[177] Moreover, there are discrepancies between the text of the two letters and external evidence, which have been noted by the editors of

Martin Luther's *Werke: Kritische Gesammtausgabe*. In particular, Luther is cited as writing in his letter to Sobek that Cahera had not only suggested the letter to the city council of Prague, *De instituendis ministries Ecclesiae*, but that he also had supplied the missive's substantive ideas. While it seems rather unlikely that Luther would let somebody dictate the content of his major pronouncements, it also appears that Cahera was not in Wittenberg in November 1523 when Luther wrote the letter to the city fathers of Prague, but had returned to Bohemia in mid-summer. In addition, Cahera's name was not mentioned in Luther's epistle, *De instituendis ministries Ecclesiae*.[178] It may be noted in this connection that fictitious letters, written as literary exercises or satires, have bedeviled the history of Bohemia in other instances.[179]

An assessment of the response to the crisis over the Articles of 1524 leaves an impression, not of Utraquism's weakening or erosion, but of its affirmation and further retrenchment in Bohemia. Even writers who were convinced that a Lutheran offensive in the 1520s fatally undermined the established Utraquist Church could not maintain that the post-1524 resurgence of Utraquism was due merely to the political pressure of Pašek of Vrat and his associates. This is further confirmed by the fact that popular dissatisfaction with alleged Lutheran trends preceded the election of Pašek as mayor of Prague in March 1524. It was the electorate, not the king or a coup d'état, that placed Pašek at the helm of the town government.[180] The common people of Prague were reported to show rather coarsely their displeasure to the clergy suspected of Lutheran leanings. According to a report, these protesters "threw dirt on some of them, exposed their buttocks at others, . . . and on passing bumped them with their shoulders . . ." Also insulting songs were composed and sung about known or suspected Lutherans.[181] One of these songs claimed that the Lutheran faith was even a "worse whore than that of the Roman pope."[182] The Bohemian Diet proceeded to dispel any remaining suspicions that there might have been an infiltration of Lutheran ideas into Utraquism, and it reaffirmed its attachment to Utraquist orthodoxy in February 1525. Above all, the Diet made up for the deficiency of the Candlemas Day Articles (noted by Krofta), and restated explicitly the Utraquist adherence to an episcopally ordained sacramental priesthood, thus clearly rejecting the idea of the Lutheran ministry.[183]

The vogue of Utraquism in Bohemia and its ultimate independence from a particular political or personal leadership was further substantiated by the startling developments of 1528. In a dramatic turn of the wheel of fortune, Pašek and Cahera were removed from office by an unusual intervention of Bohemia's new Habsburg king, Ferdinand I, who replaced the mild-mannered Louis upon the extinction of the Hungaro-Bohemian branch of the Jagellon dynasty in 1526. Acting to reassert royal prerogatives, Ferdinand also permitted the return to Prague of the exiles, who had been victimized by the persecution of 1524–1525. Crowning his exceptional display of monarchical authority, the king instead banished Cahera from the country in 1529, and Pašek from Prague a year later.[184] The image of a Lutheran steamroller in the early 1520s is also blunted by the fact that the alleged pioneers of Lutheranism in Bohemia were found to be genuine Utraquists during the formal processes of rehabilitation of the former exiles following Pašek's exile.[185]

Neither the change in public authority, nor the return of the exiles, was followed by any noticeable Lutheran upsurge. While the Unity of Brethren continued to maintain its lively contacts with Luther,[186] there was little evidence of Lutheranism's influence on mainline Utraquism during the 1530s. It would not be until 1543 that another wave of interest in Luther's teachings would affect theological discussions in the Utraquist Consistory.[187] Eduard Winter is the only historian who maintained that Lutheranism gained strength in Bohemia in the late 1520s, but as noted earlier, the sole basis for his position was his questionable interpretation of the correspondence between Šimon of Habry and Jan of Německý Brod.[188]

Failed Rapprochement with Rome

Having dealt with the claim that the Utraquist Church felt a compulsion to turn Lutheran, let us now examine the opposite claim, namely that the Utraquists wished to reunite with the Roman Church in order to stem the tide of the Protestant Reformation.[189] This is the thesis of Eduard Winter, who maintains that the "Lutheran threat" to Utraquism was so strong that its leaders were compelled to seek protection from Rome.[190] This idea is firmly entrenched in mainstream historical writing, which has asserted that the opponents of the Articles of 1524 desperately desired a reunion with Rome; its pursuit was decided at the Bohemian Diet in February 1525.[191]

In a paradoxical way, the emergence of the Protestant Reformation lessened the urgency of a modus vivendi with the Roman Church with a significant neutralization of the terror-inspiring apparatus hitherto at the disposal of Rome. Luther's defiance of the Roman Church, and getting away with it, took out the teeth from the traditional spiritual weapons of the

Roman Curia, which included various types of anathemas, excommunications, and interdicts. They were still imposed, but with lesser effect. Next, the joining of other nations outside Rome's jurisdiction lessened the sting or even the threat of accusations of schism or heresy against the Czechs. From another angle, however, it might have appeared that the time for negotiations might be propitious in 1525. Faced with the threat of a grievous defection in Germany, Rome might have been more forthcoming and even eager to reconcile with Bohemia. Erasmus and his acquaintances in the Roman Curia had also counseled an approach, modeled on the Compactata, for a rapprochement between Rome and the Lutherans.[192] Such attempts would actually follow in the form of several loose agreements between Rome and the Lutherans, particularly the Interims of Regensburg (1541) and of Augsburg (1548). In the end, however, such qualified and ambiguous agreements would prove no more effective than the Compactata.

The initiative of 1525 for a rapprochement with the Utraquists, in fact, came from the Roman side. While the Utraquists were now less pressed to regularize their relations with Rome, the latter had a more positive incentive to seek a modus vivendi with the Utraquists. The Roman propagandists' attempt to discredit Luther by linking him with Hus proved counterproductive; if anything it pushed Luther into greater radicalism and made his cause more popular. The new task of damage control led to an effort to split the Czechs as much as possible from Luther's cause by convincing the Utraquists that Luther departed from several traditional doctrines of Christianity cherished by them.[193] The first to manifest this concern was Hieronymus Emser, who traveled in Bohemia in the service of Duke Georg, but the new line was adopted most noticeably by Cochlaeus.[194] Emser warned the Czechs against being misled by Luther particularly in his message *De disputatione lipsicensi ad Boemos obiter deflexa est* (1519).[195] A Roman apologist, Hieronymus Dungersheim noted already in the fall of 1519 that Luther's attitude toward the papacy did not stem from the Utraquists, but from the more radical Picards.[196] As mentioned earlier, Luther himself indeed entered the picture. Fearing, on his part, that an agreement between Rome and the Utraquists might weaken the cause of reformation in Germany, he addressed on July 15, 1522, a plea reminding the Bohemian estates of their grievances against the papacy.[197] When the Diet at Nuremberg failed in April 1524 to take decisive measures against Luther, according to the Edict of Worms, the papal legate Lorenzo Campeggi was authorized by Pope Clement VII to open discussions with the Utraquists for reconciliation with Rome.[198] The pope greeted the anti-Lutheran campaign in

Prague as one of the most significant events of his pontificate, indicating the importance that the Curia attached to the divergence between Luther and the Bohemians.[199] The Roman Curia welcomed the opening of negotiations with the Utraquists in February 1525, as an event offsetting Luther's defection in Germany.[200]

In May and June 1525 an effort toward rapprochement with the Roman Church occurred through reopening the issue of the Compactata in order to gain papal recognition. These negotiations were carried out at the royal court in Buda, the principal residence of Louis, who (like his father Vladislav II) was simultaneously the king of Hungary and Bohemia. According to Skýbová, Lev of Rožmitál and his faction, on regaining their posts in February 1525, used the negotiation to strengthen their power position in Bohemia.[201] The idea of seeking recognition of the Compactata was embedded in the coronation oath of the Bohemian kings, and also implied an effort to restore an archbishop of Prague who would ordain Utraquist clergy. Thus, Vladislav II had previously sought to reopen negotiations with the Roman Curia in that regard. The immediate impetus to Louis's attempt dated to his extended stay in Prague in 1522.[202]

The Roman side was represented at Buda by the Cardinal Legate Lorenzo Campeggi and by the Archbishop of Esztergom, Ladislaus Szalkán. The Bohemian side was led by Lev of Rožmitál and Pašek of Vrat, although Administrator Cahera with his counterpart Jan Žák, the *sub una* administrator, were also included in the delegation. The discussions of the Utraquists' reconciliation with Rome failed when it became clear that (1) Rome would not sanction any liturgical deviations except the lay chalice; and (2) the Utraquists refused to repudiate their past stances on ecclesiastical discipline and liturgy, or to swear an unconditional submission and obedience to Rome. A positive result of the Buda pourparler was the pledge of mutual tolerance between the Utraquists and the adherents of Rome in Bohemia. Lev of Rožmitál and Pašek of Vrat promised that each side would regard the other as true Christians, not as heretics.[203] In a way, they reconfirmed the provision of Kutná Hora of 1485.

For once, Bartoš Písař seemed to be correct in his assessment of the negotiations at Buda. Critical of Lev and his Prague allies, he took a stand against the need to seek confirmation of the Compactata in 1525, based on the following considerations: (1) the Roman theologians did not mean to keep their promises; (2) it was not necessary to keep others from slandering the Czechs, since especially in Germany no one paid attention to the papal anathemas.[204] Eventually, even the presence of Lutherans inside

Bohemia could and would be used to strengthen the Utraquists in their resistance to royal pressure to submit to Rome. It prepared the way to the future political alliances of the Utraquists with the Lutherans (and through them with the Brethren), which would reach its culmination in the 1609–1620 period. Thus, in a curious way, the Utraquists had become an even less suitable instrument for Bohemia's Catholic monarchs to shore up Rome's authority after the outbreak of the Lutheran Reformation than they had been before.

Bohemia's Legacy of the First Encounter with Luther

The impression that Luther's teaching had a fundamental impact on religious life in Bohemia in the 1520s owes much to two flawed pieces of evidence: Pašek's anti-Lutheran persecutions of 1524–1528, and the bias of the principal narrative account by Bartoš Písař. Pašek's anti-Lutheran hounding bestowed on the Lutheran movement much more importance than it deserved, inasmuch as the religious issues were used largely as a smokescreen for the repression of political opponents. The biases and low theological *niveau* of Bartoš's account were recognized even by historians receptive to the idea of a Lutheran upsurge. Commentators such as Tomek, Šimák, and G. P. Mel'nikov recognized that the chronicler was prejudiced in the extreme and they warned that the veracity of his testimonies required more than the usual grain of salt.[205] In particular, his boundless hatred for Cahera urged him to exaggerate the pre-1524 Lutheran offensive so that Cahera's participation in the post-1524 anti-Lutheran campaign might make his villain appear so much more despicable in the role of a turncoat.[206]

Moreover, the image of a Lutheran upsurge in the 1520s was given a life of its own by historians and propagandists of the Roman Church on one side, and those of the Lutheran movement on the other. Both sides drew comfort, albeit illusory, from the idea that Luther's impact undermined Utraquism's *via media*. On the Roman side, it was Václav Hájek of Libočany, who in his notorious *Kronika česká* (Bohemian Chronicle) (1541) claimed that priests who refused to follow Luther's teaching were expelled from Prague in 1523. Without any mention of the anti-Lutheran persecution under Pašek, he maintained on the contrary that Administrator Cahera still praised Luther's teaching in 1525.[207] The Counter-Reformation author, Symeon Evstachyus Kapihorský, in his *Hystoria kláštera Sedleckého* (History of the Sedlec Monastery) (1630), apparently based on Hájek's account, claimed that Cahera in his "scandalous sermons" in 1525 publicly extolled Luther, calling him a saint. Another Roman priest, Jindřich Ondřej Hoffman in his *Ocularia. Aneb oči sklenné* (Spectacles or the Glassy Eyes of an Old Bohemian) (1637) repeated Hájek's account, adding his own with an evident dose of *Schadenfreude:* "[A]nd that is how Luther's religion began in Bohemia, and Hus's—once considered the best—was held in contempt."[208] Czech Lutheran writers in the late sixteenth and early seventeenth centuries made a similar historiographical (mis)use of the Cahera episode. Authors such as Matěj Kolín of Chotěřina (1574), and especially Zacharyáš Bruncvík (1613), would point to the Candlemas Articles as evidence that the Bohemian Reformation embraced much of Luther's teaching as early as the 1520s.[209] These assertions, in turn, tended to affect modern conceptions of the developmental thrust of the Bohemian Reformation after Luther's emergence. The main consequence of the encounter with Lutheranism, allegedly embodied in the Articles of 1524, was, however, and as we have argued, not for the mainline Utraquist Church that continued in reality to cling steadfastly to the traditional *via media,* but for subsequent Czech historical writing that overstated the role of the Protestant Reformation at the expense of Utraquism. It is relevant to point out that Erasmus had faced a similar double jeopardy. His criticisms of the Roman Church were taken out of context by propagandists for both the Roman and the reformed side to obscure his irenic thrust and show him as a follower of Luther.[210]

There were undoubtedly genuine converts to Lutheranism in Bohemia in the 1520s, but—except for the German speakers who converted from the Roman Church—there were only individual and unorganized defectors from Utraquism, such as the abovementioned Sobek of Kornice and Oldřich Velenský. As both the response of 1524 and the situation after Pašek's downfall in 1528 indicate, the bulk of the population and the priesthood remained loyal to the traditional Utraquist Church. Moreover, the Utraquist Consistory would underscore its traditionalist ecclesiastical orientation by reopening negotiations (futile, but symbolic) for a modus vivendi with the Roman Church at Buda in 1525.[211] If, as Hrejsa has claimed, Utraquism was mobilized or energized by its encounter with Luther, it was not through adoption of, or amalgamation with, the Lutheran Reformation, but through a reassertion in confrontation with Luther of its own true self, and through a reaffirmation of the traditional *via media.* Somewhat irreverently, one may say that the Utraquists played the same trick on Luther that Luther played on Hus. While Luther paid homage to Hus without intending to honor his doctrinal conservatism, the Utraquists praised Luther without embracing his doctrinal radicalism.

Czech historians from Palacký through Janáček and Macek could not deny the failure, if not the illusory nature, of the first attempt at a Lutheran takeover in Bohemia. Admitting the continued strength of Utraquism, their teleological interpretations of history made them view the outcome in a negative light as a victory of reaction and as a setback for the idea of progress. Palacký set the tone of much subsequent historiography by regretting that the conservatism of the common people in the 1520s did not permit an advance from Utraquism to Lutheranism.[212] Janáček deplored that "the Utraquists [in the 1520s], to whom the majority of the nation belonged, ... were capable of turning their back on Luther and reject[ing] . . . a linkage with the European Reformation." As a result, "the theoretical means, offered by the Lutheran Reformation, for a recuperation of Bohemian Utraquism . . ." was lost.[213] He added with regret that: "The tenacity of Utraquism was remarkable, and in no way explicable by the King's support or by the personal interest of a certain part of clergy . . . [I]t stemmed from [the society's] insufficient interest in a more progressive and activist religious ideology."[214]

To these stern judgments one can retort that Utraquism's first confrontation with the Lutheran Reformation was not devoid of benefits even from the viewpoint of what might be considered "modern" or "progressive." As Eberhard noted in his analysis, the Candlemas Day Articles evince strong elements of tolerance and open-mindedness. Eberhard contrasted the Utraquist spirit of forbearance specifically with the intolerant self-righteousness of the German Reformation.[215] Like the Church of England, their later counterpart on the *via media,* the heirs of the Bohemian Reformation demonstrated the possibility of keeping the essentials of an ancient Christian orthodoxy, while tolerating a considerable degree of theological "laissez-faire." Unlike the fully reformed denominations, the Utraquists did not feel the need of a demonstratively rigid orthodoxy on selected issues in order to counterbalance the rejection of a substantial part of traditional fundamentals.[216] As noted earlier, Luther himself was appalled by the freedom of theological discussion and preaching in Utraquist Bohemia in 1523.[217] Luther's own enthusiasm for book burning, on the other hand, was likely to repel the Utraquist clergy who still deplored the memory of Archbishop Zajíc's consignment of Wyclif's works to the flames in 1410.[218] Moreover, it seems no longer necessary to assume an incompatibility between religious conservatism and civic liberalism. The following observation, which was made concerning the representative of the Church of England's *via media,* could perhaps fittingly apply to the Utraquists as well: "[Richard] Hooker maintained continuity with the past, looked at the old ways as preferable, would maintain the historic episcopate and traditional worship, but with his views of the freedom of reason he opened a door to the future."[219] Recent research has challenged the view of the Protestant (Lutheran and Calvinist) Reformation as a "half-way house" from medieval superstition to "the age of reason."[220]

In conclusion, let us return to the results of Luther's early encounter with the Bohemian Utraquists. The latter's response to Luther was that he performed a useful service in helping to neutralize the power of the papacy, and in breaking the isolation of the Bohemians. Beyond that Luther was fine for the Germans, who would also stop calling the Czechs heretics, but there was little indication that the Czechs should adopt or otherwise directly benefit from the substance of the Saxon reformer's teachings. For the Czechs, his significance was to make more plausible the idea that the Bohemians were God's chosen nation, and that their Reformation had been a righteous cause. As for Luther, he had an incentive to encourage and praise the Bohemian Utraquists to keep them from making a deal with Rome that could leave his German religious revolt in isolation. Furthermore, his insistence on the orthodox character of the articles, for which Hus was condemned at Constance, served to undermine the validity of Rome's magisterial authority and thus to blunt the credibility of its judicial sanctions against him. As for the substance of Hus's reformist vision, Luther felt that the Bohemian was a timid tinkerer who had misdirected his efforts toward patching up the old ecclesiastical machinery, instead of being a bold inventor who scrapped the old model and designed an altogether new one.

4

Bohuslav Bílejovský and the Geography of Utraquist Ecclesiology

A distinguishing mark of Czech religious history is that after the onset of the Protestant Reformation, unlike certain other preexisting religious dissenters, the Utraquists remained attached to their fourteenth-century reformist roots. Accordingly, their objective was still to purify the institutional structure of the medieval Church of certain bureaucratic abuses and materialistic accretions, and they resisted the calls of Luther's and Calvin's followers to dispense with the historical edifice altogether. Thus, the Utraquists came to occupy a middle position between the Church of Rome and the post-1517 fully reformed churches, and in their *via media* also came to resemble the Church of England with its "Anglicanism" evolving during the sixteenth century. The sixteenth-century Utraquists' perception of their Church's position between the existing Church of Rome and the fully reformed Protestant churches, as well as its sense of participation in the traditional Church of Western Christendom, was most systematically and directly treated and exposed by the prominent, yet neglected theologian Bohuslav Bílejovský (c. 1480–1555), a member of the Consistory. His work offers a unique prism through which to view and interpret the ecclesiology of Utraquism that was distinctive, yet endowed with aspects of ecumenical significance. At the start, two basic points should be stressed. First, despite perceiving the Roman center as morally corrupt, the Utraquists still considered themselves an integral part of the Western, indeed Roman, Church. Second, certain liturgical failings, such as the lack of communion in both kinds for the laity and the infants, were viewed as symptoms of this corruption, and hence their practice, on which the Utraquists insisted, was to be a restoration, not an innovation.

Bílejovský expressed his views in the *Kronyka česká* (Bohemian Chronicle), published in Nuremberg in 1537,[1] and his opus has paradoxically attracted severe criticism from modern Czech historians who have tended to devalue Bílejovský's work as a highly idiosyncratic phenomenon. On the one hand, he was blamed for being unbearably old-fashioned, if not outright reactionary, when not embracing wholeheartedly the Protestant Reformation and preferring instead to maintain the traditional Utraquist *via media.* On the other hand, he was virtually accused of national treason for his alleged derivation of the Bohemian Reformation from Eastern Orthodoxy and thus calling into question Czech civilization's association with the West of which most of these critics were almost inordinately proud.[2] Even discounting the national bias, however, such experienced scholars as Antonii Florovskii, Howard Kaminsky, and František Šmahel accept the allegation that Bílejovský sought to derive Utraquism from the Eastern or Byzantine Orthodox Church.[3] Actually, Bílejovský's work—as a more careful study has shown[4]—should not be regarded as a frivolous exercise, but as a semi-official statement of the mature Utraquist Church, which sought to set the course for the church for the second century of its existence, based on a review and systematization of the theological and liturgical experiences of the first.

The journey of historical exploration undertaken in this chapter seeks to analyze the nature of the neglected Utraquist *via media,* as exemplified by Bílejovský, and to see Utraquism as a Central European phenomenon that was kindred in its relative gentleness and reasonableness to the Church of England with which the former shared not only its theological centrism, but also its roots in the pre-Protestant reform movement of the fourteenth century, based on the universities of Prague and Oxford and including the influence of John Wyclif. In a sense, Bílejovský's task was comparable to that subsequently begun by John Jewel and John Whitgift, and completed by Richard Hooker on behalf of the Church of England. It was to provide a theological, more specifically ecclesiological, rationale for his church hitherto evolving largely in an ad hoc manner.[5] In other words, Bílejovský's *Bohemian Chronicle* served a purpose for the Utraquist Church in Bohemia that was similar to the service performed by Hooker's *Laws of Ecclesiastical Polity* (1593)[6] for the Church of England. The similarity between Utraquism and the Ecclesia Anglicana has been noted, but not explored, by Jarold Zeman and Antony Black.[7] Moreover, this chapter seeks to show that Bílejovský, far from promoting ties with Eastern or Byzantine Christianity, constantly affirmed the derivation of the Utraquist Church in Bohemia from a distinctly Western Christian tradition.

Pristine Western Church

As Richard Hooker (like his precursor Bishop John Jewel in *An Apology of the Church of England,* 1562)[8] did on behalf of the Church of England, so Bílejovský did in defining the complex relationship (one is almost tempted to say the love–hate relationship) between the Utraquist Church and the Church of Rome. According to Bílejovský, the Church in Bohemia historically evolved in full harmony with the Roman See and was administered by bishops, often named by the popes. He expressed a high regard for the popes who had properly guided the general (*obecná,* i.e., catholic) holy church, and with a few exceptions, like that of Pope Liberius (352–366 A.D.), effectively opposed several heresies arising mainly in the East among the Greeks. He is not even disturbed by papal schisms. When there were two or three of them, the popes still continued to keep Christians correctly adhering to matters essential to salvation.[9] This was a traditional Utraquist attitude, expressed in the previous century, for instance, by Václav Koranda the Younger, Rokycana's successor as administrator of the Utraquist Church.[10] A similar view was present within emerging Anglicanism. Thus, Hooker "was therefore quite prepared to admit that the medieval Church ruled from Rome was part of the true Church, instead of being an anti-Christian organization which had oppressed and forced underground the only true Christians . . ."[11] As Bílejovský claimed continuity between the Utraquist Church and the preexisting Church in Bohemia, so Hooker would also admit a direct relationship between the contemporary Church of England and its pre-reformation predecessor.

In defining Utraquism's stand vis-à-vis the Church of Rome, for Bílejovský, of course, the most visible issue, and the entry point for other disagreements, was the onset of Rome's insistence on communion in one kind (*sub una specie*) for the laity. Prior to that, when the entire Western Church under Rome's jurisdiction received communion in both kinds (*sub utraque specie*) the Czechs had no problem in remaining in full harmony with Rome. Accordingly, the Czechs received communion sub utraque from the time of the introduction of Christianity in the days of the first Christian rulers Bořivoj and St. Ludmila.[12] Here he reaffirmed the assertions of Jan Rokycana concerning communion sub utraque by Sts. Ludmila and Wenceslaus.[13] According to Bílejovský, it was virtually impossible to determine the exact time and reason for the Roman Church's fateful departure from the established tradition and its embracing a form of communion flatly contradicting Christ's precepts, unambiguously recorded in the Scriptures.[14]

In looking into the timing and causes of the communion sub una, Bílejovský maintained that until the twelfth century the entire Western Church was sub utraque. In particular, he stressed Pope Gelasius I's (492–496) condemnation of the "splitting" of the sacrament of the altar as a great sacrilege. Contained in the Decretum of Gratian, Distinctio 2, c. 12 (*Comperimus*), Gelasius's decree, since its use by Jakoubek in 1414, has served as one of the basic arguments for the practice of communion sub utraque in the Western Church.[15] According to Bílejovský, even under Innocent III (1198–1216) communion sub una, if it occurred, had to be practiced in secret. It appeared that it was Thomas Aquinas, followed by Nicholas of Lyra (c. 1270–c. 1349), who undertook openly the defense of the misguided practice, though both of them also testified that communion sub utraque had been practiced by the early church. On the responsibility of Aquinas and Lyra, he shares the views that Václav Koranda had expressed earlier. Bílejovský seems to suggest that 1283 was the year when the first evidence of corruption began to manifest itself in the Western Church.[16] Interestingly, this date comes very close to 1277, when according to Steven E. Ozment, relying on Etienne Gilson, the Roman Church suffered a measure of corruption by embracing a rigid authoritarianism manifest in the practice of silencing instead of debating dissent.[17] On the issue of communion, however, Bílejovský also claims that long afterward the popes and cardinals, particularly in Rome at Easter, still distributed sub utraque to laymen.[18]

Even on the Roman side, as the discussions with the Utraquists at the Council of Basel had shown, theologians were unable to demonstrate when and where the communion sub una originated, which in itself was a strong argument, in Bílejovský's eyes, for its illegitimacy. The lack of official decrees "defining the eucharistic mode until the fifteenth century" is also noted by John M. Klassen.[19] Bílejovský argued that since the communion sub utraque was solemnly instituted by Jesus Christ, as recorded in the Scripture, followed by the Apostles, the primitive (*prvotní*) church, and a long succession of bishops, popes, doctors, priests, and monks, it would seem logical that its discontinuation, and its replacement by communion sub una, would have required another solemn act of equal standing with the gospel record of the Last Supper to legitimize the new practice. There was no such solemn act.[20] Bílejovský returns to this argument elsewhere. The champions of communion sub una claimed that their belief was so old that they did not know by whom, where, and when it had begun. With more than a touch of irony, he asks: "Perhaps, it was before the world was here, and there was no human being to accept it and to remember it? . . . Then it did not originate with Christ the Lord."[21] After all, there was the Holy Writ from which it was possible to learn the beginning of all religious fundamentals, such as the creation of the world, the birth of Adam, and the birth of Christ, as well as the institution at the Last Supper of the sacrament of the altar at which Christ distributed sub utraque.[22] While unambiguously commanding communion sub utraque, the Scriptures said nothing about the origin of communion sub una. Bílejovský does not openly call the communion sub una heretical, but his anonymous colleague, the author of the Utraquist homiliary of 1540, does so explicitly.[23]

Bílejovský also sought evidence on the acceptance of communion for infants and young children in the Western Church. He related that St. Adalbert (Vojtěch), at one point bishop of Prague in the tenth century, and subsequently, as a missionary, introduced the custom of communion for infants right after baptism into Hungary where the custom was maintained, at least for royal infants, until 1235. Bílejovský claimed that Pope Innocent III upheld the practice of communion for infants, as well as communion sub utraque. He also points out that Nicholas of Lyra (whom he otherwise regards a champion of communion sub una) cites St. John in 1327 (vi, 52–59) on the issue of communion for little children as an essential complement to baptism, as the Greek Church still recognized.[24] This principle was endorsed by the author of the homiliary of 1540,[25] and generally adopted and put into practice by the Utraquist Church from 1417 into the seventeenth century.[26] Václav Koranda, and Bílejovský's colleague, Pavel Bydžovský, were particularly avid advocates of the practice.[27]

Bílejovský felt strongly the need to defend the Bohemians against the suggestion that they had lost the right to communion sub utraque since they had actually adopted communion sub una in the fourteenth century. Hence, so their opponents claimed, the Czechs' situation was fundamentally different from that of the Greeks who had never stopped to receive sub utraque.[28] According to Bílejovský, the truth was that his countrymen had not stopped receiving communion sub utraque voluntarily. Under Charles IV, Archbishop Arnošt of Pardubice first began to introduce restrictions, and full-force pressure from above against communion sub utraque was unleashed only after the death of Archbishop Jan Očko of Vlašim (1380).[29] At that point a campaign of coercion was launched to enforce communion sub una. Priests, who could not be bribed, were pressured into conformity through the threats of losing their parishes; the simple faithful were intimidated with a total denial of the sacraments, including baptisms, if they opposed communion sub una. Succumbing to such terrorism could not be confused with a voluntary acceptance, maintains Bílejovský. Moreover, there was an almost immediate opposition to the malpractice arising under Jan Milíč of Kroměříž and Matěj of Janov, and a reversal was to occur within barely twenty years since the death of Očko, under Jakoubek of Stříbro (by 1414).[30] The pressure against the communion sub utraque, that Bílejovský described as affecting both the clergy and the laity, seems to correspond more with the situation in 1419 under Wenceslaus IV who—after an initial period of toleration—had decreed a suppression of utraquism.[31]

In fact, Bílejovský was almost certainly wrong in seeking to narrow to a few decades the period between the discontinuation of the communion sub utraque and its restoration under Jakoubek. Josef Kalousek, for example, cites instances of communion sub una in Bohemia for 1253, 1267, and 1281. There are no documented cases of lay communion from the cup according to the Roman rite for Bohemia in the fourteenth century. Kalousek even censures Bílejovský for an intentional falsification of evidence, particularly a bull of 1401 by Boniface IX for Kutná Hora, to prove the existence of communion sub utraque in Bohemia in the fourteenth century, while Krofta considers Kalousek's judgments excessively harsh.[32] There were other instances of insertions and alterations of earlier texts by the Utraquists without subjecting them to the same degree of moral indignation and scathing attacks by subsequent critics.[33] The editor of the 1816 edition of *Kronyka Cýrkevní*, Josef Skalický, moreover, suggests that Bílejovský mistook for communion sub utraque references to the "reception of the body and blood of the Lord" (*přijímání těla a krve Páně*), a formula, although technically correct, that was used—in a potentially confusing way—by the Roman Church to describe the communion sub una.[34]

In any case, the minimization of the hiatus in Bohemia between the discontinuation and the resumption of communion sub utraque was not an idiosyncratic effort on Bílejovský's part. Instead, as Krofta has shown, Bílejovský puts forth a conviction perpetuated in the Utraquist Church at least since the religious settlement under Archbishop Jan Rokycana in the mid-fifteenth century. Thus, Václav Koranda also claims in his 1493 work *O svátosti oltářní* (On the Sacrament of the Altar) that communion from the chalice had been available for the laity in Bohemia as late as the reign of Charles IV, and even for a while longer, in such localities as the church of the Prague castle and in certain monasteries. On these points Koranda cites, rather surprisingly, the authority of Rokycana who allegedly had been informed about such practices by surviving credible witnesses.³⁵ Helena Krmíčková, however, has recently pointed out another dating problem in Rokycana's testimony concerning the practice of utraquism in Bohemia, especially his attribution of utraquism advocacy to Matěj of Janov, which Koranda also shares.³⁶

In the final analysis, however, Bílejovský's main point was that the change from sub utraque to sub una had occurred in Bohemia only after several centuries of sub utraque practice and that the change was illegitimate in any case. Thus, ultimately, the length of the discontinuity, while significant, was not really the crucial issue. The crux of the matter was that there was no evidence for a theologically or juridically lawful institution of communion sub una in Bohemia. Had it occurred legitimately, there would have to be some official act on record authorizing this practice, such as an entry into the Tables of the Land (*desky zemské*), or a parchment provided with seals, such as the text of the Compactata of Basel. There was no such document.³⁷

Bílejovský had two other reasons for emphasizing the continuity of communion sub utraque in the Church in Bohemia. In the first place, he sought to refute what he considered slanderous assertions by adherents to the Roman Curia that their faith was older and that of the Utraquists dated only from the time of Hus and Jan Žižka.³⁸ Like the Church of England, the Utraquists considered themselves a legitimate continuation of the medieval Church.³⁹ As noted earlier, the term *hussiti,* in fact, seemed to be a favorite one of opprobrium used by the Roman Curia to designate the Utraquists,⁴⁰ while the courteous form was *communicantes sub utraque.*⁴¹ In the second place, Bílejovský sought to establish the Utraquists' right to the possession of Bohemian churches against the assertion of their opponents that they had been usurped from the faithful of the Roman Church to which they rightfully belonged. He pointed out that from the start of Christianity in Bohemia, since the days of Sts. Ludmila and Wenceslaus, the churches built in towns and villages by nobles, gentry, and burghers had been intended to distribute communion sub utraque. Hence, from the St. Vitus Cathedral in Prague to the churches in the smallest villages, all were legitimate possessions of the Utraquists. In other words, the legacy of Bohemian Christianity belonged rightfully to the communicants sub utraque; the communicants sub una had been the usurpers.⁴² Of course, the Utraquist challenge on the question of sub una had the wider implication of charging the Church of Rome with a lax or cavalier attitude toward biblical injunctions.

Ecclesiastical Authoritarianism to the Right

In continuing to define the relationship between Utraquism and the Church of Rome, Bílejovský links with the error of lay communion sub una two other features that made the Roman Church objectionable to the Utraquists: excessive love of earthly possessions, and the penchant for the exertion of secular (physical) power. These objections among the traditional tenets of Utraquism, embedded in the Compactata, were almost certainly connected with denunciation of priestly wealth and governing power—of the Caesarean or imperial hierarchy and clergy—by John Wyclif, about whose influence on Utraquism more will be said later.[43] These issues, however, also preoccupied Hus's Bohemian precursors, particularly Milíč, and Hus himself.[44] According to Bílejovský, it was in large part clergy indolence that had led to the abandonment of communion sub utraque in the first place. He cited Hus chastising such vices as avarice, simony, gluttony, fornication, pride, idleness, and neglect of religious functions among the clergy. He himself further denounced unworthy priests who, instead of preaching and serving the faithful, were interested only in collecting parish incomes, plentiful eating and drinking, and sexually enjoying their young housekeepers, as well as "the lord abbots" who "transformed monastic religion into earthly dignities."[45]

Within the context of sixteenth-century Utraquism, the author of the homiliary of 1540 seconds Bílejovský's opposition to the clerical enrichment and ecclesiastical ostentation. He denounces those who "wish to please God by building churches from the yield of robberies, namely from what they had robbed from the poor and the widows. But the more so they incite God to wrath because they wish to make Him an accomplice in their unrighteousness and oppressions."[46] The same author also warns against the exploitation of the cult of saints by priests for their personal enrichment. In general, concerns with material property should not distract the proper priests who, like the apostles, should be satisfied with bare necessities.[47]

Regarding the second subsidiary objection to the practices of the Roman Church, the inappropriate and unseemly use of physical force was epitomized, for Bílejovský, in the campaign against Utraquism, particularly in Pope Martin V's (1417–1431) sponsorship of several crusades against Bohemia and his grants of indulgences to the crusaders who would murder adherents to the divinely ordained communion sub utraque. In 1421, Martin indeed issued an a priori pardon for any crimes committed by the participants in the military expeditions against Bohemia. Bílejovský likens to the perverts of Sodom and Gomorrah the papally anointed thugs, who were ready to kill young and old, and rape virgins and married women, whose only fault was their scrupulous adherence to the Gospel commands.[48] Incidentally, Martin V, as Cardinal Oddo of Colonna, had been in charge of the initial judicial proceedings against Hus that led to the Bohemian reformer's excommunication in February 1411.[49] He had also participated in the sentencing of Jan Hus at Constance in 1415, and subsequently as pope, was virtually obsessed by the idea of extirpating the Utraquists.

For his misguided application of secular power, Bílejovský called Martin "an enemy of Christ," although he stopped short of ascribing to him the metaphysical or cosmological attributes of an authentic "Antichrist." The Utraquists did not share the zeal of Luther and his followers for identifying the pope with the horned beast of the Apocalypse (Rev 12.3), nor the view of Hus's mentor, Wyclif, who had claimed that Pope Innocent III (1198–1216) inaugurated the age of the Antichrist with the mendicant orders instituted by the pope as the Antichrist's pseudo-apostles.[50] In other words, for the Utraquists, as for (proto-)Anglicans like Hooker, the pope did not assume the status of "that man of sin . . . the son of perdition" of Saint Paul's epistle (2 Thes 2.3, see also 1 Jn 4.3).[51] Nor is the pope castigated by an application of other powerful biblical image of evil and corruption, namely that of the Whore of Babylon (Rev 17).[52] Among other reasons, the Utraquists had no need, as reformers elsewhere may have had, to use apocalyptic imagery in order to wean believers from ingrained habits of obedience to the Roman See. The course of the Bohemian Reformation had supplied the Czechs with more than enough genuine historical grievances against the papacy. Rather than in line with the censures of Wyclif or Luther, the Utraquists' denunciations were in line with those of the fourteenth-century orthodox critics of the papacy, such as Bridget of Sweden.[53] Thomas A. Fudge has advanced an intriguing suggestion that might lead to the conclusion that the Utraquists regarded the degraded papacy as a victim, rather than an incarnation, of the Antichrist.[54]

Thus, in a human, not a diabolical sense, other fifteenth-century popes than Martin, according to Bílejovský, were also less concerned—as successors of the apostles should be—with the welfare of Christians, and more interested in power and domination, "utilizing and inciting secular states to serve their will rather than God's will, so that they may grow ever more proud in their dominion."[55] The theologian probably had in mind in particular the excommunication of the Bohemian King, George of Poděbrady, by

Pope Paul II in 1466, combined with an exhortation of the neighboring monarchs for yet another crusade against Utraquism. Hus himself saw the two main clerical vices (attachment to power and wealth) neatly combined in Pope John XXIII's war against King Ladislas in 1412 declared to enforce the collection of feudal dues.[56] Examples of papal errors could be extended further into the past; Pavel Bydžovský, like Bílejovský, cited the case of Liberius and his involvement with Arianism, and added the sponsorship of the Nestorians by Pope Anastasius II (A.D. 496–498).[57]

A third subsidiary objection to the Church of Rome, clearly brought up by Bílejovský, was its opposition to liturgical use of vernacular languages. In this he again continues the established Utraquist tradition.[58] According to Bílejovský, the liturgy was sung in Czech language since the beginning of Christianity in Bohemia. After Sts. Cyril and Methodius, the vernacular singing was augmented by St. Adalbert (Vojtěch; a figure distinctly of Western Roman ecclesiastical orientation), cultivated in the Sázava monastery by St. Procopius and his successors, and finally by the monks of the Slavic abbey of Emmaus in Prague. Bílejovský claims that, despite the opposition of the champions of Latin, the Czech liturgical chant was generally used in the churches of Bohemia until the reign of Charles IV (1346–1378).[59] There were occasional setbacks. Thus, German monks who used Latin were settled in the Sázava Monastery in the eleventh century to replace the Czech-speaking denizens. Bílejovský recounts the legend, based in part on the fourteenth-century Chronicle of So-Called Dalimil, and also contained in the *Kališnický pasionál z roku 1495*,[60] that thereupon the monastery's dead founder St. Procopius made three ghostly appearances exhorting the Germans to leave. When his admonitions failed, he materialized temporarily and expelled the intruders by wielding his abbatial staff and inflicting deep cuts on these promoters of Latin.[61] The line of continuity in the development of Czech liturgical chant that Bílejovský postulates, of course, must be considered more symbolic or allegorical than real. It reflects an ideal ancestral line on which the Utraquists wished to be seen.

According to Bílejovský, it was only with the terrorist enforcement of communion sub una that the campaign against Czech in the liturgy started in earnest in the late fourteenth century. During this ecclesiastical vandalism, liturgical books were destroyed or mutilated, just like centuries previously when a certain Alchymus in Jerusalem had sought to destroy the books of the Prophets. The insistence on Latin, Bílejovský maintains, reflected the Italian hubris of the papal establishment, and the Germans, always eager to please those perceived as their superiors, became dedicated apostles of

Latinization.⁶² It was absurd to argue, as some had done, that the use of Czech or other vernaculars had led to heretical writings. Bílejovský asked: Had not Greek and Latin been used to express the most horrendous heresies, against which the Fathers of the Church had to defend the true faith? Closer to home, he also pointed out that Latin was used for heretical writings, as by Nicholas Biskupec of Pelhřimov to compose the Taborite *Acta,* and by the Bohemian Brethren for their theological works, including an *Apology,* recently published in Nuremberg.⁶³ For Bílejovský, heresy stemmed, not from the language, but from "evil heart" and "perverted reason."⁶⁴ Favoring the liturgical use of the Czech language was typical of the Utraquist Church. Václav Koranda devotes an entire section of his major treatise of 1493 to this topic.⁶⁵ Even more dramatically, the author of the homiliary of 1540 evoked the biblical image of the Philistines who filled in the wells of Abraham's and Isaac's shepherds. So the opponents of vernacular tongues tried to block "with Latin like with wisps of straw" the fountains of the Apostles' teachings in order to stop the flow of the waters of salvation and to keep the people from imbibing from these salutary springs.⁶⁶

Inasmuch as the Germans are assigned a significant role in the issues surrounding the use of liturgical languages, it is relevant to note the rather peculiar nature of Bílejovský's attitude toward the Czechs' Teutonic neighbors. He does not express dislike of them, or anger against them. He seems to convey the notion that, as undomesticated strangers, they simply could not help ending up on the wrong side doing the wrong things, whether by championing Latin liturgy and communion sub una, or by destroying a large section of Prague in 1419 at the behest of Queen Sophie, Wenceslaus IV's widow.⁶⁷ Moreover, he does not make them directly responsible for the anti-Bohemian crusades, claiming that the crusaders spoke no fewer than thirty-five different languages.⁶⁸

Bílejovský viewed the course of the Bohemian religious wars of the early fifteenth century as a sure sign that the Utraquist critique of the Roman Church was correct. Only divine favor could explain the repeated victories of the relatively small Czech forces against the enormous European hosts mobilized by Martin V's papacy. God fought his own battle through his small Czech flock, as he had done through the Israelites in the Old Testament times. Here Bílejovský followed the established Utraquist viewpoint. Already the *Husitská kronika* (Hussite Chronicle) declared concerning God's role in the battle of Vítkov in 1420 that "Not their power was victorious, it was He who—despite their low numbers—gave them victory over the enemy."[69] Repeatedly, according to Bílejovský, from the siege of Prague in 1420 to the invasion of Domažlice in 1431, the Lord struck terror in the hearts of the crusaders, led by cardinals, papal legates, and bishops. As a result—often on hearing their religious battle hymns before the Czechs came in sight—these invaders, whom Bílejovský characterizes as cutthroats, rapists, and arsonists, turned and ran, even—he adds with a Chaucer-like earthiness—soiling their pants from fear.[70] In this context, the Utraquists were ready to acclaim the military genius of Jan Žižka, while deploring the drastic iconoclasm and doctrinaire biblicism of the Taborites. Thus, the author of the homiliary of 1540 refers to Žižka as "the audacious and brave man" whom God sent as a whip against those who persecuted the truth and suppressed justice.[71] Thus, Hus himself made a comparison between the situation of the Jews under the Persian Empire and the Czechs under the Holy Roman Empire, with each nation defending its own language against alien encroachments. The comparison between the Utraquists and the ancient Hebrews would continue throughout the sixteenth century.[72]

Despite his emphasis on the historical Bohemian roots of Utraquism, Bílejovský did not regard his church simply as a national religion. He also saw the Utraquist Church as a receptacle for and guardian of an uncorrupted Western Christianity endowed with a universal mission. In seeing the reformed church of Bohemia as an integral part of the Western Church, he followed the tradition of Utraquism going back to Jan Hus.[73] Bílejovský also retained, in a somewhat muted form, the Czech religious messianism that had glowed more fiercely in the early stages of the Bohemian Reformation and, indeed, in the convictions of Jan Hus himself.[74] Above all, he saw the recovery of both kinds of lay communion as symptomatic of Utraquism's overarching ecumenical objective that marked its communicants as a people chosen to inspire and lead Western Christendom on a pilgrimage of return to the authentic forms of Christian faith and worship.[75] Influence of the Bohemian Reformation was felt in neighboring lands, including Poland and Hungary, and even Romania.[76] For instance, Bílejovský's learned colleague Pavel Bydžovský (mentioned earlier) illustrated a broad geographic sweep when discussing the adoration of the host with his examples ranging from Bohemia to Italy, the Netherlands, and France.[77] The stirrings of national messianism, viewing the English as the people chosen by God to purify the Church, were also present in the English Reformation, although less pronounced in (proto-)Anglicanism than in the works of Puritan writers such as John Foxe and John Bale.[78] In Hooker, as well as in his Anglican successors such as Archbishop William Laud, the focus on the contemporary national church tended to mute somewhat the universalist emphasis on ecclesiastical reform.[79]

In this light, it might be possible to review the issue whether the Bohemian Reformation was primarily a religious or a national movement, a question that also lay at the heart of the famous controversy between Masaryk and Pekař on the meaning of Czech history.[80] The Utraquists' self-image was of the Czechs as a chosen people destined to cleanse universal Christianity, a view that compounded or fused the universal religious and the national aspect.

Although not despairing of the ultimate rehabilitation of the Church of Rome, Bílejovský in the meantime openly invited Roman-style communicants to join the Utraquists, independently of the papacy, and participate in the inspiring task of purifying Christendom, assuring them that Utraquism, in fact, represented the uncorrupted form of Roman Christianity.[81] There was therefore an irenic quality to his approach based on the need to appeal to reason that was the property of all men and that precluded narrow dogmaticism.[82] With a proselytizing intent, Bydžovský sponsored and published German translations of sermons and other theological works by Utraquist classics, namely Hus, Jakoubek, and Jan of Příbram, for the use of Germans who lived in Bohemia, but had not yet acquired a reading facility in Czech.[83] There was, in fact, some evidence of German interest in Utraquism.[84] Bílejovský's vibrant message conveys a sense of genuine institutional purpose and conceptual vitality, and belies the critics' image of the Utraquist Church as a stagnant, if not ossified, institution.

Biblical Reductionism on the Left

If Richard Hooker, as well as John Jewel and John Whitgift, on behalf of the Church of England saw the opposition on the left mainly in the Puritans, Bílejovský focused on the Bohemian Brethren as Utraquism's radical challengers. As noted earlier, the Unity of Bohemian Brethren, a relatively small but zealous and devout sect, had emerged in Bohemia in 1457. Against the Utraquist *via media,* the Brethren revived in some respects the theological radicalism of the Taborites, and perpetuated the latter's questioning of the apostolic, sacramental, and liturgical principles of traditional Christianity.[85]

Bílejovský sought the root of the Bohemian Brethren's religious orientation in the legacy of the sect of the Picardi; hence he persists in calling the

Brethren Picardi or Pikarts. According to Bílejovský, the Pikarts had made their appearance in Prague in 1418 and gained their most important Czech convert in Martin Húska (or Loquis).[86] Mainly from this source sprang the various erroneous teachings initially manifest within the Taborite wing in the Bohemian Reformation. Here Bílejovský followed a Utraquist tradition dating at least to 1420 when John of Příbram had already applied the label of Pikarts to the radical Taborites.[87] Bílejovský cataloged the Pikarts' false teachings. Their key errors were the denial of transubstantiation and sacramental priesthood. Other sacraments, such as confirmation and confession, as well as purgatory and prayers for the dead, were also rejected. The traditional liturgy was abolished, including the use of holy water, blessed oils, sacred books, and special vestments or vessels. The invocation of saints and dedication to them of churches, chapels, or altars, were condemned as blasphemies. These radicals also denied the authority of the church fathers and doctors, even if the latter's writings were in full conformity with the Scripture.[88] This reproach had a long history. Already at the Synod of 1420 (Hádání u Zmrzlíků), the Taborites had been charged with holding a conviction that "the letters, teachings and collected sermons of holy doctors, . . . recognized by the early Church, such as Dionysius, Origen, Cyprian, Chrysostom, Jerome, Augustine, Gregory and others, should not be read, or studied, or invoked for confirmations of the Scriptures' meaning."[89] Bílejovský himself cites with approval a wide range of patristic and scholastic literature. Bydžovský does the same, and characteristically refers to St. Ambrose (339–397 A.D.) as "the great and excellent doctor of the Holy Roman Church."[90] This was fully in the tradition of the Bohemian Reformation. Hus, his precursors, and Jan Rokycana after them, all recognized the validity of patristic literature, decrees of ecumenical councils, and canon law, as long as their positions did not contradict the Scripture.[91]

These radical ideas, according to Bílejovský, inspired the Taborite iconoclasm of the 1420s when armed hosts of gentry and peasantry proceeded to demolish ecclesiastical buildings, not exempting Utraquist ones, under the excuse of extirpating idolatry. Assaulting churches and chapels, the radical Taborites ruined altars (engaging in a curious practice of cutting off their corners), smashed chalices and monstrances, stepped on consecrated bread, and spilled consecrated wine on the ground. Missals were thrown into the mud under wagon wheels, and church vestments re-sown into common clothes. The iconoclasts used the holy oils to waterproof their footwear, and defecated into baptismal founts.[92]

As an exception to condemning the Taborites' religious terrorism,

Bílejovský seeks to justify the destruction of monasteries during the early stages of the Bohemian Reformation. According to him, the monks proved to be incorrigible opponents of utraquism. Failing to respond to earnest exhortations and admonitions, they persisted in casting their anathemas against the Utraquists and favoring the foreign invaders. Hence, the Utraquists had little choice but to neutralize these—to use a modern military metaphor—fifth columnists in order to prevent the monasteries' employment as shelters or points of support for the genocidal campaigns of the crusaders.[93] Aside from the antimonastic views of Wyclif, the Utraquists' sentiments (voiced by Bílejovský) were probably engendered by the conspicuous role of the monastic orders, first the Cistercians, then the Dominicans, in the suppression of dissent at the behest of the papacy, especially from the time of the Albigensian Crusades (1209–1229) on.[94]

Bílejovský's tendency to look askance at Taborite militarism, if it went beyond what was seen as the legitimate defense of the Bohemian Reformation, appears to be typical of sixteenth-century Utraquism. Aside from the rejection of Taborite religious radicalism, perceived as the source of meaningless violence, the negative view of Taborite warfare was also a legacy of the memories of suffering and destruction seen as increasingly arbitrary and purposeless once detached from its original defensive motivation. For instance, Taborite warfare is also strongly condemned, especially with reference to the 1440s, as largely unnecessary and purely destructive, by a later prominent Utraquist writer Blažej Nožička z Votína, writing in 1566. Nožička likewise emphasizes the detrimental effect of the ideas of the Taborites and their partners, the Orebites, in inciting violence and dissension in the very center of the Bohemian Reformation movement.[95] Similarly, in his edition and translation of Georg Lauterbeck's treatise on government (Prague, 1584), Daniel Adam of Veleslavín includes an emphatic warning against unrestrained warfare, preferring two years of negotiations to one of armed conflict.[96]

Bílejovský relates the religious outlook of the Bohemian Brethren to the Pikart doctrines, coupling this with a curiously insistent denial that the former were influenced by the Waldensians. Commenting on the public emergence of the Brethren, which he dates to 1479 (thirty-five years after the routing of the Taborites), Bílejovský writes: "[T]hey are again called Pikarts, though for a long time, by those ignorant of history, they were counted as Waldensians; however, nothing that is Waldensian was theirs."[97] Most of the third book of his *Kronyka Cýrkevní* is dedicated to establishing the connection between the Brethren and the Pikarts. Interestingly, Bílejovský's colleague and theological ally, Pavel Bydžovský, while agreeing with placing the Brethren outside the pale of traditional Christianity, sees their origin exactly in the medieval Waldensian sect.[98]

A delicate problem for Bílejovský in seeking to navigate past the Charybdis of religious radicalism was to define the attitude of the Utraquist Church toward John Wyclif and his teaching, inasmuch as the orthodoxy of his views had been questioned and the Taborites, the spiritual ancestors of the Brethren, had tended to appeal to his authority.[99] Yet, Wyclif could not be condemned without disparaging the most distinguished son of the Utraquist Church, Jan Hus, who had been sent to the stake in 1415 for refusing to renounce Wyclif without an open debate on where his use of Wyclif contravened the Scripture.[100] Happily, some of Wyclif's doctrines had been subject in Bohemia in 1427 to a sanitizing exegesis by Peter Payne, an English follower of Wyclif and a prominent figure in the Bohemian Reformation.[101] A reliance on Payne's interpretations substantially eased Bílejovský's task, and his attitude toward Wyclif did not follow the negative opinion of Jan of Příbram, but rather the more generous view of the Utraquist mainstream, epitomized by Jakoubek of Stříbro and Jan Rokycana.[102] Bílejovský denied that Wyclif's influence had caused Jan Hus to waver on the issue of the Eucharist.[103] At the same time, he deplored the consignment of Wyclif's works to the flames in Prague in 1410 by Archbishop Zbyněk Zajíc of Hasenburk, whom he considered an ignorant oaf who "in a silly way . . . caused many difficulties to the learned students, bachelors, and masters, who were steeped in godly truths, and to spite them he ordered Wyclif's books (not understanding them himself) to be burnt in their presence in his court yard."[104]

Bílejovský assessed the principal issues of Wyclif's beliefs in his commentary on the Diet of 1444, which routed the Taborites.[105] He attributed to Payne (and by implication to Wyclif) an orthodox view of the Eucharist acknowledging the physical presence of Christ therein. He quotes Payne as asserting: "I believe that the real Body of Christ, born of Virgin Mary, martyred on the cross, is according to its substance and real being in every visible aspect of the sacrament."[106] According to Bílejovský, Payne advocated the retention of the seven sacraments, appealing to Wyclif's *Trialogus*: "Master Peter Engliš [Payne] confirmed this approval of the sacraments . . . when he testified about the seven sacraments that they should be held and preserved. And for this he adduced Master John Wyclif that the latter had thus maintained in the *Trialog,* in the 1. 2. and 3. chapter."[107]

Also, according to Bílejovský, in *On the Worldly Dominion* (De Civili

Dominio), Wyclif affirmed the existence of the purgatory: "[I]n the books *On the Worldly Dominion* he [Wyclif] derives purgatory from St. Paul's letter to the Corinthians in the New Testament . . ."[108] Further, he cites Peter Payne's references to Wyclif in the *Decalog* (De Mandatis Divinis) to show his master's belief in the efficacy of prayers and other charitable deeds for the dead: "Master Peter Engliš [Payne] . . . states the following: The purgation of souls that have left the body should be accepted . . . , and one should pray and perform other charitable acts for these souls. He backs this up by Wyclif in the *Dekalog* and several other books."[109] These were significant issues for Bílejovský, inasmuch as the related beliefs in purgatory and prayers for the dead had occupied an important place in Utraquist theology. Early in the Bohemian Reformation in 1415, Nicholas of Dresden had condemned both, as profit-making inventions to augment clerical incomes from masses for the dead. This view, however, was reversed two years later by Jakoubek of Stříbro, then the authoritative Utraquist theologian who had become convinced about the ancient Christian origins of these beliefs.[110]

Continuing, within the context of the Diet of 1444, his defense of Wyclif against misuses by the Taborites, Bílejovský cites Payne's references to Wyclif's *Trialogus* on the efficacy of saints' intercessions: "Those can beg for our sins, who had their own—to the extent that they had any—washed off by their blood. . . . Master Peter Engliš [Payne] backs this up by Master John Wyclif in the *Trialogus,* chapter 31."[111] Likewise, he refers to Wyclif concerning the preservation of traditional Christian liturgy and other customs sanctioned by tradition, citing from the evangelical doctor's *On Papal Domination* (De Potestate Papae). Some rules depended, Bílejovský maintained, on the guidance of the Holy Spirit for the homely reason that the Bible would reach a simply unmanageable elephantine size were it to specify every detail of the Christian order: "[P]roper ecclesiastical customs should be observed, even if not explicitly contained in the Holy Scriptures . . . because too large and heavy would be Christ's Testament, if all such customary particulars were written down in it. Thus it should be believed that the Holy Ghost had communicated to the Christians all the necessary matters. . . . Thus far Wyclif." In this implicit rejection of the Lutheran principle of sola scriptura Bílejovský expresses a Utraquist attitude that coincides with the *via media* of the Church of England. Hooker would similarly caution on the limitation of the Scriptures as follows: "Others . . . growe likewise unto a daungerous extremitie, as if scripture did not onely containe all things in that kinde necessary, but all things simply. . . . And as incredible praises geven unto men do often abate and impaire the credit of their deserved commendation; so we must likewise take great heede, lest in attributing unto scripture more than it can have, the incredibillitie of that do cause even those thinges which indeed it hath most aboundantly to be lesse reverendly esteemed."[112] Finally, Bílejovský cites the authority of Payne that Wyclif advocated the use of special liturgical vestments at mass and at other Christian rituals: "Peter Engliš [Payne] . . . says that Christian priests when they serve mass or conduct divine services, should use vestments instituted for that service, and he backs this up with Master Wyclif."[113]

It is important to note, however, that the courteous treatment of Wyclif by the Utraquist theologians remained far from full-fledged endorsement. Thus, Bílejovský's earlier mentioned colleague Pavel Bydžovský also claims an orthodox position for Wyclif on the Eucharist, quoting him as saying in an Easter sermon that "a believing Christian accepts it on faith that a complete Body of Christ, and his Blood and soul are in every, even the smallest, part of the sacrament." Like Bílejovský, he quotes Wyclif "because some boast and say that they believe as he had believed so that having read his true and Christian speech they might indeed, with the help of the Divine Lord, so believe." Bydžovský, however, adds these words of caution about Wyclif: "God forbid that we should follow him in all things . . ."[114] As noted earlier, the Utraquists did not share Wyclif's view of the pope as the Antichrist. The author of the homiliary of 1540 rejected Wyclif's contention that a priest in sin could not validly consecrate the Eucharist.[115] Despite these caveats, Utraquist priests apparently still used Wyclif's works in the first half of the sixteenth century.[116] This, together with a fairly copious study of Luther's translated works,[117] points to a considerable open-mindedness (not shirking from opposing viewpoints) on the part of the Utraquists in this period. This was despite their basic aversion to the characteristic doctrines of the German Reformation, particularly the principles of sola fide and sola scriptura, and their continuing commitment to the traditional beliefs and practices of the apostolic and sacramental Christianity of the Western style.

An Outsider to the East

Having spoken of Bílejovský's attitude toward the Church of Rome on the one hand, and toward the Taborites/Bohemian Brethren on the other, let us now sum up the particularly sensitive issue of his attitude toward Eastern Orthodoxy that seems to lie at the heart of much of the negative criticism surrounding his *Chronicle*. Contrary to what has been said on this issue by his critics, Bílejovský actually kept his distance from Rome's twin sister of the East. It is for him neither a peculiarly Slavic, nor a uniquely admirable and orthodox establishment. When he speaks of the Eastern Church, he presents it as a by and large Greek institution which, although preserving the correct form of communion and endowed with outstanding theologians, had also fallen into early heresies. Moreover, in some instances the Eastern Church had to be rescued from error by the popes.[118]

Conversely, when Bílejovský speaks of extra-Bohemian Slavic elements in Czech ecclesiastical history, such as the Christianizing mission of Cyril and Methodius in the ninth century, or the settlement of Slavic monks in the Emmaus Monastery of Prague by Charles IV in the fourteenth, he does not refer to the Orthodox Church. Instead, he confines these Slavic aspects to the orbit of Western Christendom. For him, Sts. Cyril and Methodius were dispatched by the pope and the cardinals; the monks of Emmaus were the spiritual progeny of St. Jerome, a distinctly Western/Latin Church father, moreover hailing for Bílejovský, like the monks, from the ultra-Catholic Croatia.[119] It is, therefore, misleading to attribute to Bílejovský the authorship of a "Cyrilomethodian theory" of the origins of Bohemian Utraquism, if it implied an Eastern Orthodox causation of the practice.[120] According to Bílejovský, Cyril and Methodius served as agents of the then-existing Western practice, and their Eastern provenance was accidental and for the purpose of communion in both kinds irrelevant.

The absence of concrete religious linkages with the Orthodox East, however, did not imply that the Czech reading public was unaware of the Czechs' ethnic kinship with the Orthodox Slavs, such as the Serbs and the Russians, or of the concept of "Slavdom." The kinship, however, was perceived as linguistic, not religious. This would be pointed out by Daniel Adam of Veleslavín in his introduction to the Czech translation of Aleksander Gwagnin's *Sarmatiae Europeae descriptio* (1578) and *Gesta praecipua tyrannisque ingens Monarchae Moscoviae* (1581) as *Kronika Moskevská* by Matouš Hosius, which would appear in 1589.[121] Veleslavín added that the Russians or Muscovites were so little known partly because of their remoteness and inclement climate, partly because of the lack of any notable achievements on their part.[122]

With respect to Orthodoxy, Bílejovský furthermore consistently maintains that the communion sub utraque was always administered in the Church of Bohemia according to the Western, not the Orthodox, rite. The earlier Roman practice, which Utraquism restored, was drinking from the cup.

According to the Byzantine rite, both species were distributed together on a spoon. Likewise in the Eucharistic ritual, the Utraquists according to the Western norm, maintained the use of unleavened bread and condemned the use of leavened bread that was prescribed in the Eastern Church.[123] Similarly, Bydžovský derived the traditional Utraquist practice of distributing communion to infants from an earlier (but illegitimately interrupted) practice of the Roman Church, not from the current usage of Eastern Orthodoxy. He stresses the views of St. Cyprian, whom the Roman Church views as almost equal to St. Peter in merit, that newborn infants in their innocence were more worthy of communion than older persons who were usually laden with sins.[124] According to Bydžovský, the Church of Rome had observed the communion of infants since primitive times, as attested by the doctors of the Church, by the Decretum of Gratian in mid-eleventh century, and as late as 1243 by the testimony of Pope Innocent IV, contained in his *Summa* in chapter thirty-nine concerning the sacraments.[125] In the previous century, Koranda likewise traced communion sub utraque from the chalice for wine to an earlier Western tradition, embraced by the bishops of Rome.[126] Both Bydžovský and Koranda refer to the *Pontificals* and *Agenda,* the ritual manuals of the archdiocese of Prague, to substantiate their claims of an earlier communion for infants in the Roman Church.[127] The Utraquist theologians stood on solid historical ground in their assertion that infant communion was practiced in the Western Church "until at least the twelfth century and then in some places until the fourteenth."[128] Finally, the Utraquist mass had the form and the tenor of a Western rite. The one element that it shared with the Byzantine rite and which was absent in the Roman one, the *epiclesis* (or an invocation of the Trinity before consecration), might have been derived from the Mozarabic rite of Spain.[129]

In addition, as noted earlier, Bílejovský argued consistently with his Western orientation (and also, as it turns out, with the conclusions of modern musicologists), and identified the liturgical chant adopted by the Utraquists as Czech and of the Western Roman type, and not as a variant of the Old Slavonic chant of the Eastern Orthodox Church. As Francis Dvornik and Josef Vašica pointed out, even Cyril and Methodius probably introduced in Bohemia and Moravia the so-called liturgy of St. Peter (a Slavic translation of the contemporary Roman rite) rather than the Byzantine Rite.[130] Recent research has also suggested that the emergence of Bohemo-Slavonic liturgical and legendary texts in the early Middle Ages in the tenth through the eleventh centuries was a phenomenon analogous to the emergence of similar texts in Old High German and in Anglo-Saxon in the eighth and ninth centuries. All these epiphanies occurred in the orbit of the Western Church, and all succumbed to the same triumphal advance of Latin.[131]

It was, in fact, because the Utraquists insisted so firmly on participating in the Western Church that the satisfaction of their demand for sub utraque created such difficulty from the viewpoint of the Roman Curia. If they were within the Eastern Church, their *desideratum* could have been more easily accommodated under the "Unia" formula, under which, for instance, the Byzantine rite Ukrainians and Belarussians would be permitted lay communion of both kinds after pledging allegiance to Rome according to the Union of Brest (1596). Also it was their sense of belonging to the Western Christendom that kept the Utraquists insisting on having priests ordained by bishops in communion with the see of Rome. Thus historically they recognized that the Church of Bohemia had been from the very beginning a part of the Western ecclesiastical jurisdiction (or patriarchate), based on Rome, and that this was true, as Bílejovský explicitly and correctly pointed out, despite the seemingly Eastern Orthodox character of the mission of Sts. Cyril and Methodius of 863 A.D. It was also true that the Utraquists would accept and even seek ordinations at the hands of Byzantine-rite Roman bishops, and that the Roman Curia in condoning this practice treated the Utraquists in this period as quasi-Uniates (from the death of Bishop Sancturian to the restoration of the archbishop in Prague). From the Utraquist point of view, however, all this was done not out of preference for the Eastern rite per se, but simply for the practical reason that the Byzantine-rite Roman prelates would not require the candidates to abjure communion sub utraque, as the Latin-rite Roman bishops might.[132] Thus, even this practice reflected a loyalty to the authentic Western practice, as the Utraquists understood it, and not a preference for the Eastern rite. The Roman authentication of their episcopal authority was an asset that outweighed the liability of those prelates' adherence to the alien Byzantine rite.

Bílejovský, as a spokesman for traditional Utraquism, did not imply, much less assert, a direct historical connection between the original medieval Christianity of Bohemia, and hence the Bohemian Reformation, on the one hand, and the Eastern Orthodox Church on the other. The belief in an organic Eastern Orthodox connection was not entertained by the traditional Utraquists, but was unequivocally postulated, as Kamil Krofta points out, only in the seventeenth century by the Czech Lutheran exile, Pavel Stránský in his notable work *Respublica Bojema* (Leyden, 1634), and subsequently by the world-famous bishop of the Unity of Bohemian Brethren, Jan A. Komenský (Comenius), in *Ecclesiae slavonicae brevis historiola* (Amsterdam, 1660). Paradoxically, it was these paragons of Western-style Protestantism, who unabashedly sought the pedigree of the Bohemian Reformation in Eastern or Byzantine Orthodoxy. It is symptomatic of the animus against Bílejovský, however, that at least one critic blames him for having misled Stránský, and presumably Comenius, into a belief in the Orthodox connection.[133] Since Stránský did use Bílejovský for Czech ecclesiastical history, he might have been in fact the first historian to misinterpret Bílejovský on the Orthodox connection.[134]

Ironically, it was also the Church of England that with its more extreme antipapalism was tempted under James I and Charles I to experiment with what from the viewpoint of its Western roots could be regarded as a miscegenation with, or a contamination by, the Eastern Church.[135] The (proto-) Anglicans were even earlier interested in Eastern liturgical texts, particularly the liturgy of St. James, to establish the ancient origins of the mass in controversies with the Calvinists.[136] In any case, seeking rapprochement with the Orthodox Church was not a particularly promising route even for churches like the Old Catholics who adhered to the historic apostolic succession and recognized the church councils of the first millennium. In a somewhat simplistic way, the Eastern Church tended to find them even more abhorrent than the Roman Church, regarding them as schismatics to the second degree.[137]

To compound the irony, Bílejovský's distinct detachment from Eastern Orthodoxy contrasts with the warmer feelings that the Utraquists had entertained for the Orthodox in the mid-fifteenth century and which were discussed earlier.[138] Changed conditions explain the subsequent diminution of the Utraquists' interest in the Orthodox Church. The fall of Constantinople to the Turks in 1453 caused the prestige of Orthodoxy to plummet. This catastrophe also ended any chance that a Utraquist reconciliation with Rome might become a part of a grander union between Rome and Byzantium. For the rest of the fifteenth century, however, sporadic expressions of Utraquist sympathy for the Orthodox Church still appeared.[139] In a broader sense, an appeal to the status of the Greek or Orthodox Church was the standard weapon for those who revolted against the idea of the papal monarchy. Above all, Luther played the Greek card against the claim of papal supremacy, particularly at the Leipzig disputation with Eck in 1519, and of course he was beyond suspicion of seeking to derive the origins of German Christianity from Eastern Orthodoxy.[140]

As for the Utraquists, however, even in the sixteenth century their attitude toward the Eastern Orthodox Church did not coincide with the Rome's view of the Orthodox as inferior schismatics. Without wishing to compromise in any way their Roman roots and credentials, or seeking their origins in the Eastern Church, as an institution particularly suitable for the Slav nations or for any other reason, the Utraquists retained from the fifteenth century a recognition of Orthodoxy's essential equality with Rome and of its religious authenticity. Independently of the East–West jurisdictional division, which they accepted and observed, the Utraquists also continued to acknowledge the major contributions of the Greek Church fathers that had become a common possession of traditional Christianity, benefiting the Western Church as well as the Eastern one. Thus, Viktorin Kornelius of Všehrdy stressed the value of learning from the Greek fathers in the introduction to his translation of a treatise of John Chrysostom in 1495, and with his colleague Řehoř Hrubý of Jelení translated other works of Greek patristics, particularly by St. Basil.[141] Bílejovský himself cited Greek patristic literature in the *Kronyka,* referring particularly to Eusebius, John Damascene, Origen, and Pseudo-Dionysius.[142] His colleague and contemporary, Pavel Bydžovský, deferred to the views of Basil the Great, Cyprian, Cyril of Jerusalem, John Chrysostom, John Damascene, Origen, and Theophylactus of Ochryda on such issues as communion sub utraque, the real presence of Christ in the Eucharist, and the principles of apostolic succession and sacramental priesthood.[143] Bydžovský also published a translation of the canon of the Greek mass into Czech in 1549, although this elicited much contemporary critical dismay even in Utraquist circles.[144] It is also true that subsequently the Utraquists would publish Eusebius's *Ecclesiastical History* in 1594 with its strong orientation to the Eastern Church and with its almost total ignorance of the rise and development of the Latin Church. The appearance under the same auspices and in the same year of the *Ecclesiastical History* of Cassiodorus, however, can be viewed as redressing the balance to give its due to the Church of the West.[145] The Utraquists' special reverence for the Greek fathers was not unique in the sixteenth century among those who felt themselves firmly rooted within the Western Church. The humanists, in particular Erasmus and his friends, flaunted their preference for the Greek fathers, often together with contempt for the scholastics. Thus, Jacopo Sodaleto claimed that even St. Augustine occasionally misinterpreted the Pauline epistles because of his limited knowledge of Greek.[146]

Whatever may have been the Utraquist attitude toward the Greek Church, by the turn of the sixteenth century the rituals and customs of the Orthodox Church of Muscovy, were presented as something exotic, if not bizarre, in the abovementioned *Kronika Moskevská*. For instance, the dogmatic insistence on the sign of the cross from right to left is considered absurd, and the rejection of the *filioque* from the creed as doctrinally unsound.[147] At the same time, the Utraquist townspeople did not hide their abhorrence of the Tsarist tyranny under which the contemporary Russian Orthodox Christians were forced to live. The *Kronika Moskevská* included in its subtitle the following description of its contents: "Also about the unheard of tyranny of Ivan [the Terrible] Vasilevich the Prince of Moscow which, in our memory, he has exercised over his subjects."[148]

A Kindred *Via Media* to the West

As noted previously, instead of a kinship with the Eastern or Byzantine Church, there is actually a closer relationship between Utraquism, as represented by Bílejovský and his colleagues, and the Church of England, as it had emerged from the Elizabethan settlement, exemplified by Richard Hooker, the star disciple of John Jewel and John Whitgift. This similarity was already broached in the broad sense of the adherence to the *via media* and the exercise of reason vis-à-vis authority and private inspiration in religious matters. Let us now turn to more specific features.

While navigating between the Scylla of Rome and the Charybdis of Wittenberg (and Geneva),[149] both Utraquism and the Church of England embraced the traditional apostolic, sacramental, and liturgical tenets of Christianity, and defended the traditional tripod of Western Christendom, namely the Bible, Aristotelian rationalism (in its scholastic and patristic incarnation), and the extra-biblical ecclesiastical tradition. At the most fundamental level, the Utraquists shared with the Ecclesia Anglicana an endorsement of the role of reason against sola scriptura, and an insistence on the observance of the law against the principle of solafideism.[150]

Like Bílejovský (and the Utraquists in general), although in opposition to Rome, Hooker set out to justify the ancient principles of Christianity against the reformed churches in his magisterial *The Laws of Ecclesiastical Polity*.[151] This was his guiding position: "As farre as they followe reason and truth, we feare not to tread the selfe same steppes wherin they have gon, and to be theire followers. Where Rome keepeth that which is ancienter and better, others whome we much more affect leavinge it for newer and changinge it for worse; we had rather followe the perfections of them whome we like not, than in defects resemble them whome we love."[152] Arguing against both Lutherans and Puritans, Hooker opposed the notion that the Roman Church should be entirely destroyed. Instead, the reformist task consisted for him in purging the historical church of Western Christendom of certain grave blemishes introduced mostly in the late Middle Ages. As he declares in his sonorous Elizabethan prose: "The indisposition therfore of the Church of Rome to reforme hir selfe must be no stay unto us from performing our duetie to God; even as desire of retaining conformitie with them could be no excuse if we did not performe that duetie. Notwithstanding so far as lawfullie we may, we have held and doe hold fellowship with them."[153] Hooker was, in fact, restating the proposition advanced by Jewel in the *Apologia* that a national church had the right, indeed duty, to seek needed reforms, if the Roman center failed to heed the need.[154] As Diarmaid MacCulloch points out: "Hooker was even ready to say that the contemporary Roman Church was part of the visible church despite its errors."[155] This view comes close to Bílejovský's historical argument that the Utraquists represented the true Western Roman Church and pioneered in its purification. Despite its national roots, Hooker also entertained ecumenical aspirations for the Ecclesia Anglicana.[156]

Doctrinally, Hooker's works, like those of the Utraquist theologians, came close enough to the Roman point of view for Pope Clement VIII to praise Hooker's intellectual acumen and express a wish to see his writings translated into Latin (according to Isaac Walton and Bishop Henry King), and for King James II to claim that reading Hooker's treatise aided his conversion to the Roman Church.[157] His Puritan opponent, Travers, charged in *A Supplication to the Privy Counsel* that Hooker "made false claims about the Church of Rome, seeing it as a Christian church in which many people are still being saved and that in essential matters stands in agreement with the Church of England," and furthermore alleged that Hooker expressed himself in the style of a scholastic theologian reminiscent of the days of the Catholic Queen Mary.[158] Against Travers, Hooker also defended the doctrine of justification, held by the Roman Church, as essentially correct.[159] As to Travers's accusations, Hooker in fact entertained a high regard not only for the methodology, but also the substance, of medieval scholasticism, in particular the teachings of Thomas Aquinas. In this regard he appeared to go beyond his own mentor Bishop Jewel who was willing to admit appeal only to the first six centuries of Christian literature.[160] Hooker surpassed even the Utraquists who seemed somewhat more cautious in endorsing the attainments of medieval scholastics. Václav Koranda the Younger, for instance, considers Aquinas an opportunistic apologist for certain errors of the Roman Church, above all, the communion sub una specie. Bílejovský views

Nicholas of Lyra in a similarly negative light.[161] Otherwise, however, unless a particular writer contradicts clear provisions of a scriptural text, Bílejovský does support the Christian authenticity of the recognized corpus of not only patristic, but also scholastic literature.[162]

While the similarities between Utraquism and proto-Anglicanism were striking and affected the fundamentals, there were also differences that could not be overlooked. One of them was the Utraquist emphasis on spreading the word of God. The requirement of preaching the word of God freely was originally put forward by Hus's precursors, such as Jan Milíč of Kroměříž, and by Hus himself, and put into practice at the Bethlehem Chapel in 1491. It passed into the mainstream of Utraquism through its incorporation into the basic Utraquist creeds, the Four Articles of Prague of 1419 (as Article One), and the Compactata (as Article Two).[163] In the English Reformation, there were attempts to control the contents of sermons, such as by issuing official homiliaries in 1547 and 1571.[164] Later in the sixteenth century, the emphasis on preaching was regarded with suspicion as a desideratum of the Puritans.[165] A related issue was access to the Bible. Article 10 of the Utraquist Candlemas Day Articles of 1524 provided that every pious man should study the Bible and teach it to his wife and children,[166] while Henry VIII's Act for the Advancement of True Religion of 1543 restricted lay reading of the Scripture to the upper classes.[167] In the realm of liturgy, the Utraquists relied on the fourteenth-century missal, pontifical, and agenda of the archdiocese of Prague,[168] which were more distinctly medieval than the Anglicans' *Book of Common Prayer.* Yet, the latter was traditional enough to be viewed as an abomination by the Puritans.

More importantly from the viewpoint of ecclesiology, the Church of England—especially because of its own bishops—was, of course, institutionally more independent from the Roman Church than the Utraquists were. The issue of the episcopate reflected in part differences in the view of the bishops' role. The Church of England stressed its administrative function by which the prelates maintained doctrinal orthodoxy, particularly keeping Puritan inroads contained.[169] The principle of historical apostolic succession seemed secondary, perhaps at times inessential. Thus, Cranmer as early as 1540 emphasized the bishops' jurisdictional power to maintain authority, which derived from secular rulers, while the exercise of sacerdotal power conveyed to the Church by Christ appeared secondary.[170] The Utraquists feared the bishops' administrative power as a potential threat of bureaucratic coercion from Rome. All important to them was the possession of priestly power flowing through the bishops as authentic successors of the

Apostles, and thus guarantors of true priesthood. As for the exercise of administrative responsibility, the Utraquists felt most comfortable with entrusting it to the priests of the Consistory chaired by the administrator. Looking at the issue of ecclesiastical governance the other way around, Utraquism historically represented a revolt of the priesthood against not only the papacy, but also against the episcopate (after the failure of Rokycana's archiepiscopal consecration, and the misadventures with Bishop Philip of Sidon in 1505).[171] Rejecting administratively (although not sacramentally) both papalism and episcopalism, the system might be best characterized by the old-fashioned term of presbyterialism.[172] All this led to a rather unusual separation between ordination and jurisdiction (or between the sacramental and administrative powers) at the diocesan level. While the administrative power rested with the Utraquist Consistory (as a partial heir of the archbishopric of Prague's jurisdiction), the sacramental power was furnished by random bishops, provided that they were in communion with the see of Rome.

The issue of the episcopate in part also reflected a difference between the Utraquists and the Church of England in the perception of the papacy. The Church of England's position (like that of the full-fledged Protestants) represented a view that the rupture of relations with Rome was more or less complete. The position of the Utraquists was that the existing rupture was caused by Rome (by Pope Pius II's abrogation of the Compactata in 1462), not by the Utraquist Church, and hence, at least theoretically, there was a state of perennial, often dormant, negotiations over differences in biblical interpretations of the Christian faith and liturgy.[173] In the interim, however, the Utraquists insisted on clerical ordinations by bishops (usually outside of Bohemia) who were not only canonically consecrated, but also by and large in communion with the see of Rome.[174] Thus while questioning Rome's authority in ecclesiastical governance, particularly its zest for micromanagement, and Rome's claims to absolute infallibility in biblical interpretation, the Utraquists evidently acknowledged the Roman See as the fountainhead of sacerdotal power, at least as far as Western Christendom was concerned. This conclusion is supported by Bydžovský's equation of "Roman" priestly ordination (*kněží římského svěcení*) with a proper ordination (*kněží řádně svecení*).[175] The bond between the Utraquists and Rome persisted in consequence of the central position of the Eucharist and of frequent communion in the Utraquist liturgy. Their insistence on a canonically consecrated Eucharist led to a corresponding insistence on a canonically ordained priesthood. This fact, in turn, conditioned the Roman Curia's reciprocal view of the Utraquist priesthood. While the Anglican orders, both episcopal and presbyterial, would be regarded as null and void, the Roman Church recognized the Utraquist clergy as validly ordained priesthood despite Rome's abomination of Hus and the Bohemian Reformation.[176]

In consequence of their stand on the historical apostolic succession, after the emergence of Lutheranism the Utraquists found themselves in a complicated situation that had its own logic. After excoriating the papacy's exercise of power for its perfidy and brutality for a hundred years, they had to adopt, in part, a novel role of defending the substance of the papacy, as Bílejovský did, against the Lutherans who threatened its very existence.[177] This became necessary in order to preserve the availability of papal spiritual power as a guarantee of the apostolic succession in the Western Church. Against the adherents of the Roman Church, however, the Utraquists still resisted any extension of the papacy's administrative or judicial powers into Bohemia. The continued resolve in this respect was based on the illegitimate use of such powers in the trial of Jan Hus, and in the subsequent crusades against Bohemia sponsored by the papal Curia.[178] In this regard, the Utraquists' situation vis-à-vis Rome resembled a qualified separation or a high degree of autonomy more so than a full-fledged divorce, or one might say that while the *Anglicana Ecclesia* chose the left side of the *via media*, the Utraquists chose the right. The Utraquists' esteem for Thomas More and John Fisher may be seen as a graphic reflection of this difference.[179] In that sense the Utraquists similarly differed from other later churches, like the Dutch and German Old Catholics or the Polish National Catholics who, although embracing apostolic and sacramental principles, would maintain a full separation or schism from the Roman See.

The complex, yet not incomprehensible ambiguity in the Utraquists' relation to the papacy has lain at the heart of the unfortunate and largely artificial distinction between "Old" and "New" Utraquism that has plagued the study of Bohemian Reformation ever since the injection of these terms into historical discourse by Ferdinand Hrejsa in 1912. Almost any Utraquist theologian or spokesperson could be labeled as an Old Utraquist, or virtually an adherent of the Roman Church, if the focus were on the source of sacerdotal power, or he/she could be called a quasi-Lutheran Neo-Utraquist, if the spotlight shifted to the categorical rejection of papal administrative and judicial jurisdiction.[180] In other words, the Utraquists, while firmly rejecting an inquisitorial pope, would cautiously and with reservations tolerate a pastoral pope. This nuanced attitude was not idiosyncratic or unprecedented, but came close to, for instance, the views on the role of the papacy advanced by Marsilio of Padua and William Ockham earlier in the fourteenth century.[181]

On the issue of the relationship between the state and church, there were, however, in Bohemia only echoes—albeit distinct ones—of the Caesaropapist arrangement (royal supremacy over the church) so ardently advocated by Hooker. In a way, the Utraquists' marked dependence on state authority was the natural consequence of the Wyclifite opposition to the political and economic power of the clerical establishment that the Utraquists shared to some extent with the Church of England. If ecclesiastics were to abstain scrupulously from the exercise of judicial jurisdiction (except in matrimonial cases and matters of internal clerical discipline), and from property accumulation to sustain it, then almost of necessity there had to be an intensified reliance on state power for the protection of the church and enforcement of its decrees. Yet, the Utraquists have been subjected to considerable criticism by historians for resorting to royal protection and assistance, which was seen as more incongruous in their case than for the Ecclesia Anglicana, inasmuch as, except for George of Poděbrady (1458–1471), they depended on monarchs who were unalloyed adherents of the Roman Curia.[182] A partially analogous situation would have arisen for the Church of England had it remained under the rule of the recusant James II and of his like-minded son and grandson.

Nevertheless, in Bohemia the kings from Sigismund of Luxembourg (1436–1437) through Maximillian II (1564–1576) swore according to the Compactata of 1436 to uphold the Utraquist Church, regardless of its relation with the papacy. Like Queen Elizabeth I of England a century later (in 1570 at the hands of Pius V), the Utraquist king, George of Poděbrady, suffered the ultimate humiliation when Pope Paul II in 1465 declared him heretic deprived of his throne, and his subjects absolved from allegiance to him. George had found his Philip II in Matthias Corvinus, the king of Hungary, while—unfortunately for him—the hussars of the Magyar host did not suffer from the same ineptitude as the Spanish captains of the Invincible Armada, and caused a temporary loss of Moravia from the bond of the Bohemian Kingdom. Unlike Elizabeth, George had the additional disadvantage of being unable to contain the sedition of the Roman Church's domestic adherents.[183] As for the Utraquist Church, there was no appeal from the decisions of its Consistory to the papal Curia, at first, under King Sigismund's imperial charter of the Bohemian Church's ecclesiastical liberties, dated January 6, 1436, and later supplemented by a specific decree of the Bohemian Diet in 1531.[184] The Utraquist Consistory remained from 1564 until 1609 typically in administrative subordination to the Bohemian Royal Chancery, not to the then-restored Roman archbishop of Prague, although it continued to style itself "Consistory of the Archbishopric of Prague for Communicants in Both Kinds" (*konsistoř arcibiskupství pražského pod obojí přijímajících*).[185] Until 1562, the administrator and the Consistory were appointed primarily by the Bohemian Diet, subsequently by the King and his officials without any formal reference to the papal Curia or to the archbishop.[186] The royal authority was considered competent to resolve jurisdictional issues between the Consistory and the Roman archbishop, as well as ecclesiastical issues between the Consistory and local governments, such as the town of Hradec Králové.[187] In their last stand in the aftermath of the Battle of White Mountain, the Utraquist clergy appealed for protection to the royal governor Count Karel of Lichtenstein in 1621.[188] Like the English Parliament in the sixteenth century would do for the Ecclesia Anglicana, so the Bohemian Diet issued major disciplinary and liturgical rules for the Utraquist Church as legislative enactments in the fifteenth century, although the latter would object to parliamentary laymen actually composing confessional texts touching on the issues of dogma in the sixteenth century.[189] Also, in a sense the initial success of the Bohemian Reformation had depended on royal authority when King Wenceslaus IV protected the reformers who in turn supplied him with ideological (Wyclifite) tools for constraining the archbishops of Prague and other prelates, especially in the period from 1403 to 1412.[190] Already then the Czech reformers argued that it was up to the king to purify the Church: "[H]e should root out simony, fornication, prostitution, excess of worldly goods, and worldly dominion of the clergy."[191] In 1411, Wenceslaus curtailed the payment of rents by towns to ecclesiastical institutions, and coerced Archbishop Zbyněk Zajíc to cancel an interdict imposed on Prague.[192]

Yet, Bílejovský's and Hooker's churches clearly parted ways in their respective perceptions of the monarch's ecclesiastical role. The monarch in Bohemia could be said to act as a defender of the faith for the Utraquist Church, but the Anglican concept of the monarch as the actual head of the church[193] would have been alien to the Utraquists, although the view of royal supremacy was far from clear-cut in the English Church.[194] It was less an ideal in itself than a compromise solution where to locate ecclesiastical authority with the papacy discredited and genuine general councils unavailable.[195] In addition to their less autonomous institutional framework, the Utraquists, compared with the Ecclesia Anglicana, had the ultimately critical disadvantage in that they lacked the support of at least a preponderance of the country's sociopolitical elites that would enable the Church of England to withstand both the Puritan challenge of Cromwell and the Roman challenge of James II. While the Utraquist Church of Bohemia enjoyed solid support among the Czech commoners,[196] many nobles, aside from those fully loyal to the Roman Curia, would gravitate toward Lutheranism or radical sectarianism by the turn of the sixteenth century.

A Paragon of Utraquism

Assessing the general significance of Bílejovský, first, he may be seen as a Czech Richard Hooker (or possibly a Czech John Jewel) whose objective was the daunting task of charting more clearly the correct path for the Utraquist Church between the biblical deviations of the Church of Rome and the stark biblicism of the full-fledged Reformation, exemplified by the Unity of Bohemian Brethren. In the second place, on closer examination, he did not suffer from an identity crisis (between the East and the West), but located the Church of Bohemia squarely in the bosom of Western Christianity, and there is no reason to question the sincerity of his assertion that the Utraquists were "the true Romans,"[197] who were at the time more truly Catholic than the pope. Bílejovský shared with Hooker not only the grim view of what they considered the foibles of the Roman Church, but also the implied hope of its salvageability.

5

Pavel Bydžovský and Utraquism's Second Confrontation with Luther

Historians concerned with the later phases in the Bohemian Reformation have treated Pavel Bydžovský (1496–1559) in a highly critical manner. Together with his contemporary and colleague, Bohuslav Bílejovský, this prominent Utraquist ecclesiastic has been viewed as a narrow-minded hinderer of progress in his leadership of the opposition to a full-fledged Protestant transformation in the 1530s and 1540s of the Utraquist Church. The purpose of this chapter is to place Bydžovský's stand on Lutheranism in a new perspective. This augmented understanding may also shed some light on the behavior of Utraquist ecclesiastics, especially the administrator Jan Mystopol (1542–1555, 1562–1568), as well as Mystopol's predecessor, Havel Cahera (1523–1529), whom historians have censured for performing intellectually inexplicable and morally inexcusable reversals between favoring and opposing Lutheran teachings, and thus for having brought discredit on the Utraquist Church during the second quarter of the sixteenth century.[1] Finally, Bydžovský will emerge as one of the key figures of Utraquism and, together with Bílejovský, its theological pacesetter in the sixteenth century and beyond.

Bydžovský in Historiography

One of the leading Czech encyclopedias characterizes Bydžovský's position in a typical way: "Being a dedicated proponent of Utraquism, his entire activity was directed against Luther's teaching that was beginning to spread in Bohemia."[2] Bydžovský's critics have focused mainly on two topics: his collaboration in 1537 with Johann Faber (or Fabri), the bishop of Vienna, and on his role in frustrating the Lutheran takeover of the Utraquist Consistory in 1543:

> Bydžovský in his zeal was not choosy about his means. While Bílejovský turned his dislike against the Brethren, Bydžovský attacked primarily Luther's adherents, though he detested the Brethren as well. Preaching before the general public he accused the masters of Prague University of Lutheran leanings, and he complained to Faber, the Roman bishop of Vienna, that Luther's teachings had influenced the Consistory. He sought to promote the established Utraquist faith by reporting to King Ferdinand, for instance, the decisions of a Utraquist synod of 1543 that favored adopting changes in religious rituals advocated by Luther. In his sermons he praised King Ferdinand as a defender of the Utraquist faith.[3]

In the first controversial episode involving Bydžovský in 1537, Bishop Faber, a prelate of the Roman Church, was brought to Bohemia by King Ferdinand I as a confidant and advisor on religious affairs. Faber published a pamphlet, *Confutatio gravissimi erroris,*[4] arguing that the Czechs were embracing religious innovations and straying from the orthodox teachings of traditional Utraquism. He praised Utraquist theologians, such as Jan of Příbram, for upholding Christ's entire presence in each of the two species of the Eucharist at the Synod of 1421, and for promulgating orthodox definitions of the sacrament of the altar at the Synods of 1429 and 1432.[5] Faber stressed the role of Jan Rokycana in the Compactata, which had been negotiated with the Council of Basel in 1436.[6] The Compactata had brought peace between Bohemia and the Church of Rome until their revocation by Pope Pius II in 1462. According to Faber, the Picards, Waldensians, Lutherans, and even the Zwinglians tended to invoke Hus's name, but in fact the Bohemian reformer had not provided any support for their heresies.[7] The Viennese bishop was truly delighted that Hus did not accept even Wyclif's concept of remanence.[8] Faber reproached the Czechs for their current betrayal of Jan Hus's reform Catholicism in favor of outright heresy, urging them to abandon the aberrant path and to seek a new reconciliation with the universal Church.[9] His assessment of Hus was, in fact, unusually generous coming as it did from a German spokesman for the Roman Church. In contrast, for instance, his theological confrere and Luther's famous opponent, Johannes Cochlaeus, would refer to Hus in 1549 as worse than the pagans, Turks, Tartars, or Jews.[10]

Nevertheless, the Czechs considered Faber's missive a national insult.

As a consequence, at the session of the Bohemian Diet on January 24, 1538, he was subjected to such invectives as a scoundrel (*lotr, padouch*) and as "a devil's blacksmith (*čertův kovář*)," who forged plots against the Utraquists.[11] Demands were also raised ranging from his expulsion from Bohemia to an immediate defenestration. Luckily, the German prelate was in safe hiding.[12] When bailiffs arrived at bookstores, sent by the Prague city council to seize and burn the offending pamphlet, it was discovered that the populace had already looted and destroyed virtually all copies.[13] Parenthetically, however, it may be noted that at least one copy did survive and is now deposited in the National Library in Prague; also a manuscript Czech translation, under the title *O potupení bludu,* is available in the State Research Library in Olomouc.[14] During the public outcry against Faber's pamphlet, the suspicion arose that an expert in Utraquist theology who opposed the influence of Lutheran ideas must have initiated Faber, an outsider, into the specifics of the early history of Utraquism. The ensuing investigation focused on Bydžovský who, in fact, readily admitted having done so when summoned and questioned by the Utraquist Consistory on February 23, 1538.[15] Faber's references to Luther's critique of the Brethren, and to the Brethren's objection to the adoration of the Eucharist,[16] are, in fact, themes developed by Bydžovský in his writings, as noted below. Faber, however, also had direct knowledge of the Brethren's Confession of 1535, which Ferdinand I had referred to him for analysis and expert opinion.[17]

The second episode revolved around a convocation of Utraquist clergy, summoned by the administrator and the Consistory on or about April 25, 1543, in the College of Charles University, including priests not only of Prague, but also those from other parts of Bohemia. Three questions were submitted to this gathering, the answer to which would determine Utraquist or Lutheran direction: (1) the mass as a sacrifice or not a sacrifice; (2) propriety or impropriety of invocation of the saints; and (3) justification before God through good deeds or merely by faith without deeds.[18] According to the historical record of the Unity of Bohemian Brethren, "Poznamenání a spolu shromáždění některých věcí pamětihodných přítomným i budoucím" (Notation and Collection of Matters Memorable for the Present and the Future Generations), which is the main available source for these events, the initiative came from a party that called itself Evangelical (*evangelitská*) and included the administrator, Jan Mystopol; Václav Mitmánek, a member of the Consistory; and, as a lay sponsor, the Moravian baron, Jan of Pernštejn.[19] These discussions, however, were cut short by an edict of Ferdinand I of June 15, 1543. The King simply ordered the Consistory not to deviate from the Utraquist tradition as it was established in the fifteenth century.[20] Again according to the Brethren's history, Pavel Bydžovský figured prominently among the Utraquist ecclesiastics who persuaded the king to thwart by decree the objectives of the Evangelical faction.[21] Even the otherwise unfriendly Josef Janáček, however, recognizes that the preservation of Utraquism was not due merely to royal intervention: "[Utraquism] remained attached to the old national traditions and its internal and external weakness did not exclude an existential tenacity that by no means was a mere posturing out of inertia."[22]

Although the tenor of the Unity's account is considered clearly tendentious, the basic facts have been accepted, perhaps somewhat incautiously, as authentic by modern historians from Václav V. Tomek to Winifried Eberhard.[23] Curiously, the Brethren's attitude was even less sympathetic to the Evangelicals than to the Utraquists, and was clearly marked by *Schadenfreude* over the setbacks of the former.[24] The episode of 1543, as described, bears an interesting resemblance to an effort a few years earlier by Cromwell and Cranmer to Lutheranize the Church of England against the opposition of high churchmen led by Edward Lee, the archbishop of York. This happened at the ecclesiastical Synod of late 1537, which was recently reconstructed by Diarmaid MacCulloch.[25] Neither event resulted in the embracing of Luther's teaching by the two respective churches.

Luther in Bydžovský's Published Works

Now let us consider how Bydžovský treated Luther in his theological works. In view of the above depiction of Bydžovský's allegedly strong aversion to Lutheranism, it might be assumed that his theological writings would contain vehement attacks on the German reformer and his teachings. Therefore, it comes as a surprise to find references to Luther and Melanchton in tones of praise and respect. This happened fairly often and usually within the context of Bydžovský's pointing out that the theological views of the two German reformers were preferable to those of the Unity of Bohemian Brethren. The Utraquist theologian, in fact, paid unusual attention to this domestic sect, and to highlighting its differences vis-à-vis Lutheranism. It may have been, in part, a preventive tactic, so that in the event the Lutherans received some degree of official recognition, the Unity would not be covered. As indicated above, the Brethren would repay, or more than repay, his persistent, though relatively temperate, critique. Their unique historical literature mercilessly satirized him as a mindless bigot, buffoon, and royal bootlicker, affecting his reputation negatively for almost half a millennium.

Above all, Bydžovský cited approvingly Luther's and Melanchton's opinions on the nature of the Eucharist, namely the bodily (as distinct from merely spiritual, or merely figurative) presence of Christ in the sacrament of the altar. In *Knížky o přijímání Těla a Krve Pána našeho Jeříše Krysta pod obojí způsobou* (The Booklets About the Reception of the Body and Blood of Our Lord Jesus Christ in the Both Kinds),[26] he focused on Article X of the Augsburg Confession, after arguing for communion in both kinds for the laity on the basis of the Old and the New Testaments, the Church Councils, the Greek and Latin Fathers, the medieval doctors of the Church, and canon law, as well as the classics of the Utraquist tradition (particularly, Jan Milíč of Kroměříž, Matěj of Janov, Jan Hus, Jakoubek of Stříbro, Martin Lupáč, Jan Rokycana, and Václav Koranda, Jr.).[27] The last section of his work, referring to the Augsburg Confession, was entitled, "And here is posited a hundred times better confession of faith about the Body and the Blood of the Lord than the members of Waldenisian Sect profess in their temples."[28] In opposition to the views of the Brethren, to whom of course he referred under the term Waldensian Sect, he lauded the Lutheran Eucharistic belief.

For a clarification of Bydžovský's argument, a few words of explanation concerning the Unity's understanding of the Eucharist may be in order.[29] After an initial hesitation, the Brethren had, under the impact of the German Reformation, adopted a Eucharistic position halfway between Luther's and Zwingli's, embodied in the work of their authoritative theologian, Brother Lukáš of Prague, which was published in 1525, and entitled *Spis dosti Činící těm, jenž o svátosti těla a krve Páně méne než pravda Čtenie smysliti káže smyslí, pravíc ji znamením tolko a ne pravdou býti* (A Treatise Responding to Those Who Concerning the Sacrament of the Body and Blood of Christ Contrive a Corruption Lesser than the Truth of Scripture, Saying That It Is a Sign Only and Not the Truth). Lukáš here endorsed an older Taborite formula, according to which Christ was present in the sacrament "sacredly, spiritually, powerfully, and truly." As Říčan explained:

> The first two terms rejected the physical understanding of the presence of Christ and the last two rejected an opinion which was merely . . . figurative. Thus the Unity . . . at the same time rejected Luther's opinion,

according to which Christ was all there.... The Unity likewise rejected the figurative interpretation of Zwingli, which denied a sacramental character to the Lord's Supper...."[30]

Against the Brethren's definition, Bydžovský emphasized with particular approval the following statement from Article X of the Augsburg Confession: "[W]e profess that we hold that at the Lord's Supper the Body and the Blood of Christ are really and substantially present. And that precisely those two under the forms of Bread and Wine are given to those who receive the Sacrament."[31]

In *Tato Knižka toto try ukazuje* (This Book Contains a Triple Lesson),[32] Bydžovský focused on defending the adoration of the Eucharist. Again he argued on the basis of the Old and the New Testaments, the Church Councils, the Greek and Latin fathers, the medieval doctors of the Church, and canon law, as well as prominent mainline Utraquist theologians. At the conclusion of his discussion he turned once more to Luther and Melanchton, and emphasized that they likewise agreed that the sacrament should be adored and prayed to. Bydžovský in this connection cited from a pamphlet that Luther had addressed to the Brethren, *Von anbeten des Sakraments des heyligen leychnams Christi,* published in 1523, and dedicated to "Meinen lyben herrn und freunden den Brudern, genant Valdenser, ynn Behemen und Mehren."[33] Referring to this pamphlet, he wrote: "Behold, Luther states that a man of faith cannot, without sin, deny honor and adoration to the Divine Body and Blood."[34] Bydžovský connected the Brethren's refusal to adore the sacrament with their lack of recognition of the bodily presence of Christ in the Eucharist, and cited Luther in chastising them: "[I]n your booklets ... it is stated that Christ is not present substantially and naturally in the sacrament, and also that he should not be adored. That upsets us Germans very much [Což námi niemcy welmi pohybuje]."[35] In the same connection, Bydžovský commented on another of Luther's works, *Enchyridion piarum precationum:* "According to Luther, who separates divinity from humanity, reveals himself as Antichrist, and a more cruel man than the prostitute who did not allow that her bastard son be split in two before King Solomon."[36] Bydžovský also repeated, from his *Knížky o přijímání Těla a Krve,* the lengthy citation and praise of Article X of the Augsburg Confession, concluding: "Not only Melanchton, but also the enlightened [German] Princes [*vosvícená Knížata*] recognize *corporaliter Christum esse in sacramento.*"[37] He was referring to the princely signatories of the Augsburg Confession, namely John, duke of Saxony; elector George, margrave of Brandenburg;

Ernest, duke of Lüneburg; Philip, landgrave of Hesse; John Frederick, duke of Saxony; Francis, duke of Lüneburg; and Wolfgang, prince of Anhalt.[38]

In *Tento spis ukazuje, že Biskupové Biskupa, a Biskup kněží, a kněží od řádných Biskupů svěceni Těla a krve Boží posvěcovati mají* (This Treatise Shows that a Bishop should be Consecrated by Other Bishops, a Priest Ordained by a Bishop, and the Body and Blood of God Consecrated by Priests Properly Ordained by a Bishop), Bydžovský returned for the third time to the praise of Article X of the Augsburg Confession, and to Luther's message to the Brethren, as well as his *Enchyridion piarum precationum.* He stressed that the cited evidence on the issue of the bodily presence of Christ in the Eucharist contradicted the Brethren's claim that they followed the "most learned men in Germany [nejučenější w niemcych], Luther and Melanchton," and believed the same as "those two German doctors [tiech doktoruo dwau niemeckých]."[39] He further referred to Melanchton's booklet endorsing the traditionally orthodox Eucharistic views of seven (four Greek and three Latin) Church fathers. Apparently, he had in mind the German reformer's *Sententiae sanctorum patrum de coena Domini,*[40] and he challenged the Brethren to produce a Czech translation of this treatise that he would then publish at his own expense. Otherwise, he had to assume that they merely hid behind Melanchton, "as a serpent would under green grass."[41] He noted that in answering Luther's pamphlet of 1523, the Brethren had already rejected the adoration of the Eucharist.[42] Thus, the Brethren did not follow Luther in what was true and faithful, but only in his deviations; while the faithful accepted him where he was in harmony with the Church.[43]

Despite Bydžovský's relatively frequent and almost excessively profuse praise of Luther and Melanchton, it does become clear, on deeper probing in his works, that he indeed rejected the basic framework of Lutheran doctrines whenever they differed from the tenets of traditional mainline Utraquism. Without mentioning Luther or Melanchton by name, he took a firm stand against the crucial Lutheran doctrine of justification sola fide. In a refreshing change, he no longer argued against the Brethren (happily, they also objected to solafideism).[44] Instead, he dedicated a pamphlet to refuting the views of "New Believers" (*nowowercy*), presumably Czech Lutherans, who opposed the religious requirement of good works.[45] In his writings of the 1540s, Bydžovský seemed to avoid the term "Lutheran," but in his Latin treatise of 1554 he would speak of Lutherans or of New Evangelicals.[46] Luther clearly opposed the observance of Lent and other fasts, as well as the veneration of saints and images. What were Bydžovský's views?

In his *Spis o postu* (A Treatise About the Fast), the argument focused on the defense of fasting, but it touched on other good works as well, and also—reflecting a disagreement with the Lutheran sola scriptura position—on the obligatory character of extra-biblical ecclesiastical rituals. In support of fasting, Bydžovský began his Old Testament references with Exodus (34:27) when God responded to the Jews so long as "having faith in [Him], they practised fasts and good deeds,"[47] and followed up with Daniel (9:3, 10:2–3), Ezra (8:21), Joel (2:15), Jonah (3:4–10), and the Psalms (35:13, 109:24).[48] As for the New Testament, he relied mainly on St. Paul's admonition in 2 Corinthians (6:4–5).[49] From patristic literature, Bydžovský cited Ambrose, Augustine, and Jerome on the meritorious character of mandatory fasting which, however, had to be combined with sinlessness; otherwise, he warned in the words of Sts. Isidore and John Chrysostom, one "resembles the devils who neither eat nor drink, but are constantly in sin."[50] For the culminating period of fasting and other good deeds, the Lenten period, Bydžovský endorsed the rituals that the Church had established to mark the occasion: "[T]he Holy Church, that is our mother, wishing to lead her sons and daughters to the safeguarding of this Lent and fast, established various songs and prayers, different for each day. To promote piety and penance a different part of the Scripture and a different Epistle are read each day so that the people, hearing God's word selected from the Old and the New Testament, would amend their lives through fasting, alms-giving, and prayers."[51] In other words, Bydžovský enumerated the whole roster of good deeds. He went on to admonish against rejecting good traditional customs, based on ordinances of the Church and the Christian Councils, which aimed at augmenting the praise of God.[52]

In order to place Bydžovský's view on justification in the Utraquist context, it should be pointed out that the requirement of good deeds was, indeed, firmly embedded in the Utraquist tradition. The Utraquist Church had affirmed the observance of traditional fasts at the St. James Day Synod of 1434, and again at the Synod of Kutná Hora in 1441.[53] The articles proclaimed by the Consistory on July 18, 1526, specified the observance of traditional fasts and feast days.[54] The Utraquist pastor of Habry, Šimon, appealed in 1528 in defense of fasting, almsgiving, and prayers, and against Lutheran challenges of the need for good deeds, to the injunction of the "holy doctors" and of "the law of God" (*zákon Boží*): *elemosinam date, jejunate, orate!*[55] Similarly, the author of the notable Utraquist homiliary (*postilla*) of 1540 explicitly opposed Luther's stand on justification, and asserted that faith alone was not sufficient without complementation by good deeds.[56] Unlike the practice of the Roman Church, however, the performance of good deeds was not to be an occasion for fleecing the faithful for the purposes of architectural splendor or military (mis)adventures.[57] One can see this going back to Hus's controversy with the Roman Curia over the marketing of indulgences in 1412. The Consistory's official instruction to the church in Kadaň of September 4, 1548, specifically enjoins the observance of established fasts, together with the celebration of feast days.[58]

In his pamphlet, *Čechové milí Čechové* (Oh, Czechs, Dear Czechs),[59] again without mentioning Luther, Bydžovský defended another traditional area of religious practice resolutely rejected by the German reformer, namely, the invocation of saints and the veneration of images. In his reticence, he likewise avoided commenting on the iconoclasm of the Brethren. It may have been because Luther himself approved of the Brethren's stand on this issue, praising them in his missive *Von anbeten des Sakraments des heyligen leychnams Christi:* "that they believed well about God in the Trinity, that they forsook obedience to the pope and the bishops, that they did not invoke the Mother of God or the saints . . ."[60] Bydžovský presumably lacked any interest in discussing the areas of agreement between the German reformer and the Brethren.

On the invocation of saints, Bydžovský resorted to the authority of Jan Hus, who incidentally was himself venerated as a saint by the Utraquist Church together with several other Utraquist martyrs, despite the lack of papal canonization.[61] The abovementioned Consistory's instruction to Kadaň explicitly mentions the feast day of St. Master Jan Hus (*sv. mistra Jana Husy*).[62] Bydžovský pointed to the fact that Jan Hus, in his *Výklad na přikázání Boží* (Explanation of the Divine Commandments), had also asked for the intercessions of Sts. Bernard and John Chrysostom, writing: "Oh my dear St. Bernard what a difficult task you have placed on me wherefore I, lacking in courage, implore you and your comrade John to intercede before God the Lord for me that he may assist me not to be afraid, but courageously to write and preach the truth that you both had written."[63] Hus's firm veneration of the Virgin Mary also relied on the views of St. Bernard.[64]

The tradition of Utraquism on the veneration of saints, exemplified by Bydžovský, reflected, in fact, the characteristic *via media*. On the one hand, at the Synod of Kutná Hora in 1441, the Utraquist Church had reaffirmed the veneration of saints, the practice of which had been denounced by the Taborite theologians, especially Mikuláš of Pelhřimov.[65] In 1466, for instance, Pikart converts (presumably the Brethren) to Utraquism were required to declare the following in Our Lady Before the Týn (cathedral) in Prague: "The Virgin Mary and other heavenly saints, also praying to our Lord

Jesus Christ..., help the sinful penitents... and it is proper and worthy to ask for their assistance."[66] On the other hand, the Utraquists—in a tradition going back to Matěj of Janov in the late fourteenth century[67]—had called for moderation in the veneration of the saints, and had adopted a particularly reserved attitude toward the saints' relics, which Jan Rokycana counseled to be discreetly locked away rather than publicly exhibited.[68] Basing himself on the teachings of Jan Hus and Matěj of Janov, Martin Žatecký outlined the Utraquist teaching on the veneration of saints in a pamphlet of 1517.[69] As another illustration of the Utraquist attitude, the author of the sermon collection of 1540 asserted that the condition of sainthood stemmed from the subject's relationship to Christ, not from papal canonization, and warned against reliance on the saints, including Mary, for aid in salvation (if personal merit was lacking), or for assistance in realizing merely material gains.[70]

On the veneration of images, Bydžovský again quoted Jan Hus, who in *Výklad na přikázání Boží,* chapter 35, in his discussion of the subject of idolatry, viewed religious paintings and sculptures as helpful aids in uplifting the mind to the objects they depicted, although, of course, not as foci of adoration or prayer in themselves.[71] On the issue of images, Bydžovský once more confirmed the characteristic stance of the Utraquist Church. On the whole, the Utraquists tended to steer a middle course between barrenness and flamboyance on the question of ecclesiastical decorations and art. Against the iconoclastic tendencies of the Taborites that had led them to deny the need even for ecclesiastical edifices, the mainline Utraquist Church admitted paintings and sculptures on altars, thus reaffirming the decisions of the early St. Wenceslaus Day Synod of 1418.[72] The veneration of images was likewise justified in the Compactata with reference to canon law.[73] Administrator Václav Koranda, Jr. (1471–1497) confirmed this cautious, but not negative, attitude vis-à-vis the images.[74] Among the preserved graphic examples of Utraquist veneration of images are the late fifteenth-century wall paintings in St. James's Church of Kutná Hora, featuring particularly Christ as infant Jesus and as the Man of Sorrows, and the Virgin Mary in Annunciation and Assumption scenes.[75] It was clearly one thing to say, as the Utraquists did, that the veneration of saints and images should not be a money-making occasion for the Church, and another, as Luther did, that such practices were at best irrelevant, at worst blasphemous.

In two of his treatises Bydžovský found himself at odds with significant aspects of Luther's Eucharistic doctrine. It happened explicitly in his *Odvolání jednoho Bratra z Roty Pikhartské,*[76] and implicitly in *Dět'átka a neviňátka hned po přijetí křtu sv. Tělo a Krev Boží, že přijímati mají.*[77] In the former work, originally published in 1559, he turned once more against the innovators who deviated from the path of Utraquism. These conceited individuals thought of themselves as instruments of enlightenment (*domnívajíce se býti jako paprskové jasní sluneční*), but actually they confused the youth in schools and even in higher education, leading others to a disdain toward the rites helpful to salvation. In particular, Bydžovský censured the Lutherans' rejection of the adoration of the host outside the Eucharistic service. The Utraquists traditionally performed this ritual with enthusiasm, especially in the elaborately festive Corpus Christi processions. In line with their advocacy of communion *sub utraque,* the Utraquists carried not only the host in a monstrance, but also the consecrated wine in a chalice, during the Corpus Christi processions.[78] Referring to the innovators, Bydžovský stated: "[T]hey do not light the candles for honoring the Body of God, as though in the procession the Body of God were not truly the Body of God . . ."[79]

In the last part of the treatise Bydžovský gives examples tending to demonstrate the continued real presence of Christ in the Eucharist after the ceremonies of the Last Supper. He retells the legend about an attempted desecration of the host in Kutná Hora in 1482, when unbelievers removed a host, exposed for adoration, from the monstrance. The host was found two years later in an unclean place, but miraculously undefiled, not even gnawed by mice. The parishioners in reparation erected a special altar for the exposition of the host and conducted weekly processions in honor of the Eucharist.[80] He adds nine other stories concerning the marvels and benefits connected with the adoration of the exhibited Eucharist. Ranging widely in time from St. Augustine to St. Louis of France and Charles V, and in space from Bohemia to Italy and Burgundy, they include a naively charming tale of bees that, out of an alleged innate respect for the divine, constructed an elaborate tabernacle out of honeycombs around a host.[81]

The treatise *Děťátka a neviňátka hned po přijetí křtu sv. Tělo a Krev Boží, že přijímati mají,* published in 1541, was entirely devoted to the cherished Utraquist practice of infant communion, which the Lutherans resolutely opposed.[82] This topic is of particular interest. An examination of Bydžovský's treatise shows that the Utraquist tenet was not just a whim or perverse oddity (in questionable taste), but had substantial erudition and notable theological depth behind it.[83] It is true that Bydžovský did not argue explicitly against the Lutheran stance, but once again directed his strictures against the position of the Brethren who, according to him, held that children should be admitted to communion only after the age of twelve.[84] In the long run, however, the attitude toward communion for infants came to constitute for almost a century one of the most visible marks of liturgical distinction between Utraquism and Lutheranism in Bohemia.

In his treatise, Bydžovský proceeded to cite the reasons for the communion for infants from his standard set of sources. He argues primarily from direct precedents, and secondarily from the signs of God's respect and favor for human infants. From the Old Testament, Bydžovský focuses on three symbolic episodes (or prophetic parables) foreshadowing the communion of infants. The first symbolic lesson was the incidents of manna from heaven and water from the rock during the Exodus (Ex 16:4, 31; 17:6). The manna and the water were provided for all, the children as well as the adults. The second symbolic event was a banquet (Esth 1:5) that the Persian King Ahasuerus gave in the city of Susa "for all the people . . . both great and small." Bydžovský tell us that in this biblical account, according to Albert the Great's interpretation, the king stood for Christ who at the Last Supper offered his body and blood not just to the adults, but also to children. As a bonus in favor of the Utraquist desideratum of communion sub utraque, Bydžovský further quotes Albert in reference to Ahasuerus's banquet that a plentiful feast without sufficient drink would have been defective and inadequate. As a third parable, Bydžovský cites God's giving food and drink to Adam immediately after his birth through creation (Gen 1:29, 2:10).[85]

Among the Old Testament sources, Bydžovský next turned to the witness of the Prophets. He cited the testimony of Isaiah (Isa 49:22): "[T]hey shall bring your sons in their arms, and your daughters shall be carried on their shoulders." Bydžovský identified with the view of Nicholas of Lyra for whom Isaiah's statement prefigured the apostolic times when parents would carry infants yet unable to walk, not only to be baptized, but also to participate in the Lord's Supper. In those days, according to Thomas Aquinas in his *Compendium theologiae veritatis* (chapter thirteen), baptism, confirmation, and communion were given in immediate sequence to all who accepted the Christian faith. Dionysius the Areopagite (or Pseudo-Dionysius) had also postulated in his book, *The Ecclesiastical Hierarchy,* the necessity of the immediate communion following baptism and confirmation inasmuch as it was the Eucharist that perfected the other sacraments. Bydžovský then turned to the testimony of King David in the Psalms that God gave food to all, which must have meant infants as well.[86]

The New Testament indicated the worth and dignity of small children, symbolized above all by Christ's initial arrival on earth as a baby in the crèche of Bethlehem. Bydžovský cited the view of Martin Lupáč that thereby Christ signified that "he was the food not only for those of a grown-up age, but also for infants," and further that "these infants immediately after baptism—having been born anew from the water and the Holy Spirit—should be carried to the Divine feast."[87] In addition, Bydžovský cited Matthew (18:2–6) on "unless you . . . become like children, you will never enter the kingdom of heaven"; Luke (18:15–17) on "Let the little children come to me . . .; for it is to such as these that the kingdom of God belongs. . . . [W]hoever does not receive the kingdom of God as a little child will never enter it"; and John (6:53) on "Very truly, I tell you, unless you eat the flesh of the Son of Man and drink his blood, you have no life in you."[88]

Moreover, in both the Old and the New Testaments, God was recorded as bestowing a special favor on infants still in their mothers' wombs, as on the Prophet Jeremiah (Jer 1:5) and on John the Baptist (Luke 1:41, 44). God similarly blessed others soon after birth. Above all, Bydžovský cited the incident in the temple (Mat 21:15–16) when the chief priests and the scribes were scandalized by children's cries, addressing Jesus: "Hosanna to the Son of David." He quoted Christ's response that God invited praise for Himself "out of the mouths of infants and nursing babies." Bydžovský also recounts legends from early Christian history in which babies only one month old gave significant testimony or praise to God. In view of his high regard for babies and infants, the Czech theologian maintained, the Lord must have deemed them worthy of, and hence included them in, his invitation to the communion table, and it was not up to the world to deny this grace to them.[89]

Arguing that in the primitive church priests "distributed the Body of God and His holy blood to little children," Bydžovský highlighted the authority of Pseudo-Dionysius. In his *The Ecclesiastical Hierarchy* (chapter seven), the alleged disciple of St. Paul confronted those who cited the lack of understanding on the infant's part as a bar to receiving communion. According to Bydžovský, the theologian of the ancient Church set aside this objection by pointing out that, in any case, many divine things were not comprehensible to humans or even to angels, but only to the "supreme Divine Wisdom."[90] He gave as his source Dionysius's collected works, edited by Jacques Le Fèvre d'Étaples, and published in Paris in 1505.[91]

Among the Greek doctors, Bydžovský called attention to John Chrysostom's homilies and Bessarion's treatise on the Eucharist for injunctions that an infant's communion should follow the baptism. Before discussing the

Latin doctors, Bydžovský paused to emphasize that their testimony was particularly important. It demonstrated that the infant communion was not an oddity of the Greek Church, but to the contrary a universal Christian obligation germane also to the Latin Church, which until relatively recently had practiced it. Conversely, its abandonment was one of the signs of the Church of Rome's fallibility.[92] He focused on the views of Sts. Cyprian and Augustine. For St. Cyprian, the newborn infants in their innocence were more worthy of communion than the sinful adults.[93] The Church taught, according to St. Augustine, that through baptism infants were included among the believers; hence communion could not be denied to them on the pretext of an incapacity to believe in Christ. Bydžovský further mentioned Remigius of Rouen's *Feria,* and Rabanus Maurus's *De institutione clericorum,* mandating communion as a natural and logical completion of the baptismal rite.[94]

From among the more recent Western theologians, he referred to Nicholas of Lyra and—more surprisingly—to Thomas Aquinas, citing again the angelic doctor's interpretation of Isaiah as prophesying the administration of confirmation and communion immediately after baptism. Above all, Bydžovský noted the testimony of Pope Innocent IV, contained in his *Summa* in chapter thirty-nine concerning the sacraments and dating to 1243. This showed, according to Bydžovský, that the Church of Rome had observed the communion of infants from primitive times, as attested by the doctors of the Church, until the mid-thirteenth century.[95] As for recent history, demonstrating the practice under the aegis of the Western Church, he noted, like Bílejovský, the alleged giving of communion to princely infants in the royal families of medieval Poland and Hungary.[96]

Canon law was for Bydžovský another major source of cogent arguments to document that infant communion had enjoyed traditional acceptance specifically in the Western Church into the second millennium of Christianity. After all, its classical formulation in the Decretum of Gratian dated to the mid-eleventh century. From canon law, he cited from Distinctio 4, Canon "Si qui vel hi qui," which provided that those who after baptism and confirmation were unable to walk, either because of young age or handicap, should be carried to receive communion. If the infant could not receive the wine directly from the chalice, it could be administered together with the bread on a spoon. Further, Distinctio 4, Canon "Eccles," stated that lack of understanding did not bar infants from the body and blood of Christ, the reception of which enabled the attainment of eternal life.[97]

Aside from surveying the traditional sources of Christian practices for the validity of infant communion, with an emphasis on the Western Church, or the patriarchate of Rome, Bydžovský likewise sought witnesses within the Bohemian milieu. Relying on Václav Koranda and his book *Traktát o velebné a božské svátosti oltářní,* published in 1493, he refers to old liturgical books of the archbishopric of Prague, known as the *Pontificals* and *Agenda,* presumably at least from the fourteenth century. The *Pontificals,* which contained rites for ordinations and consecrations reserved to bishops, and were almost identical for Prague, Rome, and Litomyšl, there was a provision for infant communion. Referring to Holy Saturday, the *Pontificals* specified that children baptized on that day should not receive any other food until given the communion. Bydžovský then notes a provision, commonly contained in the *Agenda* (subsequently known as *Rituale*), which were used by priests to administer sacraments and blessings and to conduct processions and exorcisms. Written in an ancient script, these manuals—according to Bydžovský—were still available in many churches of Bohemia, and stipulated that after baptism, if a bishop was present, the baby (having been clothed) should be confirmed, and given the consecrated bread and wine by the bishop.[98]

Bydžovský then highlighted the landmark decisions of the Utraquist Church from the Diets of 1421 and 1426 that mandated infant communion. He also called attention to a reaffirmation of this provision by the convocation of clergy under Administrator Martin Klatovský in Prague on August 24, 1539, and noted the published version of its decisions (in Czech and in Latin), which he recommended for purchase to his readers, particularly in view of their low price.[99] Bydžovský also brought up the arguments in favor of infant communion advanced by Martin Lupáč in a treatise, prepared for King George of Poděbrady, and by Koranda in his *Traktát o velebné a božské svátosti oltářní.* He quotes mainly from Lupáč, who recapitulated the exegesis of Thomas Aquinas on the words of Pseudo-Dionysius, the views of St. Augustine, and the words of Christ on the need and rewards of eating his body and drinking his blood without any limitation as to the recipient's age.[100] He quotes Koranda that, although an infant was saved by baptism alone, the Eucharist added a quantum leap in holiness.[101]

At the conclusion of the treatise Bydžovský provided instructions for parents concerning infant communion. Included were points such as proper removal, if a baby pushed a fragment of the host onto his lip after communion, and an injunction against natural food until after the infant's post-communion nap.[102] At the very end, Bydžovský appended a hymn celebrating the communion of infants.[103]

In another theological work, Bydžovský clearly found himself at odds with Luther's concept of the common priesthood of the faithful.[104] In *Tento spis ukazuje,* which was devoted to the nature of ministry in the church, he embarked on the defense of special orders for sacramental priests and bishops based on the historic apostolic succession. In a way, this treatise may be viewed as a response to the well-known pamphlet that Luther had written for the city council of Prague in 1523, *De instituendis ministries Ecclesiae, ad clarissimum senatum Pragenum Bohemiae,*[105] in which he reminded the Bohemians of the hostility of Rome to their reformation, and urged them to create a reformed ministry based on the idea of the general priesthood of all believers. In defending the historic apostolic succession, Bydžovský once again sought evidence in the Old and the New Testaments, the decrees of the Councils, the Greek and Latin fathers and doctors of the Church, and canon law, as well as in the writings of the traditional Utraquist theologians. He displayed formidable knowledge of canon law, adducing at least twelve Distinctiones and Causae from the Decretum of Gratian, particularly those defining the respective status of bishops and priests (Causa 1 and 24,[106] Distinctio 92 and 95[107]) and those bearing on the proper consecration of the Eucharist (Distinctio 2[108]). The very fact of resorting to arguments from canon law revealed Bydžovský's incompatibility with Luther, who had denounced this type of legislation as "summa injuria tyrannis."[109] In this Bydžovský followed in the tradition of the Bohemian Reformation. Hus, for instance, referred in his writings to the Decretum of Gratian more often than to any other source except the Scripture.[110]

Pursuing his argument further on the priestly issue from Greek patristic literature, Bydžovský cited John Chrysostom and Theophylactus of Ochryda as affirming the traditional view of the superiority of bishops over priests because of the former's ability to ordain priests and consecrate bishops and other powers that ordinary priests lacked.[111] Among the Latin fathers he quoted to the same effect were Pope Leo I, Ambrose, Remigius, and Augustine, and he added that Jerome had seen a foreshadowing of the distinction between bishops and priests in the Old Testament differentiation between Aaron and his sons on the one hand, and the Levites on the other.[112] As for the Utraquist classics, he referred to the views of Matěj of Janov, Jan Hus, Jakoubek of Stříbro, and particularly Jan of Příbram, that only priests who had been ordained by bishops according to the power of the keys entrusted by Christ to the apostles and their successors could validly consecrate the Eucharist.[113]

It seems that Bydžovský also drew support for his views on priestly powers from the work of Carlo Cappello, *Epitome apostolicarum constitutionum*.[114] Cappello, a Venetian humanist author, who served as a senator in his native city and also as ambassador to the Imperial court in the 1530s, presents in his book early Christian views, translated from Greek, on sacramental priesthood, and on the division between the ranks of bishops and priests. Truhlář lists an edition of this work by Bydžovský in the original Latin and dedicated to Václav Subul, pastor in Týn, but without an indication of the place or year of publication.[115]

While upholding the principles of apostolic succession and priestly sacramental power, Bydžovský argued explicitly within the context of invalidity of priesthood, and hence of sacraments, within the Unity of the Brethren.[116] Although resolute in its argument, his rhetoric was couched more in a tone of sorrow than of anger.[117] He returned in *Dět'átka a neviňátka* to the point of the Brethren's lack of valid sacraments because their priests were deprived of proper episcopal ordinations.[118] Surprisingly, he did not take the opportunity in *Tento spis ukazuje* to analyze, and presumably to reject, the Lutheran view of the priesthood and the hierarchy. On the contrary, as noted earlier, he used the occasion to launch once more into warm praises of Lutherans' Eucharistic views. The question, indeed, arises whether—despite his firsthand and thorough knowledge of certain fundamental documents of Lutheranism—he, in fact, fully understood the Lutherans' rejection of the principle of apostolic succession and of a separate order of sacramental priesthood.[119] This possibility, however, seems unlikely, inasmuch as already in 1528—Bydžovský wrote in 1543—Šimon, the Utraquist pastor of Habry, had expressed doubts about the nature of the Lutheran ministry, claiming that among the Lutherans, laymen pretended to ordain other laymen to the priesthood.[120] Similarly, Bydžovský's contemporary, the author of the homiliary of 1540, while denying that the power of the keys (i.e., the source of priestly power) was an exclusive property of the bishops of Rome, rejected the Lutheran idea that Christ entrusted this privilege indiscriminately to common believers.[121] The probable answer is that once again Bydžovský did not wish to call attention to the similarity between the Unity and the Lutherans, this time in the abandonment of the principle of apostolic succession. Moreover, the lack of canonical priesthood would undermine the validity of the actual status of their Eucharist, though not necessarily of what the Lutherans said about the Eucharist.

Bydžovský and Luther

After analyzing Bydžovský's works, it does not appear that his attitude toward Luther and Lutheranism was one of an utter rejection and abomination, as may be suggested by a reading of the Brethren's narrative of the events of 1543–1544, which has influenced subsequent historians. Bydžovský viewed Lutheranism in a relatively open-minded way as a movement kindred to Utraquism. One can speculate that this sense of kinship was facilitated because in the documents of the 1530s, particularly the Augsburg Confession, the Lutherans tended to argue from traditional Christian positions, and to gloss as much as possible over aspects of more radical departures from the apostolic, sacramental, and liturgical principles of medieval Christianity.[122] Thus, Bydžovský could feel that, unlike the Brethren or the adherents of the Roman Curia, the Lutherans were in the same league with the Utraquists: The Lutherans, like the Utraquists, were questioning certain ills of the Roman Church starting from the traditional benchmark, although their diagnosis differed.

On the contrary, the Brethren—in his judgment—derived from the medieval Waldensian sect, and therefore did not even share in the traditional Church, including the historic Church of Bohemia and its own transformation in the Bohemian Reformation. He went as far as to label as spurious the Unity's claims to the heritage of such luminaries of the Bohemian Reformation as Matěj of Janov, Jan Hus, Jakoubek, Jan of Příbram, and Martin Lupáč.[123] Curiously, Bydžovský's colleague and theological ally, Bílejovský, while in agreement with placing the Brethren outside the pale of traditional Christianity, categorically denied that their sect originated from the Waldensians,[124] and traced their roots instead to the sect of the Picardi, or Beghardi, who had allegedly made their first appearance in Prague in 1418, and had injected their idiosyncratic influence into the Bohemian religious maelstrom through their Czech convert, Martin Húska.[125] While Bydžovský ignored the likely connection between the Brethren and the Taborites, Bílejovský viewed the Taborites as the transmission belt of what he considered pseudo-Christian doctrines, from the Picardi to the Brethren.[126]

In Bydžovský's basically friendly disposition toward Lutheranism, however, there were also important qualifications. While kindred, the Lutheran Reformation, compared to Utraquism, was the product of a distinctly different geographic and intellectual milieu, as well as being a relative latecomer to the world stage. His prescription for the Utraquist Church was that Luther might be welcomed, but not embraced. It was not primarily a matter of ethnic or linguistic intolerance. To the contrary, Bydžovský sponsored and published German translations of sermons and other theological works by Utraquist classics, namely Hus, Jakoubek, and Jan of Příbram, for the spiritual edification of Germans who lived in Bohemia, but had not yet acquired reading competence in Czech.[127] This is not to say, however, that the Utraquists were unaware that full-fledged Lutheranism had a strong appeal for the Germans of the Bohemian Lands. Such an attraction had been noted, for instance, in the Moravian town of Jihlava by 1528.[128]

The most serious reservation vis-à-vis Luther that emerges from Bydžovský's theological writings is the unmistakable, albeit usually implicit, assumption of the German reformer's unacceptable radicalism. For Bydžovský, Lutheranism tended to overstep the boundaries that had marked the fifteenth-century reform movement. That movement had inspired Utraquism, with a limited reformism by and large shared with the Church of England. Luther did not just reject the fruits of the clerical hubris of the late medieval papacy, that is, its straying toward secular dominion and material wealth. He went beyond this in seeking to deconstruct what were for the Utraquists the sound parts of the apostolic Christian ecclesiastical tradition. Bydžovský clearly demonstrated, in arguing theological propositions, that, in addition to the Bible and the early Church Councils, he also recognized sources whose authority was largely incompatible with the Lutherans' sola scriptura viewpoint. These included the Greek and Latin fathers, the medieval doctors of the Church, canon law as embodied in the Decretum of Gratian, and (with some exceptions) the medieval Councils, as well as the mainstream (high church) theologians of the Bohemian Reformation of the fourteenth and the fifteenth centuries. Curiously, in his Czech writings of the 1530s and 1540s, Bydžovský mentioned Luther by name when agreeing with him, but usually did not name him when arguing against his doctrines. Despite this tactfulness or circumspection, however, he made it explicitly clear that, in his opinion, Luther in certain matters deviated from religious truth and faith and was out of harmony with the traditional Christian church.[129]

On the whole, Bydžovský's attitude appeared to be that the Utraquists, while to a certain extent sympathizing with Luther, ultimately did not really need him. As for the points of agreement with Luther, such as the real presence of Christ in the Eucharist and the lay communion in both kinds, they had their own theologians to instruct them, from Matěj of Janov and Jan Hus through Jakoubek of Stříbro and Jan of Příbram to the "venerable priest" (*poctivý kněz,* as Bydžovský insisted on styling him) Martin Lupáč, and Jan Rokycana. Even in these respects, he undoubtedly considered the theological formulations of the Utraquist classics superior to those of the German reformers. He lauded the Eucharistic stance of Luther and Melanchton mainly in contrast to that of the Unity.

Incidentally, through Bydžovský's theological discussions, including a review of the Utraquist theology during the first century of its existence, he in fact helped to set the theological canon and agenda for the Utraquist Church for its second century. During his service as a priest, particularly after the Lutheran challenge had subsided by 1544, he augmented his contribution in that regard by training those who would fill the ranks of the Utraquist clergy in the next generation. Bydžovský helped to prepare theology students for examinations before the Consistory, prior to their departure for ordination in Italy.[130] One of his grateful disciples, Jakob Srnec of Varvažov, dedicated to his mentor, whom he called a man of rare honesty, the following verses as a New Year's Day present (1557):

Tu primus fueras studiorum, Paule, meorum
autor, Mecaenas tu mihi primus eras.
Tu primus dederas stimulum atque in carmina vires,
O et praesidium dulce decusque meum.
Me commendarat sancto tibi pectore primus
Marchio Quercenus, candor amorque meus . . .[131]

In a broader perspective, the theological works of Bydžovský, together with Bílejovský's *Kronyka česká,* came to constitute a kind of benchmark at the midpoint of what would turn out to be the span allotted to the Utraquist Church for its development. Both Bydžovský and Bílejovský would be, in fact, cited as authoritative Utraquist theologians in the confessional statements of the Utraquist Church in 1572 and 1575.[132] References by Jesuit Václav Šturm to Bydžovský as a Utraquist authority in his *Krátké ozvání* (1584) also attests to his long range influence.[133]

As for the points of disagreement with Luther, such as the sacramental priesthood, solafideism, and the veneration and invocation of Mary and the saints, Bydžovský's attitude toward the Lutherans paralleled the future Anglicans' view of their disagreements with fellow Protestants. This may be summed up by the famous statement of another proponent of the *via media,* Richard Hooker: "As farre as they followe reason and truth, we feare not to tread the selfe same steppes wherin they have gon, and to be theire followers. Where Rome keepeth that which is ancienter and better, others whome we much more affect leavinge it for newer and changinge it for worse; we had rather followe the perfections of them whome we like not, than in defects resemble them whome we love."[134] One can cite, as another parallel with Bydžovský's treatment of Luther, Hooker's courteous treatment of Calvin about whom he spoke with respect in the Preface to *Of the Laws of Ecclesiastical Polity,* while, at the same time, outlining or implying his profound disagreements with the great French theologian.[135] Bydžovský's characterization of Luther and Melanchton as "the most learned men in Germany" (*nejučeniejši w niemcych*)[136] can stand side by side with Hooker's description of Calvin as "I thinke incomparably the wisest man that ever the [F]rench Church did enjoy, since the houre it enjoyed him."[137] Hooker could regard Calvin as "wise," "of great capacity," and "deserving of honors," while at the same time distancing himself from his own Puritan compatriots who, he felt, surrounded Calvin's writings with an aura of infallibility,[138] and claim that Calvin's ecclesiastical regime at Geneva was "little better than popish tyranny disguised and tendered . . . under a new form."[139] Similarly, Bishop Jewel, one of the architects of the Church of England's *via media* and Hooker's mentor, could refer to Luther and Zwingli as "those excellent men, sent by God for the enlightenment of this world."[140] On the Czech side, one may also cite the earlier example of Jan of Příbram, who was not suspected of great fondness for John Wyclif, of referring to the latter in the 1420s as *doctor evangelicus* and *ille sanctus doctor.*[141] Also Erasmus's counsel of moderation in religious discussions is of relevance here, considering his profound influence on the intellectual life of Bohemia in the sixteenth century. The Dutch sage cites the examples of Christ, St. Paul, and St. Augustine as masters of gentle polemics.[142] He also avowed his interest in discussing religious problems with Lutherans without worrying about their denominational labels. Still in 1523 he would be glad to talk with Luther himself, and with hope (in the spirit of St. Paul) that he might still be diverted from his erroneous course. After all, according to Erasmus, Luther was not all wrong: "It cannot be denied that Luther has drawn attention to many abuses which it is in the interest of Christendom to rectify, and which the world could endure no longer."[143] It would be logical to assume that some of Erasmus's tolerant spirit rubbed off on the Bohemian Utraquists, considering their high admiration for him. Inasmuch as Erasmus's good temper and civility had influenced theological discourse in England, particularly Jewel and probably Hooker as well, the Dutch sage may be considered partly responsible for the similarity between Utraquism and the Ecclesia Anglicana in their tradition of civility and tolerance.[144]

In his late treatise in Latin of 1554, Bydžovský indicated that his ultimate choice for the correct course of church renewal in Germany was Georg Witzel, and he recommended the latter to the Lutherans.[145] Witzel, an ordained priest, married and served as Lutheran minister in Saxony in the 1520s. Rejoining the Roman Church as a married lay preacher after the Augsburg Confession in 1530, and living mainly in Dresden, Berlin, and Mainz, Witzel proposed a remaking of the Roman Church in a way that to some extent resembled the Bohemian Reformation, including a liberal ecclesiology (based on patristics and eschewing scholastic formulae), lay communion sub utraque, vernacular liturgy, and de-emphasis on the veneration of saints.[146] Having visited Bohemia in the early 1540s, he gained the favor of Ferdinand I (as subsequently of Maximilian II).[147] Bydžovský's attention might have been drawn to Witzel also by Bishop Faber, who had been Witzel's sponsor since the mid-1530s.[148] The Utraquist translator of Robert Barnes's *Vitae Romanorum Pontificum,* and Bydžovský's contemporary, Šimon Ennius Klatovský was likewise familiar with Witzel's irenic position.[149] Subsequently, Witzel prepared for Ferdinand I a formula of concord (*Pro concordia Ecclesiae repurgandae ac restituendae*) for presentation to the Diet of Augsburg in 1555. Not surprisingly, in view of his liberal ecclesiology, he remained an opponent of the Council of Trent until his death in 1573.[150] Witzel's interest in Eastern liturgies, including the mass of St. Chrysostom and of St. Basil, might have influenced Bydžovský in his translation of the canon of the Greek mass into Czech in 1549.[151] Witzel's contemporary irenic theologian, the Croatian bishop Andreas Dudič, likewise was interested in Greek liturgy and copied the liturgy of Saint James from a manuscript in London in 1555.[152] In any case in 1554, Bydžovský exhorted any Evangelicals or Lutherans (*Euangelicastros, intelligo Luteranos*) who might be in Bohemia, to listen to Witzel's voice.[153] To the extent that Utraquism felt responsible for a general reform of the Western Church, as far as the Germans were concerned, Bydžovský recommended that they learn either from the translations of Hus, Jakoubek, and Příbram, or the exhortations of Witzel.

It is further significant for the assessment of Utraquist ecclesiology that Bydžovský included his endorsement of Witzel in the same pamphlet as his eulogies of Thomas More and Bishop John Fisher, recognizing in them kindred reformist spirits despite their more pronounced papalism. Paradoxically, More and Fisher gave up their heads for the pope as the chief of the sacramental system in the Western Church, while they wished to abolish his role as the monarch of an ecclesiastical state. In this, in fact, their position resembled that of the Utraquists, and abrogated the seeming contradiction of their praise by Bydžovský. In other words, like the Utraquists, the two English martyrs were opponents of papal monarchism.[154] Fisher, moreover, shared with Bydžovský and Witzel an interest in the liturgy of the Eastern Church. At his request, Erasmus furnished a new Latin translation of St. John Chrysostom's liturgy, eventually published in Paris in 1537.[155]

If one looks at the other side of the equation—the two Englishmen's attitude toward Bohemia—More seemed to have a dim view of Jan Hus, placing him (although Hus was not considered as pestilent as Luther) together with other heretics who were, or soon would be, burning in hell.[156] The Bohemians (as well as the Greeks) were lesser heretics than Luther.[157] Apparently under the influence of Aeneas Silvio Piccolomini's (later Pope Pius II) story of the Adamites in *Historia Bohemica,* More assumed that sexual licentiousness was a significant strand in the early Bohemian Reformation.[158] Fisher's attitude was rather equivocal. He used Bohemia's example as a deterrent to reducing the liberty and authority of the clergy in England in 1530, apparently also inspired by Piccolomini's *Historia Bohemica,* which was influential in England for its accounts of the Bohemians' confiscations of ecclesiastical estates.[159] Yet, he also acknowledged that the Church of Bohemia and the Greek Church, as well as those of "India, Persia, Egypt [and] Africa," were more schismatic than heretical.[160] Nevertheless, the statutes for St. John's College at Cambridge, inspired by Fisher in 1530, included the "Hussites" with the heresies of "the Lutherans, Oecolampadians, Anabaptists, Wycliffites . . . and all the others who do not think in a Catholic way . . ." It seems that Fisher rather perceptively distinguished between the heretical "Hussites" (presumably the radicals of the Bohemian Reformation) and the schismatic Church of Bohemia.[161] His attitude toward Hus was somewhat ambiguous, as it is apparent from his assertion that the Bohemian's condemnation could not be blamed on the pope, inasmuch as his judges were at odds with the Holy See, and thus could not be seen as acting to curry its favor.[162]

The Utraquist Church and Luther

What can Bydžovský's experience teach us about the impact of Luther on the Bohemian Reformation in the second quarter of the sixteenth century? It may be argued that the character of Bydžovský's encounter with Lutheranism could help to lessen the puzzle of the alleged vacillation of

Utraquist ecclesiastics, particularly Mystopol, and even his predecessor Cahera. As noted above, historians have censured the two for fickleness, opportunism, venality, or character deficiency for having warmly endorsed Luther at one time (Mystopol before 1544, Cahera before 1524), and for having opposed his ideas with determination at another time.[163] If a person like Bydžovský, with an established reputation as a stalwart of Utraquist orthodoxy and as a stern sentinel against Lutheran intrusions, could display an open fondness for certain aspects of Luther's and Melanchton's teachings, then conversely those who became known for their fondness for Lutheran ideas might have at the same time maintained an overriding loyalty to the Utraquist tradition.

There were others whose devotion to Utraquism was beyond any doubt, yet who uttered high praises of Luther while clearly rejecting his basic doctrines. Thus, while he explicitly opposed Luther's solafideism and his rejection of the veneration and invocation of Mary and the saints,[164] the Utraquist author of the sermon collection of 1540 praised Luther's Eucharistic beliefs, including the adoration of the sacrament of the altar, as superior to the Eucharistic views of Zwingli, Oecolampadius, and the Brethren. In addition, the author asserted that Luther displayed greater wisdom than several of the popes in his understanding of the requirements of the law of God concerning the communion sub utraque.[165] Like Bydžovský, he cited the presentation of Eucharistic issues in Luther's *Enchyridion piarum precationum* approvingly.[166] A similar attitude of respectful open-mindedness emerged from the controversy of 1528 between the previously mentioned Šimon of Habry and another Utraquist priest, Jan of Německý (now Havlíčkův) Brod. Jan pointed out that he agreed with Luther only on matters in harmony with the Church (e.g., the Eucharistic matters), when responding to Šimon who had castigated him for his attachment to Luther's teachings. Jan's standpoint closely resembled that of Bydžovský.[167] Another theologian with impeccable credentials of orthodox Utraquism, and the subsequent administrator of the Consistory (1572–1581), Jindřich Dvorský of Helfenburk, sought to satisfy his curiosity about the substance and methods of religious studies in Lutheran Germany from 1534 to 1538. Visiting mainly Meissen and Saxony, at the University of Wittenberg he met Melanchton with whom he subsequently corresponded. Nevertheless, as a member of the Consistory from 1539, Dvorský firmly opposed any religious innovations, including Lutheran.[168] Jan the Elder of Valdštejn, certainly an individual with an unblemished Utraquist track record, also received correspondence from Melanchton.[169] From the opposite shore, one may cite the case of Pavel Paminondas, a Czech priest, who converted from Utraquism to the *sub una*. While hardly susceptible to any Crypto-Lutheran allegiance, he would nevertheless praise Luther highly in his *Písničky křest'anské* (Prague, 1596) for his agreement with certain doctrines of the Roman Church, in particular the bodily presence of Christ in the Eucharist.[170]

In a more remote way, there could also be an analogy between the Utraquists' expressions of respect for Luther, and Richard Hooker's courteous treatment of Calvin, combined in both cases with firm commitments to the *via media*.[171] It would seem that a facile and rather abstract categorization of individuals as Lutherans has run the risk of overlooking the actual complexity and ambiguity of commitment. Before the religious lines had congealed, a certain amount of exploratory examination of ideas need not be regarded as something reprehensible, but rather as a sign of healthy open mindedness and intellectual curiosity that moreover in the case of the Utraquists resonated with the injunction to preach the word of God freely. One may even wonder whether the Lutheran propositions of April 25, 1543, were not submitted to the convocation of the Utraquist clergy more in the tradition of the academic disputations of the late medieval tradition, as something to be discussed and rejected, rather than as serious proposals to be discussed for adoption. Moreover, the Utraquists did not feel bound by the papal proclamation of Luther as an excommunicated heretic, who therefore could not be treated courteously. They were not compelled, morally or legally, to subscribe to the papal bulls of excommunication *Exsurge Domine* (June 15, 1520) and *Decet Romanum Pontificem* (January 3, 1521), which imposed on the German reformer the stigmas of heretic and criminal. To the contrary, the Utraquists disapproved of such heavy-handed ways of dealing with dissent ever since it had been applied in papal dealings with Hus and the Bohemian Reformation.

Two additional considerations may be advanced to support the possibility of merely a superficial attraction of Lutheranism for the Utraquist theologians who historians have presumed were won over to the side of the German Reformation. In the first place, much of the seeming enthusiasm for Luther on the part of the Utraquist ecclesiastics need not have reflected an acceptance of the specifics of his theological stance. It is very likely that this positive attitude, like Bydžovský's (and also Bílejovský's[172]), stemmed—as pointed out earlier—from a generalized sense of relief that the Germans would now have no reason to castigate the Czechs for heresy because of their own revolt against Rome.

In the second place, in view of Bydžovský's announced readiness to publish in Czech a pamphlet by Melanchton, even translating Luther's and kindred works by others need not have implied a substantial agreement with the corpus of his teachings.[173] If Bydžovský's rejection of Lutheranism was not without significant reservations, the question may well be asked whether the alleged endorsement of Luther's teaching by some of his colleagues might not have conversely contained major reservations.

From the overall context it appears that individuals like Mystopol were never fully committed Lutherans. Far from a readiness to abandon Hus and the Utraquist heritage, they were merely interested in exploring, testing, or discussing some aspects of Lutheran principles. Thus, during the beginning of the alleged ascendancy of Lutheran influences in the Consistory, a convocation of Utraquist clergy in Prague adopted on August 24, 1539, a set of Fifteen Articles (*Artykulowe a snessenij Knězstva pod obogij Spuosobau*) that affirmed certain practices rejected by Luther, such as the sacrifice of the mass, observance of fasts and holidays, invocation of the saints, and prayers for the dead.[174] Simultaneously, as Bydžovský pointed out in his treatise *Děťátka a neviňátka,* the convocation of the Utraquist clergy in 1539 reaffirmed the long-standing Utraquist practice of communion for infants, which was repugnant to the Lutherans and explicitly rejected by them.[175] At the height of its initiatives, the so-called Evangelical party under Mystopol put forth in 1544 a proposal that contradicted one of Lutheranism's cardinal tenets, the common priesthood of the faithful. Adhering to the traditional Utraquist belief in the principle of apostolic succession, the gathering called for a canonical consecration of the archbishop of Prague whom it proposed to elect.[176] The alleged inspirer of the Evangelical trend of 1539–1544, Václav Mitmánek, found it expedient, if not necessary, to obtain a priestly ordination in Italy from a bishop who was presumably in communion with the see of Rome.[177] The assumption of a limited, or even superficial, influence of Lutheranism on men like Mystopol and Cahera would, in the first place, tend to restore their moral and intellectual integrity in assessing their ultimate reaffirmation of traditional Utraquism. In the second place, this assumption would diminish the impression of ideological confusion and strife in Bohemia in the wake of the Lutheran Reformation. It would also strengthen the image of the Utraquist Church's stability during the second quarter of the sixteenth century.

In this context, it is possible to cite other examples of religious denominations praising, or even propagating, each other's writings without eroding their own doctrinal bases. Examples are the interest of the Czech Lutherans of the early seventeenth century in Puritan and other Calvinizing English theologians. Several works by William Perkins, including his *Anatomia conscientiae,* were translated, edited, and published by Czech Lutherans between 1610 and 1620.[178] The prolific Lutheran theologian, Zacharyáš Bruncvík, particularly in his *Zrcadlo Kacířství* (1613) and *Kšaftu Večeře Páně* (1614), praised, cited, and drew upon such Calvinizing theologians as Robert Abbot, Laurence Humphrey, Thomas Morton, Matthew Sutcliffe, and William Whitaker.[179] Shifting from the Lutheran to the Calvinist side of the equation, the Puritan theologians could praise Luther without compromising their Calvinism.[180] The Calvinist court chaplain of Frederick of Palatinate, Abraham Scultetus, in his sermon at his master's coronation as Bohemian king on October 24, 1619, could eulogize the crypto-Lutheran archbishop of Canterbury, Thomas Cranmer, again without any suspicion of himself turning Lutheran.[181]

Upon assessing Utraquism's encounter with Luther, it can be said that, despite an initial outburst of relief, the overall impact of Lutheranism on mainline Utraquism appears to have been one of disappointment. At first, it might have seemed that the German Reformation would confirm the truth of the Bohemian Reformation. Prior to Luther, the conviction of Utraquist righteousness had been based ultimately, although somewhat narrowly and precariously, on the signs of a special divine approval. Such was the Utraquist interpretation of the meaning of Jan Hus's followers' ability to defy militarily the rest of Christendom under Rome's jurisdiction in 1415–1437. The German defection from Rome had held out a promise that the perception of Christian righteousness, as interpreted by the Utraquists, would receive a broad acceptance. These hopes were soon derailed. From the Utraquist point of view, far from becoming more open-minded under the impact of the German Reformation, the managers of Rome's ecclesiastical policy were clinging even more stubbornly to their misperceptions of the law of God (contradicting the explicit gospel text), and the truth of Lutheranism manifestly failed to coincide with the truth of Utraquism. It is possible to argue that the main thrust of Utraquism (a purification of the medieval Church from its misdeeds) was diametrically opposed to the main thrust of Lutheranism (the ultimate irrelevance of good deeds to salvation). The stability of its own 150 years of tradition, combined with the removal of the most glaring abuses characteristic of the late medieval Church, seems to have also immunized the Bohemian Church against the appeal of sixteenth-century Protestant teachings.

The Utraquists and the Roman Curia

Let us now examine the other side of the ledger, namely the suspicion that Bydžovský and his colleagues wished to merge with the Roman Church. While informally the Utraquists kept the sacerdotal tie with Rome by having their priests ordained by bishops in communion with Rome, it was obvious that there was no question of their willingness to reconcile with the Roman Curia formally, that is in the administrative and judicial sense, except on their own terms. The failure of the negotiations conducted in Buda in the spring of 1525 between the Utraquist Consistory and the papal legate, Lorenzo Compeggi, had confirmed the status quo for the mid-sixteenth century.

Faber's pamphlet, with which Bydžovský was indirectly involved, was not an isolated phenomenon, but fitted into the context of a more generalized effort to keep the Czechs from allying with Luther. It reflected, in a large part, the conspicuous zigzag that the Roman Curia executed in its attitude toward Utraquism in the aftermath of the German Reformation. Rome's initial reaction was to discredit Luther by linking him with Hus. This was the line pursued by the polemicists on Rome's behalf, especially by Johann Eck at the Leipzig debate of 1519 and Nuncio Girolamo Aleandro at the Diet of Worms in 1521. This stratagem proved counterproductive; if anything, it pushed Luther into greater radicalism and made his cause even more popular. The Roman policymakers, therefore, shifted gears. The new approach to damage control called for weakening the dissidents by separating the Bohemians as much as possible from Luther's cause. The aim was to convince the Czechs that Luther was a dangerous heretic who had departed from several traditional doctrines of Christianity that the Utraquists cherished.[182] This approach was adopted on behalf of Rome in the 1520s by Hieronymus Dungersheim,[183] Hieronymus Emser,[184] and Johannes Cochlaeus.[185] In 1525, as noted earlier, even Bishop John Fisher in faraway England called attention to the fact that Luther was more radical than Hus, and the two were not in mutual agreement.[186]

Faber's irenic view was perpetuated by his successor as Bishop of Vienna, Friedrich Nausea, who continued his patronage of Georg Witzel, and supported the Utraquist author and translator of Barnes's *Chronicles,* Šimon Ennius Klatovský.[187] Faber together with Nausea and Witzel acquired the reputation of irenic or mediating theologians (Vermittlungstheologen) between Rome and the Reformation. Cochlaeus, on the other hand, continued his interest in the Utraquists on a more devious basis, seeking to sow discord between them and the followers of Luther. In his play, *Ein heimlich gespraech von der tragedia Johannis Hussen 1538,* written in response to Johann Agricola's *Tragoedie von Johann Hus* (1537), a dramatization of the trial in Constance, Cochlaeus used his own drama to underscore the differences between Luther and Hus. He had Luther proclaim that Hus might have been evangelical in his critique of the pope's indulgence in worldly luxury, as well as in his attacks on the greed and whoremongering of the priests, but nevertheless he had remained entirely papist in many of the articles of his teaching and personal belief. The heavy-handed satire further portrayed Luther as demanding a dire punishment of Agricola for his glorification of Hus.[188]

Cochlaeus continued his effort to separate Hus from Luther in his magnum opus, *Historiae Hussitarum libri duodecim.* Although not published until 1549, much of the book was composed in the 1530s. By 1534 he had reached the year 1457 in his account, and in 1537 he published an extract under the title, *Wahrhaftige Historia von Magister Johannes Hus.*[189] He again followed in the footsteps of earlier authors, such as Hieronymus Emser, by trying to demonstrate to the Bohemians how far Luther diverged from the beliefs of Utraquism. In a letter of July 1534, Cochlaeus confided to Nuncio Pier Vergerio his intention to revise the manuscript to be even friendlier to the Czechs. He would take Luther at his word when the German reformer had stated in 1520 that "si ille [Hus] fuit haereticus, ego plus dicies haereticus sum."[190] Ironically, Cochlaeus's attempts to portray the Utraquist theologians in a relatively favorable light—although largely in contrast to Luther—would eventually earn his history a place on the index of prohibited books in the reign of Pope Sixtus V (1585–1590).[191]

Tradition of Tolerance:
The Compactata and the Peace of Kutná Hora

Inside Bohemia, in the early and mid-sixteenth century, the discourse of theologians sub una continued to be conciliatory toward their compatriots sub utraque, reflecting the spirit of the agreements following the settlement of the Bohemian religious wars. The coexistence of Utraquism and those under the Roman Curia was explicitly codified by the Peace of Kutná Hora of 1485, after having been informally observed since the adoption of the Compactata of Basel in 1436. These legal instruments prohibited accusations of heresy and mutual vilification between the two religious groups.[192]

Conscious of its weakness, after the failure of its sedition under George of Poděbrady, the party sub una tried to avoid any outright confrontation and showed considerable political and diplomatic skills in seeking compromises. Its leaders also tended to be less than enthusiastic about the nuncios' periodic suggestions for a more active policy against the religious dissidents, whether Utraquists, Lutherans, or Brethren.[193] In fact, they were willing to share with the Utraquists what would later become known as an anti-ultramontane position.[194] Without resorting to crass economic determinism, it might be suggested that the reluctance of the nobles sub una to submit fully to the Roman Curia's will also derived from their material interests. Their earlier seizures of ecclesiastical estates were safeguarded by a political system that eliminated direct papal jurisdiction. These (mis)appropriations occurred during the wars of the Bohemian Reformation, allegedly to protect Church lands from religious dissidents.[195]

An example of this type of tolerant and cooperative attitude on the Roman side was Tomáš Bavorovský (d. 1562). Starting as a priest sub una in Plzeň (1546–1552), he was then appointed a canon in the chapter at St. Vitus Cathedral of Prague, finally serving as dean of the chapter in 1559–1561. His principal work, the homiliary *Postila česká* (1557), reflected his conciliatory attitude. The Utraquists were, for him, true Christians, unlike the Zwinglians, Lutherans, or the Brethren who rejected the doctrine of real presence. Accordingly, Bavorovský admonished his flock to: "Think well of them, . . . and love them like brothers." Even their insults should not be answered in kind, but borne patiently.[196]

There were also notable cases of cooperation between the sub una and sub utraque on both an individual and an institutional basis. Bavorovský had a close personal relationship with Jan Straněnský (fl. 1545–1584), a Utraquist scholar who wrote a preface to his *Postila*. In his own introduction to the homiliary, Bavorovský called Straněnský "a faithful colleague and at the same time a dear brother in Christ the Lord," who not only edited the work, but also prepared a voluminous index.[197] Straněnský in his introduction to the *Postila,* addressed an admonition to properly ordained priests, including presumably the sub una. Aside from the predictable stress on learning and proper care of their congregations, Straněnský introduced the characteristically Utraquist injunction against the clergy's involvement with earthly affairs, condemning particularly a preoccupation with commerce or agriculture.[198] In an earlier book, *Kázání o svatém pokání* (Sermon on the Holy Penance) (1552), Bavorovský also referred to Straněnský as "my dear friend," to whom he had sent the manuscript of this work to prepare it for publication. Straněnský also helped to arrange publication of his writings partly with Gunther in Olomouc, and partly with Melantrich in Prague.[199]

At the institutional level, the Utraquist Consistory appeared to cooperate with the Consistory sub una in assessing religious literature. Thus, Bavorovský's book, *Kázání o svatém pokání,* was submitted for approval to both consistories. Its colophon stated that the publication took place "after an examination and with the approval of the Reverend Lord Administrators of the parties sub una and sub utraque of the Archbishopric of Prague."[200] That such cooperative arrangements were not unusual is indicated by the grievance of the Utraquist Consistory that the *Kronika česká* (Bohemian Chronicle) (1543) of Václav Hájek of Libočany had not been submitted for its examination before publication.[201] According to Jiří Pešek, censorship of theological books was entrusted jointly to the two consistories.[202] It is likely that the two religious groups shared certain of the pre-Tridentine liturgical books such as the incunabula of the late fifteenth century, published apparently in Plzeň.[203] In a way, this guarded cooperation reflected the injunctions of the Compactata of 1436, which in effect established two Catholic Churches in Bohemia, in an apt phrase of Jarold K. Zeman.[204] Even though the Holy See disavowed the document in 1462, the Compactata continued to form a part of Bohemia's constitutional law until 1567 and, in an altered form, also thereafter. The conciliatory tone on the Roman side owed much to Jindřich Skribonius, administrator sub una in 1555–1561 and an advocate of peaceful coexistence.[205] The Utraquist Consistory sought to reciprocate in the mid-1560s and stop abusive language toward the sub una by its own clergy.[206]

In contrast, a sterner attitude toward Utraquism prevailed under the Bishop of Olomouc, Jan Dubravius (Jan Skála z Doubravky), in neighboring Moravia. The bishop had visited Prague in 1543 where he met with the administrator and the members of the Utraquist Consistory, as well as with the faculty of the University of Prague. In August 1544, he followed up his visit with a letter of advice to the Consistory, ominously calling attention to the forthcoming Church gathering that was to meet in Trent in 1545. In particular, he admonished the Utraquists to seek an archbishop in agreement with the projected Council.[207] In Dubravius's view the current Utraquist autonomy was untenable and he proposed a humble and full submission to the Roman Curia as the only feasible solution. In particular, he objected to ordinations of Utraquist priests by bishops outside of Bohemia,[208] and suggested a settlement on the basis of Compactata, as interpreted by Rome.[209] A contrite attitude, such as urged by Dubravius, in fact ran contrary to the

Utraquist basic conviction that it was the papal Curia not the Utraquist Church that was in error on the crucial issues, such as lay communion and ecclesiastical governance.

However, Dubravius's judgment of the Utraquist Church was not entirely negative. Unlike Faber, who had some doubts on that score, Dubravius definitely considered Utraquists a part of the Roman Catholic Church, albeit in danger of crossing the line into heresy.[210] The bishop of Olomouc also acknowledged the Utraquists' genuine grievances against the Council of Constance for its treatment of the Czech nation's leaders (presumably Hus and Jerome), as well as against the pope who called them heretics, and launched destructive assaults on their country. Dubravius appreciated the fact that despite these provocations and injuries from the Roman Curia, the Utraquists remained loyal to the valid priesthood and to the historical roots of their faith.[211]

In a way, the courteous tone adopted by Bydžovský and his colleagues toward the Lutherans paralleled the attitude of the two established churches of Bohemia toward each other. It did not signify agreement or readiness to merge under existing circumstances. The tone was set by the legal system of the Kingdom of Bohemia, and was observed by the Utraquists and the adherents of the Roman Curia, or the sub una during much of the sixteenth century.

6

The Utraquist Consistory, the Archbishop of Prague, and a Brief Honeymoon

The purpose of this chapter is to take another measure of the distinctive status of the Bohemian Church half a century after the onset of the Protestant Reformation in light of many historians' doubts about the viability of its centrist position. The object is to assess its stability and soundness as it continued to steer its *via media* with respect to both German Lutheranism and the Roman Curia with a focus on one of the crucial junctions in its development, namely its confrontation with the restored Roman archbishopric of Prague in the 1560s. The processes of the archbishopric's restoration, as well as of gaining the highly qualified papal permission for lay communion *sub utraque* in Bohemia, have been fully covered, most recently by Kavka and Skýbová.[1] What remains obscure is the institutional and, especially the doctrinal, response of the Utraquist Church to these events. The topic merits examination, particularly in view of the claim frequently encountered in historical literature, that the archiepiscopal appointment spelled an effective ecclesial end of Utraquism with one wing drawn to Luther's teachings and the other toward a merger with the Roman Church.[2] The title of Kavka and Skýbová's abovementioned monograph, *Husitský epilog* (Hussite Epilog) implies the belief that the events around the appointment of the archbishop represented the final act in the drama of Bohemian Utraquism.

Ordination of Utraquist Clergy: 1539–1561

First, let us examine the genesis of the concept of a Roman archbishop in Prague from the Utraquist perspective. This involves, above all, a restatement of the Utraquist Church's unshakable attachment to the ecclesiastical principle of historic apostolic succession.³ The stance related integrally to the Utraquists' emphatic allegiance to the liturgical and sacramental practices of the medieval Church, particularly the Eucharist, which represented the centerpieces of their worship. The validity of the liturgy and the sacraments depended on priests who were ordained by canonically consecrated bishops. Thus, the Church observed the traditional, essentially Roman, liturgical Christian year, as well as the traditional form of the mass that it frequently celebrated. The Utraquists preserved virtually all components of the Roman mass, namely, the Introit, the Kyrie Eleison, the Gloria, the Epistle, the Alleluia with the Gradual, the Sequence, the Gospel, the Creed, the Offertory, the Preface, the Sanctus, the Canon of Consecration, the Lord's Prayer, the Agnus Dei, Communion, and Blessing.⁴ In 1525, 1539, and again in 1549, the Utraquist Church formally affirmed against the Lutherans its adherence to the seven sacraments recognized by the Roman Church.⁵

The liturgical year of the Utraquists followed the traditional Roman temporal cycle, as well as the more subordinate sanctoral cycle specifying the feast days of saints.⁶ Utraquist priests also said masses for the dead.⁷ Both Czech and Latin were employed as liturgical languages. David R. Holeton did not find any substantial differences when he compared the Eucharistic rite in a standard Utraquist missal, the *Misál Kutné Hory,* copied by Jan of Humpolec in 1483, with the *Missale Pragensis* (1503) in use by the Roman Church in Bohemia.⁸ Such differences as there were leaned toward greater antiquity, not toward the innovations of the sixteenth-century Reformation.⁹ A certain simplification of ritual, in particular the absence of multiple celebrants, was explicable by the reduction in the number of priests under Utraquism.¹⁰ In addition to the missals, the Utraquists referred to other pre-Tridentine liturgical books of the Roman Church, in particular the *Pontificals* and the *Agenda.*¹¹ The classical formulation of canon law, the Decretum of Gratian, was also in use.¹²

The Utraquist insistence on ordination of priests by canonical bishops has puzzled Protestant and secular historians who tended to see in it an unwillingness to break a useless, if not harmful habit, a spirit of residual servility to the Roman ecclesiastical establishment, or a response to the demands of the Habsburg kings.¹³ The reasons, however, were not deviant or sinister, but traditionally theological. The transmission of sacramental power depended on a historically uninterrupted transmission of the apostolic office. In the Utraquists' view, without this basis of apostolic succession, there were no valid sacraments, no true church, and no real Christian life. Lacking their own authentic hierarchy, once Archbishop of Prague Konrad of Vechta, who joined the Bohemian Reformation, had died in 1431, the Utraquists relied for the ordination of their priests on itinerant bishops from Italy who occasionally had taken up residence in Bohemia during the fifteenth century. Subsequently, after the turn of the century, Utraquist candidates were sent abroad at great expense (most often to Venice) to obtain major orders from cooperating prelates.[14] The reason for the suitability of Venice might have been its tradition of relative religious tolerance and its assertive autonomy against papal Rome's efforts at rigid control. Jean Bodin chose Venice for its tolerant reputation as the setting of his famous *Colloquium Heptaplomeres,* a freewheeling discussion among representatives of seven religious faiths or philosophical orientations. Even the Venetian Inquisition enjoyed a reputation of administering slaps on the wrist rather than sending its suspects to the stake.[15] The penchant for ecclesiastical autonomy was evident in the sixteenth century, and it would assume a dramatic form in the defection of Archbishop Marco Antonio De Dominis in the early seventeenth century against papal ascendancy, manifested in heavy-handed interventions in Venetian ecclesiastical administration.[16] As for the preparation of the Utraquist candidates for ordination, although the University of Prague lacked a theological faculty since the fifteenth century, the philosophical faculty (or the faculty of arts) provided theological training. Professors, such as Jan Hortensius (1501–1557) and Jan of Kolín (?–1563), engaged in public lecturing until the mid-sixteenth century. Subsequently, others provided tutorials for Utraquist theology students.[17]

A major problem developed in 1543 when Dionysius de Franciscis, a Greek bishop under Roman jurisdiction, who regularly ordained Utraquists in the monastery of Sancta Maria del Horto,[18] was removed from Venice. Not finding Dionysius there, three candidates turned for ordination to a Roman-rite bishop, and on May 23, had to obtain absolution from the Consistory for the reception of communion *sub una.*[19] In response to this predicament, an assembly of the clergy and estates sub utraque proposed to elect an archbishop of Prague locally, and to ask the king to secure papal approval for his consecration.[20] For the meantime, Ferdinand I was asked to induce the bishops of Olomouc to perform the ordinations as the Compactata had stipulated, but in fact the bishops had traditionally declined to comply.[21] Bishop Jan Dubravius (1541–1553) followed his precursors' example in refusing to ordain Utraquist priests despite the formal request of the Bohemian Diet of June 15, 1543,[22] although otherwise he maintained correct relations with the Utraquists and did not interfere with the jurisdiction of the administrator. His advice was to seek an archbishop for Prague in connection with the forthcoming Council of Trent that would at long last open in December 1545.[23]

In February 1544, Ferdinand I helped to remove the obstacles to the ordination of Utraquist clergy in Venice.[24] Bishop Titus Cheronensus, also at Sancta Maria del Horto in Venice, apparently replaced Dionysius. On March 30, 1549, the Consistory sent him a request for holy oils, accompanied by a gift of twelve knives. The bishop's desire for a good and elegant horse (*bonum equum et elegantem*), however, could not be fulfilled a year later.[25] The Consistory's records show that between 1539 and 1555, more than 170 Utraquist priests were ordained in Venice.[26] In the meantime, on May 2, 1548, the Consistory had likewise appealed to the bishop of Vienna, Friedrich Nausea (c. 1496–1552), a court preacher and councilor of Ferdinand I since 1534, to ordain five candidates to the priesthood, and—like certain bishops in Italy—waive the requirement of communion sub una. Erasmus was a good friend of Frederick Nausea, whose interests at the Habsburg court he tried to promote through mediation by Cardinal Campeggi.[27] Nausea's patronage of Georg Witzel also attested to his irenic disposition. At least four priests were ordained by this prelate in 1550 and 1551.[28] František Tischer notes that in 1555, Ferdinand I induced Bishop Marek Kuen of Olomouc to ordain priests in Prague. It is not clear, however, whether the priests were Utraquist or sub una.[29]

Accessions of Roman priests also provided a steady influx to augment the ranks of Utraquist clergy. At least twenty-seven such converts originally ordained by bishops in Cracow, Esztergom, Poznań, Słupsk, Vienna, Wiener Neustadt, and Wrocław, are on record as joining the Utraquist priesthood from 1539 to 1555. Inasmuch as the Utraquist Church was charged with sheltering runaway monastics, it should be noted that only seven in this sample were formerly monks.[30] There was also some movement in the opposite direction.[31] On the whole, however—contrary to the view of Václav Novotný[32]—the existing system of recruitment seemed to provide a sufficient number of Utraquist clergy. It can be added that the Utraquist Church was rather parsimonious in its use of clergy, pruning off any excess in the Wyclifite spirit. Thus in 1533, Nuncio Pier Vergerio expressed his astonishment that in 1533 only six priest vacancies occurred in all of Bohemia.[33] In 1566, Archbishop Brus would even complain that the Consistory had more priests than it could accommodate in parishes under its jurisdiction.[34]

Nevertheless, King Ferdinand I wished to transcend the improvised arrangements for Utraquist ordinations, and promised in 1545 to secure the appointment of a regular archbishop in Prague who would be in communion with Rome, yet who would be authorized to ordain Utraquist clergy. The pattern for this unusual, even somewhat bizarre, arrangement began to emerge at the Bohemian Diet of August 1545 when the estates, both sub utraque and sub una, jointly asked for a bishop who would ordain priests, suggesting a Roman prelate, Jan Horák, who served as preceptor of young archdukes and as provost of Litoměřice. Horák seemed a suitable mediating figure due to his spiritual kinship and correspondence with Erasmus, Witzel, and Nausea. According to the Utraquist theory (in relation to Rome), this bishop would have a very narrow role, essentially that of ordaining the priests, but the power of appointing them to specific churches and of administrative and judicial jurisdiction over their respective clergy would belong mainly to the Utraquist and Roman consistories.[35] It was in a way a revival of the arrangement maintained under Archbishop Konrad of Vechta at the dawn of Utraquism, when the prelate was restricted to ordaining clergy, while the actual governance of the Church was entrusted to the administrators. Presumably, a similar pattern prevailed with the three Roman bishops who resided in Bohemia to serve the Utraquists in the fifteenth century.[36]

This arrangement more or less replicated the Utraquist view of the ecclesiastical establishment at its highest level: While the papal judgment could not be admitted in the matter of governance, the pope's sacerdotal power was indispensable for proper ecclesiastical functioning. While the Utraquist missals still might contain prayers for the pope in deference to his spiritual function,[37] the exclusion of papal administrative and judicial jurisdiction as far as the Church of Bohemia was concerned dated to January 6, 1436, and was reaffirmed by the estates sub utraque on March 17, 1547, by arguing that the exercise of papal authority had caused considerable harm to the country from judicial murders to massive invasions by marauding crusaders under Pope Martin V, and the efforts to depose the Utraquist King George of Poděbrady by Pope Paul II (reminiscent of papal efforts to depose Queen Elizabeth of England a century later).[38] As if to underscore the harm done by the papacy to the Bohemian cause, the scathing denunciations of Utraquism by Pope Paul II (1464–1471) appeared in Prague in Czech translation in the year of the Bohemian Diet's debates on papal authority.[39] The Utraquists expected the bishop of Rome to sanctify, but not to govern, as formulated by Václav Koranda the Younger in 1496 in his *Odpověd' na matrykát bosákův*.[40] This attitude was also reflected in the Utraquists' interest in Lorenzo Valla's *De falso credita et ementita*

Constantini donatione declamatio (1440), which was translated into Czech by Řehoř Hrubý of Jelení shortly after 1500.[41] Valla had demonstrated the spurious quality of the document, which was to substantiate the papal claim to a temporal dominion. The Utraquist stand was not inconsistent with their adherence to canon law inasmuch as Gratian's Decretum did not contain an authorization of papal infallibility and sovereignty.[42] If, as Brian Tierney suggests, the pope's ecclesiastical power had three components—magisterium, jurisdiction, and holy orders[43]—then the Utraquists accepted the third, and rejected the second. As for the first, they accepted it even in matters that were extra-biblical, unless they actually contradicted the Scripture (as in the denial of lay chalice and communion for infants).

Such a view of the papacy likewise resembled the stances of Marsilio of Padua in his famous *Defensor pacis* (1324), and of William of Ockham in his *Octo quaesitones super potestate ac dignitate papali*, or *De potestate pontificum et imperatorum* (between 1339 and 1342).[44] A bull of 1377 by Pope Gregory XI accused Wyclif of adherence to the condemned ideas of Marsilio. Ockham's influence on Wyclif is doubtful, inasmuch as his nominalist epistemology clashed with Wyclif's radical metaphysical realism.[45] There is some indication of Marsilio's possible direct influence on Hus.[46] As noted earlier, the limited view of papal powers was also consistent with the liberal ecclesiology of Thomas More. According to Brendan Bradshaw, for instance, despite his acknowledgment of papal primacy *iure divino,* More did not seek "to place this doctrine at the center of his discussion or to expand it into an assertion of jurisdictional sovereignty or of magisterial infallibility." More rejected "the late medieval clericalist ecclesiology, moulded by the canonists and the scholastics, and preoccupied with the categories of power, authority, and institutional function"; instead, he drew on a patristic ecclesiological tradition "populist and communitarian in orientation." His liberal and reformatory proclivities were obscured by his subsequent opposition to Luther, and he was saddled with an undeserved image of a rabid clericalist authoritarian.[47] In other words, More's proposed course resembled what the Utraquists had practiced, namely to defy the papacy in its juridical aspect without seeking to abolish it in its sacramental part. Ultimately, he had to object—risking his neck—when Henry VIII, Thomas Cromwell, and Thomas Cranmer had crossed this line.[48] Within the Bohemian context, this interpretation makes acceptable the otherwise startling admiration for More by such papal minimalists as Pavel Bydžovský and Šimon Ennius Klatovský.[49] More's views of the papacy also paralleled those of his friend and correspondent, Erasmus.[50] To contextualize Utraquist liberal ecclesiology, it is relevant to mention the reformist ideas of the lay theologian, Georg Witzel, who visited Prague in early 1540s and, as mentioned earlier, was favorably discussed by Bydžovský in 1554.[51]

It might then be concluded that an outcome lacking a regular governing bishop for the Utraquists was seen by the Utraquist Church not just as an emergency measure dictated by necessity, but rather, on the whole, as an acceptable, or even preferable, solution. The absence of such a functionary would permit the settling of ecclesiastical governance in the customary, neighborly, almost homey spirit that had developed over the last century and a half. On the contrary, the emergence of a governing bishop, a monarchal figure dependent on the wishes of the Roman Curial *nomenklatura,* would tend to unbalance this established, and reasonably effective, organization of authority. The progress of papal imperialism and its tightening of the Holy See's control over Bohemia's episcopate can be traced in the titles of the fourteenth century when Bishop Jan of Dražice (1301–1343) was styled *dei gracia Pragensis episcopus,* and his successor Arnošt of Pardubice (1344–1364) *dei **et apostolice sedis** gracia Pragensis ecclesie archiepiscopus.*[52] The proposed Utraquist solution would be likewise consistent with the traditional opposition to the Caesarian clergy (or objections to the exercise of temporal power by ecclesiastical personnel) stemming from the fourteenth-century reform (partly Wyclifite) roots of Utraquism, and it would be consonant with the early course of the Bohemian Reformation with its determination to thwart the exercise of papal juridical and administrative power in Bohemia. This principle was tested in a modified, yet dramatic, form in 1505 when Philip of Villanova (formally the Bishop of Sidon), who as the resident Italian bishop served the Utraquists, wished to declare an interdict in Prague because of a priest's arrest by the town government (reflecting the Utraquists' abandonment of clerical immunity from secular courts). Pavel of Žatec, the Utraquist administrator, assisted by his retired predecessor Koranda, overruled the bishop's anathema, which was a weapon in the Roman Church's arsenal particularly distasteful to the Utraquists. It reminded them of the Church's claims to the exercise of temporal power and the resulting heavy-handed proceedings against the Bohemian Reformation in the fifteenth century, such as the imposition of interdict on Prague by Archbishop Zbyněk Zajíc in 1411.[53] Already Wyclif had criticized the liberal use of excommunications and anathemas by the hierarchy of the Roman Church.[54] In 1505, the Consistory proceeded to wrest the seal of the archbishopric of Prague from Philip and to send him eventually to reside in Kutná Hora for the remainder of his service.[55] This episode indicates that the absence of bishops among the Utraquists occurred only in part by default. From another viewpoint, it reflected the Utraquist distrust of an administrative hierarchy. Organizationally, its outlook was not "episcopalian," based on power transfer from the pope to the bishops, or on a revolt of the bishops against the pope, but rather it assigned the locus of administrative authority to the simple priesthood. Although from the sacramental point of view the Utraquists were not only "espiscopalians," but even "papists," from the organizational point of view the Utraquists, while rejecting papalism, did not champion episcopalism like the Anglicans, but rather they found most congenial what may be perhaps called sacerdotalism, that is administrative power in the church vested in the priests and exercised through the Consistory.

The assertion that the failure to receive a regular bishop and become fully integrated into the hierarchical structure of the Roman Church could be viewed as a defeat for Utraquism only by those historians who postulated the existence of an imaginary "Old Utraquism," namely of a movement yearning to be fully fused with the Roman Church, if only the "technicality" of communion sub utraque were granted by the Roman Curia.[56] In fact, the Utraquist stand contradicted the entire concept of the medieval monarchical power structure of the papacy. Nothing short of renouncing this power apparatus by the papal establishment would satisfy the Utraquist reformist stance.[57] Moreover, the Utraquist concern for ecclesiastical reform was not confined to the national sphere, but in its ecumenicism embraced all of Western Christendom.

In 1556, the Utraquist type of solution concerning the dispensation of episcopal power received another impetus from consultations between the Royal Lieutenant of Bohemia, Ferdinand I's son Archduke Ferdinand, and the highest officials of the land, the judges of the Court of the Land, and the members of the Royal Council. These dignitaries collectively urged the appointment of a bishop in Bohemia who—like the bishop in Venice—would be authorized by the pope to ordain priests both sub una and sub utraque. Thus, more priests could be placed in office because of lesser expense.[58] In January 1558, Ferdinand I himself repeated his promise to intervene in Rome for the appointment of such a bishop.[59] The system, originally proposed by the Utraquists and endorsed by Ferdinand I, would be actually tested with the restoration of the Roman archbishopric of Prague in 1561 that promised to furnish once again a Roman prelate who would ordain Utraquist clergy in Prague. In that year the pope approved the appointment of Antonín Brus (1561–1580) as the Roman Catholic archbishop of Prague.[60]

Testing Lutheran Ideas

Before proceeding to explore the confrontation of the Utraquists with the Roman archbishop, let us examine the character of the Utraquist Consistory and the Bohemian Church it governed in light of the dire predictions of the Church's imminent demise, voiced in the historical literature on Utraquism. As noted previously, in the mirror of conventional historiography, the Utraquist Church at this point was on the verge of disintegration, with one part just about to turn its back on Rome entirely, embracing the principles of German Lutheranism, and another part just about to be entirely co-opted by the Roman Curia.

Let us consider first the supposed turn toward German Lutheranism. As in the 1520s and early 1540s, it was alleged that in the mid–1550s[61] the Utraquist Church strongly inclined toward embracing Lutheran doctrines and thus was ready to abandon its traditional *via media*. These assumptions rested largely on the allegations against the leadership of the Utraquist Church from priest Havel Gelastus Vodňanský, a member of the Consistory until 1554, who had contributed to the temporary deposition of Administrator Jan Mystopol, accusing him in 1554–1555 of adherence to errors and erring clergy.[62] Despite an admonition from Ferdinand I in 1559, Gelastus periodically continued to voice charges against Administrator Matěj Dvorský, and against certain professors of the University of Prague, particularly for denying him the right to deliver lectures in theology.[63] Finally in January 1562, Gelastus and twenty-two clerical associates submitted to Ferdinand I a new complaint,[64] accusing twenty-three Utraquist priests of deviating from Utraquism and supporting Lutheran innovations.[65] Among the latter were the three under consideration in the election of 1562 for administrator: Matěj Lounský, Jan Mystopol, and Martin Mělnický. Incidentally a future administrator, Jindřich Dvorský (appointed in 1572) was included among the accusers. Responding to Gelastus, the accused solemnly declared their orthodoxy, by affirming their adherence to the decisions of the Utraquist synods of 1421 and 1524. Kamil Krofta suggests that the endorsement of the decisions of 1524 implied an agreement with Lutheran principles.[66] Subsequently, however, my re-examination of the synodal articles of 1524, found them free of any specifically or peculiarly Lutheran doctrines.[67] According to Krofta, Matěj Lounský was the least orthodox among the three candidates for the office of administrator. This was based on Matěj's profession of faith in 1562 when he conceded that he qualified the belief in the assistance of saints, though he had not ridiculed their veneration.

Matěj also admitted preaching against fasting, and against the belief in the Assumption of the Blessed Virgin Mary.[68] Thus for Krofta, Matěj was a less attractive candidate from Ferdinand I's point of view than was Mystopol, despite Mystopol's earlier alleged interest in Lutheran doctrines, as well as the earlier accusations by Gelastus that had resulted in his removal from the administratorship in 1555.[69]

Were the allegations of Crypto-Lutheranism justified? It appears that the discussions within the body of Utraquist theologians, as reported in the substantive sources, moved safely within established traditions and did not, in fact, cross the boundary toward outright Lutheranism. Thus, the alleged transgressions did not involve the cardinal issues that would have moved the adherents into the Lutheran fold: the mass as a sacrifice, the distinct order of priesthood (nobody suggested that the Utraquist would depart from canonical ordination and accept Lutheran-style ministry), the historic apostolic succession, or man's cooperation with grace in his salvation (or salvation through faith manifest in good deeds). Issues that were raised involved the degree of saint veneration (including the litanies), clerical marriages, the character of fasting, celebration of feast days, or the bodily assumption of the Blessed Virgin as a dogma. None of those went beyond the bounds of traditional Christian orthodoxy, and thus were all negotiable without implying a commitment to the Lutheran stance. Moreover, the principal suspect, Matěj Lounský traced his caution about invocation of the saints to the early Utraquist tradition. This cautious attitude can be, in fact, documented by the pamphlet of Martin Žatecký, *Knížka proti ošemetné poctě a pokryté Svatých,* originally published in 1517.[70] Concerning his disbelief in the Assumption, Matěj pointed out correctly that the matter was still disputed by the Church doctors.[71]

Raising subordinate or secondary issues of potential Lutheran significance in the 1550s and 1560s appears to have continued the efforts that had occurred in the 1520s and 1540s. The object was responding to the challenges of the German Reformation without disturbing the essential framework of Utraquism. Moreover, this approach harmonized with the principle of the free teaching of the word of God, enshrined in the basic confessional documents of Utraquism, especially the Four Articles of Prague and the Compactata. Not even Ferdinand I apparently considered the accusations by Gelastus and his associates particularly serious.[72]

Another act that some might consider as evidence of the appeal of Lutheranism was the translation by Šimon Ennius Klatovský of Robert Barnes's *Vitae Romanorum Pontificum* (Basel, 1535, and Wittenberg in 1536), published in 1565.[73] Barnes has, in fact, earned a reputation of an, almost notoriously, dedicated English Lutheran. He also holds the distinction of being one of the few Lutheran martyrs. The book, which attracted the particular attention of the Utraquists, however, focused on questioning the legitimacy and value of the historical exercise of the popes' authority, and its object was to bolster the Henrician rejection of papal supremacy as part of nascent Anglicanism. It did not concern any specifically Lutheran doctrines. The skepticism about the popes' governing function within the Church was, of course, also a perspective that the Utraquists had found traditionally congenial, and that would be shared eventually with the Church of England. The same was true of Barnes's efforts to portray the exercise of temporal power by the popes as a basic reason for the decline of the Roman Church.[74] Luther, for his part, as he noted to Barnes, did not need Barnes's historical arguments, because he felt that he had discredited the institution of the papacy sufficiently on biblical grounds as the Antichrist by, among others, pinning on the popes the odious label of the "man of sin" of St. Paul's Epistle (2 Thes 2.3).[75] The peccadilloes and transgressions of the individual popes were theologically irrelevant, if the entire office was illegitimate.[76] The Utraquists, to the contrary, had justified the office of the pope on biblical grounds, and were ready to welcome a catalog of the popes' historical misdeeds to document their assertion that the popes had misused their office to accumulate unwarranted powers and wealth. Despite their theological necessity, the popes could not be trusted with the administrative and judicial powers that the late medieval scholasticism had assigned to them.

Moreover, the publication of Barnes's book in Czech was timed to coincide with the restoration of the Roman archbishopric in Prague and the implanting in Bohemia of the missions of those ardent champions of papal supremacy, the Jesuit fathers. Thus, the Czech version of Barnes's work can be viewed as helping to mobilize theological resources by the Utraquists for the coming encounters with, and challenges of, the agencies of the Roman Curia. Barnes's animus against papal intervention in secular affairs came out very clearly, for instance, in the lengthy treatment of Gregory VII of the Canossa fame.[77] The use of Barnes for such a purpose is further indicated by an addition to the translated text of an original section, presumably by Ennius, covering the period from Lucius III (1181–1185) to Pius IV (1559–1565), which emphasized particular Utraquist grievances against the popes, as well as against the General Councils of the period.[78] Thus, the Utraquist interest in Barnes probably should not be seen as stemming from a historical or theological connection with Luther or his heritage. Instead, the significance of this episode was to show the Utraquists imbibing from the same source as the germinating Anglicanism. It would be also in line with the Utraquists' earlier interest in Valla's discrediting of the Donation of Constantine. It is significant in that regard that the Czech translation omits Luther's preface, which appeared in the original Latin editions of Barnes's history (1535 in Basel, and 1536 in Wittenberg). It contained Luther's characterization of the pope as the Antichrist,[79] a stand with which neither the Utraquists, nor the Anglicans, would unequivocally associate.

In the part that Ennius added to Barnes's original text, it is true that he praised both Luther and Melanchton, and took pride in Luther's lauding of Hus.[80] As discussed earlier, however, speaking respectfully of the founders of Lutheranism without endorsing their particular views was fairly common in Utraquism. Above all, one can cite the praises of Luther and Melanchton in the 1540s in the works of that quintessentially orthodox Utraquist, Pavel Bydžovský.[81] As a parallel, praise for Luther or Calvin was also voiced by proto-Anglican theologians, such as Jewel and Hooker, who were dedicated to the *via media* and, like the Utraquists, opposed to the full-fledged Protestant reformation. It is relevant to point out that Ennius likewise admired as "noble and learned" (*vznešený a učený*),[82] Thomas More who, if anything, was famous as an archenemy of Luther's solafideism. Moreover, this placed him in the same league with the quintessential Utraquist Bydžovský who was likewise a fan of More, as well as Fisher. In addition, the Roman Bishop of Vienna, Friedrich Nausea, belonged among Ennius's patrons in the late 1540s during the latter's brief stay in the Austrian capital.[83] Nausea, the successor of Faber, and also Faber's follower as a patron of Georg Witzel, points to the *via media* between Rome and Wittenberg.[84] Ennius likewise highlighted Witzel's irenic position in his entry on Pope Paul III.[85] In conclusion, Ennius expressed a fervent wish that the ongoing Council of Trent would result in a reunion of divided Christendom.[86] It is true that Jan Martínek claims that Ennius wrote notes into Eneas Silvia's *Epistulae familiares* (Nuremberg, 1481), which revealed sympathy for Luther's teaching and a low opinion of Utraquism, including ridicule of Rokycana. The force of this evidence is much diminished by doubts whether (and if so which) the glosses are actually by Ennius, and by the fact that they contradict his opinions in the published works.[87]

In the introduction, Ennius stated fairly explicitly both his objective and his conclusion for undertaking the edition of Barnes's work. According to him, Henry VIII commissioned Barnes to test the correctness of Luther's proposition that the popes had acted as the Antichrist.[88] Ennius did not accept this simple equation. He accepted the papal role in succession to that of Apostle Peter, which he saw as that of good and faithful shepherds acting by the grace of, and illumination from, the Holy Spirit. He censured, however, the attempts of some popes to force certain human inventions, which actually opposed the law of Christ, on the faithful. The view did not deviate significantly from the established Utraquist view of the purposes, weaknesses, and lapses of the papacy.[89]

What was, however, of paramount significance was that when the dust had settled and the air had cleared, the Consistory clearly reaffirmed the Utraquist Church's continued adherence to its apostolic and sacramental roots, and its immunity to the Lutheran reforms in a letter to Maximillian II of January 13, 1570.[90] The Consistory explicitly condemned the following propositions as erroneous and pernicious: (1) that faith alone justified and that good deeds had no bearing on salvation; (2) that the number of sacraments was limited to two only; (3) that Christian ministers did not differ significantly from laymen, lacking any God-given sacramental powers, or powers to remit sins, or to reenact Christ's sacrifice in the mass; (4) that the Eucharist should not be exhibited on altars or in processions; (5) that holidays and fasts historically ordained by the Church should not be observed; (6) that prayers for the dead practiced from the very inception of the Christian faith should be rejected; (7) that the liturgies sung in the holy general (*obecná*, i.e., catholic) Church from time immemorial should be abandoned, and should be arbitrarily replaced by currently composed hymns; and (8) that "the bishops are regular Anti-Christs and [that] the priests who receive from them the office of holy priesthood, [are the] Anti-Christ's priests."[91] Thus, the governing body of the Utraquist Church unequivocally rejected once more point by point virtually all the cardinal provisions of the Augsburg Confession, each and every one of Lutheranism's proposed principal emendations of medieval Christianity.

Diplomatic Contests with the Archbishop, the Roman Curia, and the Jesuits

Let us now turn to the charges emanating from the other point of view, not that the leadership of the Utraquist Church was turning Lutheran, but to the contrary, that it was becoming co-opted by the Roman Church. Frederick G. Heymann speaks of the vanishing "borderline between Old Utraquists and Catholics" in the 1560s.[92]

It has been claimed that by mid-sixteenth century, Utraquism's religious practices were "hardly distinguishable from lukewarm Catholicism. It is well known that attempts had been made to effect its quiet return to the Roman Church."[93] Negative images of the toadyism and submissiveness of Utraquist ecclesiastics to Roman prelates were sometimes based on misinformation, or on misinterpretation of common courtesy (deriving from the gentleness and reasonableness of the *via media*), or—most likely—on misperception of negotiating tactics.

The charges of willingness virtually to fuse with the Roman Church have first of all centered on the initiatives of Ferdinand I in 1549. He then pressured the convocations of the clergy and of the estates sub utraque to reaffirm the points of agreement with the Church of Rome concerning liturgy and sacraments in order to pave the way for the episcopal appointment by the pope. Using the Compactata as a criterion, one of the demands was abandonment of communion of infants, which the Compactata did not specifically approve but left as an open issue. In response to this pressure, the Utraquist Consistory indicated its good will, while at the same time deploying its two-pronged resistance to royal requests that could not be flatly contradicted. One mode was using alibis, that is, seeking an excuse by reference to the intense opposition of the believers, and thereby making a change virtually unenforceable. The other mode was procrastination, promising a gradual change over an unrealistically long period of time[94] so that the communion of infants and other Utraquist deviations from the contemporary Roman Church would continue until the end of Utraquism in 1621.[95] The critics have tended to take the excuses at face value, and have claimed that the leaders of Utraquism were, in fact, eager to merge with the Roman Church and only the fear of their flock's reaction kept them from doing so. They were portrayed as both cowards and deceivers, and the "people" as heroes of the anti-Roman resistance.

Such tactics of making promises, not intended to be kept, in order to gain desired concessions, were a common practice in the sixteenth century, and apparently not considered particularly reprehensible, although they may have shocked nineteenth-century moralists and historians. The Roman Church, for its part, engaged in such devious tactics as a matter of course. Already the grant of the Compactata to the Utraquists was intended as a ruse to gain gradually the Bohemians' full conformity with the Roman Church. Thus, Juan de Palomar, who as Cardinal Giuliano Cesarini's right-hand man was one of the chief negotiators at Basel, said concerning the Czechs: "It is, therefore, necessary to deal with them with cleverness and a good subterfuge, like with a horse or a mule to be tamed. One has to deal with them affably, until the halter is placed on their neck."[96] Jan Rokycana, as early as February 14, 1437, pointed out the duplicity of the Council of Basel in its dealings with the Utraquists, and he repeated these complaints in April and May of that year. Among the promises given to the Utraquists by the Council was consecration of Rokycana as archbishop, and the ordination of Utraquist clergy by the bishop of Olomouc. Neither promise was kept.[97] Similarly, Pius II abrogated the Compactata on March 11, 1462, on the pretense that their relevance was not for all times, but limited to the generation of 1436.[98] No great devotee of Utraquism, Josef Pekař, characterizes Pius II's act as "indeed, a true felony."[99] According to Karel Stloukal, the instructional manual for papal diplomats in the late sixteenth century "did not prohibit the nuncio to lie, only to let himself be caught lying."[100] Thus, the Utraquists played the customary diplomatic games with the archbishops, the nuncios, and the Jesuits. It was almost a matter of each party trying to outwit the other.[101]

An illustration of this tactic on the Roman side is also provided by a memorandum that Archbishop Brus sent to Emperor Ferdinand on May 28, 1563. The object was to outline a strategy for bringing the Utraquists into conformity with the Roman Church. According to this early statement, the proposed ordination of Utraquist clergy by the Archbishop of Prague and other bishops of Roman obedience was to be used as a first step in overcoming the other obstacles to a full unity of which the most important were communion for infants and small children, veneration of Jan Hus as a saint, and the jurisdictional autonomy of the Utraquist Consistory. The Archbishop was aware of the difficulty of eliminating such distinctive marks, not only because of the clergy's attitude, but even more because of the common believers' attachment to these practices. He suggested overcoming some of this resistance by means of a deception (*sancta aliqua deceptione*), for instance, by substituting for the veneration of Hus another Utraquist holiday that would be acceptable to the Roman Church, such as the Transfiguration on Mount Tabor.[102] The Roman hierarchy would perpetuate this devious approach to solving the religious problems in Bohemia, as evident from the statement of Prague Archbishop Johann Lohelius writing to the papal nuncio on August 22, 1614, about the Czechs: "This nation is by nature impetuous and wild, it cannot be overwhelmed by reasonable arguments, and if it is not overcome by goodness and kindness, it will become recalcitrant..."[103]

Secular, otherwise entirely respectable, rulers also routinely practiced various forms of dissimulation in religious matters. Thus, Elizabeth I of England, after her accession to the throne in 1559, sought to keep alive the expectations of a reunion of the English Church with Rome, but as John E. Booty points out such hopes were "based upon such tenuous evidence as rumors at court and abroad and *the deliberately misleading statements* [my emphasis] which the Queen made to over-anxious ambassadors."[104] Earlier and closer to home, George of Poděbrady, a champion of Utraquism, swore secretly before Czech and Hungarian prelates on May 7, 1458, the eve of his coronation as the king of Bohemia, promising obedience to, and union with, the Holy See, as well as suppression of heresies among his subjects. Moreover, the Curial diplomats, whose assistance he needed to assert authority over non-Utraquist Silesia, were ready to accept, at least temporarily, this highly dubious pledge. The nuncios sought to calm the skeptics by comparing George to the king of Bosnia who vacillated between the Bogomil heresy and the Roman Church.[105]

One prominent episode of alleged near fusion of the Utraquists with the Roman Church was based on misinformation. The original claim on the basis of Johann Schmidl's eighteenth-century account[106] was that Administrator Mystopol's ties with the Jesuits (to whom he entrusted the education of two of his sons) and the Roman archbishop went to the point of his unconditionally joining the Roman Church in 1572 and promising to take the entire Utraquist Church with him.[107] In reality, Mystopol had been dead for four years by 1572, and apparently had no sons. According to reliable records, his relations with the Jesuits were not only free of any intent of submission but, in general, rather distant.[108] What really happened was that Mystopol registered a boy, a remote relative or a servant, in the Jesuit school to learn music. The youngster recited poems with fellow pupils at the feast of Corpus Christi in May 1567. Somewhat earlier the administrator met two Jesuits by chance in the office of the Royal Chancery, shook hands with them, and spoke politely about the boy, promising to visit the Jesuit rector in order to check on the youngster's progress.[109]

Another instance of erroneous attribution of Roman beliefs is in the case of Blažej Nožička of Votín, a prominent Utraquist layman, who in his *Knížka proti bludům* (1566) devotes much space to chastising the Taborites and the Brethren for their theological errors.[110] In a sound Utraquist tradition he also denounces the Lutheran sola fide position.[111] Catholic apologists have seized upon his praise of Ferdinand I for the latter's willingness to safeguard the freedom of communion sub utraque under the Compactata, and "to secure therefor a concession [*povolení*] from the highest Bishop."[112] However, this position was no different from that of the Utraquist decisions of 1539 and 1545. Furthermore, against the authoritarianism of the Roman Curia, Nožička reaffirms the rule of reason, embodied in the Judge of Cheb of 1432, for the interpretation of the Christian tradition.[113] The latter he sees expressed primarily in the definitions that were adopted a thousand years earlier, and thus he implies a distinct skepticism—characteristic of Utraquism—about the papal and conciliar decisions that were proclaimed subsequent to the eleventh-century transformation of the papacy into an imperial and imperious power structure.[114] In fact, when he defends traditional Christian rituals against Luther's challenges, he argues on the basis of patristic literature of the first millennium of the Christian era.[115]

There is nothing in Nožička's position that would indicate his readiness to repudiate traditional Utraquism, or to view the bishop of Rome not as a pastor only, but also as a governor, judge, or commander. Catholic historians have also stressed the endorsement of Nožička's work by Archbishop Brus. One must, however, bear in mind that the book was written during the relatively brief honeymoon period between the Utraquist Consistory and the archbishop in the mid-1560s. Brus then expected to entice the Consistory into fully rejoining the Roman Church, and the Utraquists assumed that Brus could be cajoled into supplying episcopal services while preserving the ecclesial status quo. In his rejoicing over the appointment of Archbishop Brus, Nožička did not go beyond the sentiments, voiced by Administrator Mystopol, upon the ordination of twelve Utraquist priests in January 1566: "[T]he entire Consistory rejoices greatly that God, the Lord, has deigned to turn to us and to our nation, so that what has not been for many years that this land would have its own archbishop, it has one now . . ."[116] The cross-assessment of theological literature between the sub utraque and the sub una had an earlier tradition in Bohemia, resting apparently on the principle of religious peace. Thus, the theologian sub una, Tomáš Bavorovský, submitted his book, *Kázání o svatém pokání*, published in 1552, for approval to both consistories. As noted earlier, its colophon stated that the publication took place "after an examination and with the approval of the Reverend Lord Administrators of the parties sub una and sub utraque of the Archbishopric of Prague."[117]

The most serious charge of fusion, an alleged agreement to merge fully with the Roman Church, was advanced by historians concerning the events of August 1566. Prior to ordaining thirty Utraquist priests on August 13, the archbishop insisted on promises, repeated before the Royal Lieutenant of Bohemia, Archduke Ferdinand, that the Consistory owed him obedience in view of his episcopal authority, and that it intended to gradually remove its practices objectionable to the Roman Curia, starting with the communion for infants.[118] These events in any case were alleged to have transpired in secret, and were never promulgated, much less implemented. Thus, even if the report were true in part or in toto, the subsequent course of events showed that the Consistory had not intended to fulfill such obligations extracted under duress.[119] The Utraquist engagements, if actually made, would fall in the category of what, on the opposite side, Archbishop Brus called *sancta aliqua deceptio*. It showed that both sides were able players of the diplomatic game.

Surprising as it might seem, it is even possible that the negotiations in the 1560s were conducted in good faith. Terms like "Catholic faith," "Catholic church," or "the books and rubrics of the archbishopric of Prague," could and did cause confusion.[120] Above all, the exact meaning of "submission" did not seem to have been fully clarified (in a way definitely unacceptable to the Utraquists) until 1571–1572, as a result of the negotiations between Administrator Jindřich Dvorský of Helfenburk and Archbishop Brus, discussed below. The problem of the meaning of "submission" was illustrated as early as the 1430s when Aeneas Sylvius in his famous chronicle has Jan Rokycana promise obedience to the Roman Church (*oboedentiam Romanae ecclesiae*) on behalf of the Utraquist clergy in 1436, yet several months later he has Rokycana attacking the Roman Curia (*Romanam curiam praetermisit*) in public sermons.[121] The Utraquist negotiators might have viewed the agreements with Rome as halfway settlements, like the Compactata, which concealed disagreements on certain issues, such as the comparative merits of the communion sub una and sub utraque, or put certain issues on hold, such as the communion for infants.[122] Erasmus had counseled such an approach, modeled on the Compactata, for a rapprochement between Rome and the Lutherans.[123] Unfortunately, from the viewpoint of the Utraquists, Rome had become increasingly resistant to these loose covenants during the second half of the sixteenth century. There seemed to be two main reasons for the change. First, the several loose agreements with the Lutherans, particularly the Interims of Regensburg (1541) and of Augsburg (1548) proved ineffectual. Second, the Council of Trent in its aftermath required rigid and unambiguous definitions and commitments.

The Archbishop and the Utraquist Ordinations, 1564–1572

Uneasy attempts at a symbiotic coexistence had begun in earnest in 1564 when, under pressure from Ferdinand I,[124] the pope permitted lay communion in both kinds for the Utraquists, and authorized the ordination of Utraquist clergy by Brus, the Roman Catholic archbishop appointed to the restored see of Prague in 1561.[125] In addition, Brus appealed in 1564 to the bishop of Olomouc, Marek Kuen (who incidentally was reluctant to recognize Brus as his ecclesiastical superior) to apply the newly approved rules to issues concerning the Utraquists in Moravia who were under the jurisdiction of the Prague Utraquist Consistory.[126] After some delay, Brus ordained twelve Utraquist priests in January 1565, requiring only a promise of preserving the rules of the Utraquist Church and due respect for the archbishop.[127] Before the next ordinations in August 1566, however, he developed serious scruples about the propriety of the procedures. In particular, he was worried by the Utraquists' laxity on auricular confession, their administration of communion to small children and infants (the belief in its necessity had been anathematized by the Council of Trent against the Utraquists), and, above all, the Consistory's insubordination.[128] The prelate indeed feared that if he continued the Utraquist ordinations, he would incur the danger of suspension from office or even excommunication by Rome.[129]

At the crux of the breakdown of cooperation between Brus and the Utraquist churchmen was the conflict in the perception of their proper mutual relationship. As the archbishop explained to King Maximillian II, who had replaced Ferdinand I on the throne in 1564, in a letter on February 19, 1566, the Consistory begged him to spare it and not to send the decrees of the Council of Trent since it would not know what to do with such documents. When he sent them under imperial seal the papal permission for communion sub utraque and the accompanying provisions, the Consistory returned the packet after some delay still sealed with a notation that the documents did not concern it. The archbishop further complained that, despite his requests, the members of the Consistory would not meet with the cardinals and nuncios visiting Prague. In particular, they ignored his request to plead the cause of the ordinations with Cardinal-Legate Giovanni F. Commendone who stayed with him an entire week. In addition, the administrator and his colleagues objected to Brus's giving instructions to the candidates for priesthood in opposition to their practices such as the communion for infants.[130]

The Consistory's reactions, as described by the archbishop, have often been characterized by historians as capricious, illogical, naive, or churlish. In reality, such behavior was consistent with the Consistory's established attitude and had definite logic and reasons. On one hand, it represented once more a recognition of the papal and episcopal function in priestly ordination, and, on the other hand, the rejection of the claims of popes, Roman Curia officials, or Church Councils to administrative or judicial powers over the Bohemian Utraquist Church.[131] Thus, Brus also complained in 1566 that the Consistory simply wished him to ordain their priestly candidates, without in any way instructing or admonishing them. In addition to barring his jurisdiction from its own traditional sphere, the Consistory attempted to encroach on his own by appointing Utraquist priests to parishes that had been hitherto sub una.[132] Similarly, the Consistory and the priests of Prague rejected the archbishop's request for special prayers in July 1565 on the grounds that the Utraquist clergy did not owe him administrative obedience.[133] The reluctance to deal with Curial representatives, lest it be interpreted as administrative subordination, could be traced all the way back to the conclusion of the Compactata, when the legate of the Council of Basel, Bishop Philibbert, had difficulties in relating to the Utraquist clerical establishment in 1436–1439.[134]

More specifically, with respect to the papal decrees on communion sub utraque, a theological issue was at stake in addition to the administrative and juridical ones. By returning the documents unopened, the Consistory meant to signal a denial of the need of papal permission for practice, viewed as based on the Bible and hence beyond the pope's authority to permit, deny, or alter. Moreover, the refusal to acknowledge the papal documents permitting communion sub utraque was important to the Consistory for two other related reasons: (1) since the papacy still generally insisted on communion sub una, accepting the dispensation could be construed as implying an agreement with what was seen as an illegitimate or even heretical position of the papacy on the issue[135]; (2) accepting the permission would imply a consent that it was in the power of the papacy to deny the communion sub utraque since what was granted could also be withdrawn.[136] The latter interpretation was, in fact, the avowed view of the Roman Curia.[137]

The powerful theological and devotional underpinning of lay communion in two kinds was strongly illustrated by the collection of prayers and meditations, gathered by Utraquism's stalwart champion, the supreme chamberlain (*nejvyšší komorník*), Jan of Valdštejn the Elder, and published posthumously under the title *Modlitby (a řeči) pobožné* in 1576.[138] Thus, the paramount role of the blood of Jesus in the Christian scheme of salvation is underscored by a lengthy reflection on Christ's shedding of blood for the forgiveness of sins on seven symbolic occasions: at the circumcision, at the prayer in the Garden, during the flagellation, during the crowning with thorns, during the removal of the garments, during the way of the cross, and at the crucifixion.[139] Similarly, a prayer for the salvation of the soul dramatically underscores the role of Christ's blood in the work of redemption. Referring to the blood springing from Jesus' pierced side after the crucifixion, Valdštejn's petition continues: "Oh, the Son of the living God, wash off and remove by your most holy and dearest Blood all the stains of my soul and body. Cleanse away with your dearest blood all the wrong thoughts that are empty, vain, useless, or detrimental. Wash off with your dear blood all my wrong acts so that I may serve you, my Lord God, from this time until the end of ages, receive the forgiveness of sins, attain the eternal life . . ."[140]

For the Utraquists, the act of permitting the lay chalice may have been theologically meaningful from the erroneous standpoint of the Roman Curia. It was irrelevant, or even theologically vitiated, from the viewpoint of the Utraquists. This stand could be clearly traced to the Utraquists' response to the abrogation of the Compactata by Pius II in 1462. In his statement *Contra papam,* Martin Lupáč argued that by his act the pope harmed himself and the Roman Church, not the Utraquists. The latter would continue to observe the law of God without the Compactata, while the Roman Church could have been led to the true faith by them.[141] Hence, fundamental issues, not petty differences, were at stake, and at the heart of the confrontation between papal Rome and Utraquist Prague. From the Utraquist point of view, the acceptance of papal permission would have meant an implicit acknowledgment of the right of an erring human institution over the infallibility of a divine commandment. One may wonder how under such conditions Rome and its bishops could still bestow proper priestly ordinations in the eyes of the Utraquists. Here another principle came to the rescue. An ecclesiastic in sin could still validly exercise God-given sacramental powers. The reader might find this view shockingly mechanistic. Nevertheless, this anti-Donatist stance was basically in harmony with the teaching on the transmission of sacramental power by the Roman Church. Thus, the Utraquists, in this regard at least, acted as good Catholics. This discriminating or nuanced attitude may be illustrated by Pavel Bydžovský's view of Pius II whom the Utraquists had strong reasons to dislike and resist. Bydžovský nevertheless praised the pope for his faith in the power of the Eucharist when "though old so that his hands shook" he offered to carry the sacrament at the head of a Christian host, if it marched to confront the Turks.[142] Similarly, Erasmus, who was highly influential in Utraquist Bohemia, found a way of combining a highly critical view of certain popes with a moderate attachment to the role of the papacy.[143] A certain parallel can also be drawn between the subsequent Jansenists' early eighteenth-century attitude toward the providential role of even the "bad" episcopate and that of the Utraquists. Even though the Jansenists regarded the existing Roman episcopacy as substandard, their attachment to the integrity of the existing system induced them not to follow an invitation of the Dutch Old Catholics into a schismatic, albeit orthodox, episcopate, and they preferred to tolerate the "bad" bishops in communion with Rome.[144]

Under these circumstances, unwilling to engage in direct discussions with the Curia, lest it appeared to recognize Roman administrative and juridical jurisdiction over itself, the Consistory sought to enlist intermediaries on the issue of the ordinations. Somewhat later in 1571, it would try to gain the Jesuits' assistance to plead its cause in Rome.[145] Not surprisingly, the Jesuit fathers turned out to be an inappropriate choice to undertake mediation. In monitoring Brus's conduct in office, the Society of Jesus of Prague had in fact greeted the initial papal concession, to put it mildly, with deep skepticism and had, in particular, opposed Utraquist ordinations, comparing them maliciously, but picturesquely, to releasing foxes into a chicken coop.[146] It is possible that the Utraquists regarded the appeal to the Jesuits as simply a pro forma gesture that they made to avoid the appearance of an absolute unwillingness to communicate with the Holy See. Archbishop Brus, for his part, urged Maximillian II in 1566 to negotiate with the nuncio or directly with the Pope on the matter of Utraquist ordinations.[147]

The last Utraquist ordinations that Brus would, in fact, perform under pressure from Archduke Ferdinand and King Maximillian II were those of the thirty priests on August 13, 1566,[148] following the Consistory's promise of submission in the same month, discussed earlier. The Consistory's noncompliance with those assurances was subsequently confirmed by Archbishop Brus in his letters of July 21, 1568, to King Maximillian II and to the papal nuncio,[149] as well as in his letter of November 18, 1568, to Cardinal Commendone in answer to Pope Pius V's inquiries about the impropriety of Utraquist ordinations in 1565 and 1566.[150]

Without yielding on the issue of submission to the administrative establishment of the Roman Church, the Utraquist Consistory, in vain, appealed to Brus on August 9, 1568, to complete his ordination of several Utraquist candidates on grounds more or less independent of the juridical framework of the Roman Church. The first argument was made on the basis of Brus's implied obligation to exercise, not to withhold, his God-given episcopal power, in the sense of St. Matthew's injunction (5:15) of not hiding one's light under the bushel basket. The second argument was made on the basis of Brus's presumed interest in safeguarding the flock under the care of the

Consistory from godlessness and sectarianism for lack of proper shepherds.[151] Likewise in December 1568, Maximillian II urged Brus to continue with the ordinations and, at the same time, instructed his councilor, Sinckmoser, to request a dispensation for Brus from the Curia for that purpose.[152] Responding to Maximillian's notification of April 14, 1569, about seeking a papal indulgence, the archbishop once more on May 12, 1569, explained at great length his qualms about the propriety of ordaining Utraquist priests.[153] Thereupon, on June 1, 1569, the king acknowledged the gravity of Brus's reservations, and postponed the matter for the time being,[154] as he also notified the Royal Council of Lieutenancy in Prague on October 3, 1569.[155]

An abortive attempt to restore the Utraquist ordinations by Brus followed the appointment of Jindřich Dvorský of Helfenburk as the new Utraquist Administrator in 1571. The Archbishop initially enjoyed good relations with Dvorský, although presumably he did not take seriously the assurances of submission, similar to those of his predecessors in 1566, that Dvorský allegedly had given in 1571.[156] The cause of ordinations had made significant progress by the summer of 1572 when there seemed to be a satisfactory resolution of issues, such as the candidates' belief in the invocation of saints, prayers for the dead, and the view of the mass as a sacrifice. In December, however, the papal nuncio insisted on a profession of faith by the candidates, prescribed by the Council of Trent, which the Utraquist Consistory found unacceptable, presumably mainly for its stress on an unequivocal and complete subordination to Rome. Brus felt unable to proceed any further without incurring excommunication from the Roman Church.[157]

Thus, after 1566 the Utraquists resorted again to bishops outside Bohemia, especially to Passau, Olomouc, Wrocław, and Poznań, and later also to Nitra. Occasional accessions of Roman priests also continued to replenish the Utraquist clergy's ranks.[158] The archbishop, however, continued to supply the Consistory, for the purposes of sacramental activities, with holy oils requiring episcopal consecrations, especially those used in baptism.[159] Evidently, this transaction could be performed more discreetly than the ordination of clergy. More interestingly, it also implied that he was not utterly out of sympathy with the Utraquists. All this shows that an arrangement based on the Roman Curia's views on the ordinations of Utraquist priests, and on lay communion sub utraque, was simply unacceptable to the Utraquists. The most tangible result was to give a fictitious substance to the historiographical construct of "Old Utraquism." These alleged Old Utraquists, differing from Rome only on the lay communion sub utraque, were an extremely rare species, if they existed at all. The bulk of the Czech people were simply Utraquists rejecting both the authoritarianism of the Roman Church and the hallmarks of Lutheranism, based on the principles of sola fide and sola scriptura.

Neither Luther, Nor Rome

Historians who were impatient to see the Utraquist Church disappear have often pointed to the 1560s as a crucial landmark in the demise of Utraquism. Some have maintained that the Utraquist Church virtually vanished through a cooptation of its leadership by the Roman Church.[160] Others saw its virtual end in an irresistible attraction of Lutheran doctrines for the Utraquist clergy.[161] Neither of these scenarios was in fact correct. The reservation of the Utraquist leaders toward the Roman Curia prevented a symbiotic relationship with the Roman archbishop, and the Utraquist Church continued to maintain its administrative and judicial independence of the Roman Church throughout the rest of the sixteenth and into the seventeenth century. The alleged Lutheran influences on certain Utraquist leaders, on a closer examination, involved secondary matters, not the core doctrines of the sacramental and ecclesiological faith. Thus, it is not necessary to conjure up a struggle between an imaginary Old Utraquism and an unlikely Neo-Utraquism, or to postulate a chaotic oscillation between Rome and Wittenberg within Utraquism. The Utraquist Church, in fact, continued to maintain its steady course, the *via media* vis-à-vis Roman authoritarianism on the right, and with respect to Lutheran biblical reductionism on the left.

This is not to say that by the late 1560s there were not individual Czech theologians accepting authentic Lutheranism, just as there were atypical cases of Czech champions of the Counter-Reformation. There was also the significant group of the Unity of Brethren that stood close to the Protestant Reformation. It is, however, one thing to recognize the existence of such anomalies (to borrow František Šmahel's term from another context), and another matter to present them as the norm of Czech society. What can be said, as indicated by the conclusions of this chapter, is that the theological mainstream, flowing out of the Bohemian Reformation and represented by the Consistory, remained loyal to Utraquism as defined by Jakoubek of Stříbro, Jan of Příbram, and Jan Rokycana in the fifteenth century, and reaffirmed in the face of the Protestant Reformation by Bohuslav Bílejovský and Pavel Bydžovský in the 1530s and 1540s.[162] The Utraquists, despite their relative latitudinarianism, remained essentially united on this platform, and the twentieth-century attempts to divide them into Quasi-Catholic Old and Quasi-Lutheran New Utraquists should be viewed, in agreement with Josef Pekař, as unhelpful, even misleading, and ultimately impossible.[163]

7

The Plebeianization of Utraquism: The Controversy over the Bohemian Confession of 1575

The proposal of 1575 to adopt as a law of the land the so-called Bohemian Confession (modeled on the Augsburg Confession) preoccupied the Bohemian Diet, which sat, with two interruptions, from February 21 to September 27. The move represented the high point of the attempts to legitimize Lutheranism and the Unity of Brethren in Bohemia in the sixteenth century. If adopted, the law would have terminated the existing monopoly of mainline Utraquism, administered by a Consistory and defined by the Four Articles of Prague (1419) and subsequent confessional statements, as the only legitimate religion for those dissenting from the Roman Curia.[1] The parliamentary move to give legal recognition to the Lutherans and the Brethren, which also required the monarch's consent, was timed to coincide with the hour of need of the reluctant King Maximillian II (1564–1576). As the year 1575 opened, the king, who was simultaneously the Holy Roman Emperor, was eager to placate the Bohemian estates in order to gain the Diet's consent to the coronation of his son Rudolf as the king of Bohemia. The Bohemian Crown was to be a stepping-stone to Rudolf's election as king by the Diet of the Holy Roman Empire, which was to meet in Regensburg in the fall of 1575. This, in turn, would be an essential step to the perpetuation of the Habsburg dynasty's imperial ascendancy in the Holy Roman Empire.[2]

This chapter interprets the campaign for the Bohemian Confession primarily as symptomatic of a social cleavage within Czech society between the nobility and the commoners. It seeks to answer the questions of why the religious division opened up in Czech society along social lines, why the Utraquists gave political support to the legalization of Lutheranism and the

Unity, and what the consequences of the religious cleavage were for Utraquism. It questions the widespread view of historians that the outcome of the parliamentary action of 1575 meant a virtual demise of mainline Utraquism. For instance, Kamil Krofta has maintained that henceforth the Utraquist Consistory "merely vegetated in a complete separation from, indeed in an enmity with, the large majority" of the Czech dissidents from Rome.[3] The renowned legal historian Jan Kapras has asserted that after 1575 the Utraquists were vanishing: "toward the end of the sixteenth century there were virtually no . . . Utraquists remaining . . ."[4] Alois Míka implied that the exclusion of the Compactata from the laws of the land in 1567 already symbolized the end of Utraquism. Amazingly, he managed to give an otherwise substantial account of the events of 1575 without a single reference to the role of the Utraquist Consistory, or of Valdštejn's group. Ferdinand Hrejsa admitted the Utraquists' post-1575 existence, but he denied them the spirit of Jan Hus.[5]

Unraveling the record of the events of 1575 is at times complicated by the idiosyncratic character of the historical writings by the Unity of Brethren, which also tends to obfuscate the understanding of previous efforts to bolster Lutheranism in Bohemia in 1539–1543 (discussed in Chapter 5). To illustrate the flavor of the Brethren's narratives, one may refer to their "Diarium" of the 1575 Diet concerning King Maximillian II's reception, on March 4 or 5, of the Utraquist Consistory, which they call "the refuse" (or sewage, *colluvies*) of the Czech or Utraquist party: "[W]hen admitted before him they asked that His Majesty would not deign to abandon them that they wish to reach an agreement with the Jesuits on everything, whereupon he deigned to reply that since they were neither warm nor cold, they did not please him. Thus shamed, they left."[6] Even the proven friends of the Unity among modern historians could not credit this account. Thus, Hrejsa thinks that such a coarse and tactless treatment of the Consistory by the king unthinkable. Hrejsa also notes that the story of the insulting treatment is repeated verbatim as having occurred at another audience on March 15.[7] The Brethren evidently made considerable use of their historical writings as ramparts for launching missiles against others in the form of unwavering stereotypical images.[8]

Krofta cites a similarly offensive statement concerning the Utraquist Consistory that the Brethren's diary attributed to Maximillian II when the king allegedly sent a message to the estates on August 24 that the Consistory would "gradually perish on its own, when there is nobody to administer it, and its current members die out."[9] A continuing leitmotif from the history of 1539–1543 is a negative view of the Lutherans whom the Brethren seemed to abominate even more, if possible, than they did the Utraquists, although in this latter period there can be little doubt about the Lutherans' loyal support of the Unity's cause. Apparently, the straitlaced Brethren viewed the Lutheran precept of sola fide as a license for amoral behavior. Unlike the events of 1539–1543, for the proceedings of the 1575 Diet there are, however, alternate sources to serve as possible correctives for the Brethren's accounts, particularly in the "Diarium" of Sixt of Ottersdorf.[10]

A Religious Cleavage

The genesis of the parliamentary encounter at the Diet of 1575 between the urban advocates of Utraquism and barons and knights who were noble champions of Lutheranism had its proximate origin in the removal of the Compactata from the privileges of the Kingdom of Bohemia in 1567, and their replacement by a more general statement concerning the protection of the religious order established by the Diet, by agreements between the estates, and by existing orders and customs. Nevertheless, only the Roman Church and standard Utraquism were defined as "Holy Christian," while other faiths (implicitly including the Lutherans and Brethren) remained illegitimate.[11] The first attempt to legalize the exercise of Lutheran religion, or a dress rehearsal for the parliamentary events of 1575, occurred in May 1571 when the nobles under Supreme Justice (*nejvyšší sudí*), Bohuslav Felix Hasištejnský of Lobkovice, prepared a supplication to King Maximillian II for a free exercise of religion under the Augsburg Confession, citing the precedents of Upper and Lower Austria for which Maximillian had given such a concession. Lobkovice also assured the members of the Unity who were among the noble estates that the Lutherans intended to work in agreement with the Brethren.[12] The Utraquist estates under Jan of Valdštejn on May 23, 1571, asked for a rejection of the Augsburg Confession, adding petitions for ordination of Utraquist clergy by the Archbishop, banishment of clergy not under the Consistory, selection of the Consistory by the estates, and the appointment of *defensores* from the estates to watch over the interests of the Utraquist Church.

The Utraquist Consistory and the Roman Archbishop of Prague had already on May 10, independently of each other, signified their disapproval of the Augsburg Confession on the grounds that it stood for a foreign German religion. Incidentally, this recurrent characterization of Lutheranism as an alien entity by the Consistory and other champions of Utraquism was not meant primarily as an expression of xenophobia, but rather as a statement of fact that only the Utraquist and the Roman churches had legal standing on Bohemian soil. In other words, what may have been legal in the German parts of the Holy Roman Empire was not ipso facto legal in Bohemia. The Lutherans of Saxony used an analogous argument in opposing Calvinism, which was not locally sanctioned, as a "non-German" religion.[13] The king temporarily closed the religious discussion on May 29, 1571, when he went along with the Consistory's (and the archbishop's) arguments and ruled that approving the Augsburg Confession would violate his coronation oath. The latter prohibited religious innovation and protected only two parties (Utraquist and Roman) that observed traditional rules and orders.[14]

The drama of attempting to legalize the Augsburg Confession under the name of Bohemian Confession began at the Bohemian Diet of 1575, which opened its first session on February 21. The parliamentary move revealed a sharp cleavage between the two noble estates (the barons and the knights), on the one hand, and the estate of towns, on the other hand. When discussion of the religious issue opened on March 7, most barons and knights, led again by the supreme justice, Bohuslav Felix Hasištejnský of Lobkovice, proposed the adoption of the Bohemian Confession.[15] Most of the barons and knights also supported a legal recognition of the Unity of Brethren, either under the Bohemian Confession or separately.[16] According to Hrejsa, in the Diet of 1575 only two barons, in addition to the supreme chamberlain, Jan of Valdštejn, and three knights favored the maintenance of a legal monopoly of Utraquism for the dissidents from Rome.[17] Valdštejn, however, complained that the ranks of Utraquist supporters were artificially thinned. Some of the nobles (presumably knights), he contended, had tricked their constituencies into electing them by concealing their Lutheran proclivities.[18] In any case, the main initial opposition to the legalization of the Augsburg Confession emanated from the estate of towns, which was headed in the Diet by Sixt of Ottersdorf, chancellor of the Old Town of Prague, and by Pavel Kristián of Koldín, also of Prague.[19] Ottersdorf, speaking in the name of the towns, expressed their agreement with Valdštejn in favor of the established religion, Utraquism, and in opposition to any change in the legal religious status quo.[20]

The divergence in attitude toward Utraquism between the nobility and the towns, however, had deeper roots than the political maneuvering that culminated in negotiations at the Diet of 1575. These roots can be viewed as partly historical and partly social.[21] Historically speaking, virtually from the beginning, the Utraquist Church had maintained a special relationship to the towns of Bohemia, particularly those of Prague.[22] Thus, as noted earlier, the original Four Articles of Prague of 1419 in a version cited by Vavřinec of Březová were proclaimed by: "We the mayor and the councilors and elders, as well as the entire community, of our capital city of the Kingdom of Bohemia, declare in our names and those of all the faithful in this kingdom . . ."[23]

During the wars of the Bohemian Reformation, the towns of Prague held the top rank among the estates of the realm followed by the barons, the Taborite community, the knights, and the other towns.[24] As early as 1420, Prague and other towns experienced the unreliability of the higher estates, who showed much less determination than the towns to defend the Bohemian Reformation at a critical stage against the pretender King Sigismund, who had condoned the execution of Jan Hus at the Council of Constance. Hynek of Valdštejn was probably the only Czech baron who helped in the defense against Sigismund. Moreover, most of the high Czech nobles assented to Sigismund's coronation in Prague in 1420.[25] A year later, in a highly symbolic act, the leading baron of Bohemia, Čenek of Vartenberk, had to undergo the ceremony of a dramatic humiliation because of the vacillation of his estate in 1420. Kneeling before the representatives of Prague, Čenek confessed his sin against God and the city, and begged both for forgiveness. The militia of the city of Prague, rather than the nobles, secured in 1421 Kutná Hora and twenty other towns for the cause of Bohemian Reformation.[26] It was in the name of Prague in late 1420 that the Czech embassy was to negotiate in Poland for the replacement of Sigismund as the king of Bohemia by the Polish king Vladislav or the Lithuanian Grand Duke Vitold.[27] Prague was named before the barons, and Tábor before the knights and squires, in a document adopted by the assembly at Čáslav, which in 1421 nullified Sigismund's claim to the throne of Bohemia.[28] The one Utraquist king, George of Poděbrady, was crowned in 1458 at the city hall of the Old Town of Prague.[29] The Church of Our Lady before the Týn, the chief sanctuary of Utraquism (dubbed the "Utraquist Cathedral"), had been traditionally the principal church of the Prague townspeople since at least the turn of the thirteenth century.[30] In comparison with its monumental stature, the torso of the St. Vitus Cathedral, which by and large remained attached to the *sub una,* could appear as no more than an oversized chapel attached to the royal palace. It is little wonder that the city of Prague subsequently assumed a special role as a champion of Utraquism and as protector of the Consistory. The inhabitants of Prague and other towns came out strongly against the teaching of Luther as early as the 1520s, while the nobles wavered in their loyalty to Utraquism.[31] Even in 1564, the Consistory turned to the governments of the Old and New Towns of Prague in the matter of priest ordinations. The Praguers promised to intercede with the king and in the Diet to obtain the services of another prelate, if the archbishop of Prague continued to hesitate.[32]

The ascendancy of the towns in political power during the wars of the Bohemian Reformation, which was subsequently reflected in their participation in the parliamentary process, crowned the long-term efforts of townspeople under the leadership of Prague and Kutná Hora, to wrest a share of political power from the nobles, already strongly evident in the early fourteenth century in the reign of King John of Luxembourg.[33] Their success a hundred years later endowed the towns with a sense of self-confidence and a feeling of prudent distrust vis-à-vis the noble estates.[34] Voices were raised wondering whether Prague was not ready to transform Bohemia into a city state, as Florence had done with Tuscany.[35] That grandiose denouement, however, did not come to pass, and the nobles mounted a strong counteroffensives against the political influence of the towns, particularly after 1500.[36]

Nevertheless, the urban intelligentsia of Bohemia continued to exude a healthy dose of self-confidence into the sixteenth century. Some of it had a real basis as when the noble squads did not dare to challenge the town troops, led by Prague, on a campaign in southwest Bohemia in 1520.[37] At that time, representatives of towns met in congresses and formed leagues for mutual assistance.[38] On the historical level, Martin Kuthen of Špinsberk, a devoted Utraquist, could argue in his *Kronika o založení zeme české* (A Chronicle About the Founding of the Bohemian Land) (Prague, 1539) that the estate of towns was more ancient than those of the barons and the knights. The town estate originated in the foundation of Prague in 711 A.D., while the barons (*páni*) traced their origins only to the time of the legendary Duke Přemysl, and the knights to even later princely elevations. The towns in their contests with the nobility also emphasized their unique commercial and manufacturing contributions to the prosperity of the country.[39] Daniel Adam of Veleslavín considered the city of Prague a special guardian of the nation's interests.[40] On the perfidy of the nobles, Sixt of Ottersdorf in his historical work, *Knihy památné o nepokojných letech 1546 a 1547* (Memorial Books About the Troubled Years of 1546 and 1547), dwelled on the injury caused to the Bohemian towns by their alliance with the barons and the knights during the quarrel with King Ferdinand I of 1546–1547. In a cavalier manner, the nobles let the towns bear the brunt of royal retribution for what had been in fact a joint responsibility. In this case, the towns' sense of grievance was directed as much against the nobles, who betrayed them, as against the king, who actually punished them.[41] A similar distrust characterized the attitude of the inhabitants of Žatec toward the nobility.[42] The scathing attack by Marek Bydžovský against Ivan the Terrible's harsh treatment of the citizens of Novgorod, Pskov, and Tver in 1570–1571, may be seen as another reflection of the high degree of estate consciousness on the part of Utraquist townspeople, which transcended national and cultural boundaries and projected into class solidarity with colleagues in faraway Muscovy.[43]

While the special ties of the towns to the Utraquist Church are clear, the more puzzling question is the strong attraction of Lutheranism for the Bohemian nobles. What impelled most of the nobles to separate from the national community and to turn their backs on the entrenched religious traditions of the nation? Although the impression of the intensity of the nobles' interest in Lutheranism may be somewhat exaggerated due to the urban Utraquist bias manifest in the principal source for the events of 1575, namely Ottersdorf's "Diarium o sněmu 1575," it seems undeniable that a clear majority of the nobles pressed for the legalization of the Augsburg Confession.

Part of the answer may be traced exactly to the symbiosis between the towns and Utraquism. Because of the long-standing association of Utraquism with the urban commoners, some of the nobles' low regard for the common man also affected their view of the Utraquist Church. The social standing of the Utraquist ecclesiastical leadership was not likely to impress the nobility. The Roman Church, particularly in the Counter-Reformation phase, which was pioneered by the Jesuits, focused its attention on the aristocracy and gentry.[44] While the Roman archbishops were usually drawn from aristocracy, the higher Utraquist clergy was generally of non-noble origin. Utraquist ecclesiology did not even provide for bishops as governing figures, but merely as dispensers of sacraments as sacerdotal functionaries. The administration and judiciary were discharged collectively by the Consistory, which consisted of priests who were commoners. Moreover, the authority of the Utraquist ecclesiastics was based on theological learning and scholarship, not on political, diplomatic, or military skills. An overt questioning of the value of hereditary nobility and an opposition to the appointment of nobles to episcopal positions had a long tradition in the

Bohemian Reformation, stretching as far back as Vojtěch Raňkův in the late fourteenth century. Similarly, Jakoubek adopted a reserved attitude toward the privileged classes as early as his sermons of 1415 and 1416.[45] The plebeian bias of Utraquism might have well partly derived from the early Wyclifite influences.[46]

For their part, the nobles evidently found it problematic to show religious reverence to an institution staffed by those whom they perceived as socially inferior. The nobles' normal contempt for, and aversion to, the city dwellers was sharpened by the towns' acquisition of political influence in the fifteenth century, and by their role as agents of economic and cultural modernization in the sixteenth century.[47] The gradual increase in transnational loyalties and in the national heterogeneity of Bohemian nobility also widened their social distance from the towns, which acted as guardians of local national traditions. The aristocrats' sojourns abroad, particularly exposures to foreign Protestant and Catholic universities, were also a factor.[48] Janáček notes the growth of an adversarial relationship between the nobles and the townsmen during the sixteenth century, especially after 1547. Similarly, Zikmund Winter testifies to the arrogant behavior of the nobles toward the townspeople.[49] Not even the highest degree of education could absolve a townsman from the social stigma of a commoner. Petr Vok of Rožmberk nursed a feeling of humiliation because his early upbringing was entrusted briefly to a burgher of Soběslav and master of the University of Prague, Jan Makovský.[50]

An indication of social distance was the nobles' apparent inability to deal politely with the Utraquist authorities. Already in 1571, Maximillian II reprimanded the nobles for rudeness toward the Consistory. The king chastised them for writing in a menacing manner, and for addressing Utraquist administrator, Martin of Mělník, in a discourteous way, denying him his proper title.[51] Three incidents, although from later periods, are nevertheless illustrative of the nobles' skewed interaction with the personnel of the Utraquist Church. In 1589, Sidonie of Michalovice refused to recognize the jurisdiction of the Utraquist Consistory in a matrimonial case on the grounds that "the baronial and knightly estates can be summoned only to the courts of the Land and the Chamber, not to any lower courts." In her appeal to the emperor, she gratuitously added the alleged public view that the administrator and the clerk of the Consistory's court were "scoundrels and evident adulterers."[52] Also on record is the uncivil treatment of Administrator Václav Dačický by Chancellor Zdeněk of Lobkovice in 1604, when the former tried to object against the chancellor's describing his two daughters as "bastards" (*pankhartice*).⁵³ In another notable incident in 1618, two burgher women of Prague interceding with Count Heinrich Matthias von Thurn for the Utraquist priest Jan Locika of Domažlice, threatened with exile from Prague, pleaded that they had entrusted their souls to him. The count humiliated them by quipping whether the same was true of their bodies.⁵⁴ These are but two examples of the boorish behavior of Bohemian aristocrats vis-à-vis the townspeople.⁵⁵

Against this background, it is possible to speculate further about the attraction for the nobility of Lutheranism, and (for fewer of its members) of the Roman Church. Part of the answer probably lay again in the *via media*, the ecclesiological centrism of Utraquism. One may advance two basic reasons why the Utraquist Church did not appeal to the aristocracy on ecclesiastical grounds. On the one hand, unlike the Roman Church, it could not provide employment consistent with a noble status inasmuch as it embraced the ideal of clerical poverty. None among its clerical establishment could expect to lead lives worthy of nobles, as the prelates of the Roman Church were able to do.⁵⁶ On the other hand, the Utraquist authorities and their priests were unsuited for the same degree of domination as their Lutheran counterparts, inasmuch as the Utraquist clergy had the shield of a sacramental character, the ecclesiastical rules of canon law, and the constitutional guarantees of royal protection. Although the Utraquist Church had implemented the fourteenth-century reformist injunctions against clerical pride and ostentation, it had preserved much of the aura of "sacredness" of the Roman Church. It is relevant to cite in this connection the complaint of priest Jan Facilis, pastor of the church of St. Jiljí in Prague, in January 1594 against the willful entry into the parish house of the town judge with his scribe and henchmen as agents of secular law, in violation of the canons and ecclesiastical immunities (*contra canones et immunitates spirituales*).⁵⁷

Lutheranism, to the contrary, frankly vested ecclesiastical power in secular authorities with Luther himself having demonstratively burned the book of canon law together with the papal bull of his excommunication in 1520.⁵⁸ Hence, the noble laymen came to enjoy a greater pliability and a wider scope for asserting themselves in the ecclesiastical field. Thus, Vojtěch of Pernštejn (1532–1561) aspired to become a lay bishop of a Moravian Lutheran Church. Similar ambitions for personal aggrandizement and ecclesiological inventiveness could not be accommodated in the traditionalist Utraquist Church. Pernštejn may have been inspired by the "Saxon" type of reformation, according to which the prince simultaneously served as *summus episcopus,* possessing ecclesiastical, as well as secular power, or by the placement of junior princes as bishops into secularized dioceses of northern Germany. Even the Unity of Brethren looked askance at Pernštejn's freelance entrepreneurship in ecclesiology.[59] Also in a lesser matter, the Utraquist Consistory would voice its distaste over the zest with which the noble laymen threw themselves into composing the text of the Bohemian Confession in May 1575. The Utraquist Church did not endorse the writing of religious creeds by laypersons, and Utraquist authors looked askance at the tendency of "the great lords" to manipulate religious concepts to their liking.[60] In short, the aristocracy could neither use the Utraquist Church as a welfare safety net (for its junior members), nor treat its clergy as subjects. The Church did not seem to offer an adequate scope for the nobility's self-expression, self-indulgence, or exercise of influence, and the aristocrats were casting envious glances at the opportunities offered to their confreres in Lutheran and Calvinist lands abroad.[61] It has been suggested by Roman propagandists, like the energetic and vitriolic John of Capistrano in the 1450s, that the freedom from religious taxes and dues, and the right to seize ecclesiastical estates, explained in part Utraquism's appeal to the Bohemian nobles. If so, Lutheranism offered these licenses even more clearly.[62] The Lutherans merged the ecclesiastical jurisdiction with secular power, while the Roman Church had separated and juxtaposed the two and the Utraquists pursued a *via media* of a cooperative balance between the church and the state.[63]

In a prophetic way, Jan the Elder of Valdštejn saw the onset of an even more radical split between the Czech nobility and the rest of the Czech nation at the Bohemian Diet of 1575. Defending eloquently and with determination the distinctive status of the Utraquist Church, Valdštejn raised his solitary voice to warn his fellow aristocrats against an unfamiliar path by embracing the Augsburg Confession. He argued that the hundreds of thousands of Bohemian Christians would not welcome a new and alien religion, but would rather cling to the established religious order sanctified by an ancient tradition. He summed up the Utraquist position succinctly: "[T]here is nothing for us in either a German religion, or in what was published at Augsburg; ancient customs and diet decrees of the Bohemian Kingdom are good enough . . ."[64] The nobles in their elitist snobbery evidently did not care about the religious views or feelings of the common man as long as their own special interests were satisfied, and their particular tastes indulged. The disassociation of the nobility from Utraquism would be symbolized by a statement of Václav Budovec of Budov in 1603 that he knew of no one who would be adherent of the Prague Consistory among the higher estates.⁶⁵ In sum, Utraquism possessed neither the pride of the Roman Church, nor the submissiveness of Lutheranism. Parenthetically, it may be added that the denominational division along class lines was not unique to Bohemia. In England the upper classes held the more traditional (High Church) religion, while the commoners tended to the more innovative religious dissent.⁶⁶ Ireland represented the reverse (as mutatis mutandis did Bohemia).⁶⁷

Utraquist-Lutheran Entente: Its Genesis

Having opened participation in the Diet with the support of Valdštejn's adamant opposition to legalization of the Augsburg Confession and with an insistence on preserving the legal monopoly of Utraquism, towns estate executed a rapid about-face to the endorsement of the Lutheran desiderata.⁶⁸ After Maximillian II permitted on March 15 a discussion of the Bohemian Confession by the party *sub utraque,* the towns agreed to participate in a commission of six members from each estate (plus two representatives of the University of Prague), which was to compose the new religious documents. The town representatives, elected on March 17, 1575, included under the leadership of Sixt of Ottersdorf, Matěj Bydžovský of Aventin, also from the Old Town of Prague, two representatives from the New Town of Prague, and one each from Žatec and Kadaň.⁶⁹ When the Diet reassembled after a recess from March 26 to May 1, Ottersdorf participated in a commission of seven, which began its sessions on May 3 and completed the text of the Bohemian Confession and related documents on May 13.⁷⁰ On May 18, the towns estate joined the barons and knights in a petition to King Maximillian II to legalize both the Bohemian Confession and the Confession of the Unity, inasmuch as the Brethren had declined to accept the principles of Augsburg embodied in the former. The Brethren's Confession was submitted to the King separately on May 22 through their patron and Maximillian's personal physician, Dr. Johann Crato of Krafftheim.⁷¹ The towns even participated in the deputation of six from each estate, which pleaded with King Maximillian II on August 22 to reverse his decision against the legalization of the Bohemian Confession.⁷²

The question arises: Why did the town representatives change their minds and shift their parliamentary support, with an almost unseemly speed, from Valdštejn to his Lutheran confreres? It was not indeed an instantaneous mass conversion from Utraquism to Lutheranism. The reasons for the towns' new and surprising willingness to back the legalization of the Bohemian Confession should be sought in pragmatic politics, which had raised the specter of isolation in a hostile political environment. The new initiative was ultimately made possible by religious guarantees from the Lutheran estates, as well as from the monarch.

The perceptions of political danger, conducive to seeking allies, stemmed from both long-range threats and more immediate ones. There was increasing evidence of the general trend of repression against religious heterodoxy both in the Habsburg lands, and more broadly in Europe. Particularly vulnerable to persecution were religious groups that lacked legal recognition. A graphic reminder could be found in the periodic, although incomplete, campaigns against the Unity of Brethren, specifically the order of banishment from Bohemia in 1547, which the Utraquist townsmen found deplorable in its deviousness and brutal harshness.[73] A possible suppression of the Lutherans, as long as they stood outside the law, would also weaken the Utraquists' position vis-à-vis the Roman Curia. The Curial intransigence and the cavalier treatment of the Utraquists by papal nuncios in the matter of ordinations by the archbishop of Prague in the 1560s would make the Utraquists even more wary of confronting the Church of Rome alone. It has been suggested that the Utraquists felt more comfortable negotiating with the Brethren than with the Roman Curia. Although the gulf separating the two was too wide to bridge, such overtures did occur, most notably under Utraquist administrator Václav Koranda in the 1470s, and in the 1560s between the Unity's Bishop Augusta on one side, and Utraquist administrators Jan Mystopol and Martin Mělnický on the other.[74]

The awareness of vulnerability to arbitrary repression, of the danger from the Roman side, and of the potential usefulness of Lutheran help, was dramatically heightened for the Utraquists in 1571. On the pretext of searching for Lutheran and Calvinist books, royal officials intruded in the colleges of the University of Prague. The Utraquist Consistory and the university faculty lodged emphatic protests against the invasion with the royal authorities, fearing that a campaign of suppression, like those in Spain, France, and certain German provinces, might be unleashed against Utraquism in Bohemia. Eventually, the Consistory and the University rector were entrusted with evaluating the books presented for sale in Prague bookstores. Nevertheless, the episode brought home to the Utraquists the unpleasant possibility that they might be targeted in an offensive against heterodoxy launched in Romanist zeal by the Habsburg dynasty. This anxiety helped to engender a sense of political solidarity with the Lutherans and the Brethren. Moreover, the Utraquists became very much aware of the lethal events unleashed by the champions of the Roman Church a year later in 1572 on the night of St. Bartholomew (August 24) in Paris.[75] An insight into the authentic character of the risk of religious repression also comes from the comments of the papal nuncio Giovanni Dolfin. Writing from Prague to Rome on May 22, 1575, the prelate argued that, if the Bohemian Confession were fully enacted and the Lutherans and the Brethren recognized as the legitimate party sub utraque, then legally speaking the real Utraquists could be banished from the land.[76]

There were, however, more cogent arguments of proximate danger that helped to tip the scales and cause the rapid turnabout by the towns on the issue of the Bohemian Confession. These were the warnings voiced on the very first day of the religious discussions, March 7, by the barons and the knights. Directed mainly toward Ottersdorf (who had to go into temporary hiding to escape the nobles' anger), their message was that, if the towns broke the united front against the king, and thereby separated themselves from the other estates, then in isolation the fate of the towns of Austria would be theirs.[77] Indeed, in Upper and Lower Austria only the barons and the knights received religious liberty in 1568. Starting in 1577 under the leadership of Bishop Melchior Khlesl, religious dissent would be gradually suppressed in the towns of the two provinces, including Vienna.[78] The preferential treatment of the nobility was particularly pronounced in Inner Austria (Styria, Carinthia, Carniola, and Gorizia) where the governing archduke Charles denied in the 1570s religious liberties to the towns, while granting them to the nobles. This became a prelude to complete suppression of the urban dissidents from the Roman Church in the 1580s.[79] The Bohemian towns, moreover, had had a foretaste of what it meant to lose the political support of the nobility in 1547 when the king inflicted on them special penalties for the opposition of the Bohemian Diet to his pursuit of the Schmalkaldic War.[80] In fact, the encroachments on, and the intimidations of, the towns had traditionally belonged among the favorite (although double-edged) weapons of the Habsburgs' political armory, both in Austria and in Spain.

This pressure alone, however, does not supply a sufficient explanation for why the towns retreated, disclaiming any wish either to separate from the other estates, or to authorize Ottersdorf to speak in that sense.[81] Ultimately, the towns were persuaded to support the adoption of the Bohemian Confession by the nobility's assurances that the Utraquists would not be obliged to conform with the new confessional document. Lobkovice stressed that the noble Lutheran party did not seek uniformity under the Bohemian Confession for all those sub utraque.[82] Thus, the towns further agreed to participate in the elections on March 17, 1575, of members to a commission that was to prepare the new confession and church rules, but again with the proviso that the freedom to adhere to Utraquism would not be curtailed by the adoption of the proposed Bohemian Confession.[83] Town representatives received additional guarantees in that respect. In a speech on March 21, 1575, Michal Španovský, a leading proponent of the Bohemian Confession, reaffirmed earlier assurances that the nobles did not seek a change in the religious status quo. As Ottersdorf explained, the towns originally had feared the religious proposal, but since the barons and the knights introduced an interpretation that was acceptable, the towns would cooperate with the nobles.[84] Thus, the towns' parliamentary alliance with the Lutheran barons and knights was contingent on the latter's noninterference with Utraquism where it was established, especially in towns.

The townsmen, however, did not depend only on the guarantees of their noble colleagues in the Diet. There were also promises from King Maximillian II that, regardless of the status of the Bohemian Confession, he was determined to preserve undiminished the concerns of Utraquism. The king insisted on that proviso all along, and particularly at the audiences of May 22 and July 6, 1575.[85] On August 30, 1575, the Consistory and a Utraquist deputation led by Valdštejn would receive Maximillian's repeated assurances that the monarch would not permit any encroachments on the interests of Utraquism.[86] In a more general way, Maximillian II would seek to promote a spirit of cooperation among the divergent religious interests by his urging of tolerance, if not trust. As an illustration, one can take his speech at the audience of September 2, 1575, in which he emphatically called for an avoidance of conflicts between the Lutherans and the party sub una, between the Lutherans and Valdštejn's Ultra-Utraquists, and between the Lutherans and the Brethren. Despite historians' suspicions of his duplicity, hypocrisy, or lack of stamina, Maximillian apparently valued religious peace and felt a genuine revulsion against repression, such as the St. Bartholomew's Night, or the proceedings of Duke of Alba in the Netherlands in 1567–1573.[87] Whatever his innermost feelings, Maximillian undoubtedly contributed to engendering an atmosphere of confidence and forbearance that led to the political cooperation of the Utraquists with the Lutherans and the Brethren. It should also be recalled, however, that the spirit of religious forbearance in Bohemia had its distinct roots in the Peace of Kutná Hora of 1485, which required respectful relationships among parties varying in religious beliefs, at that time the adherents of Utraquism and the Roman Church.[88] It has been particularly noted that Utraquist theologians used considerable restraint in their controversial literature.

The most important result, in the light of these agreements and understandings, was that, if enacted, the Bohemian Confession and the Brethren's Confession would merely set the outer limits of the permissible deviations from the Roman Church. The legal recognition would cover the Lutherans and the Unity, but the Zwinglians, Calvinists, Anabaptists, and anti-Trinitarians (Arians) would still remain outside the pale.[89] At the same time, these laws would not compel all dissidents from the current Church of Rome to embrace these extremities (either of the Lutheran or the Unity type). Instead, the new legal order would allow for maintaining intermediate confessional positions. In other words, the *via media* of Utraquism would be safeguarded.[90] This limitation on the effectiveness of the Bohemian Confession was not necessarily clear to those outside the Bohemian parliamentary process. Such a presumably astute and sophisticated observer as the papal nuncio, for instance, in his observation (cited above) assumed that the legalization of the Augsburg Confession would be tantamount to an imposition of Lutheranism on all those sub utraque in Bohemia.[91]

The unlikely support by the Utraquist townsmen for the otherwise uncongenial legalization of the Bohemian Confession is, therefore, explicable by the fact that the Utraquists saw themselves, so to say, in the same boat with the Lutherans and the Brethren, and if the boat sank, all of them would go under. The Utraquists felt no more immune from a Gleichschaltung by the Roman Church than the other, more extreme dissidents. The king might be disposed to favor them in the short run, but for the long run he was likely to favor the Roman Curia. There was no reason to assume that the monarch would shirk from drastic measures against the Utraquist Church if proper circumstances arose. One might recall the unilateral deposition and banishment of Administrator Cahera by Ferdinand I in 1529.[92] The Utraquists saw the balance of power between the estates and the king as security for their autonomy and, indeed, for the very existence of the Utraquist Church. Therefore, an alliance with the noble Lutherans was essential, and securing it was a reasonable trade-off for supporting the distasteful Bohemian Confession.

The Utraquists' decision, in a sense, was analogous to that made on March 15 by the Brethren, who also had theological disagreements with Lutheranism, although from the opposite sides. Despite the advice of their sponsor at the royal court, Dr. Crato, the Brethren, for fear of political isolation, chose not to end their cooperation with the Lutherans.[93] Such a willingness to form defensive parliamentary alliances across confessional lines was reminiscent of the contemporary situation in the Polish *sejm* where the Catholics and the Uniates were ready to cooperate with the Eastern Orthodox in order to counterbalance the power of the king. Some of the Brethren looked more specifically at the Polish union of Sandomierz, or Consensus Sandomiriensis, of April 14, 1570, bringing the Lutherans, the Calvinists, and the Bohemian Brethren (exiled to Poland) into mutual peace and harmony, and into a political alliance, while each of the three religious denominations preserved its distinctive organization and form of worship.[94] The readiness of the Utraquists to form a political alliance in 1575 with the Lutherans and the Brethren in Bohemia in the campaign for the Bohemian Confession has been recently noted by Winfried Eberhard and by Josef Kollmann.[95]

The Bohemian estates thus displayed a high degree of statesmanship, in forging an alliance, not only across class, but also confessional, lines in order to resist the Counter-Reformation proclivities of the monarch.[96] Their political astuteness can be appreciated in comparison with the fate of religious dissent in neighboring countries where the class separation could not be bridged, as in Lower and Upper Austria, and particularly in the lands of Inner Austria.[97] This political savvy would be expressed even more strikingly by the Bohemian town estate in 1609, the next time the Bohemian Confession would become an object of discussion in the Bohemian Diet.

Valdštejn's Ultra-Utraquists as Spoilers

Jan of Valdštejn and his small Utraquist faction among the nobles played an ambiguous role at the Diet of 1575. Having taken an unequivocal stand in favor of Utraquism and against the Augsburg Confession, Valdštejn initially appeared to act, at least halfheartedly, in harmony with the urban Utraquists. Yet, in the middle of the proceedings he and his faction seemed to turn into spoilers working to upset the marriage of convenience concluded in the Bohemian Diet between the Utraquists of the towns estate, and the Lutherans and Brethren of the barons and knights estates.

On March 7, Valdštejn voiced his sharp objection to the Augsburg Confession, as formulating a religion valid in Germany, not in Bohemia, and he coupled his plea for retaining Utraquism as the sole legal confession sub utraque with a proposal for restoring the election of the Consistory by the estates.[98] After the towns changed their minds from opposing to supporting the discussion of the Augsburg Confession (in order not to break a united front with the majority of the nobles),[99] Valdštejn apparently agreed to go along with the prevalent sentiment in the Diet. The Brethrens' diarium makes the improbable claim that he was chastised in the following way by Baron of Biberštejn, a member of the Lutheran party: "[Y]ou constantly take counsel with the party *sub una* against us. You deign to be a good Christian only when listening to the priest's sermon, and as soon as he leaves the pulpit, you hold and accept, as well as act upon, all the possible idolatries and papist heresies."[100] On March 9 and 10, Valdštejn spoke in a conciliatory tone, and in favor of preserving unity. Nevertheless, the Brethren's diarium depicts him as virtually out of his mind with anger when Maximillian gave his formal consent on March 15 for the Diet to compose the Bohemian Confession.[101]

On May 22, 1575, the king summoned Valdštejn and his associates for an evaluation of the completed text of the Confession.[102] In response, the assessment, entitled "A Declaration and an Avowal of the Holy, Ancient, Catholic (*obecná*), Christian Faith of the Communicants in Both Kinds" (Ohlášení a přiznání k svaté staré obecné křesťanské víře pod obojí způsobou přijímajících), was presented to the king on June 4, 1575, by Valdštejn and several "barons, knights, and townsmen of Prague." The Brethren's account notes sarcastically that the undersigned included merely two barons, a few knights, and one townsman, Jan Krejčí of Dražice.[103] This rather curious document stated that the Bohemian Confession contained many traditional and proper articles, but also some new and inadmissible ones; in addition, many essential ecclesiastical rules and ceremonies were missing. Yet, the authors of the Confession claimed to adhere to the Consistory, and denied advocating unusual or unprecedented matters or religious innovations. Valdštejn and his colleagues, therefore, proposed that the authors and their clergy should meet in the principal church (apparently Our Lady Before the Týn) with the regular Utraquist priests, and receive from the latter, after confession, the body and blood of Christ, thus confirming their adherence to the true and legitimate Utraquist faith.[104]

Tomek's opinion is that sheer sarcasm was involved in Valdštejn's proposal, and Hrejsa does not comment.[105] If taken seriously, the suggestion might have aimed at demonstratively unmasking the Lutherans as not sharing the Utraquist faith by their refusal to partake in the suggested ceremonies. A less likely possibility is that the Valdštejn group had in mind what used to be called "occasional conformity" in England from the time of the

Glorious Revolution of 1689 until the nineteenth century, that is, paying lip service to the established religion by a periodic reception of communion. A petition added to Valdštejn's document contained his favorite and often-repeated wish for an election of the administrator and Consistory rather than an outright appointment by the king, as had become customary after 1562. The following were to participate in the election: estates sub utraque, university masters, the clergy of Prague, and representatives of provincial clergy, with the nominees confirmed by the king. The addendum also repeated a plea for the institution of laymen from each estate, who as defensores would assist the Consistory.[106]

Shortly afterward, Valdštejn and his associates abandoned their genuinely or seemingly conciliatory position (partly dictated by Maximillian II's pleas for mutual forbearance), and adopted an open and uncompromising line against approval of the Bohemian Confession. Seeking to mobilize opposition in the towns, they directly challenged the policy of town representatives in the Bohemian Diet, who, as noted above, for political reasons supported the adoption of the Bohemian Confession. Thus, Valdštejn's colleague and also a baron, Zdeněk of Vartenberk, who served as the royal captain of the New Town of Prague, on two occasions (June l0 and 13) attempted to have the general town assembly condemn the Bohemian Confession. The attempts failed, partly because the townsmen were reluctant to repudiate the stand of their Diet representatives.[107]

Valdštejn and Vartenberk mounted their most concerted action when Maximillian II was preparing to issue his final decision concerning the fate of the Bohemian Confession. On August 30, 1575, the two barons led a delegation to protest against the proposed Confession as introducing religious innovations, and urged instead a protection for only the existing religion. The group included four knights (Zdeněk Malovec of Malovice, Jan Rašín, Jan Hýsrle of Chody, and bailiff Holovský), and a substantial representation from the Old Town of Prague, including in particular, the mayor (*primas*), Jan Krejčí of Dražice, two other burghers, and a large number of maltsters (brewers). The papal nuncio estimated more than sixty participants.[108] The Brethren in their diarium implausibly maintained that the participating brewers had been deceived by the mayor about the true purpose of their audience with the king.[109]

On August 31 and September 1, Valdštejn precipitated a quarrel when the Lutheran estates tried to persuade the Roman party that the Bohemian Confession was compatible with the established faith sub utraque. Valdštejn vehemently denied the legitimacy of the Confession, maintaining (with considerable justification) that the latter fundamentally departed from the Utraquist tradition, which alone was covered by the previous legislation, as well as in agreements with the party sub una. His intervention disrupted the negotiations between the Lutherans and the Roman party. The Lutheran nobles complained to the king on September 2.[110] The king, then especially hard-pressed to secure his son's coronation, promised to reprimand Valdštejn for a breach of parliamentary etiquette, and actually did so on September 3.[111]

Thus, contrary to the view of Václav Novotný,[112] not all Utraquists were adamantly opposed to the legalization of the Augsburg Confession. Valdštejn's group represented an uncompromising purist position that contrasted with the more tolerant and pragmatic, yet traditionally Utraquist, stand adopted by the towns estate under the leadership of Sixt of Ottersdorf in the Diet of 1575. Valdštejn's purist attitudes, had they prevailed, would have led to political isolation of Utraquism's adherents. The townsmen's rejection of Valdstejn's blandishments to oppose the Bohemian Confession should not be viewed as a theological stand as an expression of sympathy for Lutheranism, but as a political stance to maintain a parliamentary alliance with the nobility.

Actually, Valdštejn's tactics played into the hands of the Roman party, which also sought to separate the Utraquists politically from the other dissidents. The Lutherans, indeed, asked the Roman faction in the Bohemian Diet, led by Baron Vilém of Rožmberk, to recognize them as belonging to the party sub utraque with which the party sub una had concluded past agreements of mutual toleration and recognition, in particular the Peace of Kutná Hora of 1485. The party sub una, however, demurred from the devious sleight of hand, and in its formal recommendation to the king concerning the Bohemian Confession on August 30, 1575, declared that the Augsburg Confession was incompatible with the laws of the land and ancient treaties and agreements that had regulated its relations with the party sub utraque. According to the Roman party, the proponents of the Augsburg Confession (under the name of the Bohemian Confession), therefore, should not be considered as covered by the established legal framework of the kingdom.[113]

Within the Utraquist milieu of Bohemia, the relationship of Valdštejn's group to Ottersdorf's Diet faction was somewhat similar to the role played in the Catholic milieu of contemporary France by the intransigent Guises faction vis-à-vis the more flexible and pragmatic *politiques* of Jean Bodin.[114]

The Consistory: A Guardian of Utraquist Orthodoxy

A division of labor—more fruitful than that between Valdštejn's noble ultras and Ottersdorf's town moderates—developed in 1575 within Utraquism between the latter and the Consistory. The towns estate in the Diet focused on creating the political preconditions for maintenance of the Utraquist faith by fortifying the scope of religious tolerance in a broader sense through forging an alliance "on the left." Hence, it supported the legitimization of the Bohemian Confession. The Consistory was concerned with preserving the specific confessional integrity of Utraquism, and thus focused on rejecting the Bohemian Confession from the doctrinal theological point of view. Thus, each side could be viewed as concerned with its own proper sphere, respectively, religious politics and religious orthodoxy. If the deputies' attitude toward the Bohemian Confession could be politically permissive, the priests' stance had to be theologically negative. If the Utraquist Church would no longer be the only officially defined and legally sanctioned body (outside the sub una), it became even more important to reemphasize its specific theological identity, especially vis-à-vis the newly proposed religious standard, the Augsburg/Bohemian Confession. Although the towns estate and the Consistory may have appeared to work at cross-purposes, each performed a meaningful function from the viewpoint of the Utraquist Church's interest and survival, and, in practice, their agendas were mutually supportive. Here again one may note an analogy with the behavior of the Brethren, among whom it was the lay noble leadership in the Diet, not the ecclesiastical establishment, which supported the alliance with the Lutherans.[115]

Standing on a theological, rather than a political platform, the Consistory's assessment of the Augsburg Confession was, therefore, consistently critical throughout the events surrounding the Diet session of 1575. Anticipating the discussion of the Augsburg Confession at the Bohemian Diet, the Consistory convoked a gathering of the clergy of Prague on September 17, 1574, warning that

> the sectarians and other enemies of ours in all regions are mobilizing to defile the true religion, our own persons and especially the Consistory, and to introduce into this Bohemian Kingdom new religious teachings, such as the Augsburg Confession. Therefore see to it that you exhort the people to prayers for His Church, and you yourselves beg the Good Lord

asking Him to foil their plans and turn them to naught, and that he should deign to confer on His Church a victory over them, inasmuch as these matters will be treated in the presence of His Imperial Majesty at the coming Diet gathering on Saint Martin's Day.[116]

According to the Brethren's diarium, after Maximillian II gave permission to the commission, elected from the Diet, to draft a Bohemian Confession on March 20, 1575, the Consistory in a state of consternation sent a supplication to the king begging for protection. Claiming that the authors of the Confession were largely sectarians and Brethren (*sektáři a sborníci*), they firmly rejected any claim by these writers to exercise authority over their (Utraquist) Church. At about the same time, the administrator preached against laymen who were composing new articles of religion, and who claimed erroneously that Christ was in their midst: "Truly He is not among them, but He has left them and is in hiding, just as He had left the temple when He was about to be stoned . . ."[117] The king urged the Consistory not to protest publicly against the preparation of the Bohemian Confession in order to preserve religious peace and calm. If the negotiators agreed among themselves, which he doubted, he would still not permit anything against the current state of religion.[118]

Having received the completed text of the Bohemian Confession, the king sent a copy of the document to the administrator, Jindřich Dvorský, and to representatives of the Utraquist clergy for evaluation on May 22, 1575.[119] On May 25, the Consistory considered the text of the Bohemian Confession and concluded unanimously that its articles were inconsistent with the traditional religion, and that in response to the king the deviations should be pointed out on the basis of earlier Diet decisions and religious treatises, as had been done previously in 1572. During the ensuing convocation of the clergy of Prague on May 27, the Consistory exhorted those present to conduct prayers for the protection of the established traditional religion in view of the current discussion of religious issues by the Diet.[120] The Consistory's formal reply to the king's request for evaluation of the Bohemian Confession was dated June 4. In the Consistory's judgment, the document had endorsed the Augsburg Confession and the Confession of the Brethren, both of which had been found contrary to "the true ancient Utraquist Christian religion, which is in agreement with the teachings of the holy prophets, of Christ the Lord, of the holy apostles, and with the teaching of the holy, catholic, apostolic Christian church" (pravé starobylé strany pod obojí křesťanské náboženství, srovnávající se s učením svatých proroků, Pána Krista, svatých apoštolů a s učením svaté obecné apoštolské církve křesťanské).[121] For the content of the latter, the Consistory referred to earlier confessional statements of the Utraquist Church and to the writings of its theologians, which had been submitted to the King in the form of extracts in a booklet in 1572. According to an independent report by a Lusatian historian Christophorus Manlius, this compendium included the classics of Utraquist theology ranging from Jan Rokycana and Jan of Příbram to Pavel Bydžovský and possibly Bohuslav Bílejovský.[122] Hrejsa assumes that the booklet was either one of Bydžovský's treatises, or Bílejovský's *Kronyka česká*.[123] In its own statement of June 4, the Consistory singled out for special censure the grant of power by the Bohemian Confession to laypersons to ordain priests and postulate theological tenets.[124]

The Consistory also entered the fray around the king's final decision on the fate of the Bohemian Confession. At an audience on August 30, 1575, the administrator and the Consistory appealed to the king to protect the Utraquist faith to which, they asserted, the majority of Bohemia's population adhered. They further cautioned that, if the Augsburg Confession were legalized, the Utraquist clergy would have to preach publicly concerning its defects, and thus, against the king's and its own wishes, disturb the tranquility of public life. In responding, Maximillian again stressed that he would not permit anything harmful to the Utraquist Church.[125] The Consistory's next appeal of September 9, 1575, asked for clarification of the king's decision that had been announced to the estates. The Consistory pleaded for protection of the existing Utraquist parishes not only in towns, but also in the countryside where the noble patrons might wish to introduce improperly ordained clergy.[126]

Paradoxically, during the events surrounding the debate about the Bohemian Confession, the Consistory was not on good terms with Valdštejn, despite his ultra-Utraquist stances. The main cause of friction was the baron's zeal for an election and oversight of the Consistory by the estates, which was emphasized in his statement of May 22.[127] The Consistory responded in its assessment of the Bohemian Confession addressed to the king and dated June 4: "Concerning the Prague Consistory and its organization . . . we hold that this Consistory is above all an office of Your Imperial Majesty, it has remained under the authority and under special protection of Your Imperial Majesty . . ."[128] If the Consistory and the clergy were subordinated to the estates, "then the clergy would be weak and very oppressed, and required to do what was ordained by the laypersons, and entirely deprived of its freedom in spiritual matters . . ."[129] In its inquiry of September 9, the

Consistory again expressed its wish that "our Consistory and its regular clergy might not be withdrawn from the hands and the protection of Your Imperial Majesty and placed under the authority of others, particular laypersons . . ."[130] The ill-wishers of Utraquism rejoiced over the overt difference of opinion between Valdštejn and the Consistory. The papal nuncio seemed to be almost beside himself with Schadenfreude when he wrote to Rome on May 22 about the friction between the Utraquist churchmen and their allegedly chief aristocratic patron.[131] Valdštejn's penchant for the institution of the defensores might have been yet another manifestation of aristocratic yearning for an intrusive role in ecclesiastical administration, which transcended denominational attachments.

Utraquist-Lutheran Entente: In Operation

Delaying three months after the submission of the Bohemian Confession on May 18, Maximillian informed the estates on August 22 that the document would not receive legal status, and as a final act, on September 2, he reemphasized his countervailing reassurance to the Lutherans and the Brethren about his intention to preserve the religious status quo, including their own churches and clergy. Although the petitions of the Lutherans did not reflect the Utraquists' specific interests, during all these proceedings the Utraquist towns estate loyally supported the noblemen's quest for the legalization of the Bohemian Confession.

On August 22, 1575, the king informed a six-member deputation of Lutheran nobles and knights, headed by Lobkovice (no representatives of towns or the Brethren were present this time), about the reasons why he would not approve either the Bohemian Confession, or the appointment of the Consistory by the estates. He cited the opposition of the party sub una and of the Utraquist Consistory, and the disagreements between the Lutherans and the Brethren, who submitted their own Confession. Above all, the King cited the existing laws of the land that he had confirmed by the coronation oath and which bound him to recognize only the Roman and Utraquist churches. He sought to avoid legal confusion, which had caused much strife in France and the Netherlands, but he was ready to give assurances that, as in the past, he would harm nobody for matters of religion. Thus, there was no need for the estates to ask for a change of the status quo. In the matter of the Consistory, Maximillian maintained that his ancestors had always appointed its membership, while the estates had performed only an advisory function in nominating possible candidates. Moreover, he could not accept a Consistory that (rather than a canonical bishop) would ordain priests.[132]

The towns again loyally joined the two nobles' estates on the same day in the appeal against this decision, with each estate sending six delegates. The spokesmen denied that there was a division among those who were not sub una on the approval of the Bohemian Confession. It was specifically affirmed that the towns agreed with the barons and the knights. It was noted that the only opposition came from two barons, Valdštejn and Vartenberk. The spokesmen also noted that the Diet of 1567 by the repeal of the Compactata had terminated the legal monopoly of Utraquism, which had been cited as a bar to the adoption of the Bohemian Confession.[133] During further discussions on August 24, 25, 26, 31, and September 1, the Lutherans asked for a separate Consistory, if the existing one should remain Utraquist. The towns continued to support the Lutherans in their repeated requests for the legalization of the Bohemian Confession, particularly in the negotiations of August 26, when Ottersdorf and Matěj Bydžovský of Aventin represented their estate.[134]

In his final solemn answer on September 2, Maximillian persisted in his decision that the Bohemian Confession could not be adopted as a law of the Diet or otherwise inserted among the laws of the kingdom, above all, because of the opposition of the party sub una. He reemphasized his promise that the Lutheran estates would not be disturbed in religious affairs, and specifically that he would not permit the Roman archbishop or the Utraquist Consistory to interfere with their clergy. He could further affirm that his son and successor would act similarly, although he did not consider the time opportune to give these assurances in writing. While he could not permit a Consistory controlled by the Diet, he repeated his offer (originally made on August 25) that several persons be selected by each of the estates who would watch over the interest of their clergy (presumably of whatever denomination) and would be authorized to complain to the king about any encroachments. To show his goodwill to the Lutherans and the Brethren, the king was particularly eager to allay any suspicion of sympathy for the alleged plan of the Holy League (between the pope and the kings of France and Spain) to exterminate the Protestants instead of conducting a crusade against the Turks. Thus, he crowned his plea by deploring the events of St. Bartholomew's Night, stressing that he had reproached the French king for events that cried out to God for punishment.[135] Subsequently, however, for diplomatic reasons, he softened the harsh censure of his Gallic confrere.[136]

When the estates, in fact, proceeded with selection of laymen who would watch over religious equity, designating them as defensores, the towns again participated in this act, although the institution was to serve the interests of the Lutherans and the Brethren, not just the Utraquists. Ottersdorf held the first place among the five defensores elected by the towns on September 13. The other two estates also elected five each on the same day.[137] However, in the end the institution came to nothing, when the estates attempted to use the defensores as ecclesiastical functionaries according to the proposals attached to the submission of the Bohemian Confession.[138] Maximilian objected both to designating these persons as defensores, and to endowing them with any authority of enforcement. Clearly, the king was not ready to sanction an institution existing prior to 1562 that Valdštejn among others wanted to restore.[139]

The events in 1575 thus resulted in a reasonable compromise. The Lutherans and the Brethren, with the support of Utraquist townsmen, obtained freedom and protection for the practice of their religion. Except for a foothold in the Consistory, the Lutheran estates secured the practical effect of the Bohemian Confession. At the same time, the Utraquist religion remained legally safeguarded in its existing form and extent. It became clear that the towns' support of the Lutheran nobles' legislative objectives would not facilitate the spread of the Augsburg Confession, and would not encroach on the established interests of the traditional Utraquist Church. As an expression of Maximilian II's determination to shield Utraquism, the Imperial Chancery, in response to a Utraquist petition of September 9, 1575, issued a decree on September 16 against the introduction of any religious innovations in royal towns.[140] This decree was reissued by the king in Regensburg after his departure from Prague on October 5. Evidently, these royal decrees were implemented in practice, particularly in Prague.[141] Prior to this, on September 26, Maximilian received Valdštejn and the Consistory in an audience, and reiterated in the presence of his son Rudolf, just crowned as king of Bohemia on September 22, his intent to safeguard the Utraquist jurisdiction. Informally, he is said to have spoken on this occasion sarcastically about the Bohemian Confession, although the portent of Maximillian's extemporaneous remark might have been distorted due to his limited knowledge of Czech and his interlocutors' ignorance of German.[142] Hrejsa, however, suggests—in flat contradiction to the Brethren's claims of his alleged contempt for Utraquism—that the King personally found the Utraquist *via media* more congenial than any other religious approach, not excluding the Augsburg Confession or the stance of the Roman Curia. In what seems an odd inversion of causality, Míka curiously maintains that Maximilian was actually forcing Utraquism on the Bohemian towns.[143]

An even more notable act, offering protection to Utraquism in the rural areas, was the clarification issued on November 30, 1575, by Maximilian II to the would-be defensores. The king stipulated that likewise in the countryside the Utraquist (or Roman) parishes could not be transformed into Lutheran ones, even on estates of Lutheran nobility. He wrote: "[C]oncerning the parishes . . . which have been traditionally . . . of [the] Catholic faith sub una, then also those *sub utraque,* which are administered by the Consistory of Prague, will remain in their original state . . ."[144] Thus, in the spirit of Peace of Kutná Hora, the nobles were enjoined from acting as manorial microreformers of religion and from imposing their favorite doctrines on their subjects who would find their seigneurs' doctrinal and liturgical preferences uncongenial.

Since Maximilian's son and successor Rudolf II (1576–1612) was bound by the same promise as his father with respect to religious toleration, the relative position of the religious groups, as it emerged from the informal settlement of 1575, would continue essentially unchanged during most of his reign (until 1609).[145] Maximilian's provisions resembled somewhat the Peace of Augsburg (1555) and the Convention of Passau (1552), which together had frozen the status of the Lutherans and the Roman Church in neighboring Germany.[146] The crucial difference, however, was that Maximilian's decrees enjoined the seigneurs, both secular and ecclesiastical, from forcing their subjects into conformity with their own religious views, thus flatly contradicting the notorious principle of *cuius regio, eius religio.* In this respect Maximilian's settlement with the Bohemians also differed substantially from the one he had recently reached with the nobility of Lower Austria through an oral promise of 1568 and the Assecuration of January 14, 1571 (incidentally issued in Prague). The barons and knights were thereby permitted to practice according to the Augsburg Confession not only in the family chapels of their castles, but also to introduce Lutheranism into the churches of their manors.[147] Perhaps, the French religious treaties between 1562 and 1598, resulting in the Edict of Nantes, offer the closest parallels to the letter and spirit of the Bohemian settlement of 1575.[148]

In surveying the aftermath of the events of 1575, it may be noted that the text of the Bohemian Confession itself had a somewhat curious history, perhaps due to Maximilian II's initial wish on September 18, 1575, not to rush into print, followed by an explicit prohibition of its printing on October 5.[149] This may be considered as a sign of his evenhandedness. At the other end of the religious spectrum, he had similarly prevented Archbishop Brus from proclaiming the Tridentine decrees of the Counter-Reformation in Bohemia through a clerical synod.[150] The publication of the Confession took place only in 1579 and in 1583, and then after a long lapse of time not until in the closing years of Rudolf II's reign in 1608, 1609, and finally in 1610, together with the Letter of Majesty, the Compromise (*Porovnání*), and other related documents.[151] German translations appeared in 1584, 1609 (in Amberg), and an official one by the Bohemian estates in 1610 (in Prague). A Latin version did not become available in print until 1614 in Frankfurt, subsequently reprinted again in Frankfurt in 1619.[152] However, what passed under the name of Bohemian Confession in Western Europe was usually not the Confession of 1575, but the Brethren's Confession published in Latin in 1573.[153] It was the Brethren's Confession that found its way into the prestigious international compendium, *Harmonia confessionum fidei, Orthodoxarum, et Reformatorum Ecclesiarum*, edited by Salnar de Castres (Geneva, 1581). This work was shortly thereafter translated into English, and published in an edition by J. F. Salvart, as *An harmony of the confessions of the faith of the christian and reformed churches* (Cambridge, 1586).[154] Thus, when Richard Hooker would refer in the *Laws of Ecclesiastical Polity* to the Bohemian Confession on the basis of *Harmonia confessionum fidei*, it was to the tenets of the Brethren of 1573, not to the 1575 version of the Czech Lutherans.[155]

The Social Cleavage

As a result of the religious split in Czech society preceding the discussion of the Bohemian Confession, the emerging fault line in the dissenting religious community crystallized two major forces in Bohemia. On one side stood the nobles with their Lutheran (and a few Calvinist) chaplains; the sectarians (mainly the Unity of Brethren); and the Lutherans of the German enclaves. On the other side stood the bulk of the Czech-speaking people of Bohemia who remained attached to Hus and to Utraquism, as defined in basic confessional documents from the Four Articles of Prague of 1419 to the Consistory's critique of the Bohemian Confession of 1575.

The controversies of 1575 revealed that the nobility, by rejecting Utraquism, had separated itself from the nation's majority, in contrast to Krofta's statement[156] that the Utraquist Church had separated itself from the vast majority of the national community. The nobility was becoming increasingly dysfunctional, unable to play well even its roles in foreign and military affairs, which allegedly legitimized its privileged status.[157] A military treatise of 1593 illustrated the defective training of aristocratic and gentry youth in physical prowess or political wisdom.[158] The nobility was also acquiring a parasitical character as it sought to evade civic responsibility and to shift national tax burdens to the townspeople, especially in 1567.[159] One may add that the nobles' coarse behavior toward the commoners disqualified them from serving as models of courtesy and gentleness. In their progressive detachment from the rest of society, the noble classes[160] were attracted to extrinsic religious models, be they the reformed churches of the north, or the Counter-Reformation of the south.[161] The productive and creative core of the country remained loyal to the homespun traditions of the Bohemian Reformation, exemplified by Jan Hus, and safeguarded by mainline Utraquism, deriving from the fourteenth-century reform movements in Prague and Oxford.

In the long run, the shift in religious orientations, made evident by the events of 1575, may be viewed as symptomatic of a more fundamental watershed in Czech history, namely the passing of intellectual leadership from the nobility to the middle classes.[162] Subsequently, it would be difficult to find much of intellectual or inspirational value in the legacy of the various noble Lichtenštejns, Pernštejns, or Rožmberks, with their contempt for the common man and their capricious narcissism.[163] It would be hard to find lasting value even in the anemic Weltschmerz of a more attractive figure like Karel the Elder of Žerotín.[164] Aside from a few exceptions, which seem to confirm the rule,[165] literary or artistic creativity was relatively rare even among the members of the lower nobility.[166] In addition to the virtual absence of intellectual production, Zikmund Winter and Zdeněk Kalista argue that the Bohemian nobles, like those of the neighboring German lands, and in contrast to the Bohemian townspeople, displayed markedly low levels of personal cultural or scholarly interest in the sixteenth century.[167] In this regard, Kalista challenged his mentor Josef Pekař who had wished to see in the nobles the paragons of Bohemia's national virtues.[168] More recently, Jiří Pešek stressed that the sixteenth-century Bohemian, like the rest of Central European nobility, had customarily remained at the level of bare literacy without any ambition for juridical or classical learning.[169]

In comparison, much more impressive, and subject to subsequent emulation, was the record of the unpretentious public-spirited men and gentle scholars of the towns, the creators of lasting intellectual values, such as the champions of Utraquism at the Diet of 1575, Sixt of Ottersdorf and Pavel

Kristián of Koldín, or other personages from the urban milieu, such as Daniel Adam of Veleslavín, Brikcí of Licko, Marek Bydžovský of Florentin, Jan Kocín of Kocinét, Mikuláš Konáč of Hodiškov, Martin Kuthen of Šprinsberk, and Prokop Lupáč of Hlaváčov. Starting in the late fifteenth century and extending throughout the rest of the Utraquist period, the urban middle classes established their leadership in the intellectual and literary life of the country.[170] The towns, especially Prague, had at their disposal in their chancelleries, schools, and churches impressive arrays of intellectuals, professionals, and experts in law and several academic disciplines.[171] The latter's sheer numbers outweighed whatever intellectual establishments even the wealthiest of nobles could assemble on their manors. The university of Prague was entirely in the service of the urban intellectual establishment.[172] Moreover, the critical mass of urban intellectual potential was increasing as the seigneurial towns during the sixteenth century were approximating the royal towns not only in the economic, but also in the cultural sphere. Prague, as well as other Bohemian towns, supported scholarship and historical writing, such as Hradec Králové, Kouřim, Louny, Písek, Rakovník, and Žatec.[173] Towns boasted significant public and school libraries.[174] The scope of educated townsmen's intellectual interest reached beyond practical knowledge of law, medicine, and technology to the sphere of pure science and scholarship in philosophy, classics, theology, linguistics, and history.[175] Erasmus listed Bohemia among the few countries where the humanities were valued and flourished.[176] Much of the urban intellectual life found expression and nourishment in the publication program of Adam of Veleslavín.[177]

The knowledge and learning embodied in the literary legacy of the urban statesmen and searchers after truth that subsequently helped to define the political culture, as well as the national consciousness of their country.[178] The prominent early awakener Josef Dobrovský called the sixteenth century the "beautiful or the golden age" (das schöne oder goldene Zeitalter) when "[t]he entire mass of the nation was stimulated to read and summoned to think. The cultivated part thought and wrote freely."[179] He celebrated the Utraquist sixteenth century for its augmentation of the Czech language and literature, and its spread of humanism and printing as the culmination of Czech intellectual development and a take-off point for further progress. In particular, much of this literary heritage would be reprinted and thus put into circulation in the early nineteenth century.

The significance of the debate over the Bohemian Confession may be summed up in four propositions. First, the discussions in 1575 revealed a religious split following social class lines. Second, the Utraquists, despite their theological proximity to the Roman Church, viewed the party sub una as their principal political opponent, and accepted the Lutherans and the Brethren as political allies. The Utraquists' notion of "no enemies on the left" subverts the assertions in historical literature that the Utraquists served the Habsburgs as an instrument of the Counter-Reformation.[180] Third, in a development that was possibly unique in contemporary Europe, the settlement of 1575 broadened the scope of political toleration of religious bodies from the Utraquists and the adherents of the Roman Church (covered by the Peace of Kutná Hora of 1485) to embrace de facto, if not de jure, the Lutherans and the Brethren.[181] Aside from the spirit of Kutná Hora, much credit for this expanded toleration belonged to Maximilian II, as both an inspirer and a guarantor of conditions under which religious permissiveness could flourish in relative peace. Finally, in contrast to the political alliance, the denouement of the religious controversy of 1575 foreshadowed the radical cultural alienation of the Bohemian nobility from the Czech commoners in Bohemia that would become strikingly apparent during the subsequent century and beyond.[182]

8

Orthodoxy and Toleration: The Utraquists and the Lutherans, 1575–1609

The purpose of this chapter is to address the controversial issue of the status of the Utraquist Church in the Kingdom of Bohemia in consequence of the drafting of the Bohemian Confession in 1575. The chronological scope is limited to the period up to 1609, when the issuance of the Letter of Majesty in 1609 would formalize and institutionalize the gentlemen's agreement of 1575 and alter the ecclesiastical structure accordingly. According to Czech historiography, the parliamentary action of 1575, which granted toleration, albeit tacit and conditional, to the Lutherans and the Unity of Brethren, represented a moment of truth for traditional Utraquism.[1] It was viewed as a golden opportunity to embrace the Lutheran Reformation and to shed the late medieval reformist tradition, based on the ecclesiology of the first millennium.

The prevailing opinion in Czech historical literature has been that the outcome of the settlement of 1575 meant a virtual demise of traditional Utraquism, either through replacement by or merger with the Lutheran religion. For instance, Václav Tomek characterized the Utraquist party as "lacking (by 1609) virtually any adherents except for those coerced and those coercing . . ." Antonín Rezek claimed that by 1575 the Utraquists "were dying out: neither the support of the Court, nor the sympathies of the Catholics were of any help." Kamil Krofta has maintained that after 1575 the Utraquist Consistory "merely vegetated in a complete separation from, indeed in an enmity with, the large majority" of the Czech dissidents from Rome. Josef Pekař declared that by the second half of the sixteenth century, a majority of Bohemia's population "adhered more or less openly and consciously to the Lutheran teaching and to clergy which was not administered by the Utraquist Consistory."[2] The editors of the prestigious series

Sněmy české od léta 1526 až po naši dobu (Bohemian Diets from 1526 to the Present) opined in 1891 that after 1593, "the clergy in the parishes ignored the rules of the Consistory. The large majority of them were ordained by German (i.e., Lutheran) consistories . . ."[3] Zdeněk Kalista saw in the 1590s only remnants of Utraquism, gradually losing power to prevent a full fusion with Lutheranism.[4] These views are also reflected in Anglophone and Teutonic historical literature. Thus, Lewis W. Spitz wrote in 1985 that: "By the end of the [sixteenth] century the burghers and nobles of Bohemia . . . were for the most part evangelical." Markus Reisenleitner spoke in 2000 about a transition to Protestantism (*ein deutlicher Übergang zum Protestantismus*) in Bohemia during the second half of the sixteenth century.[5]

In reassessing the conventional historical wisdom, the first and main objective of this chapter is to examine the evidence concerning the status of Utraquism in the period between 1575 and 1609 in a manner free as much as possible from preconceived notions. At issue is the religious affiliation and practice of some 75 to 83 percent of Bohemia's population. A distorting factor in the evaluation of the significance and size of Utraquism's following was the defection (by 1575) of the nobles from Utraquism to Lutheranism or the Unity of Brethren. This group was, of course, highly visible because of its political power and social prestige, but its actual numerical weight was slight, constituting less than 1 percent of the population with the number of families estimated at 1,400 in 1600.[6] A preconceived notion, the plausibility of Lutheranism's prevalence, was supported by an a priori assumption characteristic of the liberal and the Marxist historiography about the inevitability and virtually irresistible force of the Protestant Reformation. The evidence concerning the respective strength of classical Utraquism and of Lutheranism will be examined under three rubrics: (1) from the application of legal protection that Utraquism enjoyed in Bohemia, both in towns and in the countryside; (2) from the reports of foreigners, including the adherents of both the Roman Church and the reformed churches; and (3) from the character of the liturgical books typically used in the churches of Bohemia. For the first point, considerable use is made of the series *Sněmy české,* mentioned earlier, which as yet has not been sufficiently used for the interpretation of the Bohemian religious scene of the sixteenth century.[7]

The second objective is to explore the continuing identity of Utraquism, namely its theological *via media* between the Protestant Reformation and the post-Tridentine Roman Church. The focus will be on the confrontation of Utraquism with Lutheranism to examine the presumption of Utraquism's virtual erosion and replacement by Lutheranism, or the presumption of Utraquism's amalgamation with Lutheranism to produce a new hybrid religion of Neo-Utraquism.

The third objective is to address, at least in brief, the remarkable state of religious toleration in Bohemia after 1575, when King Maximilian II supplemented the official recognition of Utraquism and the Roman Church with a tacit protection of the Lutherans and the Brethren, within the limits of their numbers as of 1575. In part, the task is to illuminate Utraquism's share in this notable state of religious pluralism, which has by and large escaped the attention of Euro-Atlantic historical literature.[8] For the late sixteenth century, the emphasis has usually been placed on toleration in Poland, Transylvania, the Dutch Republic, and—after 1598—France.[9]

The following examination will call for a revision of the historical judgments cited near the beginning. Without seeking to detract from the respect due the two titans of Czech historiography, it will in particular emerge that Krofta's and Hrejsa's assessments of post-1575 Utraquism should be reversed or—as Marx said of Hegel—put on their feet.[10] It was not the Utraquist Consistory that separated itself from the nation, but the Lutheran nobles who separated themselves from the nation's Utraquist majority. The Utraquists had not lost the spirit of Hus, but to the contrary, the Consistory defended Hus's teachings in confrontation with the teachings of Luther. Likewise Tomek's dictum that by 1609 the Utraquist Church had only "those coerced and those coercing" should be reversed. To the extent that political power was applied, it was to restrain the would-be coercers, who were numerically weak, but politically powerful, from coercing those who were many but politically weak.

Parenthetically, the tendency for the *via media* in religion to disappear or to shrink into insignificance is not entirely unique to Czech historiography. The assertions that in the late sixteenth century there were no real Utraquists, only Lutherans ("Neo-Utraquists") and Romanists in Bohemia, find a partial parallel in English historiography. Thus, Arthur G. Dickens has similarly minimized the role of real Anglicans in Elizabethan England in favor of the relative extremes of Puritanism and Roman Catholicism: "Parker and Jewell were in very real sense forerunners of the 'balanced' Anglicanism of Hooker, yet even so the vast majority of Elizabethan Englishmen were either Roman Catholics or Anglican Puritans."[11] Patrick Collinson chimed in speaking of the Elizabethan settlement: "[I]t is not easy to identify very many Anglicans who were positively attached to those features of the church that distinguished it from other churches of the Reformation..."[12] The difference is that, while for Bohemia the skepticism about the *via media* has been the standard disposition, characteristic of Catholic, Protestant, liberal, and Marxist historians, for England it is but one among several variants.[13]

The Legal Status of Utraquism

As noted, the religious settlement of 1575 resulted in what may be considered a reasonable compromise that would safeguard the confessional status quo. The noble Lutherans and the Brethren, with the support of Utraquist townsmen in the Bohemian Diet, obtained freedom and protection for the practice of their religion. A major drawback was their failure—with the Consistory remaining Utraquist—to secure an organizational framework for the Lutheran clergy. The researches of Inge Auerbach have shown the precariousness of the organizational status of Czech Lutherans, who generated hardly any institutional infrastructure. This was largely due to their exclusion from the Consistory.[14] Consequently, there was no Lutheran forum in Bohemia to react, for instance, to the epochal conflict between the Gnesio-Lutherans and the Philippists, such as raged among the Lutherans of Lower and Upper Austria,[15] or to adopt the Formula of Concord of 1577, which terminated the intra-Lutheran dispute in Germany.[16] On the other side of the ledger, Utraquism remained legally safeguarded in its existing form and extent. Although the compromise was concluded orally and covertly under Maximilian II, and his son and successor Rudolf II (1576–1612) was not so fervent a believer in the virtue of forbearance as his father, nevertheless the new king felt bound by the gentlemen's agreement between his father and the Bohemian estates. Thus, in the eyes of the royal government, the relative position of the religious groups would continue basically unchanged during most of his reign (until 1609).[17]

As also noted in Chapter 7, the legal protection of Utraquism in the royal towns was mandated by Maximilian II's decree of September 16, 1575. Inasmuch as the towns usually could defend their religious interests, even more crucial was the guarantee of Utraquism for the countryside where the peasantry confronted their manorial lords, a guarantee embodied in Maximilian II's decree of November 30, 1575. These two decrees remained the cornerstones for the legal defense of Utraquist parishes, clergy, and rituals from 1575 to 1609. The documents stipulated that the parishes that were traditionally, and particularly in 1575, either under the Utraquist Consistory or Roman jurisdiction, should remain such. In effect, they would not be staffed by Lutheran ministers.[18] These provisions were, in a sense, an expansion of the principles of the Peace of Kutná Hora of 1485, which had guaranteed the existing ownership of churches between the Utraquists and the Roman party.[19] While the nobles were free to pursue their idiosyncratic religious preferences in their family chapels, the established religious traditions of the bulk of the Czech people were shielded against outside interference.[20] To the extent that the towns remained Utraquist and the peasants on noble estates could not be pressured into renouncing Utraquism for the religion of their seigneur, paradoxically the numerical weight of Czech Lutherans remained low, as their political weight—due to the adherence of nobles, especially the barons—had soared.[21]

The provision prohibiting the seigneurs from imposing Lutheranism on their subjects was of crucial importance in preservation of the strength of Utraquism. It can be argued that this measure more than any other had the potential to stop the Protestant steamroller in its tracks in Bohemia. In the first place, the peasantry then constituted at least 80 percent of the population.[22] In the second place, recent studies have shown that the main obstacles to the Reformation in Central Europe lay at the level of the rural parish. The interposition of Maximilian II's decree prevented the nobles from breaking down these barriers and weaning the villagers from the traditional Bohemian piety perpetuated by Utraquism. Using a more technical language, Maximilian's decrees frustrated what in recent scholarship has become known as the aristocratic model of the Reformation. This phenomenon had been particularly effective in northern Germany, and its shadow loomed large over Bohemia in view of the nobles' enthusiasm for Lutheranism. The other two models, evolved in recent studies for viewing the spread of the Reformation in Central Europe, were by and large inapplicable to Bohemia: (1) Arthur G. Dickens's urban model because of the towns' attachment to the traditional *via media* of Utraquism (reflecting a satisfaction with the early fifteenth-century Reformation); and (2) the Habsburg sovereigns' adherence to the Roman Curia, which ruled out the princely model.[23]

As noted in Chapter 1, in the eyes of older historiography, which explicitly or tacitly accepted a deterministic view of the Protestant Reformation's appeal and spread, any efforts to prevent the full consummation of this irresistible force could be viewed a priori as hopeless gestures of interference with the inevitable, and a thwarting of the true desires of the common men. The significance of the manipulative element was obscured by the assumption of a deterministic advance. Once history stopped adhering to an inevitable sweep of Hegel's absolute reason, Comte's positivist law, or Marx's economic dialectic, the issue of Protestantism's appeal could be examined in a more empirical way from the viewpoint of Rankean "wie es eigentlich gewesen" (how it really happened). It became possible to question that the common people experienced an irresistible urge to abandon the psychic appeal of elaborate ceremonialism in favor of the spartan and austere Protestant worship with "its complex and protracted sermons." The new research on England and Germany has tended to support the view that the peasantry, in fact, remained attached to traditional observances and rituals, and had to be cajoled, pressured, or tricked by the nobles into accepting the Reformation's reductionism, austerity, and discipline. The Reformation was not "a Protestant walkover, but . . . a prolonged and uphill struggle against conservative sentiment."[24] In a similar vein, Judith Maltby records the resistance of English congregations against Calvinist pastors' efforts to subvert the Anglican rituals in the early seventeenth century.[25]

In the Bohemian context, the medieval Christian ritual would enjoy an added appeal for Czech commoners. The availability of masses, ecclesiastical vestments, church decor, adoration of the Eucharist, or invocation of saints was devoid of the costs or penalties imposed by Rome. First, it was inexpensive, free of the burdensome charges in support of a lavish ecclesiastical bureaucracy and monastic establishment of the Roman Church. Both the costly clerical lifestyle and the cloistered ideal had been pruned away in the Wyclifite spirit by the early Utraquist reforms at the start of the fifteenth century. The modest cost of the Utraquist ecclesiastical establishment is documented, for instance, by Zikmund Winter. The expense was kept low, among other ways, by a parsimonious use of clergy, with normally only one priest in even a large urban parish, and with rituals usually dispensing with multiple clerical celebrants.[26] Unlike the practice of the Roman Curia, the performance of good deeds was not to be an occasion for fleecing the faithful for the purposes of architectural splendor or military (mis)adventures.[27] Second, the medieval ritual was offered in a way that was free of a menacing aspect, inasmuch as the Utraquist Church had renounced interdicts, anathemas, excommunications, and other dreaded spiritual weapons employed conspicuously by the Roman Church in the late medieval and early modern times.[28] Another liberalizing feature was the de-emphasis of auricular confession as a prerequisite for communion or as an annual obligation. This was so particularly in view of the Roman Church's use of confession as a means of disciplinary enforcement.[29]

Moreover, the Utraquist Church traditionally enjoyed and cultivated an image of a special concern for, and dedication to, the more plebeian strata of society. This tendency was rooted in Wyclif and the early egalitarianism of the Bohemian Reformation, as among the Orebites.[30] It continued with an unusual emphasis on the respectability of the common man in its theological discourse. For instance, the Utraquist priest, Vavřinec Leander Rvačovský of Rvačov, in his famous *Masopust* (Mardi Gras) (1580), went out of his way to note biblical injunctions concerning the dignity of the poor and ordinary people, such as, "Let there be not among you any difference; listen well to the little one as to the great one, to the poor one as to the rich one, without any regard for the person . . .," or "God himself, when he wishes to punish or to show mercy, shows no regard for the status of the person . . ."[31] Rvačovský made it clear that he was standing by the townsmen and the common people (*měšťané aneb lid obecní*) in relation to their feudal superiors (*vrchnosti*).[32] This populist concern was illustrated also by the Utraquist clergy's care to maintain a supply of religious books written in Czech for the use of the common people (*lidé prostější*), as, for instance, Jan Václav Cykáda, a member of the Utraquist Consistory (1605–1609), stressed in the introduction to his *Hody křesťanské* (Christian Feast Days) (1607). As if to further underline the plebeian character of his church, Cykáda portrayed an antagonistic relationship between the Utraquist priests and the manorial lords. The seigneurs in their cavalier treatment of the Utraquist clergy begrudged the village priests even the modest income from properties donated for their support. Such nobles seized parish grazing lands, gardens, and ponds, and refused to pay tithes from their produce.[33]

Thus, it might be said that the Czech commoners had the best of all possible worlds: enjoying their favorite liturgies; escaping the discipline of catechization and ban on secular festivities, which the Protestant Reformation entailed[34]; and escaping the heavy financial burden of supporting the luxuriant clerical and monastic apparatus, or facing the risk of spiritual penalties, which the Roman Church would impose. A special relationship bonded the Utraquist Church with plain Czech folks. The Czech Lutheran minister, Jan Štelcar Želetavský of Želetava, confirmed the people's attachment to the Utraquist faith, even as he ridiculed it as a blind attachment to ancestral beliefs.[35]

Disregarding the presumption of older historiography that the legal protection of Utraquism suffered from systemic ineffectiveness, if not irrationality, the actual state of Utraquism, both in the countryside and in the towns, will be addressed first; an examination of the arguments against its continuing strength follows.

Utraquists in the Countryside

On private manors, including their subject towns, the protection of Utraquism, under the royal decree of 1575, rested in the first instance in the hands of the manorial seigneurs. The nobles, whether themselves advocates of the Reformation or of the Roman Curia, actually tended to observe the injunction against forcing their subjects to renounce Utraquism. In a way, this principle had been ingrained in Bohemia since the peace of Kutná Hora of 1485, which explicitly granted the peasants the right to differ in religion from their feudal masters, and thus represented a notable reversal of the rule "cuius regio, eius religio" that would be adopted in the German lands. Recent research has also shown that, in contrast to the subsequent period, the Central European peasantry enjoyed considerable bargaining powers vis-à-vis its feudal lords in the sixteenth century, if backed by the right of appeal to the royal officials or the monarch himself.[36]

On the Roman side, such an indulgence of the seigneurs toward the religious preferences of their subjects may be inferred from the ordinance for the town of Jindřichův Hradec issued in 1597 by its new devout master Jáchym Oldřich of Hradec (1597–1604), the heir of the tolerant Adam of Hradec. The ordinance required properly ordained clergy for both those *sub una* and those *sub utraque,* participation in religious processions, and observance of fasts. All these provisions were consistent with the tenets of the Utraquist Church, but they would preclude changes in the Lutheran direction. The seigneurs also looked askance at new introductions of Unity congregations on their manors, and safeguarded the right of Utraquist parishes to have priests authorized by the Consistory.[37]

In addition to seeking voluntary compliance, the monarch watched over the preservation of Utraquism by the manorial seigneurs both by reconfirming the general decree and by interventions in specific cases. Likewise, the Consistory exercised its right to appeal to the monarch in order the protect its interests from encroachments by private landowners.[38] In 1584, Rudolf II reprimanded seigneurs who would seek to appoint Lutheran ministers to their parishes. A separate royal decree also in 1584 prohibited the spread of Unity congregations on private estates, as well as in royal towns.[39] Subsequently, in 1595 and again in 1602, he renewed Maximilian II's ordinance, as well as earlier legislation, providing that the manorial seigneurs should not tolerate other clergymen sub utraque on their manors than those administered by the Utraquist Consistory and observing the Compactata.[40] On December 16, 1603, Rudolf II requested Johanna Hrzanová of Sulevice not to permit the Brethren's worship on her estate. The same order was repeated to her and dispatched to four other landowners in March 1604. In July 1604, Rudolf II repeated the order that only priests under the archbishop (if the parish was sub una) or under the Utraquist Consistory (for sub utraque parishes) may be appointed in towns and villages on private estates.[41] In a more complicated case, in October 1604, Rudolf II admonished Karel Bechyně of Lažany not to interfere with his vassal Jeroným Puchfelder of Presoty, who wished to remove an irregular (*nepořádný*) clergyman and replace him with one under the Utraquist Consistory. In a reversed situation in November 1604, Rudolf II interceded with the town council of Dvůr nad Labem not to replace a Utraquist priest with one lacking episcopal ordination.[42]

The Utraquist Consistory also turned to private landlords to assert its right to appoint Utraquist priests to traditionally Utraquist parishes on their estates, as in April 1589 when the Catholic Vilém of Rožmberk was requested to respect its right to the village parish of Jirčany, and in June 1589 to the town church of Velvary.[43] Even the archbishops of Prague played a role in seeking to contain the spread of Lutheranism, at the expense of Utraquism, on the estates of landlords who were, or were presumed to be, adherents of the Roman Church. Thus in April 1598, Archbishop Berka admonished Petr Vok of Rožmberk to keep in the parishes that were traditionally Utraquist only such priests who were "ordained by canonical bishops and administered by the Lower (i.e., Utraquist) Consistory."[44]

In addition, the effectiveness of the restriction on Lutheran expansion on private estates was made evident by the limitation of worship by Lutheran nobles to their private chapels, thus isolating its exercise from the urban and rural population of their manors. Even then the Lutheran nobles had to strive to assert their right to such secluded sanctuaries, granted them under Maximilian II's oral dispensation of 1575. Thus, on September 30, 1601, Kašpar the Elder Belvic of Nostvice appealed to Rudolf II for his right to establish a Lutheran church for services to his family in Kynšperk against the wishes of the archbishop. In September 1602, Heinrich Reuss von Plauen claimed that as a noble of the Holy Roman Empire under the Religious Peace of 1555, he was exempt from the jurisdiction of the archbishop of Prague, and could be guided by decisions of the Lutheran Consistory in Gera, Saxony. Later the same month, Jan Fridrich Lang of Langenhart defended his small Lutheran church in Zaječice, staffed by Lutheran ministers, on the ground that it served only his family and that worship according to the Augsburg Confession had been permitted in Bohemia since 1575. In May 1604, Rudolf von Bünau auf Wesenstein und Plankenstein appealed to the elector of Saxony, Christian II, to intercede with Rudolf II so that he might erect a private Lutheran church on his estate in Březnice near Ústí nad Labem to worship with his family, as permitted by Maximilian II.[45] The effectiveness of the protection of Utraquism appeared to be confirmed by certain nobles' complaint in 1608 against the exclusion of Lutheran clergy from not only towns, but also villages, which apparently—in its rigidity—was considered a violation of the gentlemen's agreement of 1575. The protest also assailed the prohibition of German preaching in churches sub utraque both in towns and in the country.[46] Considering the improbability of German preaching by the Utraquists, the latter measure evidently aimed at checking the expansion of Lutheranism.

Utraquists in Royal Towns

By and large, Rudolf II adhered to his father's decrees of 1575 to protect the positions of Utraquism where established not only on the seigneurial, royal, and ecclesiastical manors, but also in the royal towns. The decrees remained the cornerstones for the legal defense of the established positions of Utraquism after the oral approval of the Bohemian Confession in 1575. Petr Codicillus reports that Lutheran ministers were not permitted to serve in Prague after 1575. Most notably, Rudolf II sent an edict to all royal towns, including Prague, in January and February 1589 with specific reference to Maximilian's legislation, stipulating that the Utraquist Consistory was their guide in religion, and the sole source of their clergy. No religious innovations should be admitted, and priests refusing obedience to the Consistory should be dismissed.[47] According to the French diplomat Pierre Bergeron, who stayed in Prague in July and August 1600, only Utraquist and Roman services could be publicly celebrated in Prague. The Utraquists held virtually all churches in the city, while the services of the Roman Church were restricted largely to the monasteries. Brethren could worship in Prague only secretly in private homes.[48]

The royal protection of Utraquism applied to towns other than Prague; for instance, in November 1595, Rudolf II intervened in favor of a Utraquist priest in Pradubice, in May 1596 in Tábor, and in 1589 in support of the Corpus Christi procession in Kadaň. Even when it came to an exceptional violation of the status quo, Rudolf acted in the interest of Utraquism against that of the Roman Church. In May 1594, in response to the Diet's petitions of October and November 1593, he approved the appointment of a Utraquist priest under the jurisdiction of the Utraquist Consistory in Kadaň, which traditionally had a priest sub una. The Utraquist priest still served there in 1604.⁴⁹ In 1602 Rudolf II ordered all circuit captains to proclaim the mandate against the Brethren in each town. In the same year, the king's mandate prohibited Lutherans and Brethren to serve as councilors in Prague city governments. This also seemed to indicate a strong position of Utraquists in Prague since they were able to dominate the council without other members of the party sub utraque. A year after the mandate (1603), the king issued an instruction to the subchamberlain, the chief official in charge of royal towns, which stipulated that in towns only such clergymen should be appointed to parishes sub utraque, who had a canonical episcopal ordination and observed the tenets of the Compactata, that is, were Utraquists, not Lutherans or Brethren.⁵⁰ Responding to a complaint by the Consistory, Rudolf II inquired on December 18, 1602, in the town of Kutná Hora concerning the type of ordination of the local clergy. In June 1603, Rudolf II requested the town of Sušice to remove a clergyman who had not been properly ordained, and replace him with a canonically ordained priest.⁵¹

The defense of Utraquism in royal towns was not simply a matter of royal policy, imposed on a passive or even unwilling population, as some would claim.⁵² The townsmen themselves continued to play an active part in safeguarding the Utraquist character of their communities, and thus manifesting a lively attachment to their traditional faith. As usual, the citizens of Prague took the lead. In February 1588, the deputies of Prague headed other Bohemian towns in petitioning the emperor to influence the archbishop to ordain Utraquist priests. In 1589, the delegates of the city of Prague defended the Consistory's jurisdiction in matrimonial cases. In February 1589, the New Town of Prague reaffirmed its full observance of the decree of Maximilian II of 1575, in respecting the jurisdiction of the Utraquist Consistory.⁵³ The towns, led by Prague, also assisted the Consistory in watching over the orthodoxy and the discipline of Utraquist priests. The Consistory, in turn, mandated the observance of traditional liturgies and fasts, in particular the solemn Corpus Christi processions.⁵⁴ Analogous studies have shown that in contemporary England the commitment to the Prayer Book and the episcopacy by laypeople was also a matter of sincere belief and not of political expediency.⁵⁵

The Consistory's Grievances

Not surprisingly, next to the king and his officials, the archbishops, the town councils, and the parishes themselves, the Utraquist Consistory played a conspicuous role in seeking to maintain the religious status quo, and in calling attention to real or alleged violation of the decrees of Maximilian II promulgated in 1575 for the protection of the special brand of Bohemian Christianity. Numerous petitions asking the king or his officials for relief against violations of these rights have survived. Still in the lifetime of Maximilian in July 1576, the Consistory complained against certain nobles who had introduced the Brethren's clergy and ceremonies on their estates. The administrator and the Consistory continued to voice their grievances under Rudolf II, as on October 11, 1577, when a letter addressed to the highest officials of the land reported violations of the religious status quo. Typically, the challenges stemmed from the countryside, where individual barons or knights wished to install non-Utraquist (presumably Lutheran) clergy on their estates. With respect to towns, the issues typically involved disciplinary problems of Utraquist clergy and the unauthorized openings of Unity congregations. In addition, a letter to Rudolf II of August 8, 1578, charged manorial seigneurs with a tendency of encroaching on the incomes of Utraquist clergy on their estates.[56]

Similarly, the Consistory in the two appeals to Rudolf II in June 1579, and in May 1580, asked him to safeguard its jurisdiction over traditionally Utraquist parishes. In October 1582, the Consistory defended the Utraquists' right to appoint the abbot of the Emmaus monastery. Protests against assignments of Lutheran ministers to Utraquist parishes on private estates and in towns followed in 1585. Several petitions concerning Utraquist parishes in towns were sent in 1589. More specifically, in April 1589, the Consistory asked the Highest Court Steward (*hofmistr*), Jiří the Elder of Lobkovice, to prevent assignments of Lutheran ministers in the towns of Kouřim and Vodňany. In June of the same year, the administrator and his colleagues petitioned the king to back their right, based on Maximilian II's decree of 1575, to clerical appointments in the towns of Nymburk and Velvary.[57] The Consistory had other areas of concern. Its petition to Rudolf II in January 1589 asked for protection of its jurisdiction in matrimonial cases. In May 1589, it petitioned the monarch to back its request for the participation of the inhabitants of Prague, including the guilds, university professors and students, and teachers and schoolchildren in the Utraquist Corpus Christi procession.[58]

The relative frequency and the plaintive character of the Consistory's petitions to Rudolf II have been (mis)used to portray Utraquism as a vanishing institution; that is, the entreaties for assistance have been taken as signs of an incurable weakness of Utraquism against the tide of the Lutheran reformation.[59] In evaluating the frequency of the entreaties, it is necessary to consider two aspects. First, the Consistory lacked its own enforcement apparatus. Its rejection of a governing clergy went back to its Wyclifite roots. Hence, the Consistory had to rely on lay public authorities to execute its decisions that, in turn, called for regular interactions with royal officials and town councils.[60] The frequent airing of grievances was thus a corollary of the dependence on lay administrative agencies. Second, the Consistory's complaints on closer examination involved matters more of jurisdictional form than of confessional substance. The administrator and his colleagues remained very sensitive to possible encroachments by manorial or urban authorities on their own ecclesiastical authority, and thus frequently protested slights of protocol or etiquette. Nevertheless, the Consistory indicated that even in this area—for instance, in matrimonial cases—a disregard for its jurisdiction was a rare exception, not a rule.[61]

In evaluating the plaintive character of the Consistory's entreaties, it is again necessary to put forth two considerations. First, the use of hyperboles, which could create the impression of desperation, may be viewed as a resort to poetic license in order to stir into action the inert and ultimately ambiguous monarch.[62] The starkest document in this regard claimed that there were more "Pikarts, Zwinglians, Calvinists, and Lutherans" than real Christians in Bohemian towns, and that only in some seven cities Utraquist worship was properly performed. The paranoid outpouring, presumably originating in the Consistory, is addressed to Rudolf II, but it bears no date or signature. It is questionable whether it was meant to be an authentic letter, or a mere stylistic exercise. Despite its dubious provenance, this document has been cited as the ultimate proof of Utraquism's bankruptcy.[63] As explained in the following section, this image of the situation in towns did not correspond with the actual state of affairs.

Second, the tone of exasperation in the Consistory's petitions to the king derived from a difference of perspective on the religious settlement of 1575 between the king and the Utraquist towns on the one hand, and the Consistory on the other. Rudolf II had to take into consideration his father's promises of 1575 to the nobles to tolerate Lutheranism and Unity where their adherents had existed at the time. The townsmen similarly had to honor their cooperation with the nobles of 1575 and accept dissent in religion up to, and including, the limits of the Bohemian Confession. The Consistory did not recognize the gentlemen's agreements of 1575 and instead upheld the formal view that only Utraquism was legally sanctioned in Bohemia, together with the vestiges of the Roman Church. In this sense, the Consistory could imply that its interests were not as effectively defended as under Ferdinand I.[64] This did not mean that Rudolf II was not ready to support Utraquism within the scope of Maximilian II's promise of toleration of 1575.

The Consistory and the Towns

Let us now turn to the Consistory's correspondence with the city councils that made the position of Utraquism appear more precarious than was actually warranted. One aspect was the pleading tone that characterized many of the Consistory's missives. This stance was a natural consequence of the fact that the Utraquist Church had abjured the use of peremptory commands, characteristic of the Roman Church, and preferred the mode of consensus in the conduct of ecclesiastical governance. Hence, resort to pleading by the Consistory, with the object of explanation and persuasion, and encountering counterarguments, should not be viewed as signs of diminished self-confidence, or of waning authority, but rather as a normal modus operandi.[65] The copious evidence of the Consistory's concern with matters of orthodoxy and discipline also belie the assertions in historical literature about the condition of theological and institutional chaos under the Consistory.[66] The other disturbing aspect of this correspondence, the revelation of tensions between what had seemed to be the most natural of allies, the Consistory and the town councils, requires more probing. The friction can be viewed as springing from the distinction of roles of three types. All these matters involved issues of procedure, rather than matters of religious substance.

First, there was the difference between the Consistory as the watchdog of orthodoxy, and the towns as practitioners of political pragmatism. Some of the Consistory's complaints about the towns' disloyalty in harboring improper priests stemmed once again from the fact that unlike the lay Utraquists in towns, it had not been a party to the agreement of 1575, which granted informal tolerance to the Lutherans and the Brethren. It upheld the earlier view that only the Utraquist and the sub una forms of Christianity were admissible, objecting to the presence of not only the Brethren, but also Lutherans in royal towns.[67] As a case in point, in January 1590, the Consistory charged that in addition to the proper Utraquist priests, certain towns tolerated also irregular clergy, such as Beroun, Domažlice, Nymburk, and Sušice. In January 1590, the Consistory appealed to Rudolf II against expansion of the Unity to Prague, pointing to decisions going back to 1443 and guaranteeing the city a Utraquist status. It voiced its approval of the closing of the Brethren's secret meeting place in Prague in December 1603.[68]

Second, there was the distinction between the towns' right of patronage over churches, and the Consistory's right to grant ecclesiastical powers to clergy.[69] In many cases, it appeared that in referring to the towns' predilection for heterodox clergy, the Consistory objected to such priests more on grounds of discipline rather than for their lack of Utraquist orthodoxy. The Consistory engaged in frequent disputes with the towns about the candidates to be appointed and confirmed as priests, even if the nominees of both parties were unimpeachably Utraquist. In such cases, the conditions of discipline, required by the Consistory, were specific and distinct from confessional orthodoxy, such as avoidance of pubs, houses of ill repute, and cronyism. In a particular case in 1590, the Consistory opposed the appointment of a priest requested by the parishioners of St. Jiljí in Prague, because he had engaged in tavern brawls, slanders, and unfair competition for performance of church services. He had also maintained contact with the abbot of Emmaus, who was persona non grata to the Consistory.[70] A report of March 1590 referred to the fact that certain towns maintained priests, who though canonically ordained (hence with the essential Utraquist credentials), were at odds with the Consistory. A statement of the king's Highest Court Steward (hofmistr) in March 1592 implied that the dissensions between the Utraquist leadership and some of the clergy were of administrative or disciplinary character. According to the letter, the king and the highest officials were displeased over the frequent disputes, which involved validly ordained, that is Utraquist, clergy.[71] The towns also wished to retain well-liked priests, and therefore hindered their transfers by the Consistory. In January 1603, the town council of Kutná Hora opposed the Consistory's recall of local priests, vouching for their observance of the rules of the "holy Catholic Christian Church."[72] Clerical marriage was another conspicuous issue of discipline that provoked conflict between the Consistory and the towns. Major cases cropped up in Prague and Tábor in 1590, but also earlier in other urban parishes.[73] The question of priestly celibacy involved an internal Utraquist controversy that went back to the mid-sixteenth century, and it should not be construed per se as implying a gravitation toward Lutheran allegiance.[74] In their approval of, or even preference for, married clergy, the towns of Bohemia appeared to be ahead of the Consistory.

Third, the Consistory's judicial authority, especially in matrimonial cases, could clash with the city councils' power of enforcement. The Consistory grieved over the lack of cooperation by the towns in the judicial field, in particular their failure to assist effectively in judicial proceedings and in the execution of the Consistory court's sentences or judgments. Thus, in petitions of 1589, the administrator and his colleagues charged the city of Prague with insufficient help with subpoenas of witness and enforcement of judgments in matrimonial trials, or in coercing recalcitrant clergy to appear before its court. In more serious breaches, in March 1590, the towns of Prague actually usurped ecclesiastical jurisdiction to decide matrimonial cases in town courts. The Old Town passed judgment on the validity of a marriage, and the New Town court dealt with the seduction of a maid by a burgher under the promise of nuptials.[75] The town councils of Prague and the Consistory were sensitive to mutual slights, and disputes arose from such alleged violations of protocol or etiquette. For instance, in November 1582, the city resisted the introduction of the Gregorian calendar that was mandated by the Consistory.[76] In general, the jurisdictional disputes involved quarrels within the Utraquist family, not Protestant defections.

At times the Consistory's charges drew such a bleak picture of the state of Utraquist religion in the towns that it evidently did not correspond to reality. In particular, the Consistory had a mischievous tendency to insinuate that the priests, who seemed insubordinate or undisciplined from the administrative point of view, were tainted with Pikartism, Lutheranism, or Calvinism. Such exaggerations were in line with the Consistory's implausible accusation in October 1586 that Archbishop Medek sought to appoint Lutheran ministers to Utraquist parishes.[77] The towns, in turn, might engage in reverse overstatements and accuse the Consistory of seeking to impose heretics as priests.[78] There was, however, one brief period in the early 1590s when the towns had a genuine reason to question the orthodoxy of Utraquism's top leadership. A suspicion of the administrator's defection to the Roman Church was actually borne out by the apostasy of Fabian Rezek in 1593. In that year, the estate of towns at the Bohemian Diet actually had to defend Utraquism against the administrator, who in alliance with the papal nuncio, tried to intimidate Utraquist clergy into signing a Tridentine statement opposed to Utraquist principles.[79] Earlier in 1591–1592, the erratic Rezek had been to the contrary suspected of leniency toward Lutheranism.[80] In a denouement, the Consistory categorically repudiated Rezek's personal decision of 1593, and he was replaced as administrator by the unimpeachably orthodox Václav Dačický in 1594.[81]

Despite the various tensions and conflicts with the Consistory, there were other strong indications of the towns' continuing allegiance to Utraquism. When the chips were down, the city fathers went to bat for Utraquism and the Consistory. An impressive gesture of their Utraquist loyalty was the solemn declaration by the town deputies from the highest tribune of the country, the Bohemian Diet, dated February 1588, in support of the Consistory and its rights. The collective pleas of the estate of towns in 1589 and 1590 that the archbishop resume ordination of Utraquist priests did not appear like behavior of those who cast a jaundiced eye at Utraquism and were eager to become Lutherans.[82] Subsequently, the towns were particularly influential in helping to restrain Administrator Fabian Rezek's erratic behavior in 1593 and, after his overt defection to the Roman Church, in restoring the Utraquist Consistory in 1594. The towns insisted again on the restoration of the Consistory in 1604 after Administrator Dačický's insolent removal from office by Chancellor Zdeněk of Lobkovice.[83]

In sum, to deal with the negative impression left by the Consistory's correspondence with the emperor and the town councils in 1575–1608, its character must be seen in the relevant perspective. First, the sense of urgency was designed to elicit action from the procrastinating and ultimately unfriendly emperor, not to reflect despair about an inevitable Lutheran takeover.[84] Second, the issues between the Consistory and the towns involved by and large internal administrative matters within the Utraquist family, not extra-confessional inroads from the Lutherans. Third, the large volume of correspondence reflected the Utraquists' replacement of the command mode of ecclesiastical governance, characteristic of the Roman Church, by a largely consensual method, requiring argumentation with the aim of persuasion. The exchanges between the towns and the Consistory showed that the Kingdom of Bohemia in the sixteenth century, although a happy and prosperous realm, had not yet reached the eschatological status of the Kingdom of God on earth in which all internal strife and litigation would cease (despite the original aspirations of the Bohemian Reformation). The very amount of litigation—covering, however, more than thirty years—can be taken as evidence that the mandates to protect Utraquism were taken seriously rather than that Maximilian II's decrees were mere window dressing, masking a massive Lutheran entrenchment in the towns and the countryside.

A clear affirmation concerning the actual strength and solid position of Utraquism early in the seventeenth century came from a report of December 14, 1602, by the administrator and Consistory to Rudolf II, which noted (twenty-seven years after the oral approval of the Bohemian Confession) that with the exception of three, all priests surveyed in royal towns under the Consistory's jurisdiction had proper ordination by bishops and pledged to serve "according to the missal and the rubrics" (*podle mšálu a rubriky znění se říditi a spravovati*). The exceptions were Mladá Boleslav, Týn nad Vltavou, and Kutná Hora, but even for them the Consistory had available proper priests ordained by bishops.[85] As the use of the Book of Common Prayer distinguished the Anglicans from the Puritans, so the use of the missal and the rubrics of the pre-Tridentine archbishopric of Prague distinguished the Utraquists from the Lutherans and the Brethren.[86] The report just cited contradicts two mantras of sixteenth-century Bohemian historiography that after 1575 the royal towns turned irresistibly Lutheran, and that the Utraquist clergy were a vanishing species. Even the less-than-friendly observer, Josef Janáček, admitted the continuation of Utraquism in the towns after 1600, although he referred to an "ossified Utraquism."[87]

"Skazaniia Inostrantsev"

The fact that religious services in Bohemia, outside the German-inhabited border regions, preserved their Utraquist character was witnessed by the reactions, both positive and negative, of travelers from abroad. This type of evidence, which is known in East European historiography by the technical Russian term as *skazaniia inostrantsev* (foreigners' narrations), is sometimes essential to document events in the remoter half of Europe, where internal evidence may have been altered or destroyed by the Counter-Reformation or other forces of cultural depredation. In Bohemia, the scale of destruction was impressive (and depressing).[88]

The English traveler, Fynes Moryson, records the following observations concerning the Utraquist religious practices in 1591: "For wheras the Papists giue not the Cupp to the layety, but only the bread, . . . the Hussites giue both kyndes, not only to lay men, but to very Infants, because Christ sayth, suffer little ones to come vnto mee. But still they beleeue with the Papists the Corporall eateing of the body and blood of our lord with the mouth by transubstantiation. . . . They sing the Masse in lattin, but they reade the Epistle, the Gospell, the forme of Baptisme and buyriall, in the Bohemian Tounge. . . . They agreed with the Papists for the number of Sacraments . . ."[89]

Foreign Lutheran visitors in the 1590s could barely conceal their disappointment when noting that Bohemian worship did not differ significantly from the rites of the Roman Church, except in the German-speaking enclaves, such as Jihlava, where, indeed, Lutheran liturgical practices could be observed. One of these voyagers was Henrick Kilian, a scholar and a citizen of Rostock in Mecklenburg, who passed in the course of a study tour through Bohemia and Moravia on his way from Lusatia to Austria. Kilian was scandalized by what he considered a "papist" character of religious services in the Utraquist churches of Prague, and also by finding there an evident reliance on good works instead of pure solafideism. He wrote in his travel account, dating to April 1592: "The people are papist and especially the women folk who hold more onto the works than onto the faith."[90] The north German excursionist was much better pleased with Jihlava, as he wrote: "[I]n the town of Jihlava, which is not large, but attractively built, and lies still in Moravia, there also begins all around the pure Lutheran teaching, and there is a fine, well appointed secondary school."[91]

At the other end of the religious spectrum, the essential conformity of the church services in Bohemia with those of the Roman Church, that is their Utraquist character, was noted with some wonder—even at the start of the seventeenth century—by West European Catholic travelers. Such was the experience of a French embassy under Marshall Urbain de Laval de Boisdauphin from Henry IV to Rudolf II, which spent a month from July 15 to August 15, 1600, in Prague. The secretary of the embassy, Pierre Bergeron, left the following account of the Utraquists' dominance in the Bohemian capital: "The Hussites inhabit over two thirds of the city and the rituals of their mass are virtually the same as ours. On the Feast Day of Corpus Christi they even conduct processions through the city and carry the host in the streets. The Jesuits and the others of our faith judge that they should not be impeded in adoring the host because, as far as known, it is touched by the hands of a genuine priest. . . . The Hussite priests distribute communion in both kinds. . . . The Hussites have no other images of saints than paintings on boards in their churches; they hold the chief temple of the city (i.e., Our Lady Before the Týn) and also all the other churches, while the Catholics can dispense the sacraments only in the monasteries."[92]

Although he was only spiritually a foreigner, it seems fitting to include here the testimony of the Jesuit Václav Šturm. Writing in 1584 about the attitudes of the various confessions in contemporary Bohemia, he used the term Utraquists as synonymous with "the Czechs," and the term Utraquist priests as a synonym for "Czech priests." His terminology clearly implied that it was a normal state for the Czechs to be Utraquists, and a rare or exceptional state to be a Brother, a Lutheran, or a communicant sub una. The impression that the Lutherans were not normally Czech speakers is strengthened by the Brethren's taunt that Šturm wrote in Czech (rather than

Latin or German) to avoid a dispute with the supporters of the Augsburg Confession. (To this the Jesuit disarmingly replied that he did not know German.) Apparently, the standard assumption was that the producers and consumers of Lutheran theological texts in late sixteenth-century Bohemia were mainly Bohemian Germans.[93] Moreover, when Šturm spoke of the Utraquists, he clearly did not mean the Lutherans or Crypto-Lutherans (Neo-Utraquists), inasmuch as to him the Czechs were synonymous with those Utraquists who distributed communion to infants, a practice firmly rejected by both the Lutherans and the Brethren.[94]

Liturgical Books

For the continuing integrity of Utraquism, the evidence is also supplemented and confirmed by the liturgical researches of Zikmund Winter and most recently those of David R. Holeton. The latter in particular, as a leading present-day specialist on Utraquist liturgy, has shown the prevalence of Utraquist worship in Bohemia into the seventeenth century through his unprecedented and meticulous comparative analyses of liturgical books used in Bohemian churches. Only a few points particularly germane to the topic of this study will be extracted from Holeton's rich and multifaceted work. The first is Holeton's comparison between a typical Utraquist missal from the end of the sixteenth century and another of the fifteenth: *Voltářní knihy Adama Táborského* (The Altar Books of Adam Táborský) (1588), transcribed by Václav Čáslavský of Písek, and *Misál Kutné Hory* (The Missal of Kutná Hora) (1483), transcribed by Jan of Humpolec. This points to an essential continuity of the Utraquist form of worship from the fifteenth into the sixteenth century.[95] Next comes Holeton's comparison of the Utraquist liturgical texts with Luther's *Formula missae pro ecclesia Wittemburgensis* (1523), together with other fundamental works of Lutheran liturgy, especially his *Deudsche Messe und Ordnung Gottis Diensts* (1526). This juxtaposition determined that the late sixteenth-century Utraquist texts failed to reflect the principles of Lutheran liturgy. In particular, the character of the mass as a sacrifice was clearly maintained, retaining the offertory and the canon, both banished by Luther as great abominations. Likewise, invocations of the saints and prayers for the dead remained.[96]

The distinctly Utraquist character of liturgical books used in Bohemia in the late sixteenth century is also confirmed by older research into liturgical veneration (as saints) of Jan Hus, Jerome of Prague, and other martyrs of the Bohemian Reformation. Large numbers of these have been collected in Václav Novotný's edition, "Bohoslužebná skládání o Husovi z XV a XVI století" (Liturgical Texts About Hus from the Fifteenth and the Sixteenth Centuries). The missals of the last two decades of the sixteenth century include the propers (*propria sanctorum*) for Hus as a saint, including the collects (said before the epistle), and the graduals (sung between the epistle and the gospel), which form parts of the traditional order of the mass. Hus as a saint is also the centerpiece of officia (*officium de sancto* Iohanne Hus), which normally cover the eight daily prayers traditionally required of priests in the Western Church. These are not isolated instances, but multiple cases so much more remarkable because most Utraquist liturgical books later succumbed to the Counter-Reformation mutilation. David Holeton discovered an additional liturgical text for the feast of Jan Hus and the Bohemian martyrs in a Utraquist antiphonary deposited in the Metropolitan Library of Esztergom, Hungary. The antiphonary contains complete propers for the feast day of Jan Hus, as well as a partial text for the officium, covering the first vespers, matins, and first nocturnes, and some of the second vespers.[97]

The style of liturgy is an important source of evidence for the integrity of Utraquism. It provides not just empty words or gestures, but rather signs or implications of belief. Holeton cites in that regard the dictum of Prosper of Aquitaine, "lex orandi sit lex credendi" (let the rule of prayer be the rule of belief). In other words, reversing the metaphor (appropriately to the age of the Titanic), liturgy is an integral tip of the iceberg of faith. Thus, proclaiming the body and blood of Christ would not be consistent with the denial of real presence, just as praying litanies to the saints, and including their propers in the mass, would be inconsistent with the ingrained Lutheran belief that the invocation of saints' intercession was idolatry, or even outright blasphemy.[98] So too would be the masses in honor of Jan Hus, as well as Jerome of Prague and other martyrs of the Bohemian Reformation. The Utraquists were not shy in stressing their reliance on the intercession of the saints, as Holeton notes concerning the Esztergom antiphonary: "Through fire, torture, the shafts, or drowning, [the martyrs of the Bohemian Reformation] have triumphed over death and now live to intercede for their brothers and sisters in the faith . . ."[99] The images of saints, which decorated Bohemian churches in the sixteenth century, carry the same type of message. In particular, portraits of Jan Hus adorned the altars, and his statues stood in public places in towns and villages.[100] While the veneration of Hus and the other martyrs of the Bohemian Reformation has been viewed mainly as a challenge to the Roman Curia, it was, in fact, even more an affront to the Lutheran understanding of the relationship between man and his redeemer.

Next, it is necessary to examine the argument that the evident ascendancy of Utraquist liturgy in Bohemia could be explained by the fact that it was actually Lutheran clergy that simulated the Utraquist rites. Zikmund Winter, for instance, confirmed the dominance of Utraquist rituals, vestments, and vessels in Bohemian churches into the seventeenth century, but according to him that was because Lutheran ministers were by and large willing to put up a false front. Their motive was either to please the populace, or to avoid antagonizing it. This charade was facilitated, according to Winter, by the Lutheran conviction that ceremonies were irrelevant to salvation.[101] Aside from what these assertions tell us about the actual religious preferences and beliefs of the Czech commoners, such Machiavellian explanations failed to take into account the putatively blasphemous and idolatrous character of the Utraquist ceremonies from the Lutheran point of view. What to the twentieth-century agnostic historian might have appeared as an inconsequential custom was of utmost seriousness to the sixteenth-century believer. While a manipulative attitude toward religion may have seemed plausible to the rationalists of the age of Polybius, or the age of Voltaire, it would have been abhorrent in the eyes of clergy of whatever denomination in the age of the Reformation. Czech Lutherans, in fact, explicitly condemned the use of traditional liturgical books, such as missals, breviaries, and the Agenda or Rubrics, which formed the very backbone of the Utraquist liturgy and, as pointed out earlier, their printing at the turn of the fifteenth century assured an adequate supply of these volumes. The Lutheran ministry was specifically defined in 1609 as rejecting such compendia of traditional rituals.[102] It is further ironic that those who have never tired of severely censuring Utraquism's alleged moral and intellectual laxity, or life in degradation (*život v pokleslosti*), have been willing to condone, or even applaud, a putative chicanery on the Lutheran side.[103] It is also relevant to cite the categorical refusal by the English Puritans to tolerate—for the sake of church unity—"a few ceremonies" of the Church of England, which they regarded as "the rags of Rome."[104]

It is not necessary to argue just abstractly about the implausibility of Lutherans indulging in Utraquist rituals. There are specific rejections on the Lutheran side of such duplicitous practices. Štelcar Želetavský in his *Kázání dvoje* (Two Sermons) (1586) threatened terrible divine retribution for clergymen who would knowingly engage in idolatry for a gainful purpose or to please their parishioners. In uncompromising terms, he condemned any pandering to the people's erroneous ideas, even if based on historical precedents or ancestral customs.[105]

Another Lutheran theologian, Zacharyáš Bruncvík, viewed the Utraquists' veneration of images as spiritual adultery that violated the mystical marriage between Christ and his Church. The reluctance of Lutheran pastors to perform religious rites in the Utraquist manner is attested somewhat later by the famous case of a Czech Lutheran, Jiří Dykastus. Appointed pastor of the Týn Church in 1614, he refused the congregation's demands for the traditional manner of worship, and the impasse had to be resolved by the appointment of a Utraquist chaplain.[106] The principled stand of the Lutherans indicated that the Lutherans, like the Utraquists, were learned and honest men, and not deceivers or simpletons as conventional historiography has tended to depict them.[107] In other words, if a clergyman, who was ordained by a Roman bishop, said mass in the Utraquist manner, there did not seem much ground for viewing him as a Crypto-Lutheran. Moreover, it was not the character of the ceremonies themselves, but, above all, the character of the minister's ordination that made the ceremonies authentic from the Utraquist point of view.

Utraquism's Pre-Protestant Theology

After assessing the continuing strength of Utraquism, the next major question to be confronted is whether Utraquism was straying from its *via media,* and gravitating toward an amalgamation with Lutheranism into a new syncretic religion of Neo-Utraquism. Contrary to the prevailing opinion in historical literature, it can be argued that the fundamental confessional position of Utraquism did not change during the period, bracketed by the Bohemian Confession of 1575 at one end and by the Letter of Majesty of 1609 at the other. On the theoretical or official level, this was made graphically manifest by the fact that the Utraquist Church would submit as a statement of its faith in 1609 essentially the same document as the one presented in 1575 in opposition to the Bohemian Confession.[108] Beyond that, inasmuch as the 1575 statement reflected the views and contained references to the works of Pavel Bydžovský and Bohuslav Bílejovský, it also wished to profess that the dogmatic line and the historical self-perception of Utraquism followed the tradition of the Bohemian Reformation as enshrined by the two theologians in the 1540s at the end of the first century of Utraquism's existence, and in the face of the challenges posed by the Protestant Reformation. The Consistory, of course, issued intermediate statements defining its confessional position, particularly with respect to the Lutherans and the Brethren. For instance, a notable document of this type was submitted to the Bohemian Diet in December 1586.[109] On the practical or pastoral side, Utraquism's continued independence, and the implausibility of convergence with Lutheranism, can be illustrated from theological discourse. The characteristic views of Utraquist theologians will be noted in this section, and those of their Czech Lutheran counterparts in the next section.

In examining the Utraquist adherence to the tenets of pre-Reformation Christianity in the period 1575–1609, we may point to the views of the prominent Utraquist theologian, Valentin Polon, author of the treatise, *Pomni na mne* (Remember Me) (1589). His book was an equivalent of what in sixteenth-century England was called "a Primer,"[110] containing prayers with commentaries, commentaries on the sacraments, and liturgical texts and hymns for specific occasions. In assessing his ecclesial approach, a striking aspect is his firm and unequivocal upholding of the traditional doctrine of a distinct order of sacramental priesthood against one of the cardinal Lutheran principles, the priesthood of all believers. Emphasizing the special reverence due the sacerdotal office, he exhorted the common people (*lid obecný*) "to accept from (the priest's) mouth the word of God in no other way than as from God Himself, and not to disdain his Holy Office . . . , even if held by a common person of little worth . . ."[111] Polon embraced without qualification the principle of historic apostolic succession, calling priests "present-day deputies of Christ and of the Holy Apostles" (*náměstkové Kristovi i Apoštolů Svatých nynější*). In a further contradiction of the Lutheran stance, Polon maintained that only ordination by validly consecrated bishops could confer the apostolic lineage on the clergy. As he put it, the priest received his office through the laying of hands by the bishop, and in turn accepted in front of the bishop an obligation to God to forsake the world and its enticements, and a commitment of obedience, faith and persistence to God and to His Church until the end.[112] These views coincided with the teaching of the Utraquist Consistory, which had just confirmed the traditional principle of historic apostolic succession in the statement submitted to the Bohemian Diet in December 1586. Correspondingly, the Consistory regularly held as spurious the priesthood of Lutheran ministers, who were ordained in its eyes irregularly and invalidly (*neřádně*) in Frankfurt, Leipzig, or Wittenberg.[113] In yet another contradiction of a fundamental Lutheran stand, Polon stressed that the priest, in the course of the

Eucharistic service, performed a sacrificial act on behalf of the congregation when he consecrated the body and blood of the Lord.[114] The Lutherans were, of course, adamantly opposed to viewing the Lord's Supper as a sacramental oblation, a concept inherited by traditional Christianity from Jewish sacerdotal practices.[115]

Clear statements supporting the concepts of sacramental and sacrificial priesthood are found in the work of the Utraquist theologian, Jakub Sofian Walkmberger of Walkembergk, *Advent a Štědrý den* (Advent and Christmas Eve) (1596). In this connection, he addressed the issue of the two orders of sacramental priesthood, the bishops and the priests. Sofian maintained that the ascendancy of Aron, as a bishop, over the Levites, as regular priests, foreshadowed the distinction between the two sacerdotal orders in Christianity. This analogy had appeared already in the work of Pavel Bydžovský, *Tento spis ukazuje* (1543). The latter, in turn, had credited St. Jerome with developing the parallel.[116]

While rejecting the medieval papal monarchy, the Utraquists continued to acknowledge the role of the popes in the transmission of sacerdotal power. As noted in the case of Bílejovský,[117] the assessment of papal activity, particularly during the first millennium of the Christian era, continued to be positive. Thus, Jan Kocín of Kocinét in his introduction to Cassiodorus's *Historia Cýrkevní* (Ecclesiastical History) (1594) cited with approval Leo I's backing of Bishop Theodoret of Cyr (c. 393–c. 466) in correcting the ancient heretics (followers of Arius, Eunomius, and Marcion). He also referred with respect to Pope Gregory the Great's dictum that the four Ecumenical Councils of Nicaea, Constantinople, Ephesus, and Chalcedon carried a weight comparable to that of the four gospels.[118] This attitude contrasted with Luther's view of the papacy as an agency of the Antichrist. Moreover, Gregory the Great was specifically unacceptable to the Lutherans on theological grounds.[119] While applauding certain decisions of the early Ecumenical Councils, particularly the condemnation of the monophysites and monthelites, Czech Lutherans would not think of giving any credit to the popes. Rather, Bruncvík praised "the glorious monarchs" as architects of the beneficent Councils, including Charlemagne for convoking the Council of Frankfurt in 794.[120] In an even more blatant contradiction of Luther's view of the papacy, Kocín highlighted Cassiodorus's view of papal primacy in citing the decision of the Eastern bishops to accept a decision of Julius I "because of the dignity and elevation of the Roman See."[121]

At the other end of the ecclesiastical spectrum, the Utraquist theologians seemed fond of speaking about the "primitive church" (*prvotní církev*). By this term, however, they did not mean, like the Lutherans and the Calvinists, the largely imaginary church of apostolic times, but rather, like the proto-Anglicans (of Jewel's and Hooker's stripe), the actually functioning and documented Western Church of the first millennium, that is, before the—some would say ill-advised—onset of papal monarchist entrepreneurship. The Utraquists seemed to feel most comfortable with the image of the Church as drawn in the ecclesiastical histories of Eusebius and Cassiodorus, both of which were published in Czech translation in 1594. The Church described by these chroniclers already functioned as a full-fledged hierarchical organism, but with the papacy playing a modest, perhaps even marginal role, certainly compared with the papal Befehlsstaat, which emerged in the High Middle Ages, and which the Utraquists found reprehensible.[122]

Against the Lutheran endorsement of solafideism, Utraquists maintained the contrary emphasis on the need for good works in fulfillment of the commandments and other components of the law of God. As Rudolf Říčan has astutely observed, Utraquism differed in its initial activist impulse from the more passive focus of inner liberation in Lutheranism. The former stressed the implementation of the law of God, the latter a rejoicing in the certainty of justification by faith.[123] Among the Utraquist theologians, Rvačovský was most explicit on this matter in his magnum opus, titled *Masopust* (Mardi Gras). He stressed particularly the salvific virtue of almsgiving, warning that those who would not share their worldly goods with the needy evidently had no love of God within them, and as they turned away from the poor so the Lord would avert his face from them. He added: "Alms-giving for sure liberates from all kinds of sin and from death, and does not permit the soul to descend into the darkness. Alms-giving will be of great merit in the face of God for all who practice it out of faith in Christ."[124] Prayers and other good deeds rose like incense into the heavens before God, as long as their roots were in faith and in charity. Rvačovský referred to the Gospel of Matthew (chapter 6) to connect good deeds with salvation, drawing a parallel between the conduct of a believer toward a needy neighbor, and God's attitude toward him. Mercy toward one's poor brethren for Christ's sake, assured divine mercy for the giver. He summed up the linkage thus: "[I]n sharing alms with poorer neighbors and in other holy virtues, those who walk in the faith of Our Lord Jesus Christ, and who perform such deeds from their hearts' goodness (as the fruit of the Holy Spirit), such are the sons of God, and the heirs of the Kingdom of Heaven."[125] Another Utraquist theologian, Jan Straněnský had stressed the relationship between good deeds and salvation in his compendium of spiritual exhortations, *O životě křesťanském krátké sebrání z Písem svatých* (A Brief Collection on Christian Life from the Holy Scripture) (1576). He quoted from both the Old and New Testaments on the necessity of good works (e.g., Romans 12.7, Proverbs 3.5–7, and 2 Corinthians 8.21). His treatise contained special sections on each of the three categories of good works: fasting, alms, and prayer. In a similar vein, Polon defined it as a duty of priests to serve as models for the people not only in faith, but also in good works.[126]

While staying doctrinally within traditional parameters, and eschewing the grounds of the Protestant Reformation, Utraquist practice did not turn rigid or into Janáček's "ossified Utraquism," as often charged by its historical critics, but rather underwent its own evolution.[127] It would be, in fact, difficult to apply to Utraquism Patrick Collinson's characterization of the sixteenth-century Church of England as "a kind of ecclesiastical fossil not subject to either Reformed or Tridentine reconstruction."[128] As noted earlier, one line of development led to a gradual de facto change in the Utraquist view of ecclesiastical government. The initial rejection of administrative popes was extended to cover also administrative bishops who had been originally condoned as witnessed by the election of Rokycana and his suffragans to episcopal dignities in the 1430s. A hundred years later, the Utraquist view de facto restricted also bishops to sacramental functions, as it had initially done to the popes, and church administration by a college of priests, the Consistory, appeared as the norm. The informal turning point in the Utraquist attitude was apparently the clash in 1505 between the Consistory and Philip of Villanova (formally the bishop of Sidon) who, as the resident bishop from Italy, served the Utraquists.[129]

In the later sixteenth century, another line of change in Utraquist practice was an increasing tolerance for clerical marriages, until their virtual acceptance by the end of the sixteenth century. The change occurred gradually and rather grudgingly on the part of the Consistory, which rejected married priesthood in October 1577, and did so again in a statement of December 1586 presented to the Bohemian Diet. In early 1590, the issue of celibacy still caused a dispute between the Consistory and Matouš Benešovský. In the same year, the Consistory requested a priest in Tábor to separate from his wife before his appointment to a parish in Prague.[130] Nevertheless, Nuncio Cesare Speciano reported to Rome in 1592 that most Utraquist priests lived with women. Speciano naturally, although ungallantly, viewed these ladies as "concubines," and grew indignant that at the funeral of one of them the preacher spoke of her as a legitimate spouse.[131] A significant turning point occurred in 1594 with the appointment of the Utraquist administrator, Václav Dačický, who was married (with two daughters) and tolerated married clergy. Yet, celibacy remained a live issue within Utraquism for another half a dozen years. Thus, Rudolf II's instruction to the Consistory, in a draft dated June 23, 1594, still urged prohibition of married clergy. The marriage of a Utraquist priest, Václav Rakovnický, in 1595 in the town of Rokycany led to an attempt to remove him from office by the archbishop of Prague acting in his capacity as the manorial seigneur of the town. In 1600, however, another well-known Utraquist clergyman, Jan Václav Cykáda, a member of the Utraquist Consistory (1605–1609), took a wife. According to the testimony of a French observer in the summer of the same year, Utraquist priests were generally free to marry.[132]

Despite a formal resemblance to the practices of Lutheranism, other reformed churches, or even Eastern Orthodoxy, this change did not represent a departure from the core of traditional Christianity since even in the Church of Rome the prohibition of clerical marriages was of a relatively late origin. In Bohemia, clerical marriage was common until the mid-twelfth century.[133] In other words, there is no reason to look to the example of other churches, inasmuch as priestly celibacy in the Western Church, from the viewpoint of its own orthodoxy, stemmed from a historical decision that could be changed. Clerical marriages, like the lay communion sub utraque, can be viewed as restoring an original practice of the Western Church, not as a response either to Lutheranism or to an influence of the Eastern Church.[134] Even such a staunch champion of the Roman Church as Emperor Ferdinand I, in fact, favored clerical marriages at the time of the Council of Trent in 1563.[135] A contributing factor was probably the high regard in which women were held since the beginnings of the Bohemian Reformation, starting even before Hus himself by his precursor Matěj of Janov.[136]

In an even more gradual change evident by the later sixteenth century, the Czech language surpassed Latin in Utraquist liturgical texts. There was no abrupt linguistic change, such as occurred in England in 1550.[137] Nevertheless, writing in 1589 and 1592, respectively, nuncios Antonio Puteo and Antonio Caetano found the spread of liturgical Czech quite reprehensible.[138] The vernacular intrusion, however, should not be viewed as a novelty inspired by the Lutherans' example, but rather as a return to the early phase of the Bohemian Reformation in the fifteenth century, when Czech had penetrated into various sections of the mass.[139] The intermediate resurgence of liturgical Latin in the early sixteenth century, temporarily reversing the vernacular trend, was probably due to the renewed glamour of, and infatuation with, the classical languages, aroused by the penetration of humanism into

Bohemia's educational system from the University of Prague to the local grammar schools. Indeed, in what may be considered a paradox to the second degree, according to Zikmund Winter, the sixteenth-century classicist vogue in Bohemia triggered as well an incursion of Latin into the liturgy of Czech Lutheranism.[140]

Utraquists and Lutherans

Aside from Utraquist dwellers in Czech towns and villages, there were also authentic adherents to Lutheranism in Bohemia in the late sixteenth and early seventeenth centuries. As noted earlier, their ranks appeared to be largely confined to the nobility, the barons and the knights, and to the population of the German border areas. The manorial castles, indeed, sheltered articulate Czech theologians who helped to define the boundaries separating the devotees of the Augsburg Confession from the followers of the original Bohemian Reformation. Their views showed that, just as the Utraquists did not wish to amalgamate theologically with the Lutherans, neither did the Lutherans yearn to absorb Utraquist beliefs and create a hybrid religion of Neo-Utraquism.

At the theological level, since communion sub utraque for the laity was common to the Utraquists and the Lutherans, there were two other Eucharistic aspects that clearly distinguished the two: (1) the adoration of the host outside the Eucharistic service and (2) the communion for infants, both of which the Utraquists firmly endorsed and the Lutherans just as firmly rejected. The first issue became particularly pronounced on the Feast of Corpus Christi when the Utraquists conducted festive outdoor processions in honor of the Body of Christ with the Eucharist prominently displayed for adoration.[141] When Matouš Collinus of Chotěřina, a Prague university professor and a humanist, had ridiculed the ritual as a Roman custom in 1545, it was pointed out to him in reprimand that the Eucharistic exhibitions and processions were Utraquist rites as well, and moreover that the Utraquists engaged in these practices even more ardently than the adherents of the Roman Curia.[142] Likewise, in distinction from the Roman processions, and as a sign of their devotion to a parity of the two Eucharistic species, the Utraquists carried not just the host in a monstrance, but also the chalice with consecrated wine. Also both species were solemnly carried for the anointing of the sick.[143] In addition, the Utraquists conducted four other types of processions, presumably unacceptable to the Lutherans, namely on Holy

Saturday, Palm Sunday, Candlemas Day, and Rogation Days.[144] The Lutheran animus in this regard is illustrated by the Donauwörth crisis of 1606–1607 in neighboring Bavaria, where the Lutheran majority in the town risked complete suppression rather than agree to a Corpus Christi procession by the Roman minority.[145]

The other important aspect, separating the Utraquists from the Lutherans (as well as, in this case, from the Roman Church) was the issue of communion for infants. Already Henry VIII had chided Luther for inconsistency in 1523 because he insisted on lay communion in both kinds, but rejected communion for infants.[146] Although this was one of the marks of distinction of the Bohemian Reformation, it was rescued from virtual oblivion only recently by the scholarly work of David R. Holeton. Hitherto Czech historiography had tended to pass over this aspect in silence or trivialize it as a rather embarrassing, if not repugnant or distasteful, matter.[147] It was not a merely symbolic act, but a genuine consuming of the two species by the infant.[148] The concern and respect for the child had a continuous tradition in Utraquist religious practice.[149] Far from being a trivial item, however, the infant communion was an issue of the Bohemian Reformation that had engaged the pan-European forum of the Council of Trent. The fathers of the Council deemed the matter of sufficient weight as to pronounce an anathema against those who would insist on the theological necessity of infant communion.[150] In recent times, the World Council of Churches has sponsored a revival of positive interest in the issue.[151]

As for the Lutheran opponents of the Utraquist Eucharistic practices inside Bohemia, Štelcar devoted almost his entire treatise, *Kniha nová o původu kněžství Krista Pána* (A New Book on the Origin of the Priesthood of Christ the Lord) (Prague, 1592), to denouncing what he considered to be the objectionable rite of communion for infants. Seeking to blacklist the advocates of this practice, Štelcar assembled a set of twenty works and thus unintentionally offered a handy bibliographical survey of the development of Utraquist theology on the issue at hand.[152] His spotlight fell particularly on Pavel Bydžovský to whom he attributed one quarter (five) of the items on his booklist. These included a treatise edited and published by Bydžovský and Brikcí of Licko, erroneously attributed by the editors to Jan Milíč of Kroměříž, but probably written by Jan of Příbram.[153] Some of the books listed by Štelcar have not survived, especially Jan Xenomen Rausinovský of Mazanovice, *Dar Nového léta dítkám zrozeným* (Prague, 1590), which indicated a continuing and lively Utraquist interest in this liturgical practice.[154] The abovementioned Fynes Moryson likewise noted infant communion as a common Utraquist practice in 1591.[155] The attitude toward infant communion may, therefore, be viewed as virtually a litmus test for distinguishing the Lutherans from the Utraquists.[156]

Although the clearest, the Eucharistic differences were not the only distinguishing marks between the Utraquists and the Lutherans. One can point to the markedly visible issue of the invocation of saints. In another work published in 1593, Štelcar denounced a Utraquist prayer book published in 1584 that contained litanies and prayers to the holy men and women. Similarly, he objected to the teaching of Utraquist Administrator Václav Benešovský (1581–1590) and the Consistory in 1585 on the power of the saints to intercede with God for Christians invoking their assistance. He sought to discredit the Utraquists' arguments in favor of the practice, such as that drawn from Luke (16:27–28) about the rich man imploring Abraham to save his five brothers from hellfire, or from John (5:45) about Christ's reference to the heavenly intercessions by Moses.[157] Similarly, Štelcar excoriated Administrator Benešovský for publishing in 1588 a *Traktátek o přímluvách svatých* (Little Treatise on the Intercessions of Saints) that, according to Štelcar, was thoroughly erroneous in its claims of the saints' assistance. The work "falsely alters the meaning of the holy scripture and twists it to a human meaning."[158]

Essentially, of course, Štelcar's indignation was a case of taking the matter out of context inasmuch as the Utraquists simply could not avoid invoking the saints, if for no other reason than their commitment to the traditional liturgical texts and rituals of the Western Church, particularly to the sequence of saints' feast days in the missal. The Lutherans' theologically grounded distaste for seeking intercession from the dead (i.e., the liturgical saints) at the same time tends to confirm the implausibility of the suggestions, mentioned earlier, of the Lutheran ministers' use of Utraquist missals. These liturgical texts conspicuously featured the veneration of saints, including Hus, Jerome, and the other martyrs of the Bohemian Reformation. In fact, when the holidays of Hus and Jerome were omitted from the official calendar of state holidays in 1585, the Utraquist Consistory took the lead in demanding their restoration, which happened in 1588 and in subsequent years. Curiously, in view of the previous discussion, the editor of the calendar, who was blamed for the omission, was a Lutheran, Petr Codicillus. The perpetrator was then ridiculed for his act in a popular song, and it is just possible that in this case the Roman Curia's abomination of Hus (un)happily colluded with the Lutheran distaste for the liturgical veneration of saints.[159] In the same vein, the Utraquist Consistory continued to mandate the praying of litanies. Thus, in June 1596, the Consistory issued a call for special daily prayers to the saints, as well as masses, litanies, and processions on Fridays for victory against the Turks. The Utraquists also continued to encourage in moderation the veneration of the Blessed Virgin Mary, which went back to the times of Jan of Příbram and Jan Rokycana in the early fifteenth century.[160] Characteristically, the previously mentioned Utraquist theologian Polon, included Hail Mary in his explication of the basic Christian prayers together with the Our Father, the Apostles' Creed, and the Ten Commandments.[161] The veneration of the Virgin is also documented by the wall paintings in the St. James's Church of Kutná Hora, containing Marian imagery particularly linked with the Annunciation and the Assumption. Jan of Příbram and Jan Rokycana had taught devotion to the Virgin Mary, especially in her role as the Mother of God.[162] The Utraquists also revered the early medieval saints of Bohemia—Wenceslaus, Ludmila, Vojtěch, and Procopius.[163]

Finally, Štelcar spoke very sharply against the practice of venerating religious images, and against the entire sphere of ecclesiastical art, which the Utraquists traditionally condoned, albeit again with restraint. In his *Kázání dvoje* (1586), he cited Moses' injunctions against idols as mandating an uncompromising iconoclasm (Ex 20:4–6): "You shall not make for yourself an idol. . . . You shall not bow down to them or worship them: for I the Lord your God am a jealous God . . ."[164] As mentioned earlier, the Utraquists had no compunctions about two-dimensional images of saints, including that of Hus. Another favorite image was that of an angel bringing the chalice from heaven to highlight the communion sub utraque. By the same token, the Utraquists revered sculptured images of the chalice with which they tended to replace sculptured crucifixes, especially in cross-road shrines.[165] One can cite again the mural paintings in the St. James Church in Kutná Hora which, in addition to the images of Christ and the Virgin Mary, contain conspicuous depictions of the chalice.[166]

Aside from observing the officially established principle of mutual tolerance based on the political agreements of 1575, Czech Lutherans showed some vestigial sentimental ties with the principles of Utraquism. In a cautious way, Štelcar tried to identify antecedents for Lutheranism in the original Bohemian Reformation. Praising Hus, of course, was not enough since foreign Lutherans, including Luther himself, had done so without being considered Neo-Utraquists. In particular, he claimed that the Lutheran teaching against the veneration of saints was not a novelty, but was foreshadowed in Utraquism's middle period of the fifteenth century. Štelcar argued on the basis of a pamphlet by Martin Žatecký, published originally in 1517, just at the dawn of Luther's emergence. The argument, however, was not cogent inasmuch as the Utraquists, in fact—while rejecting portrayals in sculpture—continued to signal their devotion to the saints by liturgical invocations and by adorning their churches with likenesses of holy men and women in two-dimensional paintings.[167] The printing of a Czech adaptation of Iacopo da Varagine's *Aurea legenda sanctorum seu Historia Lombardica seu Pas sionale sanctorum* as *Passional všech svatých* (Prague, 1495) testified to the fifteenth-century Utraquists' attachment to the veneration of saints. The publication substituted traditional Bohemian saints for those less well known in Bohemia, and appended an exaltation of Jan Hus and Jerome of Prague to signify their inclusion within the heavenly host.[168]

In general, links mentioned by Lutherans to the Bohemian Reformation were too insubstantial to provide support for a genuine amalgam of Czech Lutheranism and Utraquism under the theory of Neo-Utraquism. The doctrinal divide was too clear to be argued away or finessed. If, as the folk saying goes, there is no way for a woman to be just a little pregnant, there was no way for a Utraquist to be just a little Lutheran (or vice versa). The irreducible mark of a Utraquist was to believe in the apostolic episcopal succession and in sacramental priesthood. If one did so believe, there was no way that he could be considered a Lutheran. Lutheranism, if anything, stood at its core exactly for the rejection of the historical episcopate and for the endorsement of the priesthood of all believers. To repeat, the differences between Utraquism and Lutheranism were not vague or ineffable, but sharp and clearly definable. Using the biblical injunction of "every tree is known by his own fruit" (Luke 6.44), we might say, somewhat whimsically, that they produced fruit as unmistakably different from each other as apples are from oranges.

Despite much loose talk about Neo-Utraquism, no one has yet produced a Neo-Utraquist theological text, or even made a suggestion regarding along what lines a genuine dogmatic or liturgical synthesis of Utraquism and Lutheranism should proceed. The problem is how would one combine divergent views such as (1) the Utraquist emphasis on the sacramental orders of priesthood with the Lutheran belief in the priesthood of all believers; (2) the Utraquist adoration of the host outside the Eucharistic service with its Lutheran condemnation as a blasphemy; (3) the Utraquist mass as a sacrifice with the celebratory Last Supper of the Lutherans; (4) the Utraquist insistence on, with the Lutheran abhorrence of, the communion for infants; (5) the Utraquist activism in seeking to fulfill the law of God with the

Lutherans' passive acceptance of justification by Christ; (6) the Utraquist stress on the soteriological efficacy of good works with the Lutheran condemnation of them as a form of spiritual bribery; (7) the Utraquist belief in seven sacraments with the Lutheran rejection of all but two; (8) the Utraquist reliance on the intercession of saints with the Lutheran view of the practice as a form of spiritual adultery; (9) the Utraquists' veneration of the images of saints with the Lutheran condemnation as idolatry; (10) the Utraquists' acceptance of the Western Church as it had evolved during the first millennium with the Lutheran insistence on the (largely imaginary) church of apostolic times; (11) the Utraquists' retention of canon law with Luther's vesting of ecclesiastical, as well as secular authority in the state. One can name Utraquist theologians such as Jan Cykáka, Valentin Polon, Vavřinec Leander Rvačovský of Rvačov, Jakub Soffian Walkmberger of Walkmbergk, or Jan Straněnský, and one can name Lutheran theologians such as Zacharyáš Bruncvík, Jiřík Dykastus (Miřkovský), Václav Slovacius, or Jan Štelcar Želetavský of Želetava, but who can name an authentic Neo-Utraquist theologian who has meaningfully combined elements of Utraquism and Lutheranism? Neo-Utraquism, like the "purple cow" of the folk saying, seems to be a phenomenon that none have actually seen. Certain imaginary objects can at least be depicted, such as a unicorn or a three-headed dragon. In the case of Neo-Utraquism, one cannot even imagine, much less outline, the contours of the beast.[169]

The Basis of Toleration

The settlement of 1575 had resulted in a reasonably stable compromise on the Bohemian religious scene. The Lutherans and the Brethren, with the support of Utraquist townsmen, obtained freedom and protection for the practice, albeit a restricted one, of their religion. Except for a foothold in the Consistory, the Lutheran estates secured the practical aims of their campaign for the legalization of the Bohemian Confession. At the same time, the Utraquist religion remained legally safeguarded in its existing form and extent. An examination of the way these safeguards operated (presented in the first part of this chapter) leaves a clear impression that their main thrust was not to coerce the Czech common people to remain Utraquist, but to prevent the nobles or the archbishop, from coercing them to abandon Utraquism for Lutheranism or the Roman Church.

Maximilian II had played a significant role in the settlement of 1575.

The reinforced and expanded tolerance, however, could build, in Bohemia's political culture, on the earlier legal coexistence of Utraquism and the adherents of the Roman Curia, explicitly codified by the Peace of Kutná Hora of 1485, and informally observed since the adoption of the Compactata of Basel in 1436.[170] The stability of this coexistence compared favorably with the difficulties of finding a religious modus vivendi in contemporary France.[171] The pacific inclinations toward tolerance were, in turn, conditioned by the memory of the destructiveness of the internal and external conflicts of the Bohemian Reformation. Two important points should be made about the origin and the character of the Bohemian toleration after 1575. First, the agreements resulting in toleration were based on political alliances of the religious groups, not on a tendency toward their religious amalgamation. Second, Utraquism's stance of relative open-mindedness and restraint in controversy facilitated the political coexistence of the sharply defined religious groups.[172]

Manifesting considerable political prudence, the basis of the alliance among the disparate dissidents from Rome was a strategic need of common defense against the Habsburg royal government, which ultimately favored the Roman Curia. This was the reason for the political cooperation of the Utraquist townspeople with the Lutheran nobles in the Bohemian Diet. This also motivated the Lutheran aristocracy to back up the Unity of Brethren. When Rudolf II attempted to proceed tentatively against the Brethren by issuing decrees against the Picardi or Pikarts in 1584 and 1602, the noble Lutheran estates came to their assistance assuming that their turn would come next, if the Unity were suppressed.[173] A subsidiary motive for the interdenominational political alliance was the fear of Moslem advance. Thus, Jan Kocín z Kocinétu in his translation of Johannes Leunclavius, *Kronyka nová o národu tureckém* (A New Chronicle of the Turkish Nation) (1594) exhorted all Christians "who confessed the one savior, Jesus Christ" to forsake internal quarrels and bloodshed in order to unite against the common enemy, the Turks.[174] Budovec stressed the Christians' common interest in resisting Islamization in his treatise, *Antialkorán,* which was completed by 1593.[175]

The agreements by the denominational political spokesmen, however, did not reflect a mutual weakening of allegiance to the particular religious orientations. The denominations remained theologically differentiated, while coexisting within the Bohemian political context. This was shown by the discussion of the continuing theological differences between the Utraquists and the Lutherans. Each group defined its religious identity: the Utraquists in their programmatic statements of 1575 and 1609, the Lutherans in the Bohemian Confession of 1575, and the Brethren in their own Confession, originally issued in 1573. Even Polon on the Utraquist side, who exemplified the spirit of forbearance, did not hesitate to state clearly that his tolerance had not diminished his disapproval of those views that deviated from the beliefs of the "universal and apostolic" Church.[176]

Czech Lutherans, for their part, while drawing—as pointed out earlier in this article—a clear theological boundary between themselves and the Utraquists, also sharply differentiated themselves from other Protestants, including the Unity. Thus, Štelcar sternly censured the Eucharistic teachings of the Brethren, whom he called Boleslav Brethren (Bratři Boleslavští), and claimed that in refusing to adore the Eucharist, they appeared to cast doubt on the divinity of Jesus. Rather unexpectedly, the Lutheran Štelcar was ready, in this context, to commend even the Jesuit controversialist Šturm, who excoriated the Brethren's refusal to bow before the name of Jesus. In their Eucharistic stance, according to Štelcar, the Brethren opposed Luther and St. Augustine, and followed the Zwinglians, the Calvinists, and the Arians. He separately rejected the Eucharistic teachings of Karlstadt, Zwingli, Oekolampadius, and Calvin, and traced their denial of the real presence to an original error of Berengarius of Tours.[177] Another Lutheran theologian, Václav Slovacius, argued against the Brethren's refusal to bow before the name of Jesus in a treatise of 1586 (republished in 1590), and critically assessed the Calvinist view of predestination.[178]

Let us now turn to the second basic point about Bohemian toleration. Despite the clear commitment to traditional beliefs and practices, the Utraquists were especially predisposed to broad-mindedness toward other denominations. The roots of this tendency can be seen in three areas: (1) the insistence on free discussion characteristic of the Bohemian Reformation from the start; (2) in the reaction to the great destructiveness of the Bohemian wars of religion, which pointed to the dangers and limitations of the use of force and compulsion; and (3) the eschewing of the travails of "confessionalization" in the late sixteenth and early seventeenth centuries.

First, Hus and his colleagues had already embraced a significant degree of intellectual openness in the early stages of the Bohemian Reformation. Its roots have been sought in the freewheeling academic disputations at the University of Prague, as well as to the spirit of tolerance in Wyclif's theology.[179] Hus wrote a treatise in 1410 against the destruction of heretical books as contradicting both sound reason and the Church fathers.[180] His refusal to recant at the Council of Constance in 1415, unless the error of his ideas was demonstrated, earned him wide recognition as a pioneer and martyr of human rights.[181] The endorsement of a relatively free discussion of religious issues was codified in the Four Articles of Prague, in the Test or so-called "Judge" of Cheb in 1432, and in the Compactata of the Council of Basel in 1436. The use of magisterial command without a discussion, as practiced by the Roman Church, was specifically repudiated by the Utraquists first with reference to the witness of Hus, and then collectively during the Bohemian wars of religion (1420–1436).[182] The state of toleration was not necessarily regarded as something ipso facto unnatural or unendurable. Subsequently, this attitude was reinforced by embracing theologically the *via media* between Rome and the reformed churches. There was a similarity with the other pursuers of theological centrism, the proto-Anglicans, who were known for a greater intellectual tolerance than their Puritan opponents.[183]

Second, while not going as far as the Unity of Brethren, which embraced the doctrine of nonresistance to evil, the Utraquists did not hide their aversion to the use of forcible means and compulsion. The Utraquist priest Jan Bechyňka at the turn of the fifteenth century, deploring the use of force and violence, stressed the patience and tolerance of the Utraquists, which led to their peaceful co-existence with the more belligerent sub una.[184] Similarly, Bílejovský's tendency to look askance at Taborite militarism, if it had gone beyond what was seen as the legitimate defense of the Bohemian Reformation, appears to be typical of sixteenth-century Utraquism. Aside from the rejection of Taborite religious radicalism, perceived as the source of meaningless violence, the negative view of Taborite warfare was also a legacy of memories of suffering and destruction seen as increasingly purposeless, once the violence was detached from opposing the imperial and papal crusaders. A prominent Utraquist author, Blažej Nožička of Votín, writing later in 1566, strongly condemned religious warfare, especially with reference to the 1440s, as unnecessary and thus purely destructive. Nožička likewise emphasized the detrimental effect of the ideas of the Taborites and their partners, the Orebites, in inciting violence and dissension in the very center of the Bohemian Reformation movement.[185] Similarly, Daniel Adam of Veleslavín in his edition and translation of Georg Lauterbeck's treatise on government (Prague, 1584) includes a strong warning against unrestrained warfare, preferring two years of negotiations to one of armed conflict.[186]

Third, another reason for the exceptional tolerance characteristic of the Utraquists was their escape from the need of confessionalization in the late sixteenth and early seventeenth century.[187] They avoided the process by which the Protestant groups had to define themselves against each other and against the Church of Rome, and by which the latter had to adopt its own demarcations against the churches of the Reformation. The Utraquists were already secure in their own delimitation both vis-à-vis Roman authoritarianism (since the period of Hus and the Compactata), and vis-à-vis the Protestant biblical reductionism through the fifteenth-century encounters with the Taborites and the Brethren. Accordingly, in the sixteenth and early seventeenth centuries, they were spared the process of differentiation, which often led others to cast anathemas against each other, and which was the reverse of adopting tolerant attitudes.

The avoidance of confessionalization's travails can be also approached from the viewpoint of the scale of the Utraquists' reformatory action, which preserved the core Christian doctrines intact. The Bohemian Reformation may have had the character of "a political or jurisdictional schism," but not that of "a theological revolution."[188] Unlike the fully reformed denominations, the Utraquists did not feel the need of a demonstratively rigid orthodoxy on selected issues in order to counterbalance the rejection of a substantial part of the traditional fundamentals. Those who were fully reformed seemed impelled by a distinct fervor, possibly due to guilt avoidance, to draw rigid lines around the vestigial concepts of Christian orthodoxy: for instance, the Lutherans around the doctrine of real presence, and the Calvinists around that of the Trinity. One may recall in those regards the harsh self-righteous stance of the Lutherans toward the Calvinists and the Zwinglians, and that of the Calvinists vis-à-vis the Unitarians.[189] Luther himself had not set a good example in that regard by burning not only papal bulls (which might have been an appropriate gesture of defiance at the time), but also the works of his interlocutors, such as Hieronymus Emser.[190] Melanchton in his letters to Henry VIII in March and April 1539 warned against the dangers of toleration, which he perceived in the Netherlands where almost "open license" prevailed and "many among the people are becoming open atheists . . . [and] others embrace the lunatic doctrines of the Anabaptists."[191] Likewise, the Brethren were scandalized not only by what they considered the Utraquists' moral laxity, but also by the lack of their doctrinal rigor.[192] Characteristically, the papal nuncio Giovanni Dolphin shared in 1575 Luther's earlier dim view of the diversity of religious views in Bohemia, saying about the latter: "Tanto che questo paese è la vera Babilonia."[193] Since the time of Hus, there was a particular aversion to book burning among the Utraquists, newly illustrated by the resistance of the Prague University faculty in 1610 when ordered to burn a newly published volume that referred to homosexuality.[194] The Utraquists' sense of preserving the integrity of doctrinal fundamentals probably freed them, at least in part, from the compulsion of a militant assertion of orthodoxy, and led them to acquire—in their relative serenity—the aura of flexibility, latitudinarianism and, perhaps, even a gentle bemusement and bonhomie, with respect to what they regarded as the foibles of others. Although using nautical similes more suitable for insular Britain than for landlocked Bohemia, MacCullough has pointed out an analogous religious situation in England in the 1530s: "[E]vangelicals [Cranmerian Lutherans] were often more bitter about religious radicalism [the sectarians] than the traditionalists [high churchmen] were, because it revealed the insecurity of their own position: were not the radicals seeking to capsize a boat which the evangelicals themselves were already rocking?"[195]

Utraquist theologians at the turn of the sixteenth century exhibited this spirit of forbearance. It is apropos to recall in this respect the mildness with which the archetypal Utraquist, Bydžovský, in the 1540s had treated Luther's doctrines, or with which he had chided the alleged errors of the Brethren.[196] The Utraquists' continued tradition of gentleness and civility characterized the well-known response of the Utraquist administrator, Martin Klatovský, in his *Rozsuzování upřímné Artykuluov některých* (A Sincere Review of Certain Articles) (Prague, 1544) to the vitriolic attacks by the Brethren's bishop, Jan Augusta.[197] Later in the sixteenth century, Polon treated with notable magnanimity the radical dissidents of the Bohemian Reformation, recalling the time of the Utraquists' cooperation with the Taborites during the Bohemian wars of religion.[198] Although he deplored religious dissensions and upheld the ideal of a united church, Polon counseled mildness toward dissenters and reliance on divine providence, not a coercive suppression. He exhorted the inhabitants, both lay and clerical, of the Kingdom of Bohemia and its dependencies (Moravia, Silesia, and Lusatia) to "properly beg God, our Lord, by day and night to transform all the evil (with his divine aid) into good, to stop wars, to terminate dissensions, riots, conflicts, and accusations among the Christians, to calm the differences of the sectarians and the quarrels of religious dissidents, and to bring all into the unity, solidarity and unanimity of the Holy Catholic Church . . ."[199] In counseling moderation and mildness, the Utraquist theologian clearly disapproved of intemperate disputes in religion and particularly censured the use of vitriolic language.[200]

With a tolerant magnanimity, Polon's younger colleague Jan Václav Cykáda, a member of the Utraquist Consistory (1605–1609), in his work published in 1607, praised Luther for his belief in the real presence and his teaching on the adoration of the Eucharist. Cykáda also endorsed the general principle of toleration in his sermon on the parable about the enemy sowing tares among the wheat (Mt 13:25–29). Those in error should be corrected by preachers, but not suppressed by force as long as they do not commit violence against the true church.[201] The author Václav Plácel of Elbing, in his introduction to Josephus Flavius's *Historia židovská* (1592), opposed the use of violence in the spread of true religion that should occur not by an iron material sword, but through preaching of the word of God. God's teaching is also an antidote against heresies that attempt to pervert its meaning, but are in turn defeated by its power of truth and life. In the Old Testament, God preserved his people despite their many divisions and faults in religion.[202] Similarly, Jan Kocín of Kocinét in his introduction to Flavius Magnus Cassiodorus's *Historia Cýrkevní* (1594), counseled calm and self-confidence in confrontation with religious error, which could not subvert the pillar of truth. He also approved of opposing error through discussion and persuasion, as his ideal bishop, Theodoret of Cyr, had done in ancient times.[203] Some of this more indulgent attitude can also be detected in the statement concerning the Unity by the Utraquist Consistory in December 1603. The Brethren were less threatened with fire and brimstone, and more critiqued for their unattractive stance of moral rigorism and superiority, as well as for their gloomy Weltanschauung inhibiting them from the experience of joie de vivre. They were also reprimanded for their alleged praise of ignorance with respect to secular learning.[204]

Conscious of their political (not religious) interdependence with the Lutherans, the Utraquists continued to follow the vagaries of religious tolerance abroad, and disapproved of violence also against those with whom they disagreed. Thus, the university professor, Marek Bydžovský noted in his chronicle of Rudolf II's reign an alleged decree of the French king Henry III of July 18, 1585, threatening to banish the Huguenots, unless they conformed to the Roman Church by New Year's Day 1586. Under the year 1594 the same chronicler noted the complaints of German towns against encroachments on adherents to the Augsburg Confession, and he subjected to harsh criticism the alleged Spanish cruelties against Protestants in the Netherlands.[205]

Although steadfast in their particular orthodoxy, the other religious denominations, the Utraquists' fellow citizens, to a degree shared in the benign ambiance of tolerance, which also derived from Bohemia's tradition and constitutional system. Thus, the more indulgent attitude of the Czech

Lutherans became especially apparent when contrasted with the rigid and unyielding attitudes of their German confreres.[206] The Brethren came to embrace the coexistence with others in what might be considered a negative way, by default. The Unity could not expect to ever encompass all, or even a significant portion of society, because of its attachment to moral perfectionism, which, in turn, was rooted in the radical strain of the Bohemian Reformation.[207] While their spiritual ancestors, the Taborites, might have aspired to eliminate the unrighteous by force, the Brethren, having embraced rigorous pacifism, had no choice but to live peaceably alongside their sinful compatriots.[208]

Finally, for the sub una, religious tolerance in Bohemia was also a matter of legal exigency flowing out of the Peace of Kutná Hora. With the advance of the spirit of Trent, however, this stance was becoming increasingly unnatural.[209] The Bohemian Jesuit, Ondřej Modestin, translator of Campion's *Decem rationes* (1601), deplored the divisions due to religion "when diverse heresies and multiplicity of sects and schisms arose, so that not only in one country, town, or village . . . but even in a single house or hut, one dweller can hardly recognize another."[210] Nevertheless, even the authorities under the Roman Curia felt obliged to recognize the injunctions against vituperative attacks on the Utraquists, and the subsequent extension of these prohibitions in 1575 by Maximilian II to cover the Lutherans and the Brethren. In an illustrative example, Fridrich of Žerotín complained about Václav Šturm's critique of the Brethren in his *Srovnání víry a učení bratří starších* (1582), saying that "as long as he lived he never saw or heard greater lies."[211] The Bishop of Olomouc, Stanislav Pavlovský, felt the need to apologize, citing the Jesuit author's senility as an excuse.

Prevalence of Utraquism

While there are no solid demographic data, other evidence indicates that—despite the overt and covert efforts to alter the religious status quo—the prevalent mode of public worship among the Czechs into the seventeenth century remained Utraquist and did not turn Lutheran. Moreover, clear and sharp lines of demarcation continued to separate the two religious orientations. Utraquism did not amalgamate with Lutheranism, but remained steadfast on the course upon which the Bohemian Reformation had embarked in the late fourteenth century. It was the course steered by the Utraquist Consistory, which had been refined by Jakoubek of Stříbro, Jan of Příbram, and

Jan Rokycana in the fifteenth century, and reaffirmed in the face of the Protestant Reformation by Bohuslav Bílejovský and Pavel Bydžovský in the 1530s and 1540s. Its doctrinal content was expressed in the sixteenth century by the Consistory in the Articles of 1525, the Articles of 1539, in the letters to Ferdinand I of October 1549, and to Maximilian II of January 1570, as well as in official statements, mentioned earlier in this chapter, on the Bohemian Confession in 1575 and the Letter of Majesty in 1609.[212] The efforts to turn the Czechs into a Protestant nation had failed. In a development, possibly unique in contemporary Europe, however, the settlement of 1575 concerning the Bohemian Confession broadened the scope of political toleration of religious bodies from the Utraquists and the adherents of the Roman Curia (covered by the Peace of Kutná Hora of 1485) to embrace de facto, if not de jure, the Lutherans and the Brethren.

9

The Utraquists versus the Curia: Liberal or Authoritarian Church, 1575–1609

In Chapter 8, I addressed the claim of an alleged convergence between Utraquism and Lutheranism between 1575 and 1609. This chapter deals with the opposite claim of convergence between Utraquism and the Roman Church in the same period. In a book published in 1877, Klement Borový maintained that under Archbishop Martin Medek (1581–1590), "[T]he Consistory recognized the decrees of the Tridentine Council as obligatory for the Utraquists . . . and the Consistory, and its priests, no longer hesitated to recognize [the Archbishop's] higher jurisdiction . . ."[1] The editors of the prestigious series *Sněmy české* opined in 1891 that "While the Consistory members were originally Utraquists, they did not differ from the Roman Church in anything, except the communion in both kinds, and they had conformed entirely with the Catholics by 1593."[2] Pekař claimed that the advance of Lutheranism in the second half the sixteenth century forced the Utraquists ever more into the "Catholic ranks."[3] The more cautious Krofta still painted a gloomy a picture when he wrote about the Utraquist Consistory in 1575–1608: "[T]he Utraquist Consistory . . . was constantly reaching a closer rapprochement with the Church of Rome . . ."[4] and "[it] did not, therefore, disappear even after 1593, but—completely dependent on the Archbishop and on the royal government . . . it vegetated pathetically."[5] Elsewhere he stated referring to the Consistory: "[I]n the years preceding the Letter of Majesty [1609] it lost entirely its former independence, giving up step by step its old rights and peculiarities, and submitted fully to the Archbishop's obedience . . ."[6] Zikmund Winter maintained even more categorically that the Utraquist or Lower Consistory under Administrator Jan Benedikt of Prague (1605–1609) was "entirely Catholic" (*docela katolickou*).[7] Historical literature has also commonly asserted that after 1575 the Utraquists entered into a political alliance with the adherents of the Roman Curia against the Lutherans and the Brethren.[8] Speaking of the situation after 1575, Novák writes that the Utraquist Consistory increasingly "drew near the [Roman] Church and its hierarchy and was turning into their instrument" against the Bohemian Reformation.[9]

This chapter seeks to examine the interplay between the Utraquist Church and the Roman Curia from 1575 to 1609. It examines the propositions of traditional historiography about the virtual demise of the Utraquist Church because the Utraquist Consistory was entirely dominated by the Archbishop; the Utraquist clergy was compelled to affirm the Tridentine confession of faith; Utraquist priests were appointed and administered by the archbishop; and the archbishop assumed the judicial powers of the Utraquist Consistory. This investigation will demonstrate that these propositions are problematic at best. First, I will show that instead of an institutional convergence as asserted in historical literature, there was actually a further drawing apart, as the Utraquists under the Consistory maintained their adherence to a liberal ecclesiology, while the Roman Church in the Tridentine settlement reaffirmed and fortified its adherence to the authoritarian ecclesiastical Befehlsstaat that had emerged in the late Middle Ages. The differences between Utraquism and the Roman Curia, especially in ecclesiology and church discipline, were not just minor and obscure, but far-reaching and clearly definable. Second, the Utraquist Consistory maintained its independence vis-à-vis the Roman Curia throughout the entire period. The cause célèbre of the nuncio's success in securing the apostasy of Administrator Fabian Rezek in 1593 actually led to amplifying the distinctiveness and independence of Utraquism from the Roman Church in its current state, and deepened the Utraquists' suspicions of the Curia's intentions. The reports of any other submissions by administrators or the Consistory were illusory. Third, the alleged evidence of an institutional fusion due to ascendancy of the archbishops was either fended off by the Utraquists, or resulted from misperceptions of the actual state of affairs, as in the areas "Catholic" identity and clerical ordinations.

The outcome of the events of 1575–1609 was not a rapprochement between the Utraquists and the Roman Church, as the standard literature has asserted through the alleged mergers of 1589 and 1593. To the contrary, there was a reaffirmation of the paradoxical reality, clearly evident already in 1575, that the Utraquists regarded the dogmatically proximate Roman Church as a greater threat to their integrity than the dogmatically more remote reformed churches. The pragmatic alliance concluded in 1575 was not between Utraquism and the Roman Curia, but between the Utraquist townsmen and the noble coalition of Lutherans and Brethren. On the political level, while the attitude of Rome's adherents toward Utraquism was hardening after 1600, the Utraquist townsmen secured a counterbalance in their continued political cooperation with the Lutheran and Brethren's nobility, which traced its origins to 1575.

Ecclesial Incompatibility

Utraquist Critique of Roman Ecclesiology

The chief barrier to a rapprochement between the Utraquists and the Roman Curia was their divergent concepts of ecclesiology, which grew rather than diminished in the late sixteenth century as the Roman Church applied the spirit and letter of the Council of Trent. The Utraquists preserved their ecclesiological views, which originally had owed much to John Wyclif, and which in a way were at the root of incompatibility of Utraquists with Rome, particularly during the post-Tridentine phase. The rejection of worldly dominion by the clergy, as well as the rejection of ecclesiastical riches and/or splendor continued to characterize their ecclesiology. The objectionable characteristics ultimately stemmed from the medieval development of the papal monarchy with its bureaucratic apparatus of enforcement and elaborate fiscal system. Utraquist writers, therefore, tended to look back to earlier times for a proper model of ecclesiology. Although its anticipations were earlier, the theory of papal supremacy in its full-fledged form began to emerge only in Gregorian reform movement of the late eleventh century.[10] Speaking with awe and affection about the primitive church (*prvotní církev*), the Utraquists did not refer to the church of the Apostles (like the Protestants), but to the church as it had developed during the first ten centuries of Christianity.[11] In this they resembled the humanist theologians, such as Erasmus, Thomas More, and Bishop John Fisher, who looked for new inspiration toward the Greek fathers, the theological pacesetters of the first centuries of Christianity.[12] Like the humanists, the Utraquists did not seek to emulate Eastern Byzantine rituals and practices (whether ancient or contemporary), but rather hankered after the ecclesiology that responded to the Greek stimuli within the Roman patriarchate of the West during the first millennium. Aside from these considerations, even the Council of Constance referred to the church of that era as the "primitive church" (*ecclesia primitiva*), and the Compactata recognized the Utraquists as "the sons of the primitive church."[13] For comparison's sake, the architects of the English Reformation, such as Cranmer, also regarded the church of the apostolic times, idealized by the Protestant reformers, as something incomplete and imperfect.[14]

During the period under discussion, Utraquist Bohemia's interest in the history and structure of the early church was manifest in many ways, including the translations and publication of the classical ecclesiastical histories of Eusebius and Cassiodorus, as well as the Jewish history of Josephus.[15] The presentation of the early church, or its Old Testament antecedents, provided opportunities for dwelling on its model characteristics, such as the clergy's stance toward material riches and political power. Such editorializing was of importance for the affirmation of the Utraquist ecclesiological views.[16] Jan Kocín of Kocinét, translator of Cassiodorus, for instance, launched into a discussion of episcopal prerogatives and lifestyle in his preface. Deriding bishops who sought power and prestige, Kocín upheld as a model of the proper prelate the example of Theodoret of Cyr, one of the authors on whom Cassiodorus had drawn for his history: "And because the word bishop in Greek language designates less a high dignity and disposal of many incomes, but rather a life of service and diligent labor, therefore also this Theodoret thus behaved in both his office and his vocation . . ."[17] Kocín further stressed the proper bishop's disregard for material wealth by citing from a letter of Theodoret to Pope Leo: "After having been bishop for so many years, I possessed nothing of my own[,] neither a house, nor a field, nor a penny, nor a grave, rather I freely embraced poverty, and whatever property remained after my parents' death, that I immediately gave away . . ."[18] In the introduction to his translation of Josephus's history, Václav Plácel of Elbing cited reasons why priests should be excluded from positions of political power. Referring to priests' interference with secular government, he wrote:

> And so it happened always wherever the clergy, which according to their vocation should be busy with divine services and teaching the people, having neglected this, became involved with worldly matters . . . so also they wanted to stand with one leg in the church, and to be present with the other in the town halls or in the courts of kings. In consequence many strange disorders and entanglements occurred in the land and in its municipalities.[19]

The primitive church of the first millennium, which the Utraquists evidently endorsed as an ecclesiastical model, did provide a place for the pope and his office, but his role was much more modest than in the clericalist prototype of the High Middle Ages, which the Utraquists opposed.[20] Kocín characterized the proper papal status in his translation of Cassiodorus's ecclesiastical history, as illustrated by the pontiff's relationship with the bishops of the Eastern Church. On the one hand, the Roman See was entitled to recognition of its special dignity as an "Apostolic School and Mother of Piety." On the other hand, the bishops were entitled to a reciprocal respect from the Roman See. Neither party should interfere in each other's jurisdiction.[21] In a way, this pattern of relationships corresponded with the Utraquists' practice of combining determined opposition to the papacy in administrative and judicial jurisdiction with acknowledging Rome's sacerdotal role and having their priests ordained by the hierarchy in communion with the Roman See.[22]

In 1588, the Consistory once more avowed its recognition of the pope as head of the church in this limited sense. Negotiating with Nuncio Antonio Puteo, the Utraquist Consistory under Administrator Václav Benešovský expressed its readiness to promote this, albeit limited, acknowledgment more actively and have the Utraquist priests preach that the pope was the head of the church in exchange for the ordination of Utraquist priests by the archbishop of Prague.[23] The reverence shown to the office of the pope was not just a matter of courtesy, comparable to the prayers for the sultan by the Byzantine Church in the 1500s, or prayers for Joseph Stalin offered by the Russian Orthodox Church in the 1940s. Rather, it reflected recognition of the pope as the head of priesthood in the Western Church. It was the same view that caused the Utraquists to seek priestly ordinations from bishops in communion with Rome. The genuine respect for the priestly function of the bishop of Rome in the Western Church was also reflected in Pavel Bydžovský's celebration of the martyrdom of Thomas More and John Fisher, who gave up their lives rather than deny the pope's role in the Church.[24]

Not surprisingly, however, the Roman Curia, responding by a letter from the secretary of state, Cardinal Montalto (born Alessandro Damasceni Peretti), found the Utraquists' limited sacerdotal recognition of the pope's role grossly defective. Its price was a full acknowledgment and acceptance of papal jurisdiction and an unequivocal obedience to its edicts and judgments, sealed by a profession of faith according to the edicts of the Council of Trent.[25] To contextualize the Utraquist ecclesiology, it may be recalled that on the issue of the pope as the ultimate guarantor of priestly power in the Western Church, the Utraquists stood closer to Rome than the Church of England. Utraquism, however, was further away from Rome than Anglicanism on the prerogatives of bishops. While prizing them as conveyors of priestly power, the Utraquists attributed administrative and judicial jurisdiction even in spiritual matters, not to the bishops, but to the Consistory and the administrator.

Rejection of the Council of Trent and Its Fruits

As mentioned earlier, a major factor against convergence between Utraquism and the Church of Rome, and rather a factor for growing divergence, was the Council of Trent. With their ideal of the ecclesiology leaning toward the patristic age, it is understandable that the Utraquists objected to and resisted an endorsement of the Council of Trent and its fruits. The Council reaffirmed the late medieval model of the papal monarchy instead of seeking to assert a more liberal and populist ecclesiology. In other words, it offered a centralized command model, not a decentralized discursive one. The Utraquist resistance to Trent focused on four issues: the Tridentine profession of faith, liturgical reforms, the auricular confession, and communion for infants.

The refusal of the candidates for priesthood to accept the profession of faith according to the Council was the most obvious sign of Utraquist resistance to the Council's edicts. This proved a continued obstacle to the ordination of Utraquist priests by the archbishops of Prague despite assertions in literature that such priests were ordained and in fact submitted to the unpalatable oath.[26]

David Holeton's examination of the Utraquist liturgical texts in the light of the post-Tridentine liturgy of the Roman Church likewise puts to rest the suspicions of some scholars that there was a growing concurrence between Utraquism and Rome. Relying mainly on the authoritative *editio typica* of the Eucharistic Missal of Pius V (promulgated in 1570), Holeton showed that in the late sixteenth century the Utraquists continued to maintain their distance from the Tridentine reforms, and did preserve some of the traditional ritualistic diversity of the medieval Western Church of which the Church of Rome was deprived by its standardizing liturgical reform of 1570, based on the decrees of the Council of Trent. There were also some textual deviations from the pre-Tridentine Roman standard, probably inspired by a search for local or more ancient traditions. Most notably, the scenario of the Utraquist mass shifted somewhat from that of the priest's private devotion to one with more of a shared participation by the faithful.[27] The Utraquist liturgical deviations were confirmed by no less authority than

Nuncio Antonio Caetano, who pointed out in 1592 that the services were performed according to the rites of the Church of Prague, which differed from those of the Church of Rome.[28] As a separate illustration of the independence from the Tridentine reforms, the Utraquist church in Litomyšl used liturgical texts which were essentially consistent with the pre-Tridentine forms of Roman liturgy into the early seventeenth century (until 1620).[29] As additional evidence of nonconformity, the Roman Curia in a statement of 1589 objected to the use of the Czech language in the mass by the Utraquists.[30]

Another deviation from the Tridentine standard came into play in the negotiations about reconciliation with Rome in the early 1590s and concerned the administration of the sacrament of penance. Nuncio Cesare Speciano defined the Tridentine canon on the sacrament of penance (*de poenitentiae sacramento*) as requiring under the term of sacramental confession (*confessio sacramentalis*) an auricular confession (*confessio auricularis*), which he juxtaposed to the Utraquist rite of a public communal confession prior to the reception of the sacrament of the altar. An oddly unexpected interlude followed, when the Roman Curia had some qualms about Speciano's insistence on the term confessio auricolaris as not being entirely orthodox from the viewpoint of the canon law. The nuncio, however, wished to nail the concept down lest the Utraquists weasel out of it.[31] As noted later on the same topic, Speciano also censured the candidate for the archiepiscopal see of Prague, Zbyněk Berka of Dubá, for receiving communion in his youth in a Utraquist manner, not only *sub utraque,* but also without an antecedent auricular confession.[32]

The administration of communion to infants was yet another point on which the Utraquists continued to disregard an explicit injunction of the Council of Trent. The Council had pronounced anathema against those who would insist on the theological necessity of the practice.[33] The Utraquist flaunting of Trent in this respect was viewed as a serious lapse by the Curia and repeatedly brought up by the nuncios in their periodic overtures on the issue of Utraquist reconciliation.

The Utraquists were not alone among adherents to the Western Church in their opposition to the decisions of the Council of Trent. In France, a substantial group of "critical Catholics," according to Thierry Wanegffelen, "who rejected direction from the papacy and the Roman Curia . . . in the decrees of the Council of Trent, which they believed was one of many tools of papal dictation, not a true ecumenical council."[34]

Significance of Vestigial Ties

Despite the profound differences in ecclesiology, which—notwithstanding assertions in historical literature—prevented any rapprochement between Utraquism and Rome, the split between the two could not be regarded as complete and irremediable. The Utraquists felt that the separation was caused by Rome's errors, particularly the disregard for biblical injunction, mainly in the area of the Eucharist, and its insistence on the rigid apparatus of power and enforcement. The breech was epitomized by Pius II's abrogation of the Compactata of Basel in 1462. Thus, the Utraquists thought of themselves as biding their time in the midst of suspended, drawn-out—perhaps, millennial—negotiations about settling their differences with the Curia that was, as we saw, in no mood to be conciliatory. Moreover, the Utraquists retained the belief that the Roman hierarchy—despite bad popes and bad bishops—constituted the authentic priesthood in the Western Church. The Utraquist theologians also continued to derive their institutional heritage from the historical hierarchy, namely from the archdiocese of Prague of the mid-fourteenth century. The legitimacy of the Consistory was ultimately traced to the transfer of the seal of the archdiocese of Prague to the Utraquist estates by Archbishop Konrad Vechta on joining the Utraquists in 1419, and to its affirmation by the Compactata in 1436.[35] Thus, in a curious way, the Utraquist Consistory, in a parallel with the archbishop and his Consistory *sub una,* continued to exist as a quasi-legitimate part of the Roman hierarchical network.

The Curia's willingness to maintain contact and carry on sporadic negotiations with the Utraquist Consistory and its administrators reflected at least a halfhearted recognition of the legitimacy of the Utraquist institutions as partial successors of the pre-1420 institutions of the archdiocese of Prague.[36] Another formal link between the Roman Church and the Utraquist Church was, of course, the canonically authentic ordination required of the Utraquist priests by the Consistory. The authorities of the Roman Church, including the Jesuits, continued to hold the view that there was real presence in the Eucharist consecrated by the Utraquist priests, on the presumption of their ordinations by authentic bishops. We may recall Pierre Bergeron's report of 1600: "The Jesuits and the others of our faith judge that [the Utraquists] should not be impeded in adoring the host because, as far as known, it is touched by the hands of a genuine priest. . . . The Hussite priests distribute communion in both kinds . . ."[37]

In addition, the Curia and its agents gave recognition to the Utraquist Consistory on the grounds of local constitutional law, as well as for practical reasons. Thus, in 1584, Nuncio Giovanni Francesco Bonomi[38] acknowledged that the kings of Bohemia were obliged by their coronation oath to defend both the Utraquist and the Roman Church.[39] More unexpectedly, the prelates of the Roman Church recognized, as Archbishop Berka did in 1590s, that the term "Catholic religion" within the meaning of the Compactata covered the Utraquists, not just the sub una.[40] In his letter of August 1595, the archbishop spoke of the "the Catholic faith and good ancient ecclesiastical rite" shared by the adherents of Rome and the Utraquists.[41] On more practical grounds, from the viewpoint of the Curia, the unwillingness of the Utraquists to join the Protestant Reformation was a limited victory of sorts. Earlier, in the 1520s and 1530s, it had been cheered on by polemicists for Rome, such as Hieronymus Emser, Johann Faber, and Johann Cochlaeus.[42] Thus, when the chips were down, the Curia, the nuncios, and even the Jesuits favored the preservation of the Utraquist Consistory as a lesser evil, even though inconsistently they opposed ordination of Utraquist priests by the archbishop of Prague.[43]

Rome's recognition of Utraquism's quasi-orthodoxy and "Catholic" character, however, was vitiated by grave reservations. It certainly did not cover the veneration of Hus and the communion for infants, and of course it was greatly strained by the Utraquists' refusal to submit to Rome's jurisdiction, including the decrees of the Council of Trent, and by their permissiveness in theological discussions. The problematic areas were placed in focus by the paradoxical situation around Berka's consecration as archbishop of Prague by the Roman Church in 1592–1593. Although the candidate was already a high prelate sub una, Nuncio Speciano privately learned that Berka's parents had actually been Utraquists. Moreover, he and his brothers were raised as Utraquists, receiving in their childhood and youth not only communion sub utraque, but also without a previous auricular confession. Speciano's findings seriously disturbed the Curia (represented by Cardinal Gesualdo), and even Pope Clement VIII himself.[44] The archbishop-elect deeply resented and at first resisted Rome's decision that directed him to renounce under oath the Utraquist errors before his consecration. He firmly denied any current or antecedent heresy on his own part, or that of his parents or relatives. To clinch the argument, Speciano pointed out that Berka's mother was buried in the Týn church, and Berka finally consented. To spare him public humiliation, he performed the abjuration privately in the nuncio's apartment in the presence of only a notary and two witnesses. Nevertheless, he at first refused to accept the certificate of absolution, and the relations between him and the nuncio remained strained also after his consecration in October 1593.[45] Similarly, Administrator Rezek, about whom more will be said shortly, in his notorious submission to the jurisdiction of the Roman Church in September 1593, had to renounce on oath not only the very fact of schism, but also the "heresies and errors" of the Utraquists.[46] The term heresy, however, was not applied to the objectionable practices that were specifically enumerated, such as deviations in the rite of mass, celebration of the feast of Hus, lay communion sub utraque, communion for infants, communion without prior auricular confession, and carrying wine or chalice (together with bread) in Eucharistic processions or otherwise displaying it for adoration.[47]

The continuing engagement with the Roman Church helped to bolster the status of Utraquism in two significant ways. First, in taking seriously the priestly status of Utraquist clergy and giving quasi-recognition to the Consistory as a direct extension of the pre-Reformation ecclesiastical structure, the Roman Church helped to affirm the aura of the Utraquists' institutional respectability and organizational autonomy from secular authority.[48] Second, the very fact that Rome did not categorically reject the Utraquists, cutting them off as a withered branch, helped to give their mission of reforming the Western Church a degree of credibility that Utraquism would not have had if Rome had simply refused to take any notice of the Consistory. To give the Roman Church its due credit, it could be argued that, considering the temper of the times and its authoritarian character, Rome exhibited a considerable degree of patience with the Utraquists. It is also true that this grudging indulgence existed only as long as Rome did not have sufficient power to crush the Utraquist deviation. In the meantime, however, this tour de force could continue with the Utraquists defying the assertions in historical literature about making abject or even self-destructive concessions to the Curia.

Independent Ecclesiastical Jurisdiction: The Consistory

Independence Maintained: Relationships with the Chancellery and Archbishop, 1575–1592

Let us now turn to the issue of alleged subordination of the Utraquist Consistory to the archbishop and/or to the administrative/judicial apparatus of the Roman Curia in this period (1575–1609). Three points can be made about the administrative status of the Consistory: (1) it was never administratively subordinate to the archbishop or to the Curia; (2) the administrative oversight and appointment of Consistory members was performed by the monarch largely through the Chancellery; and (3) the Consistory, nonetheless, was not a creature of the royal government, but possessed its own autonomous identity rooted in the traditions of the archdiocese of Prague, substantiated by sacramental priesthood, and protected by canon law, styling itself "administrator et parochi consistorii archiepiscopatus Pragensis sub utraque communicantium."[49] The extrinsic context of the Consistory's operations passed through three phases during this period. Initially, in the late 1570s and in the 1580s, the archbishop played a limited role as an intermediary or a clearinghouse between the Consistory and the royal government. After the Rezek affair of 1592–1593, the Consistory tended to interface directly with the official royal apparatus. After 1600, it gravitated for support toward the Bohemian Diet.

In general, the 1575–1609 period witnessed continued deadlock in the relationship between Utraquism and Rome, which had set in after the reemergence of a Roman archbishop of Prague in the 1560s. Reconciliation between the two was prevented by Rome's insistence on full administrative and juridical subordination and the Utraquists' unwillingness to agree. During the 1570s and 1580s, the Utraquist Consistory maintained a posture of continuing negotiations to regularize its relationship with the archbishop. In the meantime, vis-à-vis the authorities of the Roman Church, the Utraquists continued to practice what might be described as "civil disobedience," in both senses of being courteous, as well as nonviolent. On the one hand, it had no difficulty in paying a measure of deference to the archbishop as a holder of the second degree of sacerdotal power, moreover, within the Western Church, or Patriarchate, of which they considered themselves an integral part. The Utraquists had no problem, as was the case since Příbram and even Hus, to proclaim their devotion to the Catholic Church and the Catholic faith, although these terms continued to have notably different meanings for the Consistory and for the Roman Curia. On the other hand, the Consistory found it unthinkable to place itself into administrative subordination to the archbishop, inasmuch as a profound gap continued to separate the two parties on the issue of ecclesiology. As we saw, the Curia retaliated by not permitting the archbishop to ordain Utraquist candidates to priesthood.

All during this period, the Royal Chancellery performed the selection and appointment of the administrator and other members of the Utraquist

Consistory. The Consistory recognized the administrative authority of the king, calling itself "an office of Your Imperial Highness."[50] The royal role stemmed from the coronation oath and was ultimately rooted in the Compactata. The Consistory turned readily to Rudolf II for protection against the encroachment of its rights to maintain and to administer Utraquist parishes, as in August 1578 and June 1579,[51] and also in the matter of appointment of its own membership 1585.[52] Again on October 10, 1589, the outgoing Consistory requested that the new members be installed by the king in the traditional manner, that is, in the presence of the highest officials of the land, and with a solemn reaffirmation of their ecclesiastical and judicial authority and autonomy.[53] In June 1602, Administrator Václav Dačický remonstrated with Archbishop Berka not to interfere with the jurisdiction of the Utraquist Consistory, which was "an office of His Imperial Majesty."[54]

Although the king and his officials in fact exempted the Utraquist clergy and believers from the jurisdiction of the archbishop, Rudolf II preferred the administrator and the Consistory to approach him through the archbishop rather than directly. On the appointment of Medek on February 12, 1582, he exhorted the Utraquists to recognize him in unity and love.[55] Yet, as Matoušek pointed out, the monarch also had a vested interest in excluding them from the archbishop's jurisdiction. The existing special relationship with the Consistory enabled him to wield greater influence over the Utraquists than over the archbishop's flock. In any case, the king did not give any sign of readiness to surrender the control of the Utraquist Consistory to the archbishop.[56] The administrator and the Consistory also made it clear that they regarded the prelate as an intermediary—a messenger or a mailman—rather than one with authority of his own over the Consistory.[57] The system functioned reasonably well under Archbishop Medek (1581–1590), who did the Consistory significant favors without interfering in its internal affairs, although he observed the Curia's ban on ordaining Utraquist priests.[58] On August 7, 1584, the archbishop likewise affirmed that the Utraquist Consistory could exercise ecclesiastical jurisdiction according to the canon law in a case that involved the town of Tábor.[59] Moreover, even under Medek, the Consistory could appeal directly to Rudolf II, as it did in February 1585, concerning the ordination of Utraquist clergy and the appointment of Consistory members.[60] The Utraquist deputies of Prague and other royal towns in the Bohemian Diet also petitioned Rudolf II to put pressure on Medek regarding the question of ordinations.[61] Parenthetically, it may be noted that despite Medek's evident reluctance to yield on this issue, even in 1600 there were sufficient Utraquist clergy, presumably ordained abroad.[62]

Independence Challenged:
Papal Diplomats and the Rezek Affair, 1593

The precarious equilibrium in religious affairs was threatened by the designs of papal diplomats to take advantage of the Utraquists' desire for an ordained priesthood in order to reduce the Utraquist Consistory into full submission to Rome as a prelude to its complete abolition. Although these forays failed due to Utraquists' reluctance to embark on a path of self-destruction, they were often interpreted in historical literature as signs of the Consistory's irresistible urge to fuse with Rome. Efforts to co-opt the Consistory, which would culminate in the Rezek affair of 1592–1593, had antecedents at least as far back as Archbishop Brus's negotiations with the Consistory under Administrator Jan Mystopol in 1562[63] and under Administrator Jindřich Dvorský in 1571–1572.[64] Nuncio Giovanni Dolfin referred to the possibility of union with the Utraquists in conversation with Rožmberk during the negotiations around the Bohemian Confession in July 1575. In September, he mentioned touching on the matter of submission with Administrator Dvorský. The matter, however, was not pursued further at that point.[65] The ability of the papal diplomats to intervene was, of course, limited because the laws of Bohemia denied them any direct jurisdiction within the country.[66]

Roman designs on the Utraquist Consistory gathered steam with the establishment of a permanent nunciature in Prague in the early 1580s when Rudolf II chose the city as his seat in the capacity of the Holy Roman Emperor. Two attempts of the first nuncio, Bonomi, for reconciliation of the Utraquists with Rome failed in 1582 and 1584, when the Consistory under Administrator Václav Benešovský declined unconditional submission to the papacy—including a repudiation of Jan Hus—although it pledged to maintain its adherence to the "Catholic religion."[67] The nuncio failed to pave the way by proposing several subterfuges, such as replacing infant communion with merely showing the host to the child.[68] In August 1584, the secretary of state in Rome temporarily suspended further overtures.[69] Bonomi's successor, Nuncio Germanico Malaspina, was also more skeptical about the chances of Rome's advance in Bohemia.[70] Nuncio Filip Sega in 1587 passed on to his successor, Nuncio Antonio Puteo, a new drastic prescription that would impose Rome's authority under the guise of a peaceful unification with the Utraquists. The process would be guided by a group of nine officials, called *assistentes,* three selected each by the pope, the king, and the Diet. The assistentes would command armed detachments to coerce opponents of the new order. Although Utraquists could become members, the purpose of this junta's operation—with a guaranteed majority of sub una— would be to liquidate the Utraquist Consistory and to enforce Roman uniformity in theology and liturgy, making no allowance for distinctly Utraquist beliefs, attitudes, or practices throughout the Consistory's parishes.[71] While this plan was not implemented, it revealed the radical intent and the utter inflexibility of the Holy See, and clarified the Utraquists' growing misgivings about facing the Curia alone.

Still, under Administrator Benešovský during 1587–1589, the Consistory made its own overtures for a modus vivendi to Nuncio Puteo. It would affirm its commitment to preach that the pope was head of the church and to observe "Catholic" rites in exchange for ordination of its priests by the archbishop. This led to rumors of another submission of the administrator and the Consistory to Rome. Whatever the promises may have been, however, the answer from Rome by Secretary of State Montalto to the nuncio found the proposed pledges of the Consistory defective in not defining the allegiance to the pope or the nature of "Catholic" rites strictly on Rome's terms and thus evidently eschewing Roman jurisdiction in its entirety and integrity.[72] This episode was followed by another hiatus of inactivity, characteristic of the lack of continuity in the nuncios' initiatives.[73] Writing in 1592, Nuncio Caetano identified the chief obstacles to reunion as the Utraquist clergy's objection to Roman discipline, the royal government's reluctance to abandon the Utraquist Consistory, and the support of Utraquist independence by the other religious dissidents. He proposed a devious, if not deviant, approach of first coercing the Consistory into conformity with Rome, and then using the *gegleichschaltet* institution as an instrument to induce the faithful to abandon Utraquist practices, including the lay communion sub utraque and the liturgical use of Czech.[74]

The apostasy of the Utraquist administrator Fabian Rezek constituted on the surface perhaps the most spectacular, although in its essence not the most critical, episode in the development of Utraquism in the period between the tacit toleration of the Bohemian Confession in 1575 and its overt permission by the Letter of Majesty in 1609. The event in both its genesis and its consequences needs to be set in the context of the curiously convoluted relationship between the Church of Rome and the Utraquist Church. Apparently in the summer of 1592, Rezek and Nuncio Speciano agreed on Rezek's accession to the Roman Church, which might have paved the way to Utraquism's final demise. Rezek, originally a canon of the Roman Church, joined the Utraquists shortly before his appointment as administrator in July

1590.[75] Erratically, as early as January 15, 1591, he swore an oath before Nuncio Alfons Visconti in Prague of re-submission to Rome, and shortly thereafter reneged on his promise.[76] Speciano had to proceed largely as a free-lancer inasmuch as he failed to secure significant support from either the archbishop of Prague, or from the Jesuits. Berka, of course, nursed a grudge against the papal diplomat because of Speciano's energetic pursuit of his and his family's antecedent Utraquist lapses.[77] The Jesuits of Prague failed to assist the nuncio in his dealings with the Utraquist Consistory, although Speciano had asked Cardinal Cinthio Aldobrandini, in letters of December 1592 and January 1593, to secure the cooperation of the general of the Jesuit Order.[78] Another adversary of Speciano was Melchior Klesl, bishop of Wiener Neustadt, who was Rudolf II's trusted adviser and resided in Rome in 1593. He denounced the nuncio's project as a chimerical enterprise in a letter that came to the attention of the pope, who in turn forwarded the missive to the Congregation of the Holy Office, commissioned to deal with the Rezek case.[79] Because of Rezek's record of fickleness, even Speciano did not really trust the administrator. On his renewed (third) submission to the Holy See, the papal diplomat planned to have him replaced by an authentic and reliable adherent of Rome who would then lead the Utraquist Consistory—which Speciano called "the synagogue" in private—into subordination to the archbishop.[80]

In preparation for Rezek's Canossa-like journey to the Eternal City, eventually scheduled for late summer of 1593, he and the nuncio evidently endeavored to intimidate Utraquist clergy into compromising statements of submission to Rome. An insight into these proceedings can be gleaned from a testimony that Jakub Zofian, a Utraquist priest, presented at the Old Town of Prague city hall on March 22–23, 1593, to the deputies of Bohemian towns, gathered for the sessions of the Bohemian Diet. According to Zofian, on October 17, 1592, Rezek, under pretext of dinner with a prominent layman, took him instead to the nuncio's residence. There he was threatened with expulsion from the country as a heretic if he did not take an oath affirming that Hus was justly sentenced and put to death at the Council of Constance; obedience to the pope; and that he would believe and teach about the sacraments exactly as the Roman Church commanded. He was shown a document signed by the administrator and some fifty priests, which according to Zofian, contained "the symbol of faith and several articles which were adopted at the Council of Trent." Zofian's description of the document, however, did not refer to any outright condemnation of Hus or full obedience to the pope and exact conformity with Rome on the issue of the sacraments.[81]

The Bohemian Diet responded energetically. On the initiative of the town deputies, the parliamentary body in its March session took note of Rezek and Speciano's (mis)behavior and sent a complaint to the king.[82] The emphatic response of the Diet in favor of the Consistory was particularly significant and symptomatic of a forthcoming shift in the base of the Consistory's support, which would acquire special importance in the next decade. In this connection, it is relevant to recall the ambivalent relationship between Utraquism and the Diet after 1562, when the appointment of the administrator and the Consistory had passed from the Diet to the monarch and the Chancellery. While it could always count on the loyalty of the strongly Utraquist towns, the Consistory distrusted the noble estates (barons and knights) because of their turn to Lutheranism and the Unity of Brethren. Hence, it looked askance at the Diet's standing wish to recapture the appointment and the protection of the Consistory from the king. Rudolf II, in part, played on the Consistory's apprehensions when he responded in June 1584 to the Diet's petitions for control and protection of the Consistory, presented repeatedly in 1579, 1582, and 1584.[83] While admitting the Diet's pre-1562 oversight of the Consistory, he ruled in 1584 that the right could not be restored because the current theological orientation of the noble estates was incompatible with the Consistory's status as a guardian of Utraquist orthodoxy.[84] Notwithstanding the religious divergence, however, the political alliance forged with the towns in 1575 made the nobles fairly tolerant toward Utraquism. This benign attitude, resting on collegial loyalty with the towns in the Diet, tended to grow with Rome's increasing pressure against all dissidents. Thus, largely on the initiative of town representatives, the Consistory had received, albeit limited, backing from the Diet, as in 1586 and 1588, even before the impact of the Rezek affair.[85] Despite Stloukal's assertion, the noble estates had not withdrawn their support for religious self-determination in the cities by the 1590s.[86] Writing in 1592, Nuncio Caetano identified among the chief obstacles to the abolition of the Utraquist Consistory the support of the Utraquists' independence by the other religious dissidents.[87]

As to the denouement of the Rezek affair, a group of documents originating in Rome and printed in *Sněmy české,* contains the copy of a statement, dated August 29, 1592, which was allegedly signed by Rezek and fifty Utraquist priests, and then read and approved on March 5, 1593, in the presence of seven out of twelve members of the Consistory in Charles College of the University of Prague. The statement makes the astonishing and improbable claims that the signatories agreed to the long-standing propositions of an unconditional surrender to the Curia, such as to consider Hus a heretic, to abolish his feast day, to stop infant communion, and to accept the decrees of the Council of Trent.[88] Considering the denouement of the Rezek affair, and particularly the nature of Zofian's testimony, it would seem more plausible that the fifty clergymen signed, and the rump Consistory approved, a much weaker statement of respect for the pope and bishops, and of adherence to the Catholic faith and Catholic rites. Noncommittal types of formulations, which remained safely within the bounds of Utraquist ecclesiology, were put forth by the Consistory on previous occasions in bargaining for papal permission to ordain Utraquist clergy.[89] These precedents were established in particular by the Consistory's declarations in 1566 under Administrator Jan Mystopol, in 1571 under Administrator Jindřich Dvorský of Helfenburk, and in 1587 under Administrator Václav Benešovský,[90] none of which were taken either by the Consistory or the Curia as signifying a submission to Rome's jurisdiction.

Whatever statements might have been signed or approved between the summer of 1592 and the spring of 1593, the Consistory evidently did realize that this time around the documents might not be taken simply as ritualistic reiterations of customary courtesies, but more ominously as operational instruments of Utraquism's capitulation and self-destruction. In any case, on June 19, 1593, members of the Consistory wrote to Clement VII in order to clarify the purpose of Rezek's mission to Rome. The letter stated explicitly and emphatically that the emissary was not authorized to deal with any other matter than the request for papal consent for ordination of Utraquist clergy by the archbishop of Prague.[91] The documentary collection in *Sněmy české* includes Rezek's solemn abjuration of Utraquist errors in Rome in the Congregation of the Holy Office on September 1, 1593, falsely claiming that he was authorized to do so also on behalf of the Consistory and Utraquist clergy. According to the document, his recantation took place in a semi-public manner while he knelt in a room with the door left open.[92] On his return from Rome, the Utraquist Benedict Arnold was ostracized by the Consistory, and the pastor of the church of St. Jiljí in the Old Town of Prague who sheltered him was severely reprimanded in January 1594 for harboring "an irregular runaway Roman priest."[93] Threatened by arrest and trial for overstepping his mandate in Rome, the ex-administrator sought refuge in Moravia, where he then served in Olomouc as a priest of the Roman Church.[94]

Rezek was no longer considered administrator after his abjuration even by Rome.[95] Speciano failed in his expectation that Rezek would be succeeded by a crypto-Romanist who would steer the Utraquist Consistory into oblivion through a merger with the Roman ecclesiastical apparatus. Not even Berka supported the nuncio's wish to see committed Utraquists replaced in the new Consistory by those whom Speciano considered vacillating, and the nuncio wrote the Curia to reprimand the archbishop on that score.[96] Tomáš of Soběslav, who emerged as one of the prominent ecclesiastics of Utraquism, assumed the interim leadership of the Consistory until the appointment of Václav Dačický as administrator on April 29, 1594.[97] On the order of Rudolf II, the seal of the Utraquist Consistory, the symbol of its ecclesiastical authority, which Rezek had left at the nuncio's office before leaving for his junket to Rome, was returned to the Consistory.[98] Dačický was not tainted by Speciano's sub rosa dealings with the Utraquist Consistory in 1592–1593, and received a clean bill of health as an orthodox Utraquist from a prominent layman who called him "faithful to God and his holy church and eminently well versed in the ancient ecclesiastical rites of our party sub utraque."[99]

The decisive test of the significance and effectiveness of Speciano and Rezek's maneuvers was that in the final outcome virtually no one followed Rezek into the Roman secession. The Bohemian Diet, as early as November 3, 1593, reaffirmed the administrative independence of the Utraquist Consistory from the Roman Church.[100] The denouement can be viewed as an indication of the strength rather than the weakness of Utraquism. It showed that Utraquism was firm and resilient enough to withstand such a drastic and unceremonious intrusion into its very organizational entrails. It also pointed once again to the illusory or unreal character of the image of so-called Old Utraquism, defined as full conformity with the existing Roman Church, except for the lay communion in both kinds, which was viewed in turn as a meaningless eccentricity. As for Speciano, the imperial ambassador Koraduz wrote from Rome to Rudolf II in 1595 with what was characterized as a typical Germanic bluntness (*s německou jadrností*): "[E]veryone here in general regards him as a jackass . . ."[101] As noted, even the Jesuits had distanced themselves from Speciano's connivance with Rezek as an improbable, if not outright quixotic enterprise. It would seem that Speciano shared the zeal, but not the political savvy of his early patron and lifelong role model, Archbishop Carlo Borromeo of Milan, one of the quintessential prelates of the Counter-Reformation.[102]

Independence Reaffirmed: Gravitating toward the Diet, 1594–1609

Speciano's intervention into Utraquist affairs showed that the Roman side was becoming impatient and no longer satisfied with promises and indefinite delays, but wished for a real resolution of the ecclesiological issue on its own terms. After the repudiation of Rezek's apostasy, the relationship between the Consistory and institutions of the Roman Curia became more strained, if not frigid. It was more difficult to pretend that all was well, except for minor differences.[103] The relations between the new administrator Dačický and Archbishop Berka were uneasy from the start and occasionally became confrontational, particularly in 1597 when the prelate tried to take advantage of anonymous slanderous accusations against the administrator and his wife.[104] The relationship between Utraquism and the institutions of the Roman Church was further strained after 1606, following the death of Berka. While Berka and his two predecessors were natives of Bohemia, he was succeeded as archbishop by Karl Lamberg (1607–1612), a native of Styria, who had spent much of his life in Austria and Bavaria. The three earlier archbishops seemed to show a certain residual indulgence toward Utraquism, skirting around the harsh attitude of the Curia. As noted above, Berka himself was born into a Utraquist family. His successor Lamberg appeared to be an implacably uncompromising executor of the Curia's will and immune to any sympathetic inclinations toward Utraquism. Instead of becoming more dependent on the archbishop after 1600, as the historical literature maintains, it would seem truer to say that the Consistory was becoming increasingly estranged.[105] On general constitutional grounds, in 1608 the Bohemian Diet protested the appointment of a foreigner as archbishop. Despite Rudolf II's promise that the law would be observed in the future, another candidate unfamiliar with the Czech language, Johann Lohelius, would follow Lamberg in 1612 under King Matthias.[106] The full-fledged alienation of the archbishops from the Utraquist tradition and the increased improbability of their ordaining Utraquist priests made the idea of cooperation with them or with the Curia even less promising or attractive for the Utraquist Consistory. Contributing to this detachment, the Curia once again suspended attempts to gain control over the Utraquist Consistory.[107]

In seeking external patronage between 1593 and 1609, the administrator and the Consistory began by relying even more directly and overtly on the royal government, but only to end up by 1604 finding sustenance mainly from the Bohemian Diet, thus virtually completing an odyssey begun in 1562. No longer invoking the archbishop's mediation, initially the Utraquist leaders tended to send their petitions and requests directly to the king's officials, and ultimately to Rudolf II himself.[108] This system of transactions throughout the 1590s was facilitated by the fact that the key institutions in the Bohemian state were dominated by sympathetic dissidents from Rome. In that respect, Nuncio Speciano (1592–1597), as well as his predecessor Nuncio Caetano (1591–1592), were particularly critical of the Bohemian Chancellery. Its nominal head, Adam of Hradec, although Rome's adherent, was lukewarm in religion and an alcoholic. The actual power rested with his deputy, Kryštof Želinský of Zebuzín, who according to Caetano, was a "Calvinist [i.e., a Bohemian Brother], although he claimed to be a Lutheran."[109] When Adam was appointed supreme count palatine in 1593, Želinský—without being named Chancellor—remained effectively in charge of the crucial office, which provided the liaison function between the Utraquist Consistory and the monarch. Next to Želinský the nuncios also found Jan Milner of Milhauz, secretary of the Chancellery, distinctly objectionable.[110]

The drastic change in the relationship between the Consistory and the royal government was foreshadowed by the events of August 1599 when five adherents of Rome received high official positions. The step was largely due to Rudolf II's erratic response to the lobbying of the papal diplomats, whose instructions called for removal of Lutherans and "Calvinists" (the Brethren) from the top posts in the Bohemian governmental apparatus. Among the new appointees, Zdeněk of Lobkovice became the supreme chancellor, Václav Berka of Dubá the supreme chamberlain, Adam of Šternberk the supreme judge of the land, Volf Novohradský of Kolovraty the aulic judge, and Kryštof Popel of Lobkovice the supreme court steward.[111] Both Želinský and Milner left the Chancellery and were replaced by Rome's adherents.[112] Finally, in 1600, Ferdinand Hofmann of Grýnspichl and Střechov, president of the court chamber, was replaced by a practitioner sub una, Jakub Breuner.[113]

What was even more critical was the tendency within the new generation of the nobles sub una to embrace the militant outlook of the Counter-Reformation. These new adepts no longer cherished the Bohemian tradition of cooperation across religious lines, in the spirit of the Compactata and the

Peace of Kutná Hora, which had inspired their forebears among the sub una during the second half of the sixteenth century, such as Vratislav of Pernštejn (d. 1582), Vilém of Rožmberk (d. 1592), or Adam of Hradec (d. 1596). Trying to avoid outright confrontations, the latter showed considerable skill in seeking compromises,[114] and they also tended to be less than enthusiastic about the nuncios' periodic calls for strong-arming religious dissidents, whether Utraquists, Lutherans, or Brethren.[115] Moreover, their willingness to share with the Utraquists what might be called an anti-ultramontane position[116] seeking to eliminate direct papal jurisdiction, was in part dictated by their possession of formerly ecclesiastical estates.[117] The new generation of nobles sub una were often steered toward religious consistency and militancy by the Jesuits' influence or training in their schools. Moreover, in the latter part of the sixteenth century, Rome abandoned any insistence on the return of confiscated lands, and the nobles sub una lost their vestigial inhibition against wholehearted support of the Curia.[118] The alterations in the personnel of the Chancellery were particularly ominous. Zdeněk of Lobkovice and his deputy, the new vice-chancellor Jindřich Domináček of Písnice, were both dedicated exponents of the Counter-Reformation's spirit.[119] It is hardly surprising that the contacts between the high officials and the Utraquist ecclesiastics would sour under these circumstances in the opening years of the seventeenth century.

The actual end of the Utraquists' reliance on royal officialdom and their embracing the Bohemian Diet may be dated, as noted earlier, to October 1604. The highly dramatic and symbolic act precipitating the change was the notorious insult and hardship inflicted on Administrator Dačický by Zdeněk of Lobkovice. The chancellor publicly referred to the former's daughters as "bastards" (*pankhartice*), and when the old priest objected, Lobkovice took offense and at his request Dačický was briefly jailed and deposed from office.[120] The cavalier, boorish, and brutal treatment of the administrator by the chancellor in 1604 made clear the low level of respect on the part of the government for Utraquism and its agencies. This realization helps to explain why the urban Utraquists were increasingly willing to cast their lot with other dissidents from Rome, the Lutherans and the Brethren. They feared subordination to the archbishop and a fusion with the Roman Church on its own terms, abetted by pressure from royal officials.[121]

The influence of the Diet—and the alliance of towns with nobles within it—proved most helpful, if not crucial, in the renewal and maintenance of the Utraquist Consistory, following Dačický's demise in 1604. Nuncio Giovanni Stefano Ferreri favored leaving the position of administrator vacant, or appointing an undercover sub una who—according to Speciano's earlier formula—would bring about a gradual abolition of the Utraquist Consistory. In this sense, Ferreri lobbied the leading officials, who adhered to Rome—Zdeněk of Lobkovice, and the supreme court steward, Kryštof of Lobkovice. Melchior Klesl, bishop of Vienna, joined in support of the nuncio's wishes, in an appeal to Vice-Chancellor Jindřich Domináček.[122] The Bohemian Diet, which met in February 1605, did not raise the question of vacancy in the administrator's office, but Ferreri rejoiced prematurely.[123] When the Diet met next in June, the townsmen moved to rally the noble estates behind their request for the appointment of a new administrator. Meeting in the Old Town Hall of Prague on June 6, the towns' representatives opened negotiations with the barons and the knights to launch a joint petition in the Diet that would focus on religious concessions and include also the Utraquist desiderata.[124] The mere intimation of this development sufficed to help the Utraquist cause. The royal officials feared that the Lutheran nobles' participation in a joint petition would lead to radical demands, in particular for an overt legalization of the Bohemian Confession of 1575, or for election of the administrator by the Diet.[125] Accommodating the townsmen's Utraquism, and thus aborting the joint petition, appeared a lesser evil. The government, therefore, capitulated and a new administrator, Jan Benedikt was installed on June 8, 1605—the day on which the nobles' remonstrance was expected to be filed. Despite the nuncio's last-ditch efforts, the new administrator was a genuine Utraquist, not a crypto-Romanist, who like a Judas goat would lead the Utraquist sheep into an alien fold. What capped Rome's humiliation was the fact that the archbishop was specifically barred from attending the installation ceremony on the grounds of keeping clear the lines of jurisdiction. The care to avoid even an appearance of jurisdictional contamination dramatically reaffirmed the Consistory's independence from the Roman Curia and its subordinate organs.[126] Lest it be thought that the Diet's intervention meant compromising or watering down the Utraquist character of the Consistory in a Protestant direction, it should be stressed that its membership remained unimpeachable in its Utraquist orthodoxy, a fact attested by Zikmund Winter.[127]

Thus, events were set in motion toward the denouement of 1609 when the protection of Utraquism would shift formally and legally from the royal officialdom to the Bohemian Diet. The religious alliance and modus vivendi that the estate of towns and the two noble estates had forged during the negotiations for the Bohemian Confession, continued and matured after 1575. The towns respected the nobles' right to Lutheran and Brethren ministers in their private chapels,[128] and the nobles respected the Utraquist status quo in the royal towns (and for that matter also on their own manors). These attitudes and arrangements, rooted in the Compactata and the Peace of Kutná Hora with their respect for religious pluralism, would find their most pronounced and ultimate embodiment under the Letter of Majesty in 1609. Thus, Rome's menacing attitude would eventually draw the Utraquists from the informal defense alliance of 1575 with the Lutherans and the Brethren to a formal one of 1609 under the banner of the Bohemian Confession. Inasmuch as the Roman Curia could not but look askance at the Utraquists' defensive moves, this denouement drew a deeper wedge between Rome and Utraquism. Contrary to Krofta's judgment cited earlier,[129] after 1593 the Consistory became less dependent on the Roman Church and the royal government; instead, it drew closer to the estates represented in the Diet. Similarly, contrary to the assertion of Pekař that Lutheranism's advance forced the Utraquists ever more into the "Catholic ranks,"[130] it was the Curia's intransigence that forced the Utraquists into a closer political (not doctrinal) alliance with the Protestants. After the disrespectful treatment of the Consistory by the Curia and the royal government, respectively in the Rezek and the Dačický affairs, the Utraquists could hardly rely on either institution, and their lay patrons, the townsmen, had to look for sustenance elsewhere—to the Diet.

Independent Ecclesiastical Jurisdiction: The Clergy

Appointment of Utraquist Clergy:
The Consistory and the Archbishop

Let us now turn to the alleged subordination of the Utraquist parish clergy and the laity to the jurisdiction of the Roman archbishop of Prague. Assertions of the prelate's control over Utraquist priests have focused on the issue of clerical appointments, and that of control of the laity on the assumption of authority in matrimonial litigation.

Perhaps the main argument cited in support of the archbishop's jurisdiction over Utraquist clergy was the authorization by Rudolf II granted to Medek in 1581 and to Berka in 1594 to appoint Utraquist priests not only on the archiepiscopal estates, but also on royal manors in the name of the king as a feudal seigneur.[131] Historians such as Karel Stloukal and Josef Matoušek have asserted that the archbishops thereby were given a free hand to determine the religion of the peasantry on royal estates.[132] Actually, the prelates did not receive a carte blanche to convert such parishes to sub una; their proper task was to safeguard traditionally Utraquist parishes against various patrons who might appoint Lutheran clergy in violation of Maximillian's mandate of 1575.[133] The archbishops' right to approve the appointment of priests in Utraquist parishes derived not from an ecclesiastical jurisdiction, but from a manorial jurisdiction delegated by the monarch. In such cases, the archbishops were to act as expert witnesses or referees to the fact that the proposed clergymen were properly under the aegis of the Utraquist Consistory, or they were to ask the Consistory to supply a suitable candidate.[134] Only Utraquist priests could be appointed to parishes that were traditionally Utraquist,[135] and only the Utraquist Consistory—not the archbishop—could confer ecclesiastical jurisdiction (*pravomoc*) on such Utraquist priests.[136] The Consistory's exclusive ecclesiastical authority was specifically reaffirmed in the royal charter issued to the new administrator in 1581, and is mentioned in the instructions of Caetano to Speciano in 1592.[137] The limitation on the archbishop is confirmed by Rudolf II's letter of June 23, 1598, that in assessing the situation on imperial estates, he was to proceed according to the mandates of Ferdinand I.[138]

According to this watchdog function to keep Lutheran ministers from Utraquist parishes, Archbishop Medek, for instance, conducted an examination of the royal manor of Pardubice in January 1582 to determine whether there were any priests in the Utraquist parishes who lacked an episcopal ordination.[139] Manorial officials also played a role alongside the archbishop in the appointment of priests on royal estates.[140] The normal operation of the system is illustrated by filling parish vacancies on the royal manor of Křivoklát. On April 3, 1595, Jan Hendrych Prollhofer of Purkersdorf, the captain of the manor, wrote to Archbishop Berka to follow the precedent of his archiepiscopal predecessor, and arrange with the Utraquist Consistory for priests to serve in the villages of Lišany and Mutějovice. Similarly, on a subsequent occasion, June 19, 1603, Prollhofer notified Berka about a vacancy in the town of Unhošt', and requested that the archbishop ask for a Utraquist priest from the Utraquist Consistory. At the same time, the royal captain certified that the parish was, indeed, traditionally Utraquist, having habitually received priests administered by the Consistory.[141] On a positive note, on June 10, 1603, the town council in Kostelec nad Labem thanked the archbishop for his role in the appointment of a Utraquist priest, Tobiáš Coccius Plzeňský.[142]

The bottom line is that the clergy remained authentically Utraquist and under the ecclesiastical administration of the Consistory.[143] It neither turned sub una, nor was administratively controlled by the archbishop, or any other agents of the Roman Curia. In a reversal of the medieval investiture procedure, the Utraquist Consistory could confer the ecclesiastical power, the *potestas jurisdictionis,*[144] and the archbishop the use of tangible property of the parish on behalf of the king.[145] Such crossovers of denominational lines in implementing ecclesiastical appointments were not unique at the time. Thus, the Bohemian Chancellery, was staffed—as we saw—by dissidents from Rome, and yet executed the king's policy in the appointment of the Roman archbishop of Wrocław in the 1590s. The royal officials would not appoint a Lutheran or a member of the Unity as archbishop, any more than the archbishop of Prague would appoint priests sub una to Utraquist parishes.[146] In the Bohemian case, effective safeguards were in place to keep the archbishops from exceeding their mandate and encroaching on the Utraquist parishes, instead of defending their interests. These checks and balances will be discussed later.

In a more general sense, a variety of official documents postulated the exclusiveness of the Utraquist Consistory's ecclesiastical jurisdiction over the clergy sub utraque, and defined it as equal and parallel to the archbishop's ecclesiastical jurisdiction over clergy sub una. This documentation stemmed from the Consistory, administrator, king, and archbishop. The previously quoted affirmations by the Consistory that it was "an office of the king," not of the archbishop, belonged in this category.[147] In 1589, in their letter to King Rudolf II, Consistory members referred to their exercise of full ecclesiastical jurisdiction and administration over the authentic clergy sub utraque.[148] Later, on August 18, 1589, the Consistory affirmed the principle that clergy sub utraque was under the administrator and Consistory; and only the clergy sub una under the archbishop. Hence, the Utraquist priests were not subordinated to the archbishop.[149]

In April 1598, Archbishop Berka explicitly recognized the division of jurisdiction between himself and the Utraquist Consistory, when he admonished Petr Vok of Rožmberk to keep on his estate only "priests sub una who are administered by the Upper Consistory of the archbishopric of Prague and then those sub utraque, also ordained by proper bishops and administered by the Lower Consistory."[150] Berka restated this principle when he admitted that the validly ordained clergy sub utraque should be subordinated to the Utraquist Consistory and not to himself during the convoluted proceedings against the clergyman Vít Huber in 1594–1600 on the estate of Ferdinand Hofmann of Grýnspichl and Střechov.[151] The most explicit affirmation of the two separate jurisdictions appeared in Rudolf II's letter of October 6, 1601: "[I]n this kingdom there are maintained two kinds of clergy, firstly the Catholic sub una which is directed and administered by the . . . archbishop, then sub utraque which is canonically ordained by bishops [and directed and administered] by the Lower [i.e., Utraquist] Consistory . . ."[152] In the mandate against the Brethren of July 22, 1602, Rudolf again confirmed that legitimate clergy stemmed from two distinct and separate jurisdictions, either from the archbishop of Prague or from the administrator of the Utraquist Consistory.[153]

Administrator Dačický subsequently asserted the exclusive ecclesiastical authority of the Consistory over the Utraquist clergy on June 21, 1602, in a letter addressed to Archbishop Berka. In particular, the administrator reminded Berka that he lacked the right to deal with individual Utraquist priests.[154] In June 1604, when friction developed in Kadaň between the sub una and the sub utraque, the archbishop was unable to exercise jurisdiction over the Utraquists to resolve it. The administrator and the Consistory asked the prelate not to interfere with the status quo and to wait until a royal commission had the chance to adjudicate the issues between the two parties.[155] Incidentally, the initial authorization of a Utraquist priest's post, who would serve in Kadaň under the Utraquist Consistory, had been negotiated between the king and the Bohemian Diet in 1593–1594 without any official input from the archbishop.[156] In a notable way, Berka respected the institutional independence of the Utraquist clergy in 1605. When a clerical synod met to implement the directives of the Council of Trent under the archbishop's jurisdiction, the priests who were administered by the Utraquist Consistory were not expected to, and did not, participate.[157]

There is other evidence that the Utraquist clergy and faithful were free of the archbishop's administrative authority in spiritual matters. In November 1582, the Consistory questioned Archbishop Medek's right to introduce the new Gregorian calendar.[158] On May 9, 1584, the Consistory appealed to the Count Palatine with a petition for the king to appoint new members of Consistory, thus completely bypassing the archbishop.[159] In June 1596, the Utraquist Consistory and the archbishop endorsed separately Rudolf's proclamation, which exhorted to invocation of the saints and other prayers for victory over the Turks.[160] Similarly, the Utraquist authorities in Kutná Hora ordered in July 1596 weekly litanies and processions on the basis of the king's proclamation, not at the behest of the archbishop.[161] Likewise, the request for collecting alms to care for disabled veterans of the Turkish war went directly from Rudolf II to the Utraquist administrator, not through the archbishop.[162] When in turn in June 1601, Berka issued his own order for forty-hour prayers for victory in the Turkish war, the mandate was limited to the church of the Prague castle, which was the sole parish sub una in the city.[163] In September 1604, again bypassing the prelate, Rudolf II issued a separate directive to the administrator and the Consistory to conduct daily prayers for a defeat of the Turks.[164] The temporary detention of Dačický in the care of Archbishop Berka in 1604, after his encounter with Zdeněk of Lobkovice, might have appeared as a sign of the archbishop's ascendancy over the administrator, compromising Utraquist independence. Even Zikmund Winter, however, acknowledged that Berka's role was that of king's agent, not that of an independent actor asserting jurisdiction over the Utraquist establishment.[165]

There was no clear evidence of the archbishop's encroachment on Utraquist ecclesiastical judiciary. When the Consistory appealed to the Bohemian Diet, asking for the monarch's safeguarding of Utraquism's rights, the remonstrance made it clear on December 15, 1586, that the Consistory, not the archbishop, exercised judicial power in marital lawsuits involving Utraquist spouses.[166] This fact was affirmed in the petition to the monarch by the Diet deputies of Prague and other royal towns in February 1588.[167] In a petition to Rudolf II in 1589, the Consistory referred more generally to its ecclesiastical court and its jurisdiction in both urban and rural areas.[168] Not even the papal nuncio would accept an appeal against the Consistory's decision in a marital case in 1589.[169] A curious exception might have been a request to have Rome grant dispensation for a Utraquist marriage in case of consanguinity in March 1602. It is not clear whether Rome actually acted in this matter.[170] Most blatantly, it has been asserted that after Dačický was deposed, Berka encroached on the Consistory's jurisdiction by seizing judicial authority in the matrimonial area. Such an usurpation, however, does not find support in available documents.[171] Indeed, Nuncio Ferreri's testimony bore witness to the fact that the Consistory continued, undisturbed by the archbishop, its regular judicial agenda in spiritual matters. The Curia diplomat criticized the members of the Consistory in October 1604 for acting as judges of an ecclesiastical court without holding doctoral degrees in canon law.[172]

It is difficult to see the basis of Krofta's assertion that in the 1580s the Utraquist Consistory was brought to an increasing dependence on the archbishop.[173]

Issue of "Catholic" Clergy in Utraquist Parishes

Professions of belief in the Catholic Church and, to a lesser degree, of devotion to the books and rubrics of the Archdiocese of Prague have been (mis)used by critics to attribute to the Utraquist Consistory and its clergy either an explicit desire to submit to the Roman Curia, or an aura of mendacity, reflecting intellectual dishonesty and moral spinelessness. Actually, contrary to the twentieth-century terminological usage, such professions had nothing to do with obedience to the Roman Curia or the archbishop, or with acceptance of Council of Trent edicts. When the archbishop officially maintained that only "Catholic clergy" should be appointed to Utraquist parishes, he did not mean to introduce a Tridentine Gleichschaltung into the Church of Bohemia, which—as we saw—was not within his power at the time anyway. Like the Consistory and the king, he was aware that, according to the Bohemian constitutional system deriving here largely from the Compactata, the term "Catholic religion" covered the Utraquists, and distinguished them formally from those who embraced the Augsburg Confession or another outright Protestant creed.[174] In his letter of August 1595, the archbishop made the attribution of the term "Catholic" to the Utraquists clear in his statement referring to "the Catholic faith and good ancient ecclesiastical rite" that the adherents of Rome and the Utraquists shared.[175] Rudolf II's instruction to the Utraquist Consistory of June 23, 1594, upon the appointment of Dačický, restated the legal propriety of referring to the Utraquist Church as "Catholic," asserting that the Utraquists' faith was Catholic, inasmuch as the Roman Church had recognized it as such when it granted the Compactata.[176]

Statements that the Utraquist Consistory did or should have followed the rules of the archdiocese of Prague have been erroneously cited as evidence of actual or mandated subordination to the archbishop. Thus, the stipulations that the Consistory practice observance of fasts and ceremonies according to the archdiocesan rules, as in Rudolf II's instruction of June 23, 1594, should not be construed as demanding obedience to the post-1564 edicts of the archbishops of Prague.[177] There was nothing new or compromising in this directive, inasmuch as the Utraquists had traditionally—since the fifteenth century—expressed their essential agreement with pre-Tridentine liturgical books of the Prague archdiocese.[178] We may also recall that the administrator and the Consistory considered themselves, and in Bohemia were officially recognized, as part of the historical structure of the archdiocese—as "administrator et parochi consistorii archiepiscopatus Pragensis sub utraque communicantium."[179] Rudolf's injunction was anti-Lutheran and did not coerce the Utraquists' submission to either the archbishop or the Curia. The city fathers of Kadaň used the traditional formula in 1597 to defend their priest's Utraquist orthodoxy by reference to his use of "Prague rubrics."[180] The fifteenth-century maxim was repeated when, as Nuncio Ferreri reported, the Bohemian Chancellery admonished Administrator Benedikt of Prague, on his installation in June 1605, to observe the rubrics of the archdiocese of Prague, which were considered Catholic.[181] It would be anachronistic to view this injunction as initiating or escalating pressure on the Utraquists to conform to the current rules and practices of the Roman Curia. It was already contained in the Compactata.[182]

A related error is Stloukal's assertion that in 1599 Nuncio Filippo Spinelli induced Rudolf II to appoint only "Catholic" councilors in royal towns, implying that the appointees were sub una.[183] Contrary to Stloukal, when Nuncio Spinelli noted that Rudolf insisted on "Catholic" councilors (particularly in Prague), it did not mean that the individuals in question were sub una. It meant that they were neither Lutherans nor Brethren, but observed the Compactata, and hence were Utraquist.[184] As noted earlier, from the viewpoint of the Bohemian constitutional law based on the Compactata, both the sub una and the Utraquist were subsumed under the label of "Catholic."[185] Accordingly, in his letter of May 1596, Rudolf II referred to the "holy Catholic Church" as covering not only the sub una, but also the Utraquists.[186] In this connection it may be noted that, despite the presence of the archbishop in Prague, the number of adherents to the Roman Curia did not expand significantly in the city. In 1575, Nuncio Dolfin noted their small number and the prevalence of Utraquists (hussiti).[187] The lack of sub una parishes in Prague was further documented by the vain efforts of Nuncio Bonomi in 1584, repeated by Nuncio Speciano in 1593, to establish at least two in the city, and by the testimony of Pierre Bergeron in 1600 that masses sub una were said only in the monasteries.[188]

In any case, the stalwarts of Utraquist orthodoxy, for their part, felt no inhibition or qualms in referring to their faith and to their church as "Catholic,"[189] while rejecting juridical submission to the papacy. In this sense, the Consistory pledged to observe the "Catholic religion," during its discussions with Nuncio Bonomi in 1582.[190] In two proclamations in October 1582, the Consistory spoke, respectively, of Administrator Jindřich of Helfenburk, as having died in the "true Catholic faith," and of its "faithful priests adhering to the ancient Catholic religion."[191] In a petition to the Bohemian Diet, the Consistory defined its religion in 1586 as "Christian Catholic, of one Christian faith, confirmed by the Lord Jesus and also by the Catholic Christian Church," and again referred to "our Christian Catholic religion."[192] In its statements of 1589, the Consistory emphasized its duty to defend "the true clergy and also the ancient Catholic religion sub utraque,"[193] as well as its adherence to "the rules of the ancient Church, holy, Christian and Catholic."[194] In an authoritative treatise published in the same year1589, the Utraquist theologian, Valentin Polon did not hesitate to call the Utraquists a part of not just the "universal Church" (*Církev všeobecná*), but outright of the "Catholic Church" (*Církev katolická*).[195] In December 1603, the Consistory once again defined the true clergy as "we and other Catholic priesthood."[196] In this context, if—as Zikmund Winter maintains—Tomáš of Soběslav on his appointment as administrator in 1609 took an oath to uphold the Catholic faith, he did not thereby signal an abandonment of Utraquism for Trent.[197]

Lest it be thought that the use of "Catholic" reflected a gravitation in the late sixteenth century by the Utraquists to the Roman Curia, it may be recalled that Jan of Příbram had proclaimed his love for the Catholic Church as early as the 1430s.[198] The target of his affection, of course, did not coincide with the cardinals of the Roman Curia. Similarly, Jan Rokycana maintained that, on the basis of the Compactata, the Utraquists were faithful children of the Roman Church despite their rejection of communion sub una.[199] The Utraquists considered themselves exemplary "Catholics" for the rest of the fifteenth and into the sixteenth century, relying in part on the Compactata,[200] which had retained their validity in the constitutional law of Bohemia despite their revocation by Pius II in 1462. Indeed, in the apt phrase of Reginald Betts, the Compactata had in fact legalized "two Catholic churches" in Bohemia, one sub utraque, and the other sub una.[201] Accordingly, at the Buda negotiations in 1525, Jan Pašek of Vrat and Lev of Rožmitál, respectively, on behalf of the Utraquists and of the Curia's adherents, promised that each side would regard the other not as heretics, but as true Christians, and as the sons of the same "holy Church."[202] As noted in Chapter 4, Bohuslav Bílejovský, the paragon of Utraquist orthodoxy, in his *Kronyka česká* (1537) viewed the Utraquists not just as Catholics, but also as "true Romans."[203] After 1462, the Roman Curia apparently did not feel legally bound to recognize the Utraquists as an integral part of the Roman Catholic Church, but the laws of Bohemia enjoined papal diplomats from challenging the proposition officially and overtly within the country. Indeed, it could be said that in Bohemia it would have been unlawful to maintain that either those sub una or the Utraquists were not participating in the Roman Catholic Church.

Far from fearing that by calling themselves Catholics they were poaching on the territory of the Roman Curia, the Utraquists apparently had some doubts whether the term could be properly applied to the sub una adherents of the Roman Church. Thus, a Counter-Reformation pamphlet, issued in 1625 and aimed at "conversion" of the Utraquists, would seek to reassure its readers that "the papists" were indeed Catholics in the sense of the first half-millennium of Christianity.[204] That this was not an unheard-of or preposterous question is indicated by the debating propositions, posed in England about the same time by Bishop Richard Montagu of Chichester, namely (1) whether the contemporary Church of Rome was the Catholic Church, and (2) whether the contemporary Church of England was a sound member of the Catholic Church.[205] Put in more modern terms, it is clear that in the sixteenth and seventeenth centuries, the Roman Curia or the Holy See did not hold the copyright to the term Catholic, and others could not be charged with violation of the fair use principle, or a theft of intellectual property.[206]

All this is not to say that the term had not been misused in these early times even within Bohemia. Berka at times employed the designation Catholic as synonymous with sub una in an informal and innocuous way.[207] The term was misused more culpably by Jaroslav Bořita of Martinice in 1602 and by the abbot of Broumov in 1603, who under the formula that only the Catholic religion was legitimate in Bohemia, wished to force all their subjects to become communicants sub una.[208] Ironically and perversely, Rudolf II chose to misinterpret Bořita's policy as an equivalent of the established policy on royal manors, namely that of equal protection of the sub una and the Utraquists as members of "the ancient Christian and Catholic faith."[209] These cases may be viewed as rare aberrations. More flagrantly, in their internal correspondence with the Curia, the papal nuncios tended to habitually (mis)appropriate the word "catholici" for the sub una, and to use it in contradistinction to the Utraquists, whom they called "hussiti."[210] Nevertheless, the Curia officials in the sixteenth and early seventeenth centuries were more perceptive than subsequent historians in refusing to understand the Utraquist Consistory's pledges of allegiance to "Catholic" faith and rites—for instance, in 1587–1589—as equivalent to embracing the Roman jurisdiction in its entirety and integrity.[211]

Ordination of Utraquist Clergy

A concrete point that has been raised to demonstrate the alleged fusion of Utraquism with the Roman Church in the period 1575–1609, is the text of an oath required by the archbishop of Prague from ordinands for priesthood. This document was included among those appended to the *Second Apology* of the Bohemian estates, issued in 1618 in justification of their uprising against Ferdinand II. The Apology claimed that Utraquist priests, prior to 1609, were required to take this oath. In fact, the Tridentine text posited a craven submission to the Holy See, but by itself proved little about actual Utraquist ordinations.[212] On the one hand, there is nothing new about this text. On the other hand, there is no evidence that any Utraquist priests, qua Utraquist priests, actually took the oath.

As early as the 1560s, the archbishop of Prague had come to insist on submission to the Tridentine document by any new ordinands, thereby terminating any further archiepiscopal ordinations of Utraquists in Prague in 1566.[213] In July 1575, State Secretary Tolomeo Gallio restated to Nuncio Dolfin that the archbishop of Prague could proceed with Utraquist ordinations only if the Consistory were in full accord with the Roman Church.[214] These refusals continued for the rest of Brus's episcopate and during the entire episcopate of Medek. While Brus seemed willing to proceed with the ordination if he could avoid Roman penalties, Medek actually opposed any benevolence on Rome's part, allegedly hoping to coerce the Utraquists into a full merger under his jurisdiction.[215] He did not need to worry. The Curia rejected a petition which, on the initiative of Administrator Dvorský, Rudolf II submitted through Nuncio Giovanni Morone in July 1576.[216] In 1582 and again in 1584, Nuncio Bonomi insisted that the prelate would be committing a breach of duty if he ordained Utraquist priests; unless the Consistory abandoned all differences from the Roman Church, except communion sub utraque as permitted by Pope Pius IV in 1564, and submitted fully to the archbishop.[217] Another Utraquist petition was turned down under Nuncio Puteo in 1589. This clearly contradicted Borový's assertion that specifically under Medek as archbishop, there were no significant differences between Utraquism and the Roman Church; and that the Consistory accepted the archbishop's jurisdiction.[218]

An attempt to break the deadlock on Utraquist ordinations had failed by 1597, after seven priests, ordained with papal dispensation by Berka, had reverted to Utraquist practices.[219] There is no available record that Berka's successor, Karl Lamberg (1606–1612)—as noted earlier, a Styrian untutored in the Czech language—ordained any Utraquist clergy. Thus, Utraquist priests had to receive ordination from bishops outside Bohemia, particularly in Passau, Wrocław, Olomouc, Poznań, and Nitra. Also, Roman priests, originally sub una, continued to join the Utraquist Church.[220] In June 1602, Administrator Dačický reemphasized the policy of the Consistory to appoint and confirm to Utraquist parishes only such priests who had a certificate (*testimonium*) of a proper ordination by a proper bishop.[221] The matter of episcopal ordination was taken seriously by the Consistory into the opening decade of the seventeenth century. This is attested, for instance, by the intensive search to document the priesthood of Eliáš Šud, subsequently the first administrator under the Letter of Majesty (1609–1614).[222] Utraquist priests, who were not defectors from the Roman Church, received their theological training either as apprentices from established and experienced pastors, or from individual professors of the liberal arts faculty. The mentors issued certificates of the candidates' readiness for ordination.[223] Unlike the Lutherans, the Utraquist clergy not only wore traditional liturgical vestments in churches, but also maintained the traditional externalities of the clerical state, such as distinct street attire and marks such as the tonsure and a cleanly shaven face.[224]

Despite the complications with canonical ordinations, Administrator Dačický reported on December 14, 1602, that the Utraquist Consistory had enough priests ordained by bishops to staff its parishes, and the supply continued adequately thereafter.[225] The adequacy of clerical personnel was also indicated by the smooth functioning of Utraquism's rather extensive ecclesiastical organization, which encompassed a network of forty-six deaneries, each with its subordinate parishes.[226] The operation of this structure may be illustrated by the distribution of oils, which as noted previously, the archbishops of Prague passed on to the Consistory each Easter. The canonically blessed oils, needed for the administration of baptism and extreme unction, were sent by the Consistory to Utraquist deans and, in turn, distributed by them to parish priests.[227] In addition to its size, the Utraquist Church showed its organizational vitality by introducing, in both urban and rural areas, registers of baptisms, marriages, and funerals at the turn of the sixteenth century.[228] Infrastructural strength of this kind clearly gave the lie to the image of a vanishing institution, losing the grip on its clergy and congregations.

In contrast to the massive documentation that the reluctance to make the Tridentine oath prevented the ordinations of Utraquist clergy by the archbishop, there is virtually no independent evidence that any Utraquist candidates in 1575–1609 actually did take the formidable oath appended to the

Second Apology.[229] To the contrary, there is evidence from the 1590s that such an oath was considered abhorrent by both Utraquist clergy and laity.[230] The Tridentine profession, of course, would have been made by those Utraquist priests who had received their ordination under sub una and then shifted their allegiance. These clergymen, however, could not be considered bound by a juridical submission to the Holy See once they entered the jurisdiction of the Utraquist Consistory. It is also possible that the seven priests ordained by Berka in 1597 had taken a compromising oath, but their case was highly atypical.

Remedies Against the Archbishops' Encroachments: Checks and Balances

The role assigned to the archbishops in brokering clerical appointments on royal estates was not, of course, without its risks for the interests of the Utraquist Church. The prelates were occasionally tempted to misuse the procedure for the benefit of the Roman Church. The record showed, however, that there were effective safeguards in place to keep the princes of the Church from unauthorized appointments of Roman priests. There were three agents ready to defend the integrity of Utraquist parishes: (1) the parishes themselves, rural as well as urban; (2) the managers of the royal manors, who unlike official at higher levels, continued to be drawn from the ranks of dissidents from the Roman Church; and (3) the Utraquist Consistory. All of these agents could appeal for the protection of the Utraquist character of parishes against the archbishop to the highest officials of the land, or to the king himself.

Protests by the cities of Rokycany (April 1597) and Brandýs nad Labem (May 1597) exemplified the determination of towns on royal estates to resist Berka's appointment of clergy sub una, and to insist on priests under the jurisdiction of the Utraquist Consistory.[231] In opposing the archbishop's usurpations, the city fathers could cite the edicts of recent Bohemian kings that outlawed encroachments of the sub una against the Utraquists (and vice versa). Particularly elaborate in its historical and legal argumentation was the remonstrance of the town of Brandýs nad Labem, dated June 3, 1597, which cited precedents covering archbishops Brus and Medek, and monarchs Ferdinand I, Maximilian II, and Rudolf II, as well as the laws of the land, including the Compactata, for the protection of the Utraquist religion.[232] The parishioners' complaints against the objectionable appointees, aside from the basic one of their insubordination to the Utraquist Consistory, focused on the introduction of unfamiliar rites, and the use of an incomprehensible language. The second objection apparently reflected the fact that candidates for priesthood sub una normally were not natives of Bohemia.[233] The towns on royal estates did not have to face the archbishops alone. In August 1600, Nové Strašecí turned to the manorial director to back up its right (against the archbishop's interference) to have a Utraquist priest who was under the aegis of the Consistory.[234] In May 1601, the town council of Brandýs nad Labem, having already asked for help from the captain of the manor, proceeded beyond the manorial level and appealed directly to a royal office, the Bohemian Chamber, against the archbishop's repeated refusals to appoint a Utraquist priest.[235] In May 1602, the town council of Libice asked for help from Jan of Habartice, captain of the royal manor of Poděbrady, objecting to a priest sub una whom the archbishop was forcing on them instead of a Utraquist priest.[236]

The king's manorial managers played a particularly active role in keeping the archbishops honest. In March 1600, the captain of the royal manor of Lysá, Václav Zálužský of Vostroskály, intervened against Berka's attempt to appoint a priest sub una to a traditionally Utraquist parish. In February 1601, the director (*hejtman*) of the royal manor of Křivoklát defended the right of the village of Cerhovice to a Utraquist priest in writing to the archbishop.[237] In May 1601, the captain of the royal manor of Poděbrady, Jan of Habartice, filed a similar appeal against the archbishop with the Bohemian Chamber. In January 1602, the director of the royal manor of Křivoklát wrote to the archbishop in support of the town Nové Strašecí and its request for a priest to be supplied by the Utraquist Consistory. In May 1602, the captain of the manor of Poděbrady reported to the Bohemian Chamber that the inhabitants of Libice refused to accept the priest sent by the archbishop, even if he promised to distribute communion sub utraque, because he was of Roman obedience.[238]

As for the Utraquist Consistory, it appealed, for instance, in February 1590 to the supreme court steward (*hofmistr*), Jiří the Elder of Lobkovice, asking for restoration to its jurisdiction parishes on three manors of the royal domain. There was even a curious case in October 1586 when the Consistory protested against archbishop's attempts to appoint a Lutheran minister rather than a Utraquist priests. In a similar vein, in February 1590 the Consistory complained that the archbishop tolerated Lutheran clergy on the royal manor of Pardubice.[239]

As for ecclesiastical manors, Nuncio Bonomi failed to induce the sub una cathedral chapter of Prague to remove Utraquist priests from four parishes in 1584 on the charges of concubinage. The chapter refused on the grounds that the parishioners would revolt.[240] Villagers on episcopal estates, in fact, could offer spirited resistance to the archbishop or his vassal in cases of unauthorized appointments of priests sub una, as for instance the inhabitants of Třebenice did on May 21, 1599.[241] In June 1602, Voršila Tachovská, the abbess of the convent of Týnec, complained that the subject villagers of Pozdno refused to accept a priest of Roman obedience even if he promised to distribute communion sub utraque.[242] She repeated her complaint to the archbishop a week later.[243] In January 1603, she wrote to Berka that the inhabitants of Týnec boycotted the priest sub una and insisted on the services of a Utraquist.[244]

The seigneurs of private manors were also ready to defend the right of their villagers to the services of Utraquist clergy as Zdeslav Kaplíř of Sulevice did in the village of Jenišův Újezd. The case, which had started in 1593, reached one of the central institutions of royal justice in Bohemia, the Court of the Land (Zemský soud), by 1602. There the lawsuit was still in progress in 1603, when the archbishop received a subpoena to deliver relevant documents.[245] Similarly, on March 25, 1602, and again on May 12, 1603, Marie of Šternberk intervened to remove a priest sub una from her manorial town of Nepomuk because her subjects' parish was traditionally Utraquist, and it had customarily obtained a Utraquist priest from the Consistory.[246] This step was opposed by her brother Ladislav of Šternberk.[247] In May 1603, the town council of Nepomuk requested that Ladislav not press on them a priest sub una, since they had obtained a Utraquist priest from the Consistory with the permission of his sister Marie, who was their seigneur.[248] In June 1603, Rudolf II ordered an investigation on whether the parish of Nepomuk had been traditionally sub una or Utraquist. The outcome favored the sub una.[249] Nevertheless, in September 1603, Marie of Šternberk continued to insist on keeping the priest who was under the administrator of the Utraquist Consistory in Nepomuk.[250] The king, in turn, threatened her with judicial proceedings before the Bohemian Chancellery if she did not yield.[251] In another case, in May 1603, the mayor and council of the manorial village Lochkov induced their seigneur Zikmund Smiřický of Smiřice to intervene with the archbishop to arrange with the Consistory for the appointment of a Utraquist priest in their church. The archbishop had pressed on them the unacceptable services of the abbot of the Emmaus monastery (Na Slovanech). They understood the latter to be a convert in 1591 to sub una,[252] engaging in such (mal)practices as disregard of Jan Hus's feast day, and refusal of communion for infants.[253]

Thus, on royal, ecclesiastical, and private estates the preservation of Utraquist parishes rested on a fairly elaborate and apparently effective system of checks and balances. The archbishop acted to prevent influential patrons from appointing Lutheran ministers, while he was checked from appointing priests sub una by coalitions of manorial seigneurs, manorial managers, municipal councils, and the Utraquist Consistory, each with the right of appeal to the royal government and the king. The manorial managers played a particularly important role of ombudsmen in preserving the status quo on royal estates, siding mainly with the Utraquists.[254]

The record of historical documents in *Sněmy české,* however, shows that most of the archbishops' energies in their assigned role as watchdogs over Christian orthodoxy on royal estates were not directed at surreptitiously replacing Utraquist priests with those sub una, but rather at preventing the replacement of priests sub una by Lutheran ministers in the German speaking fringes of Bohemia. The German-speaking population had shown a particular affinity for Lutheranism as early as 1523 in Prague.[255] Baron Sebastian Schlick introduced the first Lutheran preacher to his estate in the Loket area in 1521.[256] Medek and Berka tried to stave off massive Lutheranization among the German sub una in the towns and districts of Cheb and Loket.[257] Berka struggled to preserve the Roman status quo in the county of Kłodzko (Kladsko) and on the manor of Týn Horšův where Captain Melchior of Rechenberg and Vilém of Lobkovice, respectively, attempted to carry out Lutheran reformations from 1599 to1604.[258] Other areas of major concern in the same period were the royal manor of Chomutov, the town of Česká Lípa, and the Rožmberk manor under Petr Vok in Český Krumlov.[259] While the ordinary Czechs seemed to be largely satisfied with Utraquism, Lutheranism appeared virtually irresistible for the stolid Teutonic mountaineers of Loket, Žatec, Litoměřice, the Giant Mountains (Krkonoše), and Kłodzko.[260]

Syllabus of Errors

With all due apologies to Pope Pio Nono for misappropriating the title of a key document of his reign, the following syllabus of errors can be drawn up concerning the assertions about institutional ties between the Roman Curia and the Utraquists: (1) that the Utraquist Consistory was completely controlled from Rome and/or marginalized into ineffectiveness; (2) that Utraquist clergy pledged full obedience to the Curia; (3) that the archbishop of

Prague ruled over the Utraquist clergy; and (4) that the archbishop of Prague assumed from the Utraquist Consistory ecclesiastical jurisdiction over Utraquist laity. My conclusions challenge these myths of Roman ascendancy over the Utraquist Consistory, and the Roman archbishops' ecclesiastical management of Utraquist clergy and laity.

Contrary to assertions in the historical literature, the Utraquists did not rush into the embrace of the Roman Curia, but rather kept a cautious distance. Their attempts at rapprochement, motivated largely by the issue of clerical ordinations, were discouraged by the increasingly uncompromising stance on the part of the Curia, growing out of the letter and the spirit of the Council of Trent. The papal negotiators met Utraquist overtures by alternating between unyielding rigidity and aggressive schemes to co-opt and absorb the Utraquist Consistory with its infrastructure of deaneries and parishes. The aggressive forays led the Utraquist establishment to seek a counterweight in political cooperation with other dissidents from Rome, and this further increased the divide between the Utraquists and the Curia, which could not but regard the Utraquists' defensive alliance as an adulterous going to bed with the Protestant enemy. As a result, the period of 1575 to 1609 was one of growing divergence, not convergence, between Utraquism and the Roman Curia.

10

The Curia Tightens the Noose: The Advance of Confessionalization, 1575–1609

Having followed the increasing divergence between the Roman Curia and Bohemian Utraquism on the level of institutional contacts in 1575–1609, let us now examine the parallel process of discussions in theological literature in the same period. The attitude of Roman controversialists was marked by increasing rigidity, which reflected the progress of confessionalization, eventually rendering any chances of reconciliation very slim indeed.[1] The deterioration occurred in stages. For approximately two decades after 1575, the polemics of authors for the Roman side still tended to observe the restraint mandated by the Peace of Kutná Hora of 1485. Avoiding direct attacks on Utraquism, the Romanist writers sought to distinguish Hus and Utraquism as lesser evils, compared to the Unity of Brethren and the German Reformation. Toward the end of the century, however, the distinction would blur and virtually disappear into an uncompromising attitude, not only toward outright Protestantism, but also toward mainline Utraquism. This development paralleled the implementation of the Tridentine Counter-Reformation, and the countercurrent of the Utraquist leaders' political rapprochement in Bohemia with their Lutheran and Unity allies. The Roman side would evade the injunction against domestic attacks on Utraquism by translating works of foreigners, and seeking the obscurity of a provincial center for their publication. While denouncing existing Utraquism, the Roman polemicists would fabricate the image of acceptable, but imaginary, "Old Utraquists" who were satisfied with a temporary permission of lay chalice at Rome's pleasure.

The conclusion of the Council of Trent in 1563 and the subsequent tendency to apply its decrees and anathemas, foreshadowed for Bohemia the end of the era of good feelings, and the onset of a frosty relationship. The Roman Curia felt more self-confident as the religious situation stabilized. The need to hold onto Bohemia at the cost of concessions did not seem so compelling as in the immediate post-Reformation era. Moreover, new agencies were in place by the last quarter of the sixteenth century to implement the Tridentine principles, namely (1) the Jesuit order, introduced to Bohemia in 1556; (2) the archbishop of Prague, restored after a vacancy of more than a century in 1561; and (3) a permanent papal nuncio established in Prague in 1583 after the transfer of the imperial court from Vienna to the Bohemian capital.[2] There were two landmark events in the 1580s that signaled the Curia's stiffening attitude toward Bohemian exceptionalism. Pope Gregory XIII on March 15, 1580, issued a bull indiscriminately condemning the "Hussites" (the Curia's code name for the Utraquists) together with the Wyclifites, Zwinglians, Calvinists, and other heretics.[3] Even more symbolic was the ironic placement of Cochlaeus's *Historiae Hussitarum libri duodecim* (1549), a left-handed attempt to conciliate the Utraquists, on the Index of Prohibited Books by Sixtus V (1585–1590).[4] Even the writings of Pope Pius II became subject to censorship despite the Council of Trent's misgivings about condemning a pope.[5]

Foreign Hard-Liners

Unequivocal support of Tridentine conformity became evident in foreign theologians' assessment of the Bohemian Reformation. The distinction between Hus and Utraquism, on the one hand, and Protestantism on the other—once customary among irenic Roman theologians—largely disappeared. The placing of Cochlaeus's *Historiae Hussitarum* on the Index was symptomatic of denying Utraquism a more benign status.

A prime example of sweeping criticism is furnished by Petr Illicino (or Illicinus), canon in Olomouc (1570–1585). The latter served the bishop of Olomouc, Jan Mezoun (1576–1578), who was himself the product of Jesuit schools and the Roman seminary Germanicum, designed to train clerical leaders of the Counter-Reformation in Central Europe. Accordingly, upon his consecration, Mezoun opposed in 1576 a petition in favor of religious freedom, which the Moravian Diet submitted to Maximilian II in his role as the new margrave of Moravia.[6] Illicino marshaled arguments in support of Mezoun's position in a treatise, appropriately titled *Contra impiam Deoque inimicam haereticorum legem* (Against the Heretics' Law, Impious and Inimical to God) and written in 1577.[7] Arguing against freedom of religion, he did not distinguish Hus and the Utraquists from the Wyclifites, Taborites, Picards, and even the Anabaptists. The Utraquists' claims of religious freedom were comparable to those of the Calvinists in France.[8] Illicino denounced by name Hus, Rokycana, and George of Poděbrady, charged them with employing the ferocious Žižka in order to destroy the Church, and placed them in the same class with Luther, Calvin, and Zwingli.[9] In addition to religious grounds, the Italian-born canon rejected toleration for secular reasons, that is, as subversive of governmental authority. Rulers who gathered people of different religions, he argued, were deserted by all in the end.[10]

Many other foreign theologians of note pronounced uncomplimentary verdicts on Hus and the Bohemian Reformation in the last third of the sixteenth century, such as the German Jesuit Alexander Höller,[11] or the Poles Jakób Wujek z Wągrowca[12] and Bartołomiej Paprocki z Głogoł.[13] Let us, however, focus on the most distinguished one, Edmund Campion, the English Jesuit and martyr. Sent to Bohemia from Rome, where he entered the Jesuit order in 1573, Campion spent a year in Brno at the novitiate, then taught at the Jesuit College of St. Clement in Prague for six years, first rhetoric, then philosophy.[14] In the fall of 1576, he gave an opening address for the new school year at the Jesuit gymnasium in Prague in which he spoke in very harsh terms about the Bohemian Reformation, and particularly about Jan Hus. He exhorted the inhabitants of Prague to return to the spiritual traditions of their saints Wenceslaus, Vojtěch, and Procopius, or at least to those of Emperor Charles IV, instead of invoking: "some reckless preachers, or an infamous military leader [presumably Jan Žižka], or a base apostate [presumably Jan Hus], who has brought into your venerable walls so many sects, so many schisms, so much mischief and so many vices, so much dark ignorance, and yes, an entire enormity of evil."[15]

Two of the less fortunate legacies of Campion's stay in Prague merit particular mentions. One was the training of future archbishop of Prague, Johann Lohelius (1612–1622), a native of Cheb, who lived into the early years of the Counter-Reformation in Bohemia. He then became responsible for the papal prohibition of the lay chalice and for the jailing, and possibly death of the last Utraquist leader, the priest Jan Locika of Domažlice.[16] Lohelius studied rhetoric, then philosophy under Campion, having entered the Jesuit college in 1575.[17] Campion's other bequest to his host country was connected with his directorship of the first sodality of the Virgin Mary, established in Bohemia at the College of St. Clement on January 16, 1575.[18] The sodality became one of the foci of militant Counter-Reformation spirit. By 1578, it consisted of three sections, one of which grouped the elite of the Roman Church's adherents: nobles, professors, lawyers, and physicians. Several of the sodality's members would subsequently star in the Bohemian Counter-Reformation, particularly Jaroslav Bořita Martinic, Vilém Slavata, Filip Fabricius, and once more Archbishop Lohelius.[19]

While in Prague, Campion was in touch with Archbishop Brus, who occasionally consulted him on administering the *sub una,* seeing that the latter were a minority in Bohemia in a similar proportion to the Catholics in England. He ordained Campion to the priesthood in early September 1578. After the ceremony, Brus is said to have declared: "All kinds of evil invaded Bohemia because of Wyclif, an Englishman; now the Lord has furnished us with another Englishman who would heal the wounds inflicted on the Bohemians by Wyclif."[20] During Campion's last Easter in Bohemia in 1579, the archbishop chose him as a preacher in St. Vitus Cathedral for Holy Thursday.[21] Less than a year later, in early March 1580, Campion left Prague via Rome for a mission to England, where he would meet his martyrdom on the gallows, hanged as a traitor at Tyburn on December 1, 1581.[22]

Campion's influence in Bohemia continued after his death. His famous work *Rationes decem,* was translated into Czech by Jesuit Ondřej Modestin, rector of the College of St. Clement, and appeared in two editions in 1601 and 1602.[23] Campion had written this treatise in England before his arrest as a challenge to Protestant beliefs, and it was printed secretly in London, although it bore the imprint of Douay. In his book, Campion had no incentive to favor Hus over the Protestant reformers. His task was seen as an undoing of the damage caused to Christendom and Bohemia by Hus's alleged mentor, John Wyclif, as he had been reminded by Brus, as well as by the Jesuit General who had sent him to study in Prague in order to make reparations "remembering that John Wicklif[,] an Englishman[,] was the first instrument of the devil to infest in times past that noble kingdom with his pestilent heresies."[24]

Campion returned to the 1518–1521 view of the Roman Curia, voiced by Eck and Aleandro, and linking Hus organically with the Protestant Reformation. He argued that the spiritual ancestry of Luther, Zwingli, and Calvin was to be sought in Hus and Wyclif. Thus, Hus's credentials were not qualitatively different from those of earlier heretics, such as Aerius, Iovian, Vigilantius, Heldvidius, the Iconoclasts, Berangarius, Valdensians, and Lorhard, from whom Luther, Zwingli, and Calvin also "borrowed or begged certain poisonous parts of their own heretical teachings."[25] As for Hus's trial at

Constance, Campion addressed particularly the issue of the letter of safe conduct (*glejt*) because sixteenth-century Lutherans had cited its violation as a reason to stay away from the Council of Trent. According to Campion, Hus was not protected by a safe-conduct pass from the Council of Constance, but rather one from the Emperor. The Czech violated the conditions of the imperial document by his disregard for the authority of the Council by seeking to discredit it and rejecting its offer of clemency. In any case, the Church was more than the emperor and had the power to cancel his promise. As the bottom line, "the arch-heretic did not allow himself to be corrected, hence was justly burnt." For good measure, Campion also addressed the case of Jerome of Prague, Hus's fellow martyr at Constance. He came to the Council without any *glejt;* first he abjured his heresy, then again apostatized, and hence properly died at the stake.[26] Campion's impending martyrdom perhaps took some of the edge off his hearty endorsement of the gory proceedings at Constance.

Hus and Utraquism as Lesser Evils

Although a more frigid atmosphere began to prevail, Bohemian writers, who worked under the aegis of the Roman Curia, were still making some allowances for Hus and Utraquism in the last quarter of the sixteenth century. The main thrust of their critical zeal was aimed at the Unity of Brethren, and to a lesser extent at the Lutherans. The direct Roman attacks on Utraquism were left to foreign theologians, such as Campion or Wujek z Wągrowca. Translations of their works apparently evaded, rather than violated, the letter of the Bohemian law against the vilification of the *sub utraque* by the sub una, as embodied in the Compactata and the Peace of Kutná Hora.

The focus on the Brethren seemed to be conditioned by two considerations: sowing discord among the opponents, and the Brethren's relative vulnerability. In part, the aim was to alienate the Utraquists from their more radical allies, the Brethren and the Lutherans, and thus to weaken the cohesion of those who dissented from the Roman Curia. This might have paved the way to the elimination of religious dissidents in a sequential way in a process known to modern political scientists as "salami tactics." This process was favored by members of the Curia.[27] Such an approach also represented an extension of the tactics pursued by Roman polemicists such as Fabri and Cochlaeus earlier in the century. From another angle, unfriendly critiques of the Brethren were less hazardous than theological attacks against the Utraquists. In contrast to the Utraquists, whom Bohemia's constitutional law unequivocally protected against vituperation by the sub una, the legal protection of the Unity and of the Lutherans was more precarious, resting as it did, not on explicit edicts, but merely on the gentlemen's agreement of 1575 between Maximilian II and the Bohemian estates. Moreover, the Brethren became still more vulnerable because of the mandates against the "Pikarts," which Rudolf II issued in 1584 and in 1602. Although these edicts did not directly endanger the Brethren's survival, their existence made attacking the Unity less risky.[28]

Stressing the relative orthodoxy of Hus and Utraquism in contrast to the teaching of the Unity of Brethren was characteristic of the writings of Václav Šturm and Václav Brož. Their approach in a paradoxical way paralleled the earlier critique of the Brethren by the Utraquists. Thus, Šturm and Brož echoed the Utraquist theologians, such as Pavel Bydžovský in the 1540s, in excoriating the Brethren on account of their disbelief in the real presence. While the Utraquists compared the Brethren unfavorably with Luther, Šturm and Brož compared them unfavorably with Hus. Yet, Bydžovský did not mean to endorse Luther, any more than Šturm or Brož meant to endorse Hus. From the opposite point of view, both sides sought to disassociate the Brethren's origins from Hus and the Bohemian Reformation. The claims of Šturm and Brož that the Brethren stood outside the indigenous Bohemian Reformation, and actually derived their teaching from non-Bohemian sectarians, such as the Waldensians or Picardi, again echoed the earlier reproaches of mainline Utraquists, such as Bílejovský and Bydžovský.[29]

Šturm (1533–1601) earned the reputation as the foremost expert on the Brethren's theology among the Bohemian Jesuits. He also held the distinction as one of the very first Czech-speaking Jesuits, having been sent to Rome in 1555 with eleven other Bohemian youngsters to be welcomed into the order by Ignatius Loyola himself. His long stay in Olomouc facilitated his research into the Brethren's theology inasmuch as the Unity was particularly well represented in Moravia. His main polemical works were *Srovnání víry a učení bratří starších* (The Arrangement of the Faith and Teaching of the Brethren's Elders) (1582), *Krátké ozvání... proti kratičkému ohlášení Jednoty* (A Brief Response... to the Short Declaration of the Unity) (1584), and *Rozsouzení a bedlivé uvážení Velikého kancionálu* (A Study and a Careful Assessment of the Great Hymnal) (1588).[30]

Šturm had established a point of agreement with the Utraquists in the spring of 1575 over the Bohemian Confession. His critical assessment of the document, which he prepared together with his Jesuit colleague Baltazar Hostovský, pointed out its inspiration in the Augsburg Confession, and was acceptable not only to the party sub una, but also to the Utraquist Consistory.[31] The partial agreement, of course did not signify a coincidence of theological views between Šturm and the Utraquists. The Jesuit author regarded the seminal figures of the Bohemian Reformation, such as Hus or Rokycana, as far from blameless. In his *Srovnání víry a učení bratří,* Šturm classified Hus among those who could not have been inspired by the Holy Ghost. The Holy Spirit had only one voice, while the spirit of error spoke with many, often contradictory, voices: "And thus Arius once spoke with one spirit, Macedonius with another, Wyclif with another, Master Jan Hus with another, the Taborites with another, the Lutherans with another, the Zwinglians with another, your Brethren with another, and so each and every one has a different novelty, a different sect, a different priesthood, a different congregation, and none agrees with another."[32]

Nevertheless, on the whole, Šturm's polemics were not directed against the Utraquists, but focused on the Brethren. In fact, he relied on comparisons with Hus and the Utraquists to underscore the unorthodoxy of the Unity. The Brethren, for him, were breakers of Christian community to the second degree, having themselves seceded from schismatics. Along the way, Šturm inventoried the areas in which Hus's teaching was more orthodox than the Brethren's. In particular, he lauded Hus's insistence on canonical priesthood and the use of special vestments for the Lord's Supper, both of which Hus upheld and the Brethren rejected. Šturm also emphasized that Hus taught transubstantiation, while the Brethren accepted remanence. In that connection, the Jesuit invoked Jan of Příbram's defense of Hus against Peter Payne's claim that Hus fully agreed with Wyclif's Eucharistic teaching. He also contrasted the Brethren's secretiveness about their theology with Hus's openness. Hus's views could be documented by his own works, published both in Bohemia and elsewhere in Europe. Like the Utraquist theologians Bílejovský and Bydžovský before him, Šturm brought his critique to a crescendo with the charges that the Brethren wrongly claimed to be the heirs of either Hus or the Bohemian Reformation. In light of their disagreements with his teachings, the Brethren viewed Hus not as a precursor, but as an adversary. In fact, for them, Hus was no less an Antichrist than were the followers of the Holy See.[33] Šturm claimed support for this extraordinary allegation in that the Brethren's Confession of 1574 condemned both the adherents to Rome and the Utraquists—the former for their alleged idolatry, and the latter for their practice of infant communion.³⁴ Like Bydžovský before him, Šturm pointed out repeatedly that even Luther surpassed the Brethren in relative orthodoxy, and cited the Unity's theological disagreements with the German reformer, as well as with the prominent Matthias Flacius Illyricus, particularly on the issue of real presence.³⁵

Šturm's contemporary, Václav Brož, likewise a priest sub una, although not a Jesuit, also directed his polemical works primarily against the Brethren, stressing the theological differences between them and Hus.³⁶ He served as dean in Litomyšl in the 1580s, and after 1591 he held the same office in Jindřichův Hradec, where he died in 1601.³⁷ In his most significant work, *Vejstraha všem věrným Čechům* (A Warning to All Faithful Czechs) (1589), Brož focused on the orthodox character of Hus's Eucharistic views. Not relying simply on Šturm's characterizations of Hus's teaching, he went *ad fontes* and drew directly on the latter's Latin works, published in Nuremberg in 1558 by Jan Montán and Voldřich Neyber.³⁸ His treatise juxtaposed in stark contrasts Hus's orthodoxy with the errors of the Unity concerning the nature of the Eucharist, its adoration, and its consecration.³⁹ To document the Unity's side of the issue, particularly the denial of real presence and the rejection of Eucharistic adoration, he analyzed the Unity's Confession of 1561, its Letter to the Elector of Brandenburg of 1532, and particularly the texts of hymnals published in 1564 and 1581.⁴⁰ Brož held Lukáš of Prague and Jan Augusta primarily responsible for what he considered the Unity's theological aberrations.⁴¹ In conclusion, Brož, citing a statement by Jan Augusta of 1548, argued that the Brethren condemned not only those receiving communion sub una, but also the Utraquists, because of their common belief in the real presence.⁴²

In addition, Brož devoted two other treatises to the nature of lay communion. In *O Přijímání Svátosti Těla a Krve Páně* (On the Reception of the Lord's Body and Blood) (1598), in an apparent concession to the Utraquist position, he argued that both forms of lay communion, under one or two species, were theologically defensible. While he favored communion sub una, he did not reject sub utraque.⁴³ What he considered not only erroneous, but also pernicious, was the teaching that communion sub utraque was necessary for salvation, which implied a categorical rejection of communion sub una. Brož claimed that this one-sided position had led to schisms among churches, priests, and believers.⁴⁴ He also sought to contrast the orthodox Utraquist view of the real presence with the view of the Lutherans, which he—wrongly—characterized as admitting merely a spiritual presence in the Eucharist.⁴⁵

Brož's effort to balance delicately between the lay communion sub una and sub utraque provoked an anonymous polemicist to challenge his views, and he defended himself in another treatise, *Ohlášení se proti Pithartskému Netopýři* (A Remonstration Against a Pithart Bat) (1598). Škarka and Kalina have independently suggested that Brož's challenger was the writer and printer Sixt Palma Močidlanský, who in his recently published book, *Svědectví starých svatých otců* (The Witness of Ancient Holy Fathers) (1598), argued that in ancient times, the Church had in fact insisted on communion sub utraque.[46] If not a Utraquist, Palma was apparently a Lutheran. Škarka's assertion that he must have been a member of an obscure sect of Mikulášenci (Nicolaitans) seems mistaken.[47] The anonymous critic, first of all, questioned Brož's assertion about the ancient origin of the lay communion sub una, and he forced Brož to admit that it was only the recent councils of Constance, Basel, and Trent that had declared communion sub una legitimate rather than the first four ecumenical councils of Nicea, Constantinople, Ephesus, and Chalcedon.[48] Having made this damaging concession, Brož nevertheless argued that Christ himself had clearly declared communion sub una sufficient; hence, it was not a recent invention of the Roman Curia. Moreover, the underlying principle of Christ's full presence under either of the species had been admitted by all serious Christian theologians, including "the foremost teachers of the Augsburg Confession."[49] In his second major sally, the opponent taunted Brož for inconsistency, since he clearly preferred communion sub una, and yet he did not reject communion sub utraque.[50] Brož replied nonchalantly that communion sub utraque had a basis in Christ and in the Gospels, just like sub una, and there was no reason why the two modes could not coexist. His critic lacked the necessary subtlety of mind to weigh properly the relationship between the two.[51] Finally, Brož replayed the leitmotiv of sowing discord among the Roman Curia's opponents. He emphasized again that—despite the sub utraque issue—the classical Utraquist theologians, such as Hus, Jakoubek, and Rokycana, had held the correct teaching about the real presence, which the Brethren, and even the Lutherans, lacked.[52]

The Illusion of "Old Utraquism"

In contrast to the earlier willingness to make allowances for the Utraquist position, the Roman attitudes became more condemnatory at the threshold of the seventeenth century, virtually removing the possibility of a practicable modus vivendi between Tridentine Rome and Utraquist Prague. While earlier expressions of the harsh Roman view toward Utraquism had been left by and large to foreigners, writers sub una became sterner in their intransigence within Bohemia at the turn of the century. The tenor of their polemics reflected this change. First, the range of what was acceptable to Rome shrank to temporary toleration of lay chalice. Second, the whole area of concession to liberal ecclesiology (in a way the most important aspect of the Utraquist position) became foreclosed and non-negotiable. As a bottom line, acceptable Utraquism became restricted to an imaginary "Old Utraquism," satisfied with nothing more than a highly qualified and circumscribed lay communion in both kinds. This definitional restriction, in turn, could pave the way to a complete proscription and annihilation of Utraquism, inasmuch as against this mythical standard the actually existing mainline Utraquism was guaranteed to appear deviant. The latter could then be condemned by the Roman Curia without obviously violating the previous recognition of the legitimacy of Utraquism, such as in the Compactata, or without making the Habsburg monarchs guilty of contravening the oaths of their ancestors to uphold Utraquism.[53]

Looking at the deterioration from the Utraquist point of view, the Tridentine settlement moved Roman ecclesiology in exactly the wrong direction, toward a greater institutional and disciplinary rigidity. The introduction of the Index of Prohibited Books and the moves to reinvigorate the Inquisition aimed at intellectual conformity and drastic use of authority.[54] The emphasis on a virtually automatic obedience clashed with the spirit of questioning embedded in Utraquism at least since the negotiations for the Compactata at the Council of Basel and summed up in the principles of the Judge of Cheb. Another profound difference in ecclesiology was the continuing Utraquist opposition (deriving ultimately from Wyclif) against worldly domination by clergy, which condemned the use of secular power and the accumulation of material wealth by the Church. Here again the Counter-Reformation was moving in the opposite direction with its affirmation of ecclesiastical authoritarianism and baroque ostentatiousness in rituals and architecture. The impact of this authoritarian and triumphalist resurgence necessarily overshadowed the Council of Trent's attempt to check certain flagrant clerical abuses, which the Bohemian Reformation had denounced, such as simony, plural holding of benefices, and nepotism, as well as reforms in the issuing of indulgences.[55] The baroque spirit itself, which the Counter-Reformation embraced, with its emotionalism and quasi-mysticism,[56] ran counter to customary Utraquist sobriety and realism. The flamboyant veneration of saints and images, as well as monastic and other forms of asceticism, rubbed against the grain of Bohemian religious practice.

Latter-day polemics on behalf of Rome focused on two targets: on deprecating lay communion sub utraque and on attacking Jan Hus as a heretic. Modestin (1558–1602), rector of the Jesuit College of St. Clement in Prague, may serve as a notable example. As a speaker of a Slavic tongue, he had participated in the entourage of Antonio Possevino in the peace negotiations between Stephen Bathory and Ivan the Terrible in 1581, at which time he addressed the tsar and the boyars several times in Moscow.[57] As a translator and editor, he helped to communicate Rome's critical views of Utraquism to the Bohemian public. His translations included the previously mentioned homiliary of Wujek z Wągrowca (1592) and, more importantly, Campion's *Decem rationes* (1601).[58] His own contribution to the literary assault on Utraquism, which is of primary interest here, was in the preface to the first Czech edition of Campion's polemical work.[59] Denying orthodoxy to pre-Reformation Utraquism, Modestin asserted that prior to Luther's appearance, Bohemia stood out in Western Christendom as an exceptional country that had not shared the faith of the Latin Church.[60] He ridiculed the Utraquist interpretation of Christ's command at the Last Supper "You all drink from it [i.e., the chalice]," as mandating communion under the species of wine for laypeople. According to Modestin, the expression "all" could not be taken literally; otherwise, the chalice would have to be given to the Turks, Jews, pagans, children, and even to the insane, since all of them are counted as people.[61] Ironically, there is a distinct similarity between Modestin's argument against the lay chalice and that of the Lutherans, like Taciturnus, against the Utraquists' communion for infants.[62]

A particularly prominent Bohemian participant in the overtly anti-Utraquist campaign on the Roman side was Petr Linteo of Pilsenburgk, a priest in Litomyšl, and an alumnus of the Jesuit College of St. Clement in Prague. He got an early start in 1593 with a book titled *Jistá a patrná církve svaté znamení* (Certain and Distinct Signs of the Holy Church). His polemical thrust aimed first of all at discrediting the stature of Jan Hus. According to Linteo, Hus could not be a saint because he had not performed any miracles, nor had the final fire spared him—unlike the true saints who experienced fire without burning, such as Sts. Agnes and Juliana, or the three youngsters cast in the fiery furnace of Babylon (Daniel 3:24).[63] Similarly, Hus's followers and disciples were unable to perform true miracles, only seeming ones. Linteo discredited the cures and other marvelous signs allegedly attached to a site near Nymburk where the Taborites had executed a Utraquist priest in 1425. According to Linteo, the priest betrayed the Church by condoning the communion in both kinds, and could be credited only with pseudo-miracles that would be unmasked as such on the Last Judgment Day.[64] Likewise, Luther, Calvin, or their followers could not perform miracles, although they tried or pretended to do so.[65] In one respect, Linteo did admit Hus's superiority over Luther and Calvin: The Bohemian respected the authority of patristic literature, which the others debunked.[66] Nevertheless, Hus—not the Council—was responsible for his death because of his own disobedience. The clinching argument of Hus's perversity for Linteo was his alleged desire that he wished that his soul might rest after death in the same place as Wyclif's.[67]

In the same book, Linteo aimed his second principal sally at the lay communion in both kinds. In effect, he asserted that the lay chalice was illegitimate, except in the most unusual circumstances, and then only on the basis of a specific temporary papal dispensation.[68] Turning against the Utraquist view that the communion sub utraque was mandated by Christ and necessary to salvation, Linteo resorted to a pragmatic argument that God was too merciful to let some be damned because of the manner of communion. He bolstered his position against the lay chalice by rather mundane arguments, including that some communicants in delicate health might be injured by drinking or just smelling wine, and that in some regions importing wine was prohibitively expensive or climatic conditions caused wine to turn rapidly to vinegar. Linteo—perhaps with a touch of sarcasm—commended the view that had Christ intended obligatory communion in two kinds, he would have—in his mercy—substituted water for wine in view of the precarious status of the latter.[69] Linteo also rejected the historical argument that from its Christianization to the reign of Charles IV, communion sub utraque was common in Bohemia, as maintained by Utraquist theologians, in particular Bohuslav Bílejovský.[70] His stand was that in Bohemia communion sub utraque had never existed before 1414. When Jakoubek introduced the lay chalice, it was an innovation, not a restoration.[71]

In his treatise, Linteo also paid attention to other Bohemian dissidents from Rome, the Brethren and the Lutherans. Improbably, he suggested an early link of the Brethren in the 1420s with the notorious Adamites, a sect described by Howard Kaminsky as endorsing "ritual nudism and sexual emancipation."[72] Luther's cardinal fault was, according to Linteo, his limitless pride when he claimed to be a prophet of the Gospel, whose understanding was superior to all previous Christian theologians.[73] He repeated the standard charge that solafideism led to condoning immorality. In this connection, he relished Luther's alleged suggestion that unsatisfactory physical relations with a spouse justified a man's turning to a prostitute.[74] Unlike Šturm or Brož, however, Linteo no longer structured the critique of the Brethren and the Lutherans with the Utraquists in mind in order to show Utraquism in a more favorable light, or as a lesser evil, than the Unity or German Protestantism. Ultimately, Hus, Luther, and Calvin were all equally guilty of errors in his eyes. Reversing the stance of Šturm and Brož (which, in that respect, coincided with mainline Utraquist theologians), Linteo maintained that far from being Hus's opponents, the Brethren, as well as the Taborites, were in fact Hus's followers or spiritual offspring.[75] Such a frontal attack on Hus, and by implication on Utraquism, of course, represented a clear contravention of Bohemian law, and a possible explanation for the book's appearance is its publication in the obscurity of the provincial town of Litomyšl.[76] Nevertheless, Linteo would eventually become the object of brutal retribution in 1611 for his brash violation of the social peace mandated at Kutná Hora in 1485.[77]

Let us sum up the polemics of the sub una theologians with the Utraquists. To the extent that there was an interest in reconciliation in the mid-sixteenth century, the Roman approach was flawed by a fundamental dichotomy. While conceding a large measure of orthodoxy to Utraquist theology, it clung to the charge of heresy against Jan Hus, the revered martyr/saint of the Utraquist Church. This contradiction continued to vitiate any realistic attempts at a rapprochement until the denouement of 1621. Moreover, since the late sixteenth century, within the Tridentine spirit, the Curia, and both foreign and Bohemian theologians speaking on Rome's behalf, foreclosed the possibility of a realistic settlement by reducing tolerance for any Utraquist peculiarities virtually to zero, admitting at most a temporary permission of lay communion sub utraque. This solution, of course, missed the point. The key issue in the Utraquist stance was not the rite as such, but the underlying opposition to an authoritarian ecclesiology, namely the power of the ecclesiastical authorities to declare sinful something that did not oppose divine law, but actually may have been in accordance with the law of God. The image of the minimalist "Old Utraquists" who would be satisfied with the concession offered was nothing but a red herring. In fact, the Old Utraquists did not exist, and the Roman Curia was not interested in promoting the communion sub utraque in Bohemia, even as sanctioned by the papal decree of 1564. In any case, the Jesuits, after offering it briefly in Prague, soon discontinued the option. This created the impression in Bohemia that the papal concession had been abrogated.[78]

Catholicism with Liberal Ecclesiology

Let us now review the entire complex of the continuing awkward and unresolved ties between Utraquism and the Roman Curia with a focus again on the period between 1575 and 1609. The meaning of the relationship will be examined from the viewpoint of both participants. On the side of the Utraquist Church the most conspicuous aspects were the ordination of clergy by bishops in communion with the Holy See, and an insistence on belonging to the Roman Catholic Church. For both of these principles, the Utraquists have been sternly criticized, particularly by Czech historiography. The standard historical literature has usually viewed the umbilical cord of canonical priesthood that tied the Utraquists to the Roman Church, as an obstructing, and even shameful, liability.[79] The conventional historical literature also viewed the Utraquist insistence on maintaining their conceptual adherence to the Roman Catholic Church as a rather demeaning enterprise. Josef Pekař, for instance, depicted the Utraquists as standing at the Curia's door like humble petitioners asking to be tolerated, or like beggars imploring the authorities for their indulgence.[80] From the viewpoint of the Roman Curia, the Utraquists could supply a mode of reform or renewal that was an alternative to that adopted at the Council of Trent. This liberal, yet non-Protestant, model was in harmony with the ideals of other reformers who upheld the traditional orthodoxy. In addition, it had a special distinction in that it had existed as a functioning ecclesiastical community for almost two hundred years.

Contrary to conventional historiography, the Utraquists' insistence on forming an integral part of the Roman Catholic Church may be viewed as a mark of empowerment rather than a liability.[81] While in the short run this linkage might have presented a dilemma, for the long run the claim to Roman Catholic identity signaled the transcendent scope of Utraquism's historical mission. It gave the Church in Bohemia a standing, or an inside track, in seeking to reform the largest body in Western Christendom from within, instead of attacking it from the outside. Unlike (the otherwise kindred) Church of England, which had for all practical purposes retreated into national isolation, the Utraquist Church of Bohemia clung to its universal mission of which the sacerdotal link with the Roman Church was a concrete practical sign. Lapsing into Hegelian terminology, it could be said that staying within the Roman Church (and serving as its Socratic gadfly) endowed Utraquism with a world-historical role, which would be lost if it had remained an isolated provincial movement, or if it had simply merged with the Protestant mainstream. It can also be argued that remaining attached to the Roman Church—rather than turning Protestant—served a potentially useful function in the cosmic division of labor. After all, Rome was more in need of a liberal leavening than the reformed churches were, and the Utraquists thus did not engage in the proverbial carrying of coal to Newcastle.

Contrary to conventional historiography, the Utraquists did not approach Rome as humble beggars. From their own point of view, the heirs of Hus adopted the self-confident stance of the prophets of righteousness, whom God had commissioned to exhort the Roman Curia to recognize its failings and make amends. They did not plead with the Roman Church to admit them; rather they challenged the latter to listen and respond constructively to what they considered a divinely sanctioned critique.[82] In their witness, the Utraquists saw themselves as a voice of conscience on behalf of the entirety of Western Christendom, representing a constant reproach to Rome for its errant ways. The issue was not whether Rome was willing to readmit the Utraquists, but whether the Roman Church was willing to reform according to Utraquist ecclesiological prescriptions. Looking at the relationship in another way, the Utraquists did not accept that they were in schism from the true Christian Church, but rather that the schism was on the part of the Roman Church, which had repudiated the Compactata in 1462.[83] They did not feel the need to be authenticated by Rome, but that Rome needed to be authenticated by them. Rome had not rehabilitated them by its approval of the Compactata, but by adopting the latter the Church of Rome might start rehabilitating itself. As mentioned earlier, the Utraquists thought of themselves as exemplary Roman Catholics, and readily called themselves a part of the "Catholic Church" (Církev Katolická).[84]

Even if, from the viewpoint of the realpolitik—their mutual power relations—the confrontation with Rome by the Utraquists perhaps did not make much sense, it was significant as a clash of ideas. Utraquism offered to the Church of Rome an alternate model of non-Protestant reform to that which the latter embraced at the Council of Trent. It was a service that an outright Protestant movement could not provide, and indeed would not have cared to undertake, because of the Protestants' rejection of the Church as it had developed during the first millennium with the principle of historic apostolic succession and its adherence to canon law. From the beginning, the Utraquists drew support for their audacity from sacred history, the precedent of the chosen people of Israel struggling for God against discouraging odds.[85] The Utraquist stand in the sixteenth and early seventeenth centuries required a considerable degree of moral courage, inasmuch as they resisted the leadership of the Church, which they recognized as the necessary historic center of Western Christendom, and of which they themselves were a part. It was in a sense a nonviolent extension of the war that their ancestors had fought against the imperial and papal crusaders in the early years of the Bohemian Reformation. It was also a continuing and continuous reprise of the predicament that Jan Hus had experienced in a personal and more painful way at Constance, that is, the dilemma between moral conviction and established authority. Historical literature by and large has missed the inspirational side of the Utraquists' role as champions of renewal in the Roman Church. Instead, subsequent historiography seemed to be drawn to the seamy side of their relations with the Holy See, filled with a variety of deceptions and misleading moves, such as the maneuvers around Administrator Rezek's apostasy in 1592–1593.[86]

Contrary to conventional historiography, the Utraquists' stand was neither idiosyncratic nor quixotic. The Utraquists were not unique or alone in casting a jaundiced eye from the vantage point of traditional orthodoxy at the model of church renewal taking shape at the Council of Trent (1545–1563), and in this respect may be viewed as participants, albeit distinctive ones, in a more general phenomenon, sometimes called humanist Catholicism. Unlike the proponents of anathemas and exclusions, who prevailed at Trent, these reformers were advocates of dialogue and liberal moderation as a path to renewal.[87] Let us now situate the Utraquists within the landscape of these anti-Tridentine reformist trends within sixteenth-century Roman Catholicism.

To some extent, the Utraquist stance paralleled the reforms proposed by Witzel, and also endorsed by Ferdinand I.[88] Witzel, an ordained priest, married and served as Lutheran minister in Saxony in the 1520s. After the adoption of the Augsburg Confession in 1530, he rejoined the Roman Church as a married lay preacher, and lived mainly in Dresden, Berlin, and Mainz. His proposed remaking of the Roman Church resembled the goals of the Bohemian Reformation, including a liberal ecclesiology (based on patristics and eschewing scholastic formulae), lay communion sub utraque, vernacular liturgy, and de-emphasis on the veneration of saints.[89] After visiting Bohemia in the early 1540s, Witzel gained the favor of Ferdinand I, and subsequently of his son and successor, Maximilian II. Another figure in Germany seeking to mediate between Rome and the Lutherans was Hermann von Wied, archbishop of Cologne, who was also in touch with Archbishop Thomas Cranmer in England in the mid-1540s. The Curia, however, removed him from office in 1546.[90]

More surprisingly, the Utraquist prescription was likewise akin to the liberal or populist ecclesiology of Thomas More, who—according to Brendan Bradshaw—also opposed "the institutionally oriented ecclesiology of late medieval clericalism," which would triumph at Trent.[91] Paradoxically—in view of subsequent developments—in his comments on Henry VIII's critique of Luther, *Assertio septem sacramentorum* (1521), More cautioned his sovereign to be less emphatic in stressing papal primacy.[92] Specifically, he did not consider the pope superior to the general council.[93] The views of More, and also his fellow martyr John Fisher, were under the influence of the liberal ecclesiology of Erasmus,[94] and they both belonged to the circle of his correspondents, usually called the Erasmians. More and Fisher likewise shared Erasmus's interest in Greek patristics, as well as the ecclesiological ambiance of the first millennium, and defended his translation of the New Testament from Greek.[95] The deep admiration for the Greek fathers on the part of Erasmus and his circle was coupled with distinct reservations toward medieval scholastics and their ecclesiology.[96] Erasmus himself inveighed against "certain monks and theologians, who under the guise of religion established a tyrannical empire for themselves, and whose aim it was to prey upon men's souls and property alike."[97] His aversion to papal monarchism involved him in a qualified sympathy with Luther's views, and his clear-cut break with the German reformer was delayed until 1524. Even afterwards Erasmus was highly critical of the Curia establishment, which he considered corrupt and in part unchristian.[98] He also seemed rather indifferent to the restrictions or even suppression of monastic communities.[99] He continued to be attacked on the Roman side by Belgian, Spanish, and French theologians, who were particularly concerned with his reformist views on mandatory fasting, private confession, and clerical celibacy.[100] In their overall attitudes, Erasmus and the Erasmians stood close to Utraquist viewpoints. Likewise, the combination of humanism and theology that Erasmus advocated was characteristic of Utraquism.[101]

To the company of liberalization's later advocates may be added the group of the Italian *spirituali,* including Cardinal Gasparo Contarini and the poetess Vittoria Colonna, who hoped for a reform of the institutional church. Improbable as it might seem in view of the bloody image of the failed Marian Counter-Reformation in England, the spirituali grouped around Cardinal Reginald Pole during his exile in Italy.[102] The cardinal himself is said to have adhered to a Catholic humanism, seeing much that was correct in Luther's theory of salvation. He belonged among Erasmus's correspondents. Had he not missed the papal election by a single vote in 1549, the Council of Trent might have exuded more the spirit of Vatican II than that of Vatican I.[103] It is probably characteristic of his stance that he declined the Jesuits' help during the brief campaign (1553–1558) to restore the sway of the Roman Church in his homeland, despite (or perhaps because of?) his acquaintance with Loyola in Rome.[104] Among Pole's protégés in Italy was also the Hungarian bishop of Croatian origin, Andreas Dudič (Dudith) (1533–1589), successively bishop of Knin, Csanád (1562), and Pécs (1563), who accompanied the English cardinal as his secretary to England in 1553–1554 and subsequently in 1562–1563 tried to promote a liberal line at the Council of Trent on behalf of Emperors Ferdinand I and Maximilian II, including toleration of the lay chalice and clerical marriages.[105] In a way, Ferdinand I and particularly Maximilian II served as protectors of this liberal camp by surrounding themselves with the likes of Fabri, Nausea, Wiltzel, and Dudič.[106] There was also a group of Erasmus's followers in France, recently called "critical Catholics," who aside from rejecting the authoritarian ecclesiology of the Roman Curia, devised under the leadership of Bishop of Valence, Jean de Monluc, in 1557–1561 Utraquist-like reforms of the liturgy, including lay communion in both kinds and use of the vernacular in the mass. All these were suppressed by Council of Trent's decrees and regulations for their implementation by Pope Pius V.[107] Among later Catholic reformers in the second decade of the seventeenth century, the erratic Marco Antonio De Dominis, archbishop of the Croatian Split, sought to purge the Western Church of papal monarchism and restore it to episcopal collegiality of the first millennium. His critique of papal monarchism appeared in Czech translation in 1619.[108]

Within this welter of liberal, yet loyalist and orthodox, criticism of the Roman Church, the Utraquists represented, above all numerically, the most significant group. Utraquist authors were, in fact, familiar with their liberal counterparts abroad. Utraquist Bohemia showed an active interest in Christian humanism, and virtually fell in love, intellectually speaking, with Erasmus and his reformist ideas of Christian life that were often at odds with current Roman ecclesiology. Three of Erasmus's important works were translated into Czech early in the sixteenth century: *Chvála bláznovství* (Praise of Folly) by 1513, *Enchiridion militis Christiani* in 1519 in translation by Oldřich Velenský of Mnichov, and *Výklad na Otčenáš* (Explanation of the Lord's Prayer) in 1526 by Jan Mantuan and Jan Pekk in Plzeň. In addition, eight more of Erasmus's works were published in Czech translation in Bohemia in 1519–1595, some in several editions.[109] For instance, a translation of Erasmus's paraphrase of St. Matthew's gospel appeared in 1542.[110] A Bohemian humanist, Jan Šlechta of Všehrdy, corresponded with the Dutch sage and invited him to visit Prague in 1519.[111] The latter, in turn, shared Šlechta's information about the Bohemian religious situation with Thomas More.[112] In 1520, another Czech correspondent, the nobleman Arkleb of Boskovice, assured Erasmus of the popularity of his writings and the great weight his opinions carried in the country. Significantly, he supplied the Dutchman with reliable information on the character of the Bohemian Reformation.[113] Other proponents of the Roman Church's renewal were known in Bohemia and could supply support and authentication for the Utraquist *via media*.[114] For instance, in 1554, Pavel Bydžovský, the outstanding Utraquist theologian of his day, published a treatise in which he praised Witzel and exhorted any Evangelicals or Lutherans (*Euangelicastros, intelligo Luteranos*) who might be in Bohemia to listen to Witzel's voice.[115] In the same pamphlet, Bydžovský included eulogies of Thomas More and Bishop John Fisher as exemplary Christian martyrs. The Utraquist translator of Robert Barnes's *Vitae Romanorum Pontificum* (Basel, 1535), and Bydžovský's contemporary, Šimon Ennius Klatovský, was likewise familiar with Witzel's irenic position. In addition, he expressed an admiration for More.[116] The fact that More and Fisher wished to drastically diminish the papacy, yet not to see it disappear, as they demonstrated most dramatically, pointed to their kinship with the Utraquists. The latter voiced their grievance vis-à-vis the papacy even more emphatically and sharply, yet when it came to the question of its very existence, they found the office indispensable.[117]

Aside from those proponents of Roman renewal whose ideas paralleled the Utraquist ecclesiology and/or had tangential contacts with the Utraquists, there were those for whom the experience with Utraquism provided a practicable model for Rome's accommodation with the German Reformation. Particularly notable among such figures was once more Erasmus and his close Italian friend, Cardinal Jacopo Sadoleto.[118] The latter, although more cautious, was willing like Erasmus to sidetrack the scholastics and appeal directly to biblical and patristic authority on issues of ecclesiology. The cardinal had "an inveterate contempt for the scholastics and a clear preference for the Greek fathers, Chrysostom in particular..."[119] He would in turn participate after 1535 in the commission on church reform headed by Cardinal Contarini, another Erasmian who endeavored to find a modus vivendi with the Lutheran challenge, particularly at the Diet of Regensburg in 1541, offering the last chance of an amicable settlement between Rome and Wittenberg.[120]

Erasmus himself saw in Rome's replicating vis-à-vis Lutheranism the approach that it had earlier adopted toward Utraquism as a way of averting a disastrous confrontation with Luther's reform movement. In his eyes, the Compactata in particular could serve as a basis for Rome's response to the issues raised by the Reformation in Germany and in Switzerland.[121] With much interest he followed renewed Roman negotiations with the Utraquists at Buda in the spring of 1525, which were conducted by his good friend Cardinal Lorenzo Campeggi (1472–1539) as a papal legate. The Curia then hoped that a settlement with the Utraquists might offset Luther's defection in Germany by regaining Bohemia. Moreover, Campeggi and his entourage expected that eventually the Erasmian formula of a nonconfrontational approach might succeed in appeasing the dissent in Germany. This might happen if religious passions were allowed to subside through benign neglect rather than being aggravated by Rome with "excessively violent and elaborate threats."[122] Erasmus was also a good friend of Nausea, whose interests at the Habsburg court he tried to promote through mediation by Campeggi.[123] Erasmus emphasized a "Hussite" solution in his correspondence with Sadoleto in 1530.[124] In other words, Rome's treatment of the Utraquists was to be used as a recipe for damage control. It was to engage in negotiations and compromises, even if temporary, rather than risk a head-on collision.

Erasmus and his circle's views of Utraquism, however, were not just cynical or manipulative. His correspondent Maarten van Dorp had high respect for Jerome of Prague, Hus's fellow martyr at Constance, whom he called wiser than any of the Council fathers.[125] Erasmus himself maintained that the Council executed Hus and Jerome without refuting their ideas;[126] accordingly, he considered the Bohemians schismatics rather than heretics.[127] More seemed to reach the same opinion by the time he wrote *The Letter Against Frith* in 1532.[128] If from no other source than his Bohemian correspondents, Erasmus was in a position to secure reliable information about the character of the mainline Utraquist Church, in particular to distinguish it from the more radical spin-offs of the Bohemian Reformation, in particular the Taborites and the Unity of Brethren.[129] His Roman opponents in turn accused Erasmus of siding with the Utraquists in scaling down papal authority.[130]

In addition to those who saw usefulness in Utraquism in the procedural sense as an aid in finding a modus vivendi instead of a confrontation, others proposed the use of Utraquism in a substantive sense leading to a lesser or a greater degree of "Utraquistization" of the Roman Church. Peter Fraenkel suggests that the discussions preceding the Pacification of Nuremberg of 1531–1532 between the Lutherans and the Roman Church were inspired by, and aimed at, a "Utraquist settlement." In his opinion, it was particularly

Charles V who—with the advice of bishop of Augsburg, Christoph von Stadion—aimed at such a solution, including lay communion sub utraque, vernacular mass, married clergy, and a de-emphasis, if not an outright abolition, of monasticism.[131] What was relevant in the Utraquists' experience was their objection to the medieval popes' tendency to impose on the faithful rules and regulations the Bohemian reformers called "human inventions" (*nálezky lidské*), and which actually may have contradicted biblical injunctions.[132] In Utraquism, this discriminatory skepticism went back all the way to the precursors of Hus, such as Matěj of Janov who designated as "human inventions" (*adinventiones, traditiones hominum*) all that was not in straightforward harmony with the lives, practices, and examples of Christ, the apostles, and the church of the first millennium.[133]

For a time, it seemed that Charles V had successfully persuaded Pope Clement VII to attempt concessions along Utraquist lines. The emperor's ambassador Micer Mai reported on Clement's willingness in 1531 to embrace a more liberal ecclesiology by tolerating practices against church laws that were not against the law God. Cardinals Tomasso Cajetan and Pietro Accolti were commissioned to prepare background papers on the lay chalice, clerical marriages, and dispensation from the numerous laws of the Church (as distinct from the laws of God).[134] Charles V in 1531 continued to promote the Utraquist model in loosening up the obligation of obedience to Church laws that were not directly based on the law of God.[135] Ferdinand I pressed in the same direction even at the time of the Council of Trent.[136] Nevertheless, during the course of the 1530s and 1540s, the Utraquist formula proved inadequate for a settlement between Rome and Wittenberg. As Fraenkel suggested, the Lutherans' differences from Rome were not only ecclesiological, but also dogmatic.[137] The crux of the problem was that the Utraquists rejected only those extra-biblical rules and regulations that were, in their view, contrary to the Scripture, particularly those introduced after the first millennium. For the Lutherans, most of the extra-biblical tradition since apostolic times was suspect, and by and large, to be rejected.

Ultimately, all proponents of Roman renewal who preferred the scriptural theology illuminated by the insight of the Greek fathers were defeated at Trent, which rehabilitated the scholastic doctors and their authoritarian ecclesiology.[138] Instead of embracing the patristic ecclesiological tradition which was populist and communitarian in orientation, Rome decided at the Council of Trent to perpetuate and reaffirm the model of "the late medieval clericalist ecclesiology, molded by the canonists and the scholastics, and preoccupied with the categories of power, authority, and institutional function."[139] The Utraquists, however, differed from the other orthodox opponents of the Trent model in two important respects. First, Utraquism was viewed as a more radical phenomenon than was warranted. Thus, except for Erasmus and Maximilian II, the liberal reformers did not recognize it as an acceptable alternative. As pointed out earlier, the main reasons for this was its association with radical trends (particularly Taboritism) in the early stages of the Bohemian Reformation, and its unshakable commitment to the veneration of Jan Hus. As discussed previously, Hus had been shaped into a heretical icon in the eyes of the Roman Church as a result of events in Constance, and this stature was confirmed on the Reformation side by Luther's initial provocative endorsements of Hus. These reasons seemed effective, despite being specious.[140] Parenthetically, similarly unwarranted linkages of Erasmus with Luther appeared in both the Roman and Protestant literature, but still during Erasmus's lifetime. The difference was that, while Erasmus could object in person, Hus was no longer there to do so.[141] Second, unlike Erasmus, More, Witzel, or De Dominis, who offered their proposals as individuals, the Utraquists had the actual model of an ecclesiastical organization functioning for two centuries. The suggestions of men like Erasmus, More, or Witzel, some of whom incidentally were soft on Utraquism, could be simply ignored by Rome, or even placed on the Index of Prohibited Books.[142] Particularly ironic was the placement of Cochlaeus's *Historiae Hussitarum libri duodecim* (1549) on the Index by Sixtus V (1585–1590).[143] The ultimate solution of the Utraquist problem, however, would require the deconstruction of an entire church.

Universalism and Liberalism

If the Utraquist stance appears as the proverbial case of a megalomaniac tail attempting to wag the dog, in this particular instance—at least for the long run—the tail of Prague proved to be more nearly correct than the dog of Rome. It is at least arguable that, had the Roman Church listened to the strictures of Jan Hus and the Utraquist Church, it would have avoided much grief. Above all, without abandoning any essentials of Christian orthodoxy, it would not be saddled with its closed intellectual system, authoritarian bureaucratism, intolerance, and inquisitorial techniques—features which would be seen by many as distinct liabilities in post-Tridentine times. In fact, the relevance of a more liberal stance would be demonstrated in the late twentieth century by the *aggiornamento*. Within the sixteenth-century context, the attitude of the Bohemian Reformation may be regarded as a compliment to the Roman Church, ultimately acknowledging its centrality for Western Christendom. Utraquism's purpose was not to destroy the papacy, but to save it—albeit in a scaled-down form—by inducing Rome to abandon what the Utraquists viewed as the wayward path of rigorous authoritarianism. To say that the Curia did not appreciate the Utraquists' concern for the well-being of the Roman Church would be, of course, a major understatement. In fact, the Utraquist Church came to represent a well-nigh intolerable nuisance from the viewpoint of Tridentine Rome. It could be neither written off as a heretical institution, nor sidetracked—in view of its universalist pretensions—with an autonomous Uniate-like status (as, for instance, the Ruthenians by the Union of Brest in 1596). Within the sixteenth-century context, the Roman Curia rejected the Utraquist model with its liberal ecclesiology and consensual governance, which offered an un-Protestant model of renewal in line with similarly rejected ideas of humanist Catholicism represented by figures such as Thomas More, Erasmus, and Witzel.

Inasmuch as, by the latter part of the sixteenth century, neither papal pronouncements, nor the polemicists for the Roman Church drew any qualitative distinction between the Utraquists (as a lesser evil) on the one hand, and the Lutherans, Calvinists, and various sectarians on the other, it is hardly surprising that the political leaders of Utraquism came to regard the Roman Curia as the main threat to the continued existence of their religious identity. It can be argued that Rome's intolerance was more menacing for the Utraquists than for their more radical fellow dissidents, the Unity of Brethren and the Lutherans of Bohemia. A Roman Gleichschaltung would deprive the latter two of their physical abode, but would deprive the Utraquists of their distinctive essence. The Lutherans could continue to practice their religion in Brandenburg, Saxony, or Scandinavia, and the Brethren had their places of escape ready abroad, particularly in Poland. The Utraquists had nowhere to go and no alternative to seeing their faith at risk in Bohemia. This sense of danger provided the background for a tightening of the paradoxical alliance between the Utraquists and other religious dissidents in Bohemia. As explained in Chapter 11, by 1609 the largely urban leaders of the Utraquists would be ready to intensify their political cooperation with the largely aristocratic leaders of the Lutherans and the Brethren along the lines foreshadowed by the negotiations for the Bohemian Confession in 1575.

Contrary to assertions in the historical literature, realistic prospects of reconciliation of papal Rome and Utraquist Prague were not promising. The chief stumbling block was the Utraquists' universalism combined with a liberal ecclesiology that rejected the late medieval concept of the papal monarchy. The issue of universalism involved the Utraquists' insistence on forming an integral part of Western Christendom and hence on reforming the Roman Patriarchate in its entirety. Unlike the Anglicans, the Utraquists were not satisfied with the status of a separated national church, nor could they be bought off by Rome's grant of the status of a Uniate-like autocephalous community. In addition, while recognizing the pope as the head of the Western Church, they asked that the papacy accept their ecclesiological point of view, which would require nothing less than a drastic shift from a focus on imperious authority to a focus on pastoral care. The Utraquists opposed the behemoth of bureaucratic control and autocratic enforcement, and called for replacing the command mode of governance by a consensual method.

11

A Cohabitation of Convenience: The Utraquists and the Lutherans under the Letter of Majesty, 1609–1620

An important landmark in the development of Utraquism in the early seventeenth century was the full legalization of the Bohemian Confession, essentially identical with the Augsburg Confession, a step that was accompanied by formal transfer of full control over the hitherto Utraquist Consistory from the king and his officials to the Bohemian Diet, which was dominated by Lutheran nobility. Henceforth, the Consistory would administer not only the Utraquists, but also the other so-called *sub utraque* (*pod obojí*), namely the Lutherans and the Unity of Brethren, also known collectively as the party or the estates sub utraque (*strana* or *stavy pod obojí*). This occurred by decision of King-Emperor Rudolf II, incorporated in the famous Letter of Majesty of July 9, 1609. The events and factors leading to the issuance of this document have been thoroughly explored.[1] The aspect that is unclear, and which is addressed in this chapter, is the impact of the Letter and its aftermath on the state of traditional Bohemian Utraquism.

It has been virtually an article of faith with most historians that the Letter of Majesty meant the immediate and irrevocable doom of the Utraquist Church. Along these lines, Václav Tomek has written: "[T]he Utraquist party, lacking virtually any adherents except for those coerced and those coercing, disappeared [after the events of 1609] almost entirely . . ."[2] Krofta has claimed that after 1609, Utraquist institutions "were washed away entirely by the tide of the new conditions."[3] Zikmund Winter maintained that by 1609 the Utraquists had "almost entirely become [Lutheran] Protestants."[4] Josef Pekař wrote: "The remnants of the Utraquists [the Old Czech Hussites], deprived of their old Consistory, to the extent that they did not accept the Bohemian Confession, embraced an obedience to the Archbishop."[5] Finally,

Borový stated most categorically: "On the basis of Emperor Rudolf II's Letter of Majesty . . . it can be stated that the original Utraquism in the year 1609 became extinct entirely and forever."[6]

The language used in the Letter of Majesty and in its companion document, the Accommodation (*Porovnání*), seemed to support the view of those who regarded the Letter as sounding the death-knell of Utraquism. It implied an adherence to the Bohemian Confession by all those who were not *sub una*. Moreover, the assertions about Utraquism in the several documents of 1609–1618 painted a picture of them that was curiously in harmony with the fictitious images of proper Old Utraquists disseminated by propagandists of the Roman Church. The main such propositions follow: (1) Utraquist priests were ordained by the archbishop after making the Tridentine profession of faith; (2) Utraquist priests owed complete obedience to the archbishop; (3) Utraquist priests who were not administratively under the archbishop fully embraced the Bohemian Confession in 1609 (presumably turning Lutheran); and (4) the Utraquists constituted an insignificant minority in the total population.[7]

The fatal injury to Utraquism seemed also supported by the fact that the last administrator of the purely Utraquist Consistory, Tomáš of Soběslav, serving from January to July 1609, had condemned, speaking also for the Consistory, both the Lutheran Confession of Augsburg and the Confession of the Brethren on February 7, 1609. In response to an inquiry by the Bohemian royal chancery, he reiterated the objections that the Utraquist Consistory had raised against the Bohemian Confession in 1575.[8]

In light of the above, to argue about the continued health and strength of traditional Utraquism may seem like trying to square the circle or trying to prove the impossible. Yet, there is substantial evidence to support this view. What is naturally more important than the rhetoric employed by official documents is the reality allegedly covered by the two documents. In this chapter, I argue that the reality at the grassroots did not correspond with the declarations at the top.

It will be argued that support for the Bohemian Confession in 1609 meant establishing its legitimacy as an umbrella, or perhaps a fig leaf, for religious dissent from the Roman Church, not as a specific confessional creed of all those supporting its legitimization.[9] It meant that the Utraquists and the Brethren entered into a political alliance with the Lutherans for mutual protection against the party sub una, by and large favored by the king and his officials. Inasmuch as the Utraquists, like the Brethren, obviously rejected the theology of the Bohemian Confession, subscribing to the document could be viewed only as acknowledging its function as a symbol of an ecumenical alliance, uniting autonomous religious denominations into what became known as the party sub utraque. Since the Utraquists, like the Brethren, did not embrace the theology of the Bohemian Confession to become Lutherans, its text was not regarded as a compulsory theological norm, but as a definition of the outer theological limits consistent with membership in the party sub utraque. The functional value of the Bohemian Confession was thus comparable to that of the English Blasphemy Act of 1650. While the latter defined the boundary negatively by what was prohibited, the former did so positively by stating what was permissible.[10] As in 1575, so in 1609 the political support for the Bohemian Confession was not evidence of its religious acceptance. Since the early fifteenth century, a parallel situation had existed in the acceptance, and indeed support, by the party sub una of the legal validity of the Compactata without obviously embracing their religious content. Both the recognition of the "unorthodox" Compactata in 1485 by the sub una, and the recognition of the "unorthodox" Bohemian Confession in 1609 by the Utraquists and the Brethren, fit into the framework of the established Bohemian tradition of religious toleration, peace, and harmony.

Utraquism and the Letter of Majesty

The Alliance Tradition

Historically, the political alliance concluded in 1608–1609 of the urban Utraquists with the aristocratic Lutherans and the Brethren may be also be viewed as an extension of the discussions around the Bohemian Confession in 1575. As in 1575, the connection of the Lutherans and the Brethren with the nobility gave them more political power than the largely urban Utraquists could master on their own. Hence, their political weight, and thus their value as political allies, were not commensurable with their numerical strength.[11] Even Hrejsa and Krofta admit that the Utraquists not only existed, but were also able to, and did, rally to the Lutherans and the Brethren in support of the Letter of Majesty during the negotiations in 1608–1609 leading up to its adoption.[12] The process began at the session of the Bohemian Diet in May 1608, when Rudolf II's royal crown of Bohemia was jeopardized by the armed pressure of his brother Matthias. The legislative initiative emerged as a series of articles prepared by Václav Budovec of Budov, which were eventually embodied in the Letter of Majesty, reluctantly signed by Rudolf on July 9, 1609.[13]

The apprehensions of the urban representatives of Utraquism provided the answer to the puzzle of why they had agreed to support the legalization of the Bohemian Confession. According to a contemporary account, in May 1608 the barons and knights sub una approached those in the Diet administered by the existing Consistory and its priesthood, and urged them to break the alliance with the other estates sub utraque inasmuch as their own faith sharply differed from both the Augsburg and the Brethren's confessions. According to the Roman emissaries, if the Utraquists abandoned their heterodox allies, the emperor was ready to reward them with special protection of their religion, grants of high public offices, and other signs of favor. However, the Utraquists refused to revoke their consent to the legalization of the Bohemian Confession, arguing that the alliance with their heterodox confederates was essential for their own self-preservation. The Utraquists' conviction was that suppression of the Lutherans and the Brethren would be followed by disaster for themselves: "If the priests not ordained by bishops [i.e., Lutheran] and the Brethren's clergy were banished, then almost certainly the Consistorial [i.e., Utraquist] clergy would be either banned or brought under the full jurisdiction of, and into full obedience to, the archbishop."[14] Aside from its explanatory value of the Utraquists' motives in supporting the Letter, the stance of the Utraquist estates runs counter to two propositions advanced to trivialize the status of Utraquism. These theses, advanced for instance by Gindely and Krofta, postulated that the Utraquists after 1600 gave full obedience to archbishop, and that the Utraquists simply did the bidding of the royal government officials.[15]

The reasons that had induced the Utraquist townspeople to seek an alliance with the Lutheran and Unity nobles in 1575 had become even more cogent by 1608–1609, and their decision for the alliance represented, therefore, a rather realistic and astute assessment of the political dangers. As early as 1577, within the milieu of the Roman Church, the destruction of religious dissent in Bohemia had been, in fact, proposed by application of a procedure more recently known in political and social science as "salami tactics,"[16] and mentioned in Chapter 10. Nicholas Lanoy, the visiting inspector of the Austro-Bohemian Jesuit chapter, at that time counseled to proceed initially against the Brethren and other sectarians, who were disliked by both the Lutherans and Utraquists, before turning against Lutherans and eventually the Utraquists.[17] In another scenario of 1584, Nuncio Giovanni

Bonomi urged Rudolf II to expel the Pikarts and Lutherans from Bohemia, and not tolerate any ministers ordained in Leipzig or Wittenberg. Then he would be free to force the Utraquists into a full union with Rome. Bonomi's successor, Germanicus Malaspina, rejoiced over a breach between the Lutherans and the Brethren in January 1585 at the Diet, since to him the extirpation of Bohemian dissent depended on sowing discord among the various parties of the anti-Roman alliance. With the same purpose in mind, the nobles sub una urged some concessions for the Utraquists, accompanied by a severe suppression of the Brethren.[18] Nuncio Antoneo Caetano in his proposal of 1592 likewise envisioned the suppression of non-Utraquist dissidents as a prelude to pressuring the Utraquists into full conformity with Rome.[19] In another example of sowing discord, the Jesuit Václav Šturm in a treatise of 1584 dwelt heavily on the Brethren's basic theological differences with Luther.[20] Nuncio Spinelli in 1599 viewed the Brethren's suppression as the first step toward a successful Counter-Reformation.[21] In another variant of exploiting class differences among religious nonconformists, the ruling Prince Ferdinand of Inner Austria (Carniola, Carinthia, and Styria) in 1598–1601 suppressed the urban Lutherans, while the unfriendly Lutheran nobility stood indifferently by.[22]

The concept of "salami tactics" was avidly embraced by Rudolf II's entourage, and became manifest particularly in the mandates against the Pikarts in 1584 and 1602. These decrees, inconsistent with the gentlemen's agreement of 1575 under Maximilian II, promising toleration for the Brethren and the Lutherans, aimed at sharpening the differences between the Lutherans and the Brethren and between both and the Utraquists. As the town representatives would surmise in 1608, in the quotation cited earlier, the government's moves aimed at an eventual disappearance of Utraquism as well.[23]

To explain and contextualize geographically, ideologically, and historically, the Utraquists' decision to embrace an alliance with the more alien Lutherans and Brethren against the more similar Roman Church, further reasons can extrapolated or surmised from (1) the analogous behavior of religious denominations in other countries; (2) the exceptional vulnerability of Utraquism vis-à-vis the Roman Church; and (3) historical precedents within Bohemia.

The fact that the Utraquists feared the Roman party, despite their considerable similarity with the Roman Church, more than they did the less similar Lutherans and Brethren, was not an unprecedented stand. It may also be recalled that the Eastern Orthodox Church of Constantinople under Gregorios Scholarios preferred to take its chances under Turkish Islamic rule over embracing union with Rome.[24] Similarly, the Orthodox in Poland-Lithuania formed alliances in the sixteenth century with the Calvinists against the political champions of the Roman Church. Perhaps the closest parallel to the Bohemian situation could be found in Elizabethan England, where the Puritans and the Presbyterians felt the need of forming a common front with the Church of England against what they viewed as an ever-present Roman threat.[25]

In an absolute sense, the Utraquists had more to lose from victory of the Counter-Reformation than either the Brethren or the Lutherans. The Brethren had their places of exile prepared abroad (in Poland and Prussia) as a result of previous partial expulsions, especially that of 1547.[26] The spirit of Lutheranism was firmly entrenched in neighboring countries, and could not be extinguished by events in Bohemia alone. In fact, as will be shown in Chapter 12, Czech Lutherans (after a certain amount of Gleichschaltung or brainwashing) would find succor mostly among their German co-believers after 1620. For the Utraquists, however, even a theoretical possibility of continued existence was virtually precluded. Their fate would be complete physical disappearance, although their liberal ethos might continue to live on in national memory.

Going further back in history, the political alliance of the Utraquists with the Lutherans and the Brethren in 1609 may be also be viewed as analogous to the alliance between the mainline Utraquists and the Taborites during the wars of the Bohemian Reformation in 1420–1431. In fact, everybody willing to fight was welcomed, from the most fanatical sectarians to the most sedate Utraquists, in order to defeat the onslaught of the crusaders. The political bond of self-preservation operated here also despite drastic, virtually unbridgeable, theological differences. Even the opponent was the same: secular might seeking to impose the sway of the Roman Church. It may also be recalled that at the beginning of the Protestant Reformation, although the Utraquists did not embrace Luther due to profound theological differences, to an extent they tended to view Lutheranism already then as an ally against the possible ascendancy of the Roman Church. The same tendency would become particularly evident in initial negotiations concerning the Bohemian Confession in 1575.[27] It can be said that while the Utraquists' brain might have been a twin of the Roman Church, their heart was with the other Czech dissidents from Rome.

Guarantees Given the Utraquists

The Utraquist townsmen did not give their consent without guarantees. Despite some of its language, the Letter of Majesty assumed the continued coexistence of a variety sub utraque. The basic assurance came from the main architect of the arrangement under the Letter, Václav Budovec of Budov, on June 25, 1609, who specifically defined the party sub utraque that rallied under the banner of the Bohemian Confession as consisting of three distinct groups: the Utraquists, that is, those administered hitherto by the Prague Consistory; those administered by priests ordained in Germany, that is, the Lutherans; and the Brethren. Interestingly enough, the Utraquists were named first before the Lutherans and the Brethren. Budovec went on to compare, rather infelicitously, the three distinct groups among the sub utraque to the various religious orders in the party sub una that differed as to their peculiar rules and rights in clothing, food, and religious rituals. He further compared the three kinds of sub utraque to the various churches with which St. Paul had to deal in his Epistles, such as the Romans, the Corinthians, the Galatians, the Ephesians, the Colossians, and the Thessalonians. Although diverse in ritual, rules, and even doctrine, the apostle did not seek to impose uniformity on these ecclesiastical communities.[28] Budovec's speech at the Bohemian Diet on January 11, 1603, already foreshadowed his ecumenical attitude. Then, protesting the mandate against the Brethren, he stated that the various sub utraque, although differing in religion, helped each other, all were baptized in the name of the Trinity, all served the one Lord God, all fought the Turks, and all were under the same ruler. Budovec continued to stress the Christians' common interest in resisting Islamization in his treatise, *Antialkorán,* published in 1614, although originally completed in 1593.[29]

Of significance, albeit a rather ambiguous one, for the Utraquists was also a guarantee on which the royal government insisted in the form of the so-called *Porovnání,* which accompanied and qualified the Letter of Majesty. On its face, the document pledged protection of existing Utraquist priests and parishes in their beliefs and rituals. Utraquist priests could be freely appointed on both royal and private estates, and Utraquists in towns were also to have free access to their services. The government (the highest officials of the land) promised to intercede with the Roman Archbishop of Prague to ordain Utraquist priests.[30] The language of the *Porovnání* made it clear that "adherence to the Bohemian Confession" was not synonymous with acceptance of its religious doctrines. It also designated the state of belonging to any of the three types of dissidents from Rome. In that sense, the document stated that parishes that adhered to the Bohemian Confession were free to obtain services of Utraquist priests.[31] Thus, the term "Bohemian Confession" in its political use did not specify a doctrinal commitment, but a protective umbrella alike for the Lutherans, the Brethren, and the Utraquists.

It may be noted in this connection that a terminological problem arose after 1609 also from the opposite direction. The confederated dissidents from Rome, who were covered by the Letter of Majesty, began to call themselves also the party or the estates sub utraque. As those who were designated adherents to the Bohemian Confession did not turn Lutheran, but remained Utraquists, Lutherans, or Brethren, so also those who called themselves party sub utraque remained loyal to their particular denomination. The Utraquists formed a distinct, and probably the largest component, in the coalition of the party sub utraque. As noted later, the Jesuit fathers, with their Thomistic penchant for systematization, were disturbed by this complexity and would express their indignation over the absence of terminological neatness in their own *Apology* in 1618. They could not but attribute this taxonomic perversity to their opponents' lack of religious orthodoxy, manifest by a perplexity of concepts (to them) typical of heresy.

With respect to the Utraquist clergy, however, the language of the *Porovnání* lacked clarity, and introduced a degree of confusion as to the actual status of the Utraquists and their clergy. The designation used for Utraquist clergy was "the priests sub utraque ordained by the Archbishop of Prague." Since a large number of Utraquist priests must be assumed to have been ordained by bishops of the Roman Church other than the Prague archbishop, the definition sounded oddly restrictive. What is more significant, however, is that the *Porovnání* did not refer to these priests as under the *jurisdiction* of the archbishop, but merely to their *ordination* by the archbishop. Likewise, while the language of the *Porovnání* characterized the Utraquist priests as "not ordained according to the Bohemian Confession," it did not specifically deny their administrative subordination to the new Consistory.[32]

Certain other documents later reprinted in the official defense statement of the estates sub utraque for their insurrection, the so-called *Second Apology* (Druhá Apologie) of 1618, appeared to charge that the Utraquists had in fact been coerced to operate under the Roman prelate's authority. The crucial document is the instruction issued for the—as yet unreconstructed—Utraquist Consistory by Rudolf II on January 23, 1609, and included in the *Apology* as Document no. 16. It admonished the Consistory to observe the rituals of the archdiocese of Prague. On closer examination, however, it becomes clear that the injunction did not refer to the post-Tridentine usages of the Roman Church, implying obedience to the current archbishop of Prague. The instruction specifically spoke of the rubrics of Prague that the Utraquists "had always observed," that is, in defiance of the changing modes of Roman liturgy.[33] While for the Lutherans these liturgies might have been as abominable as the Tridentine ones, for the Utraquists they had been standard since the Bohemian Reformation, and in no way signified a submission to Rome's current administrative or judicial jurisdiction. Another document of the *Apology* (no. 12) cited the oath that the Archbishop required of Utraquists before priestly ordination after 1605 that pledged allegiance to the decrees of the Council of Trent and of the Prague Synod of the Roman Church in 1605. The implication was that the candidates submitted to this procedure. Another document cited by the *Apology* (Remonstrance of 1608, no. 14), however, corrects such a misinterpretation by specifying that the Utraquist candidates refused to take the oath and sought ordinations elsewhere.[34]

It was simply not the case that the Utraquists were ever administratively subordinated to the Archbishop. The periodic, but unfruitful, discussions of adjusting this relationship, which had been pursued since 1564, were largely abandoned after the fiasco of the Fabian Rezek affair, involving an apostasy to Rome of the Utraquist administrator in 1593.[35] A further cooling of relations followed the succession of Zbyněk Berka (1592–1606) as archbishop of Prague by prelates who were no longer of Czech nationality. Falling under the archbishop's power was exactly what the Utraquists were trying to avoid in accepting the invitation of the Lutherans and the Brethren, communicated by Budovec, to form a tripartite federation in 1608. A possible explanation of such counterfactual assertions in historical literature is that the alleged Utraquist priests under the archbishop's jurisdiction were those who were authorized to distribute communion in both kinds according to the Tridentine rite, on the basis of the papal dispensation of 1564. However, no self-respecting Utraquist would resort to their services, as is attested by the firm resistance to the occasional attempts of Archbishop Berka to impose Roman priests distributing communion in both kinds on traditionally Utraquist parishes in the 1600s.[36]

In view of the guarantees received by the Utraquists in 1609, one can argue that not much had substantially changed in comparison with the state of affairs since 1575. The informal recognition of the Bohemian Confession and of the Brethren's Confession now became formally legal, but the injunction against a forcible imposition of Protestant dogmas on the Utraquists was likewise overtly legalized in the *Porovnání*. The most marked change was the broadening of the Consistory to include Lutherans and Brethren, but the very existence of the division between the Lutherans and the Brethren served as a kind of additional warranty against pressure toward homogenization of all those standing formally outside the fold of the Roman Church. While historians have maintained that the Utraquists wished to unite with the Roman Church in order to stem the tide of the Protestant Reformation, the opposite was the case. Their aim was an alliance with the Protestants to protect themselves against a forced union with Rome.[37]

The Ecumenical Consistory

Historical Background

In trying to assess the impact of the situation created by the Letter of Majesty on the Utraquists, perhaps the thorniest problem is the loss of the Utraquist Consistory, and its replacement by an institution that would serve all Bohemian dissidents from the Roman Church who observed the limits of the Bohemian Confession of 1575. This new consistory will be called the joint Consistory.[38] The advantage of a joint Consistory from the Lutheran point of view is evident—it furnished an administrative center that its clergy hitherto lacked. It is less obvious, but likewise true, that the separate Utraquist Consistory also had disadvantages for the Utraquists; in its lack of social and political weight it exposed the Utraquist Church to invidious subtle, or not-so-subtle outside pressures. To explain this fragility, it is necessary to review at least briefly the situation of the Utraquist Consistory in the preceding period between 1575 and 1609.

The Utraquist Consistory as a relatively penurious plebeian institution had a vulnerable organizational structure. Its primary dependence on the monarch and his officials since 1562 (rather than on the Bohemian Diet) was turning from a factor of strength to one of considerable risk. Lacking its own apparatus for enforcement of decisions or judgments, it needed to appeal to outside agencies, which usually were not particularly sympathetic, be they the king, the highest officials of the land, or the archbishops. Its social and administrative weight was slight, even in comparison with the archbishop's establishment, which was at least underpinned by the income from his estates, although he presided over a relatively small flock. In October 1582, it even appeared that the administrator might lose his modest source of income as the abbot of the Emmaus monastery.[39] The discrepancy in power and prestige proved still riskier when the king entrusted the archbishop with protection of Utraquist parishes against Protestant encroachments. Even the royal towns, although generally loyal to Utraquism, often failed to fully cooperate with the Consistory in executing its directives.[40] Nuncio Speciano's arrangement of Administrator Rezek's apostasy in 1593 underlined the Consistory's vulnerability, despite the fact that its rapid and decisive recovery from this assault testified to its vitality and resiliency.

As discussed earlier,[41] the status of the Utraquist Consistory deteriorated further in the middle of the first decade of the seventeenth century. With respect to the government, the insolent treatment of Administrator Václav Dačický by Chancellor Zdeněk of Lobkovice in 1604 demonstrated the low regard for the Utraquist ecclesiastical establishment on the part of the king's officials, increasingly recruited from the ranks of the Roman Church. To add insult to injury, Dačický found it necessary to appeal to the archbishop to intervene in his favor with the chancellor.[42] The increasing disrespect for Utraquism was linked with the increasing willingness of the aristocrats sub una to condone their own full-fledged ecclesiastical submission to Rome compared to the more cautious attitude of the preceding generation.[43] The use of the archbishops' mediating role became even less appealing for the Consistory when Berka's death in 1606 inaugurated a series of foreigners in the archiepiscopal chair of Bohemia. Archbishops Karl of Lamberg (1607–1612) and Johann Lohelius (1612–1622) would be scrupulous executors of the Curia's will and, unlike their Czech predecessors, devoid of any vestigial sympathy for Utraquism.[44]

With the threat from the archbishop and with the king a questionable champion, the Utraquists actually had a reason to welcome protection by the joint Consistory. The noble protectors of the joint Consistory, the defensores who were backed in cases of need by the estates sub utraque, could muster enough social prestige and political muscle to stand up against the pressures of the Roman Church, and do so more dependably than the king and his entourage with their Roman sympathies and their, at best, ambiguous attitude toward authentic Utraquism.[45] There was a precedent of the Consistory's appeal for support to the Bohemian Diet as early as December 1586, when it asked the estates sub utraque to intercede on its behalf with Rudolf II.[46] Moreover, the defensores, who would oversee and support the Consistory, would include town representatives who could be presumed to favor Utraquism.

From the Utraquists' historical perspective the idea of a joint Consistory was not utterly novel. The composition of the transient body of the defensores, elected in September 1575 (with Utraquism represented by the town members), may be viewed as a prefiguration of the religious balance of power in the post-1608 Consistory. As an earlier anticipation, one may refer to the abortive discussions between Administrator Martin Mělnický and Bishop Jan Augusta in the late 1560s, which raised the possibility of a joint consistory for the Utraquists and the Bohemian Brethren. It failed then, largely due to the determined opposition of Augusta's episcopal colleague Jan Blahoslav.[47] As for other intimations, there had been approaches to the Utraquist Consistory in the late sixteenth century for adjudication of disputes involving Lutheran clergy, as well as the willingness of the Lutheran noble estates to back the urban Utraquists' Diet petition in 1590 for strengthening the Consistory and for ordination of Utraquist priests by the archbishop.[48] Above all, the new organizational constellation was adumbrated by the Utraquists' distinct gravitation to the Diet's support after 1604.

Federation of the Three Types of Sub Utraque

None of the above would have mattered, however, if the new Consistory literally insisted on imposing Lutheranism under the guise of the Bohemian Confession. In fact, it must be stressed that the new joint Consistory, which replaced the earlier Utraquist one, should not be viewed as a Protestant Holy Office enforcing doctrinal uniformity, and rather as an ecumenical council, loosely confederating and serving the Brethren, Lutherans, and Utraquists. This, of course, corresponded to the definition of the groups eventually under the Letter of Majesty by Budovec as indeed a league of three distinct and autonomous types of sub utraque. The federated character was reflected already in the composition of the commission that was to formulate the character of the new joint consistory beginning on July 30, 1609, after it had received the records and archives of the terminated Utraquist Consistory from Tomáš of Soběslav. The commission included together with four each of Lutheran and Unity clergymen also four Utraquist priests with canonical episcopal ordinations, who were hitherto administered by the Utraquist Consistory.[49] Budovec cogently expressed the basis of the coexistence of the Utraquists, Lutherans, and Brethren in a single alliance. Admitting that there was "a triple difference in orders and ceremonies within the party sub utraque in Bohemia," he affirmed that "the different orders, ceremonies and ecclesiastical disciplines among them, do not and, God willing, will not destroy the unity of divine truth . . . or the bond of Christian love among them . . ."[50] As the Brethren were to testify in retrospect, the common Consistory was a sign of solidarity and compromise, not of amalgamation.[51]

Contrary to some assertions, the Utraquist priests were free to continue the traditional rituals and to adhere to their traditional confessional statements, last summarized by Tomáš of Soběslav in 1609.[52] In this connection, it may be pointed out that the Utraquists did not require a specific "Confession," such as the Lutherans and the Brethren had in their respective confessions of 1573 and 1575. Unlike the Protestants, the Utraquists did not feel that they had departed from the universal Christian tradition; hence their theology was defined by the Councils of the first millennium and their liturgy by the fourteenth-century books of the archdiocese of Prague. To try and improve on the traditional creeds would be at best presumptuous, at worst blasphemous. Even the crucial and venerable Four Articles of Prague, later enshrined in the Compactata, were procedural (disciplinary), not substantive (doctrinal), that is, not introducing new theological matters, such as the Lutherans' solafideism or sola scriptura.[53]

The Utraquists' position under the Consistory was to some extent analogous to that of the Brethren's clergy. The Brethren did not revoke their own confession, and insisted on retaining their own priesthood, orders of worship, and their church order and discipline. While every clergyman had to subscribe to certain minimum requirements of Christian belief, he was free to pursue his proper liturgical ritual. While radical sectarianism was excluded on the one hand, the Utraquists and the Brethren could engage in their specific rites, on the other.[54] The Brethren would substantiate ex post facto their right to an autonomous organization and their own confession during their controversy with the Lutherans in the 1630s.[55] Moreover, probably because of the Brethren's theological proximity to the Calvinists, the toleration under the federated Consistory extended in practice to Calvinist ministers as well.[56] The most prominent among them was Havel Phaëton Žalanský, a prolific author and since 1610 the pastor of the prestigious church of St. Jijljí in the Old Town of Prague. This made further evident the poetic license of the assertion that all those under the Consistory subscribed theologically to the Bohemian Confession. After all, Phaëton explicitly and emphatically denied the doctrine of real presence, a stance that was anathema to the Lutherans.[57] Here again a certain parallel with the Polish union of Sandomierz suggests itself. As previously noted, the Consensus Sandomiriensis, of April 14, 1570, brought together the Lutherans, the Calvinists, and the Bohemian Brethren (exiled to Poland) into mutual peace and harmony, and into a political alliance, while each of the three religious denominations preserved its distinctive organization and form of worship. The agreement resulted in a "confederation" rather than a "union."[58]

Beyond that there is evidence that the Utraquists could find a friendly ambiance under the new arrangement of ecclesiastical administration. The estates sub utraque were willing to advocate the causes of the Utraquists in their relations with the royal government. For instance, their remonstrance to Rudolf II of 1608, repeated in the *Second Apology* of 1618 as Document 14, denounced strongly the brutal treatment of Administrator Dačický by Chancellor Lobkovice, the unreasonable promises sought by the archbishop from Utraquist priests before ordination, the omission of the holiday of Jan Hus from the calendar, and the transfer of the abbotship of the Emmaus Monastery from the Utraquists to the sub una. The estates likewise posed as advocates for Utraquism, in particular by chastising the archbishops for their hard-nosed insistence on an oath to Tridentine Decrees as a precondition for ordination of Utraquist priests, which was basically unacceptable for the Utraquists. As pointed out earlier, the remonstrance of 1608, repeated ten years later in the *Second Apology,* most significantly stressed that the Utraquist candidates did not succumb to the blandishments of the archbishop, but turned for their ordination (presumably an episcopal one) elsewhere. The statement about "priests taken from the Archbishop"—in the *Porovnání*—should probably be interpreted as reflecting the continuing hope that Archbishop might be induced to ordain Utraquist priests. It might also reflect the fact that certain priests were ordained by the archbishop, either as Utraquists (the seven under Archbishop Berka) or subsequently defected from Roman obedience. In neither case would this category of clergy be in administrative subordination to the archbishop.[59]

A puzzling element concerning the post-1609 status of Utraquist clergy is introduced by the text of the church order issued on the instruction of the estates sub utraque by the defensores after their election on January 16, 1610. This ecclesiastical regulation, addressed to the "priests of the Lord sub utraque and with heart and lips adhering to the Bohemian Confession" mandated the abandonment of specifically Utraquist liturgical practices: processions, exhibits of the host in a monstrance, elevation of the host, infant communion, and traditional liturgical books, namely missals, breviaries, and the agenda and rubrics of the archbishopric of Prague. An actual general implementation of this order, covering all the clergy administered by the Consistory sub utraque, would have been entirely unacceptable to the Utraquists. This is a situation when a document needs to be read not only between the lines, but even against the grain, as Alexandra Walsham points out in facing similar conundrums in the history of the English Reformation.[60] As just noted above, the statement is counterfactual since the Consistory in its subsequent functioning indeed covered not only the Lutherans, but also the Utraquist clergy and the Brethren. The Unity, in fact, subsequently also perpetuated its own liturgical peculiarities and disregarded the regulations of the church order.[61]

Hence the liturgical injunctions of the church order could be viewed either as mere formalities or empty phrases, or more probably as meant to bind only those clergymen who accepted the Bohemian Confession, not merely as a general umbrella of the permissible, but as their specific and full confessional statement, that is, the Lutheran clergy. The clue probably should be sought in the address of these rules to "priests of the Lord sub utraque *and* [my emphasis] with heart and lips adhering to the Bohemian Confession," if this phrase is interpreted not in a generally descriptive, but in a restrictive sense as referring only to the Lutheran clergy.[62] Such a restriction might have been logical because the Lutheran ministers had hitherto lacked a regular organization that would have issued a formal set of rules. While they had lived in a state of "lawlessness," the Utraquists, like the Brethren, had their rules formally spelled out and established, and hence did not need them issued again. The Lutheran clergy, to the contrary, until 1609 had to operate on the margins without an umbrella organization in the private churches or chapels of manorial seigneurs, or under the protection of the city councils of several German-speaking towns that recently defected from the Roman Church.[63] The latter instances involved continuous battles against the archbishop's efforts to dislodge them. It might be said that only in 1609 the Lutheran clergy had a chance to step fully out of the closet. That recognition of the legitimacy of the Bohemian Confession did not imply its observance is likewise evident from the case of Cykáda. This unimpeachably orthodox Utraquist was also said to have agreed, or even rallied, to the Bohemian Confession.[64]

Naturally there was a price to be paid by the Utraquists to their new protectors, the Bohemian estates. The nobility sub utraque received its pound of flesh through a conspicuous, although largely symbolic, display of its religious preferences with the Lutheran and Brethren's clergy featured in the Consistory and in a few prominent churches in Prague. As early as October 1609, Jan Cykáda protested against the tendency to limit the Utraquist clergy's membership in the reconstructed Consistory. Although the first administrator of the joint Consistory, Eliáš Šud of Semanín (1609–1614) was a Utraquist, he was succeeded by two Lutherans, Zykmund Crinitus (1614–1619) and Jiřík Dykastus (1619–1621). It is evidently too strong to say, as Tomek does, that after 1609 the Utraquists "played no noticeable part in the ecclesiastical administration of the party *sub utraque* . . . ,"[65] especially in view of the fact that by 1618 the unequivocal Utraquist Cykáda would be once more a member of the Consistory.[66]

Hence, the ecclesiastical leaders of Utraquism like, for practical reasons, its political leaders, could feel reasonably secure in a friendly alliance with the Lutherans and the Brethren. While the Roman Church required a full embracing of the Tridentine standard, the Lutherans and the Brethren did not demand conformity with the Bohemian Confession or another norm unacceptable to the Utraquists. Escaping the insults of royal officials and the subtle and unsubtle pressures of the archbishop to turn sub una, might be viewed as welcome relief for the Utraquists. Switching their patronage from a combination of the Roman Archbishop and the Catholic Habsburg kings to that of the Lutheran nobility need not have been such an oddity as it might have seemed to some.[67] As we shall see, it would be a mistake to impute to the Czech Lutherans, that is, the authentic believers in the Bohemian Confession, the same degree of intolerance as characterized the contemporary champions of the Counter-Reformation, such as archbishop Lohelius, or those of German Lutheranism and Calvinism, such as the notorious Matthias Hoë von Hoënegg or Abraham Scultetus.[68] The Czech Lutheran, Samuel Martinius of Dražov, stressed the need of amicable coexistence in a period of confessional diversity in his *Oratio de Concordia ecclesiae* (1618). As for the Utraquists, the idea of a joint Consistory also harmonized with their *via media* tradition of open-mindedness and tolerance with respect to diverging religious opinions. Thus, Matěj Stříbrský devoted a treatise to charity, published in 1610, which culminates in a hymn celebrating solidarity and concord among the clergy, as well as the laity.[69]

For the sake of contextualization, it may be apropos to compare the Utraquists under the Letter in 1609–1620 with the Anglicans during the Interregnum, 1648–1660. As characterized by Spurr, the latter's situation was less appealing: "[M]any parishes continued to be served by ministers who had been ordained by bishops and had served in the Church of England before 1642; such clergymen were now either gratefully embracing new religious opportunities or keeping their heads down until better times."[70] While the status of the "prayer-book men" or Anglicans was inferior to the Independents and the Presbyterians, the Utraquists—defined as those sub utraque whose priests were ordained by bishops—had enjoyed a status of equality with the Lutherans and the Brethren.

Toleration and Orthodoxy

Hitherto the argument was directed at showing that the high degree of religious toleration, the outstanding feature of Bohemia in the early seventeenth century, was viewed by the party sub utraque as a stable condition, not as a mere prelude to, or a temporary pause before, an impending Lutheran religious homogenization. It is also important to address the opposite (mis)-perception, namely that the Bohemian tolerance, in fact, reflected a religious laxness verging on nihilism. The remarkable freedom of religion in Bohemia in the opening decades of the seventeenth century is noted, among others, by the pamphlet, *Euangelische Erklerung auff die Böhaimische Apologia* (1618), which claimed (undoubtedly with some exaggeration): "What is in Bohemia freer than religion? Every house has its own order and discipline, nobody is bound to any one religion, but regrettably everyone can believe what he wants."[71] A year later a French diplomatic report marveled at the religious diversity prevalent in Bohemia.[72] Also the Jesuits commented on the religious laissez-faire in the country in their *Apology* of 1618, published in Vienna after their expulsion from Prague on the outbreak of the Bohemian Uprising. With their penchant for rigorous conformity, the happy coexistence of the three types of sub utraque—the Utraquists or Hussitas, the Lutherans, and the Brethren—struck them as most reprehensible. According to the Jesuit *Apology,* the three types of sub utraque differed among each other more than the Utraquists from the Roman Church. While the Utraquists honored the Eucharist as the body and blood of Christ in the Corpus Christi procession, their Calvinist confreres, such as Havel Phaëton Žalanský in 1618, preached that the Eucharist was just ordinary bread and wine. The *Apology* asked: "How does one know which Word of God to hold for the right one: Whether that of the Lutherans, or of the Calvinists/Picards, or of the Utraquists [Hussitarum] (which is the oldest in Bohemia)?"[73] The situation of religious pluralism was equally distasteful for the champions of thought control on the other side of the ledger, particularly the Lutherans of Saxony, whose voice was represented in Prague by Hoë from 1611 to 1613.[74] In a way, Josef Válka calls attention to this phenomenon in referring to Czech politicians' willingness to cooperate across denominational lines, but in calling them "superconfessional Christians" (*nadkonfesijní křest'ané*) he seems to imply that this meant abandoning the specificity of their religious beliefs. There is also a less drastic suggestion by František Šmahel that the Bohemian religious forbearance—as early as the peace of Kutná Hora in 1485—marked a lessening of religious dedication.[75] This, however, need not be the case.

Was there actually a diminution in particular denominational beliefs? We find, to the contrary, that the spokesmen for Utraquism uncompromisingly affirmed their creeds against the beliefs of the Lutherans and the Brethren, as in 1575 and 1609, and it would be difficult to imagine a more categorical rejection by Lutheran divines of what they interpreted as grave errors of the Brethren.[76] It is unnecessary to speak about the Brethren's disdain for the beliefs of either the Utraquists or the Lutherans. As the evidence indicates, this sense of profound religious distinctions did not appear to be weakened or diluted by the genuine cooperation of the lay leaders of Utraquism, Lutheranism, and the Unity for political objectives. Thus, the urban Utraquists, as long as their church remained protected in its original orthodoxy, did not have to feel threatened by the religious beliefs of the Lutheran nobles or the Unity sectarians, which could equally flourish in their enclosed and safeguarded domains. Within this context, the Utraquists could safely form an amicable political alliance with them against the possible aggression of the Habsburg dynasty or the Roman party. This stance did not imply a dilution or a compromise of their religious devotion, integrity, or firm orthodoxy. Similarly, on the Protestant side, the nobles' cooperation with Utraquist townsmen did not negate the theological differences between the two faiths. Thus, the Calvinist theologian, Havel Phaëton (Žalanský), was free to denounce the Utraquist practice of Eucharistic processions as the work of the Antichrist, and condemn their religious *via media* in no uncertain terms, stating: "Because Christ himself says that no one can serve two masters. And who does not gather with Christ, that one scatters. . . . In sum: those who are neither hot nor cold have no share in Christ."[77]

The spirit of genuine toleration could coexist with an undiluted, uncompromising, and fervent devotion to a particular church. In fact, the architect of the political alliance of all the sub utraque, Budovec, considered the discussion of religious issues and diversity of opinions as a hallmark of true Christianity. An imposition of doctrinal uniformity would be a sign of Islamization. Elsewhere Budovec spoke of the various churches with which St. Paul had to deal in his Epistles, like the Romans, the Corinthians, the

Galatians, the Ephesians, the Colossians, and the Thessalonians. Thus, the apostle combined with a firm attachment to definite beliefs, a tolerance for what he considered grievous errors of others. Although he detested, and even wept over, some of the customs of his correspondents, St. Paul placed love for others above all, and repudiated the use of force to achieve a singleness of rites, rules, and even doctrines.[78]

We can call on an outside witness to illustrate the mindset which holds that fervent faith is not incompatible with a willingness to accept coexistence with other faiths, which one holds utterly false. The famous seventeenth-century apostle of religious toleration in England and North America, Roger Williams, compared the church to an enclosed garden that could be kept free of weeds, while the tares may flourish freely outside its walls. He wrote: "A false religion out of the Church will not hurt the Church no more than weeds in the wilderness hurt the inclosed Garden, or poyson hurt the body when it is not touched or taken, yea and antidotes are received against it."[79] The other side of the coin, combining toleration with a dim view of faiths other than one's own, can be underscored by another citation from Williams. The Rhode Island Baptist gives the concluding verse of the parable of the wheat and the tares, the beginning of which (Mt. 13:25–29) had been used to justify toleration by Cykáda cited in chapter eight. Williams assures us that if toleration existed in this life, in the next the angels would dispose of the tares "with their sharp and cutting sickles of eternal vengeance, shall down with them, and bundle them up for the everlasting burnings" (Mt. 13:30).[80] A politically based tolerance toward other religious groups or churches need not imply a diminution of the attachment, even a rather ominous one, to the orthodoxy of one's own group or church.

For the long run in Bohemia, there was a pious wish, and possibly even a genuine expectation, that the religious divisions would not last forever. Some authors have designated the expectation of an eventual reunion of all Christians (rather than permanent division) as concordance.[81] We have noted earlier the Utraquist view of a perpetual negotiation with the Roman Church in an implied hope of opening the misguided (step)mother's eyes to the light of reason. The Letter of Majesty was formally regarded as a provisorium until a universal Christian Council would reestablish a unity of faith and practice. The Lutheran theologian Zacharyáš Bruncvík in 1614 looked forward to such an ecumenical assembly to put an end to dissensions and bloodshed among Christians.[82] Abroad, even James I of England believed in a policy of reunion first among the Protestants, and then between them and the Church of Rome.[83]

Measures of Utraquist Strength and Vitality

After examining the historical and institutional background of Utraquism's post-1609 adjustment, let us now explore the signs of its continuing strength and popularity among the Czechs of Bohemia under the Letter of Majesty against the conventional historical view of their virtual disappearance during this period.

As discussed previously, the character of the joint Consistory indicated clearly that there were Utraquist priests under the jurisdiction of the Consistory who did not subscribe to the theology and liturgy of the Bohemian Confession. Priests with unquestionably Utraquist credentials including canonical ordinations, such as Jan Cykáda, Jan Locika of Domažlice, and Matauš Pačuda, operated under the jurisdiction of the Consistory, without evidently being required to embrace theologically the Bohemian Confession. One could, perhaps, speak of political acceptance, rather than theological endorsement of the Confession on their part.[84]

Even under the Letter of 1609, the Utraquists maintained their strong presence in towns. The city councils selected their own clergymen for appointment, and sent or delivered through their deputies or envoys a request for confirmation of their candidates to the administrator and the Consistory. Because of the rooted tradition of urban Utraquism, this arrangement would favor appointment of Utraquist priests, particularly in royal towns.[85] As pointed out earlier, Prague seemed to be something of an exception in this regard. Because of the prestige value of the city and its position as the seat of the Consistory, Lutheran ministers were appointed as pastors to important churches. However, the bulk of the Prague population remained loyal to Utraquism. The Utraquist Corpus Christi processions continued with participation of the city elites, as well as the common people, although this ritual was particularly objectionable to the Lutherans.[86] Even where Lutheran ministers were appointed, Utraquist services were not eliminated. Thus, a Czech Lutheran, Jiří Dykastus, who served as pastor of the Týn Church from 1614 and later in 1619 was to become the administrator, had to employ a Utraquist chaplain who performed religious services in the Utraquist mode.[87] Distinguished Utraquist priests from other parishes also could perform religious rites in the Týn Church, as Cykáda did at he funeral of Alžběta Valdštejnská of Valdštejn on March 17, 1614.[88] Moreover, the Týn Church kept its customary Utraquist artistic decor, which strictly speaking, should have been abhorrent, particularly to the Brethren. There was no cleansing comparable to that of the Prague Cathedral by the Calvinist entourage of

King Frederick.[89] In 1617, a royal instruction also affirmed the Utraquist dominance in Prague town government, and King Matthias (1611–1619), Rudolf II's successor, included two Utraquists and merely one Lutheran in appointing a council of lieutenancy during his absence from Bohemia. In the spring of 1618, the councilmen of the Old Town of Prague participated in a Utraquist religious procession, which ran against Lutheran precepts.[90] The decree of the directors of the insurgent government, as late as June 1619, implied that the Utraquists had a predominance in the three towns of Prague.[91] As an example of a royal town's prerogative to insist on a Utraquist priest, one may cite the rejection by Tábor of a Lutheran minister in 1610 and the Consistory's consent to the appointment of Václav Krištof Unhošt'ský in 1611 and another Utraquist priest as a chaplain in 1612. Moreover, the town's grassroots initiative for a Utraquist priest contradicts the conventional claim that it was the royal government that forced Utraquism on the royal towns.[92]

In violation of the pledge of tolerating a variety of ecclesiastical rituals, the noble defensores were occasionally tempted to interfere with the performance of Utraquist rites. Such attempts had more of a nuisance value than a real effect. Thus, despite their displeasure, the solemn Utraquist procession of Corpus Christi was conducted in 1613, in which the priests offended the Lutheran, as well as Roman, sensitivities by carrying the sacrament in both kinds in public.[93] The predominance of Utraquist sentiments among the priests of Prague is indicated by their closing of ranks behind Locika in the face of a vendetta against him in the summer of 1617 for sharp public criticism of Lutheran tenets and rites. As late as April 1618, this Utraquist ecclesiastical luminary could conduct the abovementioned solemn procession in Prague with the participation of city councilmen. Displaying the sacraments, the marchers commemorated the Resurrection on Holy Saturday.[94] Even somewhat later, the Calvinist theologian Havel Phaëton (Žalanský) felt compelled to denounce the Utraquist practice of Eucharistic processions as the work of the Antichrist.[95]

Thanks in part to the *Porovnání*, Utraquism continued to be protected after 1609 in its existing positions not only in towns, but also on private estates. The principle of noninterference by feudal seigneurs with the religion of their subjects was continued under the Letter of Majesty until the Bohemian Uprising of 1618–1620. In fact, charges of the violation of this principle by the royal government figured prominently in the reasons given for the uprising by the insurgent estate in their *Second Apology* of 1618. This principle rather baffled the other European, and especially neighboring, lands where the coercion of subjects by their seigneurs was considered a norm under the proviso *cuius regio, eius religio*.[96] It showed the exceptionality of the pattern of religious toleration in Bohemia at the beginning of the seventeenth century. Utraquism remained particularly strong on royal and archiepiscopal estates despite the fact that the king once more gave Archbishop Johann Lohelius the right to appoint clergy there on October 24, 1612. A survey of the parishes in 1613 by Tobiáš Cocius for the archbishop is significant, although rather confused in indicating the Utraquist strength. It covered the deanery of Kouřim with thirty-two parishes on the ecclesiastical manor of the provostship of St. George; on three private manors of the Kolovrats, Valdštejns, and Vchynskýs; and on six royal manors of Benátky, Brandýs, Malešov, Mělník, Přerov, and Poděbrady. Only eight of the clergy were classified as Lutheran. Most of the priests were described as preserving traditional rites, hence recognizable as Utraquists. Aside from characterizing them by their rites, the survey referred to them variously as being married, using Czech as liturgical language, administering collective confessions, or as devotees of Jan Hus. Even among the eight clergymen classified as "heretics" (presumably Lutherans or Brethren), there was at least one, the pastor of Lysá, who was actually a Utraquist.[97] The status quo on royal estates might have been jeopardized after 1615, not in favor of Lutheranism, but that of the Roman side. The managers (hejtmané, purkrabí) of royal estates had traditionally played a role in protecting the Utraquist character of parishes on the manors entrusted to their care. Apparently with the approval of King Matthias, henceforth these posts went frequently to adherents of the Roman Church, who might have been less vigilant against the appointment of priests sub una into Utraquist parishes.[98]

On private estates the parishioners exercised the right to negotiate with their seigneurs about religious pastors. Thus, the inhabitants of Lomnice asked for a Utraquist priest, and those of Soběslav objected to a Lutheran pastor to their manorial lord Jan Jiří of Švamberk in 1612.[99] Utraquist clergy also guarded against the appointments of Brethren clergy to Utraquist parishes. In 1611, thirty of them, headed by the dean of Chrudim, petitioned the defensores against this practice favored by certain influential manorial seigneurs. While Josef Jireček claims that the protesters were Lutherans, the original report by Pavel Skála ze Zhoře shows that they must have been Utraquists because of their praise of the pre-1609 Consistory, an attitude virtually inconceivable among the Lutherans.[100]

The denouement of a 1618 attempt to establish a separate Utraquist Consistory also provides evidence of the strength, independence, and self-confidence of Utraquism under the institutional arrangement in existence since 1609. In this case, some dozen Utraquist priests prepared a memorandum for the royal government in 1617, asking for the erection of a separate Utraquist consistory. This proposal, eagerly welcomed, if not inspired, by the royal officials, in particular Pavel Michna of Vacinov, was shortly withdrawn on the advice of the most influential Utraquist clergy. The opposition was led by the prominent Matouš Pačuda, who may have been slated to become the administrator of the proposed ecclesiastical body.[101] The Utraquist leaders probably viewed the proposal as just another application of "the salami tactics" by the government to an ultimate solution of the problem posed by the Bohemian Reformation. The rather obscure maneuvering around the establishment (or restoration) of a consistory exclusively for the Utraquists also made evident a substantial presence of Utraquist priests under the joint Consistory. The *Second Apology* of the insurgent Bohemian estates in 1618 worried that the Utraquist priests' withdrawal would deprive the existing Consistory of much of its administrative infrastructure, particularly in Prague.[102]

There is an indication that the town leaders were involved in the discussions about a separate Utraquist consistory, but in the end a majority also decided not to break the alliance with the Lutherans and Brethren, or risk losing the nobles' patronage.[103] This decision showed that the political leaders of urban Utraquism operated independently, reflecting local interests. The towns' attitude toward the issue of the Consistory was in line with their resistance to the royal government's pleas of 1609 not to form an alliance with the Lutheran and Unity nobles, and even in line with their original decision to support the legalization of the Bohemian Confession in 1575. The moves to establish a new Consistory, promoted by the royal chancery, could be seen in this light as aimed at weakening the united front of the sub utraque, which in the long run could be lethal to Utraquism. A separate consistory could be more easily suppressed together with its parishes, through a Roman Gleichschaltung under the archbishop, inasmuch as it would lack the support of the other dissidents who would have been antagonized by the Utraquists' break with the alliance's solidarity.

As a bottom line, the fact that the Utraquist clergy and their urban sponsors, as late as 1618 and 1619, did not go along with the plan for a new Utraquist consistory suggested that the Utraquists' situation under the existing joint Consistory was on the whole acceptable. The insurgent Bohemian estates put a more ominous spin on the episode in the list of charges against the Habsburg government, contained in the *Second Apology* of 1618. The document claimed that the proposed Utraquist Consistory was to be controlled by the archbishop and its adherent priests re-ordained. A likelihood of such a proposal is most questionable inasmuch as archiepiscopal control had been always anathema to the Utraquists, and their priests were already defined, in large part, by holding canonical ordinations.[104] Not even the most naive of the royal officials could have assumed, prior to the Battle of the White Mountain in 1620, that the Utraquists were ready for an unconditional surrender.

As the original rally of Utraquist priests and towns behind the Letter of Majesty in 1609, so also the refusal of the priests and towns to do the government's bidding in 1618, clearly contradicted the *ideés fixes* of sixteenth-century Bohemian historiography that (1) Utraquism, as a mere phantom, served as a passive and obedient tool in the hands of the king's officials; and (2) that the town councils in their support of Utraquism acted merely as pliable instruments helping the government to sabotage the Protestant Reformation. The revival of the issue of a separate Utraquist Consistory under the directors of the insurgent government in December 1618 and in early 1619, however, called for caution in attributing the idea of a restored Utraquist Consistory solely to the manipulation of the royal officials under the Habsburg regime.[105]

The testimony of outside observers continued to stress the presence of Utraquism in Bohemia, as well as the loyalty of the Utraquist priests to traditional rituals and beliefs. Thus, the Jesuits in their abovementioned *Apology* of 1618 named the Utraquists in the first place under the heterodox (referring to them as "Hussitas," as opposed to "Lutheranos," and "Picarditas seu Calvinistas") and treated them as the most numerous.[106] The *Apologia* also indicated that the Utraquists had not changed their beliefs or rituals because of the joint Consistory or the recognition of the Bohemian Confession. That the priests of the Utraquists or Hussitas had not undergone a process of Lutheranization is further affirmed by the Jesuits' praise for their preserving the following orthodox beliefs and rituals, all which the Lutherans and the Brethren had rejected: "Surely Hus and the Utraquists . . . have defended the invocation of saints, the cult and veneration of holy reliques and images, the celibacy of priests . . . , the seven sacraments of the New Testament, the sacrifice of the mass, the transubstantiation of bread and wine, the purgatory, the necessity of good works for salvation, holy processions and pilgrimages . . ."[107] According to the Jesuits' testimony, the Utraquists continued to differ in 1618 more from the Lutherans and the Brethren than they did from the Roman Church.[108] The Jesuits, however, engaged in some exaggeration, and in particular, they were overgenerous in attributing to the Utraquists the belief in clerical celibacy. Nevertheless, the statement did outline the traditional essential differences separating the Utraquists from the beliefs and practices of the Lutherans (or for that matter those of the Brethren).

The testimony of another outsider, the Calvinist minister Havel Phaëton (Žalanský), indicated the continuation of Utraquist rites to the end of the Bohemian uprising. In a sermon preached rather provocatively on the feast day of Corpus Christi in 1620, Phaëton inventoried what he considered the Eucharistic malpractices of the Utraquists. Above all, he criticized their persistent participation in the Eucharistic processions and the very concept of adoring the host and the wine outside the communion service. He also denounced their view of the mass as a sacrifice, masses for the dead, depicting Christ in statues and images, and the use of special vestments and golden vessels for Eucharistic services.[109]

Perhaps the most cogent sign of Utraquism's continued importance was its vitality and popularity exactly in the seventeenth century, reliably reported in contemporary sources, which confounded historians who had been proclaiming the Utraquist Church moribund ever since 1517, and its demise has been prematurely and variously dated in historical literature to 1517, 1524, 1539, 1564, 1575, 1593, or 1609.[110] The particularly striking event that usually triggered a need for commentary was the impressive outpouring of popular support for the Utraquist Easter procession conducted in Prague by Locika in the spring of 1618.[111] The Lutherans considered this Utraquist rite not just a meaningless exercise, but a pure abomination conducive to diverse types of idolatry.[112] Hrejsa pointed out that Utraquism had "many adherents in the conservative strata of the populace." Tischer admitted that the attempts to limit traditional Utraquist ceremonies by the Lutherans collided with "the ingrained inclinations and traditions of the common people sub utraque." Eduard Winter stated categorically: "The Czech people held firmly on the traditional rituals, the Czech vespers, the high masses, the sacramental procession and others."[113] As late as January 1620, for instance, popular commotion made the town councilors of Poděbrady fear for their lives after they removed such hallmarks of Utraquism as the sacred images and liturgical vessels from the church. The amateurish iconoclasts sought to imitate the example of King Frederick's Calvinist chaplain, Abraham Scultetus, in purging the Prague Cathedral of sacred images and statues at Christmas of 1619.[114] The councilors of the Old Town of Prague revealed their Utraquist sentiments by subsequently resisting the suggestion of removing Christ's image from the Charles Bridge.[115]

The historiographic significance of the unexpected show of Utraquism's strength, on the eve and during the course of the Bohemian uprising, is perhaps best illustrated by the way in which Anton Gindely coped with this phenomenon. Gindely typically confused political support of the Bohemian Confession in 1575, and again in 1609, with broad religious acceptance. In reality, those who agreed to accept, or even to urge, the legalization of the Bohemian Confession, as discussed earlier, did not ipso facto become Lutherans. It was only from Gindely's angle of vision that the outpouring of sympathy for Utraquism in 1618 could appear virtually incomprehensible or entirely irrational. The historian tried to deal with the intractable fact of Utraquism's popularity through a Nietzschean sneer at the fickleness (*Wankelmuth*) of the common man.[116] Nevertheless, elsewhere even Gindely paid a grudging compliment to Utraquism, saying that "the banner of the ancient faith sub utraque, due to historical tradition and the remembrance of Hus, remained still ever sacred in the eyes of the multitude."[117]

Yet another concept embedded in the sixteenth-century historiography helped to exaggerate the impression of increased Lutheranization and reciprocal decline of Utraquism. This was the presumption of the virtual identity of Utraquist ritualistic and institutional views with those of the Roman Church. Thus, the intense dislike of Counter-Reformation Catholicism, particularly evident among the lower urban classes, manifested above all during the invasion of Prague by the Passauers in 1611, would be (mis)-identified ipso facto with the appeal of the German Reformation, or cited as a proof of assimilation of Utraquism with Lutheranism.[118] As pointed out repeatedly, Utraquism actually had its own long, and one might say "venerable," tradition of intense aversion to certain institutional and procedural aspects of Rome's ecclesiology, in particular monasticism, papal or episcopal executive and judicial jurisdiction, and ostentatious displays of ecclesiastical splendor or power. These attitudes were independent of, and antedated the emergence of, Luther and his teachings.

In Utraquism's historical memory, monastic orders figured as the most virulent advocates and energetic abettors of the extermination of religious dissent during the wars of the Bohemian Reformation.[119] Thus, the popular attacks on monasteries in 1611, which focused on five institutions including the Franciscans at the Church of our Lady of the Snows, had their antecedents as far back as the fifteenth century, especially in the waves of antimonastic violence in 1448 and 1483, as well as a lesser one in 1521.[120] They reflected the perennial quarrel with the Church of Rome, which was at its core ecclesiastical, not dogmatic. In the sixteenth and seventeenth centuries, monasteries were viewed as exotic islands or fortresses staffed almost entirely by unsympathetic foreigners in the midst of Czech normalcy. In 1577 and again 1590, serious attention was paid to reports that the Jesuits were preparing attacks to seize Utraquist churches.[121] Archbishop Berka, in a report to Rome on the expulsion of the Capuchins from Prague in 1600, feared that all monastics might be expelled from the city, if not slaughtered.[122]

The Utraquists' special dislike of the Jesuit order was explicable, aside from its quasi-monastic character, by its stature as the prime promoter of papal jurisdiction, and as stern opponent of any deviations from Roman practices. In addition, the Society of Jesus sponsored certain characteristics of the Counter-Reformation's thrust that ran against the grain for the Utraquists.[123] Such was, for instance, the flamboyant display of religious art. This, in turn, led the Utraquists to emphasize their traditional restraint with respect to veneration of saints and images, which dated to the fifteenth century. The reaffirmation of this stance should not be automatically construed as assimilation to Lutheranism.[124] In a way, the Jesuits inherited the role of particularly harsh opponents of Utraquism that the Franciscans had played in the latter fifteenth century. Ironically, in 1611 the Franciscans were once again the principal sufferers, while the Jesuits, thanks to their special guards, escaped relatively unscathed.[125] Thus, the expressions of popular resentment against monasticism, against the advocacy of papal administrative ascendancy, or against the flamboyance of the Counter-Reformation had deep Utraquist roots, and a Lutheran input was not necessary for their activation.

The evidence just presented points to a conclusion that the Utraquists remained substantial in numbers, in fact the largest among the three types of sub utraque between 1609 and 1620, constituting as much as two-thirds to four-fifths of the Czech-speaking population of Bohemia.[126] In assessing this evidence, one more basic question remains to be asked. How then to explain the contemporary statements that their number had been insignificant by 1609? Above all, this is implied in the text of the *Porovnání*.[127] The answer probably lies in the fact that the noble authors of such pronouncements referred to the circles of acquaintances in their own class, among whom the Utraquists were indeed grossly underrepresented. Without trying to belabor the obvious, the limitation of the nobles' social contacts is suggested, for instance, by the diaries that Adam the Younger of Valdštejn kept between 1602 and 1633. Among some five hundred personal references, there were virtually none to commoners.[128] The aristocrats were not likely to pursue acquaintances, or fraternize, with the townspeople or the peasantry. Such an impact of the nobles' social perspectives, distorting their quantitative assessment of Utraquism, is suggested by Budovec's earlier statement of 1603: "[W]e know of no one who would be adherent of the Prague Consistory here or elsewhere in the country, namely among the higher estates . . ."[129] Without taking into account the distorting lens of his social vision in Budovec's assertion of 1603, his statement about the virtual nonexistence of Utraquism would represent a blatant contradiction to his rallying cry of 1609 for the alliance of the three types of sub utraque in which he named the Utraquists in the first place.

Looking at the issue in another way, the assertions that there were virtually no Utraquists in Bohemia might acquire a spurious semblance of veracity from a recent trend in the historiography of nationalism. This school, represented by Ernest Gellner, Eric Hobsbawm, and others, has denied the existence of authentic European nations in the sixteenth century, and placed their origin in the nineteenth century.[130] If one took into account only the "feudal" nation excluding the commoners, then indeed the Utraquists would be meager in numbers in Bohemia. Only 3 percent of the nobles could be classified as Utraquists in the opening decades of the seventeenth century.[131] As noted earlier, Czech historical literature has shown a bias toward the views of the upper classes and skepticism about ordinary people's intellectual commitments in its trivialization of the popular enthusiasm for Utraquism in 1618. A similar problem has been noted recently in English sixteenth- and seventeenth-century historiography where the emphasis on the upper classes has thwarted proper understanding of the religious orientation of the populace at large, "especially the laity below the rank of the landed gentry."[132] It is ironic that Czech historians writing in the age of liberal democracy should view the religious scene through the eyes of the noble elites, which constituted less than 1 percent of the total population of Bohemia. Those writing in the era of egalitarian socialism had at least some excuse, inasmuch as a measure of contempt for the mentality of the common man was not alien to the Leninist variant of Marxism.[133]

Utraquism as a Plebeian Church

On previous occasions it has been noted that Utraquism displayed a peculiarly plebeian character, partly related to its Wyclifite roots.[134] This contrasted not only with the appeal of Lutheranism and the Roman Church to the Czech nobility, both higher and lower, but also with the streak of social snobbery in the Unity. The Brethren in this respect resembled the English Puritans whose moral rigorism served as a mark of distinction from the poverty stricken and as a license for "their efforts to discipline the poor, to curb their drunken promiscuous ways, and to instil in them respect for sobriety, property and hard work."[135] The persistence of Utraquism's plebeian thrust can be illustrated from the principal surviving work of Pačuda, one of its intellectual leaders, who as noted earlier was considered for the post of administrator had a specifically Utraquist consistory been restored in 1617. To begin with, Pačuda's populist bent can be surmised from his excoriation of the sinfulness of pride. It was not just pride in general, which would be routine for any Christian to denounce; he aimed his rhetorical firepower specifically at the hubris of the mighty, a quality that naturally tended to characterize the nobility in Bohemia as well as elsewhere.[136] Pačuda emphasized that already in prehuman history God dealt severely with the pride of the angels. Subsequently, the Lord delighted in casting down the mighty from their high places of political or military power, in humiliating those thirsting after glory. Examples were the Prince of Tyre, suffering a ghastly death at the hands of foreigners (Ezekiel 28.1–10); Sennacherib, the king of Assyria, murdered by his own two sons; King Antiochus of Syria, excluded from human society by a foul disease; and the Pharaoh, who with his entire army, perished in the Red Sea. Military power turned into weakness, heroism into cowardice, and health into sickness. Belisarius, a captain of Emperor Justinian I, having fought brilliantly in Persia, turned into a beggar after his eyes were gouged out in captivity. Pačuda, in summing up, drew on the words of Isaiah (2:13): "Thus the Lord God knows how to cut down the high cedars of Lebanon and the impressive oaks of Bashan."[137]

As a counterpoint to castigating the vice of haughtiness, Pačuda characteristically extolled the inherent virtue of physical labor, the lot of ordinary people. According to him, labor as such was not a punishment for sin. Had Adam maintained his virtue intact, he and his descendants would enjoy working and reap continuous benefits. Constructive labor would be connected with merriment, gaiety, and thanksgiving, and it would be performed in confidence that its fruits would be properly and happily utilized and augmented by one's descendants. It was sin that overlaid the essentially joyful and fruitful process of physical work with the pall of pain, calluses, and sweat, and made the resulting benefits uncertain for succeeding generations. It can be taken as another sign of his populist predilection that in calling attention to the biblical injunction that man should raise his bread by the sweat of his brow, he commented: "[S]ome interpret this text so as to mean that emperors, kings, princes, and barons should plow and till the land; the priests also should have their homesteads and, like the peasants and others, should be occupied with such work . . ."[138] Although he implied disagreement with the statement, simply raising it in the public forum may be seen as highly significant.

Against both Roman and Protestant Christianity with their patriarchal favoritism, but in the tradition of the Bohemian Reformation when women served as theological spokespersons,[139] Pačuda took up the cause of women. Like the harsh view of physical labor, so also the subordination of women to men, according to him, was an abnormal state of affairs due to Adam's downfall. Ideally, the female would be the male's equal partner, participating fully and equally in the family's decisions and enterprises. A husband would seek consultation and mutual agreement with his wife, and never simply command her to act or to desist. Pačuda emphasized that even in the fallen state, man had to treat woman with respect: "[T]he wife should not serve her husband for a foot stool, because she is not a bone taken out of his leg, but she should be his help mate because she was created from the rib bone near to his heart."[140]

The plebeian character of Utraquism, or its status as a religion of the commoners, did not, however, involve a decline in its intellectual leadership to the primitive level of unsophisticated folkish religions usually associated with the Waldensian or Lollard ministers. The Utraquist priesthood remained loyal to the traditional roots of the Bohemian Reformation, which were firmly planted in the academy. Pačuda, for one, displayed a remarkable knowledge of both Greek and Latin patristic literature, citing from Cyprian (C1v, D6v, K5v),[141] Lactantius (B6v), Eusebius (E2v), Basil the Great (B8v), Ambrose (K5r, K6r), Chrysostom (E1r), Augustine (A7v, C4r, G4v, G5r, K4v), Gregory the Great (C7v), and Bernard of Clairvaux (D5r, E4v, F3v, F8v, J6r). Incidentally, of these at least two, Gregory the Great and Bernard of Clairvaux, were theologically unacceptable to the Lutherans.[142] Pačuda also displayed familiarity with the Greek classics, such as Homer (J4r), Herodotus (J3v), Euripides (J4r), Aristotle (C2v), Diodorus Siculus (B6r), Strabo (B4r), Philon (B1v), Plutarch (C4v, J5r), and Claudian (G1v), as well as Roman classics, such as Plautus (J6r), Cicero (E5v, H7r), Ovid (C2v, G1v), Lucanus (G8r), and Lucius Apuleius (C5v). What was even more important, his citations were not merely perfunctory, mechanical or ornamental, but used creatively and effectively for purposes of illustration or amplification.

Utraquists and Lutherans: Differences

Despite the cooperation between the Utraquist townsmen and Lutheran nobles in Bohemian parliamentary politics, and the association of the Utraquist priests with the Lutheran ministers in the joint Consistory sub utraque, traditional dogmatic differences persisted. Most had been defined in the Utraquist responses to the Bohemian Confession in 1575 and 1609 and, on the Lutheran side, in the Bohemian Confession and in the works of theologians such as Jan Štelcar Želetavský of Želetava and Jiřík Dykastus between 1575 and 1608. The continuing divergence of belief and practice once more indicated that the political rapprochement was not accompanied by doctrinal assimilation. There is no evidence of a progressive amalgamation of Lutheranism with Utraquism into a new syncretic religion of neo-Utraquism.

First, a highly visible divide continued to be the Lutheran opposition to the communion of infants. Zachariáš Bruncvík in his *Kšaftu Večeře Páně* (1613) firmly rejected the practice. Jiří Taciturnus in his Lutheran catechism, somewhat misleadingly titled *Zlatý řetízek pravého katolického náboženství* (The Golden Chain of the True Catholic Religion) and published in 1616, not only condemned infant communion, but went on to compare its practice to giving communion to drunkards, persons of ill repute, the enraged, blasphemers, or heretics.[143] As Noemi Rejchrtová has pointed out, communion for infants was not an isolated precept, but rather an outgrowth of the Utraquists' profound respect for the status of children, the nature of whose faith Christ had posited as an example for adults.[144] Thus, Cykáda in a funeral sermon of October 1612 conjured up the image of toddlers in heaven happily romping around with Christ who adopts the form of a white lamb.[145] The victorious Counter-Reformation, not the Lutherans, would suppress the Utraquist rite of communion for infants.

Second, another highly visible mark of distinction was the adoration of the host outside the Eucharistic service, which the Lutherans had discarded. The Utraquists, on the other hand, performed this ritual with enthusiasm, particularly in the elaborately festive Easter and Corpus Christi processions. Such displays irritated the Lutherans particularly in 1613 and in 1618, as also the Jesuits' *Apology* of 1618 testified. As noted earlier, a particularly impressive and well-attended Easter procession of 1618 was conducted by Locika of Domažlice, then pastor of St. Nicholas in the Old Town of Prague. While at that point he became a target of Lutheran retribution, he was destined to play a martyr's role during the subsequent Counter-Reformation.[146] Thus in his person the *via media* of Utraquism achieved a particularly poignant expression. The new church order for the Lutheran clergy issued on January 16, 1610, as cited by Bruncvík in his *Kšaftu Večeře Páně* (1613), proscribed any veneration of the host outside the Lord's Supper, including in processions, a monstrance, and Christ's grave on Holy Thursday, or by elevation of the host. Bruncvík, like other Czech Lutherans, upheld the principle attributed to Melanchton that the Eucharistic transformation of bread and wine into the body and blood of Christ was a transient occurrence, not continuing past the service of Lord's Supper.[147]

Third, there was a conspicuous difference between the Utraquists and the Lutherans on the issue of the veneration and invocation of the saints, particularly with respect to Hus and other martyrs of the Bohemian Reformation. Dykastus viewed the invocation of saints as a thoroughly errant practice that contradicted the Old Testament's injunction against detracting from honor due to God. In the New Testament, John the Baptist's humility before Christ taught that religious veneration belongs to the Savior alone. A Lutheran catechism, titled *Summa náboženství pravého z Konfessí české vybraná* (The Sum of the True Religion Extracted from the Bohemian Confession) and published in 1618, referring to the issue of the invocation of saints, stated categorically: "[W]e should neither invoke the Saints, nor have recourse to them."[148] This statement challenged the centuries-long veneration of the martyrs of the Bohemian Reformation, particularly Hus, in the public worship of the Utraquist Church.[149] At the same time, it showed how far the Bohemian Confession deviated from the Utraquist tradition, and how distinctly it stood within the precincts of Augsburg. The *Summa náboženství pravého* referred respectfully to "Doctor Martin Luther" and appended his *Otázky křesťanské* (Christian Questions). In contrast, there was not even a token mention of Hus in either this catechism or that of Taciturnus. Similarly, Zykmund Critinus, a Lutheran and the administrator of the Consistory sub utraque (1614–1619), in his book of meditations, *Křesťanské dílo denní* (The Daily Christian Work) (1613), deferred to Luther as an authority on spiritual life, again without any mention of Hus.[150]

Fourth, related to rejection of the invocation of saints, was the Lutherans' opposition to religious images depicting either the Trinity or the saints. Zacharyáš Bruncvík, in his *Idolorum pia suplantatio* (1613), cited in opposition to the veneration of images particularly the edicts of the two iconoclastic Byzantine Emperors, Leo III (717–741) and Constantine V Copronymos (741–775), and those of the Council of Constantinople (or Hiereia) in 775, without noting that these decisions were subsequently reversed, particularly by the Second Ecumenical Council of Nicaea (787). In an earthy simile, he called veneration of images a spiritual adultery that violated the mystical marriage between Christ and his Church. In the *Zrcadlo Kacířství,* Bruncvík specifically denounced the depiction of the Holy Spirit as a dove, and that of Christ as a lamb, and defended an early Persian iconoclast, a certain Xeneias, as a man "enlightened by divine truth," who should not suffer vilification.[151]

Fifth, one may note a hardening of the position on the salvific role of good works in the Lutheran literature of this period. While Dykastus, writing in a book published in 1592, still praised prayer, fasting, and almsgiving as influential with the divinity, Bruncvík in his treatise of 1613 presented unambiguously the orthodox Lutheran view on justification by faith alone with a corollary dismissal of the doctrine of the purgatory. As one of his arguments, he cited Luke (16:22–25) on the postmortem fates of Lazarus, who was carried by the angels into Abraham's bosom, and the rich man, who was cast into Hades. Luke did not mention an intermediate cleansing as an option.[152]

Sixth, and undergirding the other points of difference, the Lutherans opposed the use of liturgical books that the Utraquists had employed as a basis of their traditional rites since the beginning of the Bohemian Reformation, some one hundred years before Luther. These volumes were inherited, by tradition and in fact, from the service books of the Archdiocese of Prague, dating to the mid-fourteenth century, specifically the missals and breviaries, as well as the agenda and rubrics of the archbishopric of Prague.[153] According to David Holeton, Utraquist liturgical texts were in fact incompatible with Lutheran usages. The proscription of their use was included in the abovementioned new church order for the Lutheran clergy under the Consistory sub utraque, issued in 1610.[154]

Finally, in view of the routine charges in historical literature of the Utraquists' craven submissiveness to royal authorities,[155] it is curious to note the fervor of Lutherans' commitment of loyalty to secular sovereigns under virtually any circumstances. Thus, Dykastus in his *Postylla* (1612) condemned the heretical and unfaithful (*bludní a nevěrní*) Christians who would murder such monarchs as William of Orange (1584), or Henry III (1589) and Henry IV of France (1610), or attempt to assassinate James I of England (1605). What is particularly significant is Dykastus's model of the proper attitude toward sovereigns. It was that of the early Christians who prayed for the pagan emperors set on martyring them.[156] Such a degree of devotion to state power would be hard to find in Utraquist writings. It would present a problem for the Lutheran theologians to justify the uprising against Kings Matthias and Ferdinand II.

On the whole, the Lutherans decisively discarded some of the most cherished of Utraquist practices, particularly those of infant communion, the public display of the Eucharist, the veneration of Jan Hus and other martyrs of the Bohemian Reformation, and the traditional liturgical books of the pre-Tridentine archdiocese of Prague. This stance indicated the width of the chasm that continued to separate the confessors of Augsburg—even under the label of the Bohemian Confession—from the direct heirs of the Bohemian Reformation. It was the same chasm that has been pointed out previously by Pavel Bydžovský in his writings of the 1540s, by the opponents of the Bohemian Confession in 1575, and by the Utraquist spokesmen in 1609. The new church order for Lutheran clergy of 1610 summed up the difference between the Lutherans and the Utraquists. According to this document, "the priests of the Lord *sub utraque* and with heart and lips adhering to the Bohemian Confession" should abstain from veneration of the host outside the liturgy, abandon infant communion, and avoid the traditional liturgical books of the archbishopric of Prague.[157]

Utraquists and Lutherans: Flirtations

Despite the social and economic antagonism between the towns and the nobles, political considerations led the Utraquist towns to perpetuate their political alliance with the Lutheran aristocracy until the turning point at White Mountain in 1620.[158] On the religious level, the Czech Lutherans, as discussed above, repaid the political fidelity of the Utraquists by acting in a fairly tolerant, and hence loyal, manner toward the Utraquists, even against some of the language of the Letter of the Majesty of 1609. As noted earlier, Czech Lutherans, for instance, in exceptional cases even acquiesced in sharing churches with the Utraquists, although of course with separate services. The most striking instance of this was the sharing of the prestigious Týn Church in Prague after the appointment of Dykastus as pastor in 1614. Martinius of Dražov, the prominent Lutheran pastor of St. Castulus (Haštal) in Prague since 1617, made a major speech at the University of Prague on December 9, 1616, which focused on the need of cooperation across denominational lines in order to safeguard the freedom of religion. In what may be considered an overture to the Utraquists (as well as the Brethren), he cited historical examples of peacefully resolving religious disagreements, and the disastrous consequences of the wars of religion. Martinius was to become a member of the Consistory in 1619.[159] As noted earlier, the Jesuits of Prague, in their Viennese exile in 1618 reflecting on the recent period in Bohemia, expressed their dismay that the Utraquists should form an alliance with the Lutherans and the Brethren against the Church of Rome disregarding the profound differences with their confederates, particularly on the nature and the adoration of the Eucharist.[160]

Despite their preference for the tradition of Luther over that of Hus, as preserved and cherished by Utraquism, it would not be fair to represent the Czech Lutherans as entirely rejecting the historical and cultural heritage of Bohemia. While there is little doubt about their sincere and full acceptance of the Augsburg Confession, there is also evidence that the Czech Lutherans tended to justify embracing Luther's teaching by a presumption that Hus anticipated Luther. This perpetuated the view of the supreme justice, Bohuslav Felix Hasištejnský of Lobkovice, when he proposed the adoption of the Bohemian Confession in 1575.[161] For instance, the Lutheran minister Zacharyáš Bruncvík tried to discern precedents of certain Lutheran tenets in Czech Utraquism. In his *Kšaftu Večeře Páně*, published in 1613, he sought to equate Hus's opposition to indulgences with that of Luther and Zwingli. In his *Idolorum pia suplantatio* (also from 1613), Bruncvík tried to relate Lutheran views on religious art to a statement by Jan Hus, cited by Aeneas Sylvius, and the decisions of the Utraquist Synod of 1421.[162] These arguments ignored the facts that Hus opposed only the misapplication of indulgences by Pope John XXIII, not their very existence, that Aeneas Sylvius was an unreliable witness, and finally that the Utraquists firmly believed in the veneration of saints. Similarly, the Utraquists' uncompromising view of the mass as a sacrifice belied Bruncvík's perception of the Utraquist Articles of 1524 in *Kšaftu Večeře Páně* as a Lutheran-like reform of the mass.[163] Seeking to present the Articles of 1524, which he cited from a work of Matěj Kolín of Chotěřina, as a Lutheran document, Bruncvík omitted some and (mis)interpreted others in a Lutheran sense. Above all, endorsements of infant communion; Hus's sainthood; and the theology of Hus, Jakoubek of Stříbro, and Jan Rokycana were missing; and a rejection of the traditional Western liturgical books was falsely added.[164]

The most valiant attempt to relate Luther to Hus made on the Czech Lutheran side was probably that of Martinius of Dražov, who prepared a lengthy treatise, *Hussius et Lutherus*, published in 1618, to show various external parallels in the lives of both. The crucial doctrinal comparison, however, was not fruitful. Martinius chose to compare the Bohemian Confession of 1575 with the Augsburg Confession, especially in chapter four under the heading "Doctrinae Hussii et Lutheri collatio."[165] The former, which was in fact a derivation from the Augsburg Confession, was (mis)-represented as an epitome of Hus's teachings. Martinius actually compared one Lutheran text with another rather than the teachings of Hus with Luther's. Nevertheless, as late as 1619 in an exhortation to the soldiers in the Bohemian uprising, the Lutheran theologian Jiřík Bartolomeus proudly recalled the prowess of their ancestors in the wars of the Bohemian Reformation. However, he did not draw any theological lessons from their feats, and discussed them alongside other victories against unfavorable odds due to divine aid, such as Gideon's victory over the Midianites (Judges 8.4–10) and repulsions of the Turks in 1532 and 1598.[166] At the other side of the ledger, Czech Lutherans had no compunction about their allegiance to "the authentic original Augsburg Confession (*pravé originální Konfesí Augšpurské*)," as subsequent administrator Zykmund Crinitus declared on the title page of a treatise published in 1609.[167] A catechetical version of the Bohemian Confession appeared in 1614, and again in 1620, under the frank title *Konfessí Česká pravá Aušpurská* (The Bohemian Confession, an Authentic Augsburg Confession).[168]

Czech Lutherans and Germany

While the vestigial echoes of Hus and Bohemian ways were insufficient to support the construction of neo-Utraquism, a novel synthesis of the teachings of Hus and Luther, it would not be appropriate to regard the Czech Lutherans simply as German clones who were "intellectually dependent entirely on German culture."[169] Their detachment from the current trends in German Lutheranism was indicated by lack of involvement in the epochal controversy raging between the Gnesio-Lutherans and the Philippists, or with the Formula of Concord of 1577 that terminated the intra-Lutheran dispute in Germany. This disinterest contrasted even with the involvement of their Lutheran colleagues in the Slovene lands of Inner Austria, who subscribed to the Formula in 1582. The Slovene Lutherans stood closer to the German dispute since their near-compatriot, the Croat Flacius Illyricus, led the Gnesio-Lutheran faction which by and large prevailed in the Formula of Concord.[170] The close contact of the Czech Lutherans with their German colleagues in the post-White Mountain exile made the difference more evident. This is illustrated by the experience of the abovementioned Martinius. In his subsequent stay in Saxony during the 1620s, despite a course of study at the University of Wittenberg, he would find himself unfit to serve German congregations due to limitations of language and his lack of empathy with local mentalities.[171] More generally, even their minor and relatively innocuous deviations would make the Czech Lutherans subject to harsh pressure from their German Lutheran hosts to abandon such divergences and accept a full conformity. This proscription evidently included doing no more than paying lip service to a substantial connection between the reform programs of Hus and Luther. The authoritative Saxon theologians of Wittenberg showed no inclination to have Luther share any of the limelight with Hus, as they would make clear in a statement of 1620, justifying Saxon aid to Ferdinand II to crush the Bohemian Uprising: "[F]or us as the Sons of light, it is proper . . . to multiply the said Holy Truth, which from the infinite mercy of God a hundred years ago was first introduced to no one else, but solely to us Germans and especially to the Saxon nation, [and conducted] down from heavens, through the hands of Doctor Luther, into our faithful hands."[172] The German theologians thus categorically—and one may add, quite properly—excluded Hus from any share in the revelation of the Lutheran religious truth.[173]

While the Czech Lutherans conscientiously subscribed to the tenets of the Augsburg Confession, as well as to the teachings of Luther and Melanchton, their theological apologetics and devotional literature tended to draw to a considerable degree on Transrhenish Europe. Prime examples are the moralistic works of the English Puritan divine William Perkins, which were translated into Czech between 1610 and 1620 by three clergymen: Jiří Oekonomus of Chrudim, Jan Regius of Žatec, and Simeon Valecius of Louny.[174] Among Czech theologians, the prominent Bruncvík relied largely on English dissenting divines for his encyclopedic *Zrcadlo Kacířství* (1614). He also held in high esteem the collection *Harmonia confessionum fidei, Orthodoxarum, et Reformatorum Ecclesiarum* (Geneva, 1581), and similar compendia, which prominently featured the Protestant creeds of Western Europe, particularly English, Scottish, French, Dutch, and Swiss. In his *Kšaftu Večeře Páně*, the Lutheran theologian drew on Foxe's *Book of Martyrs,* and on Laurence Humphrey's *Contra Edmundi Campioni rationes* for information on Wyclif and the Lollards.[175] The conspicuous interest in English nonconformist theology is explored more fully in a subsequent section of this chapter.

The same lack of squeamishness about Calvinism, facilitated perhaps by close contacts between the Lutheran and Brethren clergy, permitted the Lutheran nobility to select as the king of Bohemia in 1619 the Calvinist son-in-law of James I, Frederick of Palatinate, whose theological background was closer to that of the Brethren. All this showed that the Czech Lutherans did not display the same rigid intolerance as their fellow believers abroad. In fact, their attitude would be subject to scathing criticism by their above-mentioned German confrere, Hoë von Hoënegg, from 1613 the principal preacher at the court of Johann Georg, the elector of Saxony, who had resided in Prague two years previously (1611–1613) as the pastor of a German church in the Old Town.[176] As noted earlier, West European Calvinists could be, in turn—in contrast to the reserve of the German Lutherans—enthusiastic about claiming Hus for their spiritual ancestry, as witnessed above all by the martyrologies of Foxe and Crespin.

Utraquists and the Roman Church: Frigidity

Aside from the presumption that Utraquism disappeared after 1609 by coming under the aegis of the new Consistory, another scenario of Utraquism's disappearance called for its virtual fusion with the Roman Church. Thus, Glücklich wrote that after 1609, Utraquism "entered on the closest possible rapprochement" with Rome in order "to serve as a barrier against religious innovation."[177] Let us now examine these claims. While the Czech Lutherans exhibited a rather benign and tolerant attitude toward Utraquism (in contrast to their foreign, especially Saxon, confreres), the representatives of the Roman Church in Bohemia continued to display a post-Tridentine rigidity and intolerance that contrasted with the more benevolent stance earlier in the sixteenth century. The frigidity seemed to increase after the affair of the apostasy of Administrator Rezek in 1593. The unfriendly tone on the Roman side was accompanied by the more conspicuous ascendancy of foreign personnel in the hierarchy of the Roman Church in Bohemia, and in particular, the introduction of German prelates Lamberg and Lohelius to Prague after the archiepiscopate of Berka.

The more militant tone vis-à-vis Utraquism can be illustrated from the writings of the prominent theologian of the Roman Church in Bohemia, Petr Linteo of Pilzenburgk. In a head-on clash with Utraquism, Linteo focused on the alleged illegitimacy of the requirement of lay communion in both kinds. He attributed its introduction in Bohemia under Jakoubek to the work of the devil who sought to disturb the harmony in the Western Church in which, without any quarrel, the laity had received communion under the species of bread only. The devil chose as his instrument Peter of Dresden, who in turn infected Jakoubek in 1414: "[I]n front of him . . . [Peter] poured this poison out of his own mouth; having absorbed it, [Jakoubek] immediately the following day boasted to the masters and bachelors in the Great College that he had found the way of life in the Lord's Testament. He declared the customary communion sub una specie to be in error, and extolled and approved the communion sub utraque as the only means to salvation."[178] As a horrendous consequence, argued the Roman apologist, the new precept could cast doubts about salvation of the ancestors of the Czechs, and about the chances of salvation for the people in many other Christian lands where communion sub una had been practiced for centuries. Next, Linteo took the opportunity to denounce another cardinal principle of Utraquism that was objectionable to the Roman Church, namely that of searching for religious truth through free argumentation. Thus, he attributed the embracing of communion sub utraque to unrestrained power of reasoning, saying about Peter of Dresden that he was "more competent in grammar than in the Scripture," and characterizing Jakoubek as "a venturesome person and a rash logician."[179] As his trump card, Linteo brought up the allegation that Hus did not approve of the communion sub utraque. According to him, the Bohemian reformer was greatly saddened when he learned about the use of the lay chalice in his homeland while he was imprisoned in Constance. Elsewhere in his book, the Roman critic of Utraquism claimed again that Hus characterized lay communion sub utraque as an act of rashness (*všetečnost*).[180] He capped his assessment of communion sub utraque by calling its initiators "the instruments and henchmen of a satanic deception and tyranny."[181]

Turning to the Compactata issued to the Utraquists by the Council of Basle 1436 with a guarded approval of the lay communion sub utraque, Linteo claimed that the concession was invalid, inasmuch as the document did not bear the approval of the Roman Curia. That remained the case into the sixteenth century, as attested by the failure of Bohemian King Vladislav II Jagellonian (1471–1516) to obtain papal approval of the Compactata shortly before his death. Linteo characterized as legitimate only the permission of the lay chalice by Pope Pius IV, which was included in a letter dated April 16, 1564, to the electors of Cologne and Trier; archbishops of Salzburg, Prague, Bremen, and Esztergom; and the bishops of Hamburg and Jurck.[182] Even though this permission involved a disavowal of the superiority of communion sub una, Linteo still depicted the papal grant as a precarious concession that was only temporary. He proceeded to cite reasons why in any case to receive sub una was preferable to communion in both kinds, even though he acknowledged that in principle both forms were appropriate. He offered altogether ten arguments in favor of communion in one kind, stressing that the demand for communion sub utraque had opened a Pandora's box of heretical notions.[183]

The alleged fusion of the Utraquists with the Roman Church after 1609 had received a semblance of support from the documents appended to the *Second Apology* of the Bohemian estates (1618). One document in particular quoted the oath that Utraquist candidates for priesthood were supposedly required to take prior to their ordination by the archbishop of Prague.[184] The Tridentine text, as cited, in fact contained an abject promise of submission to the Holy See, but by itself proved little about actual Utraquist ordinations. I have touched on this issue previously in this chapter. On the one hand, there was nothing new about this text. As early as the 1560s, the archbishop of Prague had come to insist on submission to the Tridentine document by any new ordinands, thereby terminating any further archiepiscopal ordinations of Utraquists in Prague. Subsequently, Utraquist priests were ordained by bishops outside Bohemia, particularly in Passau, Wrocław, Olomouc, Poznañ, and Nitra.[185] On the other hand, there seems to be little independent evidence that any Utraquist candidates for priesthood actually submitted to such a requirement since the turn of the sixteenth century either before or after 1609. The Tridentine oath, of course, would have been taken by those Utraquist priests who had originally received ordination under sub una and then shifted their allegiance. These priests, however, could not be considered bound by a juridical submission to the Holy See. As an example, one can cite the case of the prominent Utraquist priest Jan Cykáda, a member of the Consistory in 1605–1609, who had been ordained by the archbishop and had served as a priest sub una during the 1590s.

In any case, the leading Utraquist theologians of the period 1609–1620, such as Pačuda, Locika, Cykáda, or Jakub Soffian Walkmberger of Walkmbergk, could not be considered lackeys of the Roman Church, any more than they could be viewed as crypto-Lutherans. As an example, the notable Utraquist pastor, Locika of Domažlice, preached so critically about the Roman Church in 1613 at his parish church in Prague that he received a formal reprimand from Administrator Crinitus, a Lutheran.[186] If, as Hrejsa maintained, the adherents of the Roman Church, guided by the nuncio and Cardinal Melchior Klesl, supported in 1618 the plan for a Utraquist Consistory as a way to weaken the united front sub utraque and bring the Utraquists into submission to the archbishop, the Utraquist priests clearly refused to swallow the bait.[187] On the popular side, the Utraquist hostility to the institutions of the Roman Church can be gleaned from the assaults on the monasteries, noted earlier, which accompanied the invasion of the Passauers in Prague in 1611. Incidentally, one of the victims of these riots was Linteo, the anti-Utraquist controversialist just cited, who was then severely beaten and died two years later possibly in consequence of his injuries.[188]

Only after the outbreak of the Bohemian Uprising in 1618, the voice of the Roman Church toward the Utraquists softened once again, reminiscent of the views expressed at the midpoint of the previous century. This occurred in the oft-cited Jesuit *Apology,* which the Society published in Vienna, first in Latin and then in a German translation, after its expulsion from Bohemia on June 1, 1618. As noted earlier, the Jesuit *Apology* praised Hus and the Utraquists for their orthodox beliefs. Nevertheless, the *Apology* remained highly ambiguous, if not contradictory, in its ultimate assessment of Utraquism. Prior to 1609, despite the evident juridical schism between the Utraquists and the Roman Curia, Roman authorities might consider the Utraquists as still essentially participants in the Catholic Church. The *Apology,* on the one hand, contrasted the Utraquists with the Lutherans and gave them credit for defending much of the "faith and institutions of the Catholic Church." On the other hand, it struck a surprisingly discordant note by clumping the Utraquists with the Lutherans and the Brethren, and labeling all, without any qualification, as non-Catholics (Acatholicos).[189]

Utraquists and the Church of England: Mutual Misperceptions

Because of the previously noted sharing of the *via media* by the Utraquists and the Church of England, it appears paradoxical that the two had little contact or even mutual knowledge, although relations between Bohemia and Britain substantially increased in the period culminating in the Bohemian Uprising. A likely explanation is that knowledge of the religious situation on each side was propagated by the religious radicals—Lutherans and the Brethren in Bohemia and nonconformists in England—and the Utraquists and proto-Anglicans tended to view each other in this distorting mirror.[190]

Except for the translation of John Jewel's *Apologia,*[191] the interest in English religious thought in Bohemia seemed focused on outright Protestant or Puritan trends, which appealed to the Lutherans and the Brethren. This was in part a result of availability. While continental Protestants had only limited interest in authentic proto-Anglicans, they favored the English nonconformists, and even printed or reprinted their writings in places like

Geneva. Continental dissemination facilitated the effect of such literature on Bohemia's Lutherans. The use of English nonconformist sources was exemplified in the treatise *Kšaftu Večeře Páně* (1613) by the Lutheran Zacharyáš Bruncvík, who relied for an explication of Wyclif on the works of Laurence Humphrey (1527–1590), an exile from the Marian Counter-Reformation.[192] Otherwise, Bruncvík cited Foxe's *Book of Martyrs* on Wyclif, a list of fifteen notable Lollards from a publication he called *Catalogus testium veritatis,* and again from Humphrey on the burning of Wyclif's books in Prague in 1410.[193] Bruncvík displayed an even broader knowledge of English religious radicalism in his *Zrcadlo Kacířství* (1614). He relied largely on such English sources (in Latin) to demonstrate that mainline Protestantism either had not embraced ancient and early medieval heresies, as charged by the Roman Church, or if it did so, such teachings were not really heretical but orthodox. The Czech Lutheran referred to the Oxonian Puritan, Robert Abbot, and even to James I's *Apology for the Oath of Allegiance* (1609) on the issues of the Antichrist and false prophets.[194] He repeatedly cited another Puritan, William Whitaker, as well as his own old favorite Humphrey, on the nature of the Church and religious rituals. The special relevance of these writers to Bohemia stemmed from their polemical sallies against Edmund Campion's *Rationes decem*. As discussed in the preceding chapter,[195] Campion had spent seven years at Jesuit colleges in Brno and Prague (1573–1580), and his important work, *Rationes decem,* had appeared twice in Czech translation early in the seventeenth century.[196] Nevertheless, Bruncvík resorted most frequently to the also Puritanically inclined Matthew Sutcliffe, and to the low churchman Bishop Thomas Morton, for their wide-ranging inventory of real or putative past deviations from the true Christian faith.[197] He featured Morton's anti-Roman polemic, *Apologia Catholica* (1606) as one of his main sources on the title page of his *Zrcadlo Kacířství*.[198] It was typical of the radical leanings of Bruncvík's English sources that Humphrey, Morton, Sutcliffe, and Whitaker, according to him, all vouched for Calvin's Christian orthodoxy. In the same context, Bruncvík countered William Gifford's equating Calvin's followers with those of Mohammed in *Calvino-Turcismus* (1603) by citing Sutcliffe's response, *De Turco-Papismo* (1604), which drew contrary parallels between Rome and Islam.[199] He also rejoiced that for Humphrey, Morton, and Whitaker, far from being a heretic, Luther was "a special vessel of God (*zvláštní nádoba Boží*)."[200]

As noted earlier, Czech Lutherans showed a lively interest in the devotional works of the Puritan William Perkins (1558–1602), among them the lengthy *Anatomia conscientiae,* which appeared in Prague in Czech translations by Oeconomus, Regius, and Valecius between 1610 and 1620. Of the three translators, Regius would continue his interest in England where he traveled for two years (1633–1635) from his post-White Mountain exile in Saxony. In *Zrcadlo Kacířství,* Bruncvík likewise referred to Perkins's rejection of purgatory.[201] As also noted earlier, Czech Lutherans shared the outrage of the English nonconformists over the alleged Gunpowder Plot of 1604–1605. Abraham Scultetus, preaching in honor of Frederick of Palatinate's coronation as Bohemian king on October 24, 1619, praised the crypto-Lutheran archbishop, Thomas Cranmer, who in repentance burned his right hand by which he had signed a statement approving of the mass. According to Frederick's court preacher, Cranmer's and others' subsequent martyrdom for their evangelical faith under Queen Mary caused the rise of the devout ranks of Protestant believers.[202]

The Bohemian focus on English religious radicalism seemed to mirror the English interest in Bohemia that centered on Taboritism and tended to (mis)perceive Hus and Jerome as proto-Protestants. The appreciation of Utraquism as a *via media* seems to have been lost.[203] Perhaps under the influence of Foxe, the Puritans appropriated Hus so convincingly that the Anglican polemicists habitually included him and Jerome of Prague in the company of proto-Protestants, such as the Albigensians, the Waldensians, the Taborites, and Wyclif. Already Henry VIII had considered Luther another Hus, speaking of a worm that metamorphosed into the dragon of the Bohemian sect.[204] The Unity of Brethren and other atypical Bohemian radicals with international connections also tended to display a misleadingly radical visage of the Bohemian Reformation in their contacts with England. Thus, a Bohemian disciple of Luther, Ulrichus Velenus, upset Bishop John Fisher in 1521 by denying St. Peter's residence in Rome. Writing a book against the "impudent" Bohemian, Fisher granted him by singling him out a distinction that he otherwise bestowed among foreign theologians only on Jacques Lefèvre d'Étaples, Luther, and Johann Oecolampadius.[205] The author was identical with Oldřich Velenský of Mnichov, an early Czech Lutheran, who became a Brother by 1530.[206] Jan Opsimates presented to James I in July 1616 a Czech version of Calvin's *Institutes,* earlier translated by Jiří Strejc. The dedicatory copy included a special Latin preface in honor of James, containing verses by scholars from Bremen, Prague, and Nuremberg.[207] The Bohemian estates' choice of a Calvinist, Frederick of Palatinate, as king in 1619 pointed in the same radical direction, even though he was James I's son-in-law. Anthony Milton relates a particularly poignant episode, which—albeit dating from the post-1620 period—evidently reflected a long-term attitudinal trend. An almanac published in London for 1631 by William Beale replaced several medieval saints in the Prayer Book Calendar by Foxe's Lollard Martyrs, Wyclif, Savonarola, as well as Hus and Jerome of Prague. An Anglican critic, John Pockington condemned the work as "a Calendar . . . wherein the Holy Martyrs and Confessors of Jesus Christ . . . are rased out, and Traitors, Murderers, Rebels, and Hereticks set in their roome."[208]

An analogous misperception seemed to have characterized the Utraquist view of the English Reformation as a more radical phenomenon than it really was. While the Lutherans honored Thomas Cranmer and the Marian martyrs, the Utraquists, as mentioned earlier,[209] went in the opposite direction to celebrate Thomas More and John Fisher, as evident from the writings of Pavel Bydžovský and Šimon Ennius Klatovský.[210] Henry VIII's full break with the papacy—compared with the Utraquists' merely partial one—undoubtedly played a role here. Ironically, the two English martyrs, who literally lost their heads for the pope, were themselves severe critics of the papal monarchism of the late Middle Ages. While upholding sacramental papacy, they actually shared the Utraquists' aversion to the heavy-handed papal quasi-governmental jurisdiction.[211] There were other misapprehensions, based on exaggerated notions of the English Reformation's radicalism. In a letter to Rudolf II of July 3, 1599, Archbishop Berka compared England to Heidelberg as a hotbed of Calvinism.[212] This skewed image of the English religious scene was partly due to the propagandists for the Roman Church. In this connection Richard Montagu argued in his *Gag for the New Gospel? No: A New Gag for the Old Goose* (1624) that the Catholics were charging the Church of England with doctrines "raked together out of the lay-stalls of deepest Puritanisme, as much opposing the Church of *England,* as the Church of *Rome.*"[213] An additional confusing element was the willingness of the English government and the anti-Puritan bishops to tolerate or even unleash Puritan propaganda when it suited their purposes. As a case in point, during the Campion affair, Puritan writers were free to generate particularly stern propaganda against the Jesuits. This involved not only Humphrey and Whitaker, but also Charke, Field, and Travers. Ironically, some suitable Puritan polemicists were suggested to royal officials, such as William Burghley, by the anti-Puritan bishop Aylmer.[214]

Although never explicitly repudiating Christian ecumenicism or catholicity, a distinct national insularity seemed to lead the Utraquists, as the Anglicans, to largely surrender the field of international contacts to their fully reformed compatriots. As Diarmaid MacCulloch points out concerning the Anglican outlook: "While strikingly universal in his view of the past, Hooker became parochial in his view of the present: a retreat from the English Protestant internationalism . . . which was alive and well in the thinking of the Puritans."[215] Thus, an opportunity for mutual recognition—if not mutual support—was lost. Moreover, because of the complexities of their differing attitudes toward the papacy, the English Reformation appeared more, and Utraquism less, radical than reality warranted. This also hindered the likelihood of mutual appreciation, or possibly Christian affection.

The Utraquists and the Bohemian Uprising

The Utraquist towns remained loyal to their alliance with the Lutheran nobles, and against their own convictions and better judgment, followed the aristocrats into the revolt against Kings Matthias and Ferdinand II in 1618 with disastrous results.[216] The reluctance of the towns was graphically described by Mikuláš Dačický, the outstanding townsman/historian.[217] After the defenestration of the two royal lieutenants, Jaroslav Bořita Martinic and Vilém Slavata, the councilors of the city of Prague disassociated themselves from the nobles' acts of violence. The *Euangelische Erklerung auff die Böhaimische Apologia* (1618) also asserts that the Prague town council objected to the defensores' action in the spring of 1618, and the towns still on the day of the defenestration, May 23, 1618, refused to join the uprising. As a replay of the situation in 1575, when the towns had initially refused to support the Bohemian Confession, the burghers once again were threatened and intimidated into alliance with the noble estates. The towns' reluctance reflected their own caution rather than royal pressure or influence. Despite the assertion that the royal government appointed many sub una into town councils, the Utraquists in fact still predominated.[218] Similarly, there is no evidence for effective intimidation of town councils by the royal judges appointed in towns by the king. The towns still counseled moderation and negotiation with the king at the Diet of August 25, 1618, when there could be no question of pressure by royal judges.[219] In the end, the traditional cooperation between the noble estates and the burghers prevailed.[220] The nobles agreed to sweeten the pill by giving the urban estate a considerable share of power in the provisional government, the Directorium, established in May 1618. The towns were assigned ten of the thirty directors who assumed power from the defenestrated royal lieutenants, and—with the

Diet—ruled the country. This gave Bohemia a brief taste of the republican form of government until August 1619.[221] In this way, the towns also attained full political equality with the nobles.[222]

The towns' reluctance to join the uprising may be in part ascribed to the Utraquists' ingrained aversion to forcible resolutions of internal or external conflicts, a tendency that had evolved in reaction to the destructiveness of the Bohemian Reformation wars in the first half of the fifteenth century, as noted in Chapter 8. Although this pacific attitude had not reached truly Tolstoyan proportions as it had in the Unity, it had found its expression in the Utraquists' notable tolerance. The Utraquist quasi-pacifism was, however, only one ideological obstacle that the Lutheran nobles had to face. The Lutheran chaplains had to justify their masters' imbroglio with an enthroned monarch against their own foreign co-religionists, such as against the taunts of the *Euangelische Erklerung* that true and sincere Evangelicals owed obedience even to evil rulers (*zlé vrchnosti*) and "whoever opposes or vituperates the sovereign, opposes God himself, [inasmuch as] the monarchs concerned bear and manifest the image of God in their persons."[223] Thus, in response to Lutheran qualms, Bartolomeus argued that a war with its perils, as a visitation from God, roused the feeling of religious awareness that tended to decline during the period of peace with its sense of security. Its incidence could be also viewed as a divine scourge in punishment for sins.[224] Not only kings or princes, but also other rulers established by God could declare war, such as feudal estates (nobles and towns), entrusted with administration of their country (which was presumably the case in Bohemia). A just war could oppose not only enemies of God, but also those who threatened the security of recognized privileges, liberties, or properties.[225]

The (mis)management of the Bohemian uprising (1618–1620) demonstrated further the dysfunctional character of the Bohemian nobility by revealing its incompetence in the direction of both diplomatic and military affairs.[226] The aristocrats demonstrated their lack of civic-mindedness even during the insurrection, endeavoring to shift the burden of taxation from themselves onto the towns.[227] The election of Frederick of Palatinate as king on August 26, 1619, deprived the townspeople of their share in central government with the consequential dissolution of the body of the thirty directors. The new high royal officials were appointed entirely from the noble estates. Soon the towns likewise lost their representation in the county governments.[228] Moreover, the Calvinist zeal of Frederick's chaplains can be viewed as an affront to the Utraquist townspeople in its challenge to their religious *via media*. Such was the iconoclastic cleansing of the Prague cathedral in cooperation with the Brethren.[229] On the diplomatic front, the Calvinist alliance yielded only assistance from the Dutch, while alienating the Lutheran countries, particularly Saxony, and leaving the Britain of James I neutral.[230]

Otherwise, however, the insurgent governments during the uprising (in both its directorial and royal phases) did not interfere with Utraquist townsmen or clergy. Religious pluralism continued under the Consistory after the uprising, as is evident from the directors' orders of July 1618 which stipulated that the administrator should prevent clashes among clergy of different convictions. The previously mentioned proceedings against Locika of Domažlice in December 1618 seem to be an isolated case of persecution of Utraquist clergy.[231] Official restrictions affected adherents of the Roman Curia, including the expulsion of the Jesuits from the country and the exclusion of sub una from the councils of royal towns. Archbishop Lohelius likewise had to seek the security of refuge in Vienna. However, the adherents of Rome who forswore the principle that "promises given to heretics need not be kept" were tolerated, including the Franciscan and Capuchin orders.[232] Thus, the phenomenon of religious toleration withstood even the test of war, and existed in stark contrast to what was to follow.

Utraquism under the Letter of Majesty

In conclusion, four propositions can be suggested as to the state of the Utraquist Church in Bohemia between 1609 and 1621. First, whether individual Utraquist priests had to promise allegiance to the Tridentine creed when ordained by the archbishop of Prague or another Roman prelate was ultimately irrelevant, because operating as a Utraquist priest implied repudiation of obedience to the bureaucratic apparatus of the Roman Church. Second, the Utraquist clergy functioned under the authority of the Consistory sub utraque, not that of the archbishop of Prague. Third, while embracing the Bohemian Confession as a symbol, the Consistory sub utraque did not enforce Lutheran ecclesiastical uniformity, but rather provided a milieu federating three types of sub utraque with distinct confessions and liturgies: the Utraquists, the Lutherans (the authentic adherents to the Bohemian Confession), and the Unity of Brethren. Fourth, the Utraquists (or Hussites as they were improperly called) constituted a substantial portion, in fact a majority, of the sub utraque among the Czech townsmen and peasants.

12

White Mountain, 1620: The Transfiguration and the Protean Legacy of Utraquism

The Battle of White Mountain on November 8, 1620, by and large ended the insurrection of the Bohemian estates against Habsburg rule. In its aftermath, the country was subject to what amounted to a revolution in religious, as well as political, matters. During the restored reign of King Ferdinand II, Bohemia witnessed an abrupt and drastic imposition of the Counter-Reformation, which proceeded in an unrestrained way due to the simultaneous introduction of royal absolutism by the victorious Habsburg.[1] Gone was the remarkable state of relative tolerance, respect for human rights, unfettered learning, and economic prosperity that hitherto had characterized the Kingdom of Bohemia. The era of Camelot was over.

On the religious front, the clergy of the Unity of Brethren and the Calvinists were expatriated as early as 1621. The banishment of German Lutheran ministers was delayed until 1622–1624 to pacify Ferdinand II's ally, the elector of Saxony, Johann Georg. In 1622, the Jesuits were authorized to supervise education and censor books. In the same year, measures were introduced to suppress Utraquism, the focus of this chapter. A campaign to convert dissidents in towns and in the countryside was launched in 1623–1624 and continued for several years. The task was entrusted to special missions supported by military detachments and directed by "reformation" commissions. Aside from imprisonment and corporal punishment, the threats of quartering of troops proved particularly effective in eliciting submission.[2] Many urban dissenters emigrated, mainly from areas bordering Saxony and Silesia. The suppression of dissent was formally legalized in 1627, when the Letter of Majesty of 1609 was explicitly abrogated and the Renewed Land Ordinance declared the Roman Catholic religion the only permissible one. The main thrust of the Counter-Reformation then turned against the nobles, who thus far had been spared. Those who did not wish to conform had to leave the country. Protestant hopes engendered during the rest of the Thirty Years' War by periodic military successes of the Swedes, and briefly also of the Saxons (who participated in the anti-Habsburg coalition between 1630 and 1635), were completely extinguished in October 1648 by the Treaty of Westphalia, which gave the Habsburgs a carte blanche to settle religious affairs in both Bohemia and Moravia. Subsequently, dissenters continued to face serious penalties, since religious heterodoxy became equated with political treason.[3]

The repression following the Battle of White Mountain has been covered in both older and recent literature.[4] Similarly, the story of the Bohemian Lutherans and Brethren in the post-White Mountain exile has received considerable attention.[5] In contrast, the story of the Utraquists has remained by and large a mystery. The aim of this chapter is to explore the consequences for Bohemian Utraquism under the following rubrics: (1) the fate of Utraquist clergy, institutions, and believers; (2) the apparently rapid and complete disappearance of Utraquism; and (3) the long-range impact and significance of Utraquism.

After the Battle of White Mountain, the Utraquists still constituted the most substantial part of Bohemia's population.[6] Their treatment thus represented the most formidable challenge that the Counter-Reformation had to face. In contrast, the problem of the Protestant groups by and large solved itself through emigration. The Lutheran nobles and townspeople (mainly from the German areas) left largely for Saxony. The Unity of Brethren, and those suspected of Calvinism, had to go farther afield to Prussia, Poland, Holland, England, and eventually to Dutch and British North America. As for the Utraquist majority, the Czech-speaking townspeople and rural folk, they had no place to go, even if they were permitted to, which in most cases they were not. There was no ecclesiastical rationale, milieu, or market abroad to which they could turn with their distinctive Bohemian brand of liberal Roman[7] Catholicism, inasmuch as no organized religious group shared it at the time. They could not run or hide, but had to stay and face the Counter-Reformation music.

In the unhappy and even perverse outcome, the Bohemian religious organism was not destroyed on the surface. Instead its spirit was altered, while the body remained. One is reminded of the phenomenon of extraterrestrial body-snatching "aliens" in contemporary American cinematography. There was relatively little change in the external appearance of the ecclesiastical framework, that is, in the modes of faith and worship. It was, however, as if an alien character had entered the familiar body. It was as if a nurturing, some would say overindulgent, mother was replaced by a suspicious stepmother, committed to chastising and castigating her flock. The spirit of reasonableness and discussion, based on the Judge of Cheb (*soudce chebský*) of 1432, the Compactata of 1436, and the Peace of Kutná Hora of 1485,[8] was replaced by that of authoritarianism and intolerance, based on the anathemas of the councils of Constance and of Trent and on the militancy of the traditionally feared monastic orders. Seen from the grassroots, the character of the clergyman as a kindly pastor and neighbor was transmuted into that of a detached spiritual inspector acting as a counterpart to the manorial bailiff who was correspondingly charged with the work of secular policing. Without any striking changes in dogma or liturgy, their church turned from a neighborly and easygoing polity into a remote and rigid police state. The process was not entirely bloodless; it required at least two prominent Utraquist victims, the priests Jan Locika of Domažlice in 1622 and Vavřinec Hanžburský of Kopeček in 1631.

In the conclusion of this chapter, several suggestions will be put forth in a speculative vein and as issues for further research. First, the Bohemian Counter-Reformation produced a national religious amnesia by which the conscious awareness of Utraquism was suppressed, but not replaced by an attachment to either the Roman Curia or one of the reformed churches. Second, the liberal substrate, albeit divorced from the original theological context, would reemerge in the Bohemian national awakening, roused by the republication of sixteenth-century literature that was originally nurtured by the Utraquist ambiance. Finally, Utraquism would continue to stand as a prototype for subsequent epiphanies of "liberal Catholicism," particularly the Josephin ecclesiastical reforms of the late eighteenth century.

What Happened to the Utraquists?

The Question of Toleration

The fate of the Utraquist Church was decided in 1621. It was true that King Ferdinand II as late as June 1620 had still entertained the idea of preserving the institution sanctioned by his grandfather, uncle, and cousins. After all, it was the Lutherans and the Unity of Brethren, not the Utraquists, who initiated and spearheaded the revolt against Habsburg rule, while the Utraquist towns initially hesitated. It was the Lutherans, not the Utraquists, who debunked the veneration of the Virgin Mary. It was the Calvinists of King Frederick's court, not the Utraquists, who destroyed the religious art in the St. Vitus Cathedral in June 1620. The victorious avenger's temporary indulgence toward the Utraquists may have also been inspired by a misplaced wish to please his Lutheran ally Johann Georg, the elector of Saxony, who had helped him to put down the Bohemian uprising.[9] Even the Jesuits advocated a more tactful and humane approach toward the Utraquists, at least before the Battle of White Mountain.[10]

An advisory commission that assembled in freshly conquered Prague in late November 1620 still recommended "the salami tactic," namely a sequential elimination of opponents. The commission counseled initially proceeding only against the Brethren and the Calvinists, and to tolerate temporarily the Lutherans and the Utraquists.[11] In early 1621, the royal governor of Bohemia, Karl Lichtenstein, also favored the maintenance of Utraquism, at least on a temporary basis, including a separate Consistory. Mainly to relieve the shortage of acceptable clergy, he proposed that those Utraquist priests who were willing to obey the archbishop, be allowed to distribute communion in both kinds, a practice conditionally permitted by Rome at the time of the Council of Trent.[12] The Czech Catholic historian Václav V. Tomek, reported the situation thus: "In the first terrible phase of a complete uprooting of the country's legal order [1621], the party of the Old Utraquists raised once more its voice. . . . Some of its priests approached the royal governor Lichtenstein, asking that they be permitted, according to the established custom, to distribute communion in both kinds . . . and to be administered by a Consistory composed of their own clergy . . ."[13]

In the aftermath of White Mountain, however, Ferdinand did not seek to tolerate Utraquism or to promote its reconciliation with the papacy (on an admittedly remote chance that a compromise could be found between Utraquist liberalism and Roman authoritarianism). Moreover, schooled in forcible suppression of religious dissent in Inner Austria, which he had previously ruled as a prince (1596–1619), Ferdinand rejected a peaceful approach toward a restoration of religious unity that was effective in neighboring Poland.[14] One need not be a committed secularist or a Protestant fundamentalist to feel dismay about the resolution of the religious conditions in Bohemia through a heavy-handed Spanish-style Counter-Reformation. The authoritarian regime indiscriminately suppressed the mainstream Utraquists together with the Protestants, that is, the largely German Lutherans and the marginal Brethren.[15] Ferdinand acted in an extraordinary way, inasmuch as by the seventeenth century the use of force to alter religious conviction no longer seemed obviously natural or normal. The principle *cuius regio, eius religio* by no means worked smoothly, much less automatically, even in the area of its chief application—among the peoples of the Empire. This was specifically demonstrated by the failure of the elector of Prussia, Johann Sigismund, to change the faith of his subjects from Lutheranism to Calvinism in 1613.[16] At the other end of Europe, the English had more sense than to apply brute force in order to "convert" the Irish, or for that matter to suppress the Roman faith anywhere in Britain, as long as its adherents promised not to condone assassinating the monarch or call her/him a heretic in public.[17] The revocation of the Edict of Nantes (1598) in 1685 would be the occasion of a major international scandal. Yet, Ferdinand II's act of outlawing religious freedom, his abrogation of the Letter of Majesty of 1609, has failed to find its proper place on the world register of history's infamous acts. There were, however, individuals on the Roman side, including Ernst Adalbert von Harrach, Lohelius's successor as archbishop of Prague (1623–1667), and the theologian Valerian Magni, who for a long time felt uneasy about the use of police and military coercion to establish the decreed orthodoxy in the Czech lands.[18]

What made the procedure particularly lacerating in Bohemia was a superimposition of national prejudice on top of Spanish-like religious zeal. The combination produced the peculiarly vengeful and spiteful character of the Counter-Reformation there. This was largely the result of the changed ethnic character of the Roman Church's leadership in the country at the turn of the century. As noted in the preceding previous chapter,[19] prior to that time, the first three archbishops of the restored see of Prague, officiating from 1564 to 1606, could be considered products of the Bohemian cultural milieu—the third, Zbyněk Berka, was even born and raised as a Utraquist. Their two successors—Karl of Lamberg and Johann Lohelius—however, were Germans who could not even speak the language of the population over whose fate they were destined to preside.

Thus, by a conjunction of circumstances, the leaders of the Roman Church in Bohemia happened to be imbued not only with a militant religious ardor, but also with peculiar ethnic grudges. They reflected the double aversion that the Catholics of the Holy Roman Empire felt against the Bohemian Reformation and its followers. First, there was a sense of national grievance, inasmuch as ethnic Germans figured conspicuously among the victims of the Taborite religious terror during the wars of the Bohemian Reformation.[20] Second, Luther had used Hus's condemnation at Constance as a weapon to undermine the credibility of the Roman Curia.[21] Thereby he opened the door to a massive defection from Rome and to a painful division of the Holy Roman Empire along religious lines. It appears that these unfriendly sentiments could only be assuaged by a total victory following the Battle of White Mountain, completely reversing the humiliations inflicted by the Bohemian Reformation.

In the context of outsiders' input into the Bohemian Counter-Reformation, it is important to consider that the archbishop of Prague, Johann Lohelius, came from the German border town of Cheb. His two chief ecclesiastical associates and allies were Casper von Questenberg, the abbot of Strahov Monastery, born in Cologne, and Johann Ernst Platejs, a holder of multiple canonries, whose father was a convert to the Roman Church from Saxony. Platejs would be linked with at least one cause celebre of Utraquist martyrdom. The historians of the Bohemian Counter-Reformation, including Anton Gindely, Ernest Denis, and Josef Pekař (none of them susceptible to xenophobia), have credited the three prelates with the principal initiatives aimed at a particularly drastic and insensitive suppression of Utraquism. Pekař was especially harsh in condemning the activities of what he considered a sinister Teutonic troika.[22] The ethnic bias was also noted on the Roman side by Anthony Bruodin, a member of the expatriated Irish Franciscan community of Strict Observance who found refuge in Prague in the 1630s. The distinguished Irish scholar saw in the implementation of the Counter-Reformation an echo, or an extension, of the Czech-German strife, dating all the way back to the time of Hus.[23]

Methods of Obliteration

Whatever benign characteristics the Counter-Reformation may have possessed elsewhere in Europe, and however many magnificent specimens of baroque architecture it may have left behind, in Bohemia the strand of ethnic antagonism synergized with an anti-heretical zeal to produce a relentless campaign toward unconditional and complete merger with the Roman Church. The Utraquists' subordination to the Curia's rule and their fusion with the organizational structure under Rome had been prematurely announced, dating variously to 1564, 1575, 1593, or 1609. Now all this would actually come to pass, not on a voluntary basis, but through coercion. The new royal absolutism removed the protective cover of the Bohemian Diet, which, together with the Utraquists' alliance with Lutherans and the Brethren, had guaranteed their security. Because of its total victory, the government, moreover, had no need to proceed with the dilatory "salami tactics," which might have bought some time for the Utraquists while their more radical religious allies were being suppressed. Ferdinand II's agents could deal with the three types of Bohemian dissidents almost simultaneously.

As had happened previously, the Bohemian nobles cavalierly let the Utraquist towns bear the immediate brunt of the physical punishments, despite their own primary responsibility for the uprising, which the towns were initially reluctant to join. Thus, their behavior repeated the pattern of 1547 when the burghers paid the price for the estates' insubordination to King Ferdinand I. During the most theatrical and gruesome Habsburg retribution for the uprising, the beheadings in the Old Town Square of Prague on June 21, 1621, of the twenty-seven victims, seventeen were townspeople and only three were barons, with the remaining seven belonging to the gentry. Many nobles escaped abroad, and some were pardoned.[24] In fact, the mainly Utraquist townspeople were repressed more severely than the largely Lutheran nobles.[25] These venomous proceedings reflected the shortsighted policy that marked the Habsburg dynasty's paranoia vis-à-vis the towns, incidentally, with disastrous consequences for the economic development of their realms. Here again the Austrian Habsburgs proved to be faithful students of the misguided lessons taught by their Spanish cousins.

Having Ferdinand II's ear, Archbishop Lohelius and the Jesuits responded with determined opposition to Lichtenstein and his secretary Pavel Michna of Vacínov, who advocated an at least temporary toleration of the Utraquist clergy with their own Consistory. Michna had, in fact, favored a purely Utraquist Consistory even before the Bohemian uprising in 1617, but at that point the Utraquist leaders had not wished to break their protective alliance with the Lutherans and the Brethren.[26] The unequal contest between Lichtenstein and Lohelius to save the Utraquists would extend until Easter 1622. In the next step in early 1621, the archbishop together with the canons of the Prague Cathedral formally rejected a distinct order of clergy that would be entitled to distribute communion *sub utraque*. This decision signaled not only that the Utraquist Church would be suppressed, but that the distribution of the Eucharist in both kinds, permitted by the papal concession of 1564, would be proscribed as well.[27] Accordingly, a convocation of clergy was held in April 1621 when the Utraquist priests (having episcopal ordination) were offered continuation in office, if first they agreed completely with the Tridentine Roman Church, and then pledged to distribute communion *sub una*. As the third and final condition, in an apparently compassionate gesture, although not a particularly gallant one, the priests were not asked to separate literally from their wives, but merely to start referring to these spouses as their housekeepers or cooks.[28] The result of this appeal remains unknown, but Platejs held another convocation of Utraquist priests in Prague in September 1621, and admonished them to declare officially that communion sub una was no less beneficial than the sub utraque; admit none to communion without a prior auricular confession; and use Latin, instead of Czech, as the liturgical language.[29]

In gradually destroying Utraquism, the archbishop and his two associates gained a powerful ally in the papal nuncio to Vienna and the Imperial Court, Carlo Caraffa, a hardliner who likewise insisted on absolute conformity and opposed any concession to the Utraquists. He valued particularly the intolerant zeal of Platejs.[30] As the next measure against Utraquism, the use of the Czech language for liturgical purposes was proscribed in October 1621.[31] The joint Consistory, which had served the Utraquists together with the Lutherans and the Brethren since 1609, was abolished in the very same year.[32] The last administrator, the Lutheran Jiřík Dykastus, was exiled from Bohemia with other Czech Protestant clergy in December 1621.[33] To forestall any semblance of compromise through the use of communion sub utraque, the Bohemian prelates turned with Caraffa's help to Rome, and rejoiced when the news arrived, dated December 22, 1621, that the Holy See had abrogated the permission of the lay chalice for Bohemia. Questenberg and Platejs were then in Vienna and sought to persuade Ferdinand II to promulgate the papal ordinance immediately despite opposition from Lichtenstein and Michna of Vacínov, who continued to favor a measure of tolerance for Utraquism.[34] The situation escalated when Lohelius, not waiting for Ferdinand's authorization, made public the prohibition of the lay chalice on February 28, 1622, declaring that the communion in both kinds for the laity, sanctioned by Pope Pius IV in 1564, was henceforth prohibited as harmful by a new decree of Pope Gregory XV.[35] The Utraquist clergy in Prague initially tried to evade the order, and Lichtenstein—in a stalling tactic on Michna's advice—granted permission for the lay communion sub utraque in at least two churches in Prague at Easter. Moreover, Michna, once more in a formal memorandum, proposed the restoration of Utraquism, as long as the priests continued to receive proper episcopal ordinations and required an auricular confession prior to communion.[36] The hardliners, of course, had made it clear earlier that even this diluted version was unacceptable. On Caraffa's complaint, Ferdinand II censured his two recalcitrant deputies in Prague, and confirmed Lohelius's edict banning the lay chalice.[37] As a result, even the minimalist concession for Utraquism was finally foreclosed.

The spiteful character of the Counter-Reformation was symbolized by Platejs's response, which marked the final prohibition of the lay chalice in a particularly humiliating way for the Utraquists. The German prelate chose to celebrate a mass with communion sub una in St. Martin's Church on March 28, 1622, because, as he said, he wished to end the Utraquist tradition in the exact spot where it was initiated by Jakoubek of Stříbro more than two hundred years earlier (in 1414).[38] On August 7, 1622, the administration of the Týn Church, the principal temple of Utraquism, was entrusted to a Roman priest, Ctibor Kotva of Freyfeld. Under the cover of darkness, on the night of January 17, 1623, Kotva together with his assistant, Jiří Fer, removed the chalice and the statue of Utraquist King George of Poděbrady from the tower of the Týn Church.[39] Soon the tombstone of Jan Rokycana, depicting him in the regalia of an archbishop, as well as his grave, were taken from the sanctuary. Also removed from the sanctuary were the remains of Utraquist Bishop Augustine Sancturien.[40] Both were burned in the churchyard. Such procedures, energetically replicated in all corners of Bohemia, rapidly eliminated or disguised Utraquism's physical memorabilia. Moreover, the Counter-Reformation disregarded the Utraquists' attachment to religious art of Gothic-like monochrome austerity and simplicity, and would replace the sacral objects, which it had destroyed, by unusual decorations in the flamboyant polychromatic baroque style.[41] Subsequent constructions would continue the work of violence against Utraquist aesthetics.[42] The entire spirit of the baroque, which the Counter-Reformation embraced with its stress on the emotional and irrational, clashed with the Utraquist spirit of sobriety and realism.[43] Thus, the flamboyant veneration of the saints and images, as well as monastic and other forms of asceticism, rubbed against the grain of Bohemian religious practice.

Whatever might have been the case elsewhere in the world of the Counter-Reformation, in Bohemia even the image of the Blessed Virgin was enlisted for an unsavory campaign. Although traditionally venerated by the Utraquists starting with Jan of Příbram and Rokycana,[44] she was now used as a symbol for Utraquism's suppression. The Utraquist mementos in the Old Town Square would characteristically be replaced—at the behest of Ferdinand II's son and successor Ferdinand III—by a Marian Column in 1652,[45] and the Roman Church made the person of Virgin Mary one of the centerpieces of proselytizing in the post-White Mountain era. As early as 1622, Archbishop Lohelius started a collection of funds that led two years later to the erection of a Marian shrine at the battlefield on White Mountain, which credited an apparition of the Virgin for the graces assuring the Habsburg victory.[46] A characteristic aspect of this new Marian emphasis was the republication in 1629 of the book by Kašpar Arsenius of Radbuza, *Pobožná knížka o blahoslavené Panně Marii* (A Devout Book About the Blessed Virgin Mary), which had originally appeared in 1613. Arsenius, then dean of the chapter at St. Vitus Cathedral, now vicar general of the archdiocese of Prague, inserted stories into the post-White Mountain edition that show how the Virgin was recruited for the cause of the Counter-Reformation. One such tale credited the survival of Jaroslav Bořita of Martinice to her special intervention after his defenestration at the start of the Bohemian uprising on May 23, 1618.[47] In an episode of particularly questionable taste, the Virgin was made to share responsibility for the Old Town executions on June 21, 1621. According to Arsenius, the beheadings reflected a divine retribution for the destruction of Marian imagery and other religious art in the St. Vitus Cathedral by the Calvinist purge on the same day the year before.[48] This campaign received support from Rome. A Carmelite monk, Dominic a Jesu Maria, attached a Marian image to his chest during the Battle of White Mountain, while he exhorted troops into battle with promises of the Virgin's assistance.[49] When Dominic brought the portrait into Rome on May 8, 1622, Pope Gregory XV ordered the icon placed in a chapel in the church of St. Paolo di Monte Cavallo, which was renamed for the Madonna della Vittoria. As Francesco Gui points out, the victory at White Mountain, celebrated under the patronage of the Virgin, became the counterpart of the great victory at Lepanto some fifty years earlier (October 7, 1571). The one had curbed the spread of religious dissent in East Central Europe, and the other had checked the expansion of Islamic heresy in the Mediterranean.[50]

Another tactic of the Counter-Reformation in Bohemia involved auricular confession. While the rite itself might have had in its essence a humane and salutary effect,[51] it was now in large part converted into an instrument of thought control. A certificate of confession became a legal requirement to be submitted annually by every inhabitant to the appropriate municipal or manorial office. The certificates were scrupulously counted and tabulated as an index of the Counter-Reformation's success. Attempts to evade the official edict led to what from the ecclesiastical point of view would be regarded as a variety of sacrilegious (or perhaps Švejkian?) behavior. The recalcitrants would offer to purchase certificates from the clergy "for money, grain, calves, geese, or other goods." Elsewhere, hardened individuals would collect certificates from numerous confessors and distribute the coveted documents to others. An evader would ask an unscrupulous friend to confess and obtain a certificate in his name.[52] The task of religious repression was, indeed, a formidable one, considering the size of the dissident population. In Prague alone, of the 120,000 inhabitants in 1620 only two thousand adhered to the Tridentine Roman Church.[53] Contrary to the earlier-noted assertions in the standard historical literature that classical Utraquism had virtually disappeared, and had been replaced by a Bohemian variant of Lutheranism (or "Neo-Utraquism") by 1609, available evidence indicates that most who were not obedient to the Roman Curia in Bohemia in 1621 were not Protestants, but Utraquists. The high proportion of Utraquists was also indicated by reported "conversion" figures. Already, in an early rehearsal of the Counter-Reformation in Český Krumlov, the Jesuits "converted" eleven Utraquists for every two Lutherans in late 1619, and seventy-one Utraquists for every thirty-three Lutherans in 1620.[54] Moreover, most of the Lutherans in Český Krumlov were probably German.

The most cogent evidence for the Utraquist preponderance, however, comes from the Roman side. Thus, the papal instruction to Nuncio Caraffa, dated April 12, 1621, emphasized the issue of the Utraquists (Hussiti), while viewing the other dissidents as marginal in post-White Mountain Bohemia. It is clear that the term Hussiti referred to the Utraquists and not to the Lutherans or crypto-Lutherans ("neo-Utraquists") since the document spoke of the Hussiti not as heretics, but as those eligible for reunion with the "Catolici," that is, mere schismatics.[55] The use of the term "Hussiti" as a synonym for the Utraquists is confirmed by Platejs, the quintessential figure of Tridentine orthodoxy. Thus, in March 1621, he made it clear that in referring to "parochi hussitici" he meant Utraquist priests who had episcopal ordination (*sacerdotes rite consecrati*).[56] Another sign that the Bohemian dissidents were considered mere schismatics by Rome was that, to legitimize their ecclesiastical status, the candidates were not required to abjure particular heresies, which would be the case with Lutherans or Calvinists. The standard Roman practice stipulated that even members of the Church of England had to submit to an open recantation of their "Protestantism" before admission to the papal fold.[57] In Bohemia, simple auricular confession and reception of communion under one species sufficed.[58] Similarly, most of the Bohemian clergy were viewed as Utraquist with canonical ordinations, even in the eyes of the most rigid Curial representatives. Thus, at the clerical convocations in Bohemia, such as the one assembled by Platejs in September 1621, clergymen were offered admission to the Roman priesthood fold without the condition of reordination.[59] This could not have applied to Lutheran ministers, who would have been instituted outside the historical episcopal framework. Technically speaking, the process of the Utraquist priests' and laypeople's integration into the Roman Curia's fold resembled more a "reunion," than a "conversion."[60]

An indication of the Utraquists' prevalence in Prague came also from the behavior of the common believers. When in 1622, the observance of the feast day of Jan Hus and the Bohemian martyrs on July 6 was prohibited without a prior public announcement, it was reported that the people of Prague gathered in droves in front of the locked churches.[61] Since Lutherans normally opposed veneration of saints, and their attitude toward honoring religious heroes such as Hus and other Bohemian martyrs was, to say the least, ambiguous, the conclusion can be drawn that most of Prague's population was Utraquist at that point. Even Pope Gregory XV was disturbed by Nuncio Caraffa's account about the enthusiasm for the feast.[62] The prevalence of Utraquists is supported by the report that more than a thousand believers came to receive communion in both kinds from Jan Locika of Domažlice earlier in the year.[63] Lutheran communicants were unlikely to be among them, inasmuch as the Evangelicals detested the Utraquist rites in general, and Locika in particular, as much as they abhorred the Tridentine masses and the clergy sub una.[64] Finally, the strength of Utraquism is indicated by the major presence of its priesthood after the Battle of White Mountain, as cited by Tomek.[65] In addition to this group of clergy, which must have been substantial, another group of six Utraquist priests had submitted unconditionally to Archbishop Lohelius in March 1621.[66]

Even after several years of Counter-Reformation suppression, there were signs of distinctly Utraquist feelings among the rural population. When rumors of renewed religious tolerance spread in 1627 in the district of Litomyšl, peasants from many villages demanded from the Catholic dean of the town masses in the Czech language and communion in both kinds.[67] In view of the Lutherans' rejection of the canonical mass, these were evidently Utraquist, not Lutheran (or "neo-Utraquist"), desiderata.

Looking at the situation from another angle, the fact that there were relatively few Czechs among the Lutheran exiles from Bohemia would indicate that most of the Bohemian Lutherans were German, while most of the Utraquists were Czechs and hence not attracted by refuge in Lutheran countries.[68] For instance, the town of Pirna in Saxony was one of the principal gathering sites for religious refugees from Bohemia, and the lists of exiles, compiled there in 1621–1639, showed a striking prevalence of German names.[69] Even making allowance for Czech speakers with German names or for Czech names mutated into German, it would still appear that most of the Lutheran exiles were Germans rather than Czechs, supporting the idea that the Czechs were mostly Utraquists rather than Lutherans in 1620.

Resistance and Collaboration

An authentic hero of the Utraquist resistance was Jan Locika of Domažlice, pastor of the principal church of Utraquism, Our Lady Before the Týn in Prague. In the absence of a Utraquist Consistory, he may be viewed as Utraquism's head or chief representative, who was also a learned man with at least two theological treatises to his credit.[70] Locika followed Lichtenstein's permission for distribution of communion sub utraque in the churches of Týn, as well as St. Henry's, at Easter of 1622 (March 27),[71] and administered communion in two kinds to more than a thousand faithful. On Easter Monday (March 28), he invited the congregation to receive communion in both kinds and declared that "some wish to prevent it, but it is more proper to obey God than people. Although they want to suppress your hereditary faith, remain faithful and do not be misled. I will stay with you of one mind like a shepherd with his flock."[72] He continued to defy the archbishop's reiterated prohibition of the lay chalice, and two weeks later he still preached fidelity to the Utraquist practices to his congregation, although anticipating his own imminent demise. A contingent of troops with loaded muskets and flaming torches, which, at the archbishop's behest, actually came to seize him in the midst of a religious service on April 10, 1622, was repelled by the assembled congregation. Despite a final attempt by Michna to protect him, Locika was captured in his lodgings three days later in the early morning of April 13. Thereupon he was deposed by the archbishop and taken to jail where he soon died.[73] He might have been beheaded in the castle of Křivolát.[74] Incidentally, in the spirit of present-day ecumenical trends, the martyrdom or near-martyrdom of Locika may suggest that his canonization would be an efficacious gesture for the Vatican to conciliate the Bohemians and make the Roman Church more fully at home in the third millennium.[75]

In a flashback, it may be seen that the mistreatment of Locika despite his promise of cooperation with the Roman Curia showed how unreliable were the offers of accommodation with the Utraquist priesthood, which Rome had proffered since the turn of the century. The witness of Locika's sacrifice also appears as a clear answer to those who would maintain that Utraquism had lost its vitality, having turned from a living organism to an inert skeleton. In his views and demeanor, he symbolized the genuineness of the

Utraquist *via media*. While opposed to Protestantism, he was no lackey of the Roman Curia. He had preached critically against the Tridentine Roman Church, while warning his followers against embracing the reformed religion, particularly Calvinism.[76] In consequence, it was hardly surprising that he would become subject to much maligning from both parties headquartered on each side of the *via media*. On the contrary, the Utraquists of Prague signified their ardent support for their spiritual leader in the face of both the Lutheran persecution in December 1618 and Lohelius's repression in April 1622.[77]

Most of the Utraquist priests had little choice but to accept assignments from the Roman Church after 1621. The incorporation of the Utraquist clergy and their congregations in the Roman ranks was a rough-and-ready process. A typical example was its application in the deaconate of Litomyšl. The dean, Vojtěch Hájek, called together the priests of the deaconate on May 23, 1622, and read them a directive that henceforth the lay communion in both kinds was proscribed. Laypersons who refused communion sub una should be denied marriages and church burials. Those turning to any remaining unauthorized priests were to be punished more severely by confiscation of property or otherwise.[78] We can assume that with rare exceptions (noted later), the priests submitted resentfully, and the Roman Church just as naturally did not trust them to advance its objectives of imposing a post-Tridentine rigid conformity. Initially, their assignments were in rural parishes, although toward the end of the 1620s a few returned to Prague.[79] As an additional precaution, they were not permitted to play any role in theological training. The Utraquist clergy had traditionally received their instructions from parish priests who served as mentors.[80] Henceforth, the education of priests was conducted by and large by the Jesuits and in strict isolation from any influence of the Bohemian Reformation. The Jesuit fathers eagerly assumed the task as soon as Ferdinand II placed the University of Prague under their control on November 10, 1622.[81] The resulting lack of training facilities was particularly detrimental in the longer run to the Utraquists because of their dependence on canonically ordained clergy. The Lutherans and the Brethren could secure clandestine services from clergy abroad.

Covert practice of the old rites by former Utraquist priests was impeded by the Counter-Reformation's enforcement system, the operatives of which, as noted earlier, were not natives with even vestigial empathy with the local ways, but harshly unsentimental outsiders.[82] Nevertheless, there were known instances of resistance and evasion, which produced yet another authentic Utraquist martyr. A former Utraquist priest who returned to Prague, Vavřinec Hanžburský of Kopeček, pastor of St. Vojtěch, continued communion sub utraque to his parishioners and issued them the officially required certificates of confession and communion sub una. His trial can be used as a prism for understanding the vulnerability of former Utraquist priests under the Counter-Reformation. First, the defendant was unjustly charged with publicly distributing communion sub utraque at Easter of 1622, although the rite was ordered (presumably at Lichtenstein's behest) by Sezima of Vrtba, the captain of the New Town of Prague. Second, Hanžburský declined to appeal to Rome against the verdict of the archiepiscopal court, which was apparently in line with the traditional Utraquist denial of papal jurisdiction, and which harkened back to Hus's refusal to recognize either papal or conciliar authority to judge him. Third, he was charged with apostasy for having rejected Roman obedience after ordination. Inasmuch as Utraquist priests in general were ordained by bishops in communion with Rome, all lived under the threat of this indictment. Sentenced to death, Hanžburský was beheaded in Prague on April 7, 1631, on a scaffold appropriately erected in front of the Týn Church, the former "cathedral" of Utraquism. His case in the archiepiscopal court was zealously promoted by the notorious Platejs who, however, lacked the courage to witness the execution, although twelve other high ecclesiastical dignitaries were present.[83] Hanžburský may be regarded, next to Locika, as one of two leading candidates for canonization in the Utraquist pantheon.

The investigative commission that "unmasked" Hanžburský claimed or suspected other cases of secret Utraquism, especially in the countryside. Thus, another priest, Havel Zemánek of Sadská, was tried also in 1630 for having issued false certificates to forty families.[84] At times, the opposition to communion sub una was so strong that even the Roman Church had to compromise and, despite overt prohibitions, temporarily tolerate lay communion in both kinds in certain localities.[85] Nuncio Caraffa reported active peasant resistance in 1625.[86] Even later, after several years of Counter-Reformation suppression, there was evidence of strong Utraquist feelings within the rural population. As noted, the villagers appealed for masses in the Czech language and communion in both kinds in the district of Litomyšl in 1627.[87] It is possible that during the brief restoration of religious freedom in Prague, when the Saxons occupied the city temporarily from November 1631 to May 1632, some of the Utraquist priests resumed church services according to the old rites. Among the restored clergy are listed two former monastics and five who reverted from the Roman Church.[88]

It appears that the Reformation Commissions pursued the Utraquists with the same vigor as the Protestants. Thus, declarations in Mladá Boleslav in 1627 lumped those "who are non-Catholic or hold schismaticall opinions" together, exhorting them to return to the bosom of the Catholic Church.[89] A related decree threatened schismatics with banishment not only from the town, but from the entire Kingdom of Bohemia.[90] As noted earlier, the term "schismatic" —in other cases "hussite"—was the Bohemian Counter-Reformation's code word for the Utraquists, while "heretic" referred to the Lutherans or other Protestants. The directives of the Reformation Commission in Prague, charged with extirpation of religious dissent in Bohemia, went into considerable detail. As an illustration, its letter of August 2, 1629, to the town council of Mělník dealt with three married women who had refused to receive communion sub una. To break resistance in such cases, the commission mandated imprisonment with a diet of bread and water and subjection to continuous exhortation of a priest. In the case of one of the women, who escaped from town, the husband was held responsible because of his alleged hesitation and lack of firmness in making his spouse conform.[91] Aside from punishments, procedures were employed to camouflage the transition from Utraquism. Thus, unconsecrated wine was offered to communicants together with the consecrated host.[92] This type of ersatz Utraquist lay communion would continue in some localities into the eighteenth century, and as a rare curiosity even into the nineteenth century.[93]

A few priests of the Utraquist Church appeared to willingly serve the new ecclesiastical regime. Two prominent ecclesiastics, who in contrast to Locika's resistance conformed and rendered an unqualified obedience to Rome, were Jindřich Hoffman and Symeon Kapihorský. Assisting their superiors, the two converts engaged in the type of campaign that did the most damage to the Czech religious consciousness in the long run. Their writings aimed at deconstruction of the religious *via media* of the Bohemian Reformation, resulting in denial of the existence of a coherent Utraquist faith. According to this Counter-Reformation version of history, the original moderate Bohemian Reformation was soon highjacked by a variety of contending religious radicals, and eventually by contending Protestants. Accordingly, Hoffman portrayed the entire era of the Bohemian Reformation as one of confusion and strife. Appealing to the witness of Václav Hájek of Libočany, a tendentious sixteenth-century writer sub una, he dated an original revolt against Hus already to the adoption of the lay communion in both kinds, which Hus had allegedly rejected.[94] Hoffman further misinformed his readers that the nation had entirely repudiated the Bohemian Reformation in 1567 when the Lutheran and Unity nobles demanded exclusion of the Compactata from the constitutional laws of the Kingdom of Bohemia. In contrast to what he portrayed as endless disputes and quarrels of the past, the Roman convert extolled the general peace and tranquility guaranteed by the Counter-Reformation's single faith.[95] Along the same lines, Kapihorský claimed that the heirs of the Bohemian Reformation rejected and abandoned Hus and his teaching in the 1520s when they allegedly rallied behind Luther.[96] According to these accounts, which constituted the more or less official scenario embraced by the Counter-Reformation, there were no orthodox Utraquists in sixteenth-century Bohemia, only Lutherans, Brethren, and other religious radicals. In a perverse way, this counterfeit image of a largely Protestant Bohemia, which erased the memory of the Utraquist *via media,* appealed also, although for opposite reasons, to the Evangelicals and the Reformed. It has continued to haunt Czech historiography to the present day.

In another example of the Counter-Reformation's distortion and misappropriation of Bohemia's religious past, Utraquist liturgical books continued in use after the purge of objectionable passages. A case in point is the Gradual of the Utraquist church in Litomyšl.[97] More generally, David Holeton called attention to the use of "sanitized" Utraquist liturgical books in the new parishes of the Roman Church: "Often, this involved little more than the excision or mutilation of the feast of Hus. The Kutná Hora Gradual . . . has had the proper for the feast excised as has the small antiphonary. . . . Other texts, like the Gradual of Martin Bachelor, have had the pages containing the feast so badly mutilated that they are unusable."[98] Apart from mutilation of texts, there was a far-reaching and persistent campaign to eliminate Utraquist literature, as well as Czech Protestant books.[99] The scale of destruction was impressive (and depressing). A single Jesuit missionary, Antonín Koniáš (1691–1760)—although undoubtedly an overachiever—was credited by his would-be hagiographer with consigning 60,000 books to the flames in the early eighteenth century. Subsequent research has scaled the figure down to a still formidable thirty thousand.[100] As a result of this destruction of books, as noted above, the contents of the two theological treatises of Locika remain unknown. Similarly, the main work of Matauš Pačuda, Utraquism's leading figure prior to Locika, is available only in one defective copy.[101]

The lack of suitable clergy militated against the possibility of Nicodemism, that is, the concealment of religious beliefs in the face of persecution, such as was practiced in Elizabethan England by both recusants and Puritans.[102]

The prospects of Utraquism's continued existence under persecution were virtually nil in Bohemia, partly due to the extreme intrusiveness of the Counter-Reformation, and partly to the Utraquist dependence on the services of canonically ordained sacramental clergy. First, the thoroughness of thought and behavior control was epitomized by the continuing requirements of confessional certificates issued by Roman priests.[103] Second, unlike their Lutheran counterparts, the Utraquists could not function without a distinct order of clergy. Even under the conditions of lesser need, the Lutherans could receive underground sustenance of ministers from surrounding areas. With their sense of distinctiveness from Eastern Orthodoxy, the Utraquist had no access to clergy ordained in the process of historical apostolic succession in the West. As pointed out earlier, there were no concrete relations with the Anglicans. The other kindred movement, that of Jansenism in the Netherlands, which opposed papal centralism and Tridentine authoritarianism, did not lead to the emergence of the Dutch Old Catholics until 1724.[104] The most that the Utraquist faithful could hope for was to find an ex-Utraquist priest who would minister to them in the Utraquist manner at the risk of his own life.[105]

The difficulty of Utraquism's long-term survival without its own clergy is illustrated by the figures of "converts" to the Roman Church in 1661–1678. If the breakdown of Bohuslav Balbín, the ranking Jesuit geographer and historian, can be trusted, the total figure included 141 Utraquists, compared to 21,757 Lutherans (presumably from the German-speaking area), out of a total of 29,588.[106] The bulk of the disgruntled Utraquists had by this time been (mis)labeled as faithful children of Rome. Nevertheless, the influence of Utraquism seemed to linger on. Surveys of library inventories of Prague burghers for 1700–1784 revealed that 42 percent of Czech-language books dated from the period before 1620 related to the Bohemian Reformation, but were not Protestant.[107] Also there is a record of surreptitious communion sub utraque having a specifically Utraquist (rather than Protestant) basis as late as 1710 in Prague.[108]

Lutherans and the Brethren

In contrast to the Utraquists, their Protestant countrymen had other places to go. Czech Lutherans sought refuge in adjacent Lutheran lands, especially in Saxony, the destination of most of the noble and middle-class emigration in 1620–1627.[109] Their German hosts required full conformity, which involved shedding any reminiscences of the Bohemian Reformation, as well as a clear separation from the Brethren and the Calvinists.[110] Only those who conformed fully with German Lutheranism could remain in Saxony, according to the Elector's edicts of January 18, 1623, and August 28, 1627. Those suspected of deviations, usually in the Calvinist direction, had to migrate farther.[111] This happened to a considerable number of Bohemian refugees, who were suspected of deviations from the articles of the Augsburg Confession in 1635. Another oath of loyalty was required from the rest in 1638.[112]

The Brethren sought refuge largely with their coreligionists in Poland. Their theologians continued to maintain intellectual ties with the English and American Puritans. In an impressive—although perhaps not the most felicitous—gesture, the Brethren had previously dedicated their Czech translation of Calvin's *Institutes* to King James I in 1616.[113] In exile, the famous bishop of the Unity, John A. Comenius, promoted the popular work *Praxis pietatis* by the Puritan theologian, Bishop Lewis Bayly (d. 1631). Comenius had a Czech translation published in Leszno, Poland, in 1630, and another in Amsterdam in 1661. What attracted the Brethren was apparently Bayly's emphasis on good deeds, especially fast and prayer, as aids to salvation—a stance that distinguished them from the Lutherans. At the other end of the spectrum, the Brethren also heartily endorsed the bishop's distaste for venerating the saints, including the Virgin Mary. The Puritans' interest in the Brethren would also lead to the story, possibly apocryphal, that the presidency of Harvard College in New England's Massachusetts was offered to Comenius in the 1640s.[114] Likewise in the post-White Mountain period, the Unity was asked to supply additional material for a new edition of Puritanism's *chef-d'oeuvre*, Foxe's martyrology, *The Acts and Monuments*.[115]

The polemics between the Lutherans and the Brethren continued abroad. The Lutherans looked askance on the relationship between the Brethren and the Puritans. In 1636, Martinius of Dražov condemned Bayly's *Praxis pietatis* of which Comenius sponsored two Czech translations published, as noted earlier. Martinius called it a gloomy book, which contained much that was misleading, questionable, and even heretical.[116] What the Lutherans found objectionable was apparently Bayly's emphasis on good deeds as aids to salvation.[117] The Brethren defended their sponsorship of Bayly's devotional text in their response to Martinius.[118] What grieved them most was that the Lutherans would question the Unity's Christian orthodoxy by citing arguments from the writings of Václav Šturm, the sixteenth-century Jesuit controversialist, although, as they pointed out, the Jesuit had been just as severe in his attacks on the teachings of Luther.[119]

Victorious Counter-Reformation?

At this point the task of reconstructing the character of Bohemian Utraquism from 1517 to 1622 has been completed. What follows will abandon the solid ground of the Rankean "wie es eigentlich gewesen" (how it really happened) for a more speculative approach, largely to suggest areas for further exploration. This exercise begins with an assessment of the Counter-Reformation's place in Bohemian history, and end with suggestions of the long-term effects of Utraquism.

It has been maintained that, thanks to the Counter-Reformation, the Czech nation was "thoroughly Recatholicized."[120] Such a dramatic conversion of ex-Utraquists from abominating the Counter-Reformation (as they had demonstrated, for instance, by sacking the monasteries in Prague in 1611[121]) to turning into its dedicated supporters seems an astonishing transformation. From such glowing descriptions, one almost gets the impression that—had it not been too early in the history of science—the Jesuit fathers had performed a feat of genetic engineering, having successfully implanted Tridentine Spanish cells into Bohemian brains. Marie-Elisabeth Ducreux, for one, has questioned the reality behind this success story: "How are we to evaluate the depth and the authenticity of this conversion that continued over a century and a half? Historically, the problem remains open. There are too many overlapping and contradictory elements in a process that was both personal and social. . . . A change of religion over an entire land is . . . the sum of thousands of individual conversions. That this was the case in Bohemia remains doubtful . . ."[122] The image of the Counter-Reformation's victory was supported, on the one hand, by the lack of resistance and, on the other, by indifference to Protestantism. The population maintained an overt conformity, without frequent application of harsh penalties or the emergence of a significant number of active resisters. The Bohemians remained relatively unresponsive to Protestant proselytizing from abroad and, ultimately, to the option of embracing the reformed faith, once it became available in the late eighteenth century. In what follows, the aim is to review what has apparently become the accepted position in Czech historiography since the 1990s,[123] and to suggest an alternate scenario for explaining Bohemia's docility under the Counter-Reformation. This topic will be approached under two rubrics: (1) the presence and pervasiveness of intimidation, and (2) the loss of collective historical memory. This examination may suggest that the impression of consent and internalization of the Counter-Reformation was more illusory than real.

As late as the eighteenth century, the Austrian government did not share the sanguine view of the Counter-Reformation's success, and continued to suspect the Bohemians of hidden heresy.[124] Constant vigilance was thought to be the price of conformity. From the viewpoint of Vienna's bureaucratic authoritarianism, religious observance was not something stemming from the grassroots, but an obligation to be exacted, policed, and enforced like the performance of serf labor, collection of taxes, or military recruitment.[125] Routine surveillance via the certificates of confession was fortified by penalties periodically announced and investigative campaigns launched. Thousands of people were intimidated by investigations at the diocesan level and had their cases either settled by ecclesiastical punishments or referred to civil authority.[126] On the ecclesiastical side, the main philosopher of the system of thought control in Bohemia, the Belgian-born Jesuit William Lamormaini, justified the use of compulsion on two grounds. First, if an individual were compelled to perform certain acts, he would gradually adopt a positive attitude and act willingly. Second, since the Bohemian dissidents—unlike the Jews or the infidels—had been baptized, the Church held a rightful jurisdiction over them, and had the authority to compel their obedience by relying on the power of the state.[127] As another sign of insecurity, the Counter-Reformation regime engaged in a continuing propaganda war against the legacy of the heterodox past. The suspicion of underground heresy, in fact, seemed to intensify with the progressive aging of the system. Warnings were issued against the legacy of Jan Hus and the Bohemian heresy,[128] and as late as 1777, the authorities of the Roman Church found it apropos to publish in Czech an extract from Florimond de Remond's *Histoire de la naissance, progrès et décadence de l'herésie de ce siècle* (Paris, 1605), under the title *Husitského v Čechách kacířství počátku, zrůstu, a pádu vejtah* (An Extract Concerning the Origin, the Growth, and the Fall of the Hussite Heresy in Bohemia).[129]

The relatively limited use of repressive violence, particularly of capital and other harsh punishments for religious transgressions during the Counter-Reformation era has been cited as evidence for the willing acceptance of the Counter-Reformation culture in Bohemia.[130] Nevertheless, a closer examination shows that, while drastic punishments were relatively infrequent, their incidence was ever present. The research of Marie-Elisabeth Ducreux into the Counter-Reformation's modus operandi revealed that between 1704 and 1781, 729 cases of heresy were referred to the Court of Appeals in Prague from the three dioceses in Bohemia. A total of forty-four death sentences were pronounced.[131]

What to make of this? The low number of victims may reflect the progression from medieval lack of sophistication to early modern subtlety, which led the practitioners of thought control to abandon mass murder for more artful means of imposing ideological conformity. Instead of wiping out the heretics, as was done in the crusades against the Albigensians and proposed during the crusades against the Bohemian dissidents in the early fifteenth century, the managers of the Counter-Reformation could employ tools developed and tested in the sixteenth century, particularly in Spain, a country on which (as noted earlier) the Austrian Habsburgs heavily depended for religious and political inspiration.[132] Consequently, the policy of the Counter-Reformation in Bohemia could get much mileage of intimidation out of a moderate but judicious use of capital or other harsh punishments.[133] It can also be argued that there was another crucial reason why the inhabitants of Bohemia exhibited docility toward the Counter-Reformation regime, which could be mistaken for acquiescence, and which was touched upon previously. It was the loss of conscious historical memory of their real religious identities—a collective religious amnesia. The evidence of their ecclesiastical past was mutilated or destroyed. From this point of view, the Czechs had been subjected to grand larceny of their religious heritage from both sides of the great religious divide. The current captor, Rome, as well as their would-be rescuers, the reformed churches, portrayed the past inhabitants of Bohemia as either true subjects of the Roman Curia, guilty only of minor misbehavior, or as true children of the Reformation, marred only by a few national oddities. The pseudo-reality of the Roman/Protestant view involved denial of the historical existence of a real Utraquist Church with its distinct ecclesiology and liturgy. Victimized by this disinformation, the disoriented Utraquists had nowhere to turn to recapture the image of their true identity. Their own traditional ecclesiology had vanished with the alienation of Utraquist clergy and institutions by the Roman Curia and, as noted earlier, the Utraquists had not been accustomed—while memory still lingered—to look abroad for kindred sojourners on the *via media.*

The counterpart to the sullen resentment of Rome's iron rule was the relatively feeble effect of Czech Lutheran emigration on the spiritual life of Bohemia. This failure also has been cited as a sign of the Tridentine Catholicism's victory.[134] The cause of this phenomenon was not necessarily the pressure or the effect of the Counter-Reformation, severe as the latter undoubtedly was. Instead, it might be attributed to the fact that the émigré propaganda did not resonate with the Czech religious mentality, which would find the full-fledged Reformation just as uncongenial as Tridentine

Catholicism. In other words, neither the Counter-Reformation nor the Protestant Reformation resonated with their customary behavior or sensitivity to ethical and aesthetic values, which had been formulated over quarter of a millennium. It is doubtful that such ingrained habits could be eradicated in the period of the Counter-Reformation's comparatively short *durée* (to take advantage of Fernand Braudel's terminology[135]). The Czechs knew what they were not, but—due to the collective religious amnesia—they did not know what they should be. As Marie-Elisabeth Ducreux has pointed out: "In this country [Bohemia] that accomplished the first Reformation in Europe a century before Luther, an obligatory conversion to Catholicism thus probably contributed to the laicization of people's consciences."[136]

This brings up for consideration the phenomenon that has been cited as foolproof evidence of the Bohemians' final conversion to Tridentine Catholicism. It was the virtually complete indifference to the Toleration Patent of Joseph II of 1781 which, following the dissolution of the Jesuit Order in 1773, permitted leaving the Roman Church for either Lutheranism or Calvinism. Less than 2 percent of the population took advantage of this option.[137] It may be argued that neither Wittenberg nor Heidelberg/Geneva could satisfy the Czechs' spiritual needs any more than Tridentine Rome. Neither of them coincided with the ideals of the autochthonous Reformation.[138] Hence it was not an attachment to the Roman Curia but the lack of appeal of the Reformed churches that kept the Bohemian populace from flocking toward them. Following this path, it might even be argued that the Czech mentality was not Protestant, but Catholic. If indeed in 1780 the Czech nation was "thoroughly Catholic," this Catholicism was not rooted in Tridentine Rome, but in the inarticulate pull of Utraquist Prague. It was not the Catholicism of Bohuslav Balbín, but that of Bohuslav Bílejovský. From another point of view, the Counter-Reformation, often referred to as "Re-Catholicization,"[139] might be more properly called "de-Catholicization" in two senses. First, it destroyed the conscious memory of Utraquist Catholicism, and second, it undermined the acceptability of any other form of Catholicism. That Tridentine Catholicism had not made a deep impression on Bohemian mentality is indicated by the fact that the country showed little resentment, much less resistance, to Joseph II's religious reforms of the 1780s, which eliminated some of the most distinctive features of the Counter-Reformation. This calm contrasted sharply with the fierce reactions provoked by Joseph's reforms in areas of incontrovertible Roman influence, such as the Austrian Netherlands, a province that might otherwise seem comparable to Bohemia.[140] In addition, Tridentine Catholicism remained virtually irrelevant to the mainstream of Bohemia's intellectual and cultural life in the nineteenth century.[141]

Thus, a case can be made that the imposed religious system, instead of being internalized, was passively resented, while the earlier predisposition to religious liberalism persisted. It might be said that the Bohemian Counter-Reformation created a Frankenstein monster in whom a transplanted Tridentine brain worked at odds with the liberal Utraquist heart. The creature—in an afterlife of Utraquism—would eventually turn against its Roman progenitors in such forms as Joseph II's ecclesiastical reforms, or the fierce anticlericalism of the nineteenth-century liberal movements. In the end, the Bohemian Counter-Reformation produced a no-win situation. Rome lost adherents, the reformed churches did not gain a significant number, and the Czechs lost conscious awareness of their authentic religious tradition. If one chose to regard history as a morality play, she or he might see in the outcome the fallacy of ends (orthodoxy) justifying the means (repression).

Afterlife of Utraquism

It appeared that the demise of Utraquism, which Czech historiography dated prematurely and variously to 1517, 1524, 1539, 1564, 1575, 1593, or 1609, did finally occur in 1622. But did it really? It may also be said that Utraquism did not die in 1622, but merely descended from the level of conscious thought into the substrate of habitual patterns of reactions and behavior at odds with the existing Gleichschaltung. This in a sense was the concern of the Habsburg bureaucrats and Curia dignitaries, who continued to worry about a hidden persistence of the resentful, and even rebellious, "Hussite" spirit among the Czech people.[142] It may be argued that the Utraquist mentality was to gain a new lease on life, rising like a phoenix from the ashes, after the hiatus of the Counter-Reformation. There appear to have been two significant manifestations of this survival and revival—one secular and fairly definite, the other religious and as yet conjectural.

The one clear effect was to animate the libertarian spirit of the Czech national awakening in the nineteenth century. The revival in its initial stage at the turn of the eighteenth century led to a massive return to the literature that had preceded the catastrophe of White Mountain and had been nurtured by the two and a half centuries of Utraquism. Once the Josephin enlightenment had discredited the world of the Counter-Reformation both intellectually and politically, creating a near intellectual tabula rasa, the void was in fact filled in Bohemia by the cultural legacy of the Utraquist era.[143] Apart from the negative condition of a cultural vacuum, the Bohemian awakeners had a positive incentive to return to the Utraquist sixteenth century. Its liberalism and tolerance harmonized with the spirit of the Enlightenment.[144] Its political and cultural values were transmitted through several channels across the hiatus between the Bohemian Reformation and the national revival. The transfer was effected by the means of reprinting sixteenth-century classics, reproducing sixteenth-century writings in school and university textbooks, celebrating the Bohemian Reformation in history and literature, and embracing as a political program the historical rights of the pre-1620 Bohemian state. The national awakening also involved the reestablishment of the sixteenth-century grammatical norms for the literary language.[145] It is possible to argue that the impact of sixteenth-century writings was more significant in the reprints of the early nineteenth century than in the originals of their own time because the greater spread of literacy and lower printing costs had made literature more widely accessible. If, as R. G. Collingwood in his *The Idea of History* has argued, in reading sources of the past the reader in effect thinks the thoughts of the writer,[146] then the Bohemian students and intellectuals of the early nineteenth century to a considerable extent acquired the habit of their sixteenth-century ancestors' thoughts.

The second posthumous role of Utraquism is of a wider significance. It involves the question of to what extent Utraquism may have provided an inspiration for the religious reforms of Josephinism. The ecclesiastical policies applied within the Habsburg Empire, including Bohemia, during the reign of Emperor Joseph II (1780–1790) in some salient aspects reproduced the approaches characteristic of Utraquism in the ecclesiastical and liturgical spheres.[147] It would be of course unduly simplistic to see the roots of the Josephin reforms only or primarily in subterranean Utraquist reverberations. Other sources, which have been suggested and examined, are, in particular, the French Enlightenment,[148] irenic German Protestant jurisprudence,[149] and Jansenism in the Austrian Netherlands.[150]

There are several standpoints, however, from which the relationship between Josephinism and Utraquism may be viewed.[151] First, there are formal resemblances. To a considerable degree, Joseph's ecclesiastical reforms—curtailment of clerical power, papal authority, church decorations and devotional practices (deemed extravagant), and monasticism—can be viewed as a victory of the Utraquist model over the Tridentine model of reform in the Roman Church.[152] Joseph's reforms and toleration were introduced in a religious context—that of the Catholic Enlightenment—rather than a secularist context, as in other areas under the previous sway of the Roman Church. Eduard Winter refers to Austro-Bohemian Josephinism as Reform Catholicism (Reformkatholizismus).[153] In a more particular parallel, both Utraquism and Josephinism resembled the *via media* of the Anglican Church, and harkened back to Wyclifite principles in opposition to clerical power and wealth, as well as monasticism, but without embracing Protestant ecclesiology.[154] Fittingly, the Holy See also drew an explicit link between Josephinism and the Bohemian Reformation. Responding to the proposal to severely circumscribe, if not eliminate, direct papal jurisdiction within the Habsburg Empire, Pope Pius VI pointed out on May 16, 1787, that such a questioning of ecclesiastical authority reflected one of Hus's articles (number 15) that was condemned at the Council of Constance in 1415.[155] In the popular mind as well the reforms harkened to the image of the Bohemian Reformation, according to which Emperor Joseph assumed the role of a second Hus. In a play on words, the emperor's name was explicated as Josep-Hus II (derived from Josephus II).[156]

Second, the Catholic Enlightenment called attention to the Bohemian Reformation and voiced approval of its critical assessments of authoritarian ecclesiology.[157] Thus, Augustin Zitte (1750–1785) wrote about Hus and his precursors in his *Lebensbeschreibung des Magisters Johannes Huss von Hussinecz* (4 vols., Prague, 1786–1790), and Kaspar Royko (1744–1819), professor of Church history at the University of Prague, displayed a liberal viewpoint of the Catholic Enlightenment in his history of the Council of Constance,[158] supporting conciliarism and opposing authoritarian tendencies (of the type that Hus criticized) and which, according to Royko, still persisted in the Church. Not surprisingly, his work drew denunciations from the papal nuncio Guiseppe Garampi.[159]

Third, the reforms of Josephinism found ready acceptance in Bohemia, and their prime inspirer, Václav Kounic (1711–1794), stemmed from the Bohemian Lands.[160] His right-hand man, Franz Joseph von Heinke, who headed the department for ecclesiastical affairs in the Austro-Bohemian Chancellery, although born in Silesia, was a graduate of the University of Prague and had served most of his life in Bohemia.[161] The ecclesiastical hierarchy in Bohemia included prominent supporters of Josephin reforms, such as the two successive bishops of Hradec Králové, Jan Leopold Hay (1980–1794) and Maria T. Trautmannsdorff (1795–1815). The latter's doctoral dissertation was proscribed by Rome.[162] Most of the writings in the spirit of liberal Catholic Enlightenment emanated from the Bohemian lands, in particular the noted writings of Royko and Zitte. Also, as noted, in Bohemia there was virtually no objection, either from the clergy or laity, to Joseph's intrusion into religious affairs, which contrasted with fierce opposition elsewhere, particularly in the Austrian Netherlands.[163]

Fourth, there was a distinct connection between the Josephin religious reforms and the renaissance of Utraquist literature. The clerical supporters of the Catholic Enlightenment guided the Czech national awakening toward a revival of the culture of the Utraquist age. This enlightened priesthood became largely responsible for the interest in sixteenth-century books and their reprinting. It was primarily Josef Dobrovský, one of the stalwarts of Josephin reformism, who defined the rationale for returning to the culture of a rather distant past. He eulogized the Utraquist sixteenth century for its promotion of the Czech language and literature, and for its promotion of humanism and printing as the culmination of Czech intellectual development. The Counter-Reformation represented for him a period of decline with a pathetic state of the Czech language and an imposition of medieval-like intellectual darkness in Bohemia. In the literature of the Counter-Reformation he saw an instrument of obscurantism and superstition.[164] Hence, the return to the sixteenth century and resumption of its ways was the clearly implied direction of further progress.[165] Other theologians in Bohemia who fostered the sixteenth-century revival shared Dobrovský's view about a special correspondence between the Enlightenment and the free discussion, humanism, and tolerance of the Utraquist age, in particular Mikuláš Adaukt Voigt, František Faustin Procházka, and Ignác Cornova.[166] The re-publication program of Czech classics in the 1780s, guided by Procházka, included sixteenth-century translations of Erasmus's *O připravení k smrti* (Preparation for Death)[167] and *Enchridion*.[168] The choice of Erasmus can be seen as an epitome of a triangular relationship among him, Utraquism, and Josephinism on the Christian humanist basis.

Fifth and last, the reform Catholicism of the Josephin era continued to be influential in Bohemia into the first half of the nineteenth century, perhaps most notably under the protection of Josef Hurdálek, bishop of Litoměřice, and through Bernard Bolzano and associates in the 1830s.[169] Later, Austrian advocates of political authoritarianism, also in the post-1848 period, continued to see a relationship between the Bohemian Reformation and Czech liberalism.[170] Even if this view is discounted for its bias, a curious symbiosis of Czech political culture with reform Catholicism may be discerned in the Bohemian context, whereby liberal Catholicism or its echoes would affect the intellectual concerns of pace-setting political leaders. This relationship is symbolized by seminal influences on Karel Havlíček

Borovský and Masaryk, the two leading writers and actors of modern Czech politics. Havlíček felt boundless admiration for Bernard Bolzano,[171] and Masaryk found his guru in Franz Brentano.[172] It would appear as though Czech political liberalism was gravitating toward its religious source or counterpart, or as if Utraquism, which had been revived in its secularized form, searched for a religious dimension in the form of liberal Catholicism.[173] This might also be viewed, in a way, as an attempt to close the circle, whereby the liberal Catholic dimension of Utraquism would return home to fructify intellectual life there or, conversely, whereby the Czech political mind groped for contact with its ultimate religious roots.

As the main conclusion, however, and this once more transcends the Bohemian context, it is plausible to argue that the idea which the Utraquists represented did not vanish with them, but kept reemerging. Echoing Marx and Engels' dictum of Europe haunted by the specter of communism, it could be said that henceforth the Roman Curia would be haunted by the specter of liberal Catholicism in such forms as Jansenism, the Union of Utrecht, Josephinism, Old Catholicism, modernism and, in a muted expression, in the nearly liberal spirit of the Second Vatican Council.[174] All these may be viewed as echoes, if not as direct consequences, of Utraquism. If the Hussite upheavals of the 1420s could be called the first in the chain of European "great revolutions,"[175] the Utraquist Church could be called the first, and perhaps—until the partial aggiornamento of the twentieth century—the most substantial or extensive of the epiphanies of "liberal Catholicism."[176] This would be the case whether or not there was an actual causal relationship between Utraquism and Josephinism. As a form of liberal Catholicism, Utraquism could also symbolize a bridge between Rome and the Reformation, a role that was once envisaged for the Utraquist *via media* by no less a figure than Erasmus and his peers who had proposed to resolve the conflict between Rome and Wittenberg by an "Utraquistization" of the Roman Church.[177]

In light of the foregoing, it could be said that in the long run Utraquism has had the last laugh. One may wonder whether Utraquism in a way did not replicate the destiny of its most illustrious member, Jan Hus, proceeding through annihilation to apotheosis. The spirit of responsible intellectual freedom and toleration of dissent represented by Utraquism may be judged as a worthwhile contribution to the intellectual treasury of civilization. The dean of North American specialists on the Bohemian Reformation, Howard Kaminsky, has said something similar about the lasting role and legacy of the Utraquists' radical cousins, the Taborites: "Tábor itself was conquered, its leaders, including Nicholas, thrown into prison, its unique reformational religion suppressed. Tabor in the diachron had tried and failed. But Tabor in the eschaton created for it by its bishop had played its role in the divine scenario with heroic vigor—a performance for the 'Ages.'"[178] Taking the cue from Kaminsky, it can be said that the physical disappearance of Utraquism was not the crucial matter. What mattered most was that in its liberalism and tolerance it had made a statement that would anticipate the wave of the future.

Epilog

The Meaning of the Bohemian Reformation

Before concluding, it may be useful to sum up the central themes of this study both within the European, and the narrower Bohemian context. From the broader European perspective, Utraquism served to provide insight in four different areas: the nature of patristic Christianity, the religious *via media,* liberal Catholicism, and religious toleration.

First, Utraquism sought to affirm the patristic ecclesiological tradition, populist and communitarian in orientation, which would replace the model characterized by Brendan Bradshaw as "the late medieval clericalist ecclesiology, moulded by the canonists and the scholastics, and preoccupied with the categories of power, authority, and institutional function."[1] When speaking of the "primitive" church (*prvotní církev*), the Utraquists—unlike the Protestant reformers (or the Taborites)—thought of the patristic church, not of the (largely imaginary) church of apostolic times.[2] Aside from replacement of the authoritarian and centralistic ecclesiology of the High Middle Ages, the revival of the Western Church of the first millennium was also signaled, on a more positive side, by the restoration of lay communion in both kinds, infant communion, and clerical marriage. This neglected aspect of Utraquism has been rediscovered and highly valued by theological scholars in North America, particularly Enrico C. Molnar and David R. Holeton, the latter of whom wrote: "I would suggest that, at least as far the Eucharist is concerned, [Bohemian Utraquism] has more to offer our own day than does much which transpired during the classical reformation of the sixteenth century. The relationship between baptism and Eucharist, Eucharist and Christian community, and Eucharist and Christian reform were all questions of primary importance to the Bohemians but largely left unasked in the sixteenth century. They are all questions which are being asked continually today."[3]

Second, Utraquism functioned as an example of the *via media* between the papal monarchism of the late Middle Ages and the biblical reductionism of the Protestant Reformation. Thus, it resembled its close historical variant, the Church of England of the Elizabethan settlement, but provided alternatives in both a liberal and a conservative direction. It was more liberal in ecclesiastical administration, rejecting not only papal, but also episcopal governance. It was more conservative in the sacramental area, retaining not only the presbyterial and episcopal, but also the papal sacerdotalism.

Third, although it did not exhaust its meaning, the conservative aspect of Utraquist sacerdotalism made it possible to regard Utraquism not only as part of the *via media,* but also as an exemplar of what later became known as "liberal Catholicism." It rejected "the institutionally oriented ecclesiology of late medieval clericalism," which would prevail at Trent,[4] but retained the fundamentals of Christian orthodoxy, including a scaled-down role for the papacy. Utraquism joined contemporary proponents of Catholic reform, particularly the Christian humanists of the Erasmian type. It prefigured, and often exceeded, future trends in Catholic renewal. This role became more significant in its concreteness, if considered in connection with Josephinism. The conspicuous efforts to modernize the Roman Church by Joseph II during the Catholic Enlightenment used, to as yet undetermined degree, the Bohemian Reformation as a model.

Fourth, Utraquism was associated with a remarkable state of religious toleration in Bohemia, especially after 1575, when the official recognition of Utraquism and the adherents of the Roman Curia with a tacit protection of the Lutherans and the Unity of Brethren (and through it of the Calvinists). This process culminated in 1609 by the overt legal equalization of all these denominations. The spirit of toleration resulted in part from the memories of destructiveness of religious intolerance, partly from the *via media* of Utraquism. Yet, another reason for the exceptional tolerance characteristic of the Utraquists was their escape from the need of confessionalization in the late sixteenth and early seventeenth century.[5] They avoided the process by which the Protestant groups had to define themselves against each other and against the Church of Rome, and by which the latter had to adopt its own demarcations against the churches of the Reformation. The Utraquists were already secure in their own delimitation vis-à-vis both Roman authoritarianism (since the period of Hus and the Compactata), and vis-à-vis the Protestant biblical reductionism through the fifteenth-century encounters with the Taborites and the Unity of Brethren. The resulting notable state of religious pluralism has by and large escaped the attention of Euro-

Atlantic historical literature.[6] Emphasis has usually been placed for the late sixteenth century on toleration in Poland, Transylvania, the Dutch Republic, and—after 1598—France.[7]

Turning then to the specifically Bohemian context, two significant conclusions emerge: a loss of religious memory due to the historical (mis)interpretation of the Bohemian Reformation; and the heritage of liberal political culture, separated from its religious moorings, through the renaissance of sixteenth-century literature during the national awakening.

The absorption of Utraquism by the Roman Church during the Counter-Reformation deprived the Czechs of their religious tradition in a particularly invidious way. Thus, in the wake of the Battle of White Mountain in 1620, the Utraquist Church was captured by the Church of Rome and during the Counter-Reformation subjected to a forcible transmutation—what might perhaps be called a "transubstantiation" —whereby much of the external form remained, but the inner substance was altered beyond recognition. Through this process, the Utraquist Church was annihilated as a specific ecclesial entity. There was nothing to survive either in exile or underground. Thus, once the Counter-Reformation had run its course and religious toleration was established in the Habsburg Empire in 1781, the churches of the Protestant Reformation had joined Rome to erase the memory of the uncongenial *via media* of Utraquism.

The literary heritage of the sixteenth century came alive during the period of the national awakening in the late eighteenth and early nineteenth centuries. The philosophical, political, and historical writers, as well as the belletrists, of the Utraquist era provided the intellectual nourishment of the nationally awakening generations. There was, however, a paradox in the revival process linked with the Bohemian Reformation. Eventually, the Czech national awakening resurrected the Utraquist sixteenth century in its civic culture, but without its religious dimension. The world that the Bohemian Reformation had created was revived as a secular order, not as a theological system. Two factors help to illuminate this oddity of outcome. First, as noted, the Counter-Reformation and the Reformation alike worked, albeit from opposite directions, to destroy the credibility and authenticity of a Christian *via media,* which Utraquism theologically represented. For the Counter-Reformation, the mainline Bohemian religion had a deficiency— for the Evangelical and the Reformed an excess—of traditional orthodoxy. Second, initially Catholicism of the Austrian Enlightenment, in the name of which the Counter-Reformation was overthrown in Bohemia, held out a promise for revival of Utraquism, both being subspecies of liberal Catholicism. The re-Tridentization of the Roman Church, starting in 1815 and moving full speed ahead (or perhaps backwards) after 1848 toward the authoritarian model, removed the possibility that the Austrian renewal of Catholicism might provide a surrogate institutional basis for a reemergence of theological Utraquism.

The principal lesson taught by Utraquism and its aftermath may be that a religion need not be radical or innovative, but can be moderate and conservative, to foster a liberal political culture. The story of the Bohemian Reformation serves as a reminder that the ideas of political liberty and human rights could emerge in harmony with a religious milieu, not necessarily in opposition to it through a secularist revolt. This can be the case even if eventually the benign liberal political culture separated itself from the religious context by which it had been originally nurtured. Thus, liberal secularists can appreciate the libertarian contribution of Hus and of his followers without sharing their commitment to orthodox Christianity.

Appendix

The Kings of Bohemia

Charles IV, 1346–1378; also Holy Roman Emperor, 1355–1378
Wenceslaus IV, 1378–1419; also Emperor, 1378–1400
Wars of the Bohemian Reformation, 1419–1434
Sigismund, 1436–1437; also Emperor, 1433–1437
Albrecht II, 1437–1439
Ladislav the Posthumous, 1453–1457
George of Poděbrady, 1458–1471
Vladislav II, Jagellon, 1471–1516
Louis, Jagellon, 1516–1526
Ferdinand I, Habsburg, 1526–1564; also Emperor, 1556–1564
Maximilian II, 1564–1576; also Emperor
Rudolf II, 1576–1611; also Emperor
Matthias, 1611–1619; also Emperor
Ferdinand II, 1619; also Emperor
Frederick of Palatinate, 1619–1620
Ferdinand II, 1620–1637; also Emperor
Ferdinand III, 1637–1657; also Emperor
Source: *Československé dějiny v datech* (Prague: Svoboda, 1986), 566.

Administrators of Consistory Sub Utraque

Křišt'an of Prachatice, 1437–1439
Jan of Příbram, 1439–1448
Jan Rokycana, 1448–1471
Václav Koranda, the Younger, 1471–1497
Jakub of Stříbro (Columbus), 1497–1499
Pavel of Žatec, 1500–1517
Matěj Korambus, 1517–1520
Václav Šišmánek, 1520–1523

Havel Cahera, jointly with Jan Kulata, Jindřich Lounský, and Jan of Český Brod, 1523–1524
Havel Cahera, 1524–1529
Vavřinec of Třeboň and Václav Aunoštský, 1529–1531
Václav Aunoštský, 1531–1539
Martin Klatovský, 1539–1541
Jan Hortensius, 1541
Jan Mystopol, 1542–1555
Jan Kolinský, 1555–1558
Matěj Dvorský of Hájek, 1555–1562
Jan Mystopol, 1562–1568
Martin Mělnický, 1568–1572
Jindřich Dvorský of Helfenburk, 1572–1581
Václav Benešovský, 1581–1590
Fabian Rezek of Strakonice, 1590–1593
Václav Dačický of Brozany, 1594–1604
Jan Benedikt Pražský, 1605–1609
Tomáš of Soběslav, 1609 (January 22 – July 30)
Source: Václav V. Tomek, "O církevní správě strany pod obojí v Čechách od r. 1415 až 1622," *Časopis českého muzea* 22 (1848), 463–468.

Administrators of Joint Consistory Sub Utraque

Eliáš Šúd of Semanin, 1609–1614
Sigmund Critinus Stříbrský, 1614–1619
Jiří Dikastus, 1619–1621
Source: ibid., 468.

Administrators of Consistory Sub Una

Jan Železný, 1421–1430; also bishop of Olomouc, 1416–1430
Konrád Zvolský of Zvole, 1430–1434; also bishop of Olomouc
Jan of Dubá and Šimon of Nymburk, 1435–1436
Philibbert, Bishop of Coutances and apostolic administrator of the see of Prague, also Conciliar Legate in Bohemia, 1436–1439; jointly with Prokop of Kladruby, bishop of Constance, 1437–1439
Prokop of Kladruby, 1439–1443
Šimon of Nymburk and Jiří of Prague, 1444–1448
Václav of Krumlov, 1449–1460
Mikuláš of Krumlov, 1461
Hilarius of Litoměřice, 1461–1467; jointly with Jan of Krumlov, 1461–1462; with Václav of Křižanov, 1462–1467
Hanuš of Kolovraty, 1468–1483; jointly with Jan of Krumlov, 1468–1481; with Václav of Planá, 1481–1483
Pavel Souček, 1486–1496
Ambrož Chrt of Plzeň, 1497–1511; jointly with Blažej of Planá, 1497–1499; with Jan of Vartenberk, 1500–1511

Arnošt of Šlejnice and Jan Žák, 1511–1525; jointly with Mikuláš Houska, 1524
Jan Fabri and Mikuláš Houska, 1525–1531
Arnošt of Šlejnice, 1531–1542
Valentin, Scholastic of St. Vitus; and Jan of Puchov, 1542–1553
Jindřich Scribonius, 1555–1561
Source: Jiří Kettner, *Dějiny pražské arcidiecéze v datech* (Prague: Zvon, 1993), 239–240.

Archbishops of Prague

Arnošt of Pardubice, 1344–1364
Jan Očko of Vlašim, 1364–1379
Jan of Jenštejn, 1379–1396
Olbram of Škoverec, 1396–1402
Mikuláš Puchník of Černice, 1402, unconsecrated
Zbyněk Zajíc of Hasenburk, 1403–1411
Albík of Uničov, 1411–1412
Konrád of Vechta, 1413–1431; Utraquist, 1421–1431
Jan Rokycana, 1435–1471; Utraquist, unconsecrated
Antonín Brus of Mohelnice, 1561–1580
Martin Medek, 1581–1590
Zbyněk Berka of Dubá, 1592–1606
Karl Lamberg, 1607–1612
Johann Lohelius, 1612–1622
Arnošt of Harrach, 1623–1667
Source: Kettner, *Dějiny pražské arcidiecéze v datech,* 237.

Resident Bishops Serving the Utraquists

Philibbert, Bishop of Coutances and apostolic administrator of the see of Prague, also Conciliar Legate in Bohemia, 1435–1439
Augustine Sancturien, Bishop of Mirandola (near Modena), 1482–1493
Philip of Novavilla, Bishop of Sidon, and Auxiliary of Modena, 1504–1507
Source: Chapter 6 of this volume.

Nonresident Bishops Serving the Utraquists

Dionysius de Franciscis, Greek Uniate Bishop, in the monastery of Sancta Maria del Horto, Venice, c. 1539–1543
Titus Cheronensus, Greek Uniate Bishop at the same location, 1543–1555
Friedrich Nausea, Bishop of Vienna, 1550–1551
Source: Chapter 6 of this volume.

Major Martyrs of Bohemian Reformation

Jan Hus, burned at the stake in Constance, Germany, on July 6, 1415
Jeroným of Prague, burned at the stake in Constance on May 30, 1416

Jan Locika of Domažlice, died in jail, or beheaded at the castle of Křivoklát, in April 1622

Vavřinec Hanžburský of Kopeček, beheaded in the Old Town Square of Prague on April 7, 1631

Notes

Preface

1. See Alexandra Walsham's review of John Christian Laursen and Cary J. Nederman, eds., *Beyond the Persecuting Society: Toleration Before the Enlightenment* (Philadelphia: University of Pennsylvania Press, 1998) in *English Historical Review* 114 (1999): 1309.

2. For an overview of the literature on this theme, see David Sorkin, "Reform Catholicism and Religious Enlightenment," *Austrian History Yearbook* 30 (1999): 187–219, and "Comments" by T. C. W. Blanning and R. J. W. Evans, *Austrian History Yearbook* 30 (1999): 221–235. On "Reform Catholicism," see also Franz A. J. Szabo, *Kaunitz and Enlightened Absolutism, 1553–1780* (Cambridge: Cambridge University Press, 1994), 211–212.

3. For an overview of this literature, see Alexandra Walsham, "The Parochial Roots of Laudianism Revisited: Catholics, Anti-Calvinists and 'Parish Anglicans' in Early Stuart England," *Journal of Ecclesiastical History* 49 (1998): 620–651; see also Judith Maltby, *Prayer Book and People in Elizabethan and Early Stuart England* (Cambridge: Cambridge University Press, 1998), 5–19.

4. John E. Booty, "Hooker and Anglicanism," in W. Speed Hill, ed., *Studies in Richard Hooker* (Cleveland: Press of Case Western Reserve University, 1972), 211.

5. Tony Claydon and Ian McBride, eds., *Protestantism and National Identity: Britain and Ireland, c. 1650–c.1850* (Cambridge: Cambridge University Press, 1998), 6.

6. On the Bohemian reform movement prior to 1415, see David R. Holeton, "The Communion of Infants and Hussitism," *Communio Viatorum* 27 (1984), especially 217–219; and Howard Kaminsky, *A History of the Hussite Revolution* (Berkeley: University of California Press, 1967), 5–96. On the early Utraquist synods, see Blanka Zilynská, *Husitské synody v Čechách, 1418–1440* (Prague: Univerzita Karlova, 1985).

7. The Unity survives in the contemporary world under the names of the Moravian Church (mainly in North America and the Caribbean), or the Church of the Bohemian Brethren (mainly in Central Europe). On its history, see Murray L. Wagner, *Petr Chelčický: A Radical Separatist in Hussite Bohemia* (Scottsdale, Pa.: Herald Press, 1983), and Rudolf Říčan, *The History of the Unity of Brethren: A Protestant Hussite Church in Bohemia and Moravia*, trans. C. Daniel Crews (Bethlehem, Pa.: Moravian Church in America, 1992).

8. Václav V. Tomek, "O církevní správě strany pod obojí v Čechách od r. 1415 až 1622," *Časopis českého muzea* 22 (1848): 365–383, 441–468; and Kamil Krofta, "Boj o konsistoř pod obojí v letech 1562–1575 a jeho historický základ," *Český časopis historický* 17 (1911): 28–57, 178–199, 283–303, 383–420. On the repudiation of the Taborites, see František Bartoš, *The Hussite Revolution, 1424–1437*, ed. John M. Klassen (Boulder, Colo.: East European Monographs, 1986), 112–18; and (for documentation) Zdeněk Nejedlý, *Prameny k synodám strany pražské a táborské (vznik husitské konfesse) v létech 1441–1444* (Prague: Královská česká společnost nauk, 1900), especially 56–95. The Taborites were defeated militarily in 1434, and suppressed in 1452.

9. "Hussiti" was the term of opprobrium favored by the Roman Curia. See Klaus Jaitner, ed., *Die Hauptinstruktionen Clemens' VIII. für die Nuntien und Legaten an den europäischen Fürstenhöfen, 1592–1605*, 2 vols. (Tübingen: Niemeyer, 1984), 1:59, 2:10; Johann Rainer, ed., *Nuntiaturberichte aus Deutschland, nebst ergänzenden Aktenstücken*, Abteilung 2, 1560–1572, Band 8 (Graz: Böhlau, 1967), 46–47; Helmut Goetz, ed., *Nuntiaturberichte aus Deutschland, nebst ergänzenden Aktenstücken*, Abteilung 3, 1572–1585, Band 6 (Tübingen: Niemeyer, 1982), 154, 365, 369; Almut Bues, ed., *Nuntiaturberichte aus Deutschland, nebst ergänzenden Aktenstücken*, Abteilung 3, Band 7 (Tübingen: Niemeyer, 1990), 49, 88. The courteous designation was "communicantes sub utraque"; see Goetz, Abteilung 3, Band 6, 467, and Abteilung 3, Band 7, 98, 376. A more neutral unofficial term was "Calixtini," used, for instance, by Bishop Jan Dubravius in 1544; see Dubravius, *Ad collegium Pragense de ecclesiae oeconomia epistola* printed in *Ioanis, Dei gratia episcopi Olomucensis, In psalmum ordine quintum ecclesiae deprecantis typum gerentem, cuius initium est: Verba mea auribus percipe, Domine, enarratio* . . . (Prostějov: Ioannes Guntherus, 1549), 3.

10. Ferdinand Seibt, "'Hussiten' als historischer Begriff," in Seibt, *Hussitica: Zur Struktur einer Revolution* (Cologne: Böhlau, 1965), 10–15.

11. On Luther as a "paradigm-changing figure," see Robert Kolb, "Altering the Agenda, Shifting the Strategy: The Grundfest of 1571 as Philippist Program for Lutheran Concord," *Sixteenth Century Journal* 30 (1999): 706.

12. In the Four Articles of Prague of 1419 (as Article One), and the Compactata of the Council of Basel (as Article Two), see Rudolf Říčan, ed., *Čtyři vyznání* (Prague: Komenského evangelická bohoslovecká fakulta, 1951), 39; Ferdinand Hrejsa, *Dějiny křesťanství v Československu*, 6 vols. (Prague: Husova ceskoslovenská evangelická fakulta bohoslovecká, 1947–1950), 2:271.

13. Kamil Krofta, "Václav Koranda mladší z Nové Plzně a jeho názory náboženské," in Krofta, *Listy z náboženských dějin* (Prague: Historický klub, 1936), 258. As a parenthetical observation, the Utraquists likewise escaped the dread engendered by the Calvinist stress on predestination. See Alexandra Walsham, "The Parochial Roots of Laudianism Revisited: Catholics, Anti-Calvinists and 'Parish Anglicans' in Early Stuart England," *Journal of Ecclesiastical History* 49 (1998): 629, and her references to Michael MacDonald, *Sleepless Souls: Suicide in Early Modern England* (Oxford: Oxford University Press, 1990), 64–67.

14. Otakar Odložilík, "Utrakvistická postilla z r. 1540," *Věstník České společnosti nauk* (1925): 15–17, 20–21; on purgatory see František M. Bartoš, *Husitská revoluce*, 2 vols. (Prague: Nakladatelství Československé akademie věd, 1965–1966), 1:21, 37.

15. The consensual system of administrative discipline was stipulated, for instance, in the Candlemas Day Articles of 1524, points 1 to 6. See Bartoš Písař, *Kronika pražská*,

ed. Josef V. Šimák (*Prameny dějin českých/Fontes Rerum Bohemicarum* 6 (Prague: Nadání Františka Palackého, 1907), 21–22.

16. On Utraquist laxity on confession, see Julius Pažout, *Jednání a dopisy konsistoře pod obojí způsobou přijímajících, 1562–1570* (Prague: Historický spolek, 1906), 342–343; Josef Matoušek, "Kurie a boj o konsistoř pod obojí za administrátora Rezka," *Český časopis historický* 37 (1931): 262–263; *Sněmy české od léta 1526 až po naši dobu*, 15 vols. (Prague: Zemský výbor, 1877–1941), 8:337.

17. See, for instance, John Spurr, *English Puritanism, 1603–1689* (New York: St. Martin's Press, 1998), 104.

18. On the concept of "confessionalization," see, for instance, Robert Bireley, *The Refashioning of Catholicism, 1450–1700: A Reassessment of the Counter Reformation* (Washington, D.C.: Catholic University of America Press, 1999), 6–8.

19. Thomas A. Fudge, "The Problem of Religious Liberty in Early Modern Bohemia," *Communio Viatorum* 38 (1996): 68–71; Václav Koranda, Jr., *Traktát o velebné a božské svátosti oltářní* (Prague: Tiskař Korandy, 1493), f. A3v–A4r.

20. Karin Maag, ed., *Reformation in Eastern and Central Europe* (Brookfield, Vt.: Ashgate, 1997), 1.

21. See, for instance, Konstantin Kristian Bidones z Bidenthalu, *Výstraha: Proti v Římsko-Katolické náboženství ubíhání všechnem k Augšpurské neb České Konfesí se přiznávajícím* . . . (N.p., 1624); František Hrubý, "Luterství a novoutrakvismus v Českých zemích v 16. a 17. století," *Český časopis historický* 45 (1939): 40 (see also 42–44).

22. Frederick G. Heymann, "The Impact of Martin Luther upon Bohemia," *Central European History* 1 (1968): 122, n. 44.

23. Malcolm Lambert, *Medieval Heresy: Popular Movements from the Gregorian Reform to the Reformation*, 2d ed. (Oxford: Blackwell, 1992), 381, n. 70. See also Winfried Eberhard, *Konfessionsbildung und Stände in Böhmen, 1478–1530* (Munich: Oldenbourg, 1981), 7.

24. Robert J. W. Evans, *Rudolf II and His World: A Study in Intellectual History, 1576–1612* (Oxford: Oxford University Press, 1973), 29 ff., especially 36–37.

25. See, for instance, Josef Válka, "Husitství a Morava," in *Jan Hus: Mezi epochami, národy a konfessemi*, ed. Jan B. Lášek (Prague: Česká křesťanská akademie, 1995), 220; František Hrubý, "Luterství a kalvinismus na Moravě před Bílou horou," *Český časopis historický* 40 (1934): 265–309; 41 (1935): 1–40, 237–268; Hrubý, "Luterství a novoutrakvismus v českých zemích v 16. a 17. století," *Český časopis historický* 45 (1939): 31–44; Anton Gindely, *Geschichte der Böhmischen Brüder*, 2d ed., 2 vols. (Prague: C. Bellmann, 1861–1862), 2:466, n. 57.

Chapter 1

1. On these characteristics, see W. David Neelands, "Hooker on Reason, Scripture and 'Tradition'," in *Richard Hooker and the Construction of Christian Community*, ed. Arthur S. McGrade (Tempe, Ariz.: Medieval and Renaissance Texts and Studies, 1997), 75–94; Diarmaid MacCulloch, "Richard Hooker's Reputation," *English Historical Review* 117 (2002), 778–779.

2. Examined against the American religious spectrum, the Utraquist Church would occupy a place in the High Church category, close to the Episcopal Church or

more particularly to its Anglo-Catholic wing. The similarity between Utraquism and Anglicanism is noted without elaboration by Jarold K. Zeman, *The Hussite Movement and the Reformation in Bohemia, Moravia and Slovakia, 1350–1650* (Ann Arbor, Mich.: Michigan Slavic Publications, 1977), xvi; and Antony Black, *Political Thought in Europe, 1250–1450* (New York: Cambridge University Press, 1992), 81. On the Anglican acceptance of Scripture, reason and tradition, see for instance, Paul Avis, *Anglicanism and the Christian Church* (Minneapolis: Fortress Press, 1989), 63–67; on the traditionalist national emphasis, Donald R. Kelley, "Elizabethan Political Thought," in *The Varieties of British Political Thought, 1500–1800*, ed. J. G. A. Pocock (Cambridge: Cambridge University Press, 1993), 71.

3. Richard Hooker, *The Folger Library Edition of the Works of Richard Hooker*, 6 vols., ed. W. Speed Hill (Cambridge, Mass.: Belknap Press of Harvard University Press, 1977–1993), 6:10.

4. For surveys of Utraquism's historiography, see Thomas A. Fudge, "The State of Hussite Historiography," *Mediaevistik* 7 (1994): 93–117, covering mainly the fifteenth century; František Šmahel, "Literatura a prameny," in Šmahel, *Husitská revoluce*, 2d ed., 4 vols. (Prague: Karolinum, 1996), 4:213–395, and "Hussitica 1994/95–1997," *Český časopis historický* 95 (1997), 704–740; Wojciech Iwańczak, "Die Hussitenrevolution in der polnischen Historiographie des 19. Jahrhunderts," *Husitství, Reformace, Renesance: Sborník k 60. narozeninám Františka Šmahela*, ed. Jaroslav Pánek, et al., (Prague: Historický ústav, 1994), 3:975–988; Arnošt Kraus, *Husitství v literatuře, zejména německé*, 3 vols. (Prague: Česká akademie pro vědy, slovesnost a umění, 1917–1924); G. I. Lipatnikova, "K izucheniiu gusitskogo dvizheniia v russkoi dorevoliutsionnoi istoriografii," in *Voprosy istorii slavian* (Voronezh) 1 (1963); Liudmila P. Lapteva, *Russkaia istoriografiia gusitskogo dvizheniia, 40–e gody XIX v.–1917 g.* (Moscow: Izdatel'stvo Moskovskogo Universiteta, 1978).

5. For negative attitudes in French and German historical writing, see Ernst Denis, *Fin de l'indépendance bohême*, 2d ed. (Paris: Librairie Leroux, 1930), 2:83, 91–94, 295–302; Winfried Eberhard, *Konfessionsbildung und Stände in Böhmen, 1478–1530* (Munich: Oldenbourg, 1981), especially, 19–25; Jean Bérenger, *A History of the Habsburg Empire, 1273–1700*, trans. C. A. Simpson (London: Longman, 1994), 176–177. For a cautionary note against the denunciations and dismissals of traditional Utraquism, see Robert J. W. Evans, *Rudolf II and His World: A Study in Intellectual History, 1576–1612* (Oxford: Oxford University Press, 1973), 29 ff., especially 36–37.

6. Ferdinand Hrejsa, *Česká konfese: její vznik, podstata a dějiny* (Prague: Česká akademie pro vědy, slovesnost a umění, 1912), 4.

7. Jaroslav Böhm, et al., *Československá vlastivěda, Dějiny* (Prague: Orbis, 1963), 1:380; see also 390. For a sampling of the almost routine denunciations of the Utraquists in Czech historiography, see Jaroslav Vlček, *Dějiny české literatury* (Prague: Československý spisovatel, 1951), 1:304–306; Zikmund Winter, *Život církevní v Čechách* (Prague: Česká akademie pro vědy, slovesnost a umění, 1895), 1:157–158; Václav Novotný, "Náboženské dějiny české ve století 16.," in *Česká politika*, ed. Zdeněk V. Tobolka, 5 vols. (Prague: Jan Laichter, 1906), 1:591; Karel Stloukal, "Počátky nunciatury v Praze: Bonhomi v Čechách, 1581–84," *Český časopis historický* 34 (1928): 256; František Bednář, "Úvodem," in Jakub Bílek, *Jan Augusta v letech samoty, 1548–1564* (Prague: Laichter, 1942), 6; Josef Janáček, *České dějiny: Doba předbělohorská*, 2 vols. (Prague: Academia, 1971–1984), especially, 1:191, n. 21 (see also 192, 198–199); František Kutnar, *Přehledné dějiny českého a slovenského dějepisectví* (Prague: Státní ped-

agogické nakladatelství, 1973), 1:53; Josef Macek, *Jean Hus et les traditions hussites: XVe–XIXe siècles* (Paris: Plon, 1973), 256–257, 259–260; Jaroslav Purš and Miroslav Kropilák, eds., *Přehled dějin Československa* (Prague: Academia, 1982), 1: pt. 2, 61–65. For deprecatory characterizations in the post-Marxist era, see Petr Čornej, ed., *Dějiny zemí Koruny české* (Prague: Paseka, 1992), 1:242. Noemi Rejchrtová, however, seeks to qualify the charge of the Utraquists' moral corruption in *Český časopis historický* 90 (1992): 125–126.

    8. Hrejsa, *Česká konfesse,* 640–658.

    9. František Palacký classifies the Lutherans as the party of progress (*pokrok*) and the Utraquists as the party of stagnation (*utkvělost*) during the 1520s in *Dějiny národu českého* (Prague: Bursík a Kohout, [1893]), 5:514.

    10. František Palacký, *Obrana husitství,* trans. and ed. František M. Bartoš (Prague: Blahoslav, 1926), 33–34.

    11. Luther's assertion that "without knowing it, we have been Hussites all along," is cited by Enrico C. S. Molnar, *The Catholicity of the Utraquist Church of Bohemia* (Sewanee, Tenn.: University Press of Sewanee, 1959), 1; see also Thomas A. Fudge, "Ansellus Dei and the Bethlehem Chapel in Prague," *Communio Viatorum* 35 (1993): 161. On the qualification, see Jaroslav Kadlec, *Přehled českých církevních dějin* (Prague: Zvon, 1991), 2:14–15.

    12. Jaroslav Pelikan, "Luther's Attitude Toward John Hus," *Concordia Theological Monthly* 19 (1948): 751–755; see also "Luther," *Encyclopedia Britannica, Macropaedia,* 15th ed. (Chicago: Encyclopedia Britannica, 1985), 11:191.

    13. On Counter-Reformation propaganda, see Antonii V. Florovskii, *Jan Hus v ruském pojetí* (Prague: Svaz ruských válečných invalidů, 1935), 30–31, and *Chekhi i vostochnye slaviane: ocherki po istorii cheshsko–russkikh otnoshenii, X–XVIII vv.* (Prague: Slovanský ústav, 1935), 1:400–401; Ralph Keen, *Divine and Human Authority in Reformation Thought: German Theologians on Political Order, 1520–1555* (Nieuwkoop: De Graaf, 1997), 240–241.

    14. See, for instance, Desiderius Erasmus, *The Correspondence,* 11 vols. (Toronto: University of Toronto Press, 1974–1994): 11:194–196. Erasmus was particularly disturbed by the assertions of his erstwhile friends, Oecolampadius and Pellicanus, that Erasmus's scholarly work had led them to embrace the Protestant position. Erasmus, *The Correspondence,* 11:xvii.

    15. *Artykulowe a snessenij Knězstva pod obogij Spuosobau: Leta Bozijho MDXXXIX,* archived in the National Library in Vienna under the notation, *Articuli Conciliabuli sub utraque specie communicantium* (Bohemice et latine, S.l., 1539, Signatura: 24 M 56). See also entry in *Tisky z let 1501–1800,* vol. 2 in 9 parts of *Knihopis českých a slovenských tisků* (Prague: Nakladatelství Československé akademie věd, 1939–1967; Dodatky, 1994, and ongoing), 2: part 1, 55, no. 269.

    16. Hrejsa, *Česká konfesse,* 672–681.

    17. Jaroslav Bidlo, "O Konfessi bratrské z r. 1573," in *Sborník prací historických k šedesátým narozeninám Jaroslava Golla,* ed. Jaroslav Bidlo, et al. (Prague: Historický klub, 1906), 246–278; Rudolf Říčan, *The History of the Unity of Brethren: A Protestant Hussite Church in Bohemia and Moravia,* trans. C. Daniel Crews (Bethlehem, Pa.: Moravian Church in America, 1992), 100.

    18. *Laws of Ecclesiastical Polity* (cited hereafter as *LEP*), VI.4.14, in Hooker, *The Folger Edition* (1981), 3:46–47; see also 6:265–266, 855. Hooker cited the Bohemian Confession from Salnar de Castres, ed., *Harmonia confessionum fidei, Orthodoxarum, et*

Reformatorum Ecclesiarum (Geneva: Petrus Sanctandreanus, 1581), 1:143, although the text of the Bohemian Confession was also available in the English translation of J. F. Salvart, ed., *An Harmony of the confessions of the faith of the christian and reformed churches* (Cambridge: Thomas Thomas, 1586), with the passage cited by Hooker on p. 219. On the history of the original compilation, see Peter Hall, trans. and ed., *The Harmony of Confessions: Exhibiting the Faith of the Churches of Christ Reformed* (London, n.p., 1842), xi–xvii.

19. Jacques B. Bossuet, *Histoire des variations des églises protestantes,* 3 vols. (Paris: Pichard, 1821), 1:13.

20. See John Foxe, *Fox's Book of Martyrs: The Acts and Monuments of the Church,* ed. John Cumming, 3 vols. (London: Chatto and Windus, 1875), 1:823–945.

21. Alexandra Walsham, "*Vox Piscis; or the Book-Fish:* Providence and the Uses of the Reformation Past in Caroline Cambridge," *English Historical Review* 114 (1999): 601–602.

22. See Thomas More's *Dialogue Concerning Heresies* (1529?), in More, *Complete Works,* 21 vols. (New Haven: Yale University Press, 1963–1997), 6: pt. 1, 315, 379, pt. 2, 473–474.

23. The catalog included "Luther, Wyclif, Hus, Melanchton, Oecolampadius, Bucer, the Augsburg Confession, Melanchton's *Apologia,* Tyndale, Barnes, Marshall, 'Raskell,' St. German, and such other heresies of Anabaptists . . . ," cited in More, *Complete Works,* 9:xlvii.

24. Rosemary O'Day, *The Debate on the English Reformation* (London: Methuen, 1986), 23. On Hus, Jerome of Prague, and Žižka, see Jean Crespin, *Histoire des Martyrs persécutez et mis à mort pour la vérité de l'évangile, depuis le temps des apostres iusques à présent (1619),* ed. Daniel Benoît, 3 vols. (Toulouse: Société des livres religieux, 1885–1889), 1:137–200.

25. On Saxon intolerance, see Hrejsa, *Česká konfesse,* 583–586; Kamil Krofta, *Bílá Hora: Kurs šestipřednáškový* (Prague: J. Otto, 1914), 231.

26. Jan Amos Komenský [Johann Amos Comenius], *The History of the Bohemian Persecution* (London: By A.A. for Iohn Walker, 1650). It was preceded by a Latin translation, *Historia persecutionum ecclesiae bohemicae* (published originally in Leiden in 1647 and 1648); see Jan Amos Komenský, *Opera omnia* (Prague: Academia, 1989), 9: pt. 1, 199–338. The Czech original was published subsequently as Jan Amos Komenský, *Historia o těžkých protivenstvích církve české hned od počátku jejího na víru Křesťanskou obrácení v létu 894 až do léta 1632 za panování Ferdinanda Druhého. S připojením historie o persekucí valdenských roku tohoto (1655) stálé* (Leszno: n.p., 1655), and the second edition (Amsterdam: Jan Paskovský, 1663); see Komenský, *Opera omnia,* 53–198.

27. Johannes Cochlaeus, *Historiae Hussitarum libri duodecim* (Mainz: Franciscus Behem, 1549), 94; Kraus, *Husitství v literatuře,* especially, 1:172–174; Jindřich Ondřej Hoffman, *Zrcadlo náboženství* (Prague: Impressí akademická, 1642), f. A2v. For Nuncio Camillo Caetano's view of Bohemia as where the Protestant "evil took its beginning," see Karel Stloukal, *Papežská politika a císařský dvůr pražský na předělu XVI. a XVII. věku* (Prague: F. Řivnáč, 1925), 156.

28. Janáček, *České dějiny,* 1: pt. 1, 187.

29. Johann Faber, *Confutatio gravissimi erroris asserentis in sacramento altaris post consecrationem nisi corpus tantum et sub specie vini non esse nisi sanguinem tantum* (Leipzig: Nicholas Wolrab, 1537).

30. Adam Tanner, *Apologia pro Societate Jesu ex Boemiae Regno ab eiusdem regni statibus religionis sub utraque, publico decreto immerito proscripta. Anno M.DC.XVIII. die VIIII Junij* (Vienna: n.p., 1618); German translation, Adam Tanner, *Verantwortung Deren von der Societät Jesu, so auss dem Königreich Bohem von desselben Reichs Ständen, so sich sub utraque nennen, durch offenes Decret ohnbillich verwiesen, im Jahr 1618. den 9. Tag Junii* (Vienna: Wolfgang Schump, 1618). The Jesuit *Apology* is cited by Winter, *Život církevní,* 1:275. See Chapter 11 for more detail.

31. See Chapter 12.

32. Bossuet, *Histoire des variations des églises protestantes,* 2:266–267, 339. See also Jiří Bílý, "Vývoj názoru na Husa a husitství ve francouzské literatuře," in *Jan Hus mezi epochami, národy a konfesemi,* ed. Jan B. Lášek (Prague: Česká křest'anská akademie, 1995), 255.

33. Paul de Vooght, *L'hérésie de Jean Huss,* 2d ed., 2 vols. (Louvain: Publications universitaires, 1975), especially 1:516. De Vooght still hedges with respect to Hus's concept of papal primacy; see De Vooght, "John Hus," in *New Catholic Encyclopedia* (New York: McGraw-Hill, 1967–1974), 7:272. See also Francis Oakley, "Councils, Western, 1311–1449," *Dictionary of the Middle Ages* (New York: Scribner's, 1983), 3:650.

34. Daniel DiDomizio, "Jan Hus's De ecclesia, precursor of Vatican II?" *Theological Studies* 60 (1999): 247–260.

35. František J. Holeček, "The Problems of the Person, the Life and the Work of Jan Hus: The Significance and the Task of a Commission of the Czech Bishops' Conference," in *The Bohemian Reformation and Religious Practice,* vol. 2: Papers from the XVIIIth World Congress of the Czechoslovak Society of Arts and Sciences, Brno, 1996, eds. Zdeněk V. David and David R. Holeton (Prague: Academy of Sciences of the Czech Republic, Main Library, 1998), 39–44.

36. Jaroslav Pánek and Miloslav Polívka, eds., *Jan Hus ve Vatikánu. Mezinárodní rozprava o českém reformátoru 15. století a o jeho recepci na prahu třetího tisíciletí* (Prague: Historický ústav, 2000), 111. The pope's statement still fell short of the full and formal vindication of Hus which had been previously anticipated; see Thomas A. Fudge, "*Infoelix Hus:* The Rehabilitation of a Medieval Heretic," *Fides et Historia* 30 (1998): 64.

37. Christopher Haigh, *English Reformations: Religion, Politics, and Society under the Tudors* (Oxford: Clarendon Press, 1993), 15–17.

38. Alexandra Walsham, "The Parochial Roots of Laudianism Revisited: Catholics, Anti–Calvinists and 'Parish Anglicans' in Early Stuart England," *Journal of Ecclesiastical History* 49 (1998): 621.

39. On the rejection of historical "metanarratives," like those of Hegel and Marx, in the era of postmodernism see, for instance, Jean-François Lyotard, *The Postmodern Condition: A Report on Knowledge,* trans. Geoff Bennington and Brian Massumi (Minneapolis: University of Minnesota Press, 1984), 34–37.

40. Louis Blanc, *Histoire de la Révolution française,* 12 vols. (Paris: Langlois and Leclercq, 1847–1862), 1:26, cited by Ludwig Häusser in *Gesammelte Schriften zur Geschichts–Literatur,* ed. Carl Pfeiffer (Berlin: Weidmann, 1869), 1:755.

41. On the misguided tendency to link the Bohemian and the German reformations, see Frederick G. Heymann, "John Rokycana: Church Reformer between Hus and Luther," *Church History* 28 (1959): 240–242, and Heymann, "The Hussite–Utraquist Church in the fifteenth and sixteenth centuries," *Archiv für Reformationsgeschichte* 52 (1961): 1–2. See also Eberhard, *Konfessionsbildung und Stände in Böhmen,* 15–18.

42. For the Aristotelian middle way in Hooker, see Diarmaid MacCulloch, *The Later Reformation in England, 1547–1603* (New York: St. Martin's Press, 1990), 99.

43. On the relationship between moral perfectionism and political totalitarianism, see, for instance, Karl R. Popper, *The Open Society and Its Enemies*, 2d ed. rev., 2 vols. (London: Routledge & K. Paul, 1952), 1:5: "Why do all these social philosophies support the revolt against civilization? . . . I am inclined to think that the reason is that they give expression to a deep-felt dissatisfaction with a world which does not, and cannot, live up to our moral ideals and to our dreams of perfection" (see also 2:59); Václav Černý, *Paměti*, 3 vols. (Brno: Atlantis, 1992–1994), 1:310; Jeffrey A. Barash, "The Sense of History: On the Political Implications of Karl Löwith's Concept of Secularization," *History and Theory* 37 (1998): 69–82; Karl Löwith, *Meaning in History* (Chicago: University of Chicago Press, 1949), especially 208–213; and Louis Dumont, *German Ideology: from France to Germany and Back* (Chicago: University of Chicago Press, 1994), 26; Zygmunt Bauman, *Modernity and the Holocaust* (Ithaca, N.Y.: Cornell University Press, 1989). Regarding modern philosophies overriding the individual, see Ann Taylor Allen, "The Holocaust and the Modernization of Gender: A Historiographical Essay," *Central European History* 30 (1997), especially 361.

44. Novotný, "Náboženské dějiny české ve století 16.," 1:627, 633, 639.

45. Tomáš G. Masaryk, *Česká otázka*, 6th ed. (Prague: Čin, 1948), 210–212.

46. This position has been articulated even by such a fair judge as Noemi Rejchrtová; see her "Role utrakvismu v českých dějinách," in *Traditio et Cultus: Miscellanea historica bohemica Miloslao Vlk dedicata*, ed. Zdeňka Hledíková (Prague: Univerzita Karlova, 1993), 74.

47. Examples are the Four Articles of Prague (1420) and the Judge of Cheb (1432), which are discussed in Chapter 2.

48. For such a reflexively negative attitude toward Eastern Orthodox influences, often under the code word of *cyrilometodějství* (Cyrillomethodianism), see, for instance, Julius Glücklich in Václav Budovec z Budova, *Korrespondence z let 1579–1619* (Prague: Česká akademie pro vědy, slovesnost a umění, 1908), xx; Kamil Krofta, "Novější bádání o Husovi a hnutí husitském," *Český časopis historický* 21 (1915): 76–77; Vlček, *Dějiny české literatury*, 1:305; Jan Jakubec, *Dějiny literatury české*, 2d ed., 2 vols. (Prague: Laichter, 1929–1934), 1:652; and Ivo Kořán, "Obraz a slovo v našich dějinách," in *Kapitoly z českého dějepisu umění*, by Rudolf Chadraba, et al. (Prague: Odeon, 1986), 1:17–18. See also Jaroslav Mezník, "Josef Pekař a historické mýty," in *Pekařovské studie*, ed. Eva Kantůrková (Prague: Academia, 1995), 78.

49. See Chapter 4.

50. See, for instance, František Kameníček, "Pod obojí (utrakvisté)," in Kameníček, *Zemské sněmy a sjezdy moravské, 1526–1628*, 3 vols. (Brno: Zemský výbor Markrabství moravského, 1900–1905), 3:418–419; Hrejsa, *Česká konfesse*, 58; Novotný, "Náboženské dějiny české ve století 16.," 1:634, 637; Kamil Krofta, "Nový názor na český vývoj náboženský v době předbělohorské," in Krofta, *Listy z náboženských dějin českých* (Prague: Historický klub, 1936), 380–381. Krofta provides a comprehensive overview of these charges in *Nesmrtelný národ: Od Bílé Hory k Palackému* (Prague: Laichter, 1940), 344–429.

51. Krofta, *Nesmrtelný národ*, 385–386.

52. For examples of such questionable behavior on the part of Nuncio Giovanni Bonhomini, see Stloukal, "Počátky nunciatury v Praze," 242, 251–252, 260, 264–265; on

Nuncio Cesare Speciano, see Josef Matoušek, "Kurie a boj o konsistoř pod obojí za administrátora Rezka," *Český časopis historický* 37 (1931): 252, 254, 262, 267, 275, 284–285; and Milena Linhartová, ed., *Epistulae et acta nuntiorum apostolicorum apud imperatorem, 1592–1628,* Tomus 4, *Epistulae et acta Antonii Caetani, 1607–1611* (Prague: Typographia rei publicae, 1932), 1:324.

53. Krofta, *Nesmrtelný národ,* 415–416.

54. Jakubec, *Dějiny literatury české,* 1:713, 721, referring to Tomáš Bavorovský, *Postila česká* (Olomouc: Jan Gunther, 1557), cf. Krofta, *Nesmrtelný národ,* 393; Hynek Hrubý, *České postilly: studie literárně a kulturně historická* (Prague: Česká společnost nauk, 1901), 182–189.

55. Bohuslav Bílejovský, *Kronyka Cýrkevní,* ed. Jozef Skalický (pseudonym for Josef Dittrich) (Prague: Fetterl z Vilden, 1816), 26; František Kavka and Anna Skýbová, *Husitský epilog na koncilu tridentském a původní koncepce habsburské rekatolizace Čech* (Prague: Univerzita Karlova, 1968), 183–184; Novotný, "Náboženské dějiny české ve století 16.," 1:631–632.

56. *Sněmy české od léta 1526 až po naši dobu,* 15 vols. (Prague: Zemský výbor, 1877–1941), 11: pt. 1, 43; Alena Pazderová, "Instrukce pražského nuncia Caetaniho pro jeho nástupce Speciana," in *Facta probant homines: Sborník příspěvků k životnímu jubileu prof. dr. Zdeňky Hledíkové,* ed. Ivan Hlaváček and Jan Hrdina (Prague: Scriptorium, 1998), 358–359. In neighboring Moravia, a colorful priestly conflict in 1575 involved the seizure of the deanery of the Olomouc Chapter by Jan Dambrowski "with the assistance of henchmen with rifles" to prevent his rival, Jan Mezoun, from assuming the deanship. Two years later, the same Mezoun, now bishop of Olomouc, was labeled a perjurer and usurper in an official document by another canon, Pawel Zajączkowski. See Bohumil Navrátil, *Biskupství olomoucké 1576–1579 a volba Stanislava Pavlovského* (Prague: Česká společnost nauk, 1909), 68, 83.

57. Winter, *Život církevní,* 1:245–246, 281, 340–341; on dissolute lives of monks, see 1:811–817.

58. For instance, Ferdinand Menčík, ed., *Zápisky kněze Václava Rosy* (Vienna: J. Paška, 1879), 19–23.

59. Their transgressions included adultery; abuse of wife; neglect of wife, children, household, parish, the poor, the ill, child instruction, preaching, study and learning, admonishing parishioners; drinking, fighting, misbehavior, unseemly appearance, abuse of sacraments; conflict with parishioners, other ministers, civil officials; absenteeism; blasphemy, slander and gossip; and financial malfeasance. See Bruce Gordon, *Clerical Discipline and the Rural Reformation: The Synod in Zurich, 1532–1580* (Bern: Peter Lang, 1992), 209–215.

60. The typical sources for the treatment of the Utraquists have been Klement Borový's *Jednání a dopisy konsistoře katolické a utrakvistické,* 2 vols. (Prague: I. L. Kober, 1868), or Julius Pažout's *Jednání a dopisy konsistoře pod obojí způsobou přijímajících, 1562–1570* (Prague: Historický spolek, 1906), especially v. The lurid cases of clerical transgressions were dredged up with great diligence and colorfully presented with definite *Schadenfreude,* for instance, by Zikmund Winter in *Život církevní v Čechách;* and by Antonín Podlaha in "Úpadek strany podobojí na sklonku XVI. století," *Sborník historického kroužku* 5 (1904): 29–36, 65–69, 161–164, 219–227.

61. The typical sources for the treatment of the Brethren have been Jaroslav Bidlo, ed., *Akty Jednoty bratrské,* 2 vols. (Brno: Matice moravská, 1915–1923); Anton Gindely,

Quellen zur Geschichte der böhmischen Brüder (Vienna: Hof und Staatsdruckerei, 1859); or "Diarium . . . Bratří českých," in *Sněmy české*, 4:392–464. On the Brethren's expressions of vengefulness, see Winter, *Život církevní*, 1:495–496.

62. "[Č]lověk nevážný, lhář, ožralec, kurevník zjevný . . ."; see Krofta, "Boj o konsistoř," 302, n. 2.

63. "Všichni kališní duchovní jsou nectní, nemravní, hrdí, pyšní, lakomí, ukrutní, nelítostiví, hánci bez dobrotivosti, bez sv. poslušenství, nesvorní, neřádní, svatokupečtí, neumělí, nečistí, smilní, cizoložní, rozkošní, hodovní, lehcí, nepobožní, šaškovní, žertýři, zaháleví, toulaví, křčemníci, hráči, žráči, zlolcjci, opilci, frcjíři, kuběnáři, pos měváčci, přemělači, utrhači, zloději, mordéři, vrchnostem a ustanovením jejich, též i obecním nepoddaní, svévolní, nezvedení, nepokojní, bouřlivý, mstiví, závistiví a krátce mnohým hříchům přivyklí, kázně Kristovy v církvi zbavení a netrestatedlní atd." Cited by Kameníček, *Zemské sněmy a sjezdy moravské*, 3:414.

64. Jan Blahoslav, *O původu Jednoty bratrské a řádu v ní*, ed. Otakar Odložilík (Prague: Česká společnost nauk, 1929), cited by Josef Janáček in *Jan Blahoslav* (Prague: Svobodné slovo, 1966), 160–161.

65. Hrejsa, *Česká konfesse*, 6, n. 1; Kamil Krofta, *O bratrském dějepisectví* (Prague: Laichter, 1946): 55–56; Bohuslav Souček, "Rukopis pražské universitní knihovny VII C 3," *Reformační sborník* 1 (1921): 55–56. See also Krofta, *Nesmrtelný národ*, 367.

66. Peter Lake, *Anglicans and Puritans? Presbyterianism and English Conformist thought from Whitgift to Hooker* (London; Boston: Unwin Hyman, 1988), 5.

67. Hooker, *The Folger Library Edition*, 1:18 (*LEP* Preface, 3.11).

68. Cited by Penry Williams in *The Later Tudors: England, 1547–1603* (Oxford: Clarendon Press, 1995), 481.

69. Hooker, *The Folger Library Edition*, 6:14; see also John S. Marshall, *Hooker and the Anglican Tradition: An Historical and Theological Study of Hooker's Ecclesiastical Polity* (Sewanee, Tenn.: University Press, 1963), 32–33.

70. Krofta, *O bratrském dějepisectví*, 54; Souček, "Rukopis pražské universitní knihovny VII C 3," 57. Nevertheless, not even Tomek could give credence to the Lutheran estates of Bohemia, who charged in 1575 that the celibate Utraquist priests routinely rented wives of their parishioners for periodic cohabitation; see Václav V. Tomek, *Dějepis města Prahy*, 12 vols. (Prague: Řivnáč, 1855–1901), 12:243.

71. Kameníček, *Zemské sněmy a sjezdy moravské, 1526–1628*, 3:419.

72. Matoušek, "Kurie a boj o konsistoř," 31, 267; Daniela Neri, ed., *Nuntiaturberichte aus Deutschland*, Dritte Abteilung, 1572–1585, 8, Band: Nuntiatur Giovanni Delfins, 1575–1576 (Tübingen: Max Niemayer, 1997), 74; also Anna Skýbová, "Cesta po Čechách v roce 1561," *Český lid* 63 (1975): 99; Hrejsa, *Česká konfesse*, 58.

73. "[H]omines nigri, ad solem et ventum indurati, aspectu taetri atque horribiles, et qui circa fumum in castris vixissent, aquilinis oculis, impexo crine, promissa barba, corporibus proceris, membris hispidis, cute adeo dura, ut ferrum quasi lorica videtur." Aeneas Sylvius Piccolomini (Pope Pius II), *Historia Bohemica/Historie Česká*, trans. and ed. Dana Martínková, Alena Hadravová, and Jiří Matl (Prague: Koniasch Latin Press, 1998), 163.

74. Such accusations have been fairly common; see, for instance, Desiderius Erasmus, *The Correspondence*, 11 vols. (Toronto: University of Toronto Press, 1974–1994), 11:194.

75. Otakar Josek, *Život a dílo Josefa Kalouska* (Prague: Historický spolek, 1922), 292,

cited by Krofta, *Nesmrtelný národ,* 350–351; Jaroslav Čechura and Jana Čechurová, eds., *Korespondence Josefa Pekaře a Kamila Krofty* (Prague: Karolinum, 1999), 87.

76. The rejection of mainline Utraquism, as something degraded or decadent, actually weakened the case for Masaryk's thesis of a link between the Bohemian Reformation and modern Czech political culture. This dim view of Utraquism led him to limit the influence of the Bohemian Reformation to the Unity and to Taboritism; see Masaryk, *Česká otázka,* 210–211.

77. Jakubec, *Dějiny literatury české,* 1:745. The linkage of Veleslavín to the Unity appears to derive from the questionable evidence presented by Anton Gindely, *Geschichte der böhmischen Brüder,* 2 vols. (Prague: C. Bellmann, 1862), 2:281. More cautiously, *Knihopis,* 1:4, calls Adam "an Utraquist who sympathized with the Bohemian Brethren," and according to Josef Hejnic and Jan Martínek, eds., *Rukověť humanistického básnictví v Čechách a na Moravě,* 5 vols. (Prague: Academia, 1966–1982), 1:38, "he acted [*vystupoval*] as a *přivrženec* [sympathizer] of the Unity of Brethren."

78. Vladmír Forst et al., eds., "Jan Kocín z Kocinétu," *Lexikon české literatury Osobnosti, díla, instituce* (Prague: Academia, 1985), 2: pt. 2, 755; Zdeněk Nejedlý, "Martin Lupáč," in *Ottův slovník naučný* (Prague: Otto, 1888–1909), 16:465. Apparently the main evidence for Lupáč's ties with the Brethren is the copying of some of his works into their *Akta;* see *Lexikon české literatury,* 2: pt. 2, 1252. The affection and reverence with which Pavel Bydžovský surrounds the memory of Lupáč would be hardly consistent with the latter's membership—even a secret one—in the Unity. See also Kamil Krofta, "Byl M. Pavel Stránský český bratr?" *Časopis českého musea* 90 (1916): 35–43; and Bruno Zwicker, "Byl Pavel Stránský český bratr?" *Český časopis historický* 39 (1933): 356–358.

79. Josef Jireček, *Rukověť k dějinám literatury české do konce XVIII. Věku,* 2 vols. (Prague: Tempský, 1875-1876), 1:v.

80. See Chapters 5 and 7.

81. For instance, Václav Koranda, Jr., in 1489 to Valentin Polon in 1589 and Jan Cykáda in 1607; see Krofta, *Nesmrtelný národ,* 381–382; Jan Václav Cykáda, *Hody křest'anské na které Bůh Otec skrze Syna svého zuve* (Prague: Impressí Šumanská, 1607), f. B1(r)–(v); Valentin Polon, *Pomni na mne: Knjžka obahující v sobě kratičká spasidedlná Naučení a sebrání . . .* (Prague: Buryan Valda, 1589), exhortations to priests, f. A6–2a–b, parents and youth, f. K5–3a—L5–1a, and laity in general, f. B2a–b.

82. Vavřinec Leander Rvačovský of Rvačov, *Masopust* (Prague: Jiří Melantrich, 1580), f. D2v.

83. Polon, *Pomni na mne,* f. A8v.

84. *Ibid.,* f. A8r–v.

85. *Ibid.,* f. A7r.

86. See Ernst Troeltsch's dry, but learned, disquisitions comparing the *Sektentypus* with the *Kirchentypus* in "Die Soziallehren der christlichen Kirchen und Gruppen," in Troeltsch, *Gesammelte Schriften,* 4 vols. (Tübingen: Mohr, 1912–1925), such as 1:407, 834–835, 967, 980. On the Brethren's moral rigorism, see, for instance, Jan V. Novák, "Spor Bratří s p. Vojtěchem z Pernštejna a na Prostějove r. 1557 a 1558," *Časopis českého musea* 65 (1891): 52.

87. For instance, Janáček, *České dějiny: Doba předbělohorská,* 2:191.

88. On the Consistory's abject and evasive dealings with Archbishops Brus and Medek, and with papal nuncios, see, for instance, Krofta, "Boj o konsistoř," 386, 391,

401–403; Matoušek, "Kurie a boj o konsistoř," 23, 27–28, 31, 252, 274, 281; Stloukal, "Počátky nunciatury v Praze," 15–6, 256; Winter, *Život církevní v Čechách*, 1:182–183, 330–334.

89. Francis Oakley, *The Western Church in the Later Middle Ages* (Ithaca, N.Y.: Cornell University Press, 1979), especially 300; "Councils, Western, 1311–1449," 3:650. In other settings, lesser pressures might have been effective. Thus, respected and respectable figures, such as Bishop Jewel and Archbishop Whitgift in Elizabethan England, were suspected of occasionally de-emphasizing their Puritan sympathies for the sake of prudence; see "Jewel," *DNB* 10:818; "Whitgift," *DNB* 21:130.

90. For the generalized accusation see, for instance, Zikmund Winter, *Zlatá doba měst českých* (Prague: Odeon, 1991), 167; Blanka Zilynská, "Svěcení kněžstva Biskupem Filibertem v Praze v letech 1437–39," *Documenta Pragensia* 9 (1991): pt. 2, 369; Denis, *Fin de l'indépendance bohême*, 1:286–287. I could find only one specific reference to such an incident, involving three ordinands in 1543, in Borový *Jednání a dopisy konsistoře katolické a utrakvistické*, 1:189. The resulting consternation in Utraquist circles indicated that such a "double apostasy" was not a habitual or normal occurrence. See also Klement Borový, "Die Utraquisten in Böhmen," *Archiv für österreichische Geschichtsforschung* 36 (1866): 264.

91. Pažout, *Jednání a dopisy konsistoře pod obojí*, 136.

92. See, for instance, Bílejovský, *Kronyka Cýrkevní*, 27.

93. Klement Borový, *Antonín Brus z Mohelnice, arcibiskup pražský* (Prague: Dědictví sv. Prokopa, 1873), 176; and Krofta, "Boj o konsistoř," 385. On the alleged sycophancy of the Utraquists see also Josef Pekař, *Žižka a jeho doba*, 4 vols. (Prague: Vesmír, 1927–1933), 3:327.

94. Kameníček, "Pod obojí (utrakvisté)," 407.

95. See, for instance, Otakar Odložilík, "Utrakvistická postilla z r. 1540," *Věstník české společnosti nauk* (1925), 26; Krofta, *Nesmrtelný národ*, 350.

96. Referring to Utraquist clergy as "sacerdoti . . . ignorantissimi," see Daniela Neri, ed., *Nuntiaturberichte aus Deutschland*, Dritte Abteilung, 1572–1585, 8, Band: Nuntiatur Giovanni Delfins, 1575–1576 (Tübingen: Max Niemayer, 1997), 74.

97. Bílejovský, *Kronyka Cýrkevní*, 88–104.

98. Pseudo-Dionysius, *Theologia vivificans. Cibus solidus. Dionysii coelestis hierarchia. Ecclesiastica hierarchia. Divina nomina. Mystica theologia. Undecim epistolae. Ignatii undecim epistolae. Polycarpi epistola una,* ed. Jacques Le Fèvre d'Étaples (In alma Parisiorum academia, Per Henricū Stephanū, 1515); see Pavel Bydžovský, *Děťátka a neviňátka hned po přijetí křtu sv. Tělo a Krev Boží, že přijímati mají* (Prague: Bartoloměj Netolický, 1541), f. B2r.

99. Bydžovský, *Děťátka a neviňátka*, f. B4r.

100. For instance, see Pavel Bydžovský, *Knijžky o přigigmánij Tiela a Krwe Pána nasseho Gežijsse Krysta . . .* (Prague: n.p., 1539), 52–55; Bydžovský, *Tato Knizka toto try ukazuge . . .* (N.p., 1542), 14–16; Bydžovský, *Tento spis ukazuge zie Biskupowee Biskupa a Biskup Kniežij . . .* (N.p., 1543), 12–15; Josef Jireček, *Rukověť k dějinám literatury české*, 1:114–115.

101. *Ottův slovník naučný*, 11:642–643.

102. *Ibid.*, 8:275.

103. Josef Hanzal, "Martin Bacháček z Nauměřic a městské školy ve středních Čechách před Bílou Horou," *Středočeský sborník historický* 10 (1975): 141–142.

104. Antonín Rybička, "Rvačovský Vavřinec Leander," *Časopis českého musea* 45 (1871): 326.

105. Mataus Pačuda, *Spis v němž se obsahuje které věci (z stran lidského pokolení) předešly příchod a narození mesiaše pravého Krista* (Prague: Matěj Pardubický, 1616), f. J3v, J4r, J5r.

106. Jiří Pešek, *Měšťanská vzdělanost a kultura v předbělohorských Čechách, 1547–1620* (Prague: Karolinum, 1993), 26–28.

107. Erasmus, *The Correspondence*, 6 (1982): 174.

108. Jan Vlk and Jaroslav Láník, eds., *Dějiny Prahy*, 2 vols. (Prague: Paseka, 1997), 1:223–224.

109. See, for instance, Henry Kamen, *The Iron Century: Social Change in Europe, 1550–1660* (New York: Praeger, 1971), 284–289. On the loss of international membership, and decline to an undergraduate or "finishing school" level, see Rainer C. Schwinges, *Deutsche Universitätsbesucher im 14. und 15. Jahrhundert: Studien zur Sozialgeschichte des Alten Reiches* (Stuttgart: Franz Steiner, 1986), especially 470–472, 495–496, and the review by John M. Fletcher in *English Historical Review* 104 (1989): 121–122. The situation would persist until the nineteenth century; see Olaf Pedersen, "Tradition and Innovation," in *A History of the University in Europe*, ed. Hilde de Ridder-Symoens (Cambridge and New York: Cambridge University Press, 1996), 2:486–487.

110. Zikmund Winter, *O životě na vysokých školách pražských: kulturní obraz XV. a XVI. století* (Prague: Matice česká, 1899), 564; Winter, *Děje vysokých škol pražských od secessí cizích národů po dobu bitvy bělohorské, 1409–1622* (Prague: Česká akademie pro vědy, slovesnost a umění, 1895), 60–62.

111. Hanzal, "Martin Bacháček z Nauměřic a městské školy," 142.

Chapter 2

1. On the Bohemian reform movement prior to 1415, see David R. Holeton, "The Communion of Infants and Hussitism," *Communio Viatorum* 27 (1984), especially 217–219; Thomas A. Fudge, *The Magnificent Ride: The First Reformation in Hussite Bohemia* (Brookfield, Vt.: Ashgate, 1998), 47–59; and Howard Kaminsky, *A History of the Hussite Revolution* (Berkeley: University of California Press, 1967), 5–96. See also Euan Cameron, *The European Reformation* (Oxford: Clarendon Press; Oxford and New York, Oxford University Press, 1991), 71–73.

2. Jana Zachová, "Waldhauser a Hus," in *Husitství, Reformace, Renesance: Sborník k 60. narozeninám Františka Šmahela*, ed. Jaroslav Pánek, et al. (Prague: Historický ústav, 1994), 1:288–289; Peter C. A. Morée, *Preaching in Fourteenth-Century Bohemia: The Life and Ideas of Milicius de Chremsir (+1374) and His Significance in the Historiography of Bohemia* (Slavkov, Czech Republic: Erman, 1999), 23–24, 63–64, 109–110.

3. See Lewis W. Spitz, *The Protestant Reformation, 1517–1559* (New York: Harper and Row, 1985), 58.

4. Francis Oakley, *The Western Church in the Later Middle Ages* (Ithaca, N.Y.: Cornell University Press, 1979), 38–39.

5. Cited by Bohdan Chudoba, *Jindy a nyní: Dějiny českého národa* (Prague: Vyšehrad, 1946), 109.

6. Otherwise, Matěj of Janov concentrated his critique of the current state of the church in the treatises "De Antichristo," and "De abhominacione in loco sancto," in the third book of his *Regulae Veteris et Novi Testamenti*. See also Matěj z Janova, *De corpore Christi*, vol. 5 of *Matthiae de Janov dicti Magister Parisiensis Regulae Veteris et Novi Testamenti*, ed. V. Kybal and O. Odložilík (Prague: Sumptibus Collegii ad Edenda Monumenta Reformationis Religionis in Bohemia Saec. XIV. et XV., 1926), v–vi. See also Peter Demetz, *Prague in Black and Gold: Scenes from the Life of a European City* (New York: Hill and Wang, 1997), 126.

7. Oakley, *The Western Church in the Later Middle Ages*, 195–196.

8. See, for instance, Howard Kaminsky, "The University of Prague in the Hussite Revolution: The Role of the Masters," in *Universities in Politics: Case Studies from the Late Middle Ages and Early Modern Period*, ed. John W. Baldwin and Richard A. Goldthwaite (Baltimore: Johns Hopkins Press, 1972), 79–80, 104–105; Michal Svatoš, ed., *1347/48–1622*, vol. 1 of *Dějiny Univerzity Karlovy* (Prague: Karolinum, 1995), 138–142; Jiří Kejř, *Kvodlibetní disputace na pražské universitě* (Prague: Univerzita Karlova, 1971).

9. The free and permissive range of these debates is illustrated from an earlier period by the proposition in a quodlibet of 1170 by the respected Paris theologian, Peter Comester, that "the devil had never done so much harm to the Church as by the prohibition of clerical marriages." Cited by Richard W. Southern, *Scholastic Humanism and the Unification of Europe* (Oxford: Blackwell, 1995), 1:145. See also István Bejczy, "Tolerantia: A Medieval Concept," *Journal of the History of Ideas* 58 (1997): 367.

10. Fudge, *The Magnificent Ride*, 51; Božena Kopičková, *Jan Želivský* (Prague: Melantrich, 1990), 18–19. Concerning defense of scholastic intellectuals by Vojtěch Raňkův against persecution, see Josef Triska, ed., *Starší pražská univerzitní literatura a karlovská tradice* (Prague: Univerzita Karlova, 1978), 40.

11. František Palacký, *Obrana husitství*, trans. and ed. František M. Bartoš (Prague: Blahoslav, 1926), 38.

12. Martin Wernisch, "Jan z Pomuka i Nepomuka, shrnutý a neuzavřený," *Folia Historica Bohemica* 17 (1994): 218.

13. Miloslav Kaňák, *John Viklef: Život a dílo anglického Husova předchůdce* (Prague: Blahoslav, 1973), 46–47.

14. Ian P. Wei, "The Self-Image of the Masters of Theology at the University of Paris in the late Thirteenth and Early Fourteenth Centuries," *Journal of Ecclesiastical History* 46 (1995), especially 430–31; Gordon Leff, "Wyclif and Hus," in *Wyclif in His Times*, ed. Anthony Kenny (Oxford: Clarendon Press, 1986), 111.

15. David R. Holeton, "Sacramental and Liturgical Reform in Late Medieval Bohemia," *Studia Liturgica* 18 (1987): 89.

16. David R. Holeton, "The Bohemian Eucharistic Movement in Its European Context," in *The Bohemian Reformation and Religious Practice*, vol. 1: Papers from the XVIIth World Congress of the Czechoslovak Society of Arts and Sciences, Prague 1994, ed. David R. Holeton (Prague: Academy of Sciences of the Czech Republic, Main Library, 1996), 29. See also Morée, *Preaching in Fourteenth-Century Bohemia*, 29–33, 52; Miloslav Kaňák, *Milíč z Kroměříže* (Prague: Blahoslav, 1975).

17. Holeton, "The Bohemian Eucharistic Movement," 30–31. On frequent communion, see also Matěj z Janova, *De corpore Christi*, 75–128; Ondřej Petrů, *Učení M. Matěje z Janova o častém sv. přijímání* (Olomouc: Krystal, 1946).

18. Matěj z Janova, *De corpore Christi*, vi–vii, xxiii.

19. Holeton, "The Bohemian Eucharistic Movement," 32; see also Tomáš Štítný, *Tomáše ze Štítného Knížky šestery o obecných věcech křestanských* (Prague: K. Jeřábková, 1852), 218–226.
20. Holeton, "The Bohemian Eucharistic Movement," 34.
21. On Hus, see David S. Schaff, *John Huss: His Life Teachings, and Death* (New York: Scribner's, 1915); Václav Novotný, *Jan Hus: Život a učení,* I. *Život a dílo,* 2 vols. (Prague: Laichter, 1919–1921); Matthew Spinka, *John Hus: A Biography* (Princeton, N.J.: Princeton University Press, 1968); Ernst Werner, *Jan Hus: Welt und Umwelt eines Prager Frühreformators,* Forschungen zur mittelalterlichen Geschichte, vol. 34 (Weimar: Böhlau, 1991); Peter Hilsch, *Johannes Hus (um 1370–1415): Prediger Gottes und Ketzer* (Regensburg: Pustet, 1999).
22. These clashes resulted from King Wenceslaus IV's Decree of Kutná Hora, which awarded a preponderance of power at the university to native Bohemians.
23. Hus de trinitate, Opp. I, 131, cited by Palacký in *Obrana husitství,* 36.
24. Jaroslav Čechura, *České země v letech 1378–1437,* vol. 2 of *Lucemburkové na českém trůně* (Prague: Libri, 2000), 124.
25. Paul de Vooght, *L'hérésie de Jean Huss,* 2d ed., 2 vols. (Louvain: Publications universitaires, 1975), 2:831–832.
26. Vilém Herold, "Wyclif's Ecclesiology and Its Prague Context," in *The Bohemian Reformation and Religious Practice,* vol. 4: Papers from the IV International Symposium on Bohemian Reformation and Religious Practice, under the auspices of the Philosophical Institute of the Academy of Sciences of the Czech Republic, held at Vila Lanna, Prague 26–28 June 2000, ed. Zdeněk V. David and David R. Holeton (Prague: Academy of Sciences of the Czech Republic, Main Library, 2002), 15–30.
27. Takashi Shogimen, "From Disobedience to Toleration: William of Ockham and the Medieval Discourse on Fraternal Correction," *Journal of Ecclesiastical History* 52 (2001): 601.
28. See, for instance, Brian Tierney, *The Idea of Natural Rights: Studies on Natural Rights, Natural Law and Church Law, 1150–1625* (Atlanta, Ga.: Scholars Press, 1997), 32, 214.
29. For instance, Josef Kalousek, *O potřebě prohloubit vědomosti o Husovi a jeho době* (Prague: Českoslovanská akciová tiskárna, 1915), 20–21.
30. Jeremy Catto, "Currents of religious thought and expression," in *The New Cambridge Medieval History* (New York: Cambridge University Press, 2000), 6:57–58.
31. De Vooght, *L'hérésie de Jean Huss,* 1:502, 507–508.
32. Tierney, *The Idea of Natural Rights,* 32, 221.
33. Desiderius Erasmus, *The Correspondence,* 11 vols. (Toronto: University of Toronto Press, 1974–1992), 3:160 (Letter from Maarten van Dorp, August 27, 1515).
34. For instance, Josef Čihula, "Martin Luther a Čechové pod obojí," *Český časopis historický* 3 (1897): 348–349.
35. Jiří Kejř, *Husův proces* (Prague: Vyšehrad, 2000), or Jürgen Miethke, "Die Prozesse in Konstanz gegen Jan Hus und Hieronymus von Prag—ein Konflikt unter Kirchenreformern?" in *Häresie und vorzeitige Reformation im Spätmittelalter,* Schriften des Historischen Kollegs, Kolloquien 39, ed. František Šmahel (Munich: Oldenbourg, 1998), 147–167, show more about the perversity of Rome's legal system than about the justice of Hus's sentence.
36. One may wonder with Matthew Spinka about what made them feel that they were authorized to deal with the devil, or that Satan would welcome such a transaction;

Matthew Spinka, *John Hus: A Biography* (Princeton, N.J.: Princeton University Press, 1968), 288. Seen in this light, Martin Luther's designation of the Council fathers for their role in Hus's demise as "Apostles of the Devil," might not have been an empty invective; Čihula, "Martin Luther a Čechové pod obojí," 348–349.

37. This is also the view of de Vooght, *L'hérésie de Jean Huss,* 1:506–508. For an alternate view of the trial, which seeks to present Hus's judges in a more favorable light, see Petr Čornej, vol. 5 of *Velké dějiny koruny české* (Prague: Paseka, 2000), 165–169.

38. David R. Holeton, "Liturgická a svátostná teologie Mistra Jana Husa," *Theologická revue* 1 (1996), 9-12; Enrico C. S. Molnar, "The Liturgical Reforms of Jan Hus," *Speculum* 41 (1966): 300–302; Ernst Werner, "Das Altarsakrament im Religionsverständnis von Jan Hus," in *Husitství, Reformace, Renesance: Sborník k 60. narozeninám Františka Šmahela,* ed. Jaroslav Pánek, et al., 3 vols. (Prague: Historický ústav, 1994), 1:317–329.

39. Holeton, "Liturgická a svátostná teologie Mistra Jana Husa," 11.

40. Gabriel Audisio, *The Waldensian Dissent: Persecution and Survival, c. 1170–c. 1570,* trans. Claire Davison (Cambridge and New York: Cambridge University Press, 1999), 78–81; Alexander Patschovsky, *Die Anfänge einer ständigen Inquisition in Böhmen: Ein Prager Inquisitoren-Handbuch aus der ersten Hälfte des 14. Jahrhunderts,* Beiträge zur Geschichte und Quellenkunde des Mittelalters, 3 (Berlin: Walter de Gruyter, 1975). See also Patschovsky, "Über die politische Bedeutung von Häresienverfolgung im mittelalterlichen Böhmen," in *Die Anfänge der Inquisition im Mittelalter: Mit einem Ausblick auf das 20. Jahrhundert und einem Beitrag über religiöse Intoleranz im nichtchristlichen Bereich,* Bayreuther Historische Kolloquien, 7, ed. Peter Segl (Cologne: Böhlau, 1993), 235–251; Rudolf Holinka, "Sektářství v Čechách před revolucí husitskou," *Sborník filosofické fakulty university Komenského v Bratislavě,* 6, no. 52 (1929): 260–267. On the problems of the Waldensians, see also Thomas A. Fudge, *The Magnificent Ride: The First Reformation in Hussite Bohemia* (Brookfield, Vt.: Ashgate, 1998), 37–41; and S. Harrison Thomson, "Pre–Hussite Heresy in Bohemia," *English Historical Review* 48 (January 1933): 23–42.

41. Božena Kopičková, *Jan Želivský* (Prague: Melantrich, 1990), 21–22; Amedeo Molnár, *Valdenští: evropský rozměr jejich vzdoru* (Prague: Kalich, 1991), 206–209.

42. Howard Kaminsky, "Chiliasm and the Hussite Revolution," *Church History* 26 (1957): 60. František Palacký defended (in 1868) the domestic origin of the Picardi, but subsequently (in 1871) reaffirmed their non-Bohemian provenance, as did subsequent historiography; see František Palacký, *Dílo,* 4 vols. (Prague: Mazáč, 1941), 3:131.

43. Kopičková, *Jan Želivský,* 182–183. On contacts with sectarians from Flanders and Picardy, see Augustin Neumann, "Francouzská hussitica," *Studie a texty k náboženským dějinám českým,* vol 3, nos. 2–4 (1923), especially 5; and Augustin Neumann, *České sekty ve století XIV. a XV* (Velehrad: Cyrilomotodějský tiskový spolek, 1920), 1–63.

44. See, for instance, František Bartoš, "Pikardi a Pikarti," *Časopis českého musea* 101 (1927): 225–250. On the presence of outside sectarians in Bohemia, see Rudolf Holinka, "Sektářství v Čechách před revolucí husitskou," *Sborník filosofické fakulty university Komenského v Bratislavě,* 6, no. 52 (1929): 125–312.

45. Murray L. Wagner, *Petr Chelčický: A Radical Separatist in Hussite Bohemia* (Scottsdale, Pa.: Herald Press, 1983), 46–55.

46. Bohuslav Bílejovský, *Kronyka Cýrkevní,* ed. Jozef Skalický (pseudonym for Josef Dittrich) (Prague: Fetterl z Vilden, 1816), 50, 105, 109; Pavel Bydžovský, *Tato Knížka toto try ukazuje* (N.p., [after 1541]), 2. Interestingly, as an outside observer, the French

bishop Jacques B. Bossuet also rejected a connection between the early Bohemian Reformation, and specifically Hus, and the Bohemian Brethren; Jacques B. Bossuet, *Histoire des variations des églises protestantes,* 2 vols. (Paris: Garnier frères, 1821), 2:273, 340. See also Jiří Bílý, "Vývoj názoru na Husa a husitství ve francouzské literatuře," in *Jan Hus mezi epochami, národy a konfesemi,* ed. Jan B. Lášek (Prague: Česká křest'anská akademie, 1995), 255.

47. On Jerome, see Reginald R. Betts, *Essays in Czech History* (London: Athlone, 1969), 195–235; Paul P. Bernard, "Jerome of Prague, Austria and the Hussites," *Church History* 27 (1958): 3–22; Renee N. Watkins, "The Death of Jerome of Prague: Divergent Views," *Speculum,* 42 (1967): 104–129.

48. Claims for the earlier introduction of the lay chalice are assessed by Helena Krmíčková in "The Fifteenth-Century Origins of Lay Communion *sub utraque* in Bohemia," in *The Bohemian Reformation and Religious Practice,* vol. 2: Papers from the XVIIIth World Congress of the Czechoslovak Society of Arts and Sciences, Brno 1996, ed. Zdeněk V. David and David R. Holeton (Prague: Academy of Sciences of the Czech Republic, Main Library, 1998, 57–65). See also Fudge, *The Magnificent Ride,* 54–55. Paradoxically, however, the adoption of the lay chalice may have been retarded by Milíč's stress on "concommitance in which both the body and blood are said to be received under each of the Eucharistic species"; Holeton, "The Bohemian Eucharistic Movement," 29, n. 34.

49. David R. Holeton, *La communion des tout-petits enfants: Étude du mouvement eucharistique en Bohême vers la fin du Moyen-Âge* (Rome: Edizioni Liturgiche, 1989); Bartoš, František, "Martin Lupáč a jeho spisovatelské dílo," *Reformační sborník* 7 (1939): 128–130. Regarding origins, see Helena Krmíčková, "Několik poznámek o přijímání maličkých, 1414–1416," *Sborník prací Filozofické fakulty Brněnské univerzity* C44 (1997): 59–69. At the end of the fifteenth century (1491), Konrad Celtis noted the Utraquist practice of infant communion; see Josef Truhlář, "Kterak se zachovali nejstarší humanisté k národu českému," *Časopis českého musea* 54 (1880): 480.

50. Raoul Naz, ed., *Dictionnaire de droit canonique* (Paris: Letouzey et Ané, 1935–1965), Fasc. 17, 1118–1123.

51. "The practice of communicating all the baptized was a logical step in the renewal of eucharistic practice.... [It] is congruent with [the Bohemians'] conviction that no distinction can be made between membership in the mystical body and access to the eucharistic body. In a church in which the Eucharist was seen as without peer in effecting the social dimension of the Kingdom, it would have been an unbearable irony should those whom Jesus offers as the ideal citizens of that Kingdom be unable to share in the eucharistic banquet which is its foretaste." David R. Holeton, "Sacramental and Liturgical Reform in Late Medieval Bohemia," *Studia Liturgica* 18 (1987): 92.

52. Jiří Kejř, *Mistři pražské univerzity a kněží táborští* (Prague: Univerzita Karlova, 1981), especially, 7-18, 57-63.

53. Fudge, *The Magnificent Ride,* 51. See also František Šmahel, "Husitské artikuly a jihlavská kompaktáta," in *Jihlava a Basilejská Kompaktáta: Sborník příspěvků z mezinárodního sympozia k 555. výročí přijetí Basilejských kompaktát, 26–28. červen 1991,* by František Šmahel, et al. (Jihlava: Muzeum Vysočiny, 1992), 11–28.

54. Kopičková, *Jan Želivský,* 30.

55. Eduard Maur, "Pavel z Olešné a jeho družina," in *Husitství, Reformace, Renesance: Sborník k 60. narozeninám Františka Šmahela,* ed. Jaroslav Pánek, et al., 3 vols. (Prague: Historický ústav, 1994), 2:449–463.

56. Kopičková, *Jan Želivský,* 101, 104–105, 107, 109, 128; Audisio, *The Waldensian Dissent,* 81–83; Fudge, *The Magnificent Ride,* 165.

57. Kopičková, *Jan Želivský,* 104, 130. See also Neumann, *České sekty ve století XIV. a XV,* 64–66.

58. Kaminsky, *A History of the Hussite Revolution,* 257.

59. Romolo Cegna, "Eglise vaudoise et Eglise taborite: La proposition d'un nouveau sacramentalisme dans le respect de l'ancienne foi," *Husitství, Reformace, Renesance: Sborník k 60. narozeninám Františka Šmahela,* ed. Jaroslav Pánek, et al., 3 vols. (Prague: Historický ústav, 1994), 2:617–618. In most recent scholarship, the influence of Taboritism on the Waldensians, however, has tended to be de-emphasized. See Kathrin Utz Tremp, *Waldenser: Wiedergänger, Hexen und Rebellen: Biographien zu den Waldenserprozessen von Freiburg im Üchtland, 1399 und 1430* (Freiburg, Switzerland: Universitätsverlag, 1999). See also the review by František Šmahel in *Český časopis historický* 98 (2000): 636; and Audisio, *The Waldensian Dissent,* 84.

60. Amedeo Molnár, "Želivský, prédicateur de la révolution," *Communio Viatorum* 2 (1959): 327; Kopičková, *Jan Želivský,* 182–183. Želivský was more moderate, especially less bloodthirsty, than the Taborites as revealed in their Twelve Articles. Moreover, he would be silenced by a secret execution in 1422. See Kopičková, *Jan Želivský,* 124.

61. Blanka Zilynská, *Husitské synody v Čechách, 1418-1440* (Prague: Univerzita Karlova, 1985), 39. This matter would also be the focus of debate between the Anglicans and the Puritans.

62. Kaminsky, "Chiliasm and the Hussite Revolution," 60–63.

63. Aeneas Sylvius Piccolomini (Pope Pius II), *Historia Bohemica/Historie česká,* trans. and ed. Dana Martínková, Alena Hadravová, and Jiří Matl (Prague: Koniasch Latin Press, 1998), 16, 116–118; see also Howard Kaminsky, "Pius Aeneas Among the Taborites," *Church History* 28 (1959): 281–309.

64. Thomas More, *Complete Works,* 21 vols. (New Haven: Yale University Press, 1963–1997), 5: pt. 1, 220–221; pt. 2, 909.

65. Zdeněk Nejedlý, *Dějiny husitského zpěvu,* 5 vols. (Prague: Nakladatelství Československé akademie věd, 1955), 5:19–95.

66. Pravoslav Kneidl, "Městský stav v Čechách v době předbělohorské" (Ph.D. diss., Univerzita Karlova, Prague, 1951), 10.

67. Robert Novotný, "Staročeský výraz hejtman: Sémantická analýza," *Marginalia historica* 4 (2001): 92–93.

68. Cited by Rudolf Říčan, ed., *Čtyři vyznání* (Prague: Komenského evangelická bohoslovecká fakulta, 1951), 39, n. 1.

69. On the Bohemian reform movement before 1415, see David R. Holeton, "The communion of infants and Hussitism," *Communio Viatorum* 27 (1984), especially 217–219; and Howard Kaminsky, *A History of the Hussite Revolution,* 5–96; Cameron, *The European Reformation,* 71–73. On the early Utraquist synods, see Zilynská, *Husitské synody v Čechách, 1418–1440.*

70. Matěj z Janova, *De corpore Christi,* viii, xxiv.

71. He would be unable to assume the throne of Bohemia until after the adoption of the Compactata in 1436.

72. Kaminsky, *History of the Hussite Revolution,* 362–375; Frederick G. Heymann, *John Žižka and the Hussite Revolution* (Princeton, N.J.: Princeton University Press, 1955); Palacký, *Obrana husitství,* 44–46. For basic documents in English trans. see

Thomas A. Fudge, *The Crusade Against Heretics in Bohemia, 1418-1437: Sources and Documents for the Hussite Crusades* (Burlington, Vt.: Ashgate, 2002).

73. František Šmahel, *Husitská revoluce,* 4 vols. (Prague: Karolinum, 1995–1996), 1:104–106. In another case of learning from history, much later Luther avoided Hus's fate by assiduously eschewing the jurisdiction of the Inquisition and other courts of the Roman Church.

74. Palacký, *Obrana husitství,* 47; Fudge, *The Magnificent Ride,* 96.

75. For an account of the Taborites' religious terrorism see, for instance, Josef Hamršmíd, "Několik slov o českém kněžstvu stol. XIV. A XV.," *Sborník historického kroužku,* Sešit 3 (1894), 40–55. Various extremist ideologies are reviewed in Kaminsky, "Chiliasm in the Hussite Revolution," 43–71.

76. Kopičková, *Jan Želivský,* 137, 185.

77. Richard Marius, *Martin Luther: The Christian Between God and Death* (Cambridge, Mass.: Harvard University Press, 1999), 176. See also Augustin Neumann, *Ožehavé kapitoly z českých dějin církevních* (Prague: Vyšehrad, 1937), 40–50.

78. The limited availability or nonexistence of facilities for humane containment of their opponents (internment or prisoner-of-war camps) helps to qualify the image of an unrestrained savagery of the repressions. Garrett Mattingly, *Armada* (Boston: Houghton Mifflin, 1959), 368–369, tells a similar chilling story of the English killing Spanish sailors shipwrecked in Ireland due to lack of detention facilities, thereby preventing the Spanish fleet from attacking England from her own backyard.

79. Rudolf Urbánek, "Český mesianismus ve své době hrdinské," in *Od pravěku k dnešku: Sborník k 60. narozeninám J. Pekaře* (Prague: Historický klub, 1930), 1:262–284.

80. Palacký, *Obrana husitství,* 41.

81. Vilém Herold defines this source more precisely as: "(1) the Platonic realism springing in many respects from St. Augustine's *Quaestio de ideis,* and (2) also the heterodox Pseudo-Dionysian Neoplatonism which Jeroným [of Prague] learned to know in Paris." Vilém Herold, "The University of Paris and the Foundations of the Bohemian Reformation," in *The Bohemian Reformation and Religious Practice,* vol. 3: Papers from the XIXth World Congress of the Czechoslovak Society of Arts and Sciences, Bratislava 1998, ed. Zdeněk V. David and David R. Holeton (Prague: Academy of Sciences of the Czech Republic, Main Library, 2000), 23.

82. Herold, "The University of Paris and the Foundations of the Bohemian Reformation," 23.

83. Šmahel, "Husitské artikuly a jihlavská kompaktáta," 11–27.

84. Amedeo Molnár, et al., *Soudce smluvený v Chebu* (Sborník příspěvků přednesených na symposiu k 550. výročí) (Cheb: n.p., 1982).

85. Šmahel, *Husitská revoluce,* 4:100–101. For Sigismund's decree, see *Archiv český* 3 (1844): 427–431. See also Winfried Eberhard, *Konfessionsbildung und Stände in Böhmen, 1478–1530* (Munich: Oldenbourg, 1981), 44–45.

86. Václav V. Tomek, *Dějepis města Prahy,* 12 vols. (Prague: Řivnáč, 1855–1901), 3:622.

87. Diarmaid MacCulloch, *Thomas Cranmer: A Life* (New Haven, Conn.: Yale University Press, 1996), 116.

88. Šmahel, *Husitská revoluce,* 4:100–101.

89. On the three bishops, see David R. Holeton, "Church or Sect: The *Jednota bratrská* and the Growth of Dissent from Mainline Utraquism," *Communio Viatorum* 38 (1996): 26. On Philibbert, see also Blanka Zilynská, "Svěcení kněžstva Biskupem

Filibertem v Praze v letech 1437–39," *Documenta Pragensia* 9 (1991): pt. 2, 361–388.

One of the Utraquist candidates for priesthood, Bohuslav Krejčí, who had to travel to Italy for ordinations, may have persuaded Bishop Philip to move to Bohemia in 1504; see Václav Hájek z Libočan, *Kronyka czeská* (Prague: Jan Ferdinand z Šenfeldu, 1819), f. 461r.

90. Václav Pavlík, "M. Jan z Rokycan, volený arcibiskup Pražský, 1397–1471," *Časopis katolického duchovenstva*, 54 (1913): 53–62, 122–131, 183–192, 279–288, 389–397, 452–459, 546–561, 659–668.

91. Kamil Krofta, "O některých spisech M. Jana z Příbramě," *Časopis českého musea* 73 (1899): 217–218.

92. On the repudiation of the Taborites, see František Bartoš, *The Hussite Revolution, 1424–1437*, ed. John M. Klassen (Boulder, Colo.: East European Monographs; distributed by New York: Columbia University Press, 1986), 112–118; and (for documentation) Zdeněk Nejedlý, *Prameny k synodám strany pražské a táborské (vznik husitské konfesse) v létech 1441–1444* (Prague: Královská česká společnost nauk, 1900), especially 56–95. Concerning theories about the Taborites' reincarnation seventy or eighty years later as Lutherans or "Neo-Utraquists," see Zdeněk V. David, "The Strange Fate of Czech Utraquism: The Second Century, 1517–1621," *Journal of Ecclesiastical History*, 46 (1995): 652–653.

93. Šmahel, *Husitská revoluce*, 4:104–105. See also Jan Chlíbec, "K vývoji názorů Jana Rokycany na umělecké dílo," *Husitský Tábor* 8 (1985): 39–58; Milena Bartlová, "The Utraquist Church and the Visual Arts Before Luther," in *The Bohemian Reformation and Religious Practice*, vol. 4: Papers from the IV International Symposium on Bohemian Reformation and Religious Practice, under the auspices of the Philosophical Institute of the Academy of Sciences of the Czech Republic, held at Vila Lanna, Prague 26–28 June 2000, ed. Zdeněk V. David and David R. Holeton (Prague: Academy of Sciences of the Czech Republic, Main Library, 2002), 215–223; Milena Bartlová, "Chrám Matky Boží před Týnem v 15. století," *Marginalia historica* 4 (2001), especially 120–130.

94. Jana Zachová and Jaroslav Boubín, "Drobné spisy Jana Příbrama na obranu katolické víry," in *Facta probant homines: Sborník příspěvků k životnímu jubileu prof. dr. Zdeňky Hledíkové*, ed. Ivan Hlaváček, et al. (Prague: Scriptorium, 1998), 529.

95. See, for instance, Chlíbec, "K vývoji názorů Jana Rokycany na umělecké dílo," 42, and also 40, 54.

96. Otakar Odložilík, "Utrakvistická postilla z r. 1540," *Věstník české společnosti nauk*, Třída filosoficko-historicko-jazykozpytná (1925), 18.

97. Chlíbec, "K vývoji názorů Jana Rokycany na umělecké dílo," 53. Elected in 1435 but never consecrated, Jan Rokycana was the second (and last) Utraquist archbishop of Prague.

98. Artur I. Ozolin, *Biurgerskaia oppozitsiia v gusitskom dvizhenii: Sotsial'no-politicheskie trebovaniia* (Saratov: Izdatel'stvo Saratovskogo universiteta, 1973), 21.

99. For a recent treatment of the monastics' role in combating heresy under papal patronage, see Agostino Paravicini Bagliani, *Il trono di Pietro: L'unersaltà del papato del Alessandro III a Bonifacio VIII* (Rome: Nuova Italia Scientifica, 1996), chapter 6.

100. *Ze starých letopisů českých*, trans. Jaroslav Porák and Jaroslav Kašpar (Prague: Svoboda, 1980), 156, 482; Tomek, *Dějepis města Prahy*, 9:351; Josef Jireček, *Rukověť k dějinám literatury české do konce XVIII. věku*, 2 vols. (Prague: Tempský, 1875), 1:144. See also Zikmund Winter, *Život církevní v Čechách* (Prague: Česká akademie pro vědy, slovesnost a umění, 1896), index references to "Slovanský klášter."

101. Zikmund Winter, *Život církevní v Čechách*, 2:692. Concerning Wyclif's antimonasticism, see, for instance, Kaňák, *John Viklef,* 35–36.
102. Klement Borový, *Jednání a dopisy konsistoře katolické a utrakvistické,* 2 vols. (Prague: I. L. Kober, 1868), 1:330, on September 25, 1555.
103. Veronika Macháčková and Antonín Mařík, "Praha v činnosti administrátorů pod jednou v letech 1450-1550," *Documenta Pragensia* 9 (1991): pt. 2, 409.
104. Concerning Jewish influences on the Waldensians and the Bohemian reformers, see Louis I. Newman, *Jewish Influence on Christian Reform Movements* (New York: Columbia University Press, 1925), 208–239, 435–453.
105. See Zdeněk V. David, "Jews in Sixteenth-Century Czech Historiography: The 'Czech Chronicle' of Václav Hájek of Libočany," *East European Jewish Affairs* 25 (1995): 25–26.
106. Amedeo Molnár, "Die Rassenfrage im Lichte der böhmischen Reformation," *Communio Viatorum* 17 (1974): 267.
107. Tomáš Pekný, *Historie Židů v Čechách a na Moravě* (Prague: Sefer, 1993), 308–329; Ruth Kestenberg-Gladstein, "Bohemia," in *Dark Ages: Jews in Christian Europe, 711–1096,* ed. Cecil Roth, revision ed. I. H. Levine (New Brunswick, N.J.: Rutgers University Press, 1966), 309–312; and literature cited in Kestenberg-Gladstein, *Neuere Geschichte der Juden in den böhmischen Ländern* (Schriftenreihe wissenschaftlichen Abhandlungen des Leo Baeck Instituts, 18) (Tübingen: Mohr, 1969), 1:vii, n. 1.
108. Salo W. Baron, *A Social and Religious History of the Jews,* 2d ed. (New York: Columbia University Press, 1969), 13:209–212; Ruth Kestenberg-Gladstein, "Hussitentum und Judentum," *Jahrbuch der Gesellschaft für Geschichte der Juden in der Čechoslovakischen Republik* 8 (1936): 1–25; Paul de Vooght, "'Universitas praedestinatorum' et 'Congregatio fidelium' dans l'ecclesiologie de Jean Huss," *Ephemerides theologicae lovanienses* 32 (1956): 487–534.
109. Ruth Kestenberg-Gladstein, "Eschatological Trends in Bohemian Jewry during the Hussite Period," in *Prophecy and Millenarianism in Honor of Marjorie Reeves,* ed. Ann Williams (Harlow, Essex, U.K.: Longman House, 1980), 241–242.
110. *Ibid.,* 243–245, 247, 249–251.
111. *Ze starých letopisů českých,* 64; see also Kestenberg-Gladstein, "Hussitentum und Judentum," 18–19; Zikmund Winter, *Kulturní obraz českých měst: Život veřejný v XV. a XVI. věku* (Prague: Matice česká, 1890), 1:211.
112. Kestenberg-Gladstein, "Eschatological Trends in Bohemian Jewry," 246.
113. Jan Heřman and Vladimír Sadek, "Hebrejský pramen o husitech," *Dějiny a současnost* 9 (1963): 5–8. There were, however, instances when Jews became incidental victims during the Hussites' struggles against their opponents, such as in Chomutov (1421) and in Prague (1422); see František M. Bartoš, *Husitská revoluce: Doba Žižkova, 1415–1424* (Prague: Nakladatelství Československé akademie věd, 1965), 120. See also the relevant literature cited by Friedrich Bezold, *K dějinám husitství* (Prague: Josef Pelcl, 1904), 36, n. 104.
114. Kestenberg-Gladstein, "Eschatological Trends in Bohemian Jewry," 245; see also Newman, *Jewish Influence on Christian Reform Movements,* 435–453.
115. Bedřich Mendl, "Z hospodářských dějin středověké Prahy," *Sborník příspěvků k dějinám hl. města Prahy* 5 (1932): 185.
116. Ondřej z Brodu, *Traktát o původu husitů,* ed. Jaroslav Kadlec (Tábor: Muzeum husitského revolučního hnutí, 1980), 7.

117. Matthew Spinka, *John Hus at the Council of Constance* (New York: Columbia University Press, 1965), 230. According to Simon M. Dubnov, *History of the Jews*, rev., 4th ed., 5 vols. (South Brunswick, N.J.: Thomas Yoseloff, 1969), 3:269: "Emperor Sigismund had demanded from the Jewish communities money to cover the expenses of the council of Constance, which had condemned Hus to be burned alive . . ."

118. Jan Hus, *Výklady*, Magistri Iohannis Hus Opera Omnia, 1 (Prague: Academia, 1975), 188–189, referring to Nehemiah, 13:23–25.

119. Kestenberg-Gladstein, "Eschatological Trends in Bohemian Jewry," 242; see also František Graus, *Struktur und Geschichte: Drei Volksaufstände in mittelalterlichen Prag* (Sigmaringen: Jan Thorbecke, 1971), 50–60.

120. Šmahel, *Husitská revoluce*, 1:153; Beda Dudík, *Mährens allgemeine Geschichte* (Brno: Verlag des mährischen Domestikalfondes, 1878), 8:208, 245.

121. Gordon Leff, "Wyclif and Hus: a doctrinal comparison," in *Wyclif in His Times*, ed. Anthony Kenny (Oxford: Clarendon Press, 1986), 105–125; Kaňák, *John Viklef*, 77–84; Betts, *Essays in Czech History* 29–62, 132–159; Paul de Vooght, "Huss et Wiclif," in de Vooght, *Hussiana* (Louvain: Publications Universitaires, 1960), 1–6; Katherine Walsh, "Wyclif's Legacy in Central Europe in the Late Fourteenth and Early Fifteenth Century," *Studies in Church History Subsidia* 5 (1987): 397–417; and David R. Holeton, "Wyclif's Bohemian Fate: A Reflection on the Contextualization of Wyclif in Bohemia," *Communio Viatorum* 32 (1989): 209–222, with a masterly contrasting portrayal of Wyclif and Hus, 217–219.

122. "The Accursed Memory," in *Wyclif in His Times*, ed. Anthony Kenny (Oxford: Clarendon Press, 1986), 160.

123. Steven Justice, *Writing and Rebellion: England in 1381* (Berkeley: University of California Press, 1994), chapter 2.

124. Herold, "The University of Paris and the Foundations of the Bohemian Reformation," 15–24.

125. Oakley, *The Western Church in the Later Middle Ages*, 195; František Šmahel, "'Doctor evangelicus super omnes evangelistas': Wyclif's Fortune in Hussite Bohemia," *Bulletin of the Institute of Historical Research* 43 (1970): 16–17.

126. Oakley, *The Western Church in the Later Middle Ages*, 196. More generally on Wyclif's influence, see Fudge, *The Magnificent Ride*, 43–47.

127. Oakley, *The Western Church in the Later Middle Ages*, 196–197.

128. Vilém Herold, "How Wyclifite Was the Bohemian Reformation?" in *The Bohemian Reformation and Religious Practice*, vol. 2: Papers from the XVIIIth World Congress of the Czechoslovak Society of Arts and Sciences, Brno 1996, ed. Zdeněk V. David and David R. Holeton (Prague: Academy of Sciences of the Czech Republic, Main Library, 1998), 25–37; Jaroslav Prokeš, "Kvodlibet Šimona z Tišnova r. 1416," *Časopis Matice moravské* 45 (1921): 46.

129. Oakley, *The Western Church in the Later Middle Ages*, 198. On Hus's expressing his own ideas in Wyclifite terminology, see also S. Harrison Thomson, ed., in Jan Hus, *Magistri Joannis Hus: Tractatus de ecclesia* (Boulder, Colo.: University of Colorado Press, 1956), ix.

130. De Vooght, *L'hérésie de Jean Huss*, 2:525.

131. Leff, "Wyclif and Hus," 119.

132. De Vooght, *L'hérésie de Jean Huss*, 2:832–833, 837. On the difference between Hus and Wyclif regarding understanding the Church's authority, see Enrico S. Molnar,

"Viklef, Hus a problém autority," in *Jan Hus mezi epochami, národy a konfesemi*, ed. Jan B. Lášek (Prague: Česká křest'anská akademie, 1995), 108–111.

133. "[Z]elator patrie ferventissimus . . ."; see Michal Svatoš, ed., *1347/48–1622*, vol. 1 of *Dějiny Univerzity Karlovy* (Prague: Karolinum, 1995), 145.

134. "Petam orationis auxilium, et regracier, quod de benedicta Anglia tanta bona per tuum laborem prestante Ihesu Christo domino Boemia iam suscepit." Václav Novotný, ed., *M. Jana Husi korespondence a dokumenty* (Sbírka pramenů českého hnutí náboženského ve XIV. a XV. století, 14, 1920), 84. On Wyche and Oldcastle, see Jan Sedlák, *Mistr Jan Hus* (Prague: Dědictví sv. Prokopa, 1915), 1:199–202; and de Vooght, *L'hérésie de Jean Huss,* 1:163–7; M. Aston, "Lollardy and Sedition, 1381–1431," *Past and Present* 17 (1960): 1–44. On Wyche, see also Christina von Nolcken, "Richard Wyche, a Certain Knight, and the Beginning of the End," in *Lollardy and the Gentry in the Later Middle Ages,* ed. Margaret Aston and Colin Richmond (New York: St. Martin's Press, 1997), especially 143; and John A. F. Thomson, *The Later Lollards, 1414–1520* (New York: Oxford University Press, 1965), 148–150.

135. Jiří Spěváček, *Václav IV, 1361–1419* (Prague: Svoboda, 1986), 448–49; Novotný, *M. Jana Husi korespondence a dokumenty,* 135. In a way, it could be argued that Grosseteste's focus on scaling down the pretensions of the papacy and insistence on moral reform was more reflective of the ideological thrust of mainline Utraquism, than the more extreme views of Wyclif that found a response in the more transient radical trends, above all in Taboritism.

136. Václav Koranda, *Manualník,* ed. J. Truhlář (Prague: Česká společnost nauk, 1888), xvi–xvii; Hans-Eberhard Hilpert, "Die Insel der Gläubigen?" in *Die Anfänge der Inquisition im Mittelalter: Mit einem Ausblick auf das 20. Jahrhundert und einem Beitrag über religiöse Intoleranz im nichtchristlichen Bereich,* Bayreuther Historische Kolloquien, 7, ed. Peter Segl (Cologne: Böhlau, 1993), 264.

137. William R. Cook, "John Wyclif and Hussite Theology, 1415–1436," *Church History* 42 (1973): 339–340. See also Betts, *Essays in Czech History,* 236–246.

138. Anne Hudson, *Lollards and Their Books* (London: Hambledon Press, 1985), 31–42; Hudson, *The Premature Reformation: Wycliffite Texts and Lollard History* (Oxford: Clarendon Press, 1988), 8, 264–266; Hudson, "The Hussite Catalogues of Wyclif's Works," in *Husitství, Reformace, Renesance: Sborník k 60. narozeninám Františka Šmahela,* ed. Jaroslav Pánek, et al., 3 vols. (Prague: Historický ústav, 1994), 1:401–417; and Hudson, "From Oxford to Prague: The Writings of John Wyclif and his English Followers in Bohemia," *Slavonic and East European Review* 75 (1997): 648–649, 653–657.

139. Matthew Spinka, "Paul Kravař and the Lollard-Hussite Relations," *Church History* 25 (1956): 24–5.

140. Josef Macůrek, "Husitství v rumunských zemích," *Časopis Matice moravské* 51 (1927): 60–61. František Bartoš claims that Constantine was Matthew the Englishman, a Czech with ties to England; see his "A Delegate of the Hussite Church at Constantinople," *Byzantinoslavica* 24 (1963): 289–292.

141. Anne Hudson, "Lollardy and Eschatology," in *Eschatologie und Hussitismus,* Internationales Kolloquium, Prague, September 1–4, 1993, ed. Alexander Patschovsky and František Šmahel (Prague: Historický ústav, 1996), 108.

142. John Foxe, *Fox's Book of Martyrs: The Acts and Monuments of the Church,* ed. John Cumming (London: Chatto and Windus, 1875), 1: 823–945.

143. George Cavendish, *Life and Death of Cardinal Wolsey,* Early English Text

Society, ed. Richard S. Sylvester (London: Oxford University Press, 1959), 180, lines 2–13, 266–268. See also More, *Complete Works,* 5: pt. 1, 220–221, pt. 2, 981.

144. Sedlák, *Mistr Jan Hus,* 1:216–217; Novotný, *M. Jana Husi korespondence a dokumenty,* 102–104; Max Lenz, *König Sigismund und Heinrich der Fünfte von England: Ein Beitrag zur Geschichte der Zeit des Constanzer Concils* (Berlin: G. Reimer, 1874), 31–32.

145. On this topic, see Roman Zaoral, "Podíl Anglie na tažení proti husitům: Poznámky k oxfordskému rukopisu Tanner 165," in *Pocta Josefu Polišenskému: sborník prací moravských historiků k 80. narozeninám Josefa Polišenského* (Olomouc: Univerzita Palackého, Filozofická fakulta, 1996), 183–188.

146. A. N. E. D. Schofield, "England and the Council of Basel," *Annuarium historiae conciliorum* 5 (1973): pt. 1, 1–117.

147. The views of Vasilii A. Elagin, Evgenii P. Novikov, Vasilii A. Bil'basov, and Aleksandr F. Gil'ferding are discussed by G. I. Lipatnikova in "K izucheniiu gusitskogo dvizheniia v russkoi dorevoliutsionnoi istoriografii," *Voprosy istorii slavian* (Voronezh), 1 (1963), especially 92; and Liudmila P. Lapteva, *Russkaia istoriografiia gusitskogo dvizheniia, 40–e gody XIX v.–1917 g.* (Moscow: Izdatel'stvo Moskovskogo universiteta, 1978), with a comprehensive bibliography, 326–332. See also Ivan S. Pal'mov, *K voprosu o snosheniiakh Chekhov–gusitov s vostochnuiu tserkov'iu v polovine XV veka* (St. Petersburg: Tipografiia Eleonskogo, 1889), 5–8; and for a succinct overview, Jiří Kořalka, *František Palacký, 1798–1876: Životopis* (Prague: Argo, 1998), 427–428.

148. František Bartoš, "Německého husity Petra Turnova spis o řádech a zvycích církve východní," *Věstník Královské České Společnosti Nauk* (1915): 1–2; Milada Paulová, "Styky českých husitů s cařihradskou církví na základě církevních poměrů byzantských," *Časopis českého musea* 92 (1918): 3; H. R. Trevor-Roper, "The Church of England and the Greek Church in the Time of Charles I," *Studies in Church History* 15 (1978): 213–240.

149. Bartoš, "Německého husity Petra Turnova spis," 2–3; Enrico C. S. Molnar, "The Restoration of Holy Communion in Both Kinds," *Anglican Theological Review* 2 (1954): 105.

150. On the domestic roots of the Utraquists' eucharistic views, see Holeton, *La communion des tout-petits enfants,* 61–66; Holeton, "Sacramental and Liturgical Reform in Late Medieval Bohemia," 87–92; and Kaminsky, *A History of the Hussite Revolution,* 97–136. In *Česká otázka. Naše nynější krise,* 6th ed. (Prague: Čin, 1948), 193–194, Tomáš G. Masaryk voiced his skepticism about the influence of Eastern Orthodoxy of the Bohemian Reformation.

151. Concerning Wyclif's influence on Jerome's mission, see Ferdinand Hrejsa, *Dějiny křest'anství v Československu* (Prague: Husova československá fakulta bohoslovecká, 1947), 2:43; and František Bartoš, *Husitství a cizina* (Prague: Čin, 1931), 72–74.

152. "De ritibus misse," in *Geschichtschreiber der husitischen Bewegung in Böhmen* (*Fontes rerum austriacarum,* 6), ed. Karl Höfler (Vienna:Hof- und Staatsdruckerei, 1865), 2:506; see also Nejedlý, *Dějiny husitského zpěvu,* 5:169–170.

153. Paulová, "Styky českých husitů," 92 (1918): 3.

154. Pal'mov, *K voprosu o snosheniiakh Chekhov-gusitov,* 15; Paulová, "Styky českých husitů," 93 (1919): 17–21; Antonín Salač, "Constantinople et Prague en 1452: Pourparlers en vue d'une union des Eglises," *Rozpravy Československé akademie věd. Řada společenských věd* 68, no. 11 (1958), especially, 1–6, 23. On contacts with the Armenians, see also Zacharyáš Bruncvík, *Testamenti nostri Iesu Christi pia et fida as-*

sertio. To jest: Kšaftu Večeře Páně svatá Starožitnost, pobožná posloupnost, dlouhověká až právě do dne soudného trvanlivost (Prague: Matěj Pardubský, 1613), 156–157.

155. A report of ordinations by an Armenian bishop, presumably in Poland, in 1499 seems particularly confused; see Noemi Rejchrtová, "Jan Bechyňka: Kněz a literát," in *Praga Mystica: Z dějin české reformace,* vol. 3 of *Acta reformationem bohemicam illustrantia,* ed. Amedeo Molnár (Prague: Kalich, 1984), 6–7.

156. Václav Pavlík, "Český král Jiří a kompaktata," *Časopis katolického duchovenstva* 51 (1910): 388–398, 486–505. On the Utraquist Consistory in the Poděbradian and Jagellonian period, see Thomas. A. Fudge, "Reform and the Lower Consistory in Prague, 1437–1497," in *The Bohemian Reformation and Religious Practice,* vol. 2: Papers from the XVIIIth World Congress of the Czechoslovak Society of Arts and Sciences, Brno 1996, ed. Zdeněk V. David and David R. Holeton (Prague: Academy of Sciences of the Czech Republic, Main Library, 1998), 67–96.

157. Josef Macek, *Víra a zbožnost jagellonského věku* (Prague: Argo, 2001), 58.

158. Koranda, *Manualník,* 50ff.; Václav Koranda, Jr., *Traktát o velebné a božské svátosti oltářní* (Prague: Tiskař Korandy, 1493), f. 01r–02v, Q7r–v. See also Noemi Rejchrtová, "Obrazoborecké tendence utrakvistické mentality jagellonského období a jejich dosah," *Husitský Tábor* 8 (1985): 66; Winfried Eberhard, "Zur reformatorischen Qualität und Konfessionalisierung des nachrevolutionären Hussitismus," in *Häresie und vorzeitige Reformation im Spätmittelalter,* Schriften des Historischen Kollegs Kolloquien 39, ed. František Šmahel (Munich: Oldenbourg, 1998), 223. The humanists Řehoř Hrubý of Jelení and Václav Písecký shared Koranda's view. The latter summed up the grievance against Rome at the turn of the century as follows: "[T]hey never wanted to grant . . . what they had promised in Basel and confirmed with their seals." Bohumil Ryba, "Václav Písecký, Eneáš Sylvius a Lukianos," *Listy filologické* 57 (1930): 145.

159. Rudolf Říčan, *The History of the Unity of Brethren: A Protestant Hussite Church in Bohemia and Moravia,* trans. C. Daniel Crews (Bethlehem, Pa.: Moravian Church in America, 1992), 117. On the Unity's origins, see Wagner, *Petr Chelčický.* See also Neumann, *České sekty ve století XIV. a XV,* 67–83.

160. Audisio, *The Waldensian Dissent,* 83–85; Amedeo Molnár, *Valdenští: evropský rozměr jejich vzdoru* (Prague: Kalich, 1991), 320–326.

161. Koranda, *Manualník,* 42–44, 121–122. For a later period, see, for instance, Jan Stanislaides, *O klanění velebné Svátosti oltářní proti pitharským bludom* (Prague: Konáč, 1515), arguing against the Brethren's assertion that the adoration of the host constituted idolatry. Mikuláš Konáč z Hodíškova, *Dialogus v kterémž Čech s Pithartem rozmlúvá, že sú se Bratří od obú stran oddělili* (Prague: Konáč z Hodíškova, 1515).

162. Říčan, *The History of the Unity of Brethren,* 66–67.

163. The sect was destined to survive in exile as the Moravian Church (Unitas Fratrum). As of 1995 it claimed more than 55,000 members in the United States, and over 4,000 in Canada. This church left an even more notable mark on the English-speaking world by influencing John Wesley on his way to Methodism.

164. Šmahel, *Husitská revoluce,* 4:102–103.

165. Rejchrtová, "Jan Bechyňka: Kněz a literát," 7.

166. *Archiv český* 4 (1846): 452–453; Anna Skýbová, "Česká šlechta a jednání o povolení kompaktát r. 1525," in *Proměny feudální třídy v Čechách v pozdním feudalismu,* ed. Josef Petráň (Prague: Univerzita Karlova, 1976), 87.

167. *Archiv český* 5 (1862): 376–377.

168. Šmahel, *Husitská revoluce,* 4:101.

169. Václav V. Tomek, "O církevní správě strany pod obojí v Čechách od r. 1415 až 1622," *Časopis českého musea* 22 (1848): 365–383, 464.

170. Emma Urbánková, "Nejstarší prvotisky českého původu," in *Knihtisk a kniha v českých zemích od husitství do Bílé hory: Sborník prací k 500. výročí českého knihtisku*, ed. František Šmahel (Prague: Academia, 1970), 24–30. For references to the traditional Utraquist liturgical books see, for instance, Václav Koranda, *Traktát o velebné a božské svátosti oltářní* (Prague: Tiskař Korandy, 1493), f. S3r–S3v.

171. In reality, only the *Statuta* were definitely printed in Plzeň. Despite their different font, it seems that the presumed sponsorship of all these tomes by the Roman Church became the principal reason for their prevalent derivation from Plzeň. Yet, some such as Pravoslav Kneidl and Anton Schubert, have disputed this conclusion; see Emma Urbánková, *Soupis prvotisků českého původu* (Prague: Státní knihovna ČSR, 1986), 215–216; Emma Urbánková, "Statuta Arnoštova: Nejstarší datovaný prvotisk českého původu," *Ročenka Státní knihovny* (1965): 57. Anton Schubert places the publication of the *Agenda* in Prague in his "Die sicher nachweisbaren Inkunabeln Böhmens und Mährens vor 1501," *Centralblatt für Bibliothekwesen* 16 (1899): 51–56, 227.

172. David R. Holeton, "Převedení liturgie do národního jazyka v Čechách: Spletitá otázka" (paper presented at Conference on Bohemian Reformation, Evangelical Theological Faculty of Charles University, Prague, March 31, 1999), 6.

173. Zdeněk Tobolka, ed., *Kališnický pasionál z roku 1495* (Prague: n.p., 1926) (Monumenta Bohemiae typographica, vol. 2).

174. Concerning the vestigial administration of the sub una after 1471, see Veronika Macháčková, "Církevní správa v době jagellonské na základě administrátorských akt," *Folia Historica Bohemica* 9 (1985): 235–290; and Macek, *Víra a zbožnost jagellonského věku*, 173–188.

175. Thomas A. Fudge, "The Problem of Religious Liberty in Early Modern Bohemia," *Communio Viatorum* 38 (1996): 68–71.

176. František Šmahel, "Svoboda slova, svatá válka a tolerance z nutnosti v husitském období," *Český časopis historický* 92 (1994): 677; Robert Kalivoda, "Husitství a jeho vyústění v době předbělohorské a pobělohorské," *Studia comeniana et historica* 13 (1983): 3–45.

177. Fudge, "The Problem of Religious Liberty in Early Modern Bohemia," 73–75.

178. On the armies of the Taborites and Orebites, see, for instance, Fudge, *The Magnificent Ride*, 170.

179. For such an opinion, see, for instance, Robert Kalivoda, *Husitské myšlení* (Prague: Filosofia, 1997), 69.

180. See, for instance, Frederick G. Heymann, "The Impact of Martin Luther upon Bohemia," *Central European History* 1 (1968): 110–111.

181. Josef Macek, *Víra a zbožnost jagellonského věku*, 59.

182. See, for instance, Georg Voigt, "Georg von Böhmen der Hussitenkönig," *Historische Zeitschrift* 5 (1861): 438–439; and Heymann, "The Impact of Martin Luther upon Bohemia," 110–111.

Chapter 3

1. Josef Čihula, "Martin Luther a Čechové pod obojí," *Český časopis historický* 3 (1897): 329.

2. Ferdinand Hrejsa, *Česká konfesse: Její vznik, podstata a dějiny* (Prague: Česká akademie pro vědy, slovesnost a umění, 1912), 4.

3. Eduard Winter, *Tausend Jahre Geisteskampf im Sudetenraum: das religiöse Ringen zweier Völker* (Salzburg: Otto Müller, 1938), 146.

4. "[D]ostala se radnice do rukou radikálního luteránského směru." Jan Vlk and Jaroslav Láník, eds., *Dějiny Prahy,* 2 vols. (Prague: Paseka, 1997), 1:348. The publication of these volumes received a subsidy from the city of Prague. See also Jiří Pešek, "Některé problémy bádání o spojené Praze let 1518–1528," *Documenta Pragensia* 4 (1984): 189–192.

5. Gustav Kawerau, *Hieronymus Emser: Ein Lebensbild aus der Reformationsgeschichte* (Halle: Verein für Reformationsgeschichte, 1898), 30–31.

6. For a comprehensive survey of these translations, see Rudolf Říčan, "Tschechische Übersetzungen von Luthers Schriften bis zum Schmalkaldischen Krieg," *Vierhundertfünfzig Jahre lutherische Reformation, 1517–1967: Festschrift für Franz Lau zum 50. Geburtstag* (Göttingen: Vanderhoeck and Ruprecht, 1967), 282–288.

7. Martin Luther, *O velebné svátosti svatého pravého těla Kristova a o bratrstvích,* trans. ([Oldřich Velenský of Mnichov?], 1520), translation of Martin Luther, *Ein Sermon von dem hochwürdigen Sacrament des heiligen waren Leichnams Christi und von den Brüderschaften. 1519,* in Luther, *Werke: Kritische Gesammtausgabe,* 113 vols. in 4 series (Weimar: Böhlau, 1883–1996) (hereafter *WA* [*Weimarer Ausgabe*]), 2:738–758.

8. Martin Luther, *Kázání velebného a nábožného otce Martina Luthera na desatero přikázání Božích, které lidu obecnému zjevně v městě Witemberce kázal jest* (Prague: Pavel Severýn z Kapí Hory, 1520), translation of Martin Luther, *Decem praecepta Wittenbergensi praedicata populo. 1518,* in *WA,* 1:398–521.

9. Ferdinand Hrejsa, *Dějiny křest'anství v Československu,* 6 vols. (Prague: Husova československá fakulta bohoslovecká, 1946–1950), 4:256.

10. Martin Luther, *O svobodě křest'anské knížka . . . kterouž Lvovi desátému papeži římskému psal* (Litomyšl: Alexander Aujezdský, 1521), translation of Martin Luther, *De Libertate Christiana,* in *WA,* 7:49–73.

11. Jaroslav Pelikan, "Luther's Negotiations with the Hussites," *Concordia Theological Monthly* 20 (1949): 502–503.

12. Thomas. A. Fudge, "Reform and the Lower Consistory in Prague, 1437–1497," in *The Bohemian Reformation and Religious Practice,* vol. 2: Papers from the XVIIIth World Congress of the Czechoslovak Society of Arts and Sciences, Brno 1996, ed. Zdeněk V. David and David R. Holeton (Prague: Academy of Sciences of the Czech Republic, Main Library, 1998), 86–88.

13. Jaroslav Kadlec, *Přehled českých církevních dějin,* 2 vols. (Prague: Zvon, 1991), 2:11; Frederick G. Heymann, "The Impact of Martin Luther upon Bohemia," *Central European History* 1 (1968): 114, 117.

14. "List od papeže Lva," in Jaroslav Kolár, ed., *Zrcadlo rozděleného království* (Prague: Nakladatelství Československé akademie věd, 1963), 52–57.

15. Martin Luther, *Před velebností císařskou i přede všemi knížaty říše k napomenutí jich odvolati knihy pod jménem jeho vydané* (Prague: Pavel Severýn z Kapí Hory, 1521), translation of Martin Luther, "Doctor Martinus red an Ro. Kay. May't, die Churfursten und Stende des Reichs," in *WA* 7:867–877; Heymann, "Impact of Martin Luther," 116. See also Martin Luther, *Pro kterou příčinu papežský a jeho následovníků knihy jest spálil tuto zvíš* (Prague: Pavel Severýn z Kapí Hory, 1521), trans. of Martin Luther, *Warumb*

des Bapsts und siner Jungernn bucher von Doct. Martino Luther vorbrant seynn, in *WA,* 7:161–182.

16. Ernst Ludwig Enders, ed., Dr. *Martin Luthers Briefwechsel* (Calw and Stuttgart: Verlag der Vereinsbuchhandlung, 1887), 2:75–77.

17. Hieronymus Emser, *De disputatione lipsicensi, quantum ad Boemos obiter deflexa est (1519). A venatione Luteriana Aegocerotis assertio (1519),* ed. Franz Xaver Thurnhofer (Münster: Aschendorf, 1921), 15, 31–32, 36.

18. Martin Luther, *De captivitate Babylonica ecclesiae praeludium. 1520,* in Luther, *WA* 6:497. See also Thomas More, *Complete Works,* 21 vols. (New Haven: Yale University Press, 1963–1997), 5: pt. 2, 928.

19. Luther, *O svobodě křest'anské,* f. C1r.

20. Martin Luther, *Výklad o Antikristu na vidění Danielovo: v osmé kapitole proroctví jeho položené* (Prague: Pavel Severýn z Kapí Hory, 1522), partial trans. of Martin Luther, *Ad librum eximii Magistri Nostri Magistri Ambrosii Catharini, defensoris Silvestri Prieratis accerimi, responsio. Cum exposita Visione Danielis viii. De Antichristo. 1521,* in *WA,* 7:698–778. The Czech version omits the initial part with Luther's answer to Ambrosius Catharinus, pseudonym of Lancelotto Politi, *Apologia pro veritate catholicae et apostolicae fidei ac doctrinae adversus impia ac valde pestifera Martini Lutheri dogmata* (1521).

21. Luther, *Výklad o Antikristu,* f. 70v.

22. *Ibid.,* f. 3r, 10r.

23. Luther, *Před velebností císařskou,* f. A5r–A5v.

24. Čihula, "Martin Luther a Čechové," 342.

25. Johann Agricola wrote his play *Tragoedie von Johann Hus* (1537) in part as a warning to those who would attend the proposed General Council by pointing to Hus's fate at Council of Constance; see Remigius Bäumer, *Johannes Cochlaeus (1479–1552): Leben und Werk im Dienst der katholischen Reform* (Muenster: Aschendorf, 1980), 113.

26. Bartoš Písař, *Kronika pražská,* in *Prameny dějin českých/Fontes rerum Bohemicarum,* ed. Josef V. Šimák (Prague: Historický klub, 1907), 6:122.

27. Heymann, "The Impact of Martin Luther," 115. The Czechs stood in confrontation with the rest of the world and felt like an island surrounded by a menacing ocean. See Ivan Hlaváček, "K dochování husitské a protihusitské polemické literatury v 15. století," in *Jihlava a Basilejská Kompaktáta: Sborník příspěvků z mezinárodního sympozia k 555. výročí přijetí Basilejských kompaktát, 26–28. červen 1991,* ed. František Šmahel, et al. (Jihlava: Muzeum Vysočiny, 1992), 29.

28. Thomas A. Fudge, *The Magnificent Ride: The First Reformation in Hussite Bohemia* (Brookfield, Vt.: Ashgate, 1998), 216–218.

29. S. Harrison Thomson, "Luther and Bohemia," *Archiv für Reformationsgeschichte* 44 (1953): 161.

30. Jaroslav Pelikan, "Luther's Attitude Toward John Hus," *Concordia Theological Monthly* 19 (1948): 747–755; Hrejsa, *Dějiny křest'anství,* 4:247; Arnošt Kraus, *Husitství v literatuře, zejména německé,* 3 vols. (Prague: Česká akademie pro vědy, slovesnost a umění, 1917–1924), 1:148, 151–153.

31. Luther, *Ein Sermon von dem hochwürdigen* in *WA,* 2:738.

32. Kraus, *Husitství v literatuře,* 1:56; Enders, *Luthers Briefwechsel,* 2:358.

33. More, *Complete Works,* 5: pt. 2, 869.

34. Martin Luther, *Contra Henricum Regem Angliae. 1522,* in *WA,* Band 10, Zweite

Abteilung, 180–182; also in More's *Responsio ad Lutherum*, in More, *Complete Works*, 5: pt. 1, 32–39.

35. Martin Luther, *Ein Sermon von dem neuen Testament, das ist von der heiligen Messe. 1520*, in *WA*, 6:351.
36. Kawerau, *Hieronymus Emser*, 46–47.
37. Bartoš Písař, *Kronika pražská*, 32.
38. Antonín Rezek, *Dějiny prostonárodního hnutí náboženského v Čechách od vydání tolerančního patentu až na naše časy* (Prague: Řivnáč, 1887), 12.
39. See also František Dvorský, ed., *Dopisy kněží Šimona z Habru a Jana faráře Německo-Brodského o rozdílech ve víře, 1528–1529*, in *Archiv český* 14 (1895): 325.
40. Luther, *Kázání . . . na desatero*, 2.
41. "[G]rewlichen lesterung, hasz und neyd auff beyder seytten . . . ," See Martin Luther, *An den christlichen Adel deutscher Nation von der christlichen Standes Besserung 1520*, in *WA*, 6:454.
42. Martin Luther, *Ad aegocerotem Emserianum M. Lutheri additio. 1519*, in *WA*, 2:661.
43. "[D]ie uns täglich 'teutsche Hund' nennen, auf ihre Sprache: 'Nicmetz piesska' . . ." See Enders, *Luthers Briefwechsel*, 2:521. The author of a recently published volume underlines the provocative character of Luther's appeal on the Bohemians' behalf: "Luther's comments about charity to the Hussites must have clanged as discordantly as a modern suggestion that Hitler might have been made more reasonable by a charitable response to his program." Richard Marius, *The Christian Between God and Death* (Cambridge, Mass.: Harvard University Press, 1999), 176.
44. Luther, *Výklad o Antikristu*, f. A5v.
45. Martin Luther, *Schreiben an die boehmischen Landstaende. 1522*, in *WA*, 10, Zweite Abteilung, 172–174.
46. Winfried Eberhard, *Konfessionsbildung und Stände in Böhmen, 1478–1530* (Munich: Oldenbourg, 1981), 127–129; Winter, *Tausend Jahre Geisteskampf*,146.
47. Luther, *Kázání . . . na desatero*, 3–4.
48. Luther, *Výklad o Antikristu*, f. A5v.
49. Luther, *Kázání . . . na desatero*,3–4.
50. *Ibid.*,2.
51. Martin Luther, *Disputatio Iohannis Eccii et Martini Lutheri Lipsiae habita. 1519*, in *WA*, 2:279; Kawerau, *Hieronymus Emser*, 30.
52. Martin Luther, *Resolutiones Lutherianae super propositionibus suis Lipsiae disputatis. 1519*, in *WA*, 2:405–406; Kraus, *Husitství v literatuře*, 1:153.
53. "Johannis Huss (cuius multo plures [articulos] nunc teneo, quam Lipsiae tenebam, ut suo die ostendam) Christianissimum esse . . ." Martin Luther, *Ad Johannem Eccium M. Lutheri epistola super expurgatione Ecciana 1519*, in *WA*, 2:702.
54. Luther, *Ein Sermon von dem hochwürdigen*, in *WA*, 2:742.
55. Martin Luther, *De captivitate Babylonica ecclesiae praeludium. 1520*, in *WA*, 5:504.
56. Luther, *An den christlichen Adel*, in *WA*, 6:456; Luther, *De captivitate*, in *WA*, 6:505.
57. "Denique Paulus et Augustinus ad verbum sunt Hussitae." "Luther an Spalatin," in *WA*, Briefwechsel, 2:42.
58. Luther, *Resolutiones*, in *WA*, 2:406; Emser, *De disputatione lipsicensi*, 36, 53, 66.

59. Desiderius Erasmus, *The Correspondence*, 11 vols. (Toronto: University of Toronto Press, 1974–1992), 8:157.

60. Čihula, "Martin Luther a Čechové," 348–349.

61. Luther, *Schreiben an die boehmischen Landstaende*, 174.

62. Martin Luther, *Von beyder gestallt des Sacraments zu nehmen 1522*, in *WA*, 10: pt. 2, 11–41. In the Czech translation (c. 1522), see f. B2v–B3r, C2v. The translation is known only in one copy (Olomouc, SK 32.115) with a missing title page and end page, so that its Czech title, the year of publication, and the name of the translator cannot be determined; see also Říčan, "Tschechische Übersetzungen," 286.

63. Edward Surtz, *The Works and Days of John Fisher: An Introduction to the Position of St. John Fischer (1469–1535), Bishop of Rochester, in the English Renaissance and Reformation* (Cambridge, Mass.: Harvard University Press, 1967), 323.

64. *Ibid.*, 316.

65. See More's letter to Erasmus of July 6, 1525, in Erasmus, *The Correspondence*, 11:188.

66. More, *Complete Works*, 6: pt. 1, 361, pt. 2, 707–708.

67. Pelikan, "Luther's Attitude," 751–752.

68. Fritz Erlenbusch, "Hus a německé protestantství," in *Co daly naše země Evropě a lidstvu*, ed. Vilém Mathesius (Prague: Evropský literární klub, 1939), 92–93.

69. Eberhard, *Konfessionsbildung*, 127. On Luther's view of Hus, see also Jaroslav Goll, "Jak soudil Luther o Husovi," *Časopis českého musea* 54 (1880): 60–80.

70. "[Q]uod olim Johannes Huss in Bohemia fuerat, hoc tu, Martine, es in Saxonia." See Enders, *Luthers Briefwechsel*, 2:79.

71. "Luther an Spalatin," *WA*, Briefwechsel, 2:42.

72. Hrejsa, *Dějiny křest'anství*, 4:252; Jan Hus, *Magistri Joannis Hus: Tractatus de ecclesia*, ed. S. Harrison Thomson (Boulder, Colo.: University of Colorado Press, 1956).

73. Martin Luther, *Von den neuen Eckischen Bullen und Lügen, 1520*, in *WA*, 6:588.

74. Čihula, "Martin Luther a Čechové," 343–344, 346.

75. Luther, *Kázání . . . na desatero*, 2–3.

76. "Ich will auch Johannem Husz keynen heyligen noch Marterer machen, wie echtlich Behemen thun . . .," Luther, *An den christlichen Adel*, in *WA*, 6:455. It is hard to understand Heymann's statement that Luther in the *Address to the Christian Nobility* most clearly glorified Hus. Heymann, "The Impact of Martin Luther," 116.

77. See note 57 above. See also Thomas A. Fudge, "*Ansellus Dei* and the Bethlehem Chapel in Prague," *Communio Viatorum* 35 (1993): 161.

78. Carter Lindberg, "A Specific Contribution of the Second Reformation," in Milan Opočenský, ed., *Toward a Renewed Dialogue: Consultation on the First and Second Reformations, Geneva 28 November to 1 December 1994* (Geneva: World Alliance of Reformed Churches, 1996), 42; see also Lindberg's review of the *Handbook of European History, 1400–1600*, vol. 2 (Leiden: Brill, 1995), in *Journal of Ecclesiastical History* 48 (1997): 560–561.

79. "Doctrina et vita sunt distinguenda. Vita est mala apud nos sicut apud papistas; non igitur de vita dimicamus et damnamus eos. Hoc nesciverunt Wikleff et Hus, qui vitam impugnarunt." Luther, *WA, Tischreden*, 1:294, n. 624; also cited in Lindberg, "A Specific Contribution," 42.

80. Gerd Roloff, "Hus in der Reformationspolemik," in *Studien zum Humanismus in den böhmischen Ländern*, Schriften des Komitees der Bundesrepublik Deutschland

zur Förderung der Slawischen Studien XI, ed. Hans-Bernd Harder and Hans Rothe (Cologne: Böhlau, 1988), 111–129; Erlenbusch, "Hus a německé protestantství," 93–94.

81. Vilém Herold, "Jan Hus—a Heretic, a Saint, or a Reformer?" *Kosmas: Czechoslovak and Central European Journal* 15, no. 1 (2001): 4.

82. Anonymous, *Die göttliche Mühle* (Zurich: Christoph Froschauer, 1521). For Erasmus's objections to the image, see Erasmus, *The Correspondence,* 8: 208–209, 415, n. 54. Like Hus, Erasmus was also subjected to Roman allegations of being Luther's precursor and/or inspirer; see Erica Rummel, "*Monachatus non est pietas:* Interpretation and Misinterpretation of a Dictum," in *Erasmus' Vision of the Church,* ed. Hilmar M. Pabel (Kirksville, Mo.: Sixteenth Century Journal Publishers, 1995), 54–55.

83. More, *Complete Works,* 5: pt. 1, 40–41.

84. Kadlec, *Přehled,* 2:11.

85. Luther, *O svobodě křest'anské,* for instance, f. A3v.

86. Rudolf Říčan, *The History of the Unity of Brethren: A Protestant Hussite Church in Bohemia and Moravia,* trans. C. Daniel Crews (Bethlehem, Pa.: Moravian Church in America, 1992), 110.

87. Luther, *Výklad o Antikristu,* f. 18r–18v, 31v; Martin Luther, *Kázání o novém zákoně aneb o posledním kšaftu Krista pána na své svaté večeři, to jest o mši svaté* (Prague: [Pavel Severýn z Kapí Hory?], 1521), f. M3r–M3v. Translation of Luther, *Ein Sermon von dem neuen Testament,* in *WA,* 5:349–378.

88. Luther, *Kázání o novém zákoně,* G1v, H3r, H4r, J1r; see also Thomas J. Davis, "'The Truth of the Divine Words': Luther's Sermons on the Eucharist, 1521–28, and the Structure of the Eucharistic Meaning," *Sixteenth Century Journal* 30 (1999): 325, n. 7.

89. Luther, *O svobodě křest'anské,* f. A2v.

90. Luther, *Výklad o Antikristu,* f. 31r–31v, see also f. 24v; Luther, *Kázání . . . na desatero,* 257–258.

91. Luther, *Výklad o Antikristu,* f. 31v.

92. Luther, *O svobodě křest'anské,* f. A3r.

93. Luther, *Výklad o Antikristu,* f. 17r–17v; Luther, *Kázání o novém zákoně,* f. K2r–K2v.

94. Luther, *O svobodě křest'anské,* f. B3v–C1r.

95. *Ibid.,* f. C1r.

96. Martin Luther, *De instituendis ministris Ecclesiae, ad clarissimum senatum Pragensem Bohemiae,* in *WA,* 12:160–96. The Czech translation appeared as Martin Luther, *O ustanovení služebníků církve slovutné poctivosti pánům panu purkmistru a radě starších i všemu lidu slovutného města Prahy hlavy království českého* (Prague: n.p., 1523).

97. Luther, *O ustanovení služebníků církve,* especially f. E2v–E3r.

98. For instance, in Luther, *Výklad o Antikristu,* f. 17r–17v. On the Utraquists' rejection of the Lutheran view of the pope as the Antichrist, see *Sněmy české od léta 1526 až po naši dobu.,* vols. 1-11, 15 (Prague: Zemský výbor, 1877-1941) (*Sněmy české*), 7:397.

99. Her famous invective admonishing the popes to return to Rome from Avignon, was cited in Chapter 2 of this volume from Bohdan Chudoba, *Jindy a nyní: Dějiny českého národa* (Prague: Vyšehrad, 1946), 109. See also Francis Oakley, *The Western Church in the Later Middle Ages* (Ithaca, N.Y.: Cornell University Press, 1979), 39.

100. Hieronymus Dungersheim, "Dialogus ad Lutherum," in Enders, *Luthers Briefwechsel,* 2:169, 176.

101. Luther, *Výklad o Antikristu,* f. 17r–17v, 54v, 70v. Interestingly enough, Konstantin Angelik, the alleged emissary of the Utraquists in Constantinople in 1452, was also to identify the pope as "the man of sins" for his many invented rules. Augustin Neumann, *K dějinám věku poděbradského* (Brno: Nákladem vlastním, 1933), 7.

102. Anna Skýbová, "Česká šlechta a jednání o povolení kompaktát r. 1525," in *Proměny feudální třídy v Čechách v pozdním feudalismu,* Acta Universitatis Carolinae, Philosophica et historica I, Studia historica XIV, ed. Josef Petráň (Prague: Univerzita Karlova, 1976), 81–112; Václav V. Tomek, *Dějepis města Prahy,* 12 vols. (Prague: Řivnáč, 1855–1901), 10:544–547, 575–582.

103. On the Utraquists' controversies with the Taborites, see Chapter 4. On controversies with the Brethren, see Fudge, "Reform and the Lower Consistory," 89–94; Jan Bechyňka, "Praga mistica," in *Praga Mystica: Z dějin české reformace,* ed. Noemi Rejchrtová, *Acta reformationem bohemicam illustrantia,* vol. 3, ed. Amedeo Molnár (Prague: Kalich, 1984), 39–40.

104. Tomek, *Dějepis města Prahy,* 10:554; Hrejsa, *Dějiny křest'anství,* 4:256.

105. On the pitfalls of the "Second Reformation," see, for instance, Lindberg, "A Specific Contribution," 39–41.

106. Hrejsa, *Dějiny křest'anství,* 4:247–48.

107. Zdeněk V. Tobolka, *Český knihtiskař Mikuláš Konáč z Hodíškova,* Monumenta Bohemiae Typographica IV (Prague: n.p., 1927), 2; cited from introduction to *O Turcích: Odkud a proč Turci slovú* (Prague: Mikuláš Konáč z Hodíškova, [1522?]), f. B4r. See also Mikuláš Konáč of Hodíškov, *List pravdy pro řád pokoj lásku a svornost Království českého a Markrabství Moravského sepsaný* (Prague: Konáč z Hodíškova, 1522), f. A4v, for two references to Luther.

108. Luther, *O svobodě křest'anské,* f. B1r, C4r. On good works (*gutt werck/dobrý skutek*), see also Luther, *Kázání o novém zákoně,* f. H3r. He was even more explicit in the first thesis of his Heidelberg Disputation of 1518: "Lex Dei, saluberrima vitae doctrinae, non potest hominem ad iusticiam promovere, sed magis obest" (The law of God, the soundest doctrine of life, is not able to lead humanity to righteousness, but rather stands in the way), cited from WA 1:353, 5–16 by Matthias Gockel, "A Reformer's dissent from Lutheranism: Reconsidering the Theology of Hans Denck, c. 1500-1527," *Archiv für Reformationsgeschichte/Archive for Reformation History* 91 (2000): 127. On the importance of the law of God for the Utraquists, see Thomas A. Fudge, "The "Law of God": Reform and Religious Practice in Late Medieval Bohemia," in *The Bohemian Reformation and Religious Practice,* vol. 1: Papers from the XVIIth World Congress of the Czechoslovak Society of Arts and Sciences, Prague, 1994, ed. David R. Holeton (Prague: Academy of Sciences of the Czech Republic, Main Library, 1996), 52–54; Fudge, *Magnificent Ride,* 157–161.

109. Winter, *Tausend Jahre Geisteskampf,* 146.

110. To borrow the words written in a different but similar context by Brendan Bradshaw, "The Controversial Sir Thomas More," *Journal of Ecclesiastical History* 36 (1985): 568.

111. See Chapter 2. On the importance of freedom in university disputations, see also Erasmus, *The Correspondence,* 8:210.

112. Cited by Fudge, *Magnificent Ride,* 72.

113. Rudolf Říčan, ed., *Čtyři vyznání* (Prague: Komenského evangelická bohoslovecká fakulta, 1951), 39; Amedeo Molnár, et al., *Soudce smluvený v Chebu* (Cheb: n.p., 1982), 9–36.

114. Josef V. Šimák, "Úvod," in Bartoš Písař, *Kronika pražská,* xxxiv.
115. Tomek, *Dějepis města Prahy,* 10:540; Bartoš Písař, *Kronika pražská,* 107–108.
116. Luther, *De instituendis ministris,* in *WA,* 12:171; in Czech translation, Luther, *O ustanovení služebníků církve,* f. A3v.
117. More, *Complete Works,* 6: pt. 1, 192, 195, 200; pt. 2, 658.
118. Václav Husa, *Tomáš Müntzer a Čechy,* Rozpravy ČSAV, 67, 1957, Společenské vědy 11, 62–79; Josef Janáček, ed., *Dějiny Prahy* (Prague: Nakladatelství politické literatury, 1964), 252. Based largely on Husa is the account of the Prague episode in Hans-Jürgen Goertz, *Thomas Müntzer: Apocalyptic Mystic and Revolutionary,* trans. Jocelyn Jaquiery, ed. Peter Matheson (Edinburgh: T & T Clark, 1993), 72–83. On Müntzer in Prague, see also George H. Williams, *The Radical Reformation,* 3d ed. (Kirksville, Mo.: Sixteenth Century Journal Publishers, 1992), 126–127.
119. Thomas A. Fudge, "The Problem of Religious Liberty in Early Modern Bohemia," *Communio Viatorum* 38 (1996): 67–70; Ernest Denis, *Fin de l'indépendance bohême,* 2d ed., 2 vols. (Paris: Librairie Leroux, 1930), 1:208–209; Šmahel, et al., *Jihlava a Basilejská Kompaktáta,* especially 11–27. For the text of the Compactata, see *Archiv český* 3 (1844): 398–444; for the text of the Peace of Kutná Hora, see *Archiv český* 5 (1862): 418–427.
120. František Palacký, *Dějiny národu českého,* 5 vols. (Prague: Bursík a Kohout, [1893]), 5:508–509.
121. Erasmus, *The Correspondence,* 8:81–82, 155–157, 202–211. On his influence in Bohemia, see Jaroslav Kolár, *Návraty bez konce: Studie k starší české literatuře,* ed. Lenka Jiroušková (Brno: Atlantis, 1999), 120, 141, 175–177.
122. Dvorský, "Dopisy kněží," 335. On Luther's insulting answer to Henry VIII, see Kawerau, *Hieronymus Emser,* 40–41. The text is in Martin Luther, *Contra Henricum Regem Angliae. 1522,* in *WA,* 10:Zweite Abteilung, 178–179.
123. Erasmus, *The Correspondence,* 8:203. For Erasmus's censure of Luther's arrogance and virulent style, see also 9:392.
124. Zdeněk V. David, "Pavel Bydžovský and Czech Utraquism's Encounter with Luther," *Communio Viatorum* 38 (1996): 42–43, 59–60.
125. Winter, *Tausend Jahre Geisteskampf,* 150.
126. Luther, *Kázání . . . na desatero,* 67; Richard Hooker, *The Folger Library Edition of the Works of Richard Hooker,* 6 vols., ed. W. Speed Hill (Cambridge, Mass.: Belknap Press of Harvard University Press, 1977–1993), 1:3. On Hooker's moderation, see also Diarmaid MacCulloch, "Richard Hooker's Reputation," *English Historical Review* 117 (2002): 791.
127. Šimák, "Úvod," ix, xiii.
128. Luther, *Kázání . . . na desatero,* introduction, 5; Říčan, *The History of the Unity of Brethren,* 148, 253.
129. Luther, *Výklad o Antikristu,* f. A2r; Říčan, "Tschechische Übersetzungen," 282–283.
130. Surtz, *The Works and Days of John Fisher,* 8–9; Ulrichus Velenus (Oldřich Velenský of Mnichov), *In hoc libello grauissimis, certissimisque, & in sacra scriptura fundatis rationibus uarije probatur, Apostolarum Petrum Romae non uenisse, neque illicit passum, proinde satis friuole, & temere Romanus Pontifex se Petri successorem inactat, & nominat* (Basel: n.p., 1520). There is also a German translation, which was probably published in Augsburg, 1521, under the title *In disem Büchlin wirt in mancherlay tapffern bestendigen und in der Scrifft gegründeten Ursachen klärlich bewert, das der hailig*

Apostel Petrus gen Rom nicht komen noch alda den Tod gelitten... See also A. J. Lamping, *Ulrichus Velenus (Oldřich Velenský) and his Treatise against the Papacy* (Leiden: Brill, 1976), 152–157.

131. For a general description of these events, see Pelikan, "Luther's Negotiations," 499–503; Eberhard, *Konfessionsbildung,* 135–139; and Tomek, *Dějepis města Prahy,* 10:535–538.

132. Pelikan, "Luther's Negotiations," 502–503; Luther, *De instituendis ministris,* in *WA,* 12:161. Concerning doubts about the character of Cahera's role, see discussion later in this chapter.

133. Hrejsa, *Dějiny křesťanství,* 4:266–268; Josef Macek, *Jagellonský věk v českých zemích, 1471–1526,* 4 vols. (Prague: Academia, 1992–1999), 3:104–105.

134. Hrejsa, *Dějiny křesťanství,* 4:270; Tomek, *Dějepis města Prahy,* 10:535–536; Bartoš Písař, *Kronika pražská,* 20–21.

135. Palacký, *Dějiny,* 5:513.

136. "Konečné vítězství mínění Luthranského se . . . předpokládalo." Tomek, *Dějepis města Prahy,* 10:536–537.

137. Anton Gindely, *Geschichte der Böhmischen Brüder,* 2d ed., 2 vols. (Prague: C. Bellmann, 1861–1862), 1:170.

138. "[Z]a vlivu prvních úspěchů reformace Luterovy..." Kamil Krofta, "Boj o konsistoř podobojí v l. 1562–1575 a jeho historický základ," *Český časopis historický* 17 (1911): 296, and also 180.

139. "[B]egann die Angleichung der utraquistischen Kirche an das Luthertum." Winter, *Tausend Jahre Geisteskampf,* 148.

140. Hrejsa, *Dějiny křesťanství,* 4:271.

141. Eberhard, *Konfessionsbildung,* 144.

142. Macek, *Jagellonský věk,* 3:315.

143. Heymann, "The Impact of Martin Luther," 119. The text of the Candlemas Day Articles is in Bartoš Písař, *Kronika pražská,* 21–25.

144. David R. Holeton, *La communion des tout-petits enfants: Étude du mouvement eucharistique en Bohême vers la fin du Moyen-Âge* (Rome: Edizioni Liturgiche, 1989); František Bartoš, "Martin Lupáč a jeho spisovatelské dílo," *Reformační sborník* 7 (1939): 128–130; Helena Krmíčková, "Několik poznámek o přijímání maličkých, 1414–1416," *Sborník prací Filozofické fakulty Brněnské univerzity* C44 (1997): 59.

145. David R. Holeton describes the manner of communion for infants, established by the Utraquist Synod of 1418, as follows: "The priest is instructed first to place a crumb of bread into the mouth of the infant then to hold the child's mouth shut (so that the bread would be swallowed). Then the priest was to take a drop of wine from the chalice on his finger and place it in the infant's mouth." See Holeton, "The Communion of Infants and Hussitism," *Communio Viatorum* 27 (1984): 222, n. 39.

146. Luther, *An den christlichen Adel,* in *WA,* 6:455.

147. Josef Šimák's assertion to the contrary is not supported by the text, Bartoš Písař, *Kronika pražská,* 23, note a.

148. Eberhard, *Konfessionsbildung,* 142–143.

149. The spirit of religious toleration had also pervaded the Peace of Kutná Hora between the Utraquists and the Roman party in 1485. On the Four Articles of Prague, the "Judge" of Cheb, the Compactata of Basel, and the Peace of Kutná Hora, see also Hrejsa, *Dějiny křesťanství,* 2:271; Fudge, "The Problem of Religious Liberty," 67–70.

150. Říčan, *The History of the Unity of Brethren,* 110.
151. Krofta, "Boj o konsistoř," 181.
152. Luther's treatise was titled *Von anbeten des Sakraments des heyligen leychnams Christi.* Lukáš of Prague replied with *Odpověď Bratří na spis M. Luthera* (1523), which rejected bowing before the sacrament under any circumstances as an idolatrous abomination. See Říčan, *The History of the Unity of Brethren,* 114. On Luther's controversies with the brethren, see also Martin Nodl, "Utrakvismus a Jednota bratrská na rozcestí: Dobový kontext náboženské konverze Jana Augusty," *Marginalia historica* 4 (2001): 144–148.
153. Hrejsa, *Dějiny křesťanství,* 4:270.
154. Pierre Costil, *André Dudith, humaniste hongrois 1533–1589: Sa vie, son oeuvre et ses manuscrits grecs* (Paris: Les Belles Lettres, 1935), 109. Also, Pope Clement VII in 1531 considered lifting the ban on clergy marriages in the West. Peter Fraenkel, "Utraquism or Co-Existence: Some Notes on the Earliest Negotiations Before the Pacification of Nuernberg, 1531–1532," *Studia theologica* 18, no. 2 (1964): 136.
155. Bartoš Písař, *Kronika pražská,* 25. Utraquists did not accept married clergy until the second half of the sixteenth century. See Říčan, *The History of the Unity of Brethren,* 319.
156. Hrejsa, *Dějiny křesťanství,* 4:273; Tomek, *Dějepis města Prahy,* 10:541.
157. Heymann, "The Impact of Martin Luther," 119.
158. Říčan, *The History of the Unity of Brethren,* 108–115, 117, 264–275.
159. Karel J. Erben, *Die Primatoren der königlichen Altstadt Prag* (Prague: F. Tempsky, 1858), 6; Macek, *Jagellonský věk,* 3:316–319.
160. Hrejsa, *Dějiny křesťanství,* 4:276; Tomek, *Dějepis města Prahy,* 10:541, 555–556.
161. Heymann, "The Impact of Martin Luther," 121; G. P. Mel'nikov, "Iz istorii obshchestvenno–politicheskoi borby Chekhii v dvatsatye gody XVI v.," *Sovetskoe slavianovedenie,* 5 (1980): 57.
162. Tomek, *Dějepis města Prahy,* 10:547–548; "Vordringen der lutheranischen Aggression . . ."; Gindely, *Geschichte,* 1:172.
163. "[D]es lutherfreundlichen Bürgermeisters von Prag Hlavsa . . ." and "Die Lutherfreunde sind ausgewiesen. Erst 1529 durften sie wieder zurückkehren." Winter, *Tausend Jahre Geisteskampf,* 149.
164. Husa, *Tomáš Müntzer,* 73.
165. František Kutnar, *Přehledné dějiny českého a slovenského dějepisectví,* 2 vols. (Prague: Státní pedagogické nakladatelství, 1973–1977), 1:52.
166. Erben, *Die Primatoren,* 6–7.
167. Eberhard, *Konfessionsbildung,* 150.
168. Macek, *Jagellonský věk,* 3:103–105, 315, 318; Šimák, "Úvod," vi.
169. Tomek, *Dějepis města Prahy,* 10:557–558, 587–588, 592–593; "Úmluva mezi Pražany a M. Brikcím," *Prameny dějin českých/Fontes rerum Bohemicarum,* ed. Josef V. Šimák (Prague: Historický klub, 1907), 6:373.
170. Macek, *Jagellonský věk,* 3:315.
171. Bartoš Písař, *Kronika pražská,* 107–108.
172. Tomek, *Dějepis města Prahy,* 10:540.
173. Janáček, *Dějiny Prahy,* 254.
174. Kadlec, *Přehled,* 2:14–15.

175. Heymann, "Impact of Martin Luther," 121.
176. The letters are preserved only in Bartoš Písař, *Kronika pražská*, 108–109; Heymann, "Impact of Martin Luther," 119, 121.
177. Tomek, *Dějepis města Prahy*, 10:569, n. 52; Macek, *Jagellonský věk*, 3:102.
178. These doubts about Cahera's role are raised by the editors of Martin Luther's *Werke: Kritische Gesammtausgabe* in Luther, *De instituendis ministris*, in *WA*, 12: 161–163.
179. See, for instance, Božena Kopičková a Anežka Vidmanová, *Listy na Husovu obranu z let 1410–1412: Konec jedné legendy?* (Prague: Karolinum, 1999); and Aleš Pořízka, "Listy na obranu Husovu ze 12. září až 2. října 1410: Konec druhé legendy?" *Český časopis historický* 99 (2001): 701–724.
180. Tomek, *Dějepis města Prahy*, 10:539–540; Kadlec, *Přehled*, 2:11; Mel'nikov, "Iz istorii obshchestvenno–politicheskoi," 55.
181. Tomek, *Dějepis města Prahy*, 10:541, n. 28, 545–546.
182. "[J]est horší nevěstka než papežova římská," in "Píseň proti Pikhartům," *Prameny dějin českých/Fontes rerum Bohemicarum*, ed. Josef V. Šimák (Prague: Historický klub, 1907), 6:367.
183. Luther, *De instituendis ministris*, in *WA*, 12:163.
184. Eberhard, *Konfessionsbildung*, 226–229; Janáček, *Dějiny Prahy*, 258–259; Erben, *Die Primatoren*, 7–8.
185. Šimák, "Úvod," vii.
186. Amedeo Molnár, "Martin Luther a Jednota bratrská," in *Praga Mystica: Z dějin české reformace*, ed. Amedeo Molnár, vol. 3 of *Acta reformationem bohemicam illustrantia* (Prague: Kalich, 1984), 122–125.
187. See Chapter 5. On Luther's contact with the Brethren in the 1530s, see Pelikan, "Luther's Endorsement," 834–836; and Říčan, *The History of the Unity of Brethren*, 148.
188. Winter, *Tausend Jahre Geisteskampf*, 150.
189. Skýbová, "Česká šlechta a jednání o povolení kompaktát," 97.
190. Winter, *Tausend Jahre Geisteskampf*, 149.
191. Jaroslav Purš and Miroslav Kropilák, eds., *Přehled dějin Československa* (Prague: Academia, 1980–1982), 1/2:529. On the event, see Tomek, *Dějepis města Prahy*, 10:544–547, 569, 572, 575–582.
192. Richard M. Douglas, *Jacopo Sadoleto, 1477–1547: Humanist and Reformer* (Cambridge, Mass.: Harvard University Press, 1959), 74; Josef Macek, "Osudy basilejských kompaktát v jagelonském věku," in *Jihlava a Basilejská Kompaktáta: Sborník příspěvků z mezinárodního sympozia k 555. výročí přijetí Basilejských kompaktát, 26–28. červen 1991* (Jihlava: Muzeum Vysočiny, 1992), 199–200. See also Alain Dufour, "Humanisme et Reformation," in Dufour, *Histoire politique et psychologie historique* (Geneva: Librairie Droz, 1966), 54.
193. Pelikan, "Luther's Attitude Toward John Hus," 757–761.
194. *Ibid.*, 757–758. On Emser, see Kawerau, *Hieronymus Emser*, 18, but Emser still denounced Hus in 1523 as an old heretic from whom Luther drew his ideas.
195. Emser, *De disputatione lipsicensi ad Boemos*, 14, 33.
196. In his *Dialogus ad Lutherum*, cited by Kraus in *Husitství v literatuře*, 1:154; Enders, *Dr. Martin Luthers Briefwechsel*, 2:176.
197. Martin Luther, *Schreiben an die boehmischen Landstaende. 1522*, in *WA*, Band 10, Zweite Abteilung, 169–174.

198. Tomek, *Dějepis města Prahy,* 10:544.
199. See reference to the pope's letter of October 6, 1524, to King Louis, in G. P. Mel'nikov, "Iz istorii obshchestvenno-politicheskoi borby Chekhii v dvatsatye gody XVI v.," *Sovetskoe slavianovedenie* 5 (1980): 58.
200. Letter from Floriano Montini to Erasmus, February 22, 1525, from Buda, in Erasmus, *The Correspondence,* 11:49.
201. Skýbová, "Česká šlechta a jednání o povolení kompaktát," 81–112; Antonín Rezek, "Příspěvky ku jednání o kompaktáta roku 1525," *Sborník historický* 2 (1884): 1–8.
202. Anna Skýbová, "Česká šlechta a jednání o povolení kompaktát r. 1525," 97.
203. Palacký, *Dějiny národu českého,* 5:531–532.
204. Bartoš Písař, *Kronika pražská,* 122.
205. Tomek, *Dějepis města Prahy,* 10:569, n. 52; Josef V. Šimák, "Ziga Vaníčkovic, účastník bouře pražské roku 1524," *Časopis českého musea* 78 (1904): 38; Mel'nikov, "Iz istorii obshchestvenno-politicheskoi," 58.
206. Šimák, "Úvod," xii, xv, xvii; see also Bartoš Písař, *Kronika pražská,* 109–111; Pešek, "Některé problémy bádání," 191.
207. Václav Hájek z Libočan, *Kronika česká,* ed. Jaroslav Kolár (Prague: Odeon, 1981), 693–694, 696.
208. Symeon Evstachyus Kapihorský, *Hystoria kláštera Sedleckého* (Prague: Pavel Sessius, 1630), 66; Jindřich Ondřej Hoffman, *Ocularia. Aneb oči sklenné starého Čecha* (Prague: Jiří Sedlčanský, 1637), 201–203.
209. *Antiqua et constans confessio fidei ecclesiae Christi in regno Boiemiae et Marchianatu Moraviae, quam vulgo partem sub utraque sacramentum venerabile corporis et sanguinis dom. Jesu Christi communicantium appellant,* with introduction by Matěj Kolín z Chotěřiny (Prague: n.p., 1574), f. E3v–F1v; Zacharyáš Bruncvík, *Testamenti nostri Iesu Christi pia et fida assertio. To jest: Kšaftu Večeře Páně svátá Starožitnost, pobožná posloupnost, dlouhověká až právě do dne soudného trvanlivost* (Prague: Matěj Pardubský, 1613), 163–169.
210. Erasmus, *The Correspondence,* 8:207–209, 415, n. 46. On the Roman side, the Curia officials Girolamo Aleandro and Alberto Pio, prince of Carpi, maintained that Erasmus was the source of Luther's heresies and ultimately of the religious upheaval in Germany. On the reformed side, Oecolampadius and Pellicanus asserted that Erasmus's teaching led them to embrace the Protestant position. See *The Correspondence,* 11:xvii, xx, 326–332.
211. Skýbová, "Česká šlechta a jednání o povolení kompaktát," 81–112; Tomek, *Dějepis města Prahy* 10:544–547, 575–582.
212. It may be recalled that Palacký classified the Lutherans of the 1520s as the party of progress (*pokrok*) and the Utraquists as the party of stagnation (*utkvělost*), in *Dějiny,* 5:514.
213. Josef Janáček, *České dějiny: Doba předbělohorská,* 2 vols. (Prague: Academia, 1971–1984), 1:192.
214. *Ibid.,* 1:199.
215. Eberhard, *Konfessionsbildung,* 142.
216. See, for instance, John Spurr, *English Puritanism, 1603–1689* (New York: St. Martin's Press, 1998), 104.
217. Luther, *De instituendis ministris,* in *WA,* 12:171; in Czech translation, Luther, *O ustanovení služebníků církve,* f. A3v. See also Jarold K. Zeman, "The Rise of Liberty in the Czech Reformation," *Central European History* 6 (1973): 131–138.

218. Bohuslav Bílejovský, *Kronyka Cýrkevní,* ed. Jozef Skalický (Josef Dittrich) (Prague: Fetterl z Vilden, 1816), 11. On the burning of Emser's books, see Kawerau, *Hieronymus Emser,* 34.

219. John E. Booty, "Hooker and Anglicanism," in *Studies in Richard Hooker,* ed. W. Speed Hill (Cleveland: Press of Case Western Reserve University, 1972), 211.

220. Alexandra Walsham, *Providence in Early Modern England* (Oxford: Oxford University Press, 1999), 334, cites primarily the work of Bob Scribner with related literature.

Chapter 4

1. The text of Bílejovský's work is available in a nineteenth-century edition edited by Jozef Skalický (pseudonym for Josef Dittrich) *Kronyka Cýrkevní* (Prague: Fetterl z Vilden, 1816). Born around 1480 in Malín near Kutná Hora, Bílejovský (pronounced Bee-lay-yof-skee) was ordained as a priest in Italy (probably in Venice) and served in Mělník, Čáslav, and Kutná Hora. Except for a brief mission to Tábor, from 1532 he lived in Prague where he was elected to the Consistory two years later and died in 1555. For biographic data on Bílejovský, see Josef V. Šimák, "Bohuslava Bílejovského Kronika česká," *Český časopis historický* 38 (1932): 92–93.

2. See, for instance, Josef Kalousek, "O historii kalicha v dobách předhusitských," in *Výroční zpráva obecního realného gymnasia v Praze na školní rok 1880/81* (Prague: n.p., 1881), 5, 18, 23; Jaroslav Vlček, *Dějiny české literatury,* 2 vols. (Prague: Ceskoslovenský spisovatel, 1951), 1:304–306; Jan Jakubec, *Dějiny literatury české,* 2d ed., 2 vols. (Prague: Laichter, 1929-1934), 1:652–653; Šimák, "Bohuslava Bílejovského Kronika česká," 102; František Kutnar, *Přehledné dějiny českého a slovenského dějepisectví,* 2 vols. (Prague: Státní pedagogické nakladatelství, 1973–1977), 1:53–54; Ivo Kořán, "Obraz a slovo v našich dějinách," in *Kapitoly z českého dějepisu umění,* 2 vols., ed. Rudolf Chadraba, et al. (Prague: Odeon, 1986), 1:17–18.

3. Antonii V. Florovskii, *Chekhi i vostochnye slaviane: Ocherki po istorii cheshsko-russkikh otnoshenii X-XVIII vv,* 2 vols. (Prague: Slovanský ústav, 1935–1947), 1:403; Howard Kaminsky, *A History of the Hussite Revolution* (Berkeley: University of California Press, 1967), 99; František Šmahel, *Husitská revoluce,* 4 vols. (Prague: Historický ústav, 1993), 1:13.

4. Kamil Krofta, "Slovo o knězi Bohuslavu Bílejovském," in Krofta, *Listy z náboženských dějin českých* (Prague: Historický klub, 1936), 293, 297–298.

5. I wish to thank once more Robert J. W. Evans for his suggesting an examination of historical and theological views of Hooker and other sixteenth-century Anglican or proto-Anglican divines for parallels with Bílejovský's concepts, and to Patricia M. Springborg for recommending participation in the Jubilee Conference on Richard Hooker, co-sponsored by the Folger Library and the National Cathedral in Washington, D.C., September 1993. On Hooker's ecclesiological task, see Donald R. Kelley, "Elizabethan Political Thought," in *The Varieties of British Political Thought, 1500–1800,* ed. J. G. A. Pocock (Cambridge: Cambridge University Press, 1993), 63–64. On his setting the "parameters" of Anglican thought, see Peter Lake, "Business as Usual? The immediate Reception of Hooker's *Ecclesiastical Polity,*" *Journal of Ecclesiastical History* 52 (2001): 456–457.

6. References to the *LEP* are to Richard Hooker, *The Folger Library Edition of*

the Works of Richard Hooker, 6 vols., ed. W. Speed Hill (Cambridge, Mass.: Belknap Press of Harvard University Press, 1977–1993).

7. Jarold K. Zeman, *The Hussite Movement and the Reformation in Bohemia, Moravia and Slovakia, 1350–1650* (Ann Arbor, Mich.: Michigan Slavic Publications, 1977), xvi; Antony Black, *Political Thought in Europe, 1250–1450* (New York: Cambridge University Press, 1992), 81.

8. John Jewel, Bishop of Salisbury, *An Apologie, or Answer in Defense of the Church of England* (1562; New York: De Capo Press, 1972). This work appeared in a Czech translation in 1619, probably too late to have a significant direct impact on the development of Utraquism, as *Apologia, to jest: Dostatečná Obrana Víry a Náboženství Cýrkví Englických* (Prague: Danyel Karel z Karlspergka, 1619).

9. Bílejovský, *Kronyka Cýrkevní,* 27.

10. Václav Koranda, Jr., *Traktát o velebné a božské svátosti oltářní* ([Prague?]: Tiskař Korandy, 1493), f. A5v.

11. Diarmaid MacCulloch, *The Later Reformation in England, 1547–1603* (New York: St. Martin's Press, 1990), 98; see also John Spurr, *English Puritanism, 1603–1689* (New York: St. Martin's Press, 1998), 82, 86–87.

12. Bílejovský, *Kronyka Cýrkevní,* 2, 28.

13. Jan Chlíbec, "K vývoji názorů Jana Rokycany na umělecké dílo," *Husitský Tábor* 8 (1985): 54.

14. Bílejovský, *Kronyka Cýrkevní,* 16.

15. *Ibid.*, 7; František M. Bartoš, *Čechy v době Husově, 1378–1415* (Prague: Laichter, 1947), 396. Pope Leo I's decree (c. 450), censuring communion only under the species of bread, provided another piece of evidence; see František M. Bartoš, *Husitství a cizina* (Prague: Čin, 1931), 86, 255.

16. Bílejovský, *Kronyka Cýrkevní,* 7–8, 16. For Václav Koranda's views, see Koranda, *Traktát o velebné a božské svátosti oltářní,* f. M5r–M6v, N8v–O1v. Josef Skalický, the editor of *Kronyka Cýrkevní,* without citing evidence, maintains that communion sub una started in the Western Church after the Fourth Council of Lateran in 1215; *Kronyka Cýrkevní,* 137. John M. Klassen maintains that "by the late thirteenth century communion in one kind was common." See his "Communion under Both Kinds," *Dictionary of the Middle Ages,* 13 vols. (New York: Scribner's, 1982–1989), 3:504.

17. Steven E. Ozment, *The Reformation in the Cities: The Appeal of Protestantism to Sixteenth-Century Germany and Switzerland* (New Haven, Conn.: Yale University Press, 1975), 2–3.

18. Bílejovský, *Kronyka Cýrkevní,* 30–31. According to Bílejovský, this practice lasted in Rome until the death of Pope Pius II in 1464; *ibid.,* 31. He also claims that as late as the 1390s, Pope Boniface IX approved communion sub utraque for the church of St. Barbara in Kutná Hora; *ibid.,* 28.

19. Klassen, "Communion under Both Kinds," 3:504.

20. Bílejovský, *Kronyka Cýrkevní,* 16–17.

21. *Ibid.,* 25.

22. *Ibid.*

23. "[C]ommunicare autem sub una specie [videtur] esse heresis." Cited by Otakar Odložilík, "Utrakvistická postilla z r. 1540," *Věstník české společnosti nauk* (1925): 5, n. 13.

24. Bílejovský, *Kronyka Cýrkevní,* 4, 7–8. On the importance and significance of communion for infants and small children in Utraquism, see David R. Holeton, "The

Communion of Infants and Hussitism," *Communio Viatorum* 27 (1984): 204–225; Holeton, "The Communion of Infants: The Basel Years," *Communio Viatorum* 29 (1986): 15–40; and Holeton, *La communion des tout-petits enfants; Étude du mouvement eucharistique en Bohême vers la fin du Moyen-Âge* (Rome: Edizioni Liturgiche, 1989), especially 235–303.

25. "[S]ic nunc turbantur, cum vident Christum nasci per predicacionem verbi eius, cum communicant corpori ac sangvini domini et ipsi pueri . . ." Odložilík, "Utrakvistická postilla z r. 1540," 7, n. 17.

26. See Holeton, *La communion des tout-petits enfants*, 83–162; Odložilík, "Utrakvistická postilla z r. 1540," 24.

27. Koranda devotes an entire section to this issue in *Traktát o velebné a božské svátosti oltářní*, f. R1r–S8v, especially f. R5r–v. Bydžovský's views are more fully developed in Chapter 5. On the Lutheran attitude, see Jan Štelcar Želetavský z Želetavy, *Kniha nová o původu kněžství Krista Pána* (Prague: Daniel Sedlčanský, 1592), f. D5–3v, f. N4–2r.

28. Bílejovský, *Kronyka Cýrkevní*, 17.

29. *Ibid.*, 8–9.

30. *Ibid.*, 9, 18. The actual time span was thirty-four years; on p. 9, Bílejovský gives the correct death date for Očko as 1380.

31. David R. Holeton, "Revelation and Revolution in Late Medieval Bohemia," *Communio Viatorum* 36 (1994): 35, 40–41.

32. Josef Kalousek, *O potřebě prohloubit vědomosti o Husovi a jeho době* (Prague: Českoslovanská akciová tiskárna, 1915), 19; and Josef Kalousek, ed., "Dvě bully dané do Kutné Hory r. 1401 a 1403," *Zprávy královské společnosti nauk: Třída Filosofie-Historie-Filologie* (1885): 141–142. In defense of Bílejovský, see Krofta, "Slovo o knězi Bohuslavu Bílejovském," 300–301.

33. Helena Krmíčková, for instance, notes that concerning the attempts to credit Matěj of Janov with advocacy of communion sub utraque: "At this time we are not surprised even by the arguments for the chalice supported by citing Janov, [as] this method was used already by Jakoubek, but the references to the chalice are ex post facto inserted in Matěj's work either as glosses, or directly through a subsequent reworking of the text." See Krmíčková, *Studie a texty k počátkům kalicha v Čechách,* Spisy Masarykovy univerzity v Brně, Filozofická fakulta, 310 (Brno: Masarykova univerzita, 1997), 8.

34. Josef Kalousek, "Ruské bádání o příčinách a účelích hnutí husitského," *Časopis českého musea* 56 (1882): 102; see also Bílejovský, *Kronyka Cýrkevní*, 138, n. 30.

35. Koranda, *Traktát o velebné a božské svátosti oltářní*, f. E3r–E3v; see also Kamil Krofta, "Václav Koranda mladší z Nové Plzně a jeho názory náboženské," in Krofta, *Listy z náboženských dějin českých* (Prague: Historický klub, 1936), 262.

36. Krmíčková, *Studie a texty k počátkům kalicha v Čechách,* 26–29; Koranda, *Traktát o velebné a božské svátosti oltářní*, f. E3r.

37. Bílejovský, *Kronyka Cýrkevní*, 18.

38. Bílejovský, *Kronyka Cýrkevní*, Introduction, 24. The Anglicans encountered similar questionings of their ecclesiastical origins; see Paul D. L. Avis, *Anglicanism and the Christian Church* (Minneapolis: Fortress Press, 1989), 179.

39. Anthony Milton, *Catholic and Reformed: The Roman and Protestant Churches in English Protestant Thought, 1600–1640* (Cambridge and New York: Cambridge University Press, 1995), 146–157.

40. For instance, Johann Rainer, ed., *Nuntiaturberichte aus Deutschland*, Abteilung

2, 1560–1572, vol. 8 (Graz: Boehlaus, 1967), 46–47; Abteilung 3, 6:154, 365, 369; Almut Bues, ed., Abteilung 3, 1572–1585, vol. 7 (Tübingen: Niemeyer, 1990), 49, 88. See also Klaus Jaitner, ed., *Die Hauptinstruktionen Clemens' VIII. für die Nuntien und Legaten an den europäischen Fürstenhöfen, 1592–1605,* 2 vols. (Tübingen: Niemeyer, 1984), 1:59, 2:710.

41. Rainer, *Nuntiaturberichte aus Deutschland,* Abteilung 3, 6:467; see also Bues, Abteilung 3, 7:98, 376.

42. Bílejovský, *Kronyka Cýrkevní,* 7, 23–25.

43. A condemnation of the temporal power and wealth of the Church was incorporated into the third article of the Compactata; see František M. Bartoš, *Husitská revoluce,* 2 vols. (Prague: Nakladatelství Československé akademie věd, 1965–1966), 2: 226. The demand for disendowment of the church was reinforced also by Wyclif's disciple, Peter Payne, who had been chosen to defend the third article at the Council of Basel; see Richard R. Betts, *Essays in Czech History* (London: Athlone, 1969), 246. On Wyclif's attitude, see also Gordon Leff, "Wyclif and Hus: A Doctrinal Comparison," in *Wyclif in His Times,* ed. Anthony Kenny (Oxford: Clarendon Press, 1986), 113; and Michael Wilks, "*Reformatio Regni:* Wyclif and Hus as Leaders of Religious Protest Movements," *Studies in Church History* 9 (1972): 90, 118.

44. Vilém Herold stressed their concentration on the denunciation of clerical power and wealth in Matthew 23:2–4, and in patristic literature, particularly by St. Gregory the Great, Pseudo-Chrysostom, and St. Bernard of Clairvaux. See Herold, "How Wycliffite Was the Bohemian Reformation?" in *The Bohemian Reformation and Religious Practice,* vol. 2: Papers from the XVIIIth World Congress of the Czechoslovak Society of Arts and Sciences, Brno 1996, ed. Zdeněk V. David and David R. Holeton (Prague: Academy of Sciences of the Czech Republic, Main Library, 1998), 28–32; and Thomas A. Fudge, *The Magnificent Ride: The First Reformation in Hussite Bohemia* (Brookfield, Vt.: Ashgate, 1998), 218–222, 226–228.

45. Bílejovský, *Kronyka Cýrkevní,* 21; see also 11, 114–115.

46. Odložilík, "Utrakvistická postilla z r. 1540," 8.

47. *Ibid.,* 16–17.

48. Bílejovský, *Kronyka Cýrkevní,* 13, 30; Jaroslav Eršil, ed., *Acta Martini V, pontificis Romani,* Part 1, 1417–1422, vol. 8 of *Monumenta Vaticana res gestas Bohemicas illustrantia (MBV)* (Prague: Academia, 1996), no. 900, 369–371.

49. Matthew Spinka, *John Hus: A Biography* (Princeton, N.J.: Princeton University Press, 1968), 114–115, 120; Fudge, *The Magnificent Ride,* 74.

50. Bílejovský, *Kronyka Cýrkevní,* 13, 30. On the Utraquists' opposition to calling the pope the Antichrist, see also *Sněmy české od léta 1526 až po naši dobu.,* vols. 1–11, 15 (Prague: Zemský výbor, 1877–1941), 7:397. Equating the pope with the Antichrist was not only a hallmark of the Lutheran reformation. Wyclif also made this claim; see Wilks, "*Reformatio Regni:* Wyclif and Hus as Leaders of Religious Protest Movements," 117. On the pope as the Antichrist for Wyclif and for the Lollards, see, respectively, Alexander Patschovsky, "'Antichrist' by Wyclif," and Anne Hudson, "Lollardy and Eschatology," both in *Eschatologie und Hussitismus,* ed. Alexander Patschovsky and František Šmahel, Internationales Kolloquium, Prague, September 1–4, 1993 (Prague: Historický ústav, 1996), 83–98 and 99–113.

51. In his reluctance to perceive the pope as the Antichrist, Bílejovský again resembles Anglican divines such as Hooker or Montagu. See Robert K. Faulkner, *Richard Hooker and the Politics of a Christian England* (Berkeley: University of California

Press, 1981), 31; Diarmaid MacCulloch, "Richard Hooker's Reputation," *English Historical Review* 117 (2002): 775; Milton, *Catholic and Reformed,* 111, 117, 119; Richard Montagu, *A Gagg for the New Gospell? No, a New Gagg for an Old Goose* (London: T. Snodham, 1624), 74–75. The English Puritans, however, delighted in denouncing the pope as the Antichrist or the Whore of Babylon. See Spurr, *English Puritanism,* 94–95; Alexandra Walsham, *"Vox Piscis; or the Book-Fish:* Providence and the Uses of the Reformation Past in Caroline Cambridge," *English Historical Review* 114 (1999): 602–604. English Lutherans, such as William Tyndale in the 1530s and also Archbishop Cranmer (in a sermon of 1536), did not hesitate to identify the pope with the Antichrist. See Diarmaid MacCulloch, *Thomas Cranmer: A Life* (New Haven, Conn.: Yale University Press, 1996), 150, 580.

52. Similarly, Erasmus refused to refer to any pope as the Antichrist. See Desiderius Erasmus, *The Correspondence,* 11 vols. (Toronto: University of Toronto Press, 1974–1994), 9:398. On the symbolism of the Antichrist, see Rosemary Muir Wright, *Art and AntiChrist in Medieval Europe* (Manchester: Manchester University Press, 1995).

53. Her invective in admonishing the popes to return from Avignon was cited earlier: "The successor of Peter is now the destroyer of souls, worse than the devil, less just than Pilate, more cruel than Judas." Bohdan Chudoba, *Jindy a nyní: Dějiny českého národa* (Prague: Vyšehrad, 1946), 109.

54. Fudge, *The Magnificent Ride,* 242.

55. "Anižť oni co o podstatné křesťanstva, jako náměstcy apoštolští, k zachování pečují v milosti, jen aby k své vůli všecky podmánili, užívajíce a popauzejíce mocý světských, aby y oni jich služebnícy a ne Boží byli, a oni v jich panství pychali." Bílejovský, *Kronyka Cýrkevní,* 37–38.

56. Paul de Vooght, *L'hérésie de Jean Huss,* 2d ed., 2 vols. (Louvain: Publications universitaires, 1975), 2:832.

57. Pavel Bydžovský, *Děťátka a neviňátka hned po přijetí křtu sv. Tělo a Krev Boží, že přijímati mají* (Prague: Bartoloměj Netolický, 1541), f. B–3v.

58. See, for instance, Koranda, *Traktát o velebné a božské svátosti oltářní,* f. T1r–V6r.

59. Bílejovský, *Kronyka Cýrkevní,* 21–22.

60. See Marie Bláhová, ed., *Kronika tak řečeného Dalimila* (Prague: Svoboda, 1977), 121; Zdeněk Tobolka, ed., *Kališnický pasionál z roku 1495,* Monumenta Bohemiae typographica, vol. 2 (Prague: n.p., 1926), f. F16v.

61. Bílejovský, *Kronyka Cýrkevní,* 20.

62. Bílejovský, *Kronyka Cýrkevní,* 22–23, 46. The "Alchymus" is probably the Hellenized member of a Jewish priestly family, Alcimus, who was appointed high priest in Jerusalem (162–160/59 B.C.) with the assistance of Demetrius I Soter, the Seleucid ruler of Syria, to combat Judah Maccabee and his followers; see *Encyclopaedia Judaica,* 2nd ed., 16 vols. (Jerusalem: Keter, 1973), 2:550.

63. Bílejovský, *Kronyka Cýrkevní,* 23. He probably refers to Nicholas's *Confessio Taboritarum* of 1431 (see Zeman, *The Hussite Movement and Reformation,* 179); and to the *Apology* of the Bohemian Brethren, published in 1511, which also attracted the attention of Erasmus and Luther (see Rudolf Říčan, et al., *Jednota Bratrská, 1457–1957: Sborník k pětistému výročí založení* [Prague: Kalich, 1956], 29).

64. Bílejovský, *Kronyka Cýrkevní,* 23. Anne Hudson describes similar arguments against the use of English for theological writings at the turn of the fourteenth century, citing in part from a manuscript in the Brno University Library. See Hudson, "Lollardy:

the English Heresy?" in Hudson, *Lollards and Their Books* (London: Hambledon Press, 1985), 157–158.

65. Koranda, *Traktát o velebné a božské svátosti oltářní,* f. T1r–V3r.
66. Odložilík, "Utrakvistická postilla z r. 1540," 20.
67. Bílejovský, *Kronyka Cýrkevní,* 8–10, 13, 27–28, 46,
68. *Ibid.,* 13.
69. Vavřinec z Březové, *Husitská kronika,* ed. Marie Bláhová (Prague: Svoboda, 1979), 88–89. See also Božena Kopičková, *Jan Želivský* (Prague: Melantrich, 1990), 94. See also Koranda, *Traktát o velebné a božské svátosti oltářní,* f. A3v.
70. *Ibid.,* 13–14.
71. Odložilík, "Utrakvistická postilla z r. 1540," 24. For an earlier view see Kamil Krofta, "O některých spisech M. Jana z Příbramě," *Časopis českého musea* 73 (1899): 213.
72. Jan Hus, *Výklady* (Magistri Iohannis Hus Opera Omnia, 1) (Prague: Academia, 1975), 188–189, referring to Nehemiah, 13:23–25; Josephus Flavius, *Historia židovská. Na knihy čtyry rozdělená,* trans. and introduction by Václav Plácel z Elbingu (Prague: Daniel Adam of Veleslavín, 1592), 2–7.
73. Kopičková, *Jan Želivský,* 20.
74. Rudolf Urbánek, "Český mesianismus ve své době hrdinské," *Od pravěku k dnešku: Sborník k 60. narozeninám J. Pekaře,* 2 vols. (Prague: Historický klub, 1930), 1:262–284, especially 263–264.
75. Bílejovský, *Kronyka Cýrkevní,* 39–41; Krofta, "Slovo o knězi Bohuslavu Bílejovském," 296–297.
76. See, for instance, Ewa Maleczyńska, *Ruch husycki w Czechach i w Polsce* (Warsaw: Ksiażka i Wiedza, 1959); Richard Pražák, "Zu den Beziehungen zwischen den Böhmischen Ländern und Ungarn zu Zeiten Matthias Corvinus," in *Matthias Corvinus and the Humanism in Central Europe,* ed. Tibor Klaniczay and József Jankovics (Budapest: Balassi Kiadó, 1994), 193–202; Josef Macůrek, "Husitství v rumuských zemích," *Časopis Matice moravské* 51 (1927): 1–98.
77. Pavel Bydžovský, *Odvolání jednoho Bratra z Roty Pikhartské,* 2d ed. (Prague: Jan Jičínský, 1588), f. C5r–D1v.
78. Rosemary O'Day, *The Debate on the English Reformation* (London: Methuen, 1986), 17, 20.
79. MacCulloch, *The Later Reformation in England,* 99; Milton, *Catholic and Reformed,* 303.
80. Zdeněk Kalista, *Josef Pekař* (Prague: Torst, 1994), 176, 180.
81. Bílejovský, *Kronyka Cýrkevní,* 27, 39–41.
82. On similar qualities in the religious attitudes of Hooker, see *The Folger Library Edition of the Works,* 6:part 1, 79–80 and the literature cited there.
83. Josef Jireček, *Rukověť k dějinám literatury české,* 2 vols. (Prague: Tempský, 1875–1876), 1:116.
84. See the Consistory's response of July 28, 1548, to a noble's request to replace the Lutheran minister on his estate with a Utraquist priest who would be able to serve a German-speaking congregation. Klement Borový, *Jednání a dopisy konsistoře katolické a utrakvistické,* 2 vols. (Prague: I. L. Kober, 1868–1869), 1:229.
85. Concerning the Unity, see also Rudolf Říčan, *The History of the Unity of Brethren: A Protestant Hussite Church in Bohemia and Moravia,* trans. C. Daniel Crews (Bethlehem, Pa.: Moravian Church in America, 1992).

86. Bílejovský, *Kronyka Cýrkevní*, 50. Kaminsky seeks to identify the "Picardi" with the "Beghardi" or the Brethren of the Free Spirit who were widespread in fourteenth-century Europe and condemned by the Council of Vienne in 1311. See Kaminsky, *A History of the Hussite Revolution*, 354–355. The term "Berghardi" had already been used as a vague term of insult for heretics by Jan Milíč of Kroměříž; see Holeton, *La communion des tout-petits enfants*, 21. The main competitors of the Picardi for ideological input into radical Taboritism were the Waldensians and the Lollards (the folkish followers of Wyclif). See Josef Pekař, *Žižka a jeho doba*, 4 vols. (Prague: Vesmír, 1927–1933), 1:15–17; and Anne Hudson, "A Lollard Compilation in England and Bohemia," in *Lollards and Their Books* (London: Hambledon Press, 1985), 31–42. To complicate the situation further, Václav Tomek identifies the forty-two men with women and children, French by nationality, who arrived in 1418 in Prague as Waldensians, who were soon suspected of heresy and called Pikarts or "bekardi"; see Václav V. Tomek, *Dějepis města Prahy*, 12 vols. (Prague: Řivnáč, 1855–1901), 3:624. As we shall see, Bílejovský, however, categorically rejects the influence of the Waldensians and, at least in part, seeks to rehabilitate Wyclif.

87. Bartoš, *Husitská revoluce*, 1:116. In his correspondence with the Brethren in 1540, Calvin questioned their designation as Pikarts; see [Jan Černý], "Poznamenání a spolu shromáždění některých věcí pamětihodných přítomným i budoucím," 1579 (manuscript, Prague Bib. Nat. XVII C 3), f. 143v. Fynes Moryson also calls the Brethren "Picards"; see Moryson, *Shakespeare's Europe: A Survey of the Conditions of Europe at the End of the 16th Century*, ed. Charles Hughes (London: Sherratt & Hughes, 1903), 277.

88. Bílejovský, *Kronyka Cýrkevní*, 51–53.

89. Vavřinec z Březové, *Husitská kronika*, ed. Marie Bláhová (Prague: Svoboda, 1979), 196–197.

90. "[V]eliký a znamenitý Doktor Římské Církve Svaté Ambrož . . ." Pavel Bydžovský, *Děťátka a neviňátka hned po přijetí křtu sv. Tělo a Krev Boží, že přijímati mají* (Prague: Bartoloměj Netolický, 1541), f. A3v.

91. Enrico S. Molnar, "Viklef, Hus a problém autority," in *Jan Hus mezi epochami, národy a konfesemi*, ed. Jan B. Lášek (Prague: Česká křesťanská akademie, 1995), 111–114.

92. Bílejovský, *Kronyka Cýrkevní*, 53, 55.

93. *Ibid.*, 25–26.

94. Šmahel, *Husitská revoluce*, 1:104–106.

95. Blažej Nožička z Votína, *Knížka proti bludům některým před tisíci lety odsouzeným* (Prague: Jan Kantor, 1566), f. K(v). Sweden is an example of another nation that turned to pacifism from, and possibly as a reaction to, an earlier history of bloodshed and military ferocity.

96. Georg Lauterbach, *Politica historica: O vrchnostech a správcích světských knihy patery*, trans. Daniel Adam of Veleslavín (Prague: Daniel Adam of Veleslavín, 1584); Kopecký, *Daniel Adam z Veleslavína* (Prague: Svobodné slovo, 1962), 25. Conversely, by the latter part of the sixteenth century, the Czechs' military reputation, acquired during the wars of the Bohemian Reformation, had markedly declined. See, for instance, Karel Stloukal, "Z diplomatických styků mezi Francií a Čechami před Bílou Horou," *Český časopis historický* (1926): 489.

97. Bílejovský, *Kronyka Cýrkevní*, 109; see also 105; and Šimák, "Bohuslava Bílejovského Kronika česká," 101. On the relationship between the Bohemian Brethren and

the Waldensians, often called Waldensian Brethren (*fratres Valdenses*), see Giovanni Gonnet and Amadeo Molnár, *Les Vaudois en Moyen Âge* (Turin: Claudiana, 1974), and Říčan, *The History of the Unity of Brethren*, 70–71.
98. Pavel Bydžovský, *Tato Knižka toto try ukazuje* (N.p., [after 1541]), 2.
99. Bílejovský, *Kronyka Cýrkevní*, 102.
100. On Wyclif's influence, see also Gordon Leff, "Wyclif and Hus," 105–125; Betts, *Essays in Czech History*, 29–62, 132–59; Vilém Herold, *Pražská univerzita a Wyclif* (Prague: Univerzita Karlova, 1985); and David R. Holeton, "Wyclif's Bohemian Fate: A Reflection on the Contextualization of Wyclif in Bohemia," *Communio Viatorum* 32 (1989): 209–222.
101. Bílejovský, *Kronyka Cýrkevní*, 90. See also Pekař, *Žižka a jeho doba*, 1: 140–141; and Ferdinand Hrejsa, *Dějiny křesťanství v Československu*, 6 vols. (Prague: Husova československá evangelická fakulta bohoslovecká, 1946–1950), 2:218–219. On Payne, see also Betts, *Essays in Czech History*, 236–246.
102. Payne together with Jakoubek defended Wyclif against Jan of Příbram's charges of Eucharistic unorthodoxy, particularly in 1426. See Bartoš, *Husitská revoluce*, 2:18, 25, 56; Kaminsky, *A History of the Hussite Revolution*, 461; William R. Cook, "John Wyclif and Hussite Theology, 1415–1436," *Church History* 42 (1973): 341–342.
103. Bílejovský, *Kronyka Cýrkevní*, 11. This was incidentally correct. Hus did not adopt Wyclif's remanentism, as shown by David R. Holeton, "Liturgická a svátostná teologie Mistra Jana Husa," *Theologická revue* 1 (1996), 9-12.
104. Bílejovský, *Kronyka Cýrkevní*, 11. On earlier ridicule of the archbishop, see Fudge, *The Magnificent Ride*, 207.
105. Bílejovský, *Kronyka Cýrkevní*, 86. See also Zdeněk Nejedlý, *Prameny k synodám strany pražské a táborské (vznik husitské konfese) v létech 1441–1444* (Prague: Královská česká společnost nauk, 1900), 168–169. The actual end of the Taborites' distinct ecclesiastical organization, of course, followed only in 1452. See Chapter 2.
106. Bílejovský, *Kronyka Cýrkevní*, 90; see also 95.
107. *Ibid.*, 99.
108. *Ibid.*
109. *Ibid.*
110. Bartoš, *Husitská revoluce*, 1:21, 37. Nicholas was immolated as a heretic in Meissen about 1416; *ibid.*, 22.
111. Bílejovský, *Kronyka Cýrkevní*, 100.
112. Hooker, *The Folger Library Edition of the Works*, 1:191–192 (*LEP* II.8.7); Bílejovský, *Kronyka Cýrkevní*, 103 (see also 102).
113. Bílejovský, *Kronyka Cýrkevní*, 104.
114. Pavel Bydžovský, *Křesťanské Víry upřímné o Těle a Krvi Boží vyznání*. (N.p., 1546), 10–11.
115. Odložilík, "Utrakvistická postilla z r. 1540," 6–7. Wyclif's contention paralleled the rigorous early Christian views of the Donatists.
116. Ferdinand Menčík, ed., *Zápisky kněze Václava Rosy* (Vienna: J. Paška, 1879), 18.
117. Rudolf Říčan, "Tschechische Übersetzungen von Luthers Schriften bis zum Schmalkaldischen Krieg," *Vierhundertfünfzig Jahre lutherische Reformation, 1517–1967 (Festschrift für Franz Lau zum 50. Geburtstag)* (Göttingen: Vanderhoeck and Ruprecht, 1967), 282–288.
118. Bílejovský, *Kronyka Cýrkevní*, 27.

119. *Ibid.*, 1, 22. The image of Cyril and Methodius as agents of the pope may be found also in Tobolka, *Kališnický pasionál z roku 1495*, 2:f. K9r. The attribution of the Slavic script and liturgy to St. Jerome was widespread. See, for instance, the assertion of Šimon Lomnický of Budeč in the introduction to his translation of Eusebius Cremonensis, *Kšaft Sv. Jeronýma sepsaný od jeho žáka* (Prague: n.p., 1613), f. A6r.

120. On the "Cyrillomethodian theory," see Helena Krmíčková, *Studie a texty k počátkům kalicha v Čechách*, Spisy Masarykovy univerzity v Brně, Filozofická fakulta, 310 (Brno: Masarykova univerzita, 1997), 3, 5, 8, 13.

121. Aleksander Gwagnin (Alessandro Guagnini), *Kronyka Moskevská*, trans. Matouš Hosius z Vysokého Mýta (Prague: Daniel Adam z Veleslavína, 1589), introduction, f. 4r–4v; *Kronyka Moskevská*, 2d ed. (Prague: Daniel Adam z Veleslavína, 1602). Its basis was apparently Aleksander Gwagnin's *Sarmatiae Europeae descriptio* (Cracow: Matthias Wirzebieta, 1578), and *Gesta praecipua tyrannisque ingens Monarchae Moscoviae nuper perpetrata* (Speyer: B. Albinus, 1581). The author, also known as Alessandro Guagnini, was a Polish warrior and historian of Italian background (1548–1614).

122. Gwagnin, *Kronyka Moskevská*, introduction, f. 5r.

123. Milada Paulová, "Styky českých husitů s cařihradskou církví na základě církevních poměrů byzantských," *Časopis českého musea* 93 (1919): 27.

124. Bydžovský, *Dět'átka a neviňátka hned po přijetí křtu sv. Tělo a Krev Boží, že přijímati mají*, f. B4r–B4v.

125. *Ibid.*, f. B3v–B4r, B7r–B7v.

126. Koranda, *Traktát o velebné a božské svátosti oltářní*, f. A5v.

127. Bydžovský, *Dět'átka a neviňátka*, f. B1r–B1v.

128. Holeton, "The Communion of Infants: The Basel Years," 35.

129. David R. Holeton, "The Evolution of Utraquist Eucharistic Liturgy: A Textual Study," in *The Bohemian Reformation and Religious Practice*, vol. 2: Papers from the XVIIIth World Congress of the Czechoslovak Society of Arts and Sciences, Brno 1996, ed. Zdeněk V. David and David R. Holeton (Prague: Academy of Sciences of the Czech Republic, Main Library, 1998), 126. Archbishop Cranmer also drew on the Mozarabic rite, as a more ancient one, for the Book of Common Prayer; Holeton, "The Evolution of Utraquist Eucharistic Liturgy," 123, n. 108.

130. Zdeněk Nejedlý, *Dějiny husitského zpěvu*, 5 vols. (Prague: Nakladatelství Československé akademie věd, 1955), 1:39; Francis Dvornik, *Byzantine Missions Among the Slavs: SS. Constantine-Cyril and Methodius* (New Brunswick, N.J.: Rutgers University Press, 1970), 111–116; Josef Vašica, *Literární památky epochy velkomoravské, 863–885* (Prague: Vyšehrad, 1995), 47–51. See also Francis Dvornik, *Les légendes de Constantin et de Méthode vues de Byzance*, 2d ed. (Hattiesburg, Miss.: Academic International, 1969), especially 295–313.

131. J. M. Clifton-Everest, "Slawisches Schrifttum im 10. und 11. Jahrhundert in Böhmen," *Bohemia* 37 (1996): 266–267. See also Václav Konzal, "Církevněslovanská literatura: slepá ulička na prahu české kultury?" in *Speculum medii aevi: Zrcadlo středověku*, ed. Lenka Jiroušková (Prague: Koniasch Latin Press, 1998), 153.

132. In the first half of the sixteenth century a large number, perhaps a majority, of Utraquist priests were ordained in Venice by the Greek bishops Dionysius de Franciscis and Titus Cheronensus in the monastery of Sancta Maria del Horto. See Tomek, *Dějepis města Prahy*, 12:235; Borový, *Jednání a dopisy konsistoře*, 1:161. See also Chapter 6.

133. Jakubec, *Dějiny literatury české*, 1:652. See also Krofta, "Slovo o knězi Bo-

huslavu Bílejovském," 300; Pavel Stránský, *Český stát. Okřik* (Prague: Státní nakladatelství krásné literatury, hudby a umění, 1953), 168–170; and Jan A. Komenský, *Stručná historie církve slovanské,* ed. Josef Hendrich (Prague: Melantrich, 1941), 24.

134. See Kamil Krofta, "Byl M. Pavel Stránský český bratr?" *Časopis českého musea* 90 (1916): 38–39. Stránský's misinterpretation of Bílejovský was noted already by Tomáš G. Masaryk, *Česká otázka. Naše nynější krise,* 6th ed., Spisy (Prague: Čin, 1948), 197–198.

135. H. R. Trevor-Roper, "The Church of England and the Greek Church in the Time of Charles I," *Studies in Church History* 15 (1978): 213–240; W. Brown Patterson, *King James VI and I and the Reunion of Christendom* (Cambridge: Cambridge University Press, 1997).

136. Pierre Costil, *André Dudith, humaniste hongrois 1533–1589: Sa vie, son oeuvre et ses manuscrits grecs* (Paris: Les Belles Lettres, 1935), 229, 231, 233. Byzantine texts, however, had little influence on Cramer's liturgical reforms; see MacCulloch, *Thomas Cranmer: A Life,* 415–416.

137. *New Catholic Encyclopedia* (New York: McGraw-Hill, 1967–1974), 10:673.

138. See Chapter 2.

139. Rudolf Urbánek, *Věk poděbradský,* 4 vols., pt. 3 of *České dějiny* (Prague: Laichter, 1915-1962), 2:614, 616–617.

140. Martin Luther, *Disputatio Iohannis Eccii et Martini Lutheri Lipsiae habita. 1519,* in Luther, *Werke: Kritische Gesammtausgabe* (Weimar: Böhlau, 1884), 2:276, 279; Luther, *Von dem Papstthum zu Rom wider den hochberühmten Romanisten zu Leipzig 1520,* in Luther, *Werke: Kritische Gesammtausgabe,* 6:287. See also Josef Čihula, "Martin Luther a Čechové pod obojí," *Český časopis historický* 3 (1897): 280–281, 337.

141. Karel J. Erben, ed., *Výbor z literatury české,* 2 vols. (Prague: Řivnáč, 1845–1868), 2:1041; Vladmír Forst, et al., eds., *Lexikon české literatury: Osobnosti, díla, instituce* (Prague: Academia, 1985), 2: pt 2, 339–340.

142. Bílejovský, *Kronyka Cýrkevní,* 88–104.

143. Pavel Bydžovský, *Knížky o přijímání Těla a Krve Pána našeho Jeříše Krysta pod obojí způsobou* ([Prague]: n.p., 1538–1539), f. 11v–14v; Pavel Bydžovský, *Tato Knizka toto try ukazuje* (N.p., [after 1541]), 9–10, 18; Pavel Bydžovský, *Tento spis ukazuje, že Biskupové Biskupa, a Biskup kněží, a kněží od řádných Biskupů svěceni Těla a krve Boží posvěcovati mají* (N.p., 1543), 6–7.

144. Borový, *Jednání a dopisy konsistoře,* 1:247; Jireček, *Rukověť k dějinám literatury české,* 1:116.

145. Pamphilus Eusebius, *Historie cýrkevní,* trans., Jan Kocín z Kocinétu (Prague: Daniel Adam z Veleslavína, 1594); Flavius Magnus Cassiodorus, Senator, *Historie cýrkevní,* trans. Jan Kocín z Kocinétu (Prague: Daniel Adam z Veleslavína, 1594).

146. Richard M. Douglas, *Jacopo Sadoleto, 1477–1547: Humanist and Reformer* (Cambridge, Mass.: Harvard University Press, 1959), 80–81.

147. Gwagnin, *Kronika Moskevská,* 105–106, 111.

148. "Též o neslýchaném Tyranství Ivana Vasiloviče Knížete Moskevského, kteréž on za paměti naší nad poddanými svými provozoval." Gwagnin, *Kronyka Moskevská,* title page, also 199–206.

149. The simile goes back at least to the early seventeenth century when Bishop Richard Montigu wrote that the Church of England had "to stand in the gapp against puritanisme and popery, the Scila and Charybdis of Ancient Piety," *DNB,* 3:713.

150. MacCulloch, *The Later Reformation in England*, 97, 99.
151. John S. Marshall, *Hooker and the Anglican Tradition* (Sewanee, Tenn.: University Press, 1963), 38–39; Avis, *Anglicanism and the Christian Church*, 51–52.
152. Hooker, *The Folger Library Edition of the Works*, 2:121 (*LEP* V.28.1).
153. *Ibid.*, 1:202 (*LEP* III.1.10).
154. "Jewel," *DNB*, 10:817
155. MacCulloch, *The Later Reformation in England*, 98.
156. H. R. Trevor-Roper, "The Good and Great Works of Richard Hooker," *New York Review of Books*, November 24, 1977, 49.
157. See Isaac Walton, "Life of Hooker," in Richard Hooker, *Works of That Learned and Judicious Divine*, 2 vols. (Oxford: Clarendon Press, 1865), 1:57, 80. *DNB*, 9:1188, misidentifies the pontiff as Clement XII. However, in "Richard Hooker's Reputation," 787–788, MacCulloch considers the papal anecdote "almost certainly spurious," as an attempt to undercut Hooker's Protestant credentials. At the other side of the debate, Lee W. Gibbs, "Richard Hooker: Prophet of Anglicanism or English Magisterial Reformer?" *Anglican Theological Reivew* 84 (2002): 943–960, critically surveys recent literature that has questioned Hooker's non-Protestant status as a representative of the Christian *via media*.
158. Hooker, *The Folger Library Edition of the Works*, 5:643. Concerning other critiques of Hooker as a Crypto-Catholic, see Peter Lake, "Business As Usual? The Immediate Reception of Hooker's *Ecclesiastical Polity*," *Journal of Ecclesiastical History* 52 (2001): 457–462.
159. Hooker, *The Folger Library Edition*, 5:237–245. Other Anglican theologians also defended the doctrine of justification, such as Richard Montague in *A Gagg for the New Gospell? No, a New Gagg for an Old Goose* (London: T. Snodham, 1624), 146–147.
160. On Bishop John Jewel, see Jewel, *Apologia pro Ecclesia Anglicana* of 1562, *DNB*, 10:817. Aquinas is, in fact, on the calendar of saints of the Episcopal Church with a feast day on January 28; *The Book of Common Prayer, According to the Use of the Episcopal Church* (New York: Seabury Press, 1979), 19. So, too, is Richard Hooker with a feast day on November 3; *The Book of Common Prayer*, 29. See also Thomas M. McCoog, "'Playing the Champion': The Role of Disputation in the Jesuit Mission," in *Reckoned Expense: Edmund Campion and the Early English Jesuits*, ed. Thomas M. McCoog (Woodbridge, UK: Boydell Press, 1996), 119. Edmund Campion, *Všech Pikartských, Luteryánských, i jináč zrotilých Prevytkantů, Hostides* (Olomouc: Jiř. Handle, 1602), 57.
161. Marshall, *Hooker*, 38; W. M. Spellman, *The Latitudinarians and the Church of England, 1660–1700* (Athens, Ga.: University of Georgia Press, 1993), 64–66; Koranda, *Traktát o velebné a božské svátosti oltářní*, f. M7; Krofta, "Václav Koranda mladší z Nové Plzně," 275; Bílejovský, *Kronyka Cýrkevní*, 7–8.
162. Bílejovský, *Kronyka Cýrkevní*, 51–53.
163. Fudge, *The Magnificent Ride*, 51, 62, 66; Rudolf Říčan, ed., *Čtyři vyznání* (Prague Komenského evangelická bohoslovecká fakulta, 1951), 39; Hrejsa, *Dějiny křest'anství v Československu*, 2:271.
164. For an attempt in 1542, see MacCulloch, *Thomas Cranmer*, 293–294; and Caroline M. Stacey, "Justification by Faith in the Two Books of Homilies, 1547 and 1571," *Anglican Theological Review* 83 (2001): 255–260, 268–270.
165. Spurr, *English Puritanism*, 52–54, 90.
166. Frederick G. Heymann, "The Impact of Martin Luther upon Bohemia," *Central European History* 1 (1968): 119; Bartoš Písař, *Kronika pražská*, in *Prameny dějin českých/Fontes rerum Bohemicarum*, ed. Josef V. Šimák (Prague: Historický spolek, 1907), 6:21–25.

167. Bible reading was "prohibited to householders under the level of yeoman, all dependents and servants, and all women, except women of gentle and noble status." MacCulloch, *Thomas Cranmer,* 310–312.

168. Bydžovský, *Dět'átka a neviňátka,* f. B1r–B1v, largely citing from Koranda, *Traktát o velebné a božské svátosti oltářní,* f. S3r–S3v.

169. Spurr, *English Puritanism,* 51. At Hampton Court in 1604, James I epitomized the Anglican view of bishops by his dictum "no bishop, no king," signifying his belief that monarchy and episcopacy stood or fell together; Spurr, *English Puritanism,* 60. On bishops in Anglicanism, see also Ephraim Radner, "Bad Bishops: A Key to Anglican Ecclesiology," *Anglican Theological Review* 82 (2000): 321–341.

170. MacCulloch, *Thomas Cranmer,* 279. See also MacCulloch, "Richard Hooker's Reputation," 777.

171. Krofta, "Václav Koranda mladší," 258; Tomek, *Dějepis města Prahy,* 10:225.

172. The generic term of presbyterialism, of course, must be distinguished from the specific designation of Presbyterianism, which did not recognize sacramental priesthood and was governed by a combination of ministers and lay elders; Spurr, *English Puritanism,* 104, 108.

173. This was the position formulated in the 1420s by Příbram and Rokycana. See, for instance, Augustin Neumann, *Z dějin bohoslužeb v době husitské* (Hradec Králové: Tiskové družstvo, 1922), 132.

174. See, for instance, Enrico S. Molnar, *The Catholicity of the Utraquist Church of Bohemia* (Sewanee, Tenn.: University Press of Sewanee, 1959), 3–5; Kamil Krofta, "Boj o konsistoř pod obojí v letech 1562–1575 a jeho historický základ," *Český časopis historický* 17 (1911): 412–413.

175. Bydžovský, *Dět'átka a neviňátka hned po přijetí křtu sv. Tělo a Krev Boží, že přijímati mají,* f. A–2v.

176. Eliška Fučíková, ed., *Tři francouzští kavalíři v rudolfínské Praze* (Prague: Panorama, 1989), 44–45, 116, n. 29. For a summary of Rome's view of Anglican orders, see, for instance, *New Catholic Encyclopedia* (New York: McGraw-Hill, 1967–1974), 1:526–527; and "The English Text of *Apostolicae Curae,*" *Anglican Theological Review* 88 (1996): 127-137.

177. See also the acceptance of the Bishop of Rome's sacerdotal power by the Utraquist writer, Nožička z Votína, *Knížka proti bludům některým před tisíci lety odsouzeným,* f. Aiii(v).

178. Krofta, "Boj o konsistoř," 189.

179. See, especially, Pavel Bydžovský, *Historiae aliquot Anglorum martyrum, quibus Deus suam ecclesiam exornare sicut syderibus coelum dignatus est* (Prague: J. Cantor, 1554).

180. See Zdeněk V. David, "The Strange Fate of Czech Utraquism: The Second Century, 1517-1621," *Journal of Ecclesiastical History,* 46 (1995): 653–654. As an example of the confusion, see Ferdinand Hrejsa, *Česká konfesse: Její vznik, podstata a dějiny* (Prague: Česká akademie pro vědy, slovesnost a umění, 1912), 59, 61; Krofta, *Boj o konsistoř,* 302–303.

181. On the Utraquist view of authority in the church, as defined by Hus and Jan Rokycana, see Enrico S. Molnar, "Viklef, Hus a problém autority," in *Jan Hus mezi epochami, národy a konfesemi,* ed. Jan B. Lášek (Prague: Česká křest'anská akademie, 1995), 109–113.

182. See, for instance, the censure of Pavel Bydžovský in Jakubec, *Dějiny literatury české,* 1:653.

183. Otakar Odložilík, *The Hussite King: Bohemia in European Affairs, 1440–1471* (New Brunswick, N.J.: Rutgers University Press, 1965), 177.

184. Šmahel, *Husitská revoluce*, 4:100–101; Krofta, *Boj o konsistoř*, 388. For Sigismund's decree, see *Archiv český* 3 (1844): 427–431. See also Winfried Eberhard, *Konfessionsbildung und Stände in Böhmen, 1478–1530* (Munich: Oldenbourg, 1981), 44–45.

185. *Sněmy české*, 11: pt. 1, 72–73, 79; Julius Pažout, *Jednání a dopisy konsistoře pod obojí způsobou přijímajících, 1562–1570* (Prague: Historický spolek, 1906), 374; Vilém Slavata, *Paměti nejvyššího kancléře království českého*, ed. Josef Jireček, 2 vols. (Prague: Kober, 1866–1868), 1:216, 219; and Karel Stloukal, "Počátky nunciatury v Praze: Bonhomi v Čechách, 1581–84," *Český časopis historický* 34 (1928): 13.

186. Pažout, *Jednání a dopisy*, 431–432; Krofta, *Boj o konsistoř*, 283–286.

187. Pažout, *Jednání a dopisy*, 273, 317, 372.

188. Václav Tomek, "O církevní správě strany pod obojí v Čechách," *Časopis českého musea* 22 (1848): 463; see also Hrejsa, *Česká konfesse*, 574–575.

189. Nejedlý, *Prameny k synodám strany pražské a táborské*, 13; Hrejsa, *Česká konfesse*, 189.

190. On Wenceslaus IV as a Czech Henry VIII, see Wilks, "*Reformatio regni:* Wyclif and Hus as Leaders of Religious Protest Movements," 130. See also Anne Hudson, *The Premature Reformation: Wycliffite Texts and Lollard History* (Oxford: Clarendon Press, 1988), 513–514, and Jan Urban, "'Kališnický' převrat na dvoře Václava IV," in *Husitství, Reformace, Renesance: Sborník k 60. narozeninám Františka Šmahela*, ed. Jaroslav Pánek, et al., 3 vols. (Prague: Historický ústav, 1994), 1:422.

191. František Palacký, *Obrana husitství*, trans. and ed. František M. Bartoš (Prague: Blahoslav, 1926), 40.

192. Kopičková, *Jan Želivský*, 108; Fudge, *The Magnificent Ride*, 75–77.

193. See, for instance, H. C. Porter, "Hooker, the Tudor Constitution, and the *Via Media*," in *Studies in Richard Hooker*, ed. W. Speed Hill (Cleveland: Press of Case Western Reserve University, 1972), 77–78.

194. O'Day, *The Debate on the English Reformation*, 166–169.

195. MacCulloch, *Thomas Cranmer*, 151.

196. Šmahel, *Husitská revoluce*, 1:352; Zikmund Winter, *Zlatá doba měst českých* (Prague: Odeon, 1991), 139–142, 144–145; Stloukal, "Počátky nunciatury v Praze," 255, 257; Anton Gindely, *Geschichte der Böhmischen Brüder*, 2d ed., 2 vols. (Prague: C. Bellmann, 1861–1862), 2:413.

197. Bílejovský states literally: "[W]e Czechs sub utraque are the true Romans" ([M]y Čechové pod obojí jsme praví Římané), *Kronyka Cýrkevní*, 27.

Chapter 5

1. Ernst Denis characterizes Mystopol as follows: "For several years the Lutheran estates appointed to the Consistory priests, favorably inclined toward the innovations. In 1541, they chose as administrator, the pastor of St. Nicholas, Jan Mystopol, whose decisiveness they fully trusted. He was another Cahera, rash and cowardly, restless and unstable. Having no true convictions nor real ability, he damaged his cause by excessive recklessness, harmed it by intolerance, and betrayed it in the time of danger." Ernst Denis, *Fin de l'indépendance bohême*, 2d ed., 2 vols. (Paris: Librairie Leroux, 1930), 1:91. Václav V. Tomek, *Dějepis města Prahy*, 12 vols. (Prague: Řivnáč, 1855–1901), 11:232–

233, writes: "Among them [i.e., Consistory members] . . ., Jan Mystopol became newly [c. 1539] notable—a man of a character strongly reminiscent of Havel Cahera, yearning for honors and power, however, devoid of firm principles or manly endurance, guided only by his own profit." On Mystopol, see also Václav Novotný, "Náboženské dějiny české ve století 16.," in Zdeněk V. Tobolka, ed., *Česká politika*, Zdeněk, 5 vols. (Prague: Jan Laichter, 1906), 1:607, 617. On Cahera, see Tobolka, 1:591, and Jaroslav Pelikan, Jr., "Luther's Negotiations with the Hussites," *Concordia Theological Monthly* 2 (1949): 499–503, as well as Chapter 3.

2. *Ottův slovník naučný* (Prague: Otto, 1888–1909), 4:999.

3. Jan Jakubec, *Dějiny literatury české*, 2d ed., 2 vols. (Prague: Laichter, 1929–1934), 1:653.

4. Johann Faber, *Confutatio gravissimi erroris asserentis in sacramento altaris post consecrationem nisi corpus tantum et sub specie vini non esse nisi sanguinem tantum* (Leipzig: Nicholas Wolrab, 1537).

5. *Ibid.*, 111–113. On the early Utraquist synods, see Blanka Zilynská, *Husitské synody v Čechách, 1418–1440* (Prague: Univerzita Karlova, 1985), 16–17, 19–21.

6. Faber, *Confutatio gravissimi erroris*, 113–114.

7. *Ibid.*, 75.

8. *Ibid.*, 19.

9. *Ibid.*, 116, 146.

10. Johannes Cochlaeus, *Historiae Hussitarum libri duodecim* (Mainz: Franciscus Behem, 1549), 94. Cochlaeus, however, at the same time was eager to separate the Utraquists from the Lutherans, and as an expert on Utraquism had been in touch with Bishop Faber in 1534; Jaroslav Pelikan, "Luther's Attitude Toward John Hus," *Concordia Theological Monthly* 19 (1948): 759.

11. [Jan Černý], "Poznamenání a spolu shromáždění některých věcí pamětihodných přítomným i budoucím," 1579 (manuscript, University Library, Prague, sign. XVII C 3), f. 93r. See also Leo Helbling, *Dr. Johann Fabri, Generalvikar von Konstanz und Bischof von Wien, 1478–1541: Beiträge zu seiner Lebensgeschichte* (Münster: Aschendorffsche Verlagsbuchhandlung, 1941), 125–126.

12. Antonín Rezek, *Biskup vídeňský Jan Faber a čeští utrakvisté* (Prague: Česká společnost nauk, Zprávy o zasedání, 1882), 401–402.

13. *Ibid.*, 402–403.

14. Under call number 35.B.167 and *signatura* M44, respectively. The copy of the *Confutatio* came to the National Library from the Jesuit College in Český Krumlov. The Czech translation of Faber's pamphlet, titled *O potupení bludu,* was arranged by Augustin Schwarzel of Třebenice in 1540, apparently in Moravské Budějovice. See Eduard Petrů, *Z rukopisných sbírek Universitní knihovny v Olomouci* (Prague: Státní pedagogické nakladatelství, 1959), 57.

15. Klement Borový, *Jednání a dopisy konsistoře katolické a utrakvistické,* 2 vols. (Prague: I. L. Kober, 1868), 1:124.

16. Faber, *Confutatio gravissimi erroris,* 118, 123, 132.

17. *Ibid.*, 131–132; Rudolf Říčan, *The History of the Unity of Brethren: A Protestant Hussite Church in Bohemia and Moravia,* trans. C. Daniel Crews (Bethlehem, Pa.: Moravian Church in America, 1992), 143–144.

18. Tomek, *Dějepis města Prahy,* 11:234.

19. [Jan Černý], "Poznamenání a spolu shromáždění některých věcí pamětihodných přítomným i budoucím," f. 196r, 224r.

20. *Ibid.*, f. 235v–236r. See also *Sněmy české od léta 1526 až po naši dobu.*, vols. 1–11, 15 (Prague: Zemský výbor, 1877–1941), 1:571–575; Tomek, *Dějepis města Prahy,* 11: 240.

21. The others were Jan Nožička, abbot of the Slav monastery, priest Bartoš, the dean of Kouřim, and priest Bohuslav the Elder; "Poznamenání a spolu shromáždění některých věcí pamětihodných přítomným i budoucím," f. 229r, also 223r, 238r.

22. Josef Janáček, *České dějiny: Doba předbělohorská,* 2 vols. (Prague: Academia, 1971–1984), 1: 198. For the Anglican position, see John S. Marshall, Hooker and the Anglican Tradition: An Historical and Theological Study of Hooker's Ecclesiastical Polity (Sewanee, Tenn.: University Press, 1963), 36, 64. On the Lutheran initiatives of 1522–1523 and 1541–1543, see Jaroslav Pelikan, "Luther's negotiations with the Hussites," Concordia Theological Monthly 20 (1949): 499–503; and S. Harrison Thomson, "Luther and Bohemia," Archiv für Reformationsgeschichte 44 (1953): 177–178.

23. See Bohuslav Souček, "Rukopis pražské universitní knihovny XVII C 3," *Reformační sborník* 1 (1921): 45–80, especially 45; and Kamil Krofta, *O bratrském dějepisectví* (Prague: Laichter, 1946), 53–54. Tomek, *Dějepis města Prahy,* 11:232–249; Winifried Eberhard, *Monarchie und Widerstand: zur ständischen Oppositionsbildung im Herschaftssystem Ferdinands I. in Böhmen* (Munich: Oldenbourg, 1985), 365–383.

24. See, for instance, "Poznamenání a spolu shromáždění některých věcí pamětihodných přítomným i budoucím," f. 237r–237v; cf. Krofta, *O bratrském dějepisectví,* 55, 57.

25. Diarmaid MacCulloch, *Thomas Cranmer: A Life* (New Haven, Conn.: Yale University Press, 1996), 185–196, especially 190–192.

26. Pavel Bydžovský, *Knížky o přijímání Těla a Krve Pána našeho Jeříše Krysta pod obojí způsobou.* ([Prague]: n.p., 1538–1539), 54 (56) folios. It contains three other items: (1) *Čechové, milí Čechové, jenž žádáte býti věrní,* f. 28v–33; (2) *Tyto knížky toto Try v sobě drží,* f. 34r–50v (34r–52v); and (3) *Spis o Postu,* f. 51r–54v (53r–56v). This work is cited from a copy in the National Museum Library in Prague (call number 36 C 2); there is no printed pagination, but folio numbers are marked in pencil. The penciled numbers are not accurate. (Number 46 is repeated twice, and a folio is skipped between penciled 50 and 51.) For the purpose of citation, the folios were renumbered, and in citations the reference is given to the penciled number with the correct number following in parentheses.

27. Bydžovský, *Knížky o přijímání Těla a Krve,* f. 19r–26r.

28. *Ibid.*, f. 26v.

29. For a discussion of the Unity's Eucharistic views and practices, see David R. Holeton, "Church or Sect? The Jednota Bratrská and the Growth of Dissent from Mainline Utraquism," *Communio Viatorum* 38 (1996): 17–24.

30. Říčan, *The History of the Unity of Brethren,* 118.

31. Bydžovský, *Knížky o přijímání Těla a Krve,* f. 27v. He cites Article X (*De Sacra Coena. Vom heilingen Abendmahl*) from the Apology of the Augsburg Confession of September 22, 1530, first printed together with the Confession of June 25, 1530, in 1531. See Ernst Wolf, *Die Bekenntnischriften der evangelisch-lutherischen Kirche,* 5th ed., ed. Hans Lietzmann (Göttingen: Vandenhoeck & Ruprecht, 1963), 247–248 (in Latin and German), and Theodore G. Tappert, trans. and ed., *The Book of Concord: The Confessions of the Evangelical Lutheran Church* (Philadelphia: Muhlenberg Press, 1959), 179–180 (in English). In praising Article X, Bydžovský did not depart from the traditional Utraquist definition of the sacrament. The original text of Article X in the *Augsburg Con-*

fession was sanctioned even by the Roman Church in *Confutatio Pontificia* of July 8, 1530; see Johann M. Reu, ed., *The Augsburg Confession: A Collection of Sources with an Historical Introduction* (Chicago: Wartburg Publishing House, 1930), 354.

32. Pavel Bydžovský, *Tato Knížka toto try ukazuje* (N.p., [after 1541]).

33. See Říčan, *The History of the Unity of Brethren*, 113. On the Eucharistic debate between Luther and the Brethren, see also Chapter 3.

34. Bydžovský, *Tato Knížka toto try ukazuje*, 24.

35. *Ibid.*, 14.

36. *Ibid.*, 15. The reference is presumably to Luther's *Enchiridion piarum precationum, cum Passionali* (Wittenberg, apud I. Lufft, 1543), containing a section "De Sacramento Altaris," but I did not succeed in locating the exact citation there.

37. Bydžovský, *Tato Knížka toto try ukazuje*, 16.

38. Cf. Bydžovský, *Knížky o přijímání Těla a Krve*, f. 26v; Tappert, *The Book of Concord*, 96.

39. Pavel Bydžovský, *Tento spis ukazuje, že Biskupové Biskupa, a Biskup kněží, a kněží od řádných Biskupů svěceni Těla a krve Boží posvěcovati mají* (N.p., 1543), 11–13.

40. Martin Luther, *Sententiae sanctorum patrum de coena Domini, bona fidae recitatae, & editae Witenbergae a Philippo Melanchtone anno 1530* (Wittenberg: n.p., 1530).

41. Bydžovský, *Tento spis ukazuje*, 12.

42. *Ibid.*, 13. He apparently refers to Lukáš of Prague, *Odpověd' Bratří na spis M. Luthera* (Litomyšl: Pavel Olivetský, 1523), which persists "to the point of harshness in rejecting bowing before the sacrament as an idolatrous abomination in the holy place, and did not tolerate any middle ground in this matter." See Říčan, *The History of the Unity of Brethren*, 114.

43. "To hle Luter, kteréhož zbornícy w prawdie a w wíře nenásleduji, než w wejstupcých, ale wierní kdež se s Cýrkwí srownáwá to přijimají." See Bydžovský, *Tento spis ukazuje*, 14.

44. In opposing Luther's solafideism, the Brethren insisted on the necessity of good works. Thus, Lukáš of Prague in his *Odpověd' Bratří na spis M. Luthera* (1523) wrote: "Although a person made righteous out of grace in Christ through the Holy Spirit is freed without works of his own, he still must not receive in vain this grace and righteousness in the covenant of the law and in consecration. There have to be works resulting out of it and along with it." Cited by Říčan, *The History of the Unity of Brethren*, 114.

45. "Sprawen jsem, že by jeden Kazatel z Nowowěrcůw kázati měl, proč jest Krystus se postil moha bez toho býti, a nic jiného w tom nespůsobil, nežli swár mezy Lidmi." See Bydžovský, *Spis o Postu*, lv. 51r–54v (53r–56v), in *Knížky o přijímání Těla a Krve*, f. 51r (53r).

46. "[N]ovos Evangelicastros (intelligo Luteranos) . . ." Pavel Bydžovský, *Historiae aliquot Anglorum martyrum, quibus Deus suam ecclesiam exornare sicut syderibus coelum dignatus est* (Prague: J. Cantor, 1554), f. B1r; see also A4v.

47. Bydžovský, *Spis o postu*, f. 51v (53v).

48. *Ibid.*, f. 51r–51v (53r–53v), 53r–53v (55r–55v).

49. "[B]ut in all things approving ourselves as the servants of God, in much patience . . . in imprisonments, in labors, in wakefulness and in many fastings . . ." *Ibid.*, f. 52r (54r).

50. *Ibid.*, f. 52v (54v). Bydžovský also dealt with the mundane objections of those

who claimed that fasting made them ill, or that—due to poverty—they lacked nourishment at any time; *ibid.*, f. 54v (56v).
51. *Ibid.*, f. 54r (56r).
52. *Ibid.*, f. 52v (54v).
53. Zdeněk Nejedlý, ed., *Prameny k synodám strany pražské a táborské (vznik husitské konfesse) v letech 1441–1444* (Prague: Královská Česká společnost nauk, 1900), 13. See also Zilynská, *Husitské synody v Čechách,* 74–76.
54. Borový, *Jednání a dopisy konsistoře,* 1:21.
55. František Dvorský, ed., "Dopisy kněží Šimona z Habru a Jana faráře Německo-Brodského o rozdílech ve víře, 1528–1529," *Archiv český* 14 (1895): 331.
56. Otakar Odložilík, "Utrakvistická postilla z r. 1540," *Věstník české společnosti nauk* (1925): 4. Odložilík tentatively identifies the author as the priest Jan at St. Henry's Church in the New Town of Prague, and a member of the Utraquist Consistory in 1534–1540.
57. *Ibid.*, 15–17, 20–21.
58. Borový, *Jednání a dopisy konsistoře,* 1:230–31.
59. Pavel Bydžovský, *Čechové, milí Čechové, jenž žádáte býti věrní,* f. 28v–33, in *Knížky o přijímání Těla a Krve*.
60. Říčan, *The History of the Unity of Brethren,* 114.
61. See David R. Holeton, "'O felix Bohemia—O felix Constantia': Liturgická úcta Mistra Jana Husa," in *Jan Hus mezi epochami, národy a konfesemi,* ed. Jan B. Lášek (Prague: Česká křest'anská akademie, 1995), 154–170; and Holeton, "The Office of Jan Hus: An Unrecorded Antiphonary in the Metropolitan Library at Esztergom," in *Time and Community,* ed. J. Neil Alexander (Washington, D.C.: Pastoral Press, 1990), 137–143. See also "Bohoslužebná skládání o Husovi z XV. a XVI. století," *Prameny dějin českých,* 8 (1932): 419–472; and Ferdinand Menčík, ed., *Zápisky kněze Václava Rosy* (Vienna: J. Paška, 1879), 40. The other martyrs included three in 1412 from Prague, and two in 1415 from Olomouc; see František M. Bartoš, *Husitská revoluce,* 2 vols. (Prague: Nakladatelství Československé akademie věd, 1965–1966), 1:31.
62. Borový, *Jednání a dopisy konsistoře,* 1:230. On reading of the Passion of Jan Hus on the eve before July 6 in Bohemian churches in the early sixteenth century, see Arnošt Kraus, *Husitství v literatuře, zejména německé,* 3 vols. (Prague: Česká akademie pro vědy, slovesnost a umění, 1917–1924), 1:153.
63. Pavel Bydžovský, *Čechové milí Čechové,* f. 32v–33r.
64. Miloslav Pazourek, "O významu mariánské úcty M. J. Husa pro ekumenismus," in *Jan Hus mezi epochami, národy a konfesemi,* ed. Jan B. Lášek (Prague: Česká křest'anská akademie, 1995), 171–172.
65. See, for instance, Jan Chlíbec, "K vývoji názorů Jana Rokycany na umělecké dílo," *Husitský Tábor* 8 (1985): 42, see also 40, 54.
66. *Ibid.*, 54.
67. Odložilík, "Utrakvistická postilla z r. 1540," 18.
68. Chlíbec, "K vývoji názorů Jana Rokycany na umělecké dílo," 53. Jan Rokycana was the second (and last) Utraquist Archbishop of Prague, elected in 1435, but never consecrated.
69. This work is known only in a later edition by Jan Štelcar Želetavský z Želetavy as Martin Žatecký, *Knížka proti ošemetné poctě a pokryté Svatých,* 2d ed. (Prague: n.p., 1593); see f. C1v–C2r.
70. Odložilík, "Utrakvistická postilla z r. 1540," 15–17, 20–21.

71. Bydžovský, *Čechové milí Čechové*, f. 28v. See Jan Hus, *Výklady* Magistri Ioannis Hus Opera omnia, vol. 1 (Prague: Academia, 1975), 137. See also David R. Holeton, "Liturgická a svátostná teologie Mistra Jana Husa," *Theologická revue* 1 (1996): 9–12.

72. See František Šmahel, *Husitská revoluce*, 4 vols. (Prague: Historický ústav, 1993), 4:104–105; Chlíbec, "K vývoji názorů Jana Rokycany na umělecké dílo," 47; Zilynská, *Husitské synody v Čechách, 1418–1440*, 31–39.

73. With reference to Distinctio 3, Canon "de consecratione," see "Compactata," in *Archiv český* 3 (1844): 454.

74. Noemi Rejchrtová, "Obrazoborecké tendence utrakvistické mentality jagellonského období a jejich dosah," *Husitský Tábor* 8 (1985): 66–67. see also Zikmund Winter, *Kulturní obraz českých měst*, 2 vols. (Prague: Matice česká, 1890), 1:442.

75. Zuzana Všetečková, "Iconography of the Mural Paintings in St. James's Church of Kutná Hora," in *The Bohemian Reformation and Religious Practice*, vol. 3: Papers from the XIXth World Congress of the Czechoslovak Society of Arts and Sciences, Bratislava 1998, ed. Zdeněk V. David and David R. Holeton (Prague: Academy of Sciences of the Czech Republic, Main Library, 2000), 129–146.

76. Only the second edition has survived: Pavel Bydžovský, *Odvolání jednoho Bratra z Roty Pikhartské*, 2d ed. (Prague: Jan Jičínský, 1588). Available in photocopy at the National Library in Prague, sign. f Zc 54.

77. Pavel Bydžovský, *Dět'átka a neviňátka hned po přijetí křtu sv. Tělo a Krev Boží, že přijímati mají* (Prague: Bartoloměj Netolický, 1541).

78. Cyril A. Straka, "Jak slavilo se Boží tělo v Praze v XVI. a XVII. století," *Časopis katolického duchovenstva* 57 (1916): 166.

79. Bydžovský, *Odvolání jednoho Bratra z Roty Pikhartské*, f. A–4r.

80. *Ibid.*, f. C5r–C6v.

81. *Ibid.*, f. C7r.

82. On its significance in early Utraquism, see Thomas A. Fudge, *The Magnificent Ride: The First Reformation in Hussite Bohemia* (Brookfield, Vt. : Ashgate, 1998), 245–246.

83. For earlier development of this practice, see David R. Holeton, *La communion des tout-petits enfants: Étude du mouvement eucharistique en Bohême vers la fin du Moyen-Âge* (Rome: Edizioni Liturgiche, 1989), especially 83–165.

84. Bydžovský, *Dět'átka a neviňátka*, f. A–2v.

85. *Ibid.*, f. A3v–A4r.

86. *Ibid.*, f. A4v. See also Pseudo-Dionysius, *Complete Works*, trans. Colm Luibheid and Paul Rorem (Mahwah, N.J.: Paulist Press, 1987), 203, 208–209.

87. Bydžovský, *Dět'átka a neviňátka*, f. A5r.

88. *Ibid.*, f. A5r–A5v.

89. *Ibid.*, f. A6v–A7r.

90. *Ibid.*, f. A5v–A6r, also B8r. See also Pseudo-Dionysius, *Complete Works*, 258.

91. Pseudo-Dionysius, *Theologia vivificans. Cibus solidus. Dionysii coelestis hierarchia. Ecclesiastica hierarchia. Divina nomina. Mystica theologia. Undecim epistolae. Ignatii undecim epistolae. Polycarpi epistola una*, ed. Jacques Le Fèvre d'Étaples (In alma Parisiorum academia, Per Henricū Stephanū, 1515); see Bydžovský, *Dět'átka a neviňátka*, f. B2r.

92. Bydžovský, *Dět'átka a neviňátka*, f. B2v–B4r.

93. *Ibid.*, f. B4r–B4v.

94. *Ibid.*, f. B5v–B7r. Remigius together with Pseudo-Dionysius, Cyprian, Augustine

and Chrysostom are the authorities cited in favor of infant communion by an early Utraquist song. See Zdeněk Nejedlý, *Dějiny husitského zpěvu* (Prague: Nakladatelství Československé akademie věd, 1954–1956), 6:231–232, cited in trans. by Fudge, *The Magnificent Ride*, 205–206.

95. Bydžovský, *Dět'átka a neviňátka*, f. A4v, B3v–B4r, B7r–B8r.
96. *Ibid.*, f. B1v–B2r.
97. *Ibid.*, f. A7r–A7v.
98. *Ibid.*, f. B1r–B1v, largely citing from Václav Koranda, *Traktát o velebné a božské svátosti oltářní* (Prague: Tiskař Korandy, 1493), f. S3r–S3v.
99. Bydžovský, *Dět'átka a neviňátka*, f. B8v–C1r. Bydžovský apparently had in mind the publication *Artykulowe a snessenij Knězstva pod obogij Spuosobau:* Leta Bozijho MDXXXIX. A copy is archived at the National Library in Vienna under the notation: *Articuli Conciliabuli sub utraque specie communicantium* (Bohemice et latine, S. l., 1539, Signatura, 24 M 56, cf. f. B3v).
100. Bydžovský, *Dět'átka a neviňátka*, f. C1v–C2r; see also Koranda, *Traktát o velebné a božské svátosti oltářní*, f. R5r–R8v.
101. Bydžovský, *Dět'átka a neviňátka*, f. C2r; Koranda, *Traktát o velebné a božské svátosti oltářní*, f. S5r.
102. Bydžovský, *Dět'átka a neviňátka*, f. C2v–C3r.
103. *Ibid.*, f. C4r.
104. See, for instance, Lewis W. Spitz, "The Universal Priesthood of Believers," in *The Abiding Word*, ed. Theodor F. Laetsch (St. Louis: Concordia Publishing House, 1946), 1:321–341.
105. Martin Luther, *Werke: Kritische Gesammtausgabe*, 113 vols. in 4 series (Weimar: Böhlau, 1883–1996), 12:160–196.
106. Bydžovský, *Tento spis ukazuje*, 6, 9, 14; cf. Emile Friedberg, ed., *Decretum Magistri Gratiani. Editio Lipsiensis Secunda post Aemilii Ludovici Richteri curas* (Leipzig: Bernhard Tauchnitz, 1879), 1: col. 359, 977–980.
107. Bydžovský, *Tento spis ukazuje*, 15; cf. Friedberg, *Decretum Magistri Gratiani*, 1:col. 317–318, 332.
108. Bydžovský, *Tento spis ukazuje, že Biskupové Biskupa,*14; cf. Friedberg, *Decretum Magistri Gratiani*, 1:col. 1343–1342.
109. Zikmund Winter, *O životě na vysokých školách pražských: kulturní obraz XV. a XVI. století* (Prague: Matice česká, 1899), 357. While Luther rejected classical canon law, the Anglican Church retained its substance after eliminating the elements of papal centralization. Gerald Bray, ed., *The Anglican Canons, 1529–1947* (Woodbridge, UK: Boydell Press, 1998); MacCulloch, *Thomas Cranmer,* 327, 351, 377, 449. See also James H. Provost, "Canon Law," *The Encyclopedia of Religion* (New York: Macmillan, 1987), 3: 70; Erwin L. Lueker, ed., *Lutheran Cyclopedia,* rev. ed. (St. Louis: Concordia Publishing House, 1975), 133. Bydžovský's and other Utraquist theologians' views of canon law may be assumed to have come close to that of Erasmus; see Wilhelm Maurer, "Erasmus und das Kanonische Recht," in *Vierhundertfünfzig Jahre lutherische Reformation, 1517–1967 (Festschrift für Franz Lau zum 50. Geburtstag)* (Göttingen: Vanderhoeck and Ruprecht, 1967), 222–232. On the bearing of canon law on ecclesiology, see also Takashi Shogimen, "The Relationship between Theology and Canon Law: Another Context of Political Thought in the Early Fourteenth Century," *Journal of the History of Ideas* 60 (1999): 417–431.

110. Jiří Kejř, "Jan Hus jako právní myslitel," in *Jan Hus mezi epochami, národy a konfesemi,* ed. Jan B. Lášek (Prague: Česká křest'anská akademie, 1995), 197.

111. He refers to Chrysostom's eleventh sermon on 1 Timothy 3, and to Theophylactus's commentaries on 1 Tim. 3, and Phil. 1; see Bydžovský, *Tento spis ukazuje,* 6.

112. Bydžovský, *Tento spis ukazuje,* 7.

113. *Ibid.,* 7–8.

114. Carolus Capello, *Epitome apostolicarum constitutionum in Creta insula per Carolum Capellium Venetum repertarum et e Graeco in Latinum translatarum (ad Johannes Cochlaeus)* (Ingolstadt: Alexander Weissenhorn, 1546). While serving as ambassador to the Imperial court, Capello developed a friendship with Bishop Faber; see *Dizionario Biografico degli Italiani* (Rome: Enciclopedia italiana, 1976), 18:768.

115. Antonín Truhlář, *Rukověť k písemnictví humanistickému, zvláště básnickému v Čechách a na Moravě ve století XVI* (Prague: Česká akademie pro vědy, slovesnost a umění, 1918), 1:174. I could not locate the edition listed by Truhlář.

116. Bydžovský, *Tento spis ukazuje,* 9–11, 13, 16. For a discussion of the Unity's complicated view of the ministry, see Holeton, "Church or Sect? The Jednota Bratrská and the Growth of Dissent from Mainline Utraquism," 24–34.

117. Bydžovský, *Tento spis ukazuje,* 10–11.

118. Bydžovský, *Dět'átka a neviňátka,* f. C3r–C3v.

119. Concerning the rejection of apostolic succession, see Curtis C. Stephan, "The Office of the Keys," in Theodor F. Laetsch, ed., *The Abiding Word* (St. Louis: Concordia Publishing House, 1946), 1:356.

120. Dvorský, *Dopisy kněží,* 334, 356.

121. Odložilík, "Utrakvistická postilla z r. 1540," 15.

122. See, for instance, Tappert, *The Book of Concord,* 24.

123. Bydžovský, *Tato Knižka toto try ukazuje,* 2. On the relationship of the Waldensians to the Taborites and the Brethren, see Gabriel Audisio, *The Waldensian Dissent: Persecution and Survival, c. 1170–c. 1570,* trans. Claire Davison (Cambridge and New York: Cambridge University Press, 1999), 78–86.

124. Bohuslav Bílejovský, *Kronyka Cýrkevní,* ed. Jozef Skalický (pseudonym for Josef Dittrich) (Prague: Fetterl z Vilden, 1816), 109 (see also 105); Josef V. Šimák, "Bohuslava Bílejovského Kronika česká," *Český časopis historický* 38 (1932): 101. On the relationship between the Bohemian Brethren and the Waldensians, often called Waldensian Brethren (*fratres Valdenses*), see Giovanni Gonnet and Amedeo Molnár, *Les Vaudois au Moyen Âge* (Turin: Claudiana, 1974), especially 154–158, 211–318; and Říčan, *The History of the Unity of Brethren,* 9–10, 47, 70–71.

125. Bílejovský, *Kronyka Cýrkevní,* 50. Howard Kaminsky, in *A History of the Hussite Revolution* (Berkeley: University of California Press, 1967), 354–355, seeks to identify the "Picardi" with the "Beghardi" or the Brethren of the Free Spirit who were widespread in fourteenth-century Europe and condemned by the Council of Vienne in 1311.

126. Bílejovský, *Kronyka Cýrkevní,* 105, 109. For Bílejovský's fuller development of the Picardi–Brethren nexus, see Chapter 4.

127. Josef Jireček, *Rukověť k dějinám literatury české do konce XVIII. věku,* 2 vols. (Prague: Tempský, 1875–1876), 1:116.

128. Dvorský, "Dopisy kněží Šimona z Habru a Jana faráře Německo-Brodského," 332.

129. Bydžovský, *Tento spis ukazuje,* 14.

130. Jireček, *Rukověť k dějinám literatury české do konce XVIII. věku*, 1:115; Borový, *Jednání a dopisy konsistoře katolické a utrakvistické*, 1:207 (see also 167, 182).

131. Jakub Srnec of Varvažov, *Apophoreta aliquot in Epiphaniis Domini, amicis dedicata a M. J. R. W.* (N.p., 1557), f. B3r. See also Josef Hejnic and Jan Martínek, eds., *Rukověť humanistického básnictví v Čechách a na Moravě*, 5 vols. (Prague: Academia, 1966–1982), 5:157–158; Truhlář, *Rukověť k písemnictví humanistickému*, 1:175.

132. Ferdinand Hrejsa, *Česká konfesse: Její vznik, podstata a dějiny* (Prague: Česká akademie pro vědy, slovesnost a umění, 1912), 188, n. 2.

133. Václav Šturm, *Krátké ozvání . . . proti kratičkému ohlášení Jednoty Valdenské neb Boleslavské* (Prague: Jiřík Dačický, 1584), 131–132.

134. Richard Hooker, *The Folger Library Edition of the Works of Richard Hooker*, 6 vols., ed. W. Speed Hill (Cambridge, Mass.: Belknap Press of Harvard University Press, 1977–1993), 2: 121 (*LEP* V.28.1).

135. Hooker, *Folger Library Edition of the Works*, 1:3–12 (*LEP* Preface 2); see also Arthur Dickens and John Tonkin, *The Reformation in Historical Thought* (Cambridge, Mass.: Harvard University Press, 1985), 68.

136. Bydžovský, *Tento spis ukazuje*, 11.

137. Hooker, *Folger Library Edition of the Works*, 1:3 (*LEP* Preface 2.1).

138. William P. Haugaard, "The Preface," in Hooker, *Folger Library Edition of the Works*, 6: pt. 1, 70. On Hooker and Calvinist orthodoxy, see also Peter Lake, *Anglicans and Puritans? Presbyterianism and English Conformist Thought from Whitgift to Hooker* (London: Unwin Hyman, 1988), 182–197.

139. Hooker, *Folger Library Edition of the Works*, 1:7 (*LEP*, Preface, 2.4). See also Diarmaid MacCulloch, "Richard Hooker's Reputation," *English Historical Review* 117 (2002): 791.

140. John Jewel, *An Apology of the Church of England*, ed. J. E. Booty (Ithaca, N.Y.: Cornell University Press, 1963), 57.

141. Kamil Krofta, "O některých spisech M. Jana z Příbramě," *Časopis českého musea* 73 (1899): 213.

142. "The spirit of Christ in the Gospels has a wisdom of its own, and its own courtesy and meekness." Desiderius Erasmus, *The Correspondence*, 11 vols. (Toronto: University of Toronto Press, 1974–1992), 8:203 (see also 81–82, 155–157, 202–205), 9:398. On his influence in Bohemia, see Jaroslav Kolár, *Návraty bez konce: Studie k starší české literatuře*, ed. Lenka Jiroušková (Brno: Atlantis, 1999), 120, 141, 175–177.

143. Erasmus, *The Correspondence*, 9:390 (see also 389).

144. Concerning Erasmus's influence on Jewel, see R. J. Schoeck, "From Erasmus to Hooker," in *Richard Hooker and the Construction of Christian Community*, ed. Arthur S. McGrade (Tempe, Ariz.: Medieval and Renaissance Texts and Studies, 1997), 66–67, 69–73.

145. Bydžovský, *Historiae aliquot Anglorum martyrum*, f. Br.

146. "Witzel," *New Catholic Encyclopedia* (New York: McGraw-Hill, 1967–1974), 14:984–985; "Witzel," *Allgemeine Deutsche Biographie*, 43:658–659.

147. Winfried Trusen, *Um die Reform und Einheit der Kirche: Zum Leben und Werk Georg Witzels* (Münster: Aschendorffsche Verlagsbuchhandlung, 1957), 22–26; Barbara Henze, *Aus Liebe zur Kirche Reform: die Bemühungen Georg Witzels (1501–1573) um die Kircheneinheit* (Münster: Aschendorff, 1995), 23 (visit to Bohemia).

148. Henze, *Aus Liebe zur Kirche Reform*, 33–34, n. 188.

149. Robert Barnes, *Kronyky. A životěsepsání nejvrchnejších Biskupů Římských*

jináč Papežů, trans. Ennius Glatouinus (Norimberk: Woldřich Nejber and Jan Montán, 1565), f. 198r–198v. This work is a translation of Robert Barnes, *Vitae Romanorum Pontificum, quos papas vocamus* (Wittenberg: Josephus Clvg [sic], 1536).
150. Trusen, *Um die Reform und Einheit der Kirche,* 31; for a general survey of his theological views, see Trusen, 40–83.
151. *Ibid.*, 65; "Witzel," *Allgemeine Deutsche Biographie,* 43:660–661; Borový, *Jednání a dopisy konsistoře,* 1:247.
152. Pierre Costil, *André Dudith, humaniste hongrois 1533–1589: Sa vie, son oeuvre et ses manuscrits grecs* (Paris: Les Belles Lettres, 1935), 228–231.
153. Bydžovský, *Historiae aliquot Anglorum martyrum,* f. Br;
154. *Ibid.*, f. B2r, B3v. On More's and Fisher's opposition to the late medieval ecclesiastical *Befehlsstaat,* see Brendan Bradshaw, "The Controversial Sir Thomas More," *Journal of Ecclesiastical History* 36 (1985): 563–564. More, in particular, has been called "a papal minimalist" in John Guy, *Thomas More* (London: Arnold, 2000), 201.
155. Trusen, *Um die Reform und Einheit der Kirche,* 65.
156. "[C]um Wicliffo, Husso, Heluidio, Arrio, Montano, et ijs omnibus pestilentiori Luthero." Thomas More, *Responsio ad Lutherum* (1523), in More, *Complete Works,* 21 vols. (New Haven, N.J.: Yale University Press, 1963–1997), 5: pt. 1, 520–521. There is no record of More's own reference to the Bohemian Reformation or to Hus in Brian Gogan, *The Common Corps of Christendom: Ecclesiological Themes in the Writings of Sir Thomas More* (Leiden: Brill, 1982).
157. More, *Responsio ad Lutherum,* in *Complete Works,* 5: pt. 1, 460–461.
158. *Ibid.*, 5: pt. 1, 220–221, pt. 2, 909. On the Adamites, see also Chapter 2.
159. George Cavendish, *Life and Death of Cardinal Wolsey,* ed. Richard S. Sylvester (London: Oxford University Press, 1959), 180, lines 2–13, 266–268. See also More, *Complete Works,* 5: pt. 1, 220–221, pt. 2, 981.
160. Edward Surtz, *The Works and Days of John Fisher: An Introduction to the Position of St. John Fischer (1469–1535), Bishop of Rochester, in the English Renaissance and Reformation* (Cambridge, Mass.: Harvard University Press, 1967), 50–51, 82–87. For reference to Fisher's warning about civic disorder caused by the followers of Hus in Bohemia, see also Maria Dowling, *Fisher of Men: A Life of John Fisher, 1469–1535* (New York: St. Martin's Press, 1999), 139.
161. Surtz, *The Works and Days of John Fisher,* 188 (see also 323).
162. *Ibid.*, 78.
163. See n. 1 above.
164. Odložilík, "Utrakvistická postilla z r. 1540," 11–13
165. *Ibid.,* 6–7, 20.
166. *Ibid.,* 7, n. 17.
167. Dvorský, "Dopisy kněží Šimona z Habru a Jana faráře Německo-Brodského," 329, 337; Bydžovský, *Tento spis ukazuje,* 14.
168. *Ottův slovník naučný,* 8:275.
169. Hejnic and Martínek, *Rukověť' humanistického básnictví,* 5:438.
170. Pavel Paminondas, *Písničky křest'anské* (Prague: Anna Šumanova, 1596), f. H3r-v.
171. On Hooker's courtesy in debate, see also Peter Lake, "Business As Usual? The Immediate Reception of Hooker's *Ecclesiastical Polity,*" *Journal of Ecclesiastical History* 52 (2001): 463–464.
172. Bílejovský, *Kronyka Cýrkevní,* 38; Kamil Krofta, "Slovo o knězi Bohuslavu

Bílejovském," in Krofta, *Listy z náboženských dějin českých* (Prague: Historický klub, 1936), 296. See also Chapter 3.

173. Bydžovský, *Tento spis ukazuje*, 12. On early translations of Luther into Czech, see Rudolf Říčan, "Tschechische Übersetzungen von Luthers Schriften bis zum Schmalkaldischen Krieg," in *Vierhundertfünfzig Jahre lutherische Reformation, 1517–1967: Festschrift für Franz Lau zum 50. Geburtstag* (Göttingen: Vanderhoeck and Ruprecht, 1967), 282–288.

174. *Artykulowe a snessenij Knězstva pod obogij Spuosobau*, f. A4r, B4r. See also *Sněmy české*, 1:463–469.

175. Bydžovský, *Dět'átka a neviňátka*, f. C–1r.

176. Tomek, *Dějepis města Prahy*, 11: 236; and Říčan, *The History of the Unity of Brethren*, 157.

177. Říčan, *The History of the Unity of Brethren*, 156.

178. William Perkins, *Anatomia conscientiae. Aneb pobožné rozbírání a vysvětlení svědomí lidského*, trans. Jan Regius (Prague: Karel Karlsperk, 1620); Perkins, *O opuštění Božím*, trans. Jiřík Oeconomus (Prague: Daniel Sedlčanský, 1610); Perkins, *Traktát trojí krátký, ku potěšení zarmoucených kajících lidí*, trans. Simeon Valecius (Prague: Matěj Pardubský, 1613); Perkins, *Traktát velmi platný a užitečný*, trans. Simeon Valecius (Prague: Matěj Pardubský, 1616).

179. Zacharyáš Bruncvík, *Pravitatis et impletatis haereticae pia et fida ostensio. To jest: Zrcadlo Kacířství: Do něhož kdo zdravě nahlídne, Allegata, u Doktorů Církve vykázaná, přeběhne, pozná, že my Katolíci pod obojí nevinně, a bez náležitého vší Svaté říše vyslyšání od některých se kaceřujeme* (Prague: Matěj Pardubický, 1614); and Bruncvík, *Testamenti nostri Iesu Christi pia et fida assertio. To jest: Kšaftu Večeře Páně svatá Starožitnost, pobožná posloupnost, dlouhověká až právě do dne soudného trvanlivost: V níž z nařízení Kristového, z učení evangelistského a apoštolského, z doktorů a sněmů osvícených, z kanonu a práv duchovních, z historií církevních, a nejvíce našich českých, etc. Náboženství naše podobojí pravé Katolické, Křest'anské a Starožitné, mocné, patrné a bez falše, od času Krista Pána, až do našeho věku, posloupně se dokazuje a dovodí* (Prague: Matěj Pardubský, 1613).

180. Bruncvík, *Zrcadlo Kacířství*, f. C4r.

181. Abraham Scultetus, *Vysvětlení Žalmu XX v Valdsaxu* (Prague: Daniel Karel z Karlsperkga, 1619), f. E1r, E2r. This theme of interdenominational contacts is more fully developed in Chapter 11.

182. Pelikan, "Luther's Attitude Toward John Hus," 757–761.

183. In Hieronymus Dungersheim, *Dialogus ad Lutherum*, cited by Kraus, *Husitství v literatuře, zejména německé*, 1:154; and Ernst Ludwig Enders, *Dr. Martin Luthers Briefwechsel* (Calv and Stuttgart: Verlag der Vereinsbuchhandlung, 1887), 2:176.

184. Hieronymus Emser, *De disputatione lipsicensi ad Boemos obiter deflexa est (1519). A venatione Luteriana Aegocerotis assertio (1519)*, ed. Franz Xaver Thurnhofer (Münster: Aschendorf, 1921), 14, 33. On Emser, see also Gustav Kawerau, *Hieronymus Emser: Ein Lebensbild aus der Reformationsgeschichte* (Halle: Verein für Reformationsgeschichte, 1898), 18, but Emser still denounced Hus in 1523 as an old heretic from whom Luther drew his ideas (46–47).

185. Pelikan, "Luther's Attitude Toward John Hus," 757–758. Cochlaeus knew about those trends in Bohemian theology, which were more radical than Utraquism. He published a book against an early Czech Lutheran, Ulrichus Velenus, who denied Peter's residence in Rome: Johannes Cochlaeus, *De Petro et Roma aduersus Velenum Lutheranum*,

libri quatuor (Cologne: Quentell, 1525). In this book, however, Cochlaeus still equated Hus with Wyclif as a heretic (f. B4v).
  186. Surtz, *The Works and Days of John Fisher,* 329.
  187. Hejnic and Martínek, *Rukověť humanistického básnictví,* 2:103; Henze, *Aus Liebe zur Kirche Reform,* 50, 81.
  188. Johannes Cochlaeus, *Ein heimlich gespraech von der tragedia Johannis Hussen 1538,* ed. Hugo Holstein (Halle a. Salle: M. Niemeyer, 1900), v, 18–19.
  189. Remigius Bäumer, *Johannes Cochlaeus (1479–1552): Leben und Werk im Dienst der katholischen Reform* (Muenster: Aschendorf, 1980), 84, 112–114.
  190. Pelikan, "Luther's Attitude Toward John Hus," 760–761.
  191. Theodor Kolde, "Cochlaeus," *Realenzyklopaedie fuer protestantische Theologie und Kirche* (Leipzig: Hinrichs, 1896–1913?), 4:200, cited by Pelikan, "Luther's Attitude Toward John Hus," 759, n. 95.
  192. Koranda, *Traktát o velebné a božské svátosti oltářní,* f. A3v–A4r; Denis, Fin de l'indépendance bohême, 2:208–209.
  193. Novotný, "Náboženské dějiny české ve století 16.," 1:634.
  194. Bruno Bernard, *Patrice-François de Neny, 1716–1784: portrait d'un homme d'état* (Brussels: Editions de l'Université de Bruxelles, 1993), 150.
  195. Anna Skýbová, "Česká šlechta a jednání o povolení kompaktát r. 1525," in Josef Petráň, ed., *Proměny feudální třídy v Čechách v pozdním feudalismu* (Prague: Univerzita Karlova, 1976), 81–82.
  196. Tomáš Bavorovský, *Postila česká* (Olomouc: Jan Gunther, 1557), f. 100r; 377v–378r.
  197. "V kteréžto práci měl jsem věrného tovaryše a spolu Bratra v Pánu Kristu milého, slovutného Jana Straněnského . . ." Bavorovský, *Postila,* f. 4v–5r.
  198. *Ibid., f.* x1r–v. (11–12).
  199. Jireček, *Rukověť k dějinám literatury české do konce XVIII. věku,* 2:246.
  200. "[S] přehlédnutím a povolením Důstojných Pánů Administrátorů strany pod Jednou i pod Obojí Arcibiskupství Pražského." Tomáš Bavorovský, *Kázání o svatém pokání* (Prague: Bartoloměj Netolický, 1552), f. Hh2v.
  201. Jaroslav Kolár, "Hájkova kronika a česká literatura," in Václav Hájek z Libočan, *Kronika česká* (Prague: Odeon, 1981), 10.
  202. Jiří Pešek, *Měšťanská vzdělanost a kultura v předbělohorských Čechách, 1547–1620* (Prague: Karolinum, 1993), 74. See also Antonín Škarka, "Ze zápasů nekatolického tisku s protireformací: Literární a tiskařská aféra z r. 1602," *Český časopis historický* 42 (1936): 2.
  203. Emma Urbánková, "Nejstarší prvotisky českého původu," in *Knihtisk a kniha v českých zemích od husitství do Bílé hory: Sborník prací k 500. výročí českého knihtisku,* ed. František Šmahel (Prague: Academia, 1970), 24–30. For references to the traditional Utraquist liturgical books, see, for instance, Koranda, *Traktát o velebné a božské svátosti,* f. S3r–S3v.
  204. Jarold K. Zeman, "The Rise of Liberty in the Czech Reformation," *Central European History* 6 (1973): 136, citing Reginald R. Betts, *Essays in Czech History* (London: University of London, Athlone Press, 1969), 264.
  205. Jan V. Novák, "Postilla česká kn. Tomáše Bavorovského," *Sborník historický* 3 (1885): 239, n. 6.
  206. See Julius Pažout, *Jednání a dopisy konsistoře pod obojí způsobou přijímajících, 1562–1570* (Prague: Eduard Grégr, 1906), 58, 69, 136.

207. Jan Dubravius (Jan Skála z Doubravky), *Ioanis, Dei gratia episcopi Olomucensis, In psalmum ordine quintum ecclesiae deprecantis typum gerentem, cuius initium est: Verba mea auribus percipe, Domine, enarratio*... (Prostějov: Ioannes Guntherus, 1549), f. R2v–R3r.
208. *Ibid.*, f. R4v–S1r.
209. *Ibid.*, f. V1r–V1v.
210. *Ibid.*, f. T4v–V1r. See also Hejnic and Martínek, *Rukověť humanistického básnictví*, 2:81–82.
211. Dubravius, *Ioanis, Dei gratia episcopi Olomucensis*, f. R4r.

Chapter 6

1. František Kavka and Anna Skýbová, *Husitský epilog na koncilu tridentském a původní koncepce habsburské rekatolizace Čech*, Práce z dějin Univerzity Karlovy, sv. 8 (Prague: Univerzita Karlova, 1968).
2. See, for instance, Ludvík Němec, "Utraquists," *New Catholic Encyclopedia* (New York: McGraw-Hill, 1967–1974), 14:505; Alois Kroess, *Geschichte der Böhmischen Provinz der Gesellschaft Jesu* (Vienna: Mayer, 1910–1938), 1:212–213; Miloš Dokulil, *Ve věci tolerance*, Spisy Pedagogické fakulty, v. 60 (Brno: Masarykova univerzita, 1995), 123; and Dokulil, "Meditace nad tolerancí," *Sborník prací Filozofické fakulty Brněnské univerzity* B42 (1995): 30.
3. On the principle of apostolic succession, see, for instance, Enrico S. Molnar, *The Catholicity of the Utraquist Church of Bohemia* (Sewanee, Tenn.: University Press of Sewanee, 1959), 3–5; Kamil Krofta, "Boj o konsistoř pod obojí v letech 1562–1575 a jeho historický základ," *Český časopis historický* 17 (1911): 412–413.
4. On the Utraquist liturgy see Molnar, *The Catholicity of the Utraquist Church of Bohemia*, 6–8; Klement Borový, *Jednání a dopisy konsistoře katolické i utrakvistické*, 2 vols. (Prague: Kober, 1868–1869), 1:133; *Artykulowe a snessenij Kněžstva pod obogij Spuosobau: Leta Bozijho MDXXXIX* (archived at the National Library in Vienna under the notation: *Articuli Conciliabuli* sub utraque *specie communicantium*, Bohemice et latine, S.l., 1539, Signatura: 24 M 56), 15.
5. Borový, *Jednání a dopisy*, 1:10–13, 250, 260–262; and Bohuslav Bílejovský, *Kronyka Cýrkevní*, ed. Jozef Skalický (Josef Dittrich) (Prague: Fetterl z Vilden, 1816), 98.
6. David R. Holeton, "On the Evolution of the Utraquist Eucharistic Liturgy: A Precursor of Western Liturgical Reform," *Studia Liturgica*, 25 (1995): 63–66.
7. Ferdinand Menčík, ed., *Zápisky kněze Václava Rosy* (Vienna: J. Paška, 1879), 23. Julius Pažout, *Jednání a dopisy konsistoře pod obojí způsobou přijímajících, 1562–1570* (Prague: Historický spolek, 1906), 437.
8. David R. Holeton, "The Evolution of Utraquist Eucharistic Liturgy: A Textual Study" in *The Bohemian Reformation and Religious Practice*, vol. 2: Papers from the XVIIIth World Congress of the Czechoslovak Society of Arts and Sciences, Brno 1996, ed. Zdeněk V. David and David R. Holeton (Prague: Academy of Sciences of the Czech Republic, Main Library, 1998), 99–101.
9. *Ibid.*, 106–107.
10. *Ibid.*, 103.
11. Pavel Bydžovský, *Děťátka a neviňátka hned po přijetí křtu sv. Tělo a Krev Boží, že přijímati mají* (Prague: Bartoloměj Netolický, 1541), f. B1r–B1v.

12. Bydžovský, *Dět'átka a neviňátka*, f. A7r–A7v, B4r; Pavel Bydžovský, *Tento spis ukazuje, že Biskupové Biskupa, a Biskup kněží, a kněží od řádných Biskupů svěceni Těla a krve Boží posvěcovati mají* (N.p., 1543), 6, 9, 14–15.

13. See, for instance, Krofta, "Boj o konsistoř," 409; Josef Macek, *Víra a zbožnost jagellonského věku* (Prague: Argo, 2001), 59.

14. Concerning the high cost of travel to Italy, see Borový, *Jednání a dopisy,* 1:205. The Brethren, who were less squeamish about jurisdictional boundaries, had sought ordinations in the fifteenth century also from Eastern Orthodox, or even Armenian, bishops in eastern Poland and Moldavia; see Jaroslav Bidlo, ed., *Akty Jednoty bratrské* (Brno: Matice moravská, 1915–1923), 1:327. On ordinations in Venice, see also Anna Skýbová, "Le ordinazioni dei sacerdoti utraquisti a Venezia nella prima metà del XVI secolo," in *Italia e Boemia nella cornice del rinascimento europeo,* ed. Sante Graciotti (Florence: Leo S. Olschki, 1999), 60–65. On the itinerant bishops of the fifteenth century, see Chapter 2.

15. Marion Leathers Kuntz, "The Concept of Toleration in the *Colloquium Heptapolomeres* of Jean Bodin," in *Beyond the Persecuting Society: Religious Toleration Before the Enlightenment,* ed. John C. Laursen and Cary J. Nederman (Philadelphia: University of Pennsylvania Press, 1998), 127–128.

16. William B. Patterson, *King James VI and I and the Reunion of Christendom* (Cambridge: Cambridge University Press, 1997), 220–224; see also Noel Malcolm, *De Dominis (1560–1624): Venetian, Anglican, Ecumenist and Relapsed Heretic* (London: Strickland and Scott Academic Publications, 1984). On the Venetian interdict, see Francis Oakley, "Complexities of Context: Gerson, Bellarmine, Sarpi, Richer and the Venetian Interdict of 1606–1607," in Oakley, *Politics and Eternity: Studies in the History of Medieval and Early-Modern Political Thought* (Leiden: Brill, 1999), 188–216.

17. Zikmund Winter, *O životě na vysokých školách pražských: kulturní obraz XV. a XVI. století* (Prague: Matice česká, 1899), 358–359. On the preparation of clergy earlier in the sixteenth century, see Josef Jireček, *Rukověť k dějinám literatury české do konce XVIII. věku* (Prague: Tempský, 1875), 1:115. On the theological lectures by Martin of Vlašim, see *Ze starých letopisů českých,* trans. Jaroslav Porák and Jaroslav Kašpar (Prague: Svoboda, 1980), 291.

18. Borový, *Jednání a dopisy,* 1:161.

19. Borový, *Jednání a dopisy,* 1:189; Václav V. Tomek, *Dějepis města Prahy,* 12 vols. (Prague: Řivnáč, 1855–1901), 11:235. For the formula of abjuration, see Klement Borový, "Die Utraquisten in Böhmen," *Archiv für österreichische Geschichtsforschung* 36 (1866): 264.

20. Tomek, *Dějepis města Prahy,* 11:236.

21. *Ibid.*, 11:239.

22. František V. Peřinka, *Dějiny města Kroměříže* (Kroměříž: Obecní rada města, 1913), 1:270–71.

23. In August 1544, Dubravius admonished the Consistory to seek an archbishop in agreement with the Council of Trent in his letter, *Ad collegium Pragense de ecclesiae oeconomia epistola* in *Ioanis, Dei gratia episcopi Olomucensis, In psalmum ordine quintum ecclesiae deprecantis typum gerentem, cuius initium est: Verba mea auribus percipe, Domine, enarratio . . .* (Prostějov: Ioannes Guntherus, 1549). See also Josef Hejnic and Jan Martínek, eds., *Rukověť humanistického básnictví v Čechách a na Moravě,* 5 vols. (Prague: Academia, 1966–1982), 2:76. See also Chapter 5.

24. Kavka and Skýbová, *Husitský epilog,* 30–31; Borový, *Jednání a dopisy,* 1:191.

25. Borový, *Jednání a dopisy,* 1:244. The request was repeated on June 26, 1549; *ibid.*, 1:248. As to the horse, the Consistory wrote on September 2, 1550, that such beasts were not native to Bohemia, and had to be imported from "Muscovy, Russia, or Prussia"; *ibid.*, 1:285. The Consistory again asked for the oils on March 10, 1551, with a gift of six ducates; *ibid.*, 1:297.

26. Josef Janáček, *Dějiny české: Doba předbělohorská,* 2 vols. (Prague: Academia, 1971–1984), 1: pt. 1, 264; David R. Holeton, "Church or Sect? The Jednota Bratrská and the Growth of Dissent from Mainline Utraquism," *Communio Viatorum* 38 (1996): 26, n. 77; Borový, *Jednání a dopisy,* 1:129, 136–137, 153–154, 157, 161. The fact that the Roman Curia did not stop the Utraquist ordinations in Venice raises the question of whether the Holy See had not tacitly treated the Utraquists at that time as if they were a Uniate church.

27. Desiderius Erasmus, *The Correspondence,* 11 vols. (Toronto: University of Toronto Press, 1974–1994), 11:322–323.

28. Borový, *Jednání a dopisy,* 1:224–225, 238–39. Concerning ordinations, see documents of August 22 and October 24, 1550 and January 7 and June 15, 1551; *ibid.*, 1:284, 289, 293, 299. On Nausea's relationship to Witzel, see Winfried Trusen, *Um die Reform und Einheit der Kirche: Zum Leben und Werk Georg Witzels* (Münster: Aschendorffsche Verlagsbuchhandlung, 1957), 25–26.

29. František Tischer, *K dějinám sporů arcibiskupův Pražských o právo metropolitní nad biskupy Olomouckými v XVI. století* (Prague: Česká společnost nauk, Věstnik, Třída filosoficko-historicko-jazykozpytná, 1905), 2.

30. Concerning complaints about harboring runaway monks, see Zikmund Winter, *Život církevní v Čechách: Kulturně-historický obraz v XV. a XVI. století,* 2 vols. (Prague: Česká akademie pro vědy, slovesnost a umění, 1895), 1:468. For secular priests, with the number of individuals (if more than one) indicated in brackets following the page number, see Borový, *Jednání a dopisy,* 1:129, 160, 163, 181, 214–215 [3], 221 [2], 242, 301, 302, 305, 314, 316–317, 318, 325–26 [2], 329 [2]; for monks, *ibid.*, 1:195, 211, 222, 248, 316, 330 [2].

31. A notable priest defector from Utraquism to the Roman Church was Václav Hájek of Libočany, author of the monumental *Kronika česká* (1541). The Utraquist Consistory referred to him as an "apostate," but it did approve the book's publication; see Jireček, *Rukověť k dějinám literatury české,* 1:219. For other cases, see Borový, *Jednání a dopisy,* 1:214; Pažout, *Jednání a dopisy,* 43, 260, 334–335.

32. Václav Novotný, "Náboženské dějiny české ve století 16.," in *Česká politika,* ed. Zdeněk V. Tobolka, 5 vols. (Prague: Jan Laichter, 1906), 1:608.

33. W. Friedensburg, ed., *Nuntiaturberichte aus Deutschland nebst ergänzenden Aktenstücken. Erste Abteilung 1533–1559. 1. Band, Nuntiaturen des Vergerio, 1533–1536* (Gotha: F. A. Perthes, 1892), 152.

34. Klement Borový, *Antonín Brus z Mohelnice, arcibiskup pražský; Historicko-kritický životopis* (Prague: Dědictví sv. Prokopa, 1873), 186.

35. *Sněmy české od léta 1526 až po naši dobu.*, vols. 1-11, 15 (Prague: Zemský výbor, 1877-1941), 1:633; Krofta, "Boj o konsistoř," 188–189; Kavka and Skýbová, *Husitský epilog,* 30–31. On Horák's irenic contacts see Barbara Henze, *Aus Liebe zur Kirche Reform: die Bemühungen Georg Witzels (1501–1573) um die Kircheneinheit* (Münster: Aschendorff, 1995), 40.

36. On the three bishops, see Holeton, "Church or Sect? The Jednota Bratrská and the Growth of Dissent from Mainline Utraquism," 26, n. 78. This pattern also prevails

in the modern Moravian Church, the descendant of the Unity of Brethren. Each of its provinces has a bishop whose function is to ordain priests, while the administrative power is vested in a synod that elects for that purpose a Narrow Council of three; "Jednota bratrská," *Katolický týdeník,* March 9, 1997, p. 4.

37. For instance, in the *Misál Kutné Hory,* copied by Jan of Humpolec in 1483; see Holeton, "The Evolution of Utraquist Eucharistic Liturgy: A Textual Study," 102.

38. František Šmahel, *Husitská revoluce,* 4 vols. (Prague: Historický ústav, 1993), 4:100–101. For Sigismund's decree of 1436, see *Archiv český* 3 (1844): 427–431; see also Winfried Eberhard, *Konfessionsbildung und Stände in Böhmen, 1478–1530* (Munich: Oldenbourg, 1981), 44–45. For the resolution of 1547, see *Sněmy české,* 2:156–157. Elizabeth was excommunicated by the bull *Regnans in Excelsis* issued by Pope Pius V on February 25, 1570.

39. Paulus II, *Odsudek víry* (Prague: Severýn, 1547). On his campaign to depose George of Poděbrady, see, for instance, Otakar Odložilík, *The Hussite King: Bohemia in European Affairs, 1440–1471* (New Brunswick, N.J.: Rutgers University Press, 1965). A harsher censure of the Pope was prefixed to the text of Paul III's bull directed against the Schmalcaldic League in July 1546. Stemming apparently from a Lutheran source in Moravia, the introduction speaks of the Antichrist who combats the true Christians; see Paulus III, *Bulle od Papeže Římského Antykrysta proti pravým křest'anům vydaná* ([Prostějov?]: n.p., 1546).

40. Václav Koranda, "Odpověd' na matrykát bosákův anno 1496 post pascha," in Koranda, *Manualník,* ed. J. Truhlář (Prague: Česká společnost nauk, 1888), 73–80.

41. *Knihy Vavřince Vally o Constantinovu nadání;* see Josef Dobrovský, *Dějiny české řeči a literatury v redakcích z roku 1791, 1792 a 1818,* ed. Benjamin Jedlička (Prague: Melantrich, 1936), 416.

42. Brian Tierney, *Origins of Papal Infallibility, 1150–1350: A Study on the Concepts of Infallibility, Sovereignty and Tradition in the Middle Ages* (Leiden: E. J. Brill, 1988), 12–13.

43. *Ibid.,* 310.

44. "Ockham," *DNB,* 14:802; William of Ockham, *A Short Discourse on the Tyrannical Government over Things Divine and Human, but Especially over the Empire and Those Subject to the Empire, Usurped by Some Who Are Called Highest Pontiffs,* ed. Artur S. McGrade, trans. John Kilcullen (New York: Cambridge University Press, 1992), written in the 1340s. For a recent treatment of the erection of the authoritarian monarchy by the popes in the twelfth and thirteenth centuries, see Agostino Paravicini Bagliani, *Il trono di Pietro: L'universalità del papato da Alessandro III a Bonifacio VIII* (Rome: Nuova Italia Scientifica, 1996), especially 91–118.

45. Margaret Harvey, "Adam Easton and the Condemnation of Wyclif, 1377," *English Historical Review* 113 (1998): 326. See also Miloslav Kaňák, *John Viklef: Život a dílo anglického Husova předchůdce* (Prague: Blahoslav, 1973), 80; Gordon Leff, "Wyclif and Hus: A Doctrinal Comparison," *Wyclif in His Times,* ed. Anthony Kenny (Oxford: Clarendon Press, 1986), 109.

46. See Paul de Vooght, *L'hérésie de Jean Huss,* 2d ed., 2 vols. (Louvain: Publications universitaires, 1975), 2:587–588; see also František Bartoš, "Marsiliův Defensor Pacis v husitské literatuře," *Časopis českého musea* 102 (1928): 13–26. On the triangular relationship among Marsilio, Wyclif, and Hus, see Enrico S. Molnar, "Viklef, Hus a problém autority," in *Jan Hus mezi epochami, národy a konfesemi,* ed. Jan B. Lášek (Prague: Česká křest'anská akademie, 1995), 106–109. For a general survey of the late

medieval critique of the papal monarchism, see Brian Tierney, *Foundations of Conciliar Theory: The Contributions of the Medieval Canonists from Gratian to the Great Schism* (New York: Cambridge University Press, 1955), especially 179–237.

47. Brendan Bradshaw, "The Controversial Sir Thomas More," *Journal of Ecclesiastical History* 36 (1985): 563–564.

48. See also John Guy, *Thomas More* (London: Arnold, 2000), 115, 178, 201–203.

49. Pavel Bydžovský, *Historiae aliquot Anglorum martyrum, quibus Deus suam ecclesiam exornare sicut syderibus coelum dignatus est* (Prague: J. Cantor, 1554) is devoted to the martyrdom of More and Fisher; Robert Barnes, *Kronyky. A žiwotuow sepsání najwrchnějších Biskupuow Římských jináč Papežůw,* trans. Šimon Ennius Klatovský (Nuremberg: Woldřich Nejber and Jan Montán, 1565), f. 195v. See also Chapter 5.

50. James D. Tracy, "Erasmus Among the Postmodernists: *Dissimulatio, Bonae Literae,* and *Docta Pietas* Revisited," in *Erasmus' Vision of the Church,* ed. Hilmar M. Pabel (Kirksville, Mo.: Sixteenth Century Journal Publishers, 1995), 17–18, 40. See also Ernest E. Reynolds, *Thomas More and Erasmus* (New York: Fordham University Press, 1965).

51. Bydžovský, *Historiae aliquot Anglorum martyrum,* f. Br.

52. Alexander Patschovsky, "Über die politische Bedeutung von Häresienverfolgung im mittelalterlichen Böhmen," in *Die Anfänge der Inquisition im Mittelalter: Mit einem Ausblick auf das 20. Jahrhundert und einem Beitrag über religiöse Intoleranz im nichtchristlichen Bereich,* ed. Peter Segl (Cologne: Böhlau, 1993), 241. See also Zdeňka Hledíková, "Pronikání kuriálního centralismu do českých zemí: Na dokladech provizních listin do roku 1342," *Český časopis historický* 88 (1990): 3–33.

53. Kamil Krofta, "Václav Koranda mladší z Nové Plzně a jeho názory náboženské," *Listy z náboženských dějin* (Prague: Historický klub, 1936), 258; Tomek, *Dějepis města Prahy,* 10:225; *Ze starých letopisů českých,* trans. Jaroslav Porák and Jaroslav Kašpar (Prague: Svoboda, 1980), 290–291.On Zbyněk, see Thomas A. Fudge, *The Magnificent Ride: The First Reformation in Hussite Bohemia* (Brookfield, Vt.: Ashgate, 1998), 75–76.

54. Harvey, "Adam Easton and the Condemnation of Wyclif," 333.

55. He died in 1507. Tomek, *Dějepis města Prahy,* 10:224, 227.

56. For a description of this phantom phenomenon, see, for instance, Otakar Odložilík, "Utrakvistická postilla z r. 1540," *Věstnik české společnosti nauk* (1925), 24–25. The one significant figure who might actually qualify as an "Old Utraquist" by this definition, could be the abovementioned Havel Gelastus Vodňanský, who died in 1577 surrounded by Jesuit fathers and fully reconciled to the Roman Church, without, however, renouncing his allegiance to the communion sub utraque. See Borový, *Antonín Brus z Mohelnice,* 59; Kroess, *Geschichte der Böhmischen Provinz der Gesellschaft Jesu,* 1:212.

57. For the degree of micromanagement practiced by the papal Curia even in the affairs of Olomouc, where the bishop was elected by the cathedral chapter, see Bohumil Navrátil, *Biskupství olomoucké 1576–1579 a volba Stanislava Pavlovského* (Prague: Česká společnost nauk, 1909), 210–212, 234–235.

58. Borový, *Jednání a dopisy,* 1:332–334.

59. *Sněmy české,* 3:7.

60. See Kavka and Skýbová, *Husitský epilog,* especially 35–158.

61. In 1549, the Consistory clearly adhered to the Articles of 1539, including the observance of fast and celebration of feast days; see Borový, *Jednání a dopisy,* 1:250, 255.

Notes to Pages 151–155 453

62. Krofta, "Boj o konsistoř," 193, n. 2; Tomek, *Dějepis města Prahy,* 12:62.
63. Tomek, *Dějepis města Prahy,* 12:84, 93, 129–130; Borový, *Jednání a dopisy,* 1:379.
64. Borový, *Jednání a dopisy,* 1:386.
65. In *Jednání a dopisy,* 1–2, Pažout gives the names of twenty-one of the accused.
66. Krofta, "Boj o konsistoř," 295–297. The response of the accused appears in *Antiqua et constans confessio fidei ecclesiae Christi in regno Boiemiae et Marchianatu Moraviae, quam vulgo partem* sub utraque *sacramentum venerabile corporis et sanguinis dom. Jesu Christi communicantium appellant,* with introduction by Matěj Kolín z Chotěřiny (Prague: n.p., 1574), f. B5((v)–C3(v). (Krofta cites this work in "Boj o konsistoř," 296, n. 4.)
67. See Chapter 3.
68. Krofta, "Boj o konsistoř," 298; Zikmund Winter, *Život církevní v Čechách: Kulturně-historický obraz v XV. a XVI. století,* 2 vols. (Prague: Česká akademie pro vědy, slovesnost a umění, 1895), 1:133.
69. Krofta, "Boj o konsistoř," 300.
70. Martin Žatecký, *Knížka proti ošemetné poctě a pokryté Svatých,* 2d ed. (Prague: n.p., 1593).
71. Winter, *Život církevní,* 1:133.
72. Borový, *Jednání a dopisy,* 1:388; Pažout, *Jednání a dopisy,* 9–11; *Sněmy české,* 3:156.
73. Barnes, *Kronyky. A žiwotuow sepsání najwrchnějších Biskupuow.*
74. Rosemary O'Day, *The Debate on the English Reformation* (London: Methuen, 1986), 10.
75. Neelak S. Tjernagel, *Lutheran Martyr* (Milwaukee, Wisc.: Northwestern Publishing House, 1982), 101.
76. Carter Lindberg, "A Specific Contribution of the Second Reformation," in Milan Opočenský, ed., *Toward a Renewed Dialogue: Consultation on the First and Second Reformations, Geneva 28 November to 1 December 1994* (Geneva: World Alliance of Reformed Churches, 1996), 42.
77. Barnes, *Kronyky. A žiwotuow sepsání najwrchnějších,* f. 97v–116r.
78. See also Miroslava Hejnová, "Barnesovy *Kroniky* a jejich české pokračování," *Folia Historica Bohemica* 13 (1990): 588–92.
79. Tjernagel, *Lutheran Martyr,* 101.
80. Barnes, *Kronyky. A žiwotuow sepsání najwrchnějších,* f. 194v–195r.
81. See Chapter 5.
82. Barnes, *Kronyky. A žiwotuow sepsání najwrchnějších,* f. 195v.
83. Hejnic and Martínek, *Rukověť humanistického básnictví,* 2:103.
84. On the triangular relationship among Fabri, Nausea, and Witzel, see Henze, *Aus Liebe zur Kirche Reform,* 50, 81.
85. Robert Barnes, *Kronyky. A žiwotuow sepsání najwrchnějších,* f. 198r–198v.
86. *Ibid.,* f. 205r–205v.
87. Jan Martínek, "Příspěvky k životopisu a charakteristice Šimona Ennia Klatovského," *Sborník Krajského vlastivědného muzea v Olomouci* 4 (1956–1958): 256–261, 266.
88. Barnes, *Kronyky. A žiwotuow sepsání najwrchnějších,* f. 2v.
89. *Ibid.,* f. 3v–4r.
90. Pažout, *Jednání a dopisy,* 435–438.

91. "[Ž]e biskupy řádný Antikristy a kněží, kteří od nich ouřad svatýho kněžství přijímají, Antikristovými kněžími býti soudí a praví." Pažout, *Jednání a dopisy,* 437.

92. Heymann, "The Impact of Martin Luther upon Bohemia," 127.

93. Jiří Pešek, "Protestant Literature in Bohemian Private Libraries *circa* 1600," in *Reformation in Eastern and Central Europe,* ed. Karin Maag (Brookfield, Vt.: Ashgate, 1997), 36.

94. *Sněmy české,* 2:604–618; Borový, *Jednání a dopisy,* 1:251, 260–267. See also Tomek, *Dějepis města Prahy,* 12:20–29.

95. Krofta, "Boj o konsistoř," 387.

96. Cited by Ferdinand Hrejsa, *Dějiny křest'anství v Československu,* 6 vols. (Prague: Husova Československá evangelická fakulta bohoslovecká, 1947–50), 2:271; and (in Latin) by Gerald Christianson, *Cesarini: The Conciliar Cardinal. The Basel Years, 1431–1438* (St. Ottilien: EOS Verlag, 1979), 118. See also František Bartoš, *The Hussite Revolution, 1424–1437,* ed. John M. Klassen (Boulder, Colo.: East European Monographs, 1986), 109.

97. František Palacký, *Obrana husitství,* trans. and ed. František M. Bartoš (Prague: Blahoslav, 1926), 56–57.

98. *Ibid.,* 58.

99. Josef Pekař, *Žižka a jeho doba,* 4 vols. (Prague: Vesmír, 1927–1933), 3:324.

100. Karel Stloukal, "Ke kritice *Hlídky,*" *Český časopis historický* 33 (1927): 469–470.

101. Concerning an earlier episode of such duplicity in 1525, see Václav Novotný, "Náboženské dějiny české ve století 16.," in *Česká politika,* ed. Zdeněk V. Tobolka, 5 vols. (Prague: Jan Laichter, 1906), 1:592.

102. Pažout, *Jednání a dopisy konsistoře,* 23–25; Krofta, "Boj o konsistoř," 386–387. See also Brus's memorandum of April 21, 1562, cited by Kavka and Skýbová in *Husitský epilog,* 69, from S. Steinherz, ed., *Nuntiaturberichte aus Deutschland, nebst ergänzenden Aktenstücken.* Zweite Abteilung, 1560–1572, Band 3: *Nuntius Delfino, 1562–1563* (Vienna: C. Gerold's Sohn, 1903), 44.

103. Fr. J. Zoubek, "O věcech církevních na Poděbradsku, 1550–1665," *Časopis českého musea* 52 (1878): 58.

104. John E. Booty, "Introduction," in John Jewel, *An Apology of the Church of England,* ed. J. E. Booty (Ithaca, N.Y.: Cornell University Press, 1963), ix.

105. František Šmahel, "Svoboda slova, svatá válka a tolerance z nutnosti v husitském období," *Český časopis historický* 92 (1994): 670.

106. Johann Schmidl, *Historia Societatis Jesu provinciae Bohemiae,* 2 vols. (Prague: n.p., 1747–1749), 1:226, 229, 314.

107. Later these allegations were applied to Administrator Dvorský; see Alois Kroesz, "Die Unterwerfung des utraquistischen Administrators Heinrich Dworský von Helfenberg unter den katholischen Erzbischof Anton Brus im J. 1572," *Zeitschrift für katholische Theologie* 34 (1910): 702–712.

108. Kroess, *Geschichte der Böhmischen Provinz,* 1:121.

109. Krofta, "Boj o konsistoř," 300–301.

110. Blažej Nožička z Votína, *Knížka proti bludům některým před tisíci lety odsouzeným* (Prague: Jan Kantor, 1566), f. B1r, C3r, K1v, K3r.

111. *Ibid.,* f. C3r.

112. For an attempt to highjack Nožička for Rome, see Antonín Podlaha, "Tři čeští laikové, jakožto literární obránci víry katolické ve století XVI. a XVII.: Blažej Nožička

z Votína, Jakub Horčický z Tepence, Jan Benedikt Smolík," *Sborník historického kroužku* Sešit 5 (1896): 5; Nožička, *Knížka proti bludům,* introduction, 2.

113. "Jestli že bych pak v toto mé vyznání vče pobloudil . . . a kdo mi lepší smysl Slovem Božím a Písmem Svatým v Obecném smyslu ukázal chci rád napraviti a pravdě míst dáti." Nožička, *Knížka proti bludům,* f. A3v.

114. Nožička, *Knížka proti bludům,* f. A3r.

115. For instance, *ibid.,* f. H4r.

116. Pažout, *Jednání a dopisy,* 138.

117. "[S] přehlédnutím a povolením Důstojných Pánů Administrátorů strany pod Jednou i pod Obojí Arcibiskupství Pražského." Tomáš Bavorovský, *Kázání o svatém pokání* (Prague: Bartoloměj Netolický, 1552), f. Hh2v.

118. Pažout, *Jednání a dopisy,* 365; Krofta, "Boj o konsistoř," 390–391.

119. Borový, *Antonín Brus z Mohelnice,* 191.

120. See Chapter 9.

121. Aeneas Sylvius Piccolomini (Pope Pius II), *Historia Bohemica/Historie česká,* trans. and ed. Dana Martínková, Alena Hadravová, and Jiří Matl (Prague: Koniasch Latin Press, 1998), 167, 169.

122. On the equivocal character of the Compactata, see František Šmahel, "Husitské artikuly a jihlavská kompaktáta," in *Jihlava a Basilejská Kompaktáta: Sborník příspěvků z mezinárodního sympozia k 555. výročí přijetí Basilejských kompaktát, 26–28. červen 1991,* by František Šmahel, et al. (Jihlava: Muzeum Vysočiny, 1992), 11–27.

123. Richard M. Douglas, *Jacopo Sadoleto, 1477–1547: Humanist and Reformer* (Cambridge, Mass.: Harvard University Press, 1959), 74; Josef Macek, "Osudy basilejských kompaktát v jagelonském věku," *Jihlava a Basilejská Kompaktáta: Sborník příspěvků z mezinárodního sympozia k 555. výročí přijetí Basilejských kompaktát, 26–28. červen 1991* (Jihlava: Muzeum Vysočiny, 1992), 199–200. See also Alain Dufour, "Humanisme et Reformation,"in Dufour, *Histoire politique et psychologie historique* (Geneva: Librairie Droz, 1966), 54.

124. Pažout, *Jednání a dopisy,* 27–30.

125. Anton Frind, "Urkunden über die Bewilligung des Laienkelches in Böhmen unter Kaiser Ferdinand I," *Česká společnost nauk. Abhandlungen* 6, no. 6 (1873): 13–15, 34–35, 35–41.

126. Tischer, "K dějinám sporů arcibiskupův Pražských," 2; Borový, *Antonín Brus z Mohelnice,* 176–177; Frind, "Urkunden über die Bewilligung des Laienkelches," 36, 41. Concerning the opposition to the metropolitan rights of the archbishop of Prague by Bishops Marek Kuehn (1553–1565), Vilém Prusinovský (1565–1572), Jan Grodecký (1572–1574), Tomáš Albín z Helfenburka (1574–1575), Jan Mezoun (1576–1578), and Stanislav Pavlovský (1579–1598), between 1553 and 1598, see Navrátil, *Biskupství olomoucké 1576–1579,* 213–219.

127. Pažout, *Jednání a dopisy,* 115–116, 126, 138–139.

128. *Ibid.,* 342–343; Ferdinand Hrejsa, *Česká konfesse: Její vznik, podstata a dějiny* (Prague: Česká akademie pro vědy, slovesnost a umění, 1912), 20. On the anathema of the communion for infants by the Council of Trent, see David R. Holeton, "The Communion of Infants: The Basel Years," *Communio Viatorum* 29 (1986): 40, n. 99.

129. Pažout, *Jednání a dopisy,* 344.

130. Pažout, *Jednání a dopisy,* 342–344; Krofta, "Boj o konsistoř," 385; see also Frind, "Urkunden über die Bewilligung des Laienkelches," 41–42.

131. For instance, Borový, *Antonín Brus z Mohelnice,* 176, 179, 180, 187–189; Pažout, *Jednání a dopisy,* 3.

132. Pažout, *Jednání a dopisy,* 342–343; Borový, *Antonín Brus z Mohelnice,* 186.

133. The prayers were for victory over the Turks. The Consistory instead substituted litanies in Czech. Pažout, *Jednání a dopisy,* 210–211, and also 377.

134. Blanka Zilynská, "Biskup Filibert a české země," in *Jihlava a Basilejská Kompaktáta: Sborník příspěvků z mezinárodního sympozia k 555. výročí přijetí Basilejských kompaktát, 26–28. červen 1991,* by František Šmahel et al. (Jihlava: Muzeum Vysočiny, 1992), 62–63.

135. The rejection of the validity of communion sub una was reaffirmed, for instance, in 1549; see Tomek, *Dějepis města Prahy,* 12:26–27.

136. Such power was in fact implied in Pius IV's decree permitting lay communion sub utraque; see Petr Linteo z Pilzenburgku, *Krátká správa o přijímání velebné svátosti pod jednau a dvojí spůsobau* (Prague: Kargezius, 1613), 47.

137. See, for instance, Petr Linteo z Pilzenburgku, *Jistá a patrná cýrkve svaté znamení* (Litomyšl: n.p., 1593), 163–164. As early as April 1575, Nuncio Giovanni Dolfin contemplated the future withdrawal of the permission of the lay chalice; see Daniela Neri, ed., *Nuntiaturberichte aus Deutschland,* Dritte Abteilung, 1572–1585, 8, Band: Nuntiatur Giovanni Dolfins, 1575–1576 (Tübingen: Max Niemayer, 1997), 126.

138. Jan z Valdštejna, Starší, *Modlitby (a řeči) pobožné některé z písem Svatých, jiné pak z naučení Mudrců pohanských vybrané* (N.p., 1576).

139. *Ibid.,* f. E5v–E8v.

140. *Ibid.,* f. G4v–G5r.

141. Zdeněk Nejedlý, "Martin Lupáč," in *Ottův slovník naučný* (Prague: Otto, 1888–1909), 16:465; see also Amedeo Molnár, "Martin Lupáč: Modus disputandi pro fide," *Folia Historica Bohemica* 4 (1982): 161–177.

142. Pavel Bydžovský, *Odvolání jednoho Bratra z Roty Pikhartské,* 2d ed. (Prague: Jan Jičínský, 1588), f. D1v.

143. Erasmus, *The Correspondence,* 9:397–398.

144. Ephraim Radner, "Bad Bishops: A Key to Anglican Ecclesiology," *Anglican Theological Review* 82 (2000): 337–338.

145. Krofta, "Boj o konsistoř," 401; Kroess, *Geschichte der Böhmischen Provinz,* 1:209.

146. Hrejsa, *Česká konfesse,* 20; Kroess, *Geschichte der Böhmischen Provinz,* 1:206, 208; Pažout, *Jednání a dopisy,* 369.

147. Borový, *Antonín Brus z Mohelnice,* 188.

148. Pažout, *Jednání a dopisy,* 283, 296–297, 356, 365, 430. For a list of candidates, see *ibid.,* 173.

149. Borový, *Antonín Brus z Mohelnice,* 257–262; Pažout, *Jednání a dopisy,* 381.

150. Pažout, *Jednání a dopisy,* 387–388, 389–396; Borový, *Antonín Brus z Mohelnice,* 268–269.

151. Pažout, *Jednání a dopisy,* 382–383.

152. Borový, *Antonín Brus z Mohelnice,* 270; Pažout, *Jednání a dopisy,* 385.

153. Pažout, *Jednání a dopisy,* 389–396; Borový, *Antonín Brus z Mohelnice,* 192–193.

154. Pažout, *Jednání a dopisy,* 397.

155. *Ibid.,* 402.

156. Krofta, "Boj o konsistoř," 401–403; Kroess, *Geschichte der Böhmischen Provinz der Gesellschaft Jesu,* 1:211–212.

157. Borový, *Antonín Brus z Mohelnice,* 194–195, 290, 292–293; Helmut Goetz, ed., *Nuntiaturberichte aus Deutschland nebst ergänzenden Aktenstücken,* Dritte Abteilung, 1572–1585, 6, Band: Nuntiatur Giovanni Delfinos, 1572–1573 (Tübingen: Max Niemayer, 1982), 153–154, 467.

158. Borový, *Antonín Brus z Mohelnice,* 195; Pažout, *Dopisy a jednání,* 120–121, 246.

159. Borový, *Antonín Brus z Mohelnice,* 196.

160. See, for instance, Ludvík Němec, "Utraquists," *New Catholic Encyclopedia* (New York: McGraw-Hill, 1967–1974), 14:505; Novotný, "Náboženské dějiny české ve století 16.," 1:621.

161. Kroess, *Geschichte der Böhmischen Provinz der Gesellschaft Jesu,* 1:212–213; Novotný, "Náboženské dějiny české ve století 16.," 1:620.

162. On the roles of Bílejovský and Bydžovský, see Chapters 4 and 5.

163. Josef Pekař, "Note," *Český časopis historický* 39 (1933): 356, n. 1. As examples of confusion resulting from such attempts, see, for instance, Hrejsa, *Česká konfesse,* 59, 61; Krofta, "Boj o konsistoř," 302–303.

Chapter 7

1. The events of the Diet of 1575 are available in considerable detail, above all in Ferdinand Hrejsa, *Česká konfesse: Její vznik, podstata a dějiny* (Prague: Česká akademie pro vědy, slovesnost a umění, 1912), 86–94; Hrejsa, *Dějiny křesťanství v Československu,* 6 vols. (Prague: Husova Československá evangelická fakulta bohoslovecká, 1946–1950), 6:274–323; Kamil Krofta, "Boj o konsistoř podobojí v l. 1562–1575 a jeho historický základ," *Český časopis historický* 17 (1911): 404–406, 411–416; and more recently by Jaroslav Pánek, *Stavovská opozice a její zápas s Habsburky, 1547–1577* (Prague: Academia, 1982), 101–119. For earlier presentations, see also Václav Tomek, *Dějepis města Prahy,* 12 vols. (Prague: Řivnáč, 1855–1901), 12:228ff, and Anton Gindely, *Geschichte der Böhmischen Brüder,* 2d ed., 2 vols. (Prague: C. Bellmann, 1861–1862), 2:109ff. Important documentary sources are Sixt of Ottersdorfu, "Diarium o sněmu 1575, jenž zahájen byl 21. února a zavřín dne 27. září," and "Diarium Bratří českých," *Sněmy české od léta 1526 až po naši dobu.,* vols. 1–11, 15 (Prague: Zemský výbor, 1877–1941), 4, no. 88, 318–392, and 4, no. 89, 392–464, respectively.

2. Tomek, *Dějepis města Prahy,* 12:245.

3. Krofta, "Boj o konsistoř," 417; see also Hrejsa, *Česká konfesse,* 282; Josef Macek, et al., *Dějiny,* 2 parts, together vol. 2 of *Československá vlastivěda* (Prague: Orbis, 1963), 1:390.

4. Jan Kapras, *Právní dějiny zemí koruny české,* 3 vols. (Prague: Unie, 1913), 2:536.

5. "Staroutrakvisté se hlásili k dědictví Husovu . . . ale neměli již nic z jeho ducha." Hrejsa, *Dějiny křesťanství v Československu,* 6:323. Alois Míka, "Z bojů o náboženskou toleranci v 16. století," *Československý časopis historický* 18 (1970): 375, 377.

6. Hrejsa, *Česká konfesse,* 102.

7. *Ibid.,* 120–121. The statement is, however, accepted as a historical fact by the editors of *Sněmy české,* 4:136.

8. Hrejsa, *Česká konfesse,* 102. The Unity's sixteenth-century writings, and the histories in particular, might merit an examination from the viewpoint of a humoristic

temperament, which runs through Czech literature from the chronicles of Kosmas and So-Called Dalimil to Jaroslav Hašek and even the soft pornography of Vladimír Páral's novels. The Brethren's writings might assume a distinguished place in the tradition of this literary idiosyncrasy, if analyzed in the style of Robert B. Pysent's "The Baroque Continuum of Czech Literature," *Slavonic and East European Review* 62 (1984): 321–343.

9. Krofta, "Boj o konsistoř," 414; *Sněmy české*, 4:452.

10. For instance, concerning the cited incident, see *Sněmy české*, 4:368. The principal source for the religious debates and events of 1539–1543 is the Brethren's: [Jan Černý], "Poznamenání a spolu shromáždění některých věcí pametihodných přítomným i budoucím," 1579 (manuscript, Prague, Bib. Nat. XVII C 3).

11. *Sněmy české*, 3:381.

12. Hrejsa, *Česká konfesse*, 43.

13. Josef Kollmann, *Valdštejn a evropská politika, 1625–1630: Historie 1. generalátu* (Prague: Academia, 1999), 28.

14. *Sněmy české*, 11: pt. 1: 38; Hrejsa, *Česká konfesse*, 44.

15. Josef Riss, "Život a literné působení Sixta z Ottersdorfu," *Časopis českého Musea* 35 (1861): pt. 1, 82.

16. Their petition to the emperor (drafted, but not submitted) to recognize their Confession and church organization on May 14, 1575, was signed by 17 barons and 124 knights. See Tomek, *Dějepis města Prahy*, 12:236.

17. Hrejsa, *Česká konfesse*, 60.

18. *Sněmy české*, 4:374–375; Hrejsa, *Česká konfesse*, 231.

19. Pavel Kristián was the author of the famous code of municipal law, *Práva městská království českého* (Prague, 1579, 1581, 1582), which received official status in 1579. "Kristián (Glatovinus, Christianus, Koldín, z Koldína), Pavel," in *Rukověť' humanistického básnictví*, 5 vols., ed. Josef Hejnic and Jan Martínek (Prague: Academia, 1966–1982), 3:84.

20. Hrejsa, *Česká konfesse*, 111; *Sněmy české*, 4:311, 325, 395; Riss, "Život a literné působení Sixta z Ottersdorfu," 82.

21. The plebeian character of Utraquism was subject to contemporary satire: "They make preachers out of cobblers, millers, butchers, bakers, tanners, barbers, and other craftsmen. Even women are allowed to preach." See Thomas A. Fudge, *The Magnificent Ride: The First Reformation in Hussite Bohemia* (Brookfield, Vt.: Ashgate, 1998), 171, citing Václav Nebeský, "Verše na Husity: Dvě staré satyry," *Časopis českého musea* 26 (1852): 149.

22. Prague consisted of several adjacent, but autonomous municipalities, including Old Town, New Town, as well as Lesser Town, Hradčany, Vyšehrad, and the Jewish ghetto. See Frederick G. Heymann, "The Role of the Bohemian Cities During and After the Hussite Revolution," in *Tolerance and Movements of Religious Dissent in Eastern Europe*, ed. Bela K. Kiraly (New York: Columbia University Press, 1975), 27–28. See also on the linkage between towns and Utraquism, Robert Kalivoda, *Husitské myšlení* (Prague: Filosofia, 1997), 65–68.

23. Cited by Rudolf Říčan, ed., *Čtyři vyznání* (Prague: Komenského evangelická bohoslovecká fakulta), 1951, 39, n. 1; see also *Dějiny Prahy*, 2 vols., ed. Jaroslav Láník and Jan Vlk (Prague: Paseka, 1997–1998), especially 1:225.

24. Pravoslav Kneidl, "Městský stav v Čechách v době předbělohorské" (Ph.D. diss., Univerzita Karlova, Prague, 1951), 10.

25. Božena Kopičková, *Jan Želivský* (Prague: Melantrich, 1990), 81–83, 97–98, 118; František Kafka, *Poslední Lucemburk na českém trůně* (Prague: Mladá fronta, 1998), 22. On denunciations of Czech barons who "betrayed the Czech language and nation" in the Budyšínský manuscript, see Fudge, *The Magnificent Ride,* 268.

26. Beroun, Slaný, Louny, Kadaň, Chomutov, Litoměřice, Bělá, Mělník, Kostelec nad Labem, Český Brod, Kouřim, Nymburk, Kolín, Čáslav, Chrudim, Vysoké Mýto, Polička, Litomyšl, Jaroměř, and Dvůr Králové; see Kopičková, *Jan Želivský,* 140–141; Ivana Raková, "Čeněk z Vartenberka, 1400–1425: příspěvek k úloze panstva v husitské revoluci," *Sborník historický* 28 (1982): 72–73; Vavřinec z Březové, *Husitská kronika. Píseň o vítězství u Domažlic,* ed. Marie Bláhová (Prague: Svoboda, 1979), 223. The Křížovnický manuscript of the *Old Czech Annals,* in particular, dwells on the conflict between the towns and the nobility; see Miloslav Kaňák and František Šimek, eds., *Staré letopisy české z rukopisu Křížovnického* (Prague: Státní nakladatelství krásné literatury, hudby a umění, 1959). I owe this reference to Joel Seltzer. Concerning the nobles' attitude toward early Utraquism, see John M. Klassen, *The Nobility and the Making of the Hussite Revolution* (New York: Columbia University Press, 1978), 85–113.

27. Jaroslav Prokeš, "K Pálčově Replice proti čtyřem artikulům pražským," in *Z dějin východní Evropy a Slovanstva: Sborník věnovaný Jaroslavu Bidlovi k šedesátým narozeninám,* ed. Miloš Weingart, et al. (Prague: A. Belčková, 1928), 254.

28. "Zápis velikého sněmu Čáslavského proti králi Sigmundovi," *Archiv český* 3 (1844): 226–230.

29. Daniel Adam z Veleslavína, *Kalendář historický: To jest krátké poznamenání všech dnů jednokaždého měsíce přes celý rok* (Prague: Daniel Adam z Veleslavína, 1578), 131.

30. Josef Šusta, *Král cizinec,* vol. 2, pt. 2 of *České dějiny* (Prague: Laichter, 1939), 219.

31. Hrejsa, *Dějiny křesťanství v Československu,* 4:256–257.

32. Tomek, *Dějepis města Prahy,* 12:132. Hrejsa also recognizes the strength of Utraquism in royal towns; *Česká konfesse,* 59. See also Klement Borový, *Antonín Brus z Mohelnice, arcibiskup pražský; Historicko-kritický životopis* (Prague: Dědictví sv. Prokopa, 1873), 183.

33. Particularly in 1309 and 1319; see, for instance, Šusta, *Král cizinec,* 25–39, 293–295.

34. Ivan Hlaváček, "Husitské sněmy," *Sborník historický* 4 (1956): 72–74, 80–81, 89, 93–94, 99–100, 102–103.

35. Šusta, *Král cizinec,* 298.

36. Jiří Pešek and Bohdan Zilynskyj, "Městský stav v boji se šlechtou na počátku 16. století," *Folia Historica Bohemica* 6 (1984): 140–142.

37. Jiří Pešek, "Některé problémy bádání o spojené Praze let 1518–1528," *Documenta Pragensia* 4 (1984): 188.

38. Pešek and Zilynskyj, "Městský stav v boji se šlechtou na počátku 16. století," 146. On the political strength of Prague in the 1520s, see also G. P. Mel'nikov, "Iz istorii obshchestvenno-politicheskoi bor'by Chekhii v dvatsatye gody XVI v.," *Sovetskoe slavianovedenie* 5 (1980): 61.

39. Kuthen of Šprinsberk, *Kronika o založení země české,* ed. Zdeněk V. Tobolka (Prague: Odeon, 1929), f. C2(v); Pešek and Zilynskyj, "Městský stav v boji se šlechtou na počátku 16. století," 144.

40. Daniel Adam z Veleslavína, *Kalendář historický,* introduction, f. 3a–4b.

41. For instance, Sixt of Ottersdorf, *Knihy památné o nepokojných letech 1546 a 1547,* 2 vols., ed. Josef Teige (Prague: J. Otto, [1920]), 2:197–199. See also Riss, "Život a literné působení Sixta z Ottersdorfu," 163; Josef Janáček, "Královská města česká na zemském sněmu r. 1609–1610," *Sborník historický* 5 (1956): 227. Concerning other grievances against the nobles, see, for instance, P. M. Veselský, ed., "Žaloby měst na pány a rytířstvo z některých kusů jim škodných," *Časopis českého musea* 26 (1847): pt. 2, 422–440.

42. Marie Tošnerová, ed., *Paměti města Žatce, 1527–1609* (Žatec: Regionální muzeum a Městský úřad, 1996). See also review by Jaroslav Pánck in *Český časopis historický* 98 (2000): 186–187.

43. Marek Bydžovský z Florentina, *Rudolphus rex Bohemiae XXI* (manuscript, Prague, Bib. Nat. XVI G 22), f. 88/90v. Subsequently, Ivan's tyrannical and lawless treatment of Russian towns would be pilloried in the *Kronyka Moskevská,* published by Daniel Adam of Veleslavín in 1589. Aleksander Gwagnin (Alessandro Guagnini), *Kronyka Moskevská,* trans. Matouš Hosius z Vysokého Mýta (Prague: Daniel Adam z Veleslavína, 1589), 199–206 (*Kronyka Moskevská,* 2d ed. [Prague: Daniel Adam z Veleslavína, 1602].)

44. Alexandra Walsham, "The Parochial Roots of Laudianism Revisited: Catholics, Anti-Calvinists and 'Parish Anglicans' in Early Stuart England," *Journal of Ecclesiastical History* 49 (1998): 630.

45. Josef Tříška, ed., *Starší pražská univerzitní literatura a karlovská tradice* (Prague: Univerzita Karlova, 1978), 40; František M. Bartoš, ed., *Betlémská kázání Jakoubka ze Stříbra z let 1415–1416,* Theologická příloha KR 20 (Prague: n.p., 1953), 65, 114; Artur I. Ozolin, *Biurgerskaia oppozitsiia v gusitskom dvizhenii: Sotsial'no-politicheskie trebovaniia* (Saratov: Izdatel'stvo Saratovskogo universiteta, 1973), 21.

46. Some would even view Wyclif, the critic of ecclesiastical riches, as a social radical whose writings helped to inspire the English Peasant Revolt of 1381; see Anne Hudson, "*Poor Preachers, Poor Men:* Views of Poverty in Wyclif and His Followers," in *Häresie und vorzeitige Reformation im Spätmittelalter,* Schriften des Historischen Kollegs Kolloquien 39, ed. František Šmahel (Munich: Oldenbourg, 1998), 43–44, 47, 52.

47. Josef Petráň, "Skladba pohusitské aristokracie v Čechách," and Anna Skýbová, "Česká šlechta a jednání o povolení kompaktát r. 1525," in *Proměny feudální třídy v Čechách v pozdním feudalismu,* ed. Josef Petráň, Acta Universitatis Carolinae, Philosophica et historica 1 (1976), Studia historica, 14 (Prague: Univerzita Karlova, 1976), 44, 74, 83–85.

48. Jiří Kovařík, "Proměny feudální třídy v Čechách v předbělohorském období," in *Proměny feudální třídy v Čechách v pozdním feudalismu,* ed. Josef Petráň (Prague: Univerzita Karlova, 1976), especially 138–141; see also Alois Míka, "Národnostní poměry v Čechách před třicetiletou válkou," *Československý časopis historický* 20 (1972): 214–215, 217, 220, 222, 227; Josef Polišenský and Frederick Snider, "Změny ve složení české šlechty v 16. a 17. století," *Československý časopis historický* 20 (1972): 518; and František Šamalík, *Úvahy o dějinách české politiky: Od reformace k osvícenství,* 2d ed. (Prague: Victoria Publishing, 1996), 70.

49. Janáček, "Královská města česká na zemském sněmu," 248; Zikmund Winter, *Kulturní obraz českých měst: život veřejný v XV. a XVI. věku,* 2 vols. (Prague: Matice česká, 1890–1892), 1:108–111.

50. Jaroslav Pánek, "Spor o Voka z Rožmberka," *Jihočeský sborník historický* 56 (1987): 174.

51. Krofta, "Konsistoř pod obojí," 395, n. 4.

52. "[L]otři a zjevní cizoložníci." *Sněmy české*, 7:406–407.
53. *Sněmy české*, 11: pt. 1:76; Vilém Slavata, *Paměti nejvyššího kancléře království českého*, 2 vols., ed. Josef Jireček (Prague: Kober, 1866–1868), 1:47.
54. Pavel Skála ze Zhoře, *Historie česká od r. 1602 do r. 1623*, 5 vols., ed. Karel Tieftrunk (Prague, 1865–1870), 2:180–81.
55. The aristocratic contempt for the townspeople, of course, was not a monopoly of the Bohemian nobility; it was current in other European countries. For the example of Denmark, see Kollmann, *Valdštejn a evropská politika*, 58.
56. Concerning the appeal of the Catholic priesthood to the nobles during the Counter-Reformation, see for instance, Gregory Hanlon, "The Decline of a Provincial Military Aristocracy: Siena 1560–1740," *Past and Present* 155 (1997), especially 106–108; also Bohumil Navrátil, *Biskupství olomoucké 1576–1579 a volba Stanislava Pavlovského* (Prague: Česká společnost nauk, 1909), 198.
57. *Sněmy české*, 11: pt. 1, 70, n. 293.
58. "Luther, Martin," *New Catholic Encyclopedia*, 16 vols. (New York: McGraw-Hill, 1967–1974), 8:1088.
59. Jan V. Novák, "Spor Bratří s p. Vojtěchem z Pernštejna a na Prostějově r. 1557 a 1558," *Časopis českého Musea* 65 (1891): 44, 48, 54, n. 9; "Z Pernštejna, Vojtěch," *Knihopis českých a slovenských tisků*, 2 vols. (Prague: Nakladatelství Československé akademie věd, 1925–1967), 2: pt. 6, 91; Petr Vorel, *Páni z Pernštejna: Vzestup a pád rodu zubří hlavy v dějinách Čech a Moravy* (Prague: Rybka, 1999), 212–213. On the Lutheran *summus episcopus*, see Kollmann, *Valdštejn a evropská politika*, 27, 51, 57.
60. *Sněmy české*, 4:412; Hrejsa, *Česká konfesse*, 128, cf. 120–121; Václav Plácel z Elbingu, "Jakož pak obyčejně velicí Páni z náboženství hříčky sobě strojí, a v tom co se jim dobře líbí dělají," introduction, in Josephus Flavius, *Historia židovská. Na knihy čtyry rozdělená* (Prague: Daniel Adam of Veleslavín, 1592), 3.
61. Rudolf Říčan, *The History of the Unity of Brethren: A Protestant Hussite Church in Bohemia and Moravia*, trans. C. Daniel Crews (Bethlehem, Pa.: Moravian Church in America, 1992), 203.
62. Rudolf Urbánek, *Věk Poděbradský*, 4 pts., together vol. 3 of *České dějiny* (Prague: Laichter, 1915–1962), 2:560.
63. Ralph Keen, *Divine and Human Authority in Reformation Thought: German Theologians on Political Order, 1520–1555* (Nieuwkoop: De Graaf, 1997), 6, characterized the Lutheran attitude toward political power as follows: "[W]hen the Reformers appealed to secular authorities, they did so with a conception of authority that secularized the ecclesiastical order and subordinated it to the political order."
64. *Sněmy české*, 4:393.
65. "[N]evíme tu vo kom, kdo by se koncistoří Pražskou spravoval a jinde v zemi, zvláště z vyšších stavů, o nich nevíme." *Sněmy české*, 10:427.
66. Margaret Spufford, ed., *The World of Rural Dissenters, 1520–1725* (New York: Cambridge University Press, 1995).
67. Also in Poland, the nobles, but not the common people, were attracted to Lutheranism. Robert Kalivoda, *Husitská epocha a J. A. Komenský* (Prague: Odeon, 1992), 50, n. 44. On the disjuncture in religion between the upper classes and the commoners, see also Peter Burke, *Popular Culture in Early Modern Europe* (London: T. Smith, 1978).
68. *Sněmy české*, 4:394; see also Hrejsa, *Dějiny křesťanství v Československu*, 6:282.
69. *Sněmy české*, 4:328; Tomek, *Dějepis města Prahy*, 12:232–233.

70. Tomek, *Dějepis města Prahy,* 12:234–235.
71. Hrejsa, *Dějiny křest'anství v Československu,* 6:297, 300; Tomek, *Dějepis města Prahy,* 12:236.
72. Tomek, *Dějepis města Prahy,* 12:242–243.
73. Sixt of Ottersdorf, *Knihy památné o nepokojných letech 1546 a 1547,* 2: 215–219. On the background and on the Vladislav Mandate of 1508, see Kamil Krofta, "Od kompaktát k Bílé hoře," in Krofta, *Listy z náboženských dějin českých* (Prague: Historický klub, 1936), 342–343.
74. Thomas A. Fudge, "Reform and the Lower Consistory in Prague, 1437–1497," in *The Bohemian Reformation and Religious Practice,* vol. 2: Papers from the XVIIIth World Congress of the Czechoslovak Society of Arts and Sciences, Brno 1996, ed. Zdeněk V. David and David R. Holeton (Prague: Academy of Sciences of the Czech Republic, Main Library, 1998), 92-93; Kamil Krofta, "Václav Koranda mladší z Nové Plzně a jeho názory náboženské," in Krofta, *Listy z náboženských dějin* (Prague: Historický klub, 1936), 256–257; Krofta, "Boj o konsistoř," 384; *Sněmy české,* 4:411; Říčan, *The History of the Unity of Brethren,* 46.
75. The events of 1571 and 1572 receive a substantial contemporary coverage in the chronicle of the Utraquist Marek Bydžovský z Florentina, in *Svět za tří českých králů: Ferdinand, Maximilán, Rudolf II,* ed. Jaroslav Kolár (Prague: Svoboda, 1987), 128–131, 146–161, from Marek Bydžovský z Florentina, *Altera pars annalium seu eorum, quae sub Maximiliano rege contigerunt* (manuscript, Státní ústřední archiv, Prague, fond Archív vyšehradské kapituly, inv. č. 796, kniha 358), f. 158r–162v, 198v–216v; see also Tomek, *Dějepis města Prahy,* 12:239.
76. Hrejsa, *Česká konfesse,* 175.
77. *Sněmy české,* 4:395; Hrejsa, *Česká konfesse,* 111; Riss, "Život a literné působení Sixta z Ottersdorfu," 82; Václav Novotný, "Náboženské dějiny české ve století 16.," in Zdeněk V. Tobolka, ed., *Česká politika,* 5 vols. (Prague: Jan Laichter, 1906), 1:624.
78. Hrejsa, *Česká konfesse,* 325; Miloš Pojar, *Jindřich Matyáš Thurn: Muž činu* (Prague: Ivo Železný, 1998), 36.
79. See, for instance, Robert A. Kann and Zdeněk V. David, *The Peoples of the Eastern Habsburg Lands, 1526–1918* (Seattle, Wash.: University of Washington Press, 1984), 50–51; Míka, "Z bojů o náboženskou toleranci v 16. století," 375; Anton Mell, *Grundriss der Verfassungs- und Verwaltungsgeschichte des Landes Steiermark* (Graz: Universitäts-Buchhandlung Leuschner and Lubensky, 1929), 314–319; and Regina Pörtner, *Counter-Reformation in Central Europe: Styria, 1580–1630* (Oxford: Clarendon Press, 2001), especially, 93–95. In a curiously prophetic way, this Inner Austrian approach or "Styrian model" of the Counter-Reformation, the threat of which the nobles of Bohemia used in 1575 to intimidate the towns, would be eventually, indeed, applied in Bohemia in an even more forceful manner by Archduke Charles's son Ferdinand. Concerning the "Styrian model" of the Counter-Reformation, see Jaroslav Pánek, "Rekatolizace českých zemích," *Folia Historica Bohemica* 17 (1994): 336.
80. Sixt of Ottersdorf, *Knihy památné o nepokojných letech 1546 a 1547,* for instance, 2:200–202, 209–215, 222–223; Riss, "Život a literné působení Sixta z Ottersdorfu," 163.
81. Sixt himself apologized and explained that a misunderstanding caused the negative impression produced by his original statement. See *Sněmy české,* 4:395; Hrejsa, *Česká konfesse,* 111; Riss, "Život a literné působení Sixta z Ottersdorfu," 82.
82. Hrejsa, *Česká konfesse,* 104; *Sněmy české,* 4:392.

83. Tomek, *Dějepis města Prahy,* 12:232–233.
84. "Rozmluvivše volení z měst spolu, dali odpověď skrze pana Sixta z Ottersdorfu: . . . poněvadž to jináče slyší od pánův a rytířstva, . . . a poněvadž pak jinačejší oumysl Jich M. jest nežli jsou spraveni, že rádi jim v těch prácech nápomocni býti . . . chtějí." *Sněmy české,* 4:329, also 328; Krofta, *Boj o konsistoř,* 406, n. 2.
85. Hrejsa, *Dějiny křesťanství v Československu,* 6:301; Tomek, *Dějepis města Prahy,* 12: 241.
86. Hrejsa, *Česká konfesse,* 229; Hrejsa, *Dějiny křesťanství v Československu,* 6:310–311. The course of events would also show that the position of Utraquism was not diminished in the end.
87. *Sněmy české,* 4:142, 143; Josef Dostál, "Ohlas Bartolomějské noci na dvoře Maxmiliána II.," *Český časopis historický* 37 (1931): 341, 344–345.
88. Ernest Denis, *Fin de l'indépendance bohême,* 2d ed., 2 vols. (Paris: Librairie Leroux, 1930), 2:208–209.
89. Tomek, *Dějepis města Prahy,* 12:230.
90. See, for instance, Miloš Dokulil, "Meditace nad tolerancí," *Sborník prací Filozofické fakulty Brněnské univerzity,* B42 (1995): 30.
91. Hrejsa, *Česká konfesse,* 175.
92. *Ottův slovník naučný* (Prague: Otto, 1888–1909), 5:31.
93. Hrejsa, *Dějiny křesťanství v Československu,* 6:285.
94. Hrejsa, *Dějiny křesťanství v Československu,* 6:285, 287–288, 291; Jan Felin, *Rozebrání Obrany Samuela Martinia,* ed. Josef T. Müller, Spisy Jana Amosa Komenského, 6 (Prague: Česká akademie pro vědy, slovesnost, a umění, 1902), xx; Jerzy Kloczowski, *A History of Polish Christianity* (New York: Cambridge University Press, 2000), 107; W. F. Reddaway, ed., *The Cambridge History of Poland,* 2 vols. (Cambridge: Cambridge University Press, 1941–1950), 1:345.
95. Winfried Eberhard, "Stände, Herrscher und Religion in den böhmischen Ländern in der frühen Neuzeit," *Historische und Landeskundliche Ostmitteleuropa-Studien* 16 (1995): 129; Kollmann, in *Valdštejn a evropská politika,* 31, speaks about "Českou konfesi, na níž se dohodli luteráni, čeští bratři a staroutrakvisté . . ."
96. Jaroslav Pánek, "Stavovství v předbělohorské době," *Folia Historica Bohemica* 6 (1984): 170–174.
97. Kann and David, *The Peoples of the Eastern Habsburg Lands,* 47, 49–51; Pojar, *Jindřich Matyáš Thurn,* 36; Pörtner, *Counter-Reformation in Central Europe,* 27–28.
98. *Sněmy české,* 4:310, 322, 393.
99. *Ibid.,* 4:394.
100. *Ibid.,* 4:395.
101. Mercilessly, the Brethren even poked fun at his medical problem of kidney stones; see *Sněmy české,* 4:324–325, 409.
102. Hrejsa, *Česká konfesse,* 179–180; *Sněmy české,* 4:339.
103. *Sněmy české,* 4:344.
104. Hrejsa, *Česká konfesse,* 187; *Sněmy české,* 4:313, 343–344, 435.
105. Tomek, *Dějepis města Prahy,* 12:238; Hrejsa, *Česká konfesse,* 187.
106. Hrejsa, *Česká konfesse,* 187; *Sněmy české,* 4:344–345.
107. Tomek, *Dějepis města Prahy,* 12:238–239; see also Hrejsa, *Česká konfesse,* 184; *Sněmy české,* 4:341.
108. Hrejsa, *Česká konfesse,* 228; *Sněmy české,* 4:372; 4:454; Tomek, *Dějepis města Prahy,* 12:245.

109. *Sněmy české,* 4:454.
110. Tomek, *Dějepis města Prahy,* 12:246; *Sněmy české,* 4:373; 4:457.
111. Tomek, *Dějepis města Prahy,* 12:247; *Sněmy české,* 4:378.
112. Novotný, "Náboženské dějiny české ve století 16.," 1:629.
113. Tomek, *Dějepis města Prahy,* 12:245; Hrejsa, *Česká konfesse,* 178, 226, 228–229.
114. See, for instance, Gary Remer, "Bodin's Pluralistic Theory of Toleration," in *Difference and Dissent: Theories of Tolerance in Medieval and Early Modern Europe,* ed. Cary J. Nederman and John C. Laursen (Lanham. Rowman and Littlefield, 1996), 121–122; T. M. Parker, "The Papacy, Catholic Reform, and Christian Missions," in *The Counter-Reformation and Price Revolution, 1559–1610,* ed. R. B. Wernham, vol. 3 of *New Cambridge Modern History* (Cambridge: Cambridge University Press, 1968), 52–53.
115. Hrejsa, *Dějiny křesťanství v Československu,* 6:285, 287.
116. Cited by Hrejsa, *Česká konfesse,* 45.
117. *Sněmy české,* 4:412; Hrejsa, *Česká konfesse,* 128, cf. 120–121.
118. Hrejsa, *Dějiny křesťanství v Československu,* 6:285.
119. Hrejsa, *Česká konfesse,* 179–180; *Sněmy české,* 4:339.
120. Hrejsa, *Česká konfesse,* 183–184.
121. Hrejsa, *Česká konfesse,* 187–189; *Sněmy české,* 4:345–348; Slavata, *Paměti,* 1:214–217.
122. Hrejsa, in *Česká konfesse,* 188–189 (see also 89–90), cites the description from Christophorus Manlius (1546–1575), *Krátké a jisté paměti o jednání s strany náboženství, ktréž se dálo ode všech tří stavů Království českého na sněmě v Praze l. 1575* (manuscript, Görlitz, Milich Library, Cod. Chart. 4, N. 71), f. 26–28.
123. Hrejsa, *Dějiny křesťanství v Československu,* 6:303, n. 815.
124. Hrejsa, *Česká konfesse,* 187–189; *Sněmy české,* 4:345–348; Slavata, *Paměti,* 1:214–217.
125. Hrejsa, *Česká konfesse,* 228–229; Tomek, *Dějepis města Prahy,* 12:245.
126. Slavata, *Paměti,* 1:217–218
127. Hrejsa, *Česká konfesse,* 187; *Sněmy české,* 4:344–345.
128. *Sněmy české,* 4:347.
129. *Ibid.,* 4:347–348.
130. Slavata, *Paměti,* 1:218.
131. Krofta, "Boj o konsistoř," 413; Hrejsa, *Česká konfesse,* 175.
132. *Sněmy české,* 4:365–366; 4:447; Tomek, *Dějepis města Prahy,* 12:242.
133. *Sněmy české,* 4:367, 4:449–450; Tomek, *Dějepis města Prahy,* 12:242–243.
134. *Sněmy české,* 4:368–369; Daniela Neri, ed., *Nuntiaturberichte aus Deutschland,* Dritte Abteilung, 1572–1585, 8, Band: Nuntiatur Giovanni Dolfins, 1575–1576 (Tübingen: Max Niemayer, 1997), 280–282; Tomek, *Dějepis města Prahy,* 12:243–246.
135. "[J]akož pak i k tomu upřímně a věrně i králi franskému, když jest ve Vídni u J.M. byl, raditi ráčil, v tom jemu předkládajíc příčiny jeho všelijakého neštěstí strany nezdržení víry a provedení nad admirálem a jinými tak hrozného oučinku, pročež jej pán Bůh slušně pokutovati a trestati ráčí." *Sněmy české,* 4:379 (see also 4:460–462). For the complete discussions, see Daniela Neri, ed., *Nuntiaturberichte aus Deutschland,* Dritte Abteilung, 1572–1585, 8, Band: Nuntiatur Giovanni Dolfins, 1575–1576 (Tübingen: Max Niemayer, 1997), 290–293, 297; Krofta, "Boj o konsistoř," 415; Tomek, *Dějepis města Prahy,* 12:246–247. The specific reference to the French king is omitted from the German version of Maximillian's statement of September 2, 1575; see *Sněmy české,* 4:239–

242. See also Karel Stloukal, "Z diplomatických styků mezi Francií a Čechami před Bílou Horou," *Český časopis historický* 32 (1926): 480–481; 33 (1927): 471; and Dostál, "Ohlas Bartolomějské noci," 340.
136. *Sněmy české*, 4:390. See also Hrejsa, *Dějiny křesťanství v Československu*, 6:315.
137. *Sněmy české*, 4:386–387; 4:463; Riss, "Život a literné působení Sixta z Ottersdorfu," 83.
138. *Sněmy české*, 4:388; 4:463.
139. *Ibid.*, 4:390, 464; Krofta, "Boj o konsistoř," 417.
140. *Sněmy české*, 4:474, 484; Hrejsa, *Česká konfesse*, 246, 446, n. 3; Hrejsa, *Dějiny křesťanství v Československu*, 6:315.
141. Hrejsa, *Dějiny křesťanství v Československu*, 6:319–320.
142. *Ibid.*, 6:317–318; Hrejsa, *Česká konfesse*, 254.
143. Hrejsa, *Dějiny křesťanství v Československu*, 6:27; Míka, "Z bojů o náboženskou toleranci," 375. On the complexities surrounding Maximillian II's religious convictions, see Howard Louthan, *The Quest for Compromise: Peacemakers in Counter-Reformation Vienna* (New York: Cambridge University Press, 1997), 49–120.
144. "[S]trany far jich . . . kteréž sou od starodávna . . . víry katolické pod jednou bývaly, též také pod obojí, kteréž se konsistoři Pražskou spravovaly, v tom prvním způsobu zůstanou . . ." *Sněmy české*, 4:484; Tomek, *Dějepis města Prahy*, 12:256; Kamil Krofta, "Od kompaktát k Bílé hoře," in Krofta, *Listy z náboženských dějin českých* (Prague: Historický klub, 1936), 349.
145. Krofta, "Od kompaktát k Bílé hoře," 349.
146. Kollmann, *Valdštejn a evropská politika*, 28; Erwin L. Lueker, ed., *Lutheran Cyclopedia*, rev. ed. (St. Louis: Concordia, 1975), 59.
147. Walter Grossmann, "Toleration: *exercitium religionis privatum*," *Journal of the History of Ideas* 40 (1979): 129–130.
148. Gregory Champeaud, "The Edict of Poitiers and the Treaty of Nérac, or Two Steps toward the Edict of Nantes," *Sixteenth Century Journal* 32 (2001): 326–327.
149. Hrejsa, *Dějiny křesťanství v Československu*, 6:315, 319; Novotný, "Náboženské dějiny české ve století 16.," 1:630; Neri, *Nuntiaturberichte aus Deutschland . . .*, 1572–1585, 8:324.
150. Jiří Kettner, *Dějiny pražské arcidiecéze v datech* (Prague: Zvon, 1993), 176.
151. See Hrejsa, *Česká konfesse*, 672–674; "Confessio," *Knihopis českých a slovenských tisků*, 2: pt. 3, 272–275. Concerning Rudolf's religious edicts, see Chapter 11.
152. Hrejsa, *Česká konfesse*, 675–681.
153. This Latin version, published in Wittenberg, was based on a Czech original promulgated in 1564 and submitted to Maximillian II on his accession. The previous Brethren's confession was prepared in Czech in 1535 for submission to Ferdinand I, and published in Latin in 1538 also in Wittenberg; see Jaroslav Bidlo, "O Konfessi bratrské z r. 1573," *Sborník prací historických k šedesátým narozeninám Jaroslava Golla*, ed. Jaroslav Bidlo, et al. (Prague: Historický klub, 1906), 246–278. An even earlier confession, *Apologia sacrae scripturae*, was published by the Brethren in Nuremberg in 1511; see Říčan, *The History of the Unity of Brethren*, 100.
154. See Salnar de Castres, ed., "Catalogus confessionum," in *Harmonia confessionum fidei, Orthodoxarum, et Reformatorum Ecclesiarum*, 2 vols. (Geneva: Petrus Santandreanus, 1581), 1:xxii–xxiii; J. F. Salvart, ed., "A Catalogue of the Confessions," in *An harmony of the confessions of the faith of the christian and reformed churches* (Cambridge: Thomas Thomas, 1586), iv. This inclusion apparently occurred without the

Brethren's knowledge; see Rudolf Říčan and others, *Jednota Bratrská, 1457–1957: Sborník k pětistému výročí založení* (Prague: Kalich, 1956), 68.

155. *LEP,* VI.4.14., in Richard Hooker, *Folger Library Edition of the Works,* 6 vols. (Cambridge, Mass.: Belknap Press of Harvard University Press, 1977–1993), 3:46–47 (see also 6:265–266, 855). Hooker cites from chapter 5.8 of De Castres, *Harmonia confessionum fidei,* 1:143; contained also in Salvart, *An harmony of the confessions,* 219. See also Chapter 1.

156. Krofta, "Boj o konsistoř," 417.

157. For instance, Vilém of Rožmberk's and Vratislav of Pernštejn's negotiations on behalf of the Habsburgs for the Polish throne in 1572–1573 appear as a classic example of diplomatic failure. Vilém's brother, Petr Vok of Rožmberk, was unfit for a command post in Hungary during the Turkish war in 1594 result of physical weakness due to overindulgence in food, drink, and sex (allegedly with twelve concubines). See Almut Bues, *Die habsburgische Kandidatur für den polnischen Thron während des Ersten Interregnums in Polen 1572–73* (Vienna: VWGÖ, 1984), 67–78; Pánek, "Spor o Voka z Rožmberka," 172–185. Kamil Krofta, *Nesmrtelný národ: Od Bílé Hory k Palackému* (Prague: Laichter, 1940), 416–417; Josef Salaba, "Třetí legace Viléma z Rožmberka do Polska r. 1589," *Časopis českého musea* 101 (1927): 35–49; Waclaw Sobieski, "Vilém z Rožmberka a Jan Zamojski," in *Z dějin východní Evropy a Slovanstva: Sborník věnovaný Jaroslavu Bidlovi k šedesátým narozeninám,* ed. Miloš Weingart, et al. (Prague: A. Bečková, 1928), 288–291; Zdeněk Kalista, *Čechové, kteří tvořili dějiny Světa,* 2d ed. (Prague: Gramond, 1999), 22–26 (on Vilém of Rožmberk), 30–31 (on transformation of nobles from warriors to courtiers). For contemporary criticism, see Tomáš Bavorovský, *Postila česká* (Olomouc: Jan Gunther, 1557), cf. Krofta, *Nesmrtelný národ,* 393; Hynek Hrubý, *České postilly: studie literárně a kulturně historická* (Prague: Česká společnost nauk, 1901), 182–189; Jan Jakubec, *Dějiny literatury české,* 2d ed., 2 vols. (Prague: Laichter, 1929-1934), 1:713, 721. Concerning the nobility's gluttony and drunkenness, see also the testimony of Pierre Bergeron in Eliška Fučíková, ed., *Tři francouzští kavalíři v rudolfínské Praze* (Prague: Panorama, 1989), 57–59.

158. Sigmund Chotek of Chockov, "Instrukcí vojanská," *Sněmy české,* 8:419–421.

159. Kneidl, "Městský stav v Čechách v době předbělohorské," 119–122; Pánek, "Spor o Voka z Rožmberka," 173.

160. Novotný, "Náboženské dějiny české ve století 16.," 1:638–639; Anna Skýbová, "Česká šlechta a jednání o povolení kompaktát r. 1525," 91, 94, 95, 96, n. 31, 108; Krofta, *Nesmrtelný národ,* 416–422; Josef Válka, "Politická závěť Viléma z Pernštejna: příspěvek k dějinám politického myšlení doby jagellonské," *Časopis Matice moravské* 90 (1971): 63–86.

161. See, for instance, Krofta, *Nesmrtelný národ,* 178–179; Míka, "Národnostní poměry v Čechách," 226.

162. Janáček, "Královská města česká na zemském sněmu r. 1609–1610," 251.

163. Zdeněk of Lobkovice's treatment of Administrator Dačický in 1604, for instance, does not reflect the moral sensitivity of a respectable man, but rather the coarse instincts of a despot of the ilk of Ivan the Terrible.

164. See, for instance, Noemi Rejchrtová, "Listy osamělého politika," in Karel starší ze Žerotína, *Z korespondence* (Prague: Odeon, 1982), 7–38. More recently, Kalivoda has assigned to Žerotín's political "genius" the prime responsibility for the failure of the Bohemian uprising against the Habsburgs in 1618; Robert Kalivoda, *Husitská epocha a J. A. Komenský* (Prague: Odeon, 1992), 42–43, 59–60.

165. The exceptions include Václav Budovec of Budov or Kryštof Harant of Polžice and Bezdružice. Concerning the former, see Noemi Rejchrtová, in *Václav Budovec of Budov, Antialkorán* (Prague: Odeon, 1989), 10.

166. Václav Bůžek, "Literární mecenát nižší šlechty v předbělohorských Čechách," *Husitství, Reformace, Renesance: Sborník k 60. narozeninám Františka Šmahela,* 3 vols., ed. Jaroslav Pánek, et al. (Prague: Historický ústav, 1994), 3:837, 839.

167. Zikmund Winter, *Život a učení na partikulárních školách v Čechách v XV. a XVI. století: Kulturně-historický obraz* (Prague: Česká akademie pro vědy, slovesnost a umění, 1901), 765–768; Zdeněk Kalista, "Tři staré šlechtické libráře," *Časopis Společnosti přátel starožitností* 36 (1928): 153–156; see František Hrubý's review in "Zpráva," *Český časopis historický,* 35 (1929): 207. Regarding the nobles' trivial interests and limited cultural horizons, see Adam the Younger of Valdštejn, *Deník rudolfinského dvořana, 1602–1633,* ed. Marie Koldinská and Petr Mat'a (Prague: Argo, 1997), 12–13.

168. Zdeněk Kalista, *Po proudu Života,* 2 vols. (Prague: Atlantis, 1996–1997), 2: 155–156. For a more benign view of the sixteenth-century Bohemian nobility's personal and intellectual qualities, see Kamil Krofta, *Bílá Hora: Kurs šestipřednáškový* (Prague: J. Otto, 1914), 60–62. The growing divergence between the lifestyles of the townspeople and the nobles in the sixteenth century is well summarized in Josef Petráň, et al., *Dějiny Československa,* 2 vols. (Prague: Státní pedagogické nakladatelství, 1990), 1:497–501.

169. Jiří Pešek, *Mešt'anská vzdělanost a kultura v předbělohorských Čechách, 1547–1620* (Prague: Karolinum, 1993), 129.

170. Jaroslav Kolár, *Návraty bez konce: Studie k starší české literatuře,* ed. Lenka Jiroušková (Brno: Atlantis, 1999), 25, 139–140.

171. See, for instance, Jiří Pešek, "Kultura českých předbělohorských měst, 1547–1620," *Česká města v 16.–18. století: Sborník příspěvků z konference v Pardubicích 14. a 15. listopadu 1990,* ed. Jaroslav Pánek (Prague: Historický ústav, 1991), 208–209; Petr Čornej, *Rozhled, názory a postoje hisitské inteligence v zrcadle dějepisectví 15. století* (Prague: Univerzita Karlova, 1986), 5–6. Concerning Veleslavín's particularly significant contribution, see Josef Hejnic, "Daniel Adam of Veleslavín: Zu den gegenseitigen Beziehungen zwischen der tschechischen und lateinischen Literatur im letzten Viertel des 16. Jahrhunderts," in *Studien zum Humanismus in den böhmischen Ländern,* ed. Hans-Bernd Harder and Hans Rothe, Schriften des Komitees der Bundesrepublic Deutschland zur Förderung der Slawischen Studien, 11 (Cologne: Böhlau, 1988), 270–272.

172. Michal Svatoš, "Humanismus an der Universität Prag im 15. und 16. Jahrhundert," in *Studien zum Humanismus in den böhmischen Ländern,* ed. Hans-Bernd Harder and Hans Rothe, Schriften des Komitees der Bundesrepublik Deutschland zur Förderung der Slawischen Studien, 11 (Cologne: Böhlau, 1988), 203–205; Jiří Pešek, "Mešt'anská kultura a vzdělanost v rudolfínské Praze," *Folia Historica Bohemica* 5 (1983): 174–176.

173. Václav Ledvinka, "Feudální velkostatek a poddanská města v předbělohorských Čechách," Jiří Pešek, "Kultura českých předbělohorských měst, 1547–1620," and Petr Vorel, "Města jako sídla feudálních vrchností," all in *Česká města v 16.–18. století: Sborník příspěvků z konference v Pardubicích 14. a 15. listopadu 1990,* ed. Jaroslav Pánek (Prague: Historický ústav, 1991), 101, 123–124, and 204. See dedications to mayors and town councils in Brykcí z Licska, *Regule, To jest řeholy obecné z latinských učitelův práv vybrané . . .* (Prague: Bartoloměj Netolický, 1541), f. A1v; Josephus Flavius, *Historia židovská. Na knihy čtyry rozdělená,* trans. Václav Plácel z Elbingu (Prague:

Daniel Adam of Veleslavín, 1592), f. (*)2r; and Flavius Magnus Cassiodorus, *Historia Cýrkevní*, trans. Jan Kocin z Kocinetu (Prague: Daniel Adam z Veleslavína, 1594), 261, 417.

174. Pešek, *Mešťanská vzdělanost a kultura*, 66–67.

175. *Ibid.*, 26–28.

176. Desiderius Erasmus, *The Correspondence*, 11 vols. (Toronto: University of Toronto Press, 1974–1992), 6:174.

177. Mirjam Bohatcová and Josef Hejnic, "O vydavatelské Činnosti Veleslavínské tiskárny," *Folia Historica Bohemica* 9 (1985): 291–388.

178. Zdeněk V. David, "Národní obrození jako převtělení Zlatého veku," *Český časopis historický* 99 (2001): 486–518; Zdeněk Kalista, *Josef Pekař* (Prague: Torst, 1994), 162.

179. "Die ganze Masse der Nation wird zum Lesen gereizt und zum Denken aufgefordert. Der kultivirteste Theil denkt und schreibt frei." Josef Dobrovský, *Dějiny české řeči a literatury v redakcích z roku 1791, 1792 a 1818*, ed. Benjamin Jedlička (Prague: Melantrich, 1936), 46 (see also 148–149, 152).

180. As asserted, for instance, by Václav V. Tomek in "O církevní správě strany pod obojí v Čechách od r. 1415 až 1622," *Časopis českého musea* 22 (1848): 463; Novotný, "Náboženské dějiny české ve století 16.," 1:596; Krofta, *Bílá Hora: Kurs šestipřednáškový*, 222; Josef Macek, František Graus, and Ján Tibenský, eds., *Přehled československých dějin*, 4 vols. in 5 (Prague: Nakladatelství Československé akademie věd, 1958–1968), 1:335.

181. On the Peace of Kutná Hora as the political foundation of religious tolerance, see Thomas A. Fudge, "The Problem of Religious Liberty in Early Modern Bohemia," *Communio Viatorum* 38 (1996): 64–87. See also Míka, "Z bojů o náboženskou toleranci v 16. století," 371, 380.

182. See, for instance, Krofta, *Nesmrtelný národ*, 499.

Chapter 8

1. The events of the Diet of 1575 are available in considerable detail, above all in Ferdinand Hrejsa, *Česká konfesse: Její vznik, podstata a dějiny* (Prague: Česká akademie pro vědy, slovesnost a umění, 1912), 86–94; Hrejsa, *Dějiny křesťanství v Československu*, 6 vols. (Prague: Husova Československá evangelická fakulta bohoslovecká, 1946-1950), 6:274–323; Kamil Krofta, "Boj o konsistoř podobojí v l. 1562–1575 a jeho historický základ," *Český časopis historický* 17 (1911): 404–406, 411–416; and more recently by Jaroslav Pánek, *Stavovská opozice a její zápas s Habsburky, 1547–1577* (Prague: Academia, 1982), 101–119. For earlier presentations, see also Tomek, *Dějepis města Prahy*, 12 vols. (Prague: Řivnáč, 1855–1901), 12:228ff, and Anton Gindely, *Geschichte der Böhmischen Brüder*, 2d ed., 2 vols. (Prague: C. Bellmann, 1861–1862), 2:109ff. See also Chapter 7.

2. Václav V. Tomek, "O církevní správě strany pod obojí v Čechách od r. 1415 až 1622," *Časopis českého musea* 22 (1848): 462–463; Antonín Rezek, *Dějiny prostonárodního hnutí náboženského v Čechách od vydání tolerančního patentu až na naše časy* (Prague: Řivnáč, 1887), 12; Krofta, "Boj o konsistoř," 417; Josef Pekař, *Dějiny československé* (Prague: Akropolis, 1991), 91.

3. *Sněmy české od léta 1526 až po naši dobu.*, vols. 1–11, 15 (Prague: Zemský výbor, 1877–1941), 7:3.

4. "[T]rvaly i nadále značné zbytky starého husitismu, které se bránily—aspoň zpočátku—úplnému splynutí s náboženským hnutím německým . . ." Zdeněk Kalista, *Čechové, kteří tvořili dějiny světa,* 2d ed. (Prague: Gramond, 1999), 54.

5. Lewis W. Spitz, *The Protestant Reformation, 1517–1559* (New York: Harper and Row, 1985), 127; Markus Reisenleitner, *Frühe Neuzeit, Reformation und Gegenreformation. Darstellung – Forschungsüberblick – Quellen und Literatur.* Handbuch zur neueren Geschichte Österreichs Band 1. (Innsbruck: Studien Verlag, 2000), 110.

6. The proportion of the Brethren and the sub una (i.e., adherents of the Roman Curia) within Bohemia's population is not contested. It has been estimated respectively at 5 to 10 percent, and 12 to 15 percent for the second half of the sixteenth century; see, for instance, Josef Pekař, *Dějiny československé* (Prague: Akropolis, 1991), 91–92; on the nobility's numbers, see Jan Kapras, *Právní dějiny zemí koruny české,* 3 vols. (Prague: Unie, 1913), 2:436.

7. See also the witness of Josef Janáček, *České dějiny: Doba předbělohorská,* 2 vols. (Prague: Academia, 1971–1984), 1:197, n. 34.

8. For instance, there is no mention of Bohemia in N. M. Sutherland's "Persecution and Toleration in Reformation Europe," in *Persecution and Toleration,* ed. W. J. Sheils, Studies in Church History, 21 (Oxford: Blackwell, 1984), 153–162; or in Randolph C. Head, "The Transformations of the Long Sixteenth Century," in *Beyond the Persecuting Society: Toleration Before the Enlightenment,* ed. John Christian Laursen and Cary J. Nederman (Philadelphia: University of Pennsylvania Press, 1998), 95–106; John C. Laursen, *Religious Toleration: "The Variety of Rites" from Cyrus to Defoe* (New York: St. Martin's Press, 1999); see also Robert Kalivoda, *Husitská epocha a J. A. Komenský* (Prague: Odeon, 1992), 18–19.

9. For instance, Ole P. Grell, Jonathan I. Israel, and Nicholas Tyacke, eds., *From Persecution to Toleration: The Glorious Revolution and Religion in England* (Oxford: Clarendon Press, 1991), 1; C. Berkvens-Stevelinck, J. Israel, and G. H. M. Posthumus Meyjes, eds., *Emergence on Tolerance in the Dutch Republic* (Leiden: Brill, 1997), especially 3–73.

10. For the use of the metaphor, see Thomas A. Brady, Jr., *The Protestant Reformation in Germany,* Annual Lecture 1997 (Washington, D.C.: German Historical Institute, 1998), 20.

11. Arthur G. Dickens, *The English Reformation,* 2d ed. (University Park, Pa.: Pennsylvania State University Press, 1991), 368.

12. Patrick Collinson, "Puritans," *Oxford Encyclopedia of the Reformation* (New York: Oxford University Press, 1996), 3:366.

13. See, for instance, the concept of "parish Anglicans" in Alexandra Walsham, "The Parochial Roots of Laudianism Revisited: Catholics, Anti-Calvinists and 'Parish Anglicans' in Early Stuart England," *Journal of Ecclesiastical History* 49 (1998): especially 627, 630–633.

14. *Sněmy české,* 11:49; Inge Auerbach, "Die böhmischen Stände unter Rudolf II: Zwischen Polarisierung und Konsens" (paper delivered at "Kultur und Bildung im rudolfinischen Königreich Böhmen" conference, University of Passau, April 1993), see also the report on the conference in *Folia Historica Bohemica* 17 (1994): 320; Hans-Berndt Harder and Hans Rothe, eds., *Später Humanismus in der Krone Böhmens, 1570–1620,* Studien zum Humanismus in der böhmischen Ländern, vol. 4: Schriften zur Kultur der Slaven, Neue Folge der Maisk-Schriften, Band 3 (Dresden: Dresden University Press, 1998).

15. Miloš Pojar, *Jindřich Matyáš Thurn: Muž činu* (Prague: Ivo Železný, 1998), 36–37.

16. Robert Kolb, "Altering the Agenda, Shifting the Strategy: The *Grundfest* of 1571 as Philippist Program for Lutheran Concord," *Sixteenth Century Journal* 30 (1999): 705–726. The Bohemians' better-organized Lutheran colleagues in the Slovene lands of Inner Austria subscribed to the Formula in 1582; see *Zgodovina Slovencev* (Ljubljana: Cankarjeva založba, 1979), 266, 295. Bohemian theologians of the party sub una were aware of the Formula of Concord; see Petr Linteo z Pilzenburgku, *Jistá a patrná cýrkve svaté znamení* (Litomyšl: n.p., 1593), 158. Ferdinand Hrejsa refers to a local Moravian arrangement—not to the famous German document—when he mentions the Formula of Concord of 1581; Hrejsa, Česká *konfesse: Její vznik, podstata a dějiny* (Prague: Česká akademie pro vědy, slovesnost a umění, 1912), 344, 351.

17. Jaroslav Pánek, "K povaze vlády Rudolfa II. v českém království," *Folia Historica Bohemica* 18 (1997): 82; Bohumil Navrátil, *Biskupství olomoucké 1576–1579 a volba Stanislava Pavlovského* (Prague: Česká společnost nauk, 1909), 36; Kamil Krofta, "Od kompaktát k Bílé hoře," in Krofta, *Listy z náboženských dějin českých* (Prague: Historický klub, 1936), 349.

18. *Sněmy české*, 4:474, 477, 484; 11:49.

19. On this provision, see, for instance, Jan Fiala, *Hrozné doby protireformace* (Heršpice: Eman, 1997), 24; Ernest Denis, *Fin de l'indépendance bohême*, 2d ed., 2 vols. (Paris: Librairie Leroux, 1930), 2:208–209.

20. On the practice of private chapels in sixteenth-century Europe, see also Benjamin J. Kaplan, "Fictions of Privacy: House Chapels and the Spatial Accommodation of Religious Dissent in Early Modern Europe," *American Historical Review* 107 (2002): 1050–1051.

21. Concerning the political weight of the nobles in contemporary diets see, for instance, Navrátil, *Biskupství olomoucké 1576–1579*, 3.

22. Josef Macek has estimated the rural population of Bohemia in 1500 at 1,200,000 or 80 percent; the inhabitants of large and medium towns accordingly comprised 225,000 or 15 percent, and those of small towns the remaining 75,000 or 5 percent of the total. See Macek, *Jagellonský věk v českých zemích, 1471–1526*, 4 vols. (Prague: Academia, 1992–1999), 3:29.

23. C. Scott Dixon, *The Reformation and Rural Society: The Parishes of Brandenburg-Ansbach-Kulmbach, 1528–1603* (New York: Cambridge University Press, 1996), especially 2–3, 7–8, 203, 206–207; see also H. Zmorza's review of Dixon in the *English Historical Review* 112 (1997): 1270. On the urban model, see Bernd Moeller, "Stadt und Buch: Bemerkungen zur Struktur der reformatorischen Bewegung in Deutschland," in *Stadtbürgertum und Adel in der Reformation: Studien zur Sozialgeschichte der Reformation in England und Deutschland*, ed. Wolfgang J. Mommsen (Stuttgart: Klett-Cotta, 1979), 25–39; Arthur G. Dickens, *The German Nation and Martin Luther* (London: Edward Arnold, 1974), 182–184; Arthur G. Dickens and John M. Tonkin, *The Reformation in Historical Thought* (Cambridge, Mass.: Harvard University Press, 1985), 297–305; Berndt Hamm, "The Urban Reformation in the Holy Roman Empire," in *Visions, Programs, and Outcomes*, vol. 2 of *Handbook of European History, 1400–1600*, ed. Thomas A. Brady, Jr., Heiko A. Oberman, and James D. Tracy (Grand Rapids, Mich.: William B. Eerdmans, 1996), 193–194.

24. Walsham, "The Parochial Roots of Laudianism Revisited," 627; see also Christopher Haigh, *English Reformations: Religion, Politics, and Society under the Tudors* (Ox-

ford: Clarendon Press, 1993), 15–17; Haigh, ed., *English Reformation Revised* (New York: Cambridge University Press, 1987), 1–17; J. J. Scarisbrick, *The Reformation and the English People* (Oxford: Blackwell, 1984), 1, 136–161; Rosemary O'Day, *The Debate on the English Reformation* (London: Methuen, 1986), 142–147; Dixon, *The Reformation and Rural Society,* 206–207; John Craig, "Reformers, Conflict, and Revisionism: The Reformation in Sixteenth-Century Hadleigh," *Historical Journal* 42 (1999): 1–23.

25. Judith Maltby, *Prayer Book and People in Elizabethan and Early Stuart England* (New York: Cambridge University Press, 1998), 13–14. It also appears that all the Dutch did not find Calvinism irresistible and almost half of the population of the United Provinces rejected the Reformation as late as 1650 despite considerable inducements of being "compelled to be married and to have their children baptized by Calvinist preachers, and [having] to attend their sermons." See R. Po-Chia Hsia, *The World of Catholic Renewal, 1540–1770* (New York: Cambridge University Press, 1998), 84–85. See also Auke Jelsma, "The Attack of Reformed Protestantism on Society's Mentality in the Northern Netherlands during the Second Half of the Sixteenth Century," in Jelsma, *Frontiers of Reformation: Dissidence and Orthodoxy in Sixteenth-Century Europe* (Aldershot, England: Ashgate, 1998), 110.

26. Zikmund Winter, *Zlatá doba měst českých* (Prague: Odeon, 1991), 167–168; Winter, *Kulturní obraz českých měst: život veřejný v XV. a XVI. věku,* 2 vols. (Prague: Matice česká, 1890–1892), 2:576–577; David R. Holeton, "The Evolution of Utraquist Eucharistic Liturgy: A Textual Study," in *The Bohemian Reformation and Religious Practice,* vol. 2: Papers from the XVIIIth World Congress of the Czechoslovak Society of Arts and Sciences, Brno 1996, ed. Zdeněk V. David and David R. Holeton (Prague: Academy of Sciences of the Czech Republic, Main Library, 1998), 103.

27. Otakar Odložilík, "Utrakvistická postilla z r. 1540," *Věstník české společnosti nauk* (1925): 15–17, 20–21.

28. Kamil Krofta, "Václav Koranda mladší z Nové Plzně a jeho názory náboženské," *Listy z náboženských dějin* (Prague: Historický klub, 1936), 258. As a parenthetical observation, the Utraquists likewise escaped the dread engendered by the Calvinist stress on predestination. Concerning the potentially baneful effect of this doctrine, see Walsham, "The Parochial Roots of Laudianism Revisited," 629, as well as her references to Michael MacDonald, *Sleepless Souls: Suicide in Early Modern England* (New York: Oxford University Press, 1990), 64–67; and John Stachniewski, *The Persecutory Imagination: English Puritanism and the Literature of Religious Despair* (New York: Oxford University Press, 1991), especially chapter 1.

29. On Utraquist laxity on confession, see Julius Pažout, *Jednání a dopisy konsistoře pod obojí způsobou přijímajících, 1562–1570* (Prague: Historický spolek, 1906), 342–343; Josef Matoušek, "Kurie a boj o konsistoř pod obojí za administrátora Rezka," *Český časopis historický* 37 (1931): 262–263; *Sněmy české,* 8:337.

30. On Wyclif's concern for the poor, see Anne Hudson, "*Poor Preachers, Poor Men:* Views of Poverty in Wyclif and His Followers," in *Häresie und vorzeitige Reformation im Spätmittelalter,* ed. František Šmahel, Schriften des Historischen Kollegs Kolloquien 39 (Munich: Oldenbourg, 1998), 43–44, 47, 52–53; Thomas A. Fudge, *The Magnificent Ride: The First Reformation in Hussite Bohemia* (Brookfield, Vt.: Ashgate, 1998), 173–174.

31. Citing 2 Moses 23, 5 Moses 1; Vavřinec Leander Rvačovský of Rvačov, *Masopust* (Prague: Jiří Melantrich, 1580), f. 273r.

32. Rvačovský of Rvačov, *Masopust,* f. 273v–274r.

33. Jan Václav Cykáda, *Hody křesťanské* (Prague: Impressí Šumanská, 1607), f. B1v–B2r, 222. For similar charges of noble embezzlements, see the Utraquist Consistory's letter to Rudolf II of August 8, 1578, in *Sněmy české*, 5:301.

34. On Puritan stress on "discipline," see John Spurr, *English Puritanism, 1603–1689* (New York: St. Martin's Press, 1998), 52; Richard Hooker characterized Calvin's ecclesiastical regime at Geneva as "little better than popish tyranny disguised and tendered . . . under a new form"; Hooker, *The Folger Library Edition of the Works of Richard Hooker*, 6 vols., ed. W. Speed Hill (Cambridge, Mass.: Belknap Press of Harvard University Press, 1977–1993), 1:7 (*LEP*, Preface, 2.4).

35. He had an imaginary congregation address its pastor: "[I]f you wish to be with us, perform for us the ancient rituals; for we do not want to be otherwise than our ancestors." (Faráři chceš-li u nás býti, vykonávej nám staré pořádky, neb my nechceme býti jináč než jako předkové naši.) Jan Štelcar Želetavský z Želetavy, *Kázání dvoje* (Prague: [Jiří Dačický?], 1586), f. B8v.

36. Denis, *Fin de l'indépendance bohême*, 2:208–209; Robert Kalivoda, *Husitská epocha a J. A. Komenský* (Prague: Odeon, 1992), 25; Govind Screenivasan has discussed the sixteenth-century peasants' self-confidence and assertiveness in "The Social Origins of the Peasants' War of 1525 in Upper Swabia," *Past and Present* 171 (May 2001): 40–55.

37. Václav Ledvinka, "Item poddané své spravedlivě chrániti a spravovati máme . . . : K vývoji společenských a náboženských poměrů na dominiu pánů z Hradce mezi léty 1547 a 1627," in *Husitství, Reformace, Renesance: Sborník k 60. narozeninám Františka Šmahela*, ed. Jaroslav Pánek, et al., 3 vols. (Prague: Historický ústav, 1994), 3:827–828. Concerning the Unity, see *Sněmy české*, 5:488–489, 529–530.

38. *Sněmy české*, 5:197; 7:60, 454; 11: pt. 1, 40.

39. *Ibid.*, 6:507, 510.

40. *Druhá Apologie stavův království českého, tělo a krev Pána Ježíše Krista pod obojí přijímajících* (Prague: Daniel Karel z Karlspergka, 1619), 132; *Sněmy české*, 9:181. Archbishop Berka complained in September 1595 to Rudolf II about the spread of Lutheranism, but his specific examples (at the expense of sub una) were limited to cases in the German-speaking area: the manor of Chomutov and the town of (Česká) Lípa; *Sněmy české*, 9:183–184; Karel Stloukal, *Papežská politika a císařský dvůr pražský na předělu XVI. a XVII. věku* (Prague: F. Řivnáč, 1925), 200.

41. *Sněmy české*, 10:510, 585, 587, 633.

42. *Ibid.*, 10:647, 651.

43. *Ibid.*, 7:400, 407–408.

44. *Ibid.*, 9:533.

45. *Ibid.*, 10:230–231, 349–351, 355–357, 613–614.

46. *Druhá Apologie stavův království českého*, 142.

47. Petr Codicillus [Petr Kodicillus], *Orací aneb spis k stavům pod obojí v království českém, aby oni konsistoř dolejší pražskou k své správě zase obrácenou míti se snažili*, February 10, 1582, in *Sněmy české*, 6:174; also *Sněmy české*, 4:477; 7:373, 379; 11:45, n. 205, with the last reference correcting Tomek, *Dějepis města Prahy*, 12:336.

48. Eliška Fučíková, ed., *Tři francouzští kavalíři v rudolfínské Praze* (Prague: Panorama, 1989), 44–45. On the restriction of worship of the Roman Church in Prague in 1589, see also *Sněmy české*, 7:439–440. For a list of Utraquist parishes in Prague, see Klement Borový, "Die Utraquisten in Böhmen," *Archiv für österreichische Geschichts-*

forschung 36 (1866): 255. Both Administrator Dačický and Archbishop Berka were concerned about the Brethren's services in September 1598; *Sněmy české*, 9:592.

49. *Sněmy české*, 7:407; 9:202, 287; 10:617–618. Ironically, the inhabitants of Kadaň—like those of other German-speaking towns of Bohemia—apparently would have preferred a Lutheran minister; *Sněmy české*, 8:557–558.

50. *Sněmy české*, 10:357–358, 388; *Druhá Apologie stavův království českého*, 132–133, 138; see also Miloš Kratochvíl, "Staroměstská radnice v dějinách městské samosprávy," in *Staroměstská radnice a její památky*, Samosprávná knihovna hlavního města Prahy, sv. 13 (Prague: Město Praha, 1927), 37.

51. *Sněmy české*, 9:196; 10:374, 481; *Druhá Apologie stavův království českého*, 142.

52. For instance, Winter, *Zlatá doba měst českých*, 139.

53. *Sněmy české*, 7:225, 265, 370, 373; for Maximillian's decree, see *Sněmy české*, 4:477.

54. *Ibid.*, 5:701–702; 6:241–242; 7:406.

55. Maltby, *Prayer Book and People in Elizabethan and Early Stuart England*, i.

56. *Sněmy české*, 5:197–199, 301; 7:376–377; 11:40, n. 188.

57. *Ibid.*, 5:514–516; 712; 6:268, 542–543, 602–603; 7:376–377, 397, 421–423. Other towns involved were Beroun, Domažlice, Jaroměř, Nymburk, and Sušice; see *Sněmy české*, 7:436–438.

58. *Sněmy české*, 7:371–372, 404–405; 10:617–618, 630–632, 635–638.

59. For a forceful expression of such a view, see, for instance, *Sněmy české*, 7, introduction, ii, 3–4.

60. For instance, the case of the priests in Modřany and Zlatník in 1580; *Sněmy české*, 5:701, 712.

61. *Sněmy české*, 7:400–401, 453, 526.

62. For instance, *ibid.*, 5:748.

63. *Ibid.*, 7:367, 390–391.

64. *Ibid.*, 7:529–530.

65. The consensual system of administrative discipline was stipulated, for instance, in the Candlemas Day Articles of 1524, articles 1 to 6; see Bartoš Písař, *Kronika pražská*, ed. Josef V. Šimák, Fontes rerum Bohemicarum, vol. 6 (Prague: Historický klub, 1907), 21–22.

66. For instance, Rezek, *Dějiny prostonárodního*, 12–14.

67. *Sněmy české*, 7:391.

68. *Ibid.*, 7:452–455; 10:512–513.

69. On the towns' right of patronage over Utraquist churches, see Janáček, *České dějiny: Doba předbělohorská*, 1:190; Zikmund Winter, *Život církevní v Čechách: Kulturně-historický obraz v XV. a XVI. století*, 2 vols. (Prague: Česká akademie pro vědy, slovesnost a umění, 1895), 2:521–524.

70. *Sněmy české*, 7:463–464. On the method of appointment and sources of friction between the towns and the Consistory, see Borový, "Die Utraquisten in Böhmen," 253–254.

71. *Sněmy české*, 7:530. The statement was read to the administrator and to the priests of Prague churches in the Bohemian Chancery; *Sněmy české*, 8:22–23.

72. *Ibid.*, 7:488; 10:442.

73. *Ibid.*, 7:455–456; 7:464. See Petition of October 1577, concerning married priests

in Kutná Hora, Litoměřice, and Nymburk in *Sněmy české,* 5:198; see also *Sněmy české,* 5:301.

74. *Ibid.,* 7:3.

75. *Ibid.,* 7:377–379, 432–433; 531–532.

76. *Ibid.,* 7:526, 529–530; Tomek, *Dějepis města Prahy,* 12:311. See also *Sněmy české,* 6:241.

77. Cases in Kouřim, Prague, and Slaný, *Sněmy české,* 7:380; in Mělník and Prague, *ibid.,* 7:388–389; in Velvary, *ibid.,* 7:407–408; Velvary and Nymburk, *ibid.,* 7:421–423; in Nymburk and Prague, *ibid.,* 7:431–433. The statement of October 2, 1589, shows clearly that the Consistory's displeasure could affect priests, whose proper canonical ordination was beyond doubt; *ibid.,* 7:437. On Medek, see *ibid.,* 7:25; 7:465.

78. *Sněmy české,* 7:387. The Consistory noted with dismay on October 2, 1589, that the towns of Beroun, Domažlice, Jaroměř, Nymburk, and Sušice were reluctant to accept priests assigned by the Consistory on the grounds that "the Administrator [was] *sub una . . . ,*" adding "so they talk among themselves in the towns." *Sněmy české,* 7:437.

79. See the protest of October 17, 1592, by priest Jakub Zofian against Rezek's campaign in *Sněmy české,* 8:253. On Rezek's defection to Rome, see Chapter 9.

80. He was criticized at the time for insufficient rigor on a number of issues, such as supervision of clergy, observance of fasts, celebration of feast days, confession, clerical marriages, invocation of the saints, and prayers for the dead. The critique allegedly stemmed from the pen of his later successor as administrator, Tomáš of Soběslav; see *Sněmy české,* 10:55–56. Kamil Krofta established that the target of these charges was Administrator Rezek, not Administrator Dačický (as erroneously stated in the *Sněmy*), and corrected the dating from 1600 to 1590–1592; see *Sněmy české,* 11:66, n. 283; see also *Sněmy české,* 8:5, 114–115, 197.

81. *Sněmy české,* 11, pt. 1:72; Václav Novotný, "Náboženské dějiny české ve století 16.," in *Česká politika,* 5 vols., ed. Zdeněk V. Tobolka (Prague: Jan Laichter, 1906), 1:637.

82. *Sněmy české,* 7:265, 449, 487, 494; see also 11: pt. 1, 65.

83. *Ibid.,* 8:149, 242; 11 pt.1:76, 78; Hrejsa, *Česká konfesse,* 419.

84. Concerning Rudolf's tendency to procrastinate, see Pánek, "K povaze vlády Rudolfa II," 79–80.

85. *Sněmy české,* 10:371.

86. Maltby, *Prayer Book and People in Elizabethan and Early Stuart England,* 113–129.

87. See, for instance, Tomek, *Dějepis města Prahy,* 12:336–337; *Sněmy české,* 11:56. Josef Janáček's comment on *zkornatělý utrakvism* is in his "Královská města česká na zemském sněmu r. 1609–1610," *Sborník historický* 5 (1956): 229.

88. On the foreigners' narratives as a historical genre, see Vasilii O. Kliuchevskii, *Skazaniia inostrantsev* (Petrograd: n.p., 1918). It would be useful to have for Bohemia an inventory comparable to Marshall Poe's *Foreign Descriptions of Muscovy: An Analytic Bibliography of Primary and Secondary Sources* (Columbus, Ohio: Slavica Publishers, 1995); or if Werner Paravicini continued his coverage past the year 1531 in his *Europäische Reiseberichte des späteren Mittelalters: Eine analytische Bibliographie,* of which so far only Part 1 appeared, titled *Deutsche Reiseberichte,* ed. Christian Halm (Frankfurt: Peter Lang, 1994). Disappointingly, Vincy Schwarz, ed., *Město vidím veliké: Cizinci o Praze* (Prague: Borový, 1940) does not offer substantial information on the religious situation. On the destruction of books in Bohemia during the Counter-Reforma-

tion, see J. J. Hanuš, "O působení Jesuity Antonína Koniáše v literatuře české," *Časopis českého musea* 37 (1863): pt. 1, 77–90, 194–210; Jiří Bílý, *Jezuita Antonín Koniáš: Osobnost a doba* (Prague: Vyšehrad, 1996), 161–162; and Chapter 12.

89. Fynes Moryson, *Shakespeare's Europe: A Survey of the Conditions of Europe at the End of the 16th Century,* ed. Charles Hughes (London: Sherratt and Hughes, 1903), 277. See also Moryson, *An Itinerary Containing His Ten Yeeres Travell,* 4 vols. (New York: Macmillan, 1907–1908), 4:332–333.

90. "Das volck ist papistisch und sonderlich das weiberfolck, welche ohne das vielmehr von den wercken alss von dem glauben halten." See Henrick Kilian, *Reise Beschreibung,* printed as an appendix to Jaroslav Pánek, "Čechy, Morava a Lužice v německém cestopisu ze sklonku 16. století," *Folia Historica Bohemica* 13 (1990): 221.

91. "[I]n die stadt Igelau, die ist nicht gross, aber sehr schone gebawet, liegtt noch in Mehrenlandt, da gehet auch wiederumb die reine Luttersche lehre an und ist eine feine wolbestalte particular schule doselbst." Kilian, *ibid.*

92. Fučíková, *Tři francouzští kavalíři v rudolfínské Praze,* 44–45, 116, n. 29; see also Anna Skýbová, "Cesta po Čechách v roce 1561," *Český lid* 63 (1976): 99 for the reaction of papal emissaries.

93. Václav Šturm, *Krátké ozvání . . . proti kratičkému ohlášení Jednoty Valdenské neb Boleslavské* (Prague: Jiřík Dačický, 1584), 3, 19–20. Concerning the limited currency of German, it is apropos to note Erasmus's claim that he was unable to read Luther's non-Latin tracts because he did not know enough German; Desiderius Erasmus, *The Correspondence,* 11 vols. (Toronto: University of Toronto Press, 1974–1994), 9:391–392.

94. Šturm noted: "[I]f it were true what the Brethren . . . write about us, who are administered by the general Holy Christian and Catholic Church, and about those, who are administered by the Czech and Prague priests [Českými a Pražskými kněžími se spravují], then none of us can be saved. Namely, that we Romans or Papists—as they call us—are idolators, and the Czechs [Čechové] are still worse, only because they give the venerable Sacrament of the Altar . . . to little children." In Šturm, *Krátké ozvání,* 3.

95. Winter, *Zlatá doba měst českých,* 139–142, 144–145; Holeton, "The Evolution of Utraquist Eucharistic Liturgy: A Textual Study," 107–115. As of this writing, Holeton was preparing a monograph on the topic. On traditional Utraquist liturgy, see also Enrico Molnar, *The Catholicity of the Utraquist Church of Bohemia* (Sewanee, Tenn.: University Press of Sewanee, 1959), especially 6–8; David R. Holeton, "On the Evolution of the Utraquist Liturgy: A Precursor of Western Liturgical Reform," *Studia liturgica* 25 (1995): 51–67. For documentation, see Klement Borový, ed., *Jednání a dopisy konsistoře katolické i utrakvistické,* 2 vols. (Prague: Kober, 1868), 1:10–13, 260–262; and Bohuslav Bílejovský, *Kronyka Cýrkevní,* ed. Jozef Skalický (pseudonym for Josef Dittrich) (Prague: Fetterl z Vilden, 1816), 98–105.

96. Holeton, "The Evolution of Utraquist Eucharistic Liturgy: A Textual Study," 116–120.

97. "Bohoslužebná skládání o Husovi z XV a XVI století," in *Prameny dějin českých,* vol. 8, ed. Václav Novotný (Prague: Nadání Františka Palackého, 1932), especially 431–444, 458–472; David R. Holeton, "The Office of Jan Hus: An Unrecorded Antiphonary in the Metropolitan Library of Estergom," *Time and Continuity,* ed. J. Neil Alexander (Washington, D.C.: Pastoral Press, 1990), 141–142. Early evidence on the cult of Hus is gathered in Fudge, *The Magnificent Ride,* 125–135.

98. See, for instance, Peter Fraenkel, "Utraquism or Co-Existence: Some Notes on

the Earliest Negotiations Before the Pacification of Nuernberg, 1531–1532," *Studia theologica* 18, no. 2 (1964): 130, n. 2. On the Lutheran abomination of litanies, see also Diarmaid MacCulloch, *Thomas Cranmer: A Life* (New Haven, Conn.: Yale University Press, 1996), 329.

99. Holeton, "The Office of Jan Hus," 142. On Prosper, see Holeton, "The Evolution of Utraquist Eucharistic Liturgy: A Textual Study," 99.

100. Winter, *Zlatá doba měst českých,* 145–150; Jan J. Vrabec, "Příspěvek k dějinám kultu Husova na Králové-Hradecku před Bílou Horou," *Reformační sborník* 1 (1921): 32.

101. Winter, *Zlatá doba měst českých,* 139–142.

102. Zacharyáš Bruncvík, *Testamenti nostri Iesu Christi pia et fida assertio. To jest: Kšaftu Večeře Páně svatá Starožitnost, pobožná posloupnost, dlouhověká až právě do dne soudného trvanlivost: V níž z nařízení Kristového, z učení evangelistského a apoštolského, z doktorů a sněmů osvícených, z kanonu a práv duchovních, z historií církevních, a nejvíce našich českých, etc.* (Prague: Matěj Pardubský, 1613), 214–215.

103. Winter, *Zlatá doba měst českých,* 139. Concerning the stern judgments of Utraquism's moral and intellectual standing in Czech historiography, see Chapter 1.

104. Spurr, *English Puritanism,* 50.

105. Any such compromisers would face the divine wrath foretold by the Prophet: "What does now the Prophet tell to such as these: Walk in the commandments of God, and not in the commandments of your fathers, that is, not according to the rules of men. The people should also know that God hates idolatry; he prohibits it and commands idolatrous priests to be consumed by fire together with their idols, thus saying: thou shall not keep idolaters alive, their images and engravings thou shall burn." Jan Štelcar Želetavský z Želetavy, *Kázání dvoje,* f. B8v-C1r; see also f. C1v-C2r.

106. Zacharyáš Bruncvík, *Idolorum pia suplantatio. Kázání o tom, že obrazové* (Prague: Matěj Pardubský, 1613), f. C7r; Hrejsa, *Česká konfesse,* 536, n.3, 544, n. 4; "Dikastus," *Ottův slovník naučný* (Prague: Otto, 1888–1909), 7:533. See also Chapter 11.

107. See Chapter 1.

108. The statement is printed in Vilém Slavata, *Paměti nejvyššího kancléře království českého,* ed. Josef Jireček (Prague: Kober, 1866–1868), 1:214–219; and in *Sněmy české,* 4:345–348. On Neo-Utraquism see, for instance, Rudolf Říčan, *The History of the Unity of Brethren: A Protestant Hussite Church in Bohemia and Moravia,* trans. C. Daniel Crews (Bethlehem, Pa.: Moravian Church in America, 1992), 109, 153–155, 250; František Hrubý, "Luterství a novoutrakvismus v českých zemích v 16. a 17. století," *Český časopis historický* 45 (1939): 31–44; Hrejsa, *Česká konfesse,* 4ff; and Kamil Krofta, "Nový názor na český vývoj náboženský v době předbělohorské," *Český časopis historický* 20 (1914): 10–13.

109. Hrejsa, *Česká konfesse,* 187–189; *Sněmy české,* 7:61.

110. See MacCulloch, *Thomas Cranmer: A Life,* 334–335.

111. Valentin Polon, *Pomni na mne: Knijžka obahující v sobě kratičká spasidedlná Naučení a sebrání...* (Staré Město Pražské: Buryan Valda, 1589), f. Q5v.

112. "[Z]ávazek veliký svůj kněžský, kterýž učinili Bohu před biskupem, odřekše se světa a vší žádosti jeho, připovídajíc Pánu Bohu a Církvi jeho, poslušenství, víru a setrvání, a v dobrém řádu až do smrti státi..." Valentin Polon, *Pomni na mne,* f. A8v; see also f. A4v.

113. *Sněmy české,* 7:61; see also *ibid.,* 5:198–199, 300–301, 514–516, 712; 6:542–543, 602–603. The rejection of the sacramental priesthood, sustained by the historical

episcopate, apparently remains a principle with some Lutherans to this day, having aborted in 1997 an intercommunion agreement (Concordat of Agreement) between the Evangelical Lutheran Church in America and the Episcopal Church in the United States; *Anglican Theological Review* 80 (1998): 430–439.

114. "O jak milí Bratří, milí Šafáři, Kněží Boží jest potřebná věc umění a čistoty života těm, kteříž se za jiné modlí, učí a Tělo Páně a Krev *obětujíce* [my emphasis] posvěcují." Polon, *Pomni na mne,* f. A8r.

115. Based on Paul's Epistle to the Hebrews; see also MacCulloch, *Thomas Cranmer: A Life,* 464.

116. Jan Soffian Walkmberger of Walkmbergk, *Advent a Štědrý den.* (Prague: Buryán Valda, 1596), f. C4r, C8r; Pavel Bydžovský, *Tento spis ukazuje, že Biskupové Biskupa, a Biskup kněží, a kněží od řádných Biskupů svěceni Těla a krve Boží posvěcovati mají* (N.p., 1543), 7.

117. See Chapter 4.

118. Flavius Magnus Cassiodorus, *Historia Cýrkevní,* trans. Jan Kocín of Kocinét (Prague: Daniel Adam z Veleslavína, 1594), 3, 7; Bílejovský, *Kronyka Cýrkevní,* 27.

119. Erwin L. Lueker, ed., *Lutheran Cyclopedia,* rev. ed. (St. Louis: Concordia, 1975), 627.

120. Zacharyáš Bruncvík, *Mediatoris nostri Jesu Christi assertio. Kázání o jediném a nejsvětějším mezi Bohem a lidmi prostředníku* (Prague: Jiří Hanuš Landškrounský, 1612), f. A3v-A4r; Zacharyáš Bruncvík, *Pravitatis et impletatis haereticae pia et fida ostensio. To jest: Zrcadlo Kacířství: Do něhož kdo zdravě nahlídne, Allegata, u Doktorů Církve vykázaná, přeběhne, pozná, že my Katolíci pod obojí nevinně, a bez náležitého vší Svaté Říše vyslyšání od některých se kacerujeme* (Prague: Matěj Pardubický, 1614), f. A2r-A2v. Luther himself regarded the Councils of Nicea I, Constantinople I, Ephesus, and Chalcedon as "somewhat pure," although he viewed their authority inferior to the Scripture; Lueker, *Lutheran Cyclopedia,* 204.

121. Cassiodorus, *Historia Cýrkevní,*, 143.

122. The history of Eusebius appeared as Pamphilus Eusebius, *Historia Cýrkevní,* trans. Jan Kocín z Kocinétu (Prague: Daniel Adam z Veleslavína, 1594).

123. Říčan, *The History of the Unity of Brethren,* 110.

124. Rvačovský of Rvačov, *Masopust,* f. 56v.

125. *Ibid.*, f. D1r; see also f. D1v-D2r, 57r.

126. Straněnský's treatise is included in his *Zahrádka duchovní k potěšení všem věrným v zármutcích postaveným lidem z Písem svatých sebraná* (Prague: Jiřík Černý, 1576); sections concerning good deeds in general are "O dobře činění," f. S1r, and "O oběti, kteréž Bů od nás žádá," f. Q2r-Q2v; concerning prayers "O Modlitbě," f. Q2v–Q3v; concerning alms "Almužně udělování chudým," f. Q4v-Q5v, and "Bližní naše a chudé lidi sobě poručené míti a jim z lásky Křest'nské dobře činiti," f. R5r-R5v; and concerning fasting, "O postu," f. Q3v-Q4r. The reference to Polon ("příkladem víry a dobrých skutků lid předcházeti budou . . .") is from his *Pomni na mne,* f. A8v. Czech Lutherans, of course, denied the need for good works for salvation inasmuch as man was purged of all faults and transgressions by the redemptive sacrifice of Jesus. See Zacharyáš Bruncvík, *Kázání o Pravém a jediném očistci křest'anském, v němž hříchové naši, samým milosrdenstvím Božím a trvalou zásluhou Krista Pána, zde na světě, kdež čas milosti jest, se očišt'ují* (Prague: Matěj Pardubský, 1613).

127. For reference to an "ossified Utraquism," see Janáček, "Královská města česká na zemském sněmu r. 1609–1610," 229; also Jiří Pešek, "Protestant Literature in

Bohemian Private Libraries *circa* 1600," in *Reformation in Eastern and Central Europe*, ed. Karin Maag (Brookfield, Vt.: Ashgate, 1997), 36; Martin Nodl, "Utrakvismus a Jednota bratrská na rozcestí: Dobový kontext náboženské konverze Jana Augusty," *Marginalia Historica* 4 (2001): 148, speaks of sixteenth-century Utraquism as "barren."

128. Patrick Collinson, "Puritans," in *Oxford Encyclopedia of the Reformation* (New York: Oxford University Press, 1996), 3:366.

129. On this incident, see Chapter 6. See also Krofta, "Václav Koranda mladší," 258; Tomek, *Dějepis města Prahy,* 10:225; *Ze starých letopisů českých,* trans. Jaroslav Porák and Jaroslav Kašpar (Prague: Svoboda, 1980), 290–291.

130. *Sněmy české,* 5:198–199, 5:301; 7:61, 455–456, 464.

131. Josef Jireček, *Rukověť k dějinám literatury české do konce XVIII. věku,* 2 vols. (Prague: Tempský, 1875–1876), 2:207; Matoušek, "Kurie a boj o konsistoř pod obojí za administrátora Rezka," 252.

132. *Sněmy české,* 8:570–571; 9:151–152; 11: pt. 1, 72; *Tři francouzští kavalíři,* 45.

133. Peter Demetz, *Prague in Black and Gold: Scenes from the Life of a European City* (New York: Hill and Wang, 1997), 17. The Church of England had approved clerical marriages by 1549; MacCulloch, *Thomas Cranmer: A Life,* 408.

134. Noemi Rejchrtová, "Ženy na utrakvistických farách doby předbělohorské," *Husitství, Reformace, Renesance: Sborník k 60. narozeninám Františka Šmahela,* ed. Jaroslav Pánek, et al., 3 vols. (Prague: Historický ústav, 1994), 2:747–753. For an analogous development of views on clerical marriages in the Unity of Brethren, see Anna Císařová-Kolářová, *Žena v Jednotě bratrské: Zásady, postavy a dědictví* (Prague: Kalich, 1942), 91–112.

135. Pierre Costil, *André Dudith, humaniste hongrois 1533–1589: Sa vie, son oeuvre et ses manuscrits grecs* (Paris: Les Belles Lettres, 1935), 109.

136. Božena Kopičková, "Žena a rodina v husitství," *Husitský Tábor* 12 (1999): 40–41.

137. At that time all liturgical books in Latin were ordered to be burned; see MacCulloch, *Thomas Cranmer: A Life,* 455–456.

138. Matoušek, "Kurie a boj o konsistoř pod obojí za administrátora Rezka," 27, 32.

139. Holeton, "The Evolution of Utraquist Eucharistic Liturgy: A Textual Study," 123–124; David R. Holeton, "Převedení liturgie do národního jazyka v Čechách: Spletitá otázka" (paper delivered at Conference on Bohemian Reformation, Evangelical Theological Faculty of Charles University, Prague, March 31, 1999).

140. See, for instance, Zikmund Winter, *Děje vysokých škol pražských od secessí cizích národů po dobu bitvy bělohorské, 1409–1622* (Prague: Česká akademie pro vědy, slovesnost a umění, 1895), 23–30; Winter, *Život a učení,* 517–599; Winter, *Zlatá doba měst českých,* 141–142. The Church of England had adopted liturgical vernacular by 1549; MacCulloch, *Thomas Cranmer: A Life,* 410.

141. As shown by Hana Vlhová, the glamour of the holiday was also reflected in Utraquist hymnals, in particular the Hymnal of Jistebnice (*Jistebnický kancionál*); see Vlhová, "Die Fronleichnamsmesse in Böhmen: Ein Beitrag zur spätmittelalterlichen Choraltradition," *Schweizer Jahrbuch für Musikwissenschaft,* ns. 16 (1996): 13-36, as cited by Zuzana Všetečková, "The Man of Sorrows and Christ Blessing the Chalice: The Pre-Reformation and the Utraquist Viewpoints," in *The Bohemian Reformation and Religious Practice,* vol. 4: Papers from the IV International Symposium on Bohemian Reformation and Religious Practice, under the auspices of the Philosophical Institute of the Academy of Sciences of the Czech Republic, held at Vila Lanna, Prague, 26–28 June

2000, ed. Zdeněk V. David and David R. Holeton (Prague: Academy of Sciences of the Czech Republic, Main Library, 2002), 193. On Lutheran abomination of religious processions in general, see MacCulloch, *Thomas Cranmer: A Life,* 329.

142. Fučíková, *Tři francouzští kavalíři,* 45; Winter, *Děje vysokých škol pražských.* 39. On the Utraquist Corpus Christi processions in the late sixteenth century, see also Cyril A. Straka, "Jak slavilo se Boží tělo v Praze v XVI. a XVII. století," *Časopis katolického duchovenstva* 57, no. 82 (1916): 162. On the early enthusiasm for exhibition of the host, see Fudge, *The Magnificent Ride,* 102, 247.

143. David R. Holeton, "The 'Altar Book' of Adam of Tábor as a Source for Utraquist Theology" (paper presented at Symposium on Bohemian Reformation and Religious Practice, co-sponsored by Czech Academy of Sciences and Center for Medieval Studies, Prague, June 27, 2000). On the Utraquist celebration of the feast of Corpus Christi in Slaný in 1565, see Zuzana Všetečková, "Pozdně gotické nástěnné malby v kostele sv. Gotharda ve Slaném," in *Slaný, České město ve středověku* (Kladno and Slaný: Okresní úřad Kladno, Referát kultury, 1997), 22–24.

144. Winter, *Život církevní v Čechách,* 2:871.

145. Josef Kollmann, *Valdštejn a evropská politika, 1625–1630: Historie 1. generalátu* (Prague: Academia, 1999), 29.

146. Thomas More, *Complete Works,* 21 vols. (New Haven: Yale University Press, 1963–1997), 5: pt. 2, 356–359.

147. For a comprehensive survey of theological arguments in its favor, see David R. Holeton, *La communion des tout-petits enfants: Étude du mouvement eucharistique en Bohême vers la fin du Moyen-Âge* (Rome: Edizioni Liturgiche, 1989), 235–295. See also František M. Bartoš, "Martin Lupáč a jeho spisovatelské dílo," *Reformační sborník* 7 (1939): 128–130; Helena Krmíčková, "Několik poznámek o přijímání maličkých, 1414–1416," *Sborník prací Filozofické fakulty Brněnské univerzity* C44 (1997): 59.

148. As noted in chapter 3, David R. Holeton describes the manner of communicating infants, established by the Utraquist Synod of 1418, thus: "The priest is instructed first to place a crumb of bread into the mouth of the infant then to hold the child's mouth shut (so that the bread would be swallowed). Then the priest was to take a drop of wine from the chalice on his finger and place it in the infant's mouth." See Holeton, "The Communion of Infants and Hussitism," *Communio Viatorum* 27 (1984): 222, n. 39.

149. It is reflected in the writings of priest Jan Bechyňka in the late fifteenth century; see Noemi Rejchrtová, "Jan Bechyňka: Kněz a literát," in *Praga Mystica: Z dějin české reformace,* ed. Amedeo Molnár, Acta reformationem bohemicam illustrantia, vol. 3 (Prague: Kalich, 1984), 7–8. At the other end of the chronological continuum, it is probable that John Comenius's international fame as a teacher of pedagogy derived from, and reflected, the reverence for the child engendered by the Bohemian Reformation.

150. "Si quis dixerit, parvulis antequam ad annos discretionis pervenerint, necessariam esse Eucharistiae communionem: anathema sit." Cited by Noemi Rejchrtová, "Dětská otázka v husitství," *Československý časopis historický* 28 (1980): 75. See also David R. Holeton, "The Communion of Infants: The Basel Years," *Communio Viatorum* 29 (1986), 40, n. 99.

151. Geiko Müller-Fahrenholz, ed., *. . . And Do Not Hinder Them: An Ecumenical Plea for the Admission of Children to the Eucharist,* Faith and Order Paper 109 (Geneva: World Council of Churches, 1982). According to Holeton, the gospels presented the Christians "with a child as the paradigm for citizenship in God's reign." The child illustrated the qualities of deep trust, readiness to accept unmerited gifts, willingness to

suspend everyday awareness, and the capacities for joy and wonderment. Yet, despite their exemplary traits, children are not viewed as perfect, Holeton warns. He cites St. Augustine who had pointed to the existence of jealousy among the very infants. See Holeton, "Welcome Children, Welcome Me," *Anglican Theological Review,* 82 (2000): 97–101.

152. Jan Štelcar Želetavský z Želetavy, *Kniha nová o původu kněžství Krista Pána* (Prague: Daniel Sedlčanský, 1592), f. C2r—f. Q3v, especially f. D5–3v, f. N4–2r. Štelcar's book list is on f. A-B2v; and reprinted in J. J. Hanuš, "Kněz Štelcar Želetavský z Želetavy co literát český," *Časopis českého musea* 48 (1864): 280–287.

153. Jan of Příbram [Jan Milíč of Kroměříž], *Knihy o zármutcích velkých církve svaté,* ed. Pavel Bydžovský and Brikcí of Licko (Prague: Netolický, 1542), f. 57; see Štelcar, *Kniha nová o původu kněžství,* f. B1r.

154. Jan Xenomen Rausinovský z Mazanovic, *Dar Nového léta dítkám zrozeným* (Prague: Jan Jiřínský, 1590); Štelcar, *Kniha nová o původu kněžství,* f. B2v. See also *Knihopis českých a slovenských tisků,* 2 vols., vol. 2 in 9 parts (Prague: Nakladatelství Československé akademie věd, 1925-1967), no. 17.063.

155. Moryson, *Shakespeare's Europe,* 277.

156. The practice also differentiated the Utraquists from the Brethren who—despite their abomination of the sub una—were ready to commend the Romanists for refusing communion to immature children; see G. A. Skalský, "Spor Bratří s Vojtěchem z Pernštejna 1557," *Časopis českého musea* 83 (1909): 24.

157. Martin Žatecký, *Knížka proti ošemetné poctě a pokryté Svatých,* 2d ed., ed. Jan Štelcar Želetavský z Želetavy (Prague: n.p., 1593), f. A4r–A5r. In general, all Lutheran confessions rejected the saints' role as mediators of redemption, and prohibited prayers to saints; see Lueker, *Lutheran Cyclopedia,* 692.

158. Martin Žatecký, *Knížka proti ošemetné poctě a pokryté Svatých,* f. A5v–A6r. Štelcar is referring to Václav Benešovský, *Ozvání starých Čechů a Moravců před léty osmdesáti, kteréž učinili proti těm, kteříž o nich mluvili, že jsou odřezanci církve svaté* (Prague: Jan Jiřínský, 1588).

159. "Stal se Čechům protivný kus—Vyletěla jim z Prahy hus—Prodal ji mistr Kodicillus" (An unpleasant deed was committed against the Czechs; their goose (i.e., Hus) flew out of Prague; it was sold by Master Kodicillus) in Klement Borový, *Martin Medek, Arcibiskup pražský: Historicko-kritické vypsání náboženských poměrů v Čechách, 1581– 1590* (Prague: Dědictví sv. Prokopa, 1877), 78. A manuscript of the late sixteenth century has Kodicillus (died 1589) for his deed barred from heaven; Jaroslav Kolár, *Návraty bez konce: Studie k starší české literatuře,* ed. Lenka Jiroušková (Brno: Atlantis, 1999), 211. See also Jan J. Vrabec, "Příspěvek k dějinám kultu Husova na Králové-Hradecku před Bílou Horou," *Reformační sborník* 1 (1921): 33; David R. Holeton, "'O felix Bohemia— O felix Constantia': The Liturgical Commemoration of Saint Jan Hus," *Jan Hus: Zwischen Zeiten, Völkern, Konfessionen,* ed. Ferdinand Seibt (Munich: Oldenbourg, 1997), 389–397. According to Karel Stloukal, "Počátky nunciatury v Praze: Bonhomi v Čechách, 1581–84," *Český časopis historický* 34 (1928): 257, Nuncio Bonhomi was also implicated in the campaign to eliminate the Hus feast day from the calendar.

160. Zuzana Všetečková, "Iconography of the Mural Paintings in St. James's Church of Kutná Hora," in *The Bohemian Reformation and Religious Practice,* vol. 3: Papers from the XIXth World Congress of the Czechoslovak Society of Arts and Sciences, Bratislava 1998, ed. Zdeněk V. David and David R. Holeton (Prague: Academy of Sciences of the Czech Republic, Main Library, 2000), 138.

161. *Sněmy české,* 6:242; 9:202; Polon, *Pomni na mne,* f. C8r–D1r.
162. Všetečková, "Iconography of the Mural Paintings," 127–146.
163. Bílejovský, *Kronyka Cýrkevní,* 2, 21–22; Noemi Rejchrtová, "Svatý Vojtěch v zrcadle české reformace," *Teologické texty* 8, no. 3 (1997): 93–94. See also Blažej Nožička, z Votína, *Vyznání o poctivosti vzývání, přímluvě a o modlitbě za mrtvé* (Prague: Jiří Dačický, 1568), for Utraquist endorsement of invocation of the saints and prayers for the dead.
164. Štelcar, *Kázání dvoje,* f. B8v–C1r.
165. Jindřich Ondřej Hoffman, *Zrcadlo náboženství* (Prague: Impressí akademická, 1642), 221, 241. In an earlier period, attacks by Utraquists on monasteries in Prague in 1521 seemed to target three-dimensional depictions of saints; see Václav Husa, *Tomáš Müntzer a Čechy,* Rozpravy ČSAV, roč. 67 (1957), Společenské vědy, 11 seš., 74–75.
166. Všetečková, "Iconography of the Mural Paintings in St. James's Church of Kutná Hora," 129-132.
167. Martin Žatecký, *Knížka proti ošemetné poctě a pokryté Svatých,* f. A3r; Zikmund Winter, *Kulturní obraz českých měst,* 2 vols. (Prague: Matice česká, 1890), 1:442; Fučíková, *Tři francouzští kavalíři,* 45.
168. Zdeněk Tobolka, ed., *Kališnický pasionál z roku 1495,* Monumenta Bohemiae typographica, vol. 2 (Prague: n.p., 1926).
169. The text of the Bohemian Confession has been occasionally viewed in historical literature as a Neo-Utraquist document. To the small extent, however, that the text departed from its model, the Augsburg Confession, it sought to accommodate not with Utraquism, but with the views of the Unity, which actually diverged even more from Utraquism than standard Lutheranism did. Hrejsa, *Česká konfesse,* 277, 279, 663. The Czech Lutherans themselves tended to view the text as identical, or virtually identical, with the Augsburg Confession; see, for instance, Konstantin Kristian Bidones z Bidenthalu, *Výstraha: Proti v Římsko-Katolické náboženství ubíhání všechněm k Augšpurské neb české Konfesí se přiznávajícím . . .* (N.p., 1624).
170. Václav Koranda, Jr., *Traktát o velebné a božské svátosti oltářní* (Prague: Tiskař Korandy, 1493), f. A3v–A4r; Denis, *Fin de l'indépendance bohême,* 2:208–209.
171. For the period prior to the Edict of Nantes between 1562 and 1598, see Gregory Champeaud, "The Edict of Poitiers and the Treaty of Nérac, or Two Steps toward the Edict of Nantes," *Sixteenth Century Journal* 32 (2001): 319–320.
172. Images of active confessional strife are misleading. See, for instance, the following: "The pernicious polemics concerning religion still [in the sixteenth century] always spawned multiple fruits; the Catholics, Utraquists, Lutherans, Brethren, each readily proffered their confessions to the monarchs, or came out to battle each other concerning the body and blood of Christ in the sacrament of the altar, the communion of infants, the celibacy of priests, etc." Josef J. Jungmann, *Historie literatury české,* 2d ed. (Prague: Řivnáč, 1849), 127–128. On the harmonious contact of members of different denominations, see Jaroslav Kolár, "Na okraj jednoho kronikářského záznamu," in *Marginalia historica* 4 (2001): 175–179.
173. Novotný, "Náboženské dějiny české ve století 16.," 1:635–636; *Sněmy české,* 10:453, 11: pt. 1, 41–42.
174. Johannes Leunclavius, *Kronyka nová o národu tureckém na dva díly rozdělená,* trans. Jan Kocín z Kocinétu and Daniel Adam z Veleslavína (Prague: Daniel Adam z Veleslavína, 1594), f. 5r.
175. Budovec's treatise was published only in 1614. He relied heavily on Theodor

Bibliander's *Machumetis Saracenorum principiis, eiusque succesorum vitae* (Basel: J. Oporimus, 1550) for his exposition and arguments against the Koran; Václav Budovec of Budov, *Antialkorán*, ed. Noemi Rejchrtová (Prague: Odeon, 1989), 12, 364. On a higher theological plane, Budovec argued that the challenge of Islam was closely related to that of anti-Trinitarianism. The two were just different sides of the same coin. He saw Islam as a variant of the ancient Arian heresy that denied the divinity of Christ and the Trinity's existence; *Antialkorán*, 17.

176. He wrote: "[A]nd to this day—in his evil and perversity—the devil, God's enemy and ours, incites many ferocious, angry and stormy, proud and conceited people so that several groups defend their own sects which they seek to disseminate and spread far and wide, and thus to humiliate the Christian universal and apostolic Church." Polon, *Pomni na mne*, f. A5a-A5b.

177. Štelcar Želetavský z Želetavy, *Knížka o pravé a falešné církvi* (Prague: Buryán Valda, 1589), f. N1r–N2r. The reference is apparently to Václav Šturm, *Krátké ozvání . . . proti kratičkému ohlášení Jednoty Valdenské neb Boleslavské* (Prague: Jiřík Dačický, 1584). Štelcar misdates to 1154 the error of Berengarius, who lived c. 1000–1088; see his *Knížka o pravé a falešné církvi*, f. M1r-M2v.

178. Václav Slovacius, *O pokloně ve jménu Jesus, má-li činěna býti* (Prague: Jan Jičinský, [1586]), f. A2v, A8r; Slovacius, *O pokloně ve jménu Jesus*, 2d ed. (Prague: Jan Jičinský, 1590), f. A7v, A2r, (A)3r; Václav Slovacius, *Rozjímání o předzvědění a vyvolení božím lidí k věčnému spasení* (Prague: n.p., 1615), see *Knihopis českých a slovenských tisků*, n. 15.515 (no known copy). Zachariáš Bruncvík, in a treatise of 1607, strongly condemned Michael Servetus and the entire anti-Trinitarian movement, which he located mainly in Poland and Transylvania. Like Budovec, he linked the Arian heresy with Islam. He likewise embraced Luther's denunciation of Caspar Schenckfeld's teaching for its monothelitism; Zachariáš Bruncvík, *Homilia de incarnati verbi massa: To jest, Kázání o vtělení, narození a předivném andělům, lidem pak spasitelném spojení podstatném dvojího přirození Božského a lidského v jednotu osoby Pána našeho Ježíše Krista* (Prague: Typis Schumanianis, 1607), f. E2r–E3r, F2r.

179. Stephen Lahey, "Toleration in the Theology and Social Thought of John Wyclif," in *Difference and Dissent: Theories of Tolerance in Medieval and Early Modern Europe*, ed. Cary J. Nederman and John C. Laursen (Lanham: Rowman and Littlefield, 1996), 53–58.

180. Jaroslav Čechura, *České země v letech 1378–1437*, vol. 2 of *Lucemburkové na českém trůně* (Prague: Libri, 2000), 124.

181. Brian Tierney, *The Idea of Natural Rights: Studies on Natural Rights, Natural Law and Church Law, 1150–1625* (Atlanta, Ga.: Scholars Press for Emory University, 1997), 32, 214.

182. On the strain of open-mindedness and tolerance in Utraquism, see Chapter 2, and Thomas A. Fudge, "The Problem of Religious Liberty in Early Modern Bohemia," *Communio Viatorum* 38 (1996), 64-87.

183. See Spurr, *English Puritanism*, 57, 61–62; and literature cited in Sheila Lambert, "Richard Montagu, Arminianism and Censorship," *Past and Present* 124 (1989): 68, n. 118. Like the Anglican authors in the tradition of John Jewel, Richard Hooker, or Richard Montagu, so also the Utraquist Church of Bohemia fostered discussion rather than edicts, and preserved a nonconfrontational, even cordial tone in discussion with religious interlocutors. Montagu maintained that theological subjects "should, above all,

be moderately, calmely, and quietly handled"; and he exhorted the religious controversialist: "Let himselfe . . . goe honestly, sincerely, soberly, scholler-like to worke: Let him set affection, partiallity, sinister ends apart: Let him come home to the poynts controverted, without rowling, rambling, raving: joyne issue instantly with the Question where it lyeth . . ." In Montague, *A Gagg for the New Gospell? No, a New Gagg for an Old Goose* (London: printed by T. Snodham, 1624), f. 3v.

184. Rejchrtová, "Jan Bechyňka," 17–18.

185. Blažej Nožička z Votína, *Knížka proti bludům některým před tisíci lety odsouzeným* (Prague: Jan Kantor, 1566), f. K(v). Sweden is the example of another nation that turned to pacifism from, and possibly as a reaction to, an earlier history of bloodshed and military ferocity.

186. Georg Lauterbach, *Politica historica: O vrchnostech a správcích světských knihy patery,* trans. Daniel Adam of Veleslavín (Prague: Daniel Adam of Veleslavín, 1584); Milan Kopecký, *Daniel Adam z Veleslavína* (Prague: Svobodné slovo, 1962), 25. Conversely, abroad the Czechs by the latter part of the sixteenth century had seen a marked decline in their military reputation, acquired during the wars of Bohemian Reformation. Giovanni Botero, "Žádnému národu nezadají," in *Město vidím veliké: Cizinci o Praze,* ed. Vincy Schwarz (Prague: Borový, 1940), 32, is cited as writing about the Czechs unflatteringly and curiously in 1596: "Several times they showed bravery in war; now they have the reputation of good saboteurs [*záškodníků*] rather than soldiers." See also Karel Stloukal, "Z diplomatických styků mezi Francií a Čechami před Bílou Horou," *Český časopis historický* (1926): 489.

187. On the concept of "confessionalization," see, for instance, Robert Bireley, *The Refashioning of Catholicism, 1450–1700: A Reassessment of the Counter Reformation* (Washington, D.C.: Catholic University of America Press, 1999), 6–8.

188. The Laudian portrayal of Anglicanism is characterized by Walsham, "The Parochial Roots of Laudianism Revisited," 634.

189. See, for instance, Spurr, *English Puritanism,* 104. A similar phenomenon of anxiety and need to affirm a stern orthodoxy was attributed to the Council of Constance in its treatment of Jan Hus. See Chapter 2, and Paul de Vooght, *L'hérésie de Jean Huss,* 2d ed., 2 vols. (Louvain: Publications universitaires, 1975), 1:502, 507–508.

190. On the burning of Emser's books, see Gustav Kawerau, *Hieronymus Emser: Ein Lebensbild aus der Reformationsgeschichte* (Halle: Verein für Reformationsgeschichte, 1898), 34.

191. MacCulloch, *Thomas Cranmer: A Life,* 238. On the illiberal rigidity of the official Protestant churches, see also James E. Bradley and Dale K. Van Kley, eds., *Religion and Politics in Enlightenment Europe* (Notre Dame, Ind.: University of Notre Dame Press, 2001).

192. Skalský, "Spor Bratří s Vojtěchem z Pernštejna 1557," 24.

193. Daniela Neri, ed., *Nuntiaturberichte aus Deutschland,* Dritte Abteilung, 1572–1585, 8, Band: Nuntiatur Giovanni Dolfins, 1575–1576 (Tübingen: Max Niemayer, 1997), 74. See also Jarold K. Zeman, "The Rise of Liberty in the Czech Reformation," *Central European History* 6 (1973): 131–138.

194. The case involved a translation of Plutarch's *De educatione puerorum* by Jakub Krupský; see Winter, *Děje vysokých škol pražských,* 95–96.

195. MacCulloch, *Thomas Cranmer,* 145.

196. See Chapter 5.

197. Říčan, *The History of the Unity of Brethren*, 155–156.

198. In his treatise *Pomni na mne* in a dedication to Adam of Hradec, dated December 9, 1588, he celebrated the fact that it was on that day in the year 1420 that Adam's ancestor Oldřich of Hradec helped to convoke a gathering in Prague that sought to resolve the differences between Utraquist and Taborite clergy in the face of a common danger posed by the papal crusaders; see Polon, *Pomni na mne*, f. A8v–A9r.

199. Polon, *Pomni na mne*, f. A8v–A9r. According to Utraquist theology, by the term "Holy Catholic Church," Polon, of course, did not mean the administrative structure under the Roman Curia, but the Church of the Nicene Creed. On the friendly encounter of Utraquist and Taborite priests in 1420, see *ibid.*, f. club 7r.

200. Polon, *Pomni na mne*, f. A6v.

201. Cykáda, *Hody křest'anské*, 140–141, 242.

202. Flavius Josephus, *Historia židovská. Na knihy čtyry rozdělená*, trans. and intro. Václav Plácel z Elbingu (Prague: Daniel Adam of Veleslavín, 1592), 2–3, 15–16.

203. Flavius Magnus Cassiodorus, *Historia Cýrkevní*, trans. Jan Kocín of Kocinét (Prague: Daniel Adam z Veleslavína, 1594), f. 2r, 3.

204. *Sněmy české*, 10:512–513. The aversion to secular learning, which characterized the Unity in the fifteenth century, was however substantially modified subsequently; see Jan Jakubec, *Dějiny literatury české*, 2d ed., 2 vols. (Prague: Jan Laichter, 1929–1934), 1:685–690; Zdeňka Tichá, *Cesta starší české literatury* (Prague: Panorama, 1984), 185. As pointed out earlier, the Utraquists themselves did not embrace either the discipline of moral perfection or the aversion to secular enjoyments, which were characteristic especially of the Calvinist or quasi-Calvinist strands in the Protestant Reformation. For instance, the English Puritans wished to control morals by imposing rigorous discipline on the believers; see Spurr, *English Puritanism*, 52, 75.

205. Marek Bydžovský z Florentina, *Rudolphus rex Bohemiae XXI* (manuscript, Prague, Bib. Nat. XVI G 22), f. 147/154r, 305/327ff., and 313/335ff.

206. Rezek, *Dějiny prostonárodního hnutí náboženského*, 18. On the unrestrained language of Luther's own disputations, for instance, with Emser, see Gustav Kawerau, *Hieronymus Emser: Ein Lebensbild aus der Reformationsgeschichte* (Halle: Verein für Reformationsgeschichte, 1898), 38–39.

207. On German Lutherans, see Hrejsa, *Česká konfesse*, 521–522; on the Brethren, see Kamil Krofta, *O bratrském dějepisectví* (Prague: Laichter, 1946), 53–53. An exception was the lay leader of Unity, Václav Budovec of Budov; on his outstanding contribution to religious tolerance, especially in 1609, see Julius Glücklich, *O historických dílech Václava Budovce z Budova z let 1608–1610 a jejich poměru k Slavatovi, Skálovi a neznámému dosud diariu lutherána Karla Zikmundova,* Rozpravy české Akademie pro vědy, slovesnost a umění. Třída I., číslo 42 (Prague: Alois Wiesner, 1911), 68; Pavel Skála ze Zhoře, *Historie česká od r. 1602 do r. 1623*, 5 vols., ed. Karel Tieftrunk (Prague: Kober, 1865–1870), 1:108–109.

208. On the Taborite tenet calling for the extermination of the wicked, see Fudge, *The Magnificent Ride*, 172.

209. In neighboring Moravia, the position of the Holy See was articulated by the canon of the diocese of Olomouc, Petr Illicino, in 1577. In opposing the legal provision for religious freedom in Moravia, he not only rejected toleration on religious grounds, but also argued that the idea of religious tolerance was dangerous for purely secular reasons, because it was subversive of temporal authority. Rulers who gathered people of different religions ran a great risk. Those who revolted against the authority of the church

would soon challenge the authority of the state; Petr Illicino, *Contra impiam Deoque inimicam haereticorum legem, quod liceat cuique impune ac sine aliquo impedimento de fide sentire et praedicare, ut velit.* Commentarius per Petrum Illicinum, J. U. Doctorem, canonicum ecclesiae Olomucensis. Anno MDLXXVII. [Olomouc, 1577.] Manuscript, Vienna, National Library, 11623), f. 36v–37v.

210. "[P]řeveliký dým rozličného Kacířství, mnohotvářnost Sekt a Rozbrojů v Náboženství povstalo: že nepravím v jedné krajině ani v jednom Městě nebo Vsi, ale co více jí jest v jednom špatném Domku a chalupě, jeden druhého sotva může poznati." See Edmund Campion, *Spis krátký Edmunda Kampiana Societatis Jesu, Theologa a Mučedlníka Božího, ktrý ne tak dávno pro víru S. Katolickau smrt ukrutnau podstaupil: Vznešeným Doktorům a Mistrům učení Oxonienského a Kantabrigienského podaný* (Prague: Jiřík Nygrin, 1601), f. A4r.

211. "[J]est jak živ větších lží neviděl a neslyšel . . ." Jireček, *Rukověť k dějinám literatury české*, 2:277. Žerotín referred to Václav Šturm, *Srovnání víry a učení bratří starších* (Litomyšl: Andreas Graudenc, 1582).

212. For the Articles of 1525 and the letter of 1549, see Borový, *Jednání a dopisy*, 1:10–13; 260–265. For the Articles of 1539, see *Artykulowe a snessenij Knězstva pod obogij Spuosobau: Leta Bozijho MDXXXIX* (archived at National Library in Vienna under the notation *Articuli Conciliabuli sub utraque specie communicantium*, Bohemice et latine, S.l., 1539, Signatura: 24 M 56). For the letter of 1570, see Pažout, *Jednání a dopisy konsistoře*, 435–438. For the statements of 1575 and 1609, see Slavata, *Paměti nejvyššího kancléře*, 1: 214–219; and *Sněmy české*, 4:345–348.

Chapter 9

1. Klement Borový, *Martin Medek, Arcibiskup pražský: Historicko-kritické vypsání náboženských poměrů v Čechách, 1581–1590* (Prague: Dědictví sv. Prokopa, 1877), 75.

2. *Sněmy české od léta 1526 až po naši dobu.*, vols. 1-11, 15 (Prague: Zemský výbor, 1877-1941), 7:3.

3. Josef Pekař, *Dějiny československé* (Prague: Akropolis, 1991), 91.

4. "[V]ždy více se sbližovala s církví Římskou . . ." *Sněmy české*, 11:49.

5. Kamil Krofta, *Nesmrtelný národ: Od Bílé Hory k Palackému* (Prague: Laichter, 1940), 308. See also Kamil Krofta, *Majestát Rudolfa II* (Prague: Historický klub, 1909), 13.

6. Krofta, *Majestát Rudolfa II*, 22.

7. Zikmund Winter, *Život církevní v Čechách: Kulturně-historický obraz v XV. a XVI. století*, 2 vols. (Praha: Česká akademie pro vědy, slovesnost a umění, 1895), 1:333.

8. For instance, Jaroslav Pánek, "Stavovství v předbělohorské době," *Folia Historica Bohemica* 6 (1984): 189.

9. Jan Bedřich Novák, *Rudolf II a jeho pád* (Prague: Český zemský výbor, 1935), 18.

10. James H. Burns and Thomas M. Izbicki, eds. and trans., *Conciliarism and Papalism* (Cambridge: Cambridge University Press, 1997).

11. Tomáš G. Masaryk shared this error when he saw a contradiction between appeals to the prvotní církev on the one hand, and church councils and church doctors, on the other. See Masaryk, *Česká otázka. Naše nynější krize. Jan Hus,* Spisy 6 (Prague:

Masarykův ústav, 2000), 363. On the primitive church of the Utraquists, see Bohuslav Bílejovský, *Kronyka Cýrkevní,* ed. Jozef Skalický (pseudonym for Josef Dittrich) (Prague: Fetterl z Vilden, 1816), 16–17; Pavel Bydžovský, *Dět'átka a neviňátka hned po přijetí křtu sv. Tělo a Krev Boží, že přijímati mají* (Prague: Bartoloměj Netolický, 1541), f. A5v–A6r (also B8r).

12. Irena Backus, "Erasmus and the Spirituality of the Early Church," in *Erasmus' Vision of the Church,* ed. Hilmar M. Pabel, Sixteenth Century Essays and Studies, 33 (Kirksville, Mo.: Sixteenth Century Journal Publishers, 1995), 95–114; Erica Rummel, *The Humanist-Scholastic Debate in the Renaissance and Reformation* (Cambridge, Mass.: Harvard University Press, 1995), 89–91, 103–111, 134–140. On Erasmus's and Fisher's shared interest in Greek patristics and in humanistic learning see Maria Dowling, *Fisher of Men: A Life of John Fisher, 1469–1535* (New York: St. Martin's Press, 1999), 30–40.

13. "[A]by je za dobré křest'any a syny prvotní církve svaté měli." "Compactata," *Archiv český* 3 (1844): 444; Phillip H. Stump, *The Reforms of the Council of Constance, 1414–1418* (Leiden: E. J. Brill, 1994), 215, 227, 229, 269.

14. Diarmaid MacCulloch, *Thomas Cranmer: A Life* (New Haven, Conn.: Yale University Press, 1996), 280.

15. Flavius Magnus Cassiodorus, *Historia Cýrkevní,* trans. Jan Kocín of Kocinét (Prague: Daniel Adam z Veleslavína, 1594); Flavius Josephus, *Historia židovská. Na knihy čtyry rozdělená,* trans. and introduction, Václav Plácel z Elbingu (Prague: Daniel Adam z Veleslavína, 1592).

16. It did not escape the attention of later book censors of the Counter-Reformation who automatically suspected even orthodox books if they bore the names of Utraquist editors or translators; see Jiří Bílý, *Jezuita Antonín Koniáš: Osobnost a doba* (Prague: Vyšehrad, 1996), 155–156.

17. "A poněvadž jméno biskupské v jazyku řeckém, ne tak důstojenství a povýšení s užíváním mnohých důchodů, jako více služebnost a snaživou práci vyznamenává: protož i tento Theodoritus v úřadu i povolání svém tak se choval, že se při něm žádného nedostatku ani úhony nenacházelo." Cassiodorus, *Historia Cýrkevní,* 3.

18. "[B]yv biskupem tolik let, nic svého vlastního jsem neměl ani domu, ani pole, ani haléře, ani hrobu: ale že jsem dobrovolně chudobu sobě oblíbil, a což mi koli statku po rodičích zůstalo, to jsem vše hned po jejich smrti rozdal." Cassiodorus, *Historia Cýrkevní,* 4.

19. "A tak jest se všudy stávalo, kdežkoli Duchovní lidé, majíce dle povolání svého pilni býti služeb Božích a vyučování lidu, opustivše to, pletli se do světské věci, . . . tak i oni jednou nohou chtěli v kostele státi, a druhou na Rathauzích aneb na dvořích královských přítomni býti: že potom skrze to divných neřádů a spletku v zemi a obcích se nadělalo." Josephus, *Historia židovská,* 4–5.

20. On the late medieval origin of the doctrine of papal infallibility see Brian Tierney, *Origins of Papal Infallibility, 1150–1350: A Study on the Concepts of Infallibility, Sovereignty and Tradition in the Middle Ages* (Leiden: E. J. Brill, 1988), 12–13; Kathleen G. Cushing, *Papacy and Law in the Gregorian Revolution: The Canonistic Work of Anselm of Lucca* (Oxford: Clarendon Press, 1998), 11–39.

21. Cassiodorus, *Historia Cýrkevní,* 143.

22. As, for instance, Luther has pointed out; see P. Fraenkel, "Utraquism or Co-Existence: Some Notes on the Earliest Negotiations Before the Pacification of Nuernberg, 1531–1532," *Studia theologica* 18, no. 2 (1964): 129.

23. Josef Matoušek, "Kurie a boj o konsistoř pod obojí za administrátora Rezka,"

Český časopis historický 37 (1931): 27–28. The Consistory also went on the record objecting to the pope being called the Antichrist; see Sněmy české, 7:397.

24. Pavel Bydžovský, *Historiae aliquot Anglorum martyrum, quibus Deus suam ecclesiam exornare sicut syderibus coelum dignatus est* (Prague: J. Cantor, 1554), f. B2r, B3v.

25. Matoušek, "Kurie a boj o konsistoř pod obojí," 27–28.

26. See, especially, *Druhá Apologie stavův království českého, tělo a krev Pána Ježíše Krista pod obojí přijímajících* (Prague: Daniel Karel z Karlspergka, 1619), 205 (no. 27).

27. David R. Holeton, "The Evolution of Utraquist Eucharistic Liturgy: A Textual Study," in *The Bohemian Reformation and Religious Practice,* vol. 2: Papers from the XVIIIth World Congress of the Czechoslovak Society of Arts and Sciences, Brno 1996, ed. Zdeněk V. David and David R. Holeton (Prague: Academy of Sciences of the Czech Republic, Main Library, 1998), 109–110, 121–125.

28. Alena Pazderová, "Instrukce pražského nuncia Caetaniho pro jeho nástupce Speciana," in *Facta probant homines: Sborník příspěvků k životnímu jubileu prof. dr. Zdeňky Hledíkové,* ed. Ivan Hlaváček a Jan Hrdina (Prague: Scriptorium, 1998), 354.

29. Milan Skřivánek, "K náboženským dějinám východočeského města v 15. až 18. století," *Česká města v 16.–18. století: Sborník příspěvků z konference v Pardubicích 14. a 15. listopadu 1990,* ed. Jaroslav Pánek (Prague: Historický ústav, 1991), 181.

30. Matoušek, "Kurie a boj o konsistoř pod obojí," 27. See also Holeton, "The Evolution of Utraquist Eucharistic Liturgy: A Textual Study," 123.

31. Matoušek, "Kurie a boj o konsistoř pod obojí," 262–263.

32. *Ibid.,* 271, n. 3.

33. Noemi Rejchrtová, "Dětská otázka v husitství," *Československý časopis historický* 28 (1980): 75. See also David R. Holeton, "The Communion of Infants: The Basel Years," *Communio Viatorum* 29 (1986): 40, n. 99.

34. Thierry Wanegffelen, *Une difficile fidelité: Catholiques malgré concile en France, XVIe-XVII-e siècles* (Paris: Presses Universitaires de France, 1999). See also the review by Robert M. Kingdon in *Sixteenth Century Journal* 32 (2001): 570.

35. *Sněmy české,* 4:206.

36. Matoušek, "Kurie a boj o konsistoř pod obojí," 28–29.

37. Eliška Fučíková, ed., *Tři francouzští kavalíři v rudolfínské Praze* (Prague: Panorama, 1989), 45.

38. Also known as Bonhomi or Bonhomini; see *Dizionario biografico degli Italiani* (Rome: Istituto de la Enciclopedia italiana, 1960–), 12:309.

39. Karel Stloukal, "Počátky nunciatury v Praze: Bonhomi v Čechách, 1581-84," *Český časopis historický* 34 (1928): 275.

40. "[I]n hoc regno alia religio praeter antiquam catholicam sub una et alteram sub utraque communicantium toleretur . . ." Letter of Archbishop Berka to Rudolf II, September 12, 1595, in *Sněmy české,* 9:183.

41. "[K]atolickou pak víru a řád dobrej církevní starobylý v tomto království při straně pod jednou i pod obojí vždy jednostejnej . . ." *Sněmy české,* 9:178.

42. See Chapter 5, and Jaroslav Pelikan, "Luther's Attitude Toward John Hus," *Concordia Theological Monthly* 19 (1948): 757–761.

43. *Sněmy české,* 11: pt. 1, 62.

44. Matoušek, "Kurie a boj o konsistoř pod obojí," 270–271, n. 3.

45. *Ibid.,* 278–279.

46. "[A]bjuro schisma, haereses et errores Hussitarum . . ." See *Sněmy české,* 8:338.
47. *Ibid.,* 8:337.
48. On this aspect, see Chapter 7. While the Anglican orders, both episcopal and presbyterial, were regarded as null and void, the Roman Church recognized Utraquist clergy as validly ordained priesthood despite Rome's abomination of Hus and the Bohemian Reformation; Fučíková, *Tři francouzští kavalíři v rudolfínské Praze,* 44–45, 116, n. 29. On Rome's view of Anglican orders see Leo Bishop, "The English Text of Apostolicae Curae," *Anglican Theological Review* 78 (1996): 127–137.
49. For example, in 1579; *Sněmy české,* 5:516.
50. "Stolice VMCské [Vaší Milosti Císařské]," in May 1585; *Sněmy české,* 6:602.
51. "JMCská [Jeho MilostCísařská] jurisdikcí práva duchovního konsistoře naší žádnému dáti a poručiti, než že ji v rukou a moci své císařské a tolikéž VMCské [Vaší Milosti Císařské] zanechávati a nad ní zvláštní ochranu míti a držeti ráčí." *Sněmy české,* 5:302; see also *Sněmy české,* 5:514–516.
52. *Sněmy české,* 6:542–543.
53. *Ibid.,* 7:438–439.
54. *Ibid.,* 10:332–333.
55. *Ibid.,* 6:175.
56. Matoušek, "Kurie a boj o konsistoř pod obojí," 18, 30–31.
57. *Sněmy české,* 6:241
58. Borový, *Martin Medek, arcibiskup pražský,* 72–104.
59. On the investigation of a new sect in Tábor, see *Sněmy české,* 6:513.
60. *Ibid.,* 6:542–543.
61. *Ibid.,* 7:225; 7:265.
62. *Ibid.,* 10:55.
63. Julius Pažout, *Jednání a dopisy konsistoře pod obojí způsobou přijímajících, 1562–1570* (Prague: Historický spolek, 1906), 365; Kamil Krofta, "Boj o konsistoř podobojí v l. 1562–1575 a jeho historický základ," *Český časopis historický* 17 (1911): 390–91.
64. Krofta, "Boj o konsistoř," 401–403; Alois Kroess, *Geschichte der Böhmischen Provinz der Gesellschaft Jesu,* 2 vols. in 3 (Vienna: Mayer, 1910–1938), 1:211–212; Klement Borový, *Antonín Brus z Mohelnice, arcibiskup pražský; Historicko-kritický životopis* (Prague: Dědictví sv. Prokopa, 1873), 194–195, 290, 292–293; Helmut Goetz, ed., *Nuntiaturberichte aus Deutschland nebst ergänzenden Aktenstücken,* Dritte Abteilung, 1572–1585, 6, Band: Nuntiatur Giovanni Dolfinos, 1572–1573 (Tübingen: Max Niemayer, 1982), 153–154, 467.
65. Daniela Neri, ed., *Nuntiaturberichte aus Deutschland,* Dritte Abteilung, 1572–1585, 8, Band: Nuntiatur Giovanni Dolfins, 1575–1576 (Tübingen: Max Niemayer, 1997), 233, 324. The administrator at the time was not Martin Mělnický (1568–1572) as the Nuntiaturberichte erroneously assert; *ibid.,* 324, n. 5.
66. Pazderová, "Instrukce pražského nuncia Caetaniho," 355.
67. Stloukal, "Počátky nunciatury v Praze," 15, 253–257.
68. *Ibid.,* 253–254.
69. Matoušek, "Kurie a boj o konsistoř pod obojí," 22–24; Stloukal, "Počátky nunciatury v Praze," 256.
70. Stloukal, "Počátky nunciatury v Praze," 276.
71. Krofta, in *Sněmy české,* 11: pt. 1, 62, n. 273, corrects the mistake in *Sněmy české,* 5:694–699, which dates the plan to 1580 and attributes its authorship to Nuncio "Pla-

centinus." Krofta identifies the mysterious "Placentinus" as Filip Sega, who was bishop of Piacenza and a nuncio in Prague in 1586–1587.

72. Matoušek, "Kurie a boj o konsistoř pod obojí," 27–28. On another alleged submission to Rome, see *Sněmy české*, 11: pt. 1, 64.

73. Matoušek, "Kurie a boj o konsistoř pod obojí," 30.

74. *Ibid.*, 31–32.

75. Krofta, in *Sněmy české*, 11: pt. 1, 65.

76. Marek Bydžovský z Florentina, *Rudolphus rex Bohemiae XXI* (manuscript, Prague, Bib. Nat. XVI G 22), f. 205r–207r; Matoušek, "Kurie a boj o konsistoř pod obojí," 29; *Sněmy české*, 11: pt. 1, 67, n. 287. On that occasion, Visconti imposed the following penance on Rezek: to pray seven psalms every Friday for a year, and to fast every Saturday for a month in honor of the Blessed Virgin Mary; see Bydžovský z Florentina, *Rudolphus rex Bohemiae XXI*, f. 206a–b.

77. Matoušek, "Kurie a boj o konsistoř pod obojí," 280.

78. *Ibid.*, 272.

79. *Ibid.*, 282.

80. *Ibid.*, 262.

81. For Zofian's complaint to the deputies of the Bohemian Diet, see *Sněmy české*, 8:253.

82. *Ibid.* 8:149.

83. *Ibid.*, 5:302–303; Petr Codicillus, *Orací aneb spis k stavům pod obojí*, delivered on February 10, 1582, in *ibid.*, 6:166; Václav V. Tomek, *Dějepis města Prahy*, 12 vols. (Prague: Řivnáč, 1855–1901), 12:308.

84. For the rejection of the estates' petition, which had asked for the right to select the administrator and members of Consistory, and to elect defensores for protection of the Consistory, see *Sněmy české*, 6:507; see also *ibid.*, 11: pt. 1, 50–53; Tomek, *Dějepis města Prahy*, 12:318–319.

85. *Sněmy české*, 7:60–61, 7:265.

86. Karel Stloukal, *Papežská politika a císařský dvůr pražský na předělu XVI. a XVII. věku* (Prague: F. Řivnáč, 1925), 197.

87. Matoušek, "Kurie a boj o konsistoř pod obojí," 31.

88. *Sněmy české*, 8:329–340.

89. Matoušek, "Kurie a boj o konsistoř pod obojí," 274.

90. Pažout, *Jednání a dopisy konsistoře pod obojí*, 365; Krofta, "Boj o konsistoř," 390–91; Alois Kroess, "Die Unterwerfung des utraquistischen Administrators Heinrich Dworský von Helfenberg unter den katholischen Erzbischof Anton Brus im J. 1572," *Zeitschrift für katholische Theologie* 34 (1910): 711–712; *Sněmy české*, 11: pt. 1, 64.

91. *Sněmy české*, 8:274–275; 8:197–198; Tomek, *Dějepis města Prahy*, 12:359.

92. *Sněmy české*, 8:337–340.

93. *Ibid.*, 11: pt. 1, 70.

94. Bydžovský z Florentina, *Rudolphus rex Bohemiae XXI*, f. 207v–208r; Matoušek, "Kurie a boj o konsistoř pod obojí," 292.

95. *Sněmy české*, 11: pt. 1, 70.

96. Matoušek, "Kurie a boj o konsistoř pod obojí," 288–289, 291, n. 1.

97. Bydžovský z Florentina, *Rudolphus rex Bohemiae XXI*, f. 277b–278a; Tomek, *Dějepis města Prahy*, 12:364.

98. Bydžovský z Florentina, *Rudolphus rex Bohemiae XXI*, f. 207b.

99. "[P]ánu Bohu, církvi jeho svatý věrnýho a řádů starobylejch církevních strany

naší pod obojí vejborně dobře povědomýho." Statement of Jan Kobis of Bytýška, dated March 15, 1594, and quoted by Krofta, in *Sněmy české,* 11: pt. 1, 72, n. 298.

100. *Ibid.,* 8:348. In a way, the Rezek episode resembled the 1453 rejection by the Eastern Orthodox Church of Constantinople of a Roman union, negotiated by the Byzantine emperor and the patriarch, or more remotely, the refusal of the Lutheran Church of Prussia to follow its master, the elector of Brandenburg, Johann Sigismund, in his conversion to Calvinism in 1613; see Antonín Salač, "Constantinople et Prague en 1452: Pourparlers en vue d'une union des Eglises," *Rozpravy Československé akademie věd. Řada společenských věd* 68, no. 11 (1958), especially, 1–6, 23; Bodo Nischan, *Prince, People, and Confession: The Second Reformation in Brandenburg* (Philadelphia: University of Pennsylvania Press, 1994), especially 111–131.

101. "[D]en man alhie in der gemain für ein ochsen helt . . ." Cited by Stloukal, *Papežská politika a císařský dvůr,* 87.

102. Matoušek, "Kurie a boj o konsistoř pod obojí," 38–39. On Borromeo as a role model, see Joseph Bergin, "The Counter-Reformation Church and Its Bishops," *Past and Present* 165 (1999): 46, 71.

103. Matoušek, "Kurie a boj o konsistoř pod obojí," 16–41, 252–292; Stloukal, *Papežská politika a císařský dvůr,* 196–210.

104. *Sněmy české,* 9:452.

105. For a contrary assertion, see Krofta, *Majestát Rudolfa II,* 22.

106. Tomek, *Dějepis města Prahy,* 12:441, 443.

107. See instruction for Nuncio Giovanni Stefano Ferreri, dated January 20, 1604, in Klaus Jaitner, ed., *Die Hauptinstruktionen Clemens' VIII. für die Nuntien und Legaten an den europäischen Fürstenhöfen, 1592–1605,* 2 vols. (Tübingen: Niemeyer, 1984), 2:710.

108. *Sněmy české,* 11: pt. 1, 72.

109. Stloukal, *Papežská politika a císařský dvůr,* 161. See also Matoušek, "Kurie a boj o konsistoř pod obojí," 267–268, 283–284.

110. Stloukal, *Papežská politika a císařský dvůr,* 161–162, 165.

111. Zdeněk Kalista, *Čechové, kteří tvořili dějiny světa,* 2d ed. (Prague: Gramond, 1999), 55; Stloukal, *Papežská politika a císařský dvůr,* 185.

112. Stloukal, *Papežská politika a císařský dvůr,* 191–192.

113. *Ibid.,* 200–202.

114. Matoušek, "Kurie a boj o konsistoř pod obojí," 19; Stloukal, *Papežská politika a císařský dvůr,* 155–159.

115. Václav Novotný, "Náboženské dějiny české ve století 16.," in *Česká politika,* 5 vols., ed. Zdeněk V. Tobolka (Prague: Jan Laichter, 1906), 1:634.

116. Bruno Bernard, *Patrice-François de Neny, 1716–1784: portrait d'un homme d'état* (Brussels: Editions de l'Université de Bruxelles, 1993), 150.

117. These (mis)appropriations happened during the wars of the Bohemian Reformation, allegedly to protect the church lands from the religious dissidents; see Skýbová, "Česká šlechta a jednání o povolení kompaktát," 81–82.

118. On the radicalization of the nobles sub una see, for instance, Jaroslav Pánek, "Stavovství v předbělohorské době," *Folia Historica Bohemica* 6 (1984): 176, 190.

119. Stloukal, *Papežská politika a císařský dvůr,* 188–191.

120. *Sněmy české,* 11: pt. 1, 76; Vilém Slavata, *Paměti nejvyššího kancléře království českého,* 2 vols., ed. Josef Jireček (Prague: Kober, 1866–1868), 1:47; Kalista, *Čechové, kteří tvořili dějiny světa,* 63.

121. Ferdinand Hrejsa, *Česká konfesse: Její vznik, podstata a dějiny* (Prague: Česká akademie pro vědy, slovesnost a umění, 1912), 437.
122. *Sněmy české*, 11: pt. 1, 76–77.
123. *Ibid.*, 11: pt. 1, 138, 192.
124. *Ibid.*, 11: pt. 1, 247–249.
125. *Ibid.*, 11: pt. 1, 78–79, 260–263
126. *Ibid.*, 11: pt. 1, 79, 253–254. The archbishop had been present at the installation of Benedikt's predecessor Dačický; see Bydžovský z Florentina, *Rudolphus rex Bohemiae XXI*, f. 277b–278a.
127. Winter, *Život církevní v Čechách*, 1:333.
128. On the toleration of limited private preaching by the Brethren in Prague in the 1590s, see, for instance, Matoušek, "Kurie a boj o konsistoř pod obojí," 291, n. 4.
129. Krofta, *Nesmrtelný národ*, 308; also Krofta, *Majestát Rudolfa II*, 13.
130. Pekař, *Dějiny československé*, 91.
131. *Sněmy české*, 9:223; Stloukal, *Papežská politika a císařský dvůr*, 198.
132. Stloukal, *Papežská politika a císařský dvůr*, 198–199; Matoušek, "Kurie a boj o konsistoř pod obojí," 19.
133. *Sněmy české*, 9:196–197; Tomek, *Dějepis města Prahy*, 12:365.
134. *Sněmy české*, 9:22–23, 152–153; *ibid.*, 9:445. On the case of the manor of Poděbrady, January 7, 1599, see *ibid.*, 9:627; Tomek, *Dějepis města Prahy*, 12:365. See also Stloukal, *Papežská politika a císařský dvůr*, 199.
135. *Sněmy české*, 9:152–153.
136. Klement Borový, "Administráři pod obojí," *Ottův slovník naučný* (Prague: Otto, 1888–1909), 1:217; *Sněmy české*, 5:302.
137. *Sněmy české*, 5:302, 7:370; Borový, "Administráři pod obojí," 1:217; Pazderová, "Instrukce pražského nuncia Caetaniho," 354.
138. *Sněmy české*, 9:576.
139. Tomek, *Dějepis města Prahy*, 12:307.
140. See the censure of the royal captain in Lysá by Archbishop Berka on March 10, 1600, in *Sněmy české*, 10:58.
141. *Ibid.*, 9:130; 10:484–485.
142. *Ibid.*, 10:480.
143. See, for instance, *ibid.*, 10:464–465.
144. Borový, "Administráři pod obojí," 1:217. "Assigned and confirmed" (podáváni a konfirmováni) was the formula used for installation of priests by Utraquist Consistory; *Sněmy české*, 7:382. On the exclusive Consistory jurisdiction over Utraquists and distinction between secular and ecclesiastical law, see also *Sněmy české*, 7:432–433.
145. *Sněmy české*, 9:21, 22–23.
146. Stloukal, *Papežská politika a císařský dvůr*, 169; see also 177.
147. For instance, see letter to Medek of October 5, 1582, in *Sněmy české*, 6:269; also 6:602.
148. *Ibid.*, 7:370.
149. *Ibid.*, 7:432–433.
150. *Ibid.*, 9:533. The Utraquist Consistory was at times informally designated as the "Lower Consistory," and the archbishop's Consistory as the "Upper Consistory." This terminology was not based on a jurisdictional relationship, but reflected geographic location, with the administrator's Consistory downtown, and the archbishop's on top of the castle hill.

151. Stloukal, *Papežská politika a císařský dvůr*, 201.

152. "[V] tomto království dvoje pořádné kněžstvo, předně katolické pod jednou, kteréž se dotčeným arcibiskupem Pražským, druhý pak pod obojí dolejší konsistoří jsouc od pořádného biskupa svěcení, řídí a spravují, se zachovává . . ." *Sněmy české*, 10:232.

153. *Sněmy české*, 10:337.

154. *Ibid.*, 10:332–333. For an earlier statement (1597), see *ibid.*, 9:460, Dačický to Berka: "JMt spravuje svý kněží k jurisdikcí náležící a já taky svý . . ."

155. *Ibid.*, 10:617–618; see also 10:517, 611–612.

156. *Ibid.*, 8:394, 557–558.

157. Tomek, *Dějepis města Prahy*, 12:422.

158. *Sněmy české*, 6:271.

159. *Ibid.*, 6:503.

160. *Ibid.*, 9:292.

161. *Ibid.*, 9:305.

162. *Ibid.*, 9:445.

163. *Ibid.*, 10:212.

164. *Ibid.*, 10:645.

165. Winter, *Život církevní v Čechách*, 1:333.

166. *Sněmy české*, 7:61.

167. *Ibid.*, 7:225; 7:265.

168. *Ibid.*, 7:439; see also 7:370, 372.

169. *Ibid.*, 7:370.

170. Letter of Berka to Pope Clement VIII of March 11, 1602, in *ibid.*, 10:304–305. See also Berka's letter of November 9, 1602, asking Rudolf II to intervene with the pope to facilitate such dispensations; *ibid.*, 10:362.

171. For the claim, see *ibid.*, 11: pt. 1, 73–74, n. 303. The instances of the archbishop's usurpation of the Consistory's jurisdiction cited by Winter, *Život církevní v Čechách*, 1:183, 333, fall more into the category of exceptions that confirm the rule.

172. *Sněmy české*, 11: pt. 1, 76–77.

173. *Ibid.*, 11:50.

174. "[I]n hoc regno alia religio praeter antiquam catholicam sub una et alteram sub utraque communicantium toleretur . . ." In letter of Berka to Rudolf II, dated September 12, 1595, in *Sněmy české*, 9:183.

175. "[K]atolickou pak víru a řád dobrej církevní starobylý v tomto království při straně pod jednou i pod obojí vždy jednostejnej . . ." *Sněmy české*, 9:178. Perhaps he also thought about the posthumous fate of his parents.

176. *Sněmy české*, 8:570–571.

177. *Ibid.*

178. Bydžovský, *Děťátka a neviňátka*, f. B1r–B1v, largely citing from Václav Koranda, *Traktát o velebné a božské svátosti oltářní* (Prague: Tiskař Korandy, 1493), f. S3r–S3v.

179. For example, in 1579; *Sněmy české*, 5:516.

180. "Der Kaplan . . . auch in den Kirchengebräuchen consistorianisch der präger Rubriken gemäss und nicht auf kalvinisch verhalten thuet . . ." *Sněmy české*, 9:466.

181. "[C]he nel giuramento l'havevano obligato ad osservar la rubrica di Praga, cioè il rituale che è usato da catholici . . ." *Sněmy české*, 11: pt. 1, 263.

182. "[M]še (aby) zpívány neb čteny byly podle řádu římského a rubriky kostela pražského." See "Compactata," in *Archiv český* 3 (1844): 454.

183. Stloukal, *Papežská politika a císařský dvůr,* 197.

184. *Ibid.,* 197–198. Neither Tomek, nor Winter or Skála were similarly misled by the term "Catholic" (cattolici), as Stloukal himself notes; *ibid.,* 197, n. 123.

185. Parenthetically, banning Lutherans and Brethren as councilors in royal towns was Rudolf II's right even under the gentlemen's agreement of 1575, which his father, Maximillian II, negotiated with the Bohemian estates. See Chapter 7.

186. "[P]odle starobylého od církve svaté katolické nařízeného dobrého chvalitebného pořádku . . .", writing to the town of Tábor on May 4, 1596. *Sněmy české,* 9:287.

187. "Il resto del popolo, che è grandissimo, per la maggiore parte è Hussito, overo, come essi si chiamano, sub utraque." Neri, *Nuntiaturberichte aus Deutschland,* 73–74.

188. Stloukal, "Počátky nunciatury v Praze," 245, 277; Matoušek, "Kurie a boj o konsistoř pod obojí," 269; Fučíková, *Tři francouzští kavalíři v rudolfínské Praze,* 44–45, 116, n. 29.

189. Valentin Polon, *Pomni na mne: Knijžka obahující v sobě kratičká spasidedlná Naučení a sebrání . . .* (Prague: Buryan Valda, 1589), f. Club 6v, A9r–A9v.

190. Stloukal,"Počátky nunciatury v Praze," 15. A Utraquist priest, Vavřinec Leander Rvačovský of Rvačov, dedicated his famous *Masopust* (1580) "in the first place to God, our Lord, and then to the holy Catholic and Apostolic Church" ([N]ejprve Pánu Bohu a potom Církvi svaté Katolické a Apoštolské); Vavřinec Leander Rvačovský of Rvačov, *Masopust* (Prague: Jiří Melantrich, 1580), f. E1r.

191. *Sněmy české,* 6:267, 269.

192. "[K]řest'anským katolickým, jedné křest'anské víry, pánem Ježíšem i církví křest'anskou obecnou utvrzeným náboženstvím . . ." and "naším katolickým náboženstvím," on December 15, 1586. *Ibid.,* 7:61.

193. "[K]něžstvo řádné i také starobylé náboženství katolické pod obojí . . ." *Ibid.,* 7:370.

194. [Ř]řády starobylé církve svaté, křest'anské, katolické . . ." *Ibid.,* 7:405.

195. Polon, *Pomni na mne,* f. Club 6v, A9r–A9v. Polon also spoke of the Utraquist liturgy as "od Svaté Církve Katolické nařízených služeb a řádně křest'anských." *Ibid.,* f. Club 4v.

196. "[J]ako my a jiné kněstvo katolické řádně povoláni . . ." *Sněmy české,* 10:512.

197. Winter, *Život církevní v Čechách,* 1:333.

198. Příbram's treatise, "De professione fidei catholicae et eorum revocatione," is printed in Johannes Cochlaeus, *Historiae Hussitarum libri duodecim* (Mainz: Franciscus Behem, 1549), 503–547; see also František Bartoš, *Literární činnost M. J. Rokycany, M. Jana Příbrama, a M. Petra Payna* (Prague: Česká akademie nauk, 1928), 78.

199. Augustin Neumann, *K dějinám věku poděbradského* (Brno: Nákladem vlastním, 1933), 6.

200. Josef Pekař, [Note on Písecký], *Český časopis historický* 31 (1925): 211; Aeneas Sylvius Piccolomini (Pope Pius II), *Historia Bohemica/Historie česká,* trans. and ed. Dana Martínková, Alena Hadravová, and Jiří Matl (Prague: Koniasch Latin Press, 1998), xlvii, n. 204.

201. Reginald R. Betts, *Essays in Czech History* (London: University of London, Athlone Press, 1969), 264, cited by Jarold K. Zeman, "The Rise of Liberty in the Czech Reformation," *Central European History* 6 (1973): 136.

202. František Palacký, *Dějiny národu českého*, 5 vols. (Prague: Bursík a Kohout, 1893), 5:531–532. See also Chapter 3.

203. Bílejovský states literally: "[W]e Bohemians sub utraque are the true Romans" ([M]y Čechové pod obojí jsme praví Římané), *Kronyka Cýrkevní*, 27.

204. Václav Kuttemberger z Kuttembergku, *Přídavek k dokázání mocnému a podstatnému, že z potřeby spasení k přijímání pod obojí žádný zavázán není* (Prague: Pavel Sessius, 1625), f. D2v–D3v.

205. Richard Montagu, "To the Reader," in Montague, *A Gagg for the New Gospell? No, a New Gagg for an Old Goose* (London: T. Snodham, 1624), 4.

206. As another example, James I of England, for one, is reported as saying on his deathbed in 1625, after repeating the articles of the creed, that "hee beleeued them all, as they were receiued and expounded by that part of the Catholique Church which was established here in England." Cited by William B. Patterson, *King James VI and I and the Reunion of Christendom* (Cambridge: Cambridge University Press, 1997), 356, from John Williams, *Great Britains Salomon: A Sermon Preached at the Magnificent Funerall of the Most High and Mighty King, Iames . . .* (London: John Bill, 1625), 69.

207. For example, letter of October 20, 1598; *Sněmy české*, 9:593.

208. *Ibid.*, 10:315, 457–458, 514.

209. *Ibid.*, 10:316.

210. See, for instance, Neri, *Nuntiaturberichte aus Deutschland*, Dritte Abteilung, 8:224, 239, 290; *Sněmy české*, 11: pt. 1, 77, n. 311.

211. Matoušek, "Kurie a boj o konsistoř pod obojí," 27–28. On another alleged submission to Rome, see *Sněmy české*, 11: pt. 1, 64.

212. See, especially, *Druhá Apologie stavův království českého*, 205 (no. 27).

213. See chapter 6.

214. Neri, *Nuntiaturberichte aus Deutschland*, Dritte Abteilung, 8:239.

215. *Sněmy české*, 11: pt. 1, 63.

216. Matoušek, "Kurie a boj o konsistoř pod obojí," 18; See also Dolfin's negative attitude in 1575; Neri, *Nuntiaturberichte aus Deutschland*, Dritte Abteilung, 8:75.

217. Stloukal, "Počátky nunciatury v Praze," 15–16.

218. *Sněmy české*, 11:56–58.

219. *Ibid.*, 11: pt. 1, 74. See complaint of the Consistory about the anticipated shortage of Utraquist priests in October 1577 in *ibid.*, 5:198–199; repeated in August 1578, *ibid.*, 5:300.

220. See, for instance, *Sněmy české*, 7:217; Borový, *Martin Medek, Arcibiskup pražský*, 73–74; Kroess, "Die Unterwerfung des utraquistischen Administrators Heinrich Dworský," 711–712.

221. *Sněmy české*, 10:332–333.

222. Winter, *Život církevní v Čechách*, 1:334–335.

223. *Sněmy české* 9:181. See also Zikmund Winter, *Děje vysokých škol pražských od secessí cizích národů po dobu bitvy bělohorské, 1409–1622* (Prague: Česká akademie pro vědy, slovesnost a umění, 1895), 59–60; Winter, *O životě na vysokých školách pražských: kulturní obraz XV. a XVI. století* (Prague: Matice česká, 1899), 359. On the preparation of clergy earlier in the sixteenth century, see Josef Jireček, *Rukověť k dějinám literatury české do konce XVIII. věku*, 2 vols. (Prague: Tempský, 1875–1876), 1:115. On the theological lectures by Martin of Vlašim, see *Ze starých letopisů českých*, trans. Jaroslav Porák and Jaroslav Kašpar (Prague: Svoboda, 1980), 291. Apprenticeship to an experienced priest was a common way of educating candidates for priesthood

in sixteenth-century Europe; see Lewis W. Spitz, *The Protestant Reformation, 1517–1559* (New York: Harper and Row, 1985), 51. There was also some movement the other way. Priest Václav Pražský, having been removed from the parish of Stříbro by Administrator Dačický, petitioned Berka for a parish on February 9, 1597; see *Sněmy české*, 9:396.

224. Borový, *Martin Medek, Arcibiskup pražský*, 78, n. 3.

225. *Sněmy české*, 10:371. Also, on February 7, 1603, Fridrich of Opršdorf asked Berka for a priest for the town of Týniště, either sub una, or if not available, a Utraquist administered by the Consistory. This might indicate that the supply of Utraquist priests was more adequate than of those sub una; see *ibid.*, 10:450; see also *ibid.*, 11: pt. 1, 70.

226. Utraquist deaneries follow: Benešov, Beroun, Mladá Boleslav, Český Brod, Německý Brod, Bydžov, Čáslav, Domažlice, Kutná Hora, Hořice, Chrudim, Jaroměř, Jičín, Klatovy, Kolín, Kostelec nad Labem, Kouřim, Dvůr Králové, Hradec Králové (with an archdeanery), Ledeč, Litoměřice, Litomyšl, Louny, Mělník, Vysoké Mýto, Načeradec, Náchod, Nymburk, Pardubice, Pelhřimov, Písek, Polička, Příbram, Rakovník, Roudnice, Sedlčany, Slaný, Stříbro, Sušice, Tábor, Turnov, Velvary, Vodňany, Žatec, and Žlutice; Borový, *Martin Medek, Arcibiskup pražský*, 78.

227. *Ibid.*, 78–79.

228. Winter, *Život církevní v Čechách*, 2:613–614.

229. Krofta doubts its administration prior to 1609; *Sněmy české*, 11: pt. 1, 75, n. 306.

230. *Ibid.*, 11: pt. 1, 71, n. 295.

231. *Ibid.*, 9:436–437, 441–442.

232. *Ibid.*, 9:444. See also petitions of May 13, 1597, October 4, 1599, and July 18, 1601, in *ibid.*, 9:442, 699–700; 10:216–217. Berka likewise reported resistance in Pardubice in January 1600; see *ibid.*, 10:19.

233. *Ibid.*, 9:146–147, 151–152, 442.

234. *Ibid.*, 10:83–84

235. *Ibid.*, 9:476–477; 10:209.

236. *Ibid.*, 10, 216–217, 323.

237. *Ibid.*, 10:58, 194–195.

238. *Ibid.*, 10:208, 252, 324–325.

239. *Ibid.*, 7:25, 464–465.

240. Stloukal, "Počátky nunciatury v Praze," 255.

241. *Sněmy české*, 9:675–676.

242. *Ibid.*, 10:330.

243. *Ibid.*, 10:333.

244. *Ibid.*, 10:441.

245. *Ibid.*, 9:372; 10:368–370; 395–397; 446–448.

246. *Ibid.*, 10:308; 10:463.

247. *Ibid.*, 10:471, 474.

248. *Ibid.*, 10:464–465.

249. *Ibid.*, 10:482, 488.

250. September 6, 1603; *ibid.*, 10:496.

251. September 23, 1603; *ibid.*, 10:500–501.

252. May 26, 1603; *ibid.*, 10:468. See the letter of May 30, 1603, from Smiřický to Berka, in *ibid.*, 10:470.

253. He was immortalized in a popular song threatening him with hellfire for his

transgressions against Utraquism: "A ten opat slovanský—dal na vinici kopat—na svátek Jana Husi—za to do pekla musí—věčně se trápit," cited in Jireček, *Rukověť k dějinám literatury české,* 2:77. See the complaint of priest Pavel Paminondas Horský to Berka, in *Sněmy české,* 8:448.

254. Such as Pardubice, Trutnov, Kolín, Malešov, Poděbrady, Lysá, Benátky, Křivoklát, Točník, Zbiroh, Dobříš, and others; see Josef Vávra, "Počátky reformace katolické v Čechách," *Sborník historického kroužku,* Sešit 3 (1894): 40.

255. Tomek, *Dějepis města Prahy,* 10:523–524.

256. Thomas More, *Complete Works,* 21 vols. (New Haven: Yale University Press, 1963–1997), 5: pt. 2, 868.

257. *Sněmy české,* 7:432; 9:451; 10:371–373.

258. Concerning Týn Horšův, see *Sněmy české,* 9:679; 10:90–91, 543–544, 587, 625. Concerning Kłodzko, see *ibid.,* 10:64–65, 440, 443–446, 448–449, 632.

259. Concerning Chomutov, see *Sněmy české,* 9:9; 10:611, 618, 629, 640–641. Concerning Česká Lípa, see *ibid.,* 9:511; 10:90, 92. Concerning Český Krumlov, see *ibid.,* 9:682–683; 10:544–549, 584, 586.

260. Vávra, "Počátky reformace katolické v Čechách," 3. An interesting variant on the protection of subjects' religion was the insistence of Jaroslav Bořita of Martinice on July 7, 1604, that his subjects, if migrating to other manors, must remain sub una; see *Sněmy české,* 10:587, 625–627.

Chapter 10

1. Joachim Bahlcke and Arno Strohmeyer, eds., *Konfessionalisierung in Ostmitteleuropa: Wirkungen des religiösen Wandels im 16. und 17. Jahrhundert in Staat, Gesellschaft und Kultur* (Stuttgart: Franz Steiner, 1999), especially 15–19, discuss the phenomenon with respect to East Central Europe. The index, however, contains no entry under the name "Utraquists," or the misnomer "Hussites."

2. Antonín Škarka, "Ze zápasů nekatolického tisku s protireformací: Literární a tiskařská aféra z r. 1602," *Český časopis historický* 42 (1936): 2.

3. Klement Borový, *Antonín Brus z Mohelnice, arcibiskup pražský; Historickokritický životopis* (Prague: Dědictví sv. Prokopa, 1873), 227.

4. Theodor Kolde, "Cochlaeus," *Realenzyklopaedie fuer protestantische Theologie und Kirche* (Leipzig: Hinrichs, 1896–[1913?], 4:200.

5. Peter Godman, *The Saint as Censor: Robert Bellarmine Between Inquisition and Index* (Leiden: Brill, 2000), 95. Eventually Pope Pius II's *Historia Bohemiae* would find its way on the Index, at least in Bohemia; see Josef Dobrovský, *Dějiny české řeči a literatury v redakcích z roku 1791, 1792 a 1818,* ed. Benjamin Jedlička (Prague: Melantrich, 1936), 162; Derek Sayer, *The Coasts of Bohemia: A Czech History* (Princeton, N.J.: Princeton University Press, 1998), 49.

6. Bohumil Navrátil, *Biskupství olomoucké 1576–1579 a volba Stanislava Pavlovského* (Prague: Česká společnost nauk, 1909), 11–16.

7. Petr Illicino, *Contra impiam Deoque inimicam haereticorum legem, quod liceat cuique impune ac sine aliquo impedimento de fide sentire et praedicare, ut velit,* Commentarius per Petrum Illicinum, J. U. Doctorem, canonicum ecclesiae Olomucensis. Anno MDLXXVII, Olomouc, 1577 (manuscript, Vienna, National Library, 11623). A doctor of law, born in Siena, Illicino taught Greek in Cracow (1547–1549) and Roman

law at the University of Vienna (1550–1551), and spent two decades in Hungary and Slovakia before assuming his post in Olomouc; see also Navrátil, *Biskupství olomoucké 1576–1579,* 49–53.

8. Illicino, *Contra impiam Deoque inimicam haereticorum legem,* f. 3v–4r.
9. *Ibid.,* f. 32v.
10. *Ibid.,* f. 36v–37v.
11. Alois Kroess, *Geschichte der Böhmischen Provinz der Gesellschaft Jesu,* 2 vols. in 3 (Vienna: Mayer, 1910–1938), 1:204.
12. Jakób Wujek z Wągrowca, *Postila Aneb Kázání evangelitská,* 2 vols. in 4 parts (Litomyšl: Andres Graudenc, 1592), 1: pt. 1, f. 124r–132r.
13. Bartołomiej Paprocki z Glogol lived in the Bohemian lands in 1588–1610. On his critique of Bohemian Reformation from the viewpoint of the Roman Curia, see Karel Krejčí, *Bartoloměj Paprocki z Hlohol a Paprocké Vůle: Život, dílo, forma a jazyk* (Prague: Slovanský ústav, 1946), 51–52, 176–177, 246–247.
14. Antonín Rejzek, *Blahoslavený Edmund Kampián, kněz Tovaryšstva Ježíšova, pro sv. víru mučeník ve vlasti své* (Brno: K. Winiker, 1889), 92–93, 98, 103.
15. *Ibid.,* 110–111. Campion seemed to esteem Wenceslaus highly, classing him later with such exemplary Christian sovereigns, as Edward of England, Louis of France, Hermenegilda of Spain, Henry of Saxony, and Leopold of Austria; *ibid.,* 126.
16. *Ibid.,* 118–119. On Locika, see also Jaroslav Kadlec, *Přehled českých církevních dějin,* 2 vols. (Prague: Zvon, 1991), 2:74; Václav Líva, "Studie o Praze pobělohorské," *Sborník příspěvků k dějinám hl. města Prahy* 7 (1933): 22–23.
17. Bohumír J. Dlabač, *Leben des frommen Prager Erzbischofs Johann Lohelius, ehemaligen Strahower Abtes* (Prague: Christen, 1794), 11–12.
18. Rejzek, *Blahoslavený Edmund Kampián,* 155.
19. *Ibid.,* 160–162.
20. Thomas M. McCoog, ed., *The Reckoned Expense: Edmund Campion and the Early English Jesuits* (Woodbridge, Suffolk: Boydell Press, 1996), 112. See also Rejzek, *Blahoslavený Edmund Kampián,* 150; Edmund Campion, *Spis krátký Edmunda Kampiana Societatis Jesu, Theologa a Mučedlníka Božího, který ne tak dávno pro víru S. Katolickau smrt ukrutnau podstaupil: Vznešeným Doktorům a Mistrům učení Oxonienského a Kantabrigienského podaný* (Prague: Jiřík Nygrin, 1601), f, C10r.
21. See also Rejzek, *Blahoslavený Edmund Kampián,* 169.
22. *Ibid.,* 191–97. Pope Paul VI canonized him in 1970. Paradoxically—in view of the charge—he met his demise while praying for the welfare of Queen Elizabeth I; *DNB,* 3:854.
23. Campion, *Spis krátký Edmunda Kampiana Societatis Jesu;* and Edmund Campion, *Wšech Pikartských, Luteryánských, i jináč zrotilých Prevytkantů, Hostides. To jest: Deset podstatných příčin, kterýchž jistotau, velebný kněz, a zmužilosrdnatý Mučedlník Edmund Kampian, z Tovaryšstva jména Ježíšova pohnut jsa, vše víry Ržímské Odpůrce, k zjevnému před Englickau Královnau, o Víru potýkání, pobídl; Jim se pak z brlochu na světlo vyjíti nechtělo* (Olomouc: Jiř. Handle, 1602).
24. Robert Persons, "Of the Life and Martyrdom of Father Edmund Campion," *Letters and Notices* 11 (1877): 317.
25. Campion, *Spis krátký Edmunda Kampiana Societatis Jesu,* f. C4r–v.
26. *Ibid.,* f. C10v–C11r.
27. On "salami tactics" advocated for the sequential suppression of religious dissidents in Bohemia under Kings Rudolf II and Matthias, see Philip Longworth, *The Making*

of Eastern Europe: From Prehistory to Postcommunism, 2d ed. (New York: St. Martin's Press, 1997), 80, 231. The term is based on a brag by Mátyás Rákosi, the Stalinist dictator, about his way of suppressing the democratic opposition in Hungary in the late 1940s, using the simile of the Magyars' treatment of their favorite sausage. See also Chapter 11.

28. The edicts' force was blunted in two ways. First, these mandates contradicted Maximillian II's grant of tolerance of 1575, discussed in Chapter 7. Second, the Brethren rejected the designation of themselves as "Pitharts," although almost everybody else in Bohemia called them so. See *Sněmy české od léta 1526 až po naši dobu.*, vols. 1-11, 15 (Prague: Zemský výbor, 1877-1941), 11:54–56.

29. Pavel Bydžovský, *Tato knížka toto try ukazuje* (N.p., [after 1541]), 2; Bohuslav Bílejovský, *Kronyka Cýrkevní,* ed. Jozef Skalický (pseudonym for Josef Dittrich) (Prague: Fetterl z Vilden, 1816), 109 (see also 105).

30. Václav Šturm, *Srovnání víry a učení bratří starších* (Litomyšl: Andreas Graudenc, 1582); Šturm, *Krátké ozvání . . . proti kratičkému ohlášení Jednoty Valdenské neb Boleslavské* (Prague: Jiřík Dačický, 1584); Šturm, *Rozsouzení a bedlivé uvážení Velikého kancionálu od Bratří Valdenských, jinak Boleslavských, sepsaného . . .* (Prague: Burián Valda, 1588).

31. Ferdinand Hrejsa, *Česká konfesse: Její vznik, podstata a dějiny* (Prague: Česká akademie pro vědy, slovesnost a umění, 1912), 205.

32. "A protož jiným Duchem někdy mluvil Arius, jiným Macedonius, jiným Donatus, jiným Wyclif, jiným Mistr Jan Hus, jiným Táboři, jiným Luteránové, jiným Cvinglianové, jiným Bratří vaši, a tak jeden každý jinou má novotu, jinou Sektu, jinou Víru, jiné Kněžstvo, jiný zbor, a tak jiný že žádný s jiným se nesrovnává." Šturm, *Srovnání víry a učení bratří,* 103.

33. *Ibid.,* 375–378, 419.

34. Šturm, *Krátké ozvání . . . proti kratičkému ohlášení,* 3.

35. Šturm, *Srovnání víry a učení bratří,* 340, 420–422.

36. Tomáš Kalina, "Václav Brož: Několik poznámek k jeho životopisu a literární činnosti," in *Od pravěku k dnešku: Sborník prací z dějin Československých k 60. narozeninám Josefa Pekaře,* 2 vols., ed. Josef Klik (Prague: Historický klub, 1930), 1: 441.

37. *Ibid.,* 1:429–430.

38. Václav Brož (Brosius), *Vejstraha všem věrným Čechům . . . : Aby mohli znáti jakej jest rozdíl mezy Učením Mistra Jana Husy a Učením Bratří Boleslavských v Artykuli o Večeři Páně* (Litomyšl: [Andreas Graudenc?], 1589), f. A1v. Evidently he referred to J. Montanus and U. Neuber, eds., *Historia et monumenta Joannis Hus atque Hieronymi Pragensis confessorum Christi,* 2 vols. (Nuremberg: Catharina Gerlachin, 1558). The second edition appeared in 1715.

39. Brož, *Vejstraha všem věrným Čechům,* f. A1v-A3r. Kalina, "Václav Brož," 441.

40. Brož, *Vejstraha všem věrným Čechům,* f. B1v-B3v. On these sources, see Rudolf Říčan, *The History of the Unity of Brethren: A Protestant Hussite Church in Bohemia and Moravia,* trans. C. Daniel Crews (Bethlehem, Pa.: Moravian Church in America, 1992), 135, 219, 253.

41. Brož, *Vejstraha všem věrným Čechům,* f. B4v.

42. *Ibid.,* f. C1v–C2r.

43. Václav Brož, *O Přijímání Svátosti Těla a Krve Páně. Rozmlouvání mezi dvěma osobami, prosté, krátké důvěrné a pokojné* ([Litomyšl]: [Andreas Graudenc?], 1598), f. A3v–A4r.

44. *Ibid.,* f. A4v.
45. *Ibid.,* f. B4r–C1r.
46. Sixt Palma Močidlanský, *Svědectví starých svatých otců, učitelů a mučedníků Božích o důstojném přijímání těla a krve Pána Ježíše Krysta pod obojím spůsobem* (Prague: Stříbrský, 1598); Antonín Škarka, "'Pikhartský netopýř' Brosiova 'Ohlášení' a jeho anonymní polemika," *Časopis Matice moravské* 55 (1931): 61, 68; Kalina, "Václav Brož," 440.
47. Apparently unfamiliar with the standard Lutheran doctrine, Škarka justified the classification of Palma as a Mikulášenec simply on the grounds that he upheld the doctrine of general priesthood of all believers; see Škarka, "'Pikhartský netopýř' Brosiova 'Ohlášení'," 70.
48. *Ibid.,* f. B4v–C1r.
49. "[N]ejpřednější učitelové konfessí augšpurské." Brosius, *Ohlášení,* f. A4r.
50. Brosius, *Ohlášení,* f. A3r.
51. *Ibid.,* f. D1v.
52. *Ibid.,* f. B4r.
53. See, for instance, the views of Nuncio Caetani in 1592 cited in Alena Pazderová, "Instrukce pražského nuncia Caetaniho pro jeho nástupce Speciana," in *Facta probant homines: Sborník příspěvků k životnímu jubileu prof. dr. Zdeňky Hledíkové,* ed. Ivan Hlaváček and Jan Hrdina (Prague: Scriptorium, 1998), 359. An almost necessary corollary was the fabrication of another mythical entity, later to be known as "Neo-Utraquism," in which the Utraquism of the Compactata became infiltrated by—from Rome's viewpoint—corrupting Protestant elements.
54. Carter Lindberg, *The European Reformations* (Oxford: Blackwell, 1996), 7, 341–345; Godman, *The Saint as Censor,* 3–48.
55. Robert Bireley, *The Refashioning of Catholicism, 1450–1700: A Reassessment of the Counter Reformation* (Washington, D.C.: Catholic University of America Press, 1999), 49–50; Michael A. Mullett, *The Catholic Reformation* (London: Routledge, 1999), 68.
56. Zdeněk Rotrekl, *Barokní fenomén v součastnosti* (Prague: Trost, 1995), 113–115.
57. Josef Jireček, *Rukověť' k dějinám literatury české* (Prague: Tempský, 1875), 2:42; *Ottův slovník naučný* (Prague: Otto, 1888–1909), 17:492.
58. In *Postila Aneb Kázání evangelitská,* Wujek z Wągrowca marshals arguments against lay communion sub utraque in vol. 1: pt. 1, f. 124r–132r; Campion, *Spis krátký Edmunda Kampiana Societatis Jesu.*
59. Campion, *Spis krátký,* preface, f. A2r–A8v.
60. "[V]šechny Západní Krajiny, anobrž všechna Latinská Církev (kromě špatného koutu této naší Země), jedné jsou Víry, jednoho jsou vyznání byly . . ." *Ibid.,* f. A3v.
61. *Ibid.,* f. A6r.
62. Jiří Taciturnus z Háje (Hájský), *Zlatý řetízek pravého katolického náboženství . . . k dobrému mládeži školní Aušpurské konfesi* (Prague: Matěj Pardubický, 1616), f. K4, condemned infant communion, and went on to compare its practice to giving communion to drunkards, persons of ill repute, the enraged, blasphemers, or heretics.
63. Petr Linteo z Pilzenburgku, *Jistá a patrná cýrkve svaté znamení* (Litomyšl: n.p., 1593), 220–221. A second edition of Linteo's book appeared in 1725 (Prague: Wolffkang Wickhart, 1725). Subsequent citations reference the first edition.
64. *Ibid.,* 223–225.
65. *Ibid.,* 227–231.

66. *Ibid.*, 100.
67. *Ibid.*, 286–287, 291.
68. *Ibid.*, 163–164.
69. *Ibid.*, 164–165.
70. Bílejovský, *Kronyka Cýrkevní*, 2, 28.
71. Linteo z Pilzenburgku, *Jistá a patrná cýrkve svaté znamení*, 167–168.
72. Howard Kaminsky, *A History of the Hussite Revolution* (Berkeley: University of California Press, 1967), 429; Linteo z Pilzenburgku, *Jistá a patrná cýrkve svaté znamení*, 172–173. On the Adamites, see also Chapter 2.
73. Linteo z Pilzenburgku, *Jistá a patrná cýrkve svaté znamení*, 69.
74. *Ibid.*, 181.
75. *Ibid.*, 58, 63, 152, 155.
76. Such an evasion is a time-honored practice, examples of which may be found in subsequent Czech, as well as Russian, history.
77. During the attack on monasteries and other institutions sub una in Prague in 1611, Linteo was assaulted and his death in 1613 might have been related to his injuries then sustained; see Jireček, *Rukověť k dějinám literatury české*, 1:453.
78. Josef Matoušek, "Kurie a boj o konsistoř pod obojí za administrátora Rezka," *Český časopis historický* 37 (1931): 32–33, 261. In actual fact, this would not happen until the aftermath of the battle of the White Mountain in 1621; see Líva, "Studie o Praze pobělohorské," 22–23.
79. For a reference to this issue see, for instance, Noemi Rejchrtová, "Role utrakvizmu v českých dějinách," in *Traditio et Cultus: Miscellanea historica bohemica Miloslao Vlk, archiepiscopo Pragensi, ab eius collegis amicisque ad annum sexagesimum dedicata*, ed. Zdeňka Hledíková (Prague: Univerzita Karlova, 1993), 75.
80. Josef Pekař, *Žižka a jeho doba*, 4 vols. (Prague: Vesmír, 1927–33), 3:327.
81. Macek, for instance, has characterized as benighted or retarded (*zpozdilá*) the continuing Utraquist ambition to reform the Roman Church; see Josef Macek, *Víra a zbožnost jagellonského věku* (Prague: Argo, 2001), 59.
82. Bílejovský, *Kronyka Cýrkevní*, 13–14; Vavřinec z Březové, *Husitská kronika*, ed. Marie Bláhová (Prague: Svoboda, 1979), 88–89. See also Božena Kopičková, *Jan Želivský* (Prague: Melantrich, 1990), 94.
83. Amedeo Molnár, "Martin Lupáč: Modus disputandi pro fide," *Folia Historica Bohemica* 4 (1982): 161–177.
84. Valentin Polon, *Pomni na mne: Knijžka obahující v sobě kratičká spasidedlná Naučení a sebrání*... (Staré Město Pražské: Buryan Valda, 1589), f. Club 5–1b, A6–2b, A6–3a, A6–3b. As noted in Chapter 4, Bílejovský states literally: "[W]e Czechs sub utraque are the true Romans" ([M]y Čechové pod obojí jsme praví Římané); Bílejovský, *Kronyka Cýrkevní*, 27. In the ecclesiastical area, their resistance was comparable—in its tenor, if not in its results—to the political opposition of the North American colonies to the British monarch while claiming to defend the rights of Englishmen.
85. Bílejovský, *Kronyka Cýrkevní*, 14.
86. Ernst Denis, *Fin de l'indépendance bohême*, 2d ed., 2 vols. (Paris: Leroux, 1930), 2:298–301. See also Chapter 1.
87. Peter Matheson, *Rhetoric of the Reformation* (Edinburgh: T&T Clark, 1998), 215–237.
88. Winfried Trusen, *Um die Reform und Einheit der Kirche: Zum Leben und Werk Georg Witzels* (Münster: Aschendorffsche Verlagsbuchhandlung, 1957), 48–83.
89. For an overview of Witzel's theology, see Barbara Henze, *Aus Liebe zur Kirche*

Reform: die Bemühungen Georg Witzels (1501–1573) um die Kircheneinheit (Münster: Aschendorff, 1995), 91–151. See also *New Catholic Encyclopedia* (New York: McGraw-Hill, 1967–1974), 14:984–985; *Allgemeine Deutsche Biographie,* 56 vols. (Leipzig: Duncker, 1875–1912), 43:658–659.

90. Trusen, *Um die Reform und Einheit der Kirche,* 22–26; Henze, *Aus Liebe zur Kirche Reform,* 23. On Von Wied, see Diarmaid MacCulloch, *Thomas Cranmer: A Life* (New Haven, Conn.: Yale University Press, 1996), 393. Although growing out of Erasmian influences in Lower Rhineland, the situation in Cologne got out of hand in the Lutheran direction, when Von Wied entrusted the reform project in 1542 to Martin Bucer, who in turn collaborated with Melanchton. See August Franzen, *Bischof und Reformation: Erzbischof Hermann von Wied in Köln vor der Erscheidung zwischen Reform und Reformation* (Munster: Aschendorff, 1971), 80–81; see also Rainer Sommer, *Hermann von Wied: Erzbischof und Kurfürst von Köln* (Cologne: Rheinland-Verlag, 2000).

91. Brendan Bradshaw, "The Controversial Sir Thomas More," *Journal of Ecclesiastical History* 36 (1985): 564.

92. Thomas More, *Complete Works,* 21 vols. (New Haven: Yale University Press, 1963–1997), 5: pt. 2, 721; John Guy, *Thomas More* (London: Arnold, 2000), 115.

93. William B. Patterson, "Hooker on Ecumenical Relations: Conciliarism in the English Reformation," in *Richard Hooker and the Construction of Christian Community,* ed. Arthur S. McGrade (Tempe, Ariz.: Medieval and Renaissance Texts and Studies, 1997), 289; Guy, *Thomas More,* 178. This position was consistent with the canon law, Ordinary Gloss to the Decretum on Dist. 19 c. 9, cited by Brian Tierney, *Origins of Papal Infallibility, 1150–1350: A Study on the Concepts of Infallibility, Sovereignty and Tradition in the Middle Ages* (Leiden: E. J. Brill, 1988), 309–310.

94. On Erasmus's liberal ecclesiology, see, for instance, Desiderius Erasmus, *The Correspondence,* 11 vols. (Toronto: University of Toronto Press, 1974–1994), 8:207–209, 415, n. 46; Hilmar M. Pabel, "The Peaceful People of Christ: The Irenic Ecclesiology of Erasmus of Rotterdam," in *Erasmus' Vision of the Church,* ed. Pabel, Sixteenth Century Essays and Studies, 33 (Kirksville, Mo.: Sixteenth Century Journal Publishers, 1995), 57–93; Ernest E. Reynolds, *Thomas More and Erasmus* (New York: Fordham University Press, 1965).

95. Irena Backus, "Erasmus and the Spirituality of the Early Church," in *Erasmus' Vision of the Church,* ed. Hilmar H. Pabel, Sixteenth Century Essays and Studies, 33 (Kirksville, Mo.: Sixteenth Century Journal Publishers, 1995), 95–114; Wilhelm Maurer, "Erasmus und das Kanonische Recht," in *Vierhundertfünfzig Jahre lutherische Reformation, 1517–1967: Festschrift für Franz Lau zum 50. Geburtstag,* ed. Helmar Junghans, et al. (Göttingen: Vanderhoeck and Ruprecht, 1967), 222–232. On Erasmus's and Fisher's shared interest in Greek patristics and in humanistic learning, see Maria Dowling, *Fisher of Men: A Life of John Fisher, 1469–1535* (New York: St. Martin's Press, 1999), 30–40. See also Erasmus, *The Correspondence,* 8:202.

96. Erica Rummel, *The Humanist-Scholastic Debate in the Renaissance and Reformation* (Cambridge, Mass.: Harvard University Press, 1995), 89–91, 103–111, 134–140.

97. Erasmus, *The Correspondence,* 11:193.

98. *Ibid.,* 11:xii.

99. *Ibid.,* 11:xviii.

100. Particularly by Noël Béda of the University of Paris; *ibid.,* 11:xv–xvi.

101. *Ibid.,* 11:xx.

102. Francesco Gui, *L'attesa del concilio: Vittoria Colonna e Reginald Pole nel movimento degli "spirituali"* (Rome: Editoria Università Elettronica, 1997).

103. Thomas F. Mayer, "'Heretics be not in all things heretics': Cardinal Pole, His Circle, and the Potential for Toleration," in *Beyond the Persecuting Society: Toleration Before the Enlightenment,* ed. John C. Laursen and Cary J. Nederman (Philadelphia: University of Pennsylvania Press, 1998), 107–124; Mayer, *Reginald Pole: Prince and Prophet* (Cambridge: Cambridge University Press, 2000), 439; Diarmaid MacCulloch, review of *The Time Before You Die* by Lucy Beckett, in *Times Literary Supplement,* January 28, 2000, 23; Mullett, *The Catholic Reformation,* 33, 36, 43–44. For Pole's correspondence with Erasmus, see Erasmus, *The Correspondence,* 11:314–317.

104. Thomas M. McCoog, "Ignatius Loyola and Reginald Pole: A Reconsideration," *Journal of Ecclesiastical History* 47 (1996): 257–273; Thomas F. Mayer, "A Test of Wills: Cardinal Pole, Ignatius Loyola, and the Jesuits in England," in *The Reckoned Expense: Edmund Campion and the Early English Jesuits,* ed. Thomas M. McCoog (Woodbridge, Suffolk: Boydell Press, 1996), 21–37. For other essays on this topic by Thomas F. Mayer, see his *Cardinal Pole in European Context: A Via Media in the Reformation* (Burlington, Vt.: Ashgate, 2000).

105. Howard Louthan, *The Quest for Compromise: Peacemakers in Counter-Reformation Vienna* (New York: Cambridge University Press, 1997), 164. See also Pierre Costil, *André Dudith, humaniste hongrois 1533–1589: Sa vie, son oeuvre et ses manuscrits grecs* (Paris: Les Belles Lettres, 1935), 64–67 (with Pole in England); 101–117 (at the Council of Trent); 108 (lay chalice); 109, 126 (clerical marriages). Dudič eventually turned Protestant. See also Domenico Caccamo, *Eretici italiani in Moravia, Polonia e Transilvania, 1558–1611. Studi e documenti,* Corpus Reformatorum Italicorum, ed. Luigi Firpo and Giorgio Spini (Florence and Chicago: Sansoni and the Newberry Library, 1970), 109–131.

106. On Ferdinand's attitude, see also Alois Kroess, "Kaiser Ferdinand I und seine Reformationsvorschläge auf dem Konzil von Trient bis zum Schluss der Theologenkonferenz in Innsbruck," *Zeitschrift für katholische Theologie* 27 (1903): 455–490, 621–651.

107. Thierry Wanegffelen, *Une difficile fidélité: Catholiques malgré concile en France, XVIe-XVII-e siècles* (Paris: Presses Universitaires de France, 1999), 152–162.

108. Mercantonio de Dominis, *Ohlášení a zpráva* (Prague: Daniel Sedlčanský, 1619). See also William B. Patterson, *King James VI and I and the Reunion of Christendom* (New York: Cambridge University Press, 1997), 220–224; Noel Malcolm, *De Dominis (1560–1624): Venetian, Anglican, Ecumenist and Relapsed Heretic* (London: Strickland and Scott Academic Publications, 1984).

109. Jaroslav Kolár, *Návraty bez konce: Studie k starší české literatuře,* ed. Lenka Jiroušková (Brno: Atlantis, 1999), 120, 141, 175–177; *Knihopis českých a slovenských tisků,* 2 vols., vol. 2 in 9 parts (Prague: Nakladatelství Československé akademie věd, 1925–1967), nos. 2348–2369. See also Mirjam Bohatcová, "Erasmus Roterdamský v českých tištěných překladech 16.–17. století," *Časopis národního muzea, Řada historická* 155 (1986): 37–58.

110. Desiderius Erasmus, *Evangelium Ježíše Krista syna Božího podle sepsání Svatého Matouše,* trans. Jan Vartovský of Varta (Litomyšl: Ondřej Dušík, 1542).

111. Erasmus, *The Correspondence,* 6:321–23; see also 7: 89–95, 119–128.

112. More, *Complete Works,* 6: pt. 1, 192; pt. 2, 658.

113. "For pray take it as certain that, whatever opinion you come to, people in my country will easily and gladly agree with you, and will value what you say far more than if one were to confront them with decrees of the supreme pontiff or any thunderbolt of opposition launched by men." Erasmus, *The Correspondence,* 8:75–76.

114. Kolár, *Návraty bez konce,* 179.

115. Pavel Bydžovský, *Historiae aliquot Anglorum martyrum, quibus Deus suam ecclesiam exornare sicut syderibus coelum dignatus est* (Prague: J. Cantor, 1554), f. Br.

116. Robert Barnes, *Kronyky. A životů sepsání nejvrchnějších Biskupů Římských jináč Papežů,* trans. Ennius Glatouinus (Nuremberg: Woldřich Nejber and Jan Montán, 1565), f. 195v, 198r–198v.

117. If, as Brian Tierney suggests, the pope's ecclesiastical power had three components—magisterium, jurisdiction, and holy orders—then the Utraquists accepted the first with qualifications, rejected the second, and accepted the third fully. See Tierney, *Origins of Papal Infallibility,* 310. On the Utraquist view of the papacy, see also Chapter 6.

118. Richard M. Douglas, *Jacopo Sadoleto, 1477–1547: Humanist and Reformer* (Cambridge, Mass.: Harvard University Press, 1959), 74.

119. *Ibid.,* 80–81, 116.

120. Contarini showed his spirit of accommodation in negotiations at the Diet of Regensburg in 1541 when he tried to find common ground with the Lutherans on justification. See Elisabeth G. Gleason, *Gasparo Contarini: Venice, Rome, and Reform* (Berkeley: University of California Press, 1993), x, 241–245; James Atkinson, "Die römisch-katholische Kirche und die Reformation in anglikanischer Sicht," in *Vierhundertfünfzig Jahre lutherische Reformation, 1517–1967: Festschrift für Franz Lau zum 50. Geburtstag,* ed. Helmar Junghans, et al. (Göttingen: Vanderhoeck and Ruprecht, 1967), 14–15.

121. Josef Macek, "Osudy basilejských kompaktát v jagelonském věku," in *Jihlava a Basilejská Kompaktáta: Sborník příspěvků z mezinárodního sympozia k 555. výročí přijetí Basilejských kompaktát, 26–28. červen 1991* (Jihlava: Muzeum Vysočiny, 1992), 199–200. See also Alain Dufour, "Humanisme et Reformation,"in Dufour, *Histoire politique et psychologie historique* (Geneva: Librairie Droz, 1966), 54.

122. Letter from Floriano Montini (secretary to Cardinal Campeggi) to Erasmus, February 22, 1525, from Buda, in Erasmus, *The Correspondence,* 11:48–49. On Erasmus's friendship with Campeggi, see *ibid.,* 11:84, 323. On these negotiations, see Chapter 3.

123. *Ibid.,* 11:322–323.

124. Erasmus's letter to Sadoleto is cited in Douglas, *Jacopo Sadoleto, 1477–1547,* 115.

125. "[I]ndeed it is the opinion of that great man Jerome the Hussite that universities do no more good to the church of God than the Evil One himself. Nor does it move the schoolmasters in the slightest that his opinion was condemned at the Council of Constance, for it is notorious that the council did not contain a single educated man or one who knew Greek." Letter from Maarten van Dorp, August 27, 1515, in Erasmus, *The Correspondence,* 3:160.

126. *Ibid.,* 6:15.

127. Letter to Ricardo Bartolini, March 10, 1517, in *ibid.,* 4:279.

128. More, *Complete Works,* 7:257, 391. Compared with his view of the Bohemians as heretics in *Dialogue Concerning Heresies* (1529?), see *ibid.,* 6: pt. 1, 315, 379, pt. 2, 473–474.

129. See, for instance, the disquisition of Jan Šlechta of Všehrdy in his letter of October 10, 1519, to Erasmus in Erasmus, *The Correspondence,* 7: 91–94. For Erasmus's awareness of the Taborite violence, see *ibid.,* 8:25.

130. Letter of Diego Lópes Zúñiga to Juan de Vergara of May 4, 1522, in *ibid.*, 8:345; 460, n. 8.

131. Peter Fraenkel, "Utraquism or Co-Existence: Some Notes on the Earliest Negotiations Before the Pacification of Nuernberg, 1531–1532," *Studia theologica* 18, no. 2 (1964): 130, 132–134.

132. Barnes, *Kronyky. A životů sepsání*, f. 3v–4r.

133. Jana Nechutová, "Matěj of Janov and His Work Regulae Veteris et Novi Testamenti: The Significance of Volume VI and Its Relation to the Previously Published Volumes," in *The Bohemian Reformation and Religious Practice*, vol. 2: Papers from the XVIIIth World Congress of the Czechoslovak Society of Arts and Sciences, Brno 1996, ed. Zdeněk V. David and David R. Holeton (Prague: Academy of Sciences of the Czech Republic, Main Library, 1998), 16. See also František Bartoš, *Husitská revoluce*, 2 vols. (Prague: Nakladatelství Československé akademie věd, 1965–1966), 1:21, 37; and Augustin Neumann, *K dějinám věku poděbradského* (Brno: Nákladem vlastním, 1933), 7.

134. Fraenkel, "Utraquism or Co-Existence," 135–136, 144.

135. *Ibid.*, 140.

136. Miloš Pojar, *Jindřich Matyáš Thurn: Muž činu* (Prague: Ivo Železný, 1998), 14.

137. Fraenkel, "Utraquism or Co-Existence," 137, 150.

138. Douglas, *Jacopo Sadoleto, 1477–1547*, 93.

139. Bradshaw, "The Controversial Sir Thomas More," 563–564.

140. As it was pointed out, the Utraquists successively repudiated, rather than accepted, radical teachings that would have compromised their traditionalist orthodoxy— those of the Taborites, the Unity, and the Lutherans. As for Hus, his personal doctrines did not affect their theology. His name hardly ever appeared in their formal theological pronouncements. Thus, the compendium, Klement Borový, ed., *: Akta konsistoře utrakvistické*, vol. 1 of *Jednání a dopisy konsistoře katolické a utrakvistické* (Prague: I. L. Kober, 1868), contains only four references to Hus, one to books about him (174), and three about his feast day (61, 230, 264). Moreover, it is arguable, especially on the basis of Paul de Vooght's research, that there was nothing unorthodox in Hus's own writings; de Vooght, *L'hérésie de Jean Huss*, 2d ed., 2 vols. (Louvain: Publications universitaires, 1975). See also Brian Gogan, *The Common Corps of Christendom: Ecclesiological Themes in the Writings of Sir Thomas More* (Leiden: Brill, 1982), 53–54, 56.

141. Erasmus, *The Correspondence*, 8:208–209, 415, n. 54.

142. Erasmus encountered this fate at the Council of Trent; see Bireley, *The Refashioning of Catholicism*, 52. Erasmus's works were placed on the Index of 1559, and a 1566 ruling of the Holy Office made it "an error and heresy" to claim that Erasmus had not erred; see Silvana Seidel Menchi, *Erasmus als Ketzer: Reformation und Inquisition in Italien des 16. Jahrhunderts*. (Leiden: E. J. Brill, 1993), 390–391. Subsequently, in the 1580s, Cardinal Robert Bellarmine, working for the Congregation for the Index, exhibited some qualms about labeling Erasmus an outright heretic; see Godman, *The Saint as Censor*, 108–115.

143. Kolde, "Cochlaeus," 4:200.

Chapter 11

1. Anton Gindely, *Geschichte der Ertheilung des böhmischen Majestätsbriefes von 1609* (Prague: Carl Bellmann's Verlag, 1858); Kamil Krofta, *Majestát Rudolfa II*

(Prague: Historický klub, 1909); Julius Glücklich, "Koncept Majestátu a vznik *Porovnání,*" *Český časopis historický* 23 (1917): 110–128.
   2. Václav V. Tomek, "O církevní správě strany pod obojí v Čechách od r. 1415 až 1622," *Časopis českého musea* 22 (1848): 462–463.
   3. Kamil Krofta, "Od kompaktát k Bílé Hoře," *Listy z náboženských dějin* (Prague: Historický klub, 1936), 355. See also Klement Borový, *Antonín Brus z Mohelnice, arcibiskup pražský; Historicko-kritický životopis.* (Prague: Dědictví sv. Prokopa, 1873), 196; Jan Kapras, *Právní dějiny zemí koruny české,* 3 vols. (Prague: Unie, 1913), 2:536.
   4. Zikmund Winter, *Zlatá doba měst českých* (Prague: Odeon, 1991), 142.
   5. Josef Pekař, *Dějiny československé* (Prague: Akropolis, 1991), 97.
   6. "Na základě majestátu cís. Rudolfa II . . . může se říci, že starý utrakvismus rokem 1609 úplně a navždy zanikl." *Ottův slovník naučný* (Prague: Otto, 1888–1909), 1:217.
   7. See, especially, *Druhá Apologie stavův království českého, tělo a krev Pána Ježíše Krista pod obojí přijímajících* (Prague: Daniel Karel z Karlspergka, 1619), 205 (no. 27).
   8. Josef Vávra, "Katolíci a sněm český r. 1608 a 1609," *Sborník historického kroužku* Sešit 1 (1893): 15. The text of Tomáš's reply is in Vilém Slavata, *Paměti nejvyššího kancléře království českého,* 2 vols., ed. Josef Jireček (Prague: Kober, 1866–1868), 1: 214–219. Tomáš had been a part of the Consistory's apparatus for a long time, acting for instance as the clerk of the Consistory's court in 1590; see *Sněmy české,* 7:453.
   9. Ferdinand Hrejsa, *Česká konfesse: Její vznik, podstata a dějiny* (Prague: Česká akademie pro vědy, slovesnost a umění, 1912), 437.
   10. On the Blasphemy Act, see John Spurr, *English Puritanism, 1603–1689* (New York: St. Martin's Press, 1998), 120.
   11. Concerning the disproportionate weight of the nobles, particular the barons, in contemporary diets see, for instance, Bohumil Navrátil, *Biskupství olomoucké 1576–1579 a volba Stanislava Pavlovského* (Prague: Česká společnost nauk, 1909), 3.
   12. Hrejsa, *Česká konfesse,* 440; Kamil Krofta, *Nesmrtelný národ: Od Bílé Hory k Palackému* (Prague: Laichter, 1940), 310; Krofta, *Majestát Rudolfa II,* 17.
   13. Krofta, *Majestát Rudolfa II,* 16. For the text of the Diet articles of 1608, see *Druhá Apologie stavův království českého,* 153–157 (no. 15).
   14. Pavel Skála ze Zhoře, *Historie česká od r. 1602 do r. 1623,* 5 vols., ed. Karel Tieftrunk (Prague: Kober, 1865–1870), 1:111; Hrejsa, *Česká konfesse,* 437. On the towns' fear of losing religious liberty if deserted by the nobility, see also Josef Janáček, "Královská města česká na zemském sněmu r. 1609–1610," *Sborník historický* 5 (1956): 230.
   15. Krofta, *Nesmrtelný národ,* 308; Tomek, "O církevní správě strany pod obojí v Čechách," 463; Anton Gindely, *Geschichte der böhmischen Brüder,* 2d ed., 2 vols. (Prague 1861–1862), 2:413.
   16. On "salami tactics," see Philip Longworth, *The Making of Eastern Europe: From Prehistory to Postcommunism,* 2d ed. (New York: St. Martin's Press, 1997), 80, 231; and Chapter 10, n. 27.
   17. *Druhá Apologie stavův království českého,* 469–474; *Sněmy české,* 11: pt. 1, 40.
   18. On Bonomi and Malaspina, see *Sněmy české,* 11:58–60; Josef Matoušek, "Kurie a boj o konsistoř pod obojí za administrátora Rezka," *Český časopis historický* 37 (1931), 24.
   19. Matoušek, "Kurie a boj o konsistoř pod obojí," 31–32.
   20. Václav Šturm, *Krátké ozvání . . . proti kratičkému ohlášení Jednoty Valdenské neb Boleslavské* (Prague: Jiřík Dačický, 1584), 47, 84.

21. Karel Stloukal, *Papežská politika a císařský dvůr pražský na předělu XVI. a XVII. věku* (Prague: F. Řivnáč, 1925), 204.
22. Robert A. Kann and Zdeněk V. David, *The Peoples of the Eastern Habsburg Lands, 1526–1918* (Seattle, Wash.: University of Washington Press, 1984), 50; Regina Pörtner, *The Counter-Reformation in Central Europe: Styria, 1580–1630* (Oxford: Clarendon Press, 2001), 144–180.
23. *Sněmy české,* 11:54–56.
24. Spyros Vryonis, Jr., "The Byzantine Patriarchate and Turkish Islam," *Byzanto-Slavica* 57 (1996): 82–111. In what must have been one of the colossal miscalculations of the second millennium, Gregorius assumed that the Turks, unable to resist the beauty of the Orthodox service, would abandon Islam for Christianity.
25. Spurr, *English Puritanism,* 66.
26. Rudolf Říčan, *The History of the Unity of Brethren: A Protestant Hussite Church in Bohemia and Moravia,* trans. C. Daniel Crews (Bethlehem, Pa.: Moravian Church in America, 1992), 183–193, 224–249.
27. See Chapters 3 and 7.
28. Julius Glücklich, *O historických dílech Václava Budovce z Budova z let 1608–1610 a jejich poměru k Slavatovi, Skálovi a neznámému dosud diariu lutherána Karla Zikmundova,* Rozpravy české Akademie pro vědy, slovesnost a umění, Třída I., číslo 42 (Prague: Alois Wiesner, 1911), 68; Skála ze Zhoře, *Historie česká od r. 1602 do r. 1623,* 1:108–109.
29. *Sněmy české,* 10:428. Budovec once more stressed in a letter to Rudolf II delivered by him on February 19, 1603, that the different denominations of Christians were united by belief in the same God and his Son, and opposition to the Turkish pagans. See *Sněmy české,* 10:455; Václav Budovec of Budov, *Antialkorán,* ed. Noemi Rejchrtová (Prague: Odeon, 1989), 12. On the mandate of 1602, see Stloukal, *Papežská politika a císařský dvůr,* 206–208.
30. Glücklich, "Koncept Majestátu a vznik porovnání," 121–122, 127; Vávra, "Katolíci a sněm český," 12–13; Robert Kalivoda, *Husitská epocha a J. A. Komenský* (Prague: Odeon, 1992), 37–39.
31. *Druhá Apologie stavův království českého,* 205 (no. 27). See also Jaroslav Kadlec, *Přehled českých církevních dějin,* 2 vols. (Prague: Zvon, 1991), 2:61.
32. *Druhá Apologie stavův království českého,* 205. Generally, on the confusing language of the *Porovnání,* see also the comment of Josef Pekař, *Dějiny československé* (Prague: Akropolis, 1991), 97.
33. "[U]čení kteréhož se Čechové staří podobojí vědycky přidrželi," *Druhá Apologie stavův království českého,* 160.
34. *Druhá Apologie stavův království českého,* 127–130, 141.
35. Josef Matoušek, "Kurie a boj o konsistoř pod obojí za administrátora Rezka," *Český časopis historický* 37 (1931): 285–291. On the Rezek affair see also chapter 9.
36. *Sněmy české,* 10:330, 333.
37. See previously with reference to Skála ze Zhoře, *Historie česká od r. 1602 do r. 1623,* 1:111. On the alleged desire to fuse with Rome, see, for instance, Anna Skýbová, "Česká šlechta a jednání o povolení kompaktát r. 1525," in *Proměny feudální třídy v Čechách v pozdním feudalismu,* ed. Josef Petráň, Acta Universitatis Carolinae, Philosophica et historica 1 (1976), Studia historica, 14 (Prague: Univerzita Karlova, 1976), 97.
38. The official name was Consistory sub utraque (*konsistoř podobojí*). Hrejsa uses the term "new consistory"; see Hrejsa, *Česká konfesse,* 759.

39. *Sněmy české*, 6:268–269. See also about the spartan living conditions of the administrator in 1598, *Sněmy české*, 9:592; and his petition of 1582, *Sněmy české*, 6:225.

40. See Chapter 8.

41. See Chapter 9.

42. *Sněmy české*, 11: pt. 1, 76; Slavata, *Paměti nejvyššího kancléře království českého*, 1:47. On Rudolf II's favoritism of adherents of the Roman Church, Jaroslav Pánek, "K povaze vlády Rudolfa II. v českém království," *Folia Historica Bohemica* 18 (1997): 78–79; *Sněmy české*, 10:646.

43. On the issue of expropriated ecclesiastical lands, see Anna Skýbová, "Česká šlechta a jednání o povolení kompaktát r. 1525," in *Proměny feudální třídy v Čechách v pozdním feudalismu*, ed. Josef Petráň, Acta Universitatis Carolinae, Philosophica et historica 1 (1976), Studia historica, 14 (Prague: Univerzita Karlova, 1976), 81–82.

44. In contrast, as noted previously, Berka himself had been raised in his youth as a Utraquist and his episcopal consecration required a prior humiliating abjuration of religious errors; see Matoušek, "Kurie a boj o konsistoř pod obojí za administrátora Rezka," 278–279.

45. See, for instance, Rudolf II's exhortation to the Utraquist clergy and believers to respect and cherish the new archbishop Martin Medek in February 1582; *Sněmy české*, 6:175; František Tischer, *Dopisy konsistoře podobojí z let 1610–1619* (Prague: Historický spolek, 1917–1925), viii, xi.

46. *Sněmy české*, 7:60–61.

47. *Sněmy české*, 4:411; Josef Janáček, *Jan Blahoslav* (Prague: Svobodné slovo, 1966), 119–120, 146–148. See also Chapter 7.

48. *Sněmy české*, 5:748–749; 7:494.

49. Later, four professors of the Prague University, as well as another Lutheran minister, were added; see Hrejsa, *Česká konfesse*, 473–474.

50. "[J]sou v Čechách trojí mezi stranou pod obojí v řádích a ceremoniích rozdíly . . . pak rozdílné řády, ceremonie a církevní kázně mezi nimi jsou, to už jednotu pravdy Boží, . . . též ani svazek lásky křesťanské mezi nimi neboří a bohdá nezboří . . ." Glücklich, *O historických dílech Václava Budovce z Budova*, 68.

51. *Na spis proti jednotě bratrské od Samuele Martinia etc: sepsaný . . . Ohlášení* (Leszno: n.p., 1635), 43.

52. Hrejsa, *Česká konfesse*, 533. On the dealings of Matouš Pačuda with the Consistory in September 1616, see Tischer, *Dopisy konsistoře podobojí z let 1610–1619*, 405; Slavata, *Paměti nejvyššího kancléře království českého*, 1:214–219.

53. For comparative purposes, it may be noted that even the Church of England needed to produce a set of theological articles in order to accommodate certain Lutheran borrowings under Cranmer in the 1530s. See Diarmaid MacCulloch, *Thomas Cranmer: A Life* (New Haven, Conn.: Yale University Press, 1996), 162.

54. Rudolf Říčan, *The History of the Unity of Brethren: A Protestant Hussite Church in Bohemia and Moravia*, trans. C. Daniel Crews (Bethlehem, Pa.: Moravian Church in America, 1992), 331–332; Antonín Rezek, *Dějiny prostonárodního hnutí náboženského v Čechách od vydání tolerančního patentu až na naše časy* (Prague: Řivnáč, 1887), 13; Tischer, *Dopisy konsistoře podobojí z let 1610–1619*, viii. On the "unmeltable" Brethren see also Jindřich Halama, "The Crisis of the Union of Czech Brethren in the Years Prior to the Thirty Years War," *Communio Viatorum* 44 (2002): 60–65.

55. See, especially, Jan Felin, *Rozebrání Obrany Samuela Martinia*, Spisy Jana

Amosa Komenského, 6, ed. Josef T. Müller (Prague: Česká akademie pro vědy, slovesnost, a umění, 1902), 45–53, 143–146.

56. Říčan, *The History of the Unity of Brethren,* 264–275.

57. Havel Phaëton (Žalanský), *Kázání o velikých modlářských bludích, jimiž v církvi odporné nejsvětější Páně Večeře se zlehčuje a poškvrňuje* (Prague: n.p., [1620?]), f. A4v–A6r.

58. Hrejsa, *Dějiny křesťanství v Československu,* 6:285, 287–288, 291; Felin, *Rozebrání Obrany Samuela Martinia,* xx; Jerzy Kloczowski, *A History of Polish Christianity* (New York: Cambridge University Press, 2000), 107; *The Cambridge History of Poland,* 2 vols., ed. W. F. Reddaway (Cambridge: Cambridge University Press, 1941–1950), 1:345.

59. *Druhá Apologie stavův království českého,* 141, 143, 205. On Berka's Utraquist ordinations, see *Sněmy české,* 11: pt. 1, 74.

60. Zacharyáš Bruncvík, *Testamenti nostri Iesu Christi pia et fida assertio. To jest: Kšaftu Večeře Páně svatá Starožitnost, pobožná posloupnost, dlouhověká až právě do dne soudného trvanlivost: V níž z nařízení Kristového, z učení evangelistského a apoštolského, z doktorů a sněmů osvícených, z kanonu a práv duchovních, z historií církevních, a nejvíce našich českých, etc.* (Prague: Matěj Pardubský, 1613), 213–215. Hrejsa dates the church order (*církevní řád*) to 1609 and reprints it in *Česká konfesse,* 484, n. 1. See also Alexandra Walsham, "The Parochial Roots of Laudianism Revisited: Catholics, Anti-Calvinists and 'Parish Anglicans' in Early Stuart England," *Journal of Ecclesiastical History* 49 (1998): 651.

61. Hrejsa, *Česká konfesse,* 485.

62. "Protož zvláštní Instrukci Konsistořskou nám kněžím Páně pod obojím, a Konfesí české srdcem i ústy se přiznávajícím, vydati ráčili." Cited by Bruncvík, *Kšaftu Večeře Páně,* 213.

63. Hrejsa, *Česká konfesse,* 484–485; see also Chapter 8.

64. *Knihopis českých a slovenských tisků,* 2 vols., vol. 2 in 9 parts (Prague: Nakladatelství Československé akademie věd, 1925–1967), 2: pt. 2, 309.

65. Tischer, *Dopisy konsistoře podobojí z let 1610–1619,* v–vi; Hrejsa, *Česká konfesse,* 482; Tomek, "O církevní správě strany pod obojí v Čechách," 463, 468.

66. V. Bartůněk, "Táborská duchovní správa v XVII. století," *Jihočeský sborník historický* 21 (1952): 24.

67. For the Utraquists, the change of protection from the sub una adherents in the royal government to that of the noble Lutheran defensores in the Diet, might be seen as analogous mutatis mutandis to the passing of a Christian community in India from the protection of a Hindu maharajah to that of Moslem nazims or nabobs.

68. On Hoë see, for instance, Hrejsa, *Česká konfesse,* 521–522; on Scultetus, *ibid.,* 546–553.

69. Samuel Martinius z Dražova, *Oratio de concordia ecclesiae his ultimis temporibus plurimum necessaria.* (Prague: Pavel Sessius, 1617), f. B7v–C2v, C5r–C6r, D6v–D7r; Matěj Stříbrský, *Knížka spasitedlných naučení* (Prague: Daniel Sedlčanský, 1610), f. B6v.

70. Spurr, *English Puritanism,* 119; see also C. John Sommerville, "Interpreting Seventeenth-Century English Religion as Movements," *Church History* 69 (2000): 762–765.

71. *Euangelische Erklerung auff die Böhaimische Apologia* ([Vienna?]: n.p., 1618), f. B3v. On this pamphlet, allegedly by Lutherans loyal to the Habsburg dynasty, see Antonín Markus, "Stavovské apologie z roku 1618," *Český časopis historický* 17 (1911):

213–216. A Czech translation appears in Skála ze Zhoře, *Historie česká od r. 1602 do r. 1623*, 2:241–270.

72. Karel Stloukal, "Z diplomatických styků mezi Francií a Čechami před Bílou Horou," *Český časopis historický* 32 (1926): 489.

73. Adam Tanner, *Apologia pro Societate Jesu ex Boemiae Regno ab eiusdem regni statibus religionis sub utraque, publico decreto immerito proscripta. Anno M.DC.XVIII. die VIIII Junij* (Vienna: Wolfgang Schump, 1618), 18–19, 52–53.

74. Hrejsa, *Česká konfesse*, 521–522.

75. Josef Válka, "Problémy syntézy moderních českých dějin," *Husitství, Reformace, Renesance: Sborník k 60. narozeninám Františka Šmahela*, 3 vols., ed. Jaroslav Pánek, et al. (Prague: Historický ústav, 1994), 3:1052; František Šmahel, "Svoboda slova, svatá válka a tolerance z nutnosti v husitském období," *Český časopis historický* 92 (1994): 677. But see also Noemi Rejchrtová, *Václav Budovec z Budova* (Prague: Melantrich, 1984), 170.

76. On the Utraquist attitude, see Vávra, "Katolíci a sněm český," 15. The text of Tomáš's reply is in Slavata, *Paměti nejvyššího kancléře království českého*, 1:214–219. On the Lutheran attitude, see Hrejsa, *Česká konfesse*, 523–526; "Zdání o napravení spůsobu církví evangelických českých a uvedení jich v jednotu," in Skála ze Zhoře, *Historie česká od r. 1602 do r. 1623*, 2:43–49. See also Jan Štelcar Želetavský z Želetavy, *Knížka o pravé a falešné církvi* (Prague: Buryán Valda, 1589), f. M1r–M2v.

77. Phaëton (Žalanský), *Kázání o velikých modlářských bludích*, f. C6r.

78. Budovec of Budov, *Antialkorán*, 17; Glücklich, *O historických dílech Václava Budovce z Budova*, 68; Skála ze Zhoře, *Historie česká od r. 1602 do r. 1623*, 1:108–109; Rejchrtová, *Václav Budovec z Budova*, 170.

79. Roger Williams, *The Bloody Tenent of Persecution, for cause of Conscience, discussed, in A Conference between Truth and Peace* (London: n.p., 1644), 103, cited by Norah Carlin, "Toleration for Catholics in the Puritan Revolution," in *Tolerance and Intolerance in the European Reformation*, ed. Ole P. Grell and Bob Scribner (New York: Cambridge University Press, 1996), 219.

80. Cited by John Coffey, "Puritanism and Liberty Revisited: The Case for Toleration in the English Revolution," *Historical Journal* 41 (1998): 980.

81. Thomas F. Mayer, "Heretics be not in all things heretics': Cardinal Pole, His Circle, and the Potential for Toleration," in *Beyond the Persecuting Society: Toleration Before the Enlightenment*, ed. John Christian Laursen and Cary J. Nederman (Philadelphia: University of Pennsylvania Press), 1998, 107–108.

82. Krofta, *Majestát Rudolfa II*, 37; Zacharyáš Bruncvík, *Pravitatis et impletatis haereticae pia et fida ostensio. To jest: Zrcadlo Kacířství: Do něhož kdo zdravě nahlédne, Allegata, u Doktorů Církve vykázaná, přeběhne, pozná, že my Katolíci pod obojí nevinně, a bez náležitého vší Svaté Říše vyslyšání od některých se kacěřujeme* (Prague: Matěj Pardubický, 1614), f. A3v.

83. William B. Patterson, *King James VI and I and the Reunion of Christendom* (Cambridge: Cambridge University Press, 1997), especially 155–195.

84. Tischer, *Dopisy konsistoře podobojí z let 1610–1619*, 405, 412, 461 (Pačuda), 443–445 (Locika).

85. *Ibid.*, vii.

86. Symeon Evstachyus Kapihorský, *Hystoria kláštera Sedleckého* (Prague: Pavel Sessius, 1630), 93.

87. Hrejsa, *Česká konfesse*, 533, 536, n.3, 544, n. 4; "Dikastus," *Ottův slovník naučný*, 7:533.

88. Jan Václav Cykáda, *Kázání nad mrtvým tělem urozené paní, paní Alžběty Valdštejnské z Valdštejna* (Prague: Matěj Pardubský, 1614), f. A1r.

89. Milena Bartlová, "The Utraquist Church and the Visual Arts Before Luther," in *The Bohemian Reformation and Religious Practice*, vol. 4: Papers from the IV International Symposium on Bohemian Reformation and Religious Practice, under the auspices of the Philosophical Institute of the Academy of Sciences of the Czech Republic, held at Vila Lanna, Prague, 26-28 June 2000, ed. Zdeněk V. David and David R. Holeton (Prague: Academy of Sciences of the Czech Republic, Main Library, 2002), 219-223.

90. Markus, "Stavovské apologie z roku 1618," 205; Tischer, *Dopisy konsistoře podobojí z let 1610–1619*, xi; Hrejsa, *Česká konfesse*, 536.

91. J. Prokeš, ed., *Protokol vyšlé korespondence Kanceláře českých direktorů z let 1618 a 1619* (Prague: Státní tiskárna, 1934), 121 (no. 1667).

92. V. Bartůněk, "Táborská duchovní správa v XVII. století," *Jihočeský sborník historický* 21 (1952): 24–25.

93. Hrejsa, *Česká konfesse*, 485, 533, 534; Tischer, *Dopisy konsistoře podobojí z let 1610–1619*, x.

94. Hrejsa, *Česká konfesse*, 536; Tischer, *Dopisy konsistoře podobojí z let 1610–1619*, x, 446–447.

95. Phaëton (Žalanský), *Kázání o velikých modlářských bludích*, f. C6r.

96. Markus, "Stavovské apologie z roku 1618," 431; see also Krofta, *Majestát Rudolfa II*, 22.

97. Tischer, *Dopisy konsistoře podobojí z let 1610–1619*, x–xi; Hrejsa, *Česká konfesse*, 539, n. 2; Symeon Evstachyus Kapihorský, *Hystoria kláštera Sedleckého* (Prague: Pavel Sessius, 1630), 94.

98. Josef Vávra, "Počátky reformace katolické v Čechách," *Sborník historického kroužku* Sešit 3 (1894): 40. See report on the activities of Captain Zeller on the royal manor of Brandýs nad Labem in 1617 in Zikmund Winter, *Život církevní v Čechách: Kulturně-historický obraz v XV. a XVI. století*, 2 vols. (Prague: Česká akademie pro vědy, slovesnost a umění, 1895), 1:267–268. Concerning the traditional role of the manorial managers as protectors of Utraquist parishes on royal estates, see Chapter 8.

99. Josef Lintner, "Duchovní správa v Soběslavi za faráře Prokopa Cetorazského v l. 1612–1618," *Sborník historického kroužku* 8 (1899): pt. 2, 25.

100. Josef Jireček, "Literatura exulantův českých," *Časopis českého musea* 48 (1874): pt. 1, 193; Skála ze Zhoře, *Historie česká od r. 1602 do r. 1623*, 1:326.

101. Hrejsa, *Česká konfesse*, 535; Tischer, *Dopisy konsistoře podobojí z let 1610–1619*, x. For a tendentious report on this event, see also Jan Amos Komenský, *Historia o těžkých protivenstvích*, in his *Opera omnia* (Prague: Academia, 1989), 9: pt. 1, 102. Komenský's account is based, in turn, on the *Druhá Apologie stavův království českého*, 33–34.

102. *Druhá Apologie stavův království českého*, 31–32; Tischer, *Dopisy konsistoře podobojí z let 1610–1619*, x–xi.

103. *Druhá Apologie stavův království českého*, 31–32.

104. *Ibid.*, 32.

105. Prokeš, *Protokol vyšlé korespondence*, 76 (no. 876); Tischer, *Dopisy konsistoře*, 525–26.

106. Tanner, *Apologia pro Societate Jesu ex Boemiae Regno*, 18–19; Winter, *Život církevní v Čechách*, 1:275.

107. "Certe Hussius et Hussitae veteres sanctorum invocationem; cultum et venerationem sanctorum reliquarum et imaginum; caelibatum sacerdotum, monachorum, ac monialium; septem novae legis sacramenta; sacrificium missae, transubstantionem panis et vini; purgatorium; bonorum operum necessitatem ad salutem; processiones et perigrationes sacras et c. aliaq; quamplurima ex Catholicae Ecclesiae fide et instituto defenderunt, quae a recentioribus Utraquistis prorsus reijciuntur et damnantur." Tanner, *Apologia pro Societate Jesu ex Boemiae Regno*, 53. This praise of Utraquism and Hus is omitted from the German translation of the *Apologia;* see Adam Tanner, *Apologia, oder Schutzbrief der Societet Jesu* (Vienna: Wolfgang Schump, 1618), 68.

108. Tanner, *Apologia pro Societate Jesu ex Boemiae Regno*, 18–19.

109. Phaëton (Žalanský), *Kázání o velikých modlářských bludích,* f. A4v–B1v, B5r, C3r–C4r, C5v–C6r, D3v.

110. Anton Gindely, *Geschichte der böhmischen Brüder*, 2d ed., 2 vols. (Prague: C. Bellmann, 1861–2), 2:413. See also Hrejsa, *Česká konfesse*, 533–537; and Tischer, *Dopisy konsistoře podobojí*, x–xi.

111. Eduard Winter, *Tausend Jahre Geisteskampf im Sudetenraum* (Munich: Aufstieg-Verlag, 1938), 197; *Druhá Apologie stavův království českého*, 31.

112. For instance, Phaëton (Žalanský), *Kázání o velikých modlářských bludích,* f. A4v–B1v.

113. "Das tschechische Volk hing zäh an dem Althergebrachten, den tschechischen Vespern, Hochämtern, Sakramental prozessionen und anderem." Eduard Winter, *Tausend Jahre Geisteskampf im Sudetenraum* (Munich: Aufstieg-Verlag, 1938), 197; Hrejsa, *Česká konfesse,* 534; Tischer, *Dopisy konsistoře podobojí z let 1610–1619,* x.

114. Zikmund Winter, *Kulturní obraz českých měst*, 2 vols. (Prague: Matice česká, 1890), 1:442.

115. Symeon Evstachyus Kapihorský, *Hystoria kláštera Sedleckého* (Prague: Pavel Sessius, 1630), 105.

116. Gindely, *Geschichte der böhmischen Brüder,* 2:413.

117. Anton Gindely, *Dějiny českého povstání*, 4 vols. (Prague: Tempský, 1870–1880), 1:217; or in a partial English translation, Gindely, *History of the Thirty Years' War,* 2 vols. (New York: G. P. Putnam's Sons, 1884), 1:53.

118. On the description of the riots, see James R. Palmitessa, "The Prague Uprising of 1611: Property, Politics, and Catholic Renewal in the Early Years of Habsburg Rule," *Central European History* 31 (1998): 304–314; Josef Janáček, *Rudolf II. a jeho doba* (Prague: Svoboda, 1987), 477–478.

119. In his magisterial work of sixteenth-century Utraquism, Bohuslav Bílejovský explained the rationale for the destruction of monasteries during the early stages of the Bohemian Reformation, as noted in Chapter 4; see Bohuslav Bílejovský, *Kronyka Cýrkevní*, ed. Jozef Skalický (pseudonym for Josef Dittrich) (Prague: Fetterl z Wilden, 1816), 25–26. For a recent treatment of the monastics' role in combating heresy under papal patronage, see Agostino Paravicini Bagliani, Agostino, *Il trono di Pietro: L'unersaltà del papato del Alessandro III a Bonifacio VIII* (Rome: Nuova Italia Scientifica, 1996), chapter 6.

120. Václav Husa, *Tomáš Müntzer a Čechy,* Rozpravy Československé akademie věd, roč. 67 (1957), Společenské vědy, 11 seš., 74–75.

121. Josef Matoušek, "Rukopis Bydžovského z Florentina *Rudolphus rex Bohemiae XXI*," *Časopis Archivní školy* 8 (1931): 164.

122. *Sněmy české*, 7:439; 10:102.

123. For a testimony on the intense dislike of Jesuits and monks by the common people of Prague, see also *Sněmy české*, 7:439–440.

124. On the Utraquist reserve concerning the veneration of images, see, for instance, Martin Žatecký, *Knížka proti ošemetné poctě a pokryté Svatých*, 2d ed., ed. Jan Štelcar Želetavský z Želetavy (Prague: n.p., 1593), originally published in 1517.

125. On the dislike of the Franciscans, see Petr Hlaváček, "*Errores quorundam Bernhardinorum*: Franciscans and the Bohemian Reformation," in *The Bohemian Reformation and Religious Practice*, vol. 3: Papers from the XIXth World Congress of the Czechoslovak Society of Arts and Sciences, Bratislava 1998, ed. Zdeněk V. David and David R. Holeton (Prague: Academy of Sciences of the Czech Republic, Main Library, 2000), 119–126. On the protection afforded to the Jesuits, see Palmitessa, "The Prague Uprising of 1611," 309.

126. Refining these figures further is at best a risky process that involves hazardous assumptions and can offer only the most tentative results. Yet, with these caveats in mind, an attempt can be made to arrive at illustrative numbers, both relative and absolute, for Czech non-Protestant Utraquists. Václav Líva's analysis of the religious exiles from Prague after the Battle of the White Mountain, including 600 families, indicated that more than a third were Germans, and a third Brethren or Calvinists, which would leave less than a third Czech Lutherans or Neo-Utraquists; see Václav Líva, "Studie o Praze pobělohorské," *Sborník příspěvků k dějinám hl. města Prahy* 6 (1930): 413–415. Assuming that this ratio was representative of the country, the number of Czech Lutherans (or Neo-Utraquists) would comprise between 5 and 10 percent of the population, based on the percentage of the Brethren, established in Pekař, *Dějiny československé*, 91–92. According to this formula, the Brethren and Lutherans within the Czech-speaking population would together constitute between 10 and 20 percent. This would come close to the ratio of 25 Utraquist parishes to 7 Protestant ones in the ecclesiastical district (the deanery) of Kouřim in 1613, cited by Hrejsa, *Česká konfesse*, 539, n. 2. If we further accept the proportion of 12 to 15 percent of the *sub una*, cited by Pekař, *Dějiny československé*, 91–92, for the speakers of Czech, this would yield between 65 and 78 percent of Non-Protestant Utraquists among the Czech-speaking population of Bohemia with 5 to 10 percent being Lutherans or Neo-Utraquists, 5 to 10 percent Brethren, and 12 to 15 percent *sub una*. According to this formula, assuming that Bohemia on the eve of the Bohemian uprising of 1618 had 1,700,000 inhabitants [see František Kavka and Josef Válka, *Dějiny Československa, 1437–1781* 2nd ed. (Prague: Státní pedagogické nakladatelstvi, [1970]), 201] of whom 1,200,000 were Czechs, the number of Utraquists would be between 780,000 and 936,000, the number of Czech Lutherans and Brethren each between 60,000 and 120,000, and the number of Czech *sub una* between 144,000 and 180,000.

127. Krofta, *Majestát Rudolfa II*, 41.

128. Adam the Younger of Valdštejn, *Deník rudolfinského dvořana, 1602–1633*, ed. Marie Koldinská and Petr Mat'a (Prague: Argo, 1997), 400–450.

129. "[N]evíme tu vo kom, kdo by se koncistoří Pražskou spravoval a jinde v zemi, zvláště z vyšších stavů, o nich nevíme." *Sněmy české*, 10:427.

130. See also Ernest Gellner, *Encounters with Nationalism* (New York: Blackwell,

1995); *Nations and Nationalism* (Ithaca, N.Y.: Cornell University Press, 1983); Eric J. Hobsbawm, *Nations and Nationalism Since 1780,* 2d ed. (Cambridge and New York: Cambridge University Press, 1992); Eric J. Hobsbawm and Terence Ranger, eds., *The Invention of Tradition* (Cambridge and New York: Cambridge University Press, 1983).

131. Josef Pekař, *Dějiny československé* (Prague: Akropolis, 1991), 91.

132. Walsham, "The Parochial Roots of Laudianism Revisited," 621.

133. Reliable estimates indicate that in 1600 Bohemia's barons and knights comprised 1,400 families; Jan Kapras, *Právní dějiny zemí koruny české,* 3 vols. (Prague: Unie, 1913), 2:436. The classical statement of Lenin's contempt for the intelligence of the masses is enshrined in his seminal *What Is To Be Done?* (1902).

134. On Wyclif's social concerns, see Anne Hudson, "*Poor Preachers, Poor Men:* Views of Poverty in Wyclif and His Followers," in *Häresie und vorzeitige Reformation im Spätmittelalter,* ed. František Šmahel, Schriften des Historischen Kollegs Kolloquien 39 (Munich: Oldenbourg, 1998), 43–44, 47, 52–53.

135. Spurr, *English Puritanism,* 76.

136. Josef Macek, *Jagellonský věk v českých zemích, 1471–1526,* 4 vols. (Prague: Academia, 1992–1999), 2:140–141.

137. Matauš Pačuda, *Spis v němž se obsahuje které věci (z stran lidského pokolení) předešly příchod a narození mesiaše pravého Krista* (Prague: Matěj Pardubický, 1616), f. G6r–G6v, J4v–J5r.

138. *Ibid.,* f. K8v [152]. Unfortunately, Pačuda's answer to this challenging statement is unknown. The one available copy of his work, held by the Strahov Monastery Library in Prague under the call number BX VI 22, ends abruptly at this point.

139. See, for instance, Thomas A. Fudge, *The Magnificent Ride: The First Reformation in Hussite Bohemia* (Brookfield, Vt.: Ashgate, 1998), 171–172, 270–272; Aeneas Sylvio Picolomini (later Pope Pius II) noted that the women of Tábor in 1451 surpassed many Italian priests in their knowledge of the Bible; *ibid.,* 171. John Klassen in "Women and Religious Reform in Late Medieval Bohemia," *Renaissance and Reformation,* n.s. 5:4 (1981): 211–214, emphasizes the role of women during the Bohemian wars of religion. See also Noemi Rejchrtová, "K specifiku "ženské otázky v husitství," in *Žena v dějinách Prahy,* ed. Jiř Pešek and Václav Ledvinka, Documenta Pragensis, no. 13 (Prague: Scriptorium, 1996), 67–68; Božena Kopičková, "Žena a rodina v husitství," *Husitský Tábor* 12 (1999): 40–41; Kopičková, "'[Q]uod mulieres, que sunt in Cristo, in hoc tempore viros antecurrunt.' Bohemian Reformers' Radically New View of Women and Marriage? From the Late Fourteenth Century to 1419," in *The Bohemian Reformation and Religious Practice,* vol. 4: Papers from the IV International Symposium on Bohemian Reformation and Religious Practice, under the auspices of the Philosophical Institute of the Academy of Sciences of the Czech Republic, held at Vila Lanna, Prague, 26-28 June 2000, ed. Zdeněk V. David and David R. Holeton (Prague: Academy of Sciences of the Czech Republic, Main Library, 2002), 81-97.

140. Pačuda, *Spis v němž se obsahuje,* f. J8v; also J6v-K3v.

141. References in parentheses in this paragraph are to folios in Pačuda, *Spis v němž se obsahuje.*

142. Erwin L. Lueker, ed., *Lutheran Cyclopedia,* rev. ed. (St. Louis: Concordia, 1975), 86, 627.

143. "Opilých a zlopověstných, nemluvňátek, také vzteklých, též ruhače a kacíře, nechce mít pán u večeře." Jiří Taciturnus z Háje (Hájský), *Zlatý řetízek pravého katolického*

náboženství... k dobrému mládeži školní Aušpurské konfesi (Prague: Matěj Pardubický, 1616), f. K4; Bruncvík, *Kšaftu Večeře Páně,* 214–215.

144. Noemi Rejchrtová, "Svatý Vojtěch v zrcadle české reformace," *Teologické texty* 8, no. 3 (1997): 94; Rejchrtová, "Dětská otázka v husitství," *Československý časopis historický* 28 (1980): 53–77.

145. Based loosely on the Apocalypse (Rev. 14:4); see Cykáda, *Kázání nad mrtvým,* f. A3r, A4r.

146. Tanner, *Apologia pro Societate Jesu,* 18–19; Hrejsa, *Česká konfesse,* 536–537; Tischer, *Dopisy konsistoře podobojí z let 1610–1619,* x, 446–447.

147. Bruncvík, *Kšaftu Večeře Páně,* 214–215; Bruncvík, *Zrcadlo Kacířství,* f. C7r.

148. Jiřík Dykastus (Miřkovský), *Postylla: nebo Kázání krátká na evangelia svatá,* 2 vols. (Prague: Jiřík J. Dačický, 1612), 1: 24–25, 33; *Summa religionis verae ex Confessione Bohemica excerpta/Summa náboženství pravého z Konfessí české vybraná* (Prague: Pavel Sessius, 1618), f. C8.

149. Václav Novotný, ed., "Bohoslužebná skládání o Husovi z XV a XVI století," in *Prameny dějin českých* 8 (Prague: Nadání Františka Palackého, 1932), especially 431–444, 458–472.

150. "Otázky křesťanské s odpověďmi na ně od D. Martina Lutéra sepsané pro ty, jenž k Stolu Páně přistoupiti chtějí," *Summa religionis verae ex Confessione Bohemica excerpta,* f. E6v; Zykmund Crinitus, *Diarium Christianum. Křesťanské dílo denní* (Prague: Matěj Pardubický, 1613), 129.

151. Zacharyáš Bruncvík, *Idolorum pia suplantatio. Kázání o tom, že obrazové jakož svaté Trojice Boha v podstatě jediného, neviditelného a neobsáhlého, tak i jiných svatých a světic, na něž poklona, vzývání a čest Boží se přenáší, v Církvi Páně trpěni býti nemají* (Prague: Matěj Pardubský, 1613), f. C2v–C3r, C7r; Bruncvík, *Pravitatis et impletatis haereticae pia et fida ostensio. To jest: Zrcadlo Kacířství,* f. D4r, E2r.

152. Franciscus Tillemannus, *Krátký výklad aneb vysvětlení sedmi žalmův kajících svatého Davida,* trans. Jiří Dikast (Prague: Daniel Adam z Veleslavína, 1598), f. (:)a–b, (:)2a; Zacharyáš Bruncvík, *Kázání o Pravém a jediném očistci křesťanském v němž hříchové naši, samým milosrdenstvím Božím a trvalou záslouhou Krista Pána, zde na světě, kdež čas milosti jest, se očišťují* (Prague: Matěj Pardubský, 1613), f. C4v.

153. Striking evidence of the importance attached to these pre-Tridentine liturgical books is their appearance already among the Bohemian incunabula. These incunabula included the Statutes of Archbishop Arnošt of Pardubice (1476), the Prague missal (1479), and the Agenda of the Church of Prague (c. 1479). See Emma Urbánková, "Nejstarší prvotisky českého původu," in *Knihtisk a kniha v českých zemích od husitství do Bílé hory: Sborník prací k 500. výročí českého knihtisku,* ed. František Šmahel (Prague: Academia, 1970), 24–30. For references to the traditional Utraquist liturgical books, see, for instance, Václav Koranda, *Traktát o velebné a božské svátosti oltářní* (Prague: Tiskař Korandy, 1493), f. S3r–S3v; Pavel Bydžovský (Smetana), *Děťátka a neviňátka hned po přijetí křtu sv. Tělo a Krev Boží, že přijímati mají* (Prague: Bartoloměj Netolický, 1541), f. B1r–B1v; Bruncvík, *Kšaftu Večeře Páně,* 213–215.

154. David R. Holeton, "The Evolution of Utraquist Eucharistic Liturgy: A Textual Study," in *The Bohemian Reformation and Religious Practice,* vol. 2: Papers from the XVIIIth World Congress of the Czechoslovak Society of Arts and Sciences, Brno 1996, ed. Zdeněk V. David and David R. Holeton (Prague: Academy of Sciences of the Czech Republic, Main Library, 1998), 116-120; Bruncvík, *Kšaftu Večeře Páně,* 214.

155. Jaroslav Böhm, et al., *Dějiny,* 2 vols., and pt. 2 of *Československá vlastivěda*

(Prague: Orbis, 1963), 1:380; Václav V. Tomek, "O církevní správě strany pod obojí v Čechách, od r. 1415 až 1622," *Časopis českého musea* 22 (1848): 463.

156. Dykastus, *Postylla: nebo Kázání krátká na evangelia svatá,* 1: 25. Ralph Keen, *Divine and Human Authority in Reformation Thought: German Theologians on Political Order, 1520–1555* (Nieuwkoop: De Graaf, 1997), 6, characterized the Lutheran attitude toward political power: "[W]hen the Reformers appealed to secular authorities, they did so with a conception of authority that secularized the ecclesiastical order and subordinated it to the political order."

157. Cited by Bruncvík, *Kšaftu Večeře Páně,* 213–215.

158. Pravoslav Kneidl, "Městský stav v Čechách v době předbělohorské" (Ph.D. diss., Univerzita Karlova, Prague, 1951), 175.

159. Hrejsa, *Česká konfesse,* 536, n. 3, 544, n. 4; Samuel Martinius z Dražova, *Oratio de concordia ecclesiae his ultimis temporibus plurimum necessaria* (Prague: Pavel Sessius, 1617), f. B7v–C2v, C5r–C6r, D6v–D7r.

160. Tanner, *Apologia pro Societate Jesu,* 18, 28–29.

161. Josef Riss, "Život a literné působení Sixta z Ottersdorfu," *Časopis českého musea* 35 (1861): pt. 1, 82; *Sněmy české,* 4:392. See also Martinius z Dražova, *Oratio de concordia ecclesiae,* f. B4v.

162. Bruncvík, *Kšaftu Večeře Páně,* 170–171; Bruncvík, *Kázání o tom, že obrazové,* f. C4v–C5r. Bruncvík quoted Hus's alleged statement from Aeneas's *Bohemian Chronicle* as "dei et sanctorum imagines delendas"; *Kázání o tom,* f. C2r.

163. Bruncvík, *Kšaftu Večeře Páně,* 215.

164. *Ibid.,* 163–169. Matěj Kolín of Chotěřina quoted the Articles of 1524 in *Antiqua et constans confessio fidei ecclesiae Christi in regno Boiemiae et Marchianatu Moraviae, quam vulgo partem sub utraque sacramentum venerabile corporis et sanguinis dom. Jesu Christi communicantium appellant* (Prague: n.p., 1574), f. E3v–F1v. Kolín's and Bruncvík's misinterpretations are discussed in Chapter 3.

165. Samuel Martinius z Dražova, *Hussius et Lutherus, id est: collatio historica duorum fortissimorum Iesu Christi militum* (Prague: Pavel Sessius, 1618), 130–142. See also Arnošt Kraus, *Husitství v literatuře, zejména německé,* 3 vols. (Prague: Česká akademie pro vědy, slovesnost a umění, 1917–1924), 2:6.

166. Jiřík Bartolomeus, *Kázání krátké ku potěšení a napomenutí pobožným vojákům* (Hradec Králové: Martin Kleinwechter, 1619), f. B6v-B7v.

167. Zykmund Crinitus, *Spis kratičký o osobě Pána Krista* (Prague: Oldřich Valda, 1609).

168. *Confessio Bohemica, Vera Augustana in Questiones et Responsiones Resoluta, ac ante quinquennium in lingua vernacula publici iuris cum indultu Venerandi Consistorii Pragensis facta. Konfessí Česká pravá Aušpurská na otázky a odpovědi před pěti lety v jazyku českém vůbec s povolením vzácné Konsistoře Pražské vydaná* (Prague: Jan Ctibor, 1620). It also refers to the edition of 1614 of which no copy has yet been discovered; see *Knihopis českých a slovenských tisků,* no. 1597.

169. As *Ottův slovník naučný,* 24:769, characterizes the Lutheran Jan Štelcar Želetavský of Želetava.

170. Robert Kolb, "Altering the Agenda, Shifting the Strategy: The *Grundfest* of 1571 as Philippist Program for Lutheran Concord," *Sixteenth Century Journal* 30 (1999): 705–726. *Zgodovina Slovencev* (Ljubljana: Cankarjeva založba, 1979), 266, 295. Ferdinand Hrejsa refers to a local Moravian arrangement when he mentions the Formula of Concord of 1581; Hrejsa, *Česká konfesse,* 344, 351.

171. Josef Hejnic and Jan Martínek, eds., *Rukověť' humanistického básnictví v Čechách a na Moravě od konce 15. do začátku 17. století*, 5 vols. (Prague: Academia, 1966–1982), 3:270.

172. *Uvážení Kurfirstských Saských Theologův v Vitenberce na otázku zdaliby stav Říše Římskému Císaři v této nynější český válce napomáhati chtíc* . . . (N.p., 1620), f. B2r.

173. While close to historical reality, this separation of Hus from Luther need not be seen as diminishing, but actually as enhancing Hus's stature. Instead of serving as a stepping-stone to Luther (or an imperfect Luther, or a shadow Luther), the emancipated Hus becomes more of a historical figure in his own right: for the secularist a champion of liberty, and for the religiously inclined a pioneer of a tolerant *via media*.

174. William Perkins, *Anatomia conscientiae. Aneb pobožné rozbírání a vysvětlení svědomí lidského*, trans. Jan Regius (Prague: Karel Karlsperk, 1620); Perkins, *O opuštění Božím*, trans. Jiřík Oeconomus (Prague: Daniel Sedlčanský, 1610); Perkins, *Traktát trojí krátký, ku potěšení zarmoucených kajících lidí*, trans. Simeon Valecius (Prague: Matěj Pardubský, 1613); Perkins, *Traktát velmi platný a užitečný*, trans. Simeon Valecius. (Prague: Matěj Pardubský, 1616).

175. Bruncvík, *Zrcadlo Kacířství*, f. E2v; Bruncvík, *Kšaftu Večeře Páně*, 113, 115, 122.

176. Hrejsa, *Česká konfesse*, 521–522.

177. Glücklich, "Koncept Majestátu a vznik *Porovnání*," 121; see also Pekař, *Dějiny československé*, 97.

178. "[P]řed ním . . . , jed ten z oust vylil: kterýžto on do sebe přijav, hned nazejtří . . . v Velké Koleji mezi Mistry a Bakaláři tím se chlubil, že by v Zákoně Božím Cestu života nalezl. A tak navyklé pod Jednou spůsobou přijímání za bludné položil, přijímání pak pod Obojí tak zvýšil a schválil, jakoby jináč přijímající spasení býti nemohli." Petr Linteo of Pilzenburgk, *Krátká správa o přijímání velebné svátosti pod jednau a dvojí spůsobau* (Prague: Kargezius, 1613), 14–15.

179. "[V] grammatyce ovšem, ale ne v Písmech zběhlého" (Peter of Dresden); *ibid.*, 14. "[J]ako člověkem smělým a logikářem odvážlivým" (Jakoubek); *ibid.*, 15.

180. "Z čehož však Mistr Jan Hus v Konstancy v vězení, když mu to bylo oznámeno, veliký měl zármutek, a jím to vše ne k rozumu a pobožnosti, ale k všetečnosti, kterak by ho o jeho hrdlo připraviti měla, přičetl." *Ibid.*, 17 (see also 68).

181. "Ti byli přijímání pod obojí začátkové, ti satanášového v tom obmyslu a tyranství nástrojové a náhončí." *Ibid.*, 17.

182. *Ibid.*, 29–30, 38.

183. *Ibid.*, 44–48, 54, 68.

184. *Druhá Apologie stavův království českého*, 127–130.

185. Klement Borový, *Martin Medek, Arcibiskup pražský* (Prague: Dědictví sv Prokopa, 1877), 73–74.

186. Winter, *Život církevní v Čechách*, 1:272.

187. Hrejsa, *Česká konfesse*, 534–535.

188. Josef Jireček, *Rukověť k dějinám literatury české do konce XVIII. věku*, 2 vols. (Prague: Tempský, 1875–1876), 1:453.

189. Markus, "Stavovské apologie z roku 1618," 207; Tanner, *Apologia pro Societate Jesu*, 18 (see also 53: "[Q]uamplurima ex Catholicae Ecclesiae fide et instituto defenderunt").

190. For a substantial analysis of English perceptions of the Bohemian reformation,

see also Rene Wellek, "Bohemia in Early English Literature," *Slavonic and East European Review* 21 (1943): 114–146.

191. John Jewel, Bishop of Salisbury, *Apologia, to jest: Dostatečná Obrana Víry a Náboženství Cýrkví Englických* (Prague: Danyel Karel z Karlspergka, 1619), translation of John Jewel, Bishop of Salisbury, *An Apologie, or Answer in Defense of the Church of England* (London: Reginalde Wolfe, 1562; reprint, New York: De Capo Press, 1972).

192. Bruncvík, *Kšaftu Večeře Páně*, 113. He refers to Laurentius Humfredus, *Contra Edmundi Campiani rationes*, evidently citing from Laurence Humphrey, *Iesuitismi*, 2 vols. (London: Henricus Middletonus, 1582–1584). Humphrey's Protestant leanings made him clash with such conservatives in the English Church as Archbishop Parker and John Jewel, particularly over the highly symbolic and emotionally charged issue of liturgical vestments. See *DNB*, 10:246; Spurr, *English Puritanism*, 52.

193. The Lollard inventory included figures familiar from the early stages of the Bohemian Reformation, such as Ricardus With, Joannes Oldecastel, and Petrus Payne; Bruncvík, *Kšaftu Večeře Páně*, 115. See also *ibid.*, 113 (reference to Foxe), and 122 (reference to Humphrey).

194. Bruncvík, *Zrcadlo Kacířství*, f. A8r,C2r, D4v, D6v.

195. See Chapter 10.

196. While Laurence Humphrey criticized Campion in *Iesuitismi*, William Whitaker published his *Ad decem rationes Edmundi Campiani Jesuite, quibus fretus certamen Anglicanae ecclesiae ministris obtulit in causa fidei, responsio* (London: Vautrollerius, 1581). On this controversy, see also Thomas M. McCoog, "'Playing the Champion': The Role of Disputation in the Jesuit Mission," in *Reckoned Expense: Edmund Campion and the Early English Jesuits*, ed. Thomas M. McCoog (Woodbridge, UK: Boydell Press, 1996), 133–134. The Czech translation of Campion's *Decem ratioones* appeared in two editions: one in Prague (1601), another in Olomouc (1602); see Chapter 10, n. 20 and n. 23.

197. He relied on the following of Sutcliffe's works: *De Catholica, Orthodoxa, et vera Christi Ecclesia* (London: Reg. Typog., 1592); *De Monachis, eorum Institutis et Moribus* (London: per E. Bolifantum, 1600), and *De Missa Papistica, variisque Synagogae Rom. Circa Eucharistiae Sacramentum Erroribus et Coruptelis* (London: A. Islip, 1603). See Bruncvík, *Zrcadlo Kacířství*, f. A7v, B5v, B7v. Sutcliffe subsequently acted as a sponsor of the New England colonies; *DNB*, 19:176. In *Zrcadlo Kacířství*, Bruncvík has 49 references to Sutcliffe, 41 to Morton, 35 to Whitaker, and 17 to Humphrey.

198. Thomas Morton, *Apologiae Catholicae, in qua paradoxa, haereses, blasphemiae, scelera, quae Jesuitae et Pontificii alii Protestantibus impingunt, fere omnia, ex ipsorum Pontificiorum testimoniis apertis diluuntur*, 2 vols. (London: J. Norton, 1606). *DNB*, 13: 1061, cites the opinion of Morton as "belonging to that class of episcopal divines who differed in nothing considerable from the rest of the reformed churches except in church government." On the Calvinist links of Bishop Morton, see also Alexandra Walsham, "*Vox Piscis; or the Book-Fish:* Providence and the Uses of the Reformation Past in Caroline Cambridge," *English Historical Review* 114 (1999): 592.

199. Bruncvík, *Zrcadlo Kacířství*, f. B3v–B4r, C5r. He referred to William Gifford's *Calvino-Turcismus. Id est Calvinisticae perfidiae cum Mahumetana Collatio* (Antwerp: In aedibus Petri Belleri, 1597 and 1603), and to Matthew Sutcliffe's *De Turcopapismo, hoc est De Turcarum et Papistarum adversus Christi ecclesiam et fidem Conjuratione, eorumque in fidem et moribus consensione et similitudine* (London: G. Bishop, R. Newberie, & R. Barker, 1599 and 1604).

200. Bruncvík, *Zrcadlo Kacířství*, f. C4r.

201. See n. 173 above concerning the translations. On Regius in England, see Jireček, "Literatura exulantův českých," 217–219; Jireček, *Rukověť k dějinám literatury české*, 2:163; Bruncvík, *Zrcadlo Kacířství*, f. C8r, and also E1r, referring to William Perkins, *Problema de Romanae fidei ementito catholicismo* (Cambridge: Ioann Legat, 1604).

202. Dykastus, *Postylla: nebo Kázání krátká na evangelia svatá*, 1: 25; Abraham Scultetus, *Vysvětlení Žalmu XX v Valdsaxu* (Prague: Daniel Karel z Karlsperkga, 1619), f. E1r, E2r.

203. Concerning such misjudgments, see Chapter 1.

204. Gustav Kawerau, *Hieronymus Emser: Ein Lebensbild aus der Reformationsgeschichte* (Halle: Verein für Reformationsgeschichte, 1898), 41.

205. Edward Surtz, *The Works and Days of John Fisher: An Introduction to the Position of St. John Fischer (1469–1535), Bishop of Rochester, in the English Renaissance and Reformation* (Cambridge, Mass.: Harvard University Press, 1967), 8–9; Ulrichus Velenus [Oldřich Velenský of Mnichov?], *In hoc libello grauissimis, certissimisque, & in sacra scriptura fundatis rationibus uarije probatur, Apostolarum Petrum Romae non uenisse, neque illicit passum, proinde satis friuole, & temere Romanus Pontifex se Petri successorem inactat, & nominat* (Basel: n.p., 1520). There is also a German translation that was probably published in Augsburg S. Otmar in 1521, under the title *In disem Büchlin wirt in mancherlay tapffern bestendigen und in der Scrifft gegründeten Ursachen klärlich bewert, das der hailig Apostel Petrus gen Rom nicht komen noch alda den Tod gelitten* . . . See also A. J. Lamping, *Ulrichus Velenus (Oldřich Velenský) and his Treatise against the Papacy* (Leiden: Brill, 1976), 152–157.

206. Rudolf Říčan, "Tschechische Übersetzungen von Luthers Schriften bis zum Schmalkaldischen Krieg," *Vierhundertfünfzig Jahre lutherische Reformation, 1517–1967: Festschrift für Franz Lau zum 50. Geburtstag* (Göttingen: Vanderhoeck and Ruprecht, 1967), 282–283.

207. *Institutio Christianae religionis, in quatuor libros digesta, Johanne Calvino auctore, in Bohemicam vero Lingvam a Georgio Streyzio versa, et in communem usum omnium latissimae Slavonicae linguae populorum a Johanne Opsimathe edita* (Amberg: Upper Palatinate, 1615). See also E. P. Tyrrel and J. S. G. Simmons, "Slavonic Books Before 1700 in Cambridge Libraries," *Transactions of Cambridge Bibliographic Society* 3 (1963): 383, 394 (the copy is deposited in the Sidney Sussex College, Cambridge). See also E. Urbánková, "Několik poznámek k českému vydání Kalvínovy Institucae," *Literární archiv: Sborník Památníku národního písemnictví* 1 (1996), 237ff.; William B. Patterson, *King James VI and I and the Reunion of Christendom* (Cambridge: Cambridge University Press, 1997), 125.

208. Anthony Milton, *Catholic and Reformed: The Roman and Protestant Churches in English Protestant Thought, 1600–1640* (Cambridge and New York: Cambridge University Press, 1995), 314, see also 89, 293, 301, 303, 305–306. The relatively insular character of Anglicanism—contrasted with the international orientation of Puritanism—also may partly explain the problem of obtaining accurate information about mainline Utraquism. On the tension between internationalism and localism in English religious history of the early modern period, see Tony Claydon and Ian McBride, eds., *Protestantism and National Identity: Britain and Ireland, c. 1650-c.1850* (Cambridge and New York: Cambridge University Press, 1998), 12–15. Moreover, Bohemia's religious affairs

had to compete for English attention in the early seventeenth century with other parts of Europe such as Poland; Michal J. Rozbicki, "Between East-Central Europe and Britain: Reformation and Science as Vehicles of Intellectual Communication in the Mid-Seventeenth Century," *East European Quarterly* 30 (1997): 401–419.

209. See Chapters 5 and 10.

210. Pavel Bydžovský, *Historiae aliquot Anglorum martyrum, quibus Deus suam ecclesiam exornare sicut syderibus coelum dignatus est* (Prague: J. Cantor, 1554) is devoted to the martyrdom of Fisher and More; Barnes, *Kronyky. A životů sepsání nejvrchnějších Biskupů Římských jináč Papežů* (Nuremberg: Woldřich Nejber and Jan Montán, 1565), f. 195(v).

211. Brendan Bradshaw, "The Controversial Sir Thomas More," *Journal of Ecclesiastical History* 36 (1985): 563–564, and the works he cites, including Brian Gogan, *The Common Corps of Christendom: Ecclesiological Themes in the Writings of Sir Thomas More* (Leiden: Brill, 1982), and Surtz, *The Works and Days of John Fisher*.

212. *Sněmy české*, 9:682–683.

213. The italics are Montagu's; Richard Montagu, *A Gagg for the New Gospell? No, a New Gagg for an Old Goose* (London: T. Snodham, 1624), f. *2v. See also Spurr, *English Puritanism*, 81.

214. Peter Lake and Michael Questier, "Puritans, Papists, and the 'Public Sphere' in Early Modern England: The Edmund Campion Affair in Context," *Journal of Modern History* 72 (2000): 624–625.

215. Diarmaid MacCulloch, *The Later Reformation in England, 1547–1603* (New York: St. Martin's Press, 1990), 99.

216. For a recent treatment of the uprising, see, for instance, Frank Müller, *Kursachsen und der Böhmische Aufstand* (Munster: Aschendorff, 1997); and Inge Auerbach, "The Bohemian Opposition, Poland-Lithuania and the Outbreak of the Thirty Years War," in *Crown, Church and Estates: Central European Politics in the Sixteenth and Seventeenth Centuries,* ed. R. J. W. Evans and T. V. Thomas (New York: St. Martin's Press), 1991, 196–225. For earlier treatments, see Ernst Denis, *Fin de l'indépendance bohême*, 2d ed., 2 vols. (Paris: Librairie Leroux, 1930); Josef Pekař, *Bílá Hora: Její příčiny a následky* (Prague: Vesmír, 1921); Kamil Krofta, "České povstání. Bitva na Bílé Hoře," in Krofta, *Bílá Hora: Kurs šestipřednáškový* (Prague: J. Otto, 1914), 141–190; Anton Gindely, *Dějiny českého povstání*, 4 vols. (Prague: Tempský, 1870–1880), partially trans. as Anton Gindely, *History of the Thirty Years' War,* 2 vols. (New York: G. P. Putnam's Sons, 1884).

217. Kneidl, *Městský stav v Čechách v době předbělohorské,* 176; Mikuláš Dačický z Heslova, *Paměti,* ed. Antonín Rezek, 2 vols. (Prague: Matice česká, 1878–1880), 1:245.

218. Markus, "Stavovské apologie z roku 1618," 205; *Euangelische Erklerung auff die Böhaimische Apologia,* f. A3r, C1v.

219. Jaroslav Purš and Miroslav Kropilák, eds., *Přehled dějin Československa,* 2 vols. (Prague: Academia, 1980–1982), 2:95–96, 100.

220. Kalivoda, *Husitská epocha a J. A. Komenský,* 37–38.

221. Josef Janáček, "České stavovské povstání, 1618–1620: Otázky a problémy," *Folia Historica Bohemica* 8 (1985): 15–16; Jaroslav Pánek, "Republikánské tendence ve stavovských programech doby předbělohorské," *Folia Historica Bohemica* 8 (1985): 49; Kalivoda, *Husitská epocha a J. A. Komenský,* 40.

222. Miloš Pojar, *Jindřich Matyáš Thurn: Muž činu* (Prague: Ivo Železný, 1998), 31.

223. *Euangelische Erklerung auff die Böhaimische Apologia,* f. A2r.
224. Bartolomeus, *Kázání krátké ku potěšení a napomenutí pobožným vojákům,* f. A2r–A2v, C3v.
225. *Ibid.,* f. A7v, B2r.
226. Janáček, "České stavovské povstání," 20–26, 30–32. Concerning military leadership, see František Hrubý, "Nové příspěvky k historii bitvy na Bílé hoře," *Časopis českého musea* 27 (1922): 277–288.
227. For instance, František. J. Kroiher, "Nevlastenectví českých stavů nekatolických v době předbělohorské," *Sborník historického kroužku* Sešit 3 (1894), especially 69; Jaroslav Pánek, "Stavovství v předbělohorské době," *Folia Historica Bohemica* 6 (1984): 172.
228. Purš and Kropilák, *Přehled dějin Československa,* 2:104, 106; Pánek, "Republikánské tendence," 49.
229. Vincenc Kramář, *Zpustošení chrámu svatého Víta v roce 1619,* ed. Michal Šroněk (Prague: Artefactum, 1998), 41.
230. The Dutch provided a subsidy of 50,000 guilders per month, helped to raise loans for Bohemia in Amsterdam, and sent troops. About one-eighth of the army facing the emperor at the battle of the White Mountain was Dutch or paid by the United Provinces; see Jonathan Israel, *The Dutch Republic: Its Rise, Greatness, and Fall, 1477–1806* (Oxford: Clarendon Press, 1995), 469.
231. Hrejsa, *Česká konfesse,* 536–537; Tischer, *Dopisy konsistoře podobojí z let 1610–1619,* 447.
232. Prokeš, *Protokol vyšlé korespondence,* 20–21, 36 (no. 180), 76 (no. 890); Jan Fiala, *Hrozné doby protireformace* (Heršpice: Eman, 1997), 68–69; Robert Kalivoda, "Husitství a jeho vyústění v době předbělohorské a bělohorské," *Studia comeniana et historica* 13 (1983): 18. A decree by the directors in June 1618 requested the towns of Prague to stop singing songs disparaging the sub una; Prokeš, *Protokol vyšlé korespondence,* 32 (no. 109).

Chapter 12

1. For a recent commentary, see Hans-Wolfgang Bergerhausen, "Die 'Verneuerte Landesordnung' in Böhmen 1627: ein Grunddokument des habsburgischen Absolutismus," *Historische Zeitschrift* 272 (2001): 331–347, 351.
2. R. Po-Chia Hsia, *The World of Catholic Renewal, 1540–1770* (Cambridge and New York: Cambridge University Press, 1998), 76; Jaroslav Kadlec, *Přehled českých církevních dějin,* 2 vols. (Prague: Zvon, 1991), 2:78–79.
3. Václav Líva, "Studie o Praze pobělohorské," *Sborník příspěvků k dějinám hl. města Prahy,* 6 (1930): 359–362; Robert A. Kann and Zdeněk V. David, *The Peoples of the Eastern Habsburg Lands, 1526–1918,* History of East Central Europe, 6 (Seattle: University of Washington Press, 1984), 103–107; Charles Ingrao, *The Habsburg Monarchy, 1618–1815* (Cambridge and New York: Cambridge University Press, 1994), 34–38; Josef Petráň and Lydia Petráňová, "The White Mountain as a Symbol in Modern Czech History," in *Bohemia in History,* ed. Mikuláš Teich (Cambridge and New York: Cambridge University Press, 1998), 143–148.
4. Anton Gindely, *Dějiny českého povstání,* 4 vols. (Prague: Tempský, 1880); Antonín Rezek, *Děje Čech a Moravy za Ferdinanda III až do konce třicetileté války, 1637–1648* (Prague: Kober, 1890); Tomáš Bílek, *Dějiny konfiskací v Čechách po roku 1618,*

2 vols. (Prague: Řivnáč, 1882–1883); Ernest Denis, *La Bohême depuis la Montagne-Blanche*, 2 vols. (Paris: Librairie Leroux, 1903), 1:1–241; Líva, "Studie o Praze pobělohorské," 357–415, 7 (1933): 1–120, 9 (1935): 1–439; Ivana Čornejová, *Tovaryšstvo Ježíšovo: Jezuité v Čechách* (Prague: Mladá fronta, 1995); Jiří Bílý, *Jezuita Antonín Koniáš: Osobnost a doba* (Praha: Vyšehrad, 1996); Jan Fiala, *Hrozné doby protireformace* (Heršpice: Eman, 1997).

5. Ferdinand Hrejsa, *Česká konfesse: Její vznik, podstata a dějiny* (Prague: Česká akademie pro vědy, slovesnost a umění, 1912), 573–639; Eduard Winter, *Die tschechische und slowakische Emigration in Deutschland im 17. und 18. Jahrhundert* (Berlin: Akademie-Verlag, 1955); Rudolf Říčan, *The History of the Unity of Brethren: A Protestant Hussite Church in Bohemia and Moravia,* trans. C. Daniel Crews (Bethlehem, Pa.: Moravian Church in America, 1992), 345–389; Lenka Bobková, *Exulanti z Prahy a severozápadních Čech v Pirně v letech 1621–1639* (Prague: Scriptorium, 1999).

6. On the prevalence of Utraquists under kings Rudolf II and Matthias in the population of Bohemia, see Chapters 8 and 11.

7. The Utraquists regarded themselves, and were viewed under the Compactata, as an integral part of the historical Western Patriarchate of Rome, and thus as entitled to the appellation of not just the Catholic Church, but an outright Roman Catholic Church. See Chapters 9 and 10.

8. On the liberal features of Utraquism, see, for instance, Thomas A. Fudge, "The Problem of Religious Liberty in Early Modern Bohemia," *Communio Viatorum* 38 (1996): 64–87; Ernest Denis, *Fin de l'indépendance bohême,* 2d ed., 2 vols. (Paris: Librairie Leroux, 1930), 2:208–209.

9. Hrejsa, *Česká konfesse,* 572.

10. Josef Pekař, "Bílá Hora: její příčiny a následky," *Postavy a problémy českých dějin,* ed. František Kutnar (Prague: Vyšehrad, 1990), 183. For the Jesuits' praise of Utraquism in 1618, see Adam Tanner, *Apologia pro Societate Jesu ex Boemiae Regno ab eiusdem regni statibus religionis sub utraque, publico decreto immerito proscripta. Anno M.DC.XVIII. die VIIII Junij* (Vienna: Wolfgang Schump, 1618), 53. See also Zikmund Winter, *Život církevní v Čechách,* 2 vols. (Prague: Česká akademie pro vědy, slovesnost a umění, 1895), 1:275.

11. Anton Gindely, *Dějiny českého povstání,* 4 vols. (Prague: Tempský, 1880), 4:33. On "salami tactics," see Chapter 10, n. 27.

12. Gindely, *Dějiny českého povstání,* 4:433.

13. Václav V. Tomek, "O církevní správě strany pod obojí v Čechách, od r. 1415 až 1622," *Časopis českého musea* 22 (1848): 463. See also Hrejsa, *Česká konfesse,* 574–5; Anton Frind, "Urkunden über die Bewilligung des Laienkelches in Böhmen unter Kaiser Ferdinand I," *Česká společnost nauk. Abhandlungen* 6, no. 6 (1873): 42–43; Tomáš Bílek, *Reformace katolická; neboli Obnovení náboženství katolického v království českém po bitvě na Bílé Hoře* (Prague: F. Bačkovský, 1892), 15–16; Kamil Krofta, *Bílá Hora: Kurs šestipřednáškový* (Prague: J. Otto, 1914), 222.

14. See, for instance, Janusz Tazbir, "The Fate of Polish Protestantism in the Seventeenth Century," in *A Republic of Nobles: Studies in Polish History to 1864,* ed. J. K. Fedorowicz (Cambridge: Cambridge University Press, 1982), 198–217; Jerzy Kloczowski, *A History of Polish Christianity* (Cambridge and New York: Cambridge University Press, 2000), 162–163. On Ferdinand II's earlier performance in Inner Austria, see Jaroslav Pánek, "Nástup rekatolizace ve střední Evropě," in *Rekatolizace v českých*

zemích., Sborník příspěvků z konference v Jičíně, 10. září 1993, ed. Jindřich Francek (Pardubice: Městský úřad Jičín, 1995), 6-7; Regina Pörtner, *The Counter-Reformation in Central Europe: Styria, 1580–1630* (Oxford: Clarendon Press, 2001), 108–133.

15. Concerning the influence of Spanish religiosity and political style on the Austrian Habsburgs, see Francis Dvornik, *The Slavs in European History and Civilization* (New Brunswick, N.J.: Rutgers University Press, 1962), 450–452; Robert Bireley, *Religion and Politics in the Age of the Counterreformation: Emperor Ferdinand II, William Lamormaini, S.J., and the Formation of the Imperial Policy* (Chapel Hill: University of North Carolina Press, 1981), 5–6.

16. Bodo Nischan, *Prince, People, and Confession: The Second Reformation in Brandenburg* (Philadelphia: University of Pennsylvania Press, 1994), especially 111–131.

17. On the attitude of the English/British government toward domestic Roman Catholicism in the seventeenth and eighteenth centuries, see articles by John Bossy and Hugh Trevor-Roper in Ole P. Grell, Jonathan I. Israel, and Nicholas Tyacke, eds. *From Persecution to Toleration: The Glorious Revolution and Religion in England* (Oxford: Clarendon Press, 1991), 369–408. Although subject to considerable discomfort, almost half the population of Dutch Netherlands was able to retain the Roman faith in the seventeenth century; see Hsia, *The World of Catholic Renewal*, 84–85.

18. Bireley, *Religion and Politics in the Age of the Counterreformation*, 38–41; Eduard Winter, *Der Josefinismus: die Geschichte des österreichischen Reformkatholizismus, 1740–1848* (Berlin: Rütten & Loening, 1962), 10–13.

19. See Chapter 11.

20. In fact, Richard Marius recently suggested that the Catholics of the Holy Roman Empire viewed the Taborites' terror with an aversion comparable to the present-day attitude to the Nazi conduct of the Holocaust; see Marius, *Martin Luther: The Christian Between God and Death* (Cambridge, Mass.: Harvard University Press, 1999), 176.

21. Jaroslav Pelikan, Jr., "Luther's Attitude Toward John Hus," *Concordia Theological Monthly* 19 (1948): 747–763.

22. Pekař, "Bílá Hora: její příčiny a následky," 182–183. See also Josef Hanuš, *O pobělohorské protireformaci: Úvodem k českému obrození*, Universita Komenského. Bratislava, Filosofická fakulta, Sborník, 4, n. 39 (Bratislava: Universita Komenského, 1926), 16; Gindely, *Dějiny českého povstání*, 4:431.

23. Antonius Bruodinus, *Propugnaculum catholicae veritatis* (Prague: Charles and Ferdinand University Press, 1669), cited in Stanislav Sousedík, *Filosofie v českých zemích mezi středověkem a osvícenstvím* (Prague: Vyšehrad, 1997), 142, 220.

24. Pravoslav Kneidl, "Městský stav v Čechách v době předbělohorské" (Ph.D. diss., Univerzita Karlova, Prague, 1951), 177.

25. Josef Polišenský and Frederick Snider, "Změny ve složení české šlechty v 16. a 17. století," *Československý časopis historický* 20 (1972): 520, 525.

26. Hrejsa, *Česká konfesse*, 535; František Tischer, ed., *Dopisy konsistoře podobojí z let 1610–1619* (Prague: Historický spolek, 1917–1925), x. See also Chapter 11.

27. Gindely, *Dějiny českého povstání*, 4:433.

28. *Ibid.*; Denis, *La Bohême depuis la Montagne-Blanche*, 1:39.

29. Líva, "Studie o Praze pobělohorské," 7 (1933): 18.

30. Gindely, *Dějiny českého povstání*, 4:435.

31. Tomáš Bílek, *Dějiny řádu tovaryšstva Ježíšova a působení jeho vůbec a v zemích království českého zvláště* (Prague: F. Bačkovský, 1896), 491.

32. Tomek, "O církevní správě strany pod obojí v Čechách," 463.

33. Líva, "Studie o Praze pobělohorské," 7 (1933): 19.
34. Kadlec, *Přehled českých církevních dějin,* 2:74; Gindely, *Dějiny českého povstání,* 4:435.
35. Líva, "Studie o Praze pobělohorské," 7 (1933): 22–23; Tomek, "O církevní správě strany pod obojí v Čechách," 463.
36. Alois Kroess, *Geschichte der Böhmischen Provinz der Gesellschaft Jesu,* 2 vols. in 3 (Vienna: Mayer, 1910–1938), 2:166.
37. Líva, "Studie o Praze pobělohorské," 7 (1933): 23, 25.
38. *Ibid.,* 24.
39. Josef Jireček, *Rukověť k dějinám literatury české do konce XVIII. věku,* 2 vols. (Prague: Tempský, 1875), 1:400; Josef Riss, "Jan Ctibor Kotva z Freyfeldu," *Časopis českého musea* 54 (1880): 472.
40. Josef F. Jungmann, *Historie literatury české,* 2d ed. (Prague: Řivnáč, 1849), 239; Eduard Winter, *Tausend Jahre Geisteskampf im Sudetenraum* (Munich: Aufstieg-Verlag, 1938), 204.
41. On the Utraquist taste in religious decor, see Jan Chlíbec, "K vývoji názorů Jana Rokycany na umělecké dílo," *Husitský Tábor* 8 (1985): 54–56; Milena Bartlová, "The Utraquist Church and Visual Arts before Luther," in *The Bohemian Reformation and Religious Practice,* vol. 4: Papers from the IV International Symposium on Bohemian Reformation and Religious Practice, under the auspices of the Philosophical Institute of the Academy of Sciences of the Czech Republic, held at Vila Lanna, Prague, 26-28 June 2000, ed. Zdeněk V. David and David R. Holeton (Prague: Academy of Sciences of the Czech Republic, Main Library, 2002), 215-223.
42. David Smart, "View from a Prague Window: Anti-Utraquism and Baroque Architecture in Prague," *Kosmas: Czechoslovak and Central European Journal* 12, no. 2 (1997): 55–80.
43. Zdeněk Rotrekl, *Barokní fenomén v součastnosti* (Prague: Trost, 1995), 113–115.
44. Zuzana Všetečková, "Iconography of the Mural Paintings in St. James's Church of Kutná Hora," in *The Bohemian Reformation and Religious Practice,* vol. 3: Papers from the XIXth World Congress of the Czechoslovak Society of Arts and Sciences, Bratislava 1998, ed. Zdeněk V. David and David R. Holeton (Prague: Academy of Sciences of the Czech Republic, Main Library, 2000), 138.
45. Čornejová, *Tovaryšstvo Ježíšovo,* 110.
46. Smart, "View from a Prague Window," 57–58.
47. Kašpar Arsenius z Radbuzy, *Pobožná knížka o blahoslavené Panně Marii* (Prague: Pavel Sessius, 1629), f. A4v.
48. *Ibid.,* f. H4r–H5r. In this light, the removal of the Marian Column at the end of the Habsburg era in 1918 may be viewed as an act of disrespect not for the Virgin, but for the parody of her that the Bohemian Counter-Reformation had promoted. In addition, it may be seen as a long-delayed response to the removal of the chalice from the Týn Church and the desecration of the remains of Archbishop Rokycana and Bishop Sancturien. Winter, *Tausend Jahre Geisteskampf im Sudetenraum,* 204.
49. Dominic had allegedly found the image with its eyes punched out at the castle of Strakonice, and felt that the battle was fought, in part, to vindicate the desecrated icon. Jan Herain, "Z událostí po bitvě," in *Na Bílé Hoře,* ed. Josef Teige (Prague: Černý, 1911), 84.
50. Francesco Gui, *I gesuiti e la rivoluzione boema: alle origini della guerra dei trent'anni,* Studi e ricerche storiche, 137 (Milano: F. Angeli, 1989), 411–412.

51. Such is the judicious understanding of the rite, for instance, in the Anglican communion. See Howard Harper, *The Episcopalian's Dictionary* (New York: Seabury Press, 1974), 49–50.

52. Fiala, *Hrozné doby protireformace*, 97–98.

53. Bílek, *Reformace katolická*, 6.

54. Bílek, *Dějiny řádu tovaryšstva Ježíšova*, 480.

55. Klaus Jaitner, ed., *Die Hauptinstruktionen Gregors XV. Für die Nuntien und Gesandten an den europäischen Fürstenhöfen, 1621–1623*, 2 vols. (Tübingen: Niemeyer, 1997), 2:621–622.

56. Líva, "Studie o Praze pobělohorské," 7 (1933): 10, n. 37 and n. 40.

57. As required of Edmund Campion before admission to the college at Douay in 1571, see *DNB*, 3:851.

58. Fiala, *Hrozné doby protireformace*, 92. Looking at the procedure from the opposite shore, this is reminiscent of the simple admission of converts from sub una by the Utraquists. In comparison, more elaborate procedures were required by the Utraquists for the reception of members of the Unity of Brethren, such as a profession of belief in the veneration of saints. See Chlíbec, "K vývoji názorů Jana Rokycany na umělecké dílo," 54; Pavel Bydžovský, *Odvolání jednoho Bratra z Roty Pikhartské*, 2d ed. (Prague: Jan Jiřínský, 1588), available in photocopy at the National Library in Prague, sign. f Zc 54 (first edition, Prague: Jan Kantor, 1559, no copy extant).

59. For instance, Líva, "Studie o Praze pobělohorské," 7 (1933): 18.

60. Looking at the process from another side, it may be compared to the forcible reunion of the Uniates of Belarus with the Eastern Orthodoxy in 1839 and 1875. See Theodore R. Weeks, "Religion and Russification: Russian Language in the Catholic Churches of the 'Northwest Provinces' after 1863," *Kritika* 2 (2001): 93.

61. Líva, "Studie o Praze pobělohorské," 7 (1933): 27–28.

62. Pavel Balcárek, "Z korespondence Carla Caraffy, nuncia na císařském dvoře v letech 1621–1628," in *Facta probant homines: Sborník příspěvků k životnímu jubileu prof. dr. Zdeňky Hledíkové*, ed. Ivan Hlaváček and Jan Hrdina (Prague: Scriptorium, 1998), 38. As noted earlier, all Lutheran confessions, in general, rejected the saints' role as mediators of redemption and prohibited prayers to saints. See Erwin L. Lueker, ed., *Lutheran Cyclopedia* (St. Louis: Concordia, 1975), 692.

63. Winter, *Tausend Jahre Geisteskampf im Sudetenraum*, 203.

64. On the Lutheran loathing of Locika, see Winter, *Život církevní v Čechách*, 1:272; Hrejsa, *Česká konfesse*, 537, n.4; Tischer, *Dopisy konsistoře podobojí z let 1610–1619*, 447.

65. Tomek, "O církevní správě strany pod obojí v Čechách," 463. See also Hrejsa, *Česká konfesse*, 574–575; Anton Gindely, *Geschichte der Gegenreformation in Böhmen*, ed. Theodor Tupetz (Leipzig: Duncker und Humblot, 1894), 107–111; Bílek, *Reformace katolická*, 16–17.

66. Against Hrejsa's opinion (in Hrejsa, *Česká konfesse*, 575), Líva shows that the two groups were not identical, in Líva, "Studie o Praze pobělohorské," 7 (1933): 9, 11 n. 42.

67. Antonín Podlaha, ed., *Dopisy Reformační komise v Čechách z let 1627–1692* (Prague: Nákl. vlastní, 1908), 5–6.

68. Kadlec, *Přehled českých církevních dějin*, 2:83–84.

69. Bobková, *Exulanti z Prahy*, 6–131.

70. *Kázání o posledním soudu* (N.p., [1618?]), and *O užitcích velikých z útrpného*

umučení Syna Božího (N.p., 1618). The wholesale destruction of Utraquist literature during the Counter-Reformation has probably deprived us of ever knowing more about Locika's books. See *Knihopis českých a slovenských tisků,* 2 vols., vol. 2 in 9 parts (Prague: Nakladatelství Československé akademie věd, 1925–1967), 2: pt. 4 (1948), 316, nos. 4923 and 4924.

71. Líva, "Studie o Praze pobělohorské," 7 (1933): 23.
72. Tischer, *Dopisy konsistoře podobojí,* 447.
73. Hrejsa, *Česká konfesse,* 580–581; Tischer, *Dopisy konsistoře podobojí,* 447–448; Winter, *Tausend Jahre Geisteskampf,* 203; Kroess, *Geschichte der Böhmischen Provinz der Gesellschaft Jesu,* 2:167.
74. This was asserted by Pavel Skála ze Zhoře; see Skála ze Zhoře, *Historie česká od r. 1602 do r. 1623,* 5 vols., ed. Karel Tieftrunk (Prague: Kober, 1865–1870), 5:213. See also Gindely, *Dějiny českého povstání,* 4:443; Bílý, *Jezuita Antonín Koniáš,* 69.
75. On Vatican efforts to come to grips with the issues of the Bohemian Reformation in the 1990s, see František Holeček, "The Problems of the Person, the Life and the Work of Jan Hus: The Significance and the Task of a Commission of the Czech Bishops' Conference," in Zdeněk V. David and David R. Holeton, eds., in *The Bohemian Reformation and Religious Practice,* vol. 2: Papers from the XVIIIth World Congress of the Czechoslovak Society of Arts and Sciences, Brno 1996 (Prague: Academy of Sciences of the Czech Republic, Main Library, 1998), 39–47.
76. Hrejsa, *Česká konfesse,* 536–537, n. 2, n. 4; Winter, *Život církevní v Čechách,* 1:272; Tischer, *Dopisy konsistoře podobojí,* 446.
77. Hrejsa, *Česká konfesse,* 537, n.4; Tischer, *Dopisy konsistoře podobojí z let 1610–1619,* 447.
78. Gindely, *Dějiny českého povstání,* 4:444–445.
79. Winter, *Tausend Jahre Geisteskampf,* 203–204.
80. Apprenticeship to an experienced priest was a common way of educating candidates for priesthood in sixteenth-century Europe; see Lewis W. Spitz, *The Protestant Reformation, 1517–1559* (New York: Harper and Row, 1985), 51.
81. J. Ježek, "Vatikánská zpráva o reformaci a protireformaci v Čechách a zemích s nimi spojených za Ferdinanda II," *Sborník historického kroužku* 8 (1899): pt. 2, 6.
82. Líva, "Studie o Praze pobělohorské," 7 (1933): 22. Needless to say, the local population resented the outsiders. Complaints about foreign priests and monks in the Roman Church could be heard frequently in Bohemia since the late sixteenth century, not only from the Utraquists, but also from the adherents of Rome; see, for instance, *Sněmy české od léta 1526 až po naši dobu,* 15 vols. (Prague: Zemský výbor, 1877–1941), 7:439–440.
83. *Dopisy Reformační komisse v Čechách,* 138–140; Václav Líva, "Jan Arnošt Platejs z Platenštejna: Příspěvek k dějinám pobělohorské protireformace," *Časopis Matice moravské* 54 (1930): 322–327.
84. Podlaha, *Dopisy Reformační komisse v Čechách,* 194; Fiala, *Hrozné doby protireformace,* 97.
85. Zdeněk Jan Medek, *Na slunce a do mrazu: První čas josefinské náboženské tolerance v Čechách a na Moravě* (Prague: Kalich, 1982), 23–24.
86. According to Caraffa, the acts of resistance in 1625 included the murder of the Counter-Reformation activists, the noble pair Ota Jindřich of Vartenberk and his wife, and a large-scale uprising in Kutná Hora; see Balcárek, "Z korespondence Carla Caraffy," 39.

87. *Dopisy Reformační komisse*, 6.
88. Hrejsa, *Česká konfesse*, 591, n. 1. See also Antonín Rezek, *Dějiny saského vpádu do Čech a návrat emigrace* (Prague: I. L. Kober, 1889), 121–135.
89. Jan Amos Komenský (Johann Amos Comenius), *The History of the Bohemian Persecution* (London: By A.A. for Iohn Walker, 1650), 288.
90. Komenský, *The History of the Bohemian Persecution*, 290. On the forcible Counter-Reformation, for instance, Josef Hanzal, "Rekatolizace v pobělohorských městech," *Česká města v 16.—18. století: Sborník příspěvků z konference v Pardubicích 14. a 15. listopadu 1990*, ed. Jaroslav Pánek (Prague: Historický ústav, 1991), 197–202.
91. *Dopisy Reformační komisse v Čechách*, 198–199.
92. Milan Skřivánek, "K náboženským dějinám východočeského města v 15. až 18. století," in *Česká města v 16.—18. století: Sborník příspěvků z konference v Pardubicích 14. a 15. listopadu 1990*, ed. Jaroslav Pánek (Prague: Historický ústav, 1991), 185.
93. For a list of literature on the topic, see Hrejsa, *Česká konfesse*, 580, n. 4.
94. Jindřich Ondřej Hoffman, *Ocularia. A neb oči sklenné starého Čecha, které podává Čechu nynějšímu skrze něžby hleděl na předešlou staročeskou nábožnost* (Prague: Jiří Sedlčanský, 1637), 210–211.
95. *Ibid.*, 218–219, 262.
96. Symeon Evstachyus Kapihorský, *Hystoria kláštera Sedleckého* (Prague: Pavel Sessius, 1630), 66.
97. Skřivánek, "K náboženským dějinám východočeského města v 15. až 18. století," 181.
98. David R. Holeton, "'O felix Bohemia—O felix Constantia': The Liturgical Commemoration of Saint Jan Hus," *Jan Hus: Zwischen Zeiten, Völkern, Konfessionen*, ed. Ferdinand Seibt (Munich: Oldenbourg, 1997), 393, n. 37. On the mutilation of Utraquist texts, see also Thomas A. Fudge, *The Magnificent Ride: The First Reformation in Hussite Bohemia* (Brookfield, Vt.: Ashgate, 1998), 233–234.
99. Derek Sayer, *The Coasts of Bohemia: A Czech History* (Princeton, N.J.: Princeton University Press, 1998), 48–49.
100. J. J. Hanuš, "O působení Jesuity Antonína Koniáše v literatuře české," *Časopis českého musea* 37, no. 1 (1863): 77–90, 194–210; Čornejová, *Tovaryšstvo Ježíšovo*, 195–197; Bílý, *Jezuita Antonín Koniáš*, 160–163.
101. Matauš Pačuda, *Spis v němž se obsahuje které věci (z stran lidského pokolení) předešly příchod a narození mesiaše pravého Krista* (Prague: Matěj Pardubický, 1616), ends abruptly at f. K8v [152] in the one available copy of his work, held by the Strahov Monastery Library in Prague under the call number BX VI 22. While Utraquist literature was inaccessible under the Counter-Reformation, enough has survived (abroad, or in Bohemia either kept as incriminating evidence [see Bílý, *Jezuita Antonín Koniáš*, 160], or in a mutilated state) to reconstruct Utraquist ecclesiology and liturgy. An important development in that regard is the series, David R. Holeton and Anna Vlhová, eds., *Monumenta liturgica bohemica*, that was launched with Barry F. Graham, ed., *The Litoměřice Gradual of 1517* (Prague and Brno: L. Marek, 1999), as vol. 1 of the *Monumenta*.
102. So named after the disciple who visited Jesus only at night; see Andrew Pettegree, *Marian Protestantism: Six Studies* (Aldershot, Hants, Eng.: Scolar Press; Brookfield, Vt.: Ashgate, 1996), 6–7, 24–26, 53, 90–92; Perez Zagorin, *Ways of Lying: Dissimulation, Persecution, and Conformity in Early Modern Europe* (Cambridge, Mass.: Harvard University Press, 1991), 131–152, 223–233.

103. See, for instance, Podlaha, *Dopisy Reformační komisse,* 138–139, 149–150.
104. On Jansenism in the Austrian Netherlands, see Jan Roegiers, "Jansenisme en katholieke hervorming in de Nederlanden," in *Geloven in het verleden: studies over het godsdienstig leven in de vroegmoderne tijd, aangeboden aan Michel Cloet,* ed. Eddy Put, Juliette Marinus, and Hans Storme, Symbolae Facultatis Litterarum Lovaniensis. Series A, vol. 22 (Leuven: Universitaire Pers Leuven, 1996); and Craig Harline and Eddy Put, *A Bishop's Tale: Mathias Hovius among His Flock in Seventeenth-Century Flanders* (New Haven, Conn.: Yale University Press, 2000).
105. For instance, Fiala, *Hrozné doby protireformace,* 97–98.
106. Hrejsa, *Česká konfesse,* 581, n. 4.
107. Jiří Pešek, "Protestant Literature in Bohemian Private Libraries *circa* 1600," in *Reformation in Eastern and Central Europe,* ed. Karin Maag (Brookfield, Vt.: Ashgate, 1997), 49, n. 25, referring to Jiří Pokorný, "Knihy a knihovny v inventářích pražských měšťanů v 18. století, 1700–1784," *Acta Universitatis Carolinae: Historia Universitatis Carolinae Pragensis* 28/1 (1988): 56–58.
108. Marie Elisabeth Ducreux, "Reading unto Death: Books and Readers in Eighteenth-Century Bohemia," in *The Culture of Print: Power and the Uses of Print in Early Modern Europe,* ed. Roger Chartier, trans. Lydia J. Cochrane (Princeton, N.J.: Princeton University Press, 1989), 218–219.
109. Eduard Winter, *Die tschechische und slowakische Emigration in Deutschland im 17. und 18. Jahrhundert* (Berlin: Akademie-Verlag, 1955), 14.
110. The exiled Lutheran minister Martinius mentions contacts with the Puritans in this context; Samuel Martinius z Dražova, *Obrana M. Samuela Martiniusa z Dražova: Proti ohlášení starších kněží Bratrských* (Pirna: Dědici Jana Ctibora, 1636), 433. See also Lenka Bobková, "Česká exulantská šlechta v Pirně v roce 1629," *Folia Historica Bohemica* 19 (1998): 83–116.
111. Hrejsa, *Česká konfesse,* 583–584, 588–589.
112. Bobková, *Exulanti z Prahy a severozápadních Čech,* xlix.
113. E. P. Tyrrel and J. S. G. Simmons, "Slavonic Books Before 1700 in Cambridge Libraries," *Transactions of Cambridge Bibliographic Society* 3 (1963): 383, 394 (the copy is deposited in the Sidney Sussex College, Cambridge); E. Urbánková, "Několik poznámek k českému vydání Kalvínovy Instituce," *Literární archiv: Sborník Památníku národního písemnictví* 1 (1996), 237ff.; William B. Patterson, *King James VI and I and the Reunion of Christendom* (Cambridge: Cambridge University Press, 1997), 125.
114. Lewis Bayly, *Praxis pietatis. To jest O cvičení se v pobožnosti pravé knižka milostná* (Leszno: n.p., [1630?]), 284–291, 442–44. The Amsterdam edition was published by Kopydlanský in 1661. On Comenius and Harvard, see Samuel E. Morison, *The Founding of Harvard College* (Cambridge, Mass.: Harvard University Press, 1935), 243–245.
115. After the deadline was missed in 1632, the Brethren's intended contribution was published separately in an English-language edition as Komenský (Johann Amos Comenius), *The History of the Bohemian Persecution.* It was preceded by a Latin translation, *Historia persecutionum ecclesiae bohemicae* (published originally in Leiden in 1647 and 1648). See also Jan Amos Komenský, *Opera omnia* (Prague: Academia, 1989), 9: pt. 1, 199–338. The Czech original was published subsequently as Jan Amos Komenský, *Historia o těžkých protivenstvích církve české hned od počátku jejího na víru Křesťanskou obrácení v létu 894 až do léta 1632 za panování Ferdinanda Druhého. S připojením historie o persekucí valdenských roku tohoto (1655) stálé* (Leszno: n.p.,

1655), and the second edition (Amsterdam: Jan Paskovský, 1663). See also Komenský, *Opera omnia*, 9: pt. 1, 53–198.

116. See n. 114 above. Samuel Martinius z Dražova, *Pět a třidceti mocných, znamenitých a slušných důvodů a příčin pro které všickni Evangelistští Čechové za jedno býti* (Pirna: Dědici Jana Ctibora, 1635), f. G4r–G4v; he called Bayly's work: "Kniha ... velikými zmatky a bludy a urážlivými slovy naplněná ..." (A book ... filled with great confusion and heresy and offensive words); *ibid.*, f. H3r.

117. Bayly, *Praxis pietatis*, 284–291.

118. *Na spis proti jednotě bratrské od Samuele Martinia etc: sepsaný ... Ohlášení* (Leszno: n.p., 1635), 137–139.

119. *Ibid.*, 177. See also Tomáš Kalina, "Václav Brož: Několik poznámek k jeho životopisu a literární činnosti," *Od pravěku k dnešku: Sborník k 60. narozeninám J. Pekaře* (Prague: Historický klub, 1930), 1: 435–436.

120. "[N]árod důkladně rekatolizovaný...," in Noemi Rejchrtová, "Role utrakvismu v českých dějinách," in *Traditio et Cultus: Miscellanea historica bohemica Miloslao Vlk, archiepiscopo Pragensi, ab eius collegis amicisque ad annum sexagesimum dedicata*, ed. Zdeňka Hledíková (Prague: Univerzita Karlova, 1993), 76. See also Paul Shore, "The Society of Jesus and the Culture of the Late Baroque in Bohemia," *East European Quarterly* 34 (2000): 2–3; Čornejová, *Tovaryšstvo Ježíšovo*, 184–185, 191.

121. James R. Palmitessa, "The Prague Uprising of 1611: Property, Politics, and Catholic Renewal in the Early Years of Habsburg Rule," *Central European History* 31 (1998): 304–314; Josef Janáček, *Rudolf II. a jeho doba* (Prague: Svoboda, 1987), 477–478.

122. Ducreux, "Reading unto Death," 195.

123. The benign attitude toward the Counter-Reformation can be deduced, for instance, from the critical reaction that greeted the appearance of Jan Fiala's *Hrozné doby protireformace* (1997). See Tomáš Knoz, review of Miloš Pojar, *Jindřich Matyáš Thurn* (Prague, 1998) in *Časopis Matice Moravské* 119 (2000): 306.

124. Marie-Elizabeth Ducreuxová, "Čtení a vztah ke knihám u podezřelých z kacířství v Čechách 18. století," *Acta Universitatis Carolinae: Historia Universitatis Carolinae Pragensis* 2, no. 1–2 (1992): 53–54.

125. On the nexus between temporal and religious exactions, see Fiala, *Hrozné doby protireformace*, 114–115; Kadlec, *Přehled českých církevních dějin*, 2:92–93; Čornejová, *Tovaryšstvo Ježíšovo*, 191–192.

126. Ducreux, "Reading unto Death," 198–199.

127. Bireley, *Religion and Politics in the Age of the Counterreformation*, 38.

128. On failure to carry out the Counter-Reformation program fully, and on the concern with persistent "Hussite" influences, see, for instance, Kadlec, *Přehled českých církevních dějin*, 2:96–97; Winter, *Der Josefinismus: Die Geschichte des österreichischen Reformkatholizismus*, 166.

129. Florimond de Remond, *Husitského v Čechách kacířství počátku, zrůstu, a pádu vejtah* (Prague: Jan K. Hraba, [1777]), especially the anxiety over the spirit of Hus still sparking under the ashes of the Bohemian Reformation (f. A4v). See also Denis, *La Bohême depuis la Montagne-Blanche*, 1:407–421.

130. Hsia, *The World of Catholic Renewal*, 76–77.

131. Ducreux, "Reading unto Death," 198–199. Actually, the repressions may have been even more violent; see Karolina Světlá, *Z literárního soukromí a drobné práce*, 2nd ed. (Prague: L. Mazáč, 1941), 21–22.

132. See, for instance, Virgilio Pinto Crespo, "Thought Control in Spain," in *Inquisition and Society in Early Modern Europe,* ed. Stephen Haliczer (Totowa, N.J.: Barnes and Noble Books, 1987), 171–188; Dvornik, *The Slavs in European History,* 451.

133. Parenthetically—for only functional comparisons, without drawing axiological equations—one may also recall such phenomena of later Bohemian history as Reinhard Heydrich's Protectorate of World War II, or the normalization of Leonid Brezhnev in the Cold War era. The number of victims of the Nazi occupation in the Protectorate was relatively small and yet it produced the appearance of prevalent consent or even support, which is known to have been spurious. The method of Brezhnevite normalization was virtually bloodless, yet the number of individuals involved in overt resistance, let us say in Charter 77, was relatively small, and the illusory impression of broad-based assent prevailed. Some observers —somewhat roguishly—have wondered whether in history's *longue durée,* the experience under the Counter-Reformation might not have provided a training ground or a dress rehearsal for accommodation by the Bohemians to several unpalatable regimes of the future. Lonnie R. Johnson, *Central Europe: Enemies, Neighbors, Friends* (New York: Oxford University Press, 1996), 92–93.

134. Čornejová, *Tovaryšstvo Ježíšovo,* 109–110, 185, 193.

135. Braudel referred to such historical events, contrasted with the *la longue durée,* as "crests of foam that the tides of history carry on their strong backs," cited in *Blackwell's Dictionary of Historians,* ed. John Cannon (Oxford: Basil Blackwell, 1998), 50.

136. Ducreux, "Reading unto Death," 196. See also Franco Venturi, *The First Crisis,* vol. 1 of *The End of the Old Regime in Europe, 1768–1776,* trans. R. Burr Litchfield (Princeton, N.J.: Princeton University Press, 1989), 170–171.

137. Kadlec, *Přehled českých církevních dějin,* 2:161–162.

138. Marie-Elisabeth Ducreux, "Exil et conversion: Les trajectoires de vie d'émigrants tchèques à Berlin au 18e sciècle," *Annales: Histoire, Sciences Sociales* 54 (1999): 925–926.

139. See, for instance, Jindřich Francek, ed., *Rekatolizace v českých zemích.*, Sborník příspěvků z konference v Jičíně, 10. září 1993 (Pardubice: Městský úřad Jičín, 1995).

140. Janet L. Polasky, *Revolution in Brussels, 1787–1793* (Brussels: Académie royale de Belgique; Hanover, N.H.: University Press of New England, 1987), 63–69; Bruno Bernard, *Patrice-François de Neny, 1716–1784: portrait d'un homme d'état* (Brussels: Editions de l'Université de Bruxelles, 1993), 188, 192.

141. Marie-Elisabeth Ducreux, "La reconquête catholique de l'espace bohémien," *Revue des Études Slaves* 60 (1988): 685; Kadlec, *Přehled českých církevních dějin,* 2:229; Kloczowski, *History of Polish Christianity,* 162–163.

142. As during the Bohemian rural uprisings in 1775 during the reign of Maria Theresia; see Venturi, *The First Crisis* 166–167; Miroslav Toegel, et al., eds., *Prameny k nevolnickému povstání v Čechách a na Moravě v roce 1775* (Prague: Academia, 1975), 535.

143. On rejection of Counter-Reformation literature from the viewpoint of the Catholic Enlightenment for its emphasis on miracles and asceticism, see Josef Dobrovský, *Dějiny české řeči a literatury v redakcích z roku 1791, 1792 a 1818,* ed. Benjamin Jedlička (Prague: Melantrich, 1936), 54–55, 162–164.

144. Ibid., 46, 148–149, 152.

145. Hugh L. Agnew, *Origins of the Czech National Renascence* (Pittsburgh: University of Pittsburgh Press, 1993), 117, 122–123; Jaroslav Kolár, *Návraty bez konce: Studie k starší české literatuře,* ed. Lenka Jiroušková (Brno: Atlantis, 1999), 290, 294–295;

Jireček, *Rukověť k dějinám literatury,* 2:146–147; Zdeněk V. David, "Národní obrození jako převtělení Zlatého věku," *Český časopis historický* 99 (2001): 486–518.

146. R. G. Collingwood, *The Idea of History,* rev. ed. (Oxford: Clarendon Press, 1993), especially 215–219, 282–302, 441–450. On Collingwood's theory of reenactment, see also Christopher Parker, *The English Idea of History from Coleridge to Collingwood* (Burlington, VT: Ashgate, 2000), 185–186, 201, 212; Jan W. van der Dussen, *History as a Science: The Philosophy of R. G. Collingwood* (The Hague: Martinus Nijhoff, 1981), especially 93–109, 312–324; and Rex Martin, *Historical Explanation: Re-enactment and Practical Inference* (Ithaca, N.Y.: Cornell University Press, 1977), 58–60.

147. I am indebted to Franz Szabo for suggesting this relationship, although he did not bring it up in Szabo, *Kaunitz and Enlightened Absolutism, 1753–1780* (Cambridge and New York: Cambridge University Press, 1994). On the ecclesiological aspect, see reference to Hus in Ferdinand Maass, ed., *Der Josephinismus: Quellen zu seiner Geschichte in Österreich, 1760–1850,* 5 vols., Fontes rerum Austriacarum, Zweite Abteilung, Band 71–75 (Vienna: Verlag Herold, 1951–1961), 2:492–493.

148. Franz Szabo points to the French Enlightenment as the prime source of Kaunitz's ideas and hence of Joseph's religious policy. He particularly cites the influence of Diderot's *Encyclopédie,* specifically the article on ecclesiastical discipline; see Szabo, *Kaunitz and Enlightened Absolutism,* 230. For a collection of essays that, to the contrary, emphasizes the influence of orthodox Christian liberals over rationalist agnostic secularists in the Enlightenment, see James E. Bradley and Dale K. Van Kley, eds., *Religion and Politics in Enlightenment Europe* (Notre Dame, Ind.: University of Notre Dame Press, 2001), especially 1–45.

149. Contrary to Szabo, Harm Klueting sees the primary source of Josephin ecclesiastical reforms specifically in the writings of the Leipzig law professor, Christian Thomasius (1655–1728), and of the Halle law professor, Justus Henning Böhmer (1674–1749); see Klueting, "Kaunitz, die Kirche und der Josephinismus. Protestantisches landesherrliches Kirchenregiment, rationaler Territorialismus und theresianisch-josephinisches Staatskirchentum," in *Staatskanzler Wenzel Anton von Kaunitz-Rietberg, 1711–1794,* ed. Grete Klingenstein and Franz A. Szabo (Graz: Andreas Schneider, 1996), 187. Klueting firmly denies that there is any need to trace the roots of Josephism to Gallicanism, to Diderot, or to the other encyclopedists; the influence of unorthodox German Lutheran jurists provides a sufficient explanation; *ibid.*, 193–194.

150. Against the Jesuit ultramontanism, Jansenism strove to affirm local autonomy from Rome and mitigate the authoritarian interpretation of the Tridentine directives. An important adherent was the Irish-descended head of the Privy Council of the Austrian Netherlands, Patrice François de Neny. On the Austrian Netherlands, see Roegiers, "Jansenisme en katholieke hervorming in de Nederlanden," and Harline and Put, *A Bishop's Tale.* On Jansenism in the Habsburg Empire and its relationship to Josephinism, see Peter Hersche, *Der Spätjansenismus in Österreich* (Vienna: Verlag der Österreichischen Akademie der Wissenschaften, 1977), especially 313–355. On De Neny's views, see Bernard, *Patrice-François de Neny,* 147–166. On the liberal ecclesiology of Jansenism, see Dale Van Kley, *The Jansenists and the Expulsion of the Jesuits from France, 1757–1765* (New Haven, Conn.: Yale University Press, 1975), 229. On Jansenism in Bohemia, see Milan Machovec, *Josef Dobrovský* (Prague: Svobodné slovo, 1964), 26–36.

151. Historical literature thus far seems to have ignored the potential connection between Bohemian Utraquism and support for Josephinism in Bohemia. For instance, there is no mention of Bohemian influence in Elisabeth Kovács, ed., *Katholische Aufklärung*

und Josephinismus (Vienna: Verlag für Geschichte und Politik, 1979); or in Klueting, "Kaunitz, die Kirche und der Josephinismus," 186–195.

152. Klueting, "Kaunitz, die Kirche und der Josephinismus," 174–75, 182; Maass, *Der Josephinismus: Quellen,* 3:ix–x; Kadlec, *Přehled českých církevních dějin,* 2:168–169.

153. Winter, *Der Josefinismus: Die Geschichte des österreichischen Reformkatholizismus,* 357.

154. Klueting, "Kaunitz, die Kirche und der Josephinismus," 183–185; Kadlec, *Přehled českých církevních dějin,* 2: 150, 154; 163–164.

155. Maass, *Der Josephinismus: Quellen,* 2:492–493.

156. Jan Mukařovský, ed., *Dějiny české literatury,* 4 vols. (Prague: Nakladatelství Československé akademie věd, 1959–1995), 2:35.

157. František Kutnar and Jaroslav Marek, *Přehledné dějiny českého a slovenského dějepisectví,* 2d ed. (Prague: Lidové noviny, 1997), 156–157.

158. Kašpar Royko, *Geschichte der grossen allgemeinen Kirchenversammlung zu Kostniz,* 5 vols. (Graz: A. Leykam, 1781–1782; Prague: Schönfeld, 1784–1796).

159. Winter, *Der Josefinismus: Die Geschichte des österreichischen Reformkatholizismus,* 199–200.

160. Kadlec, *Přehled českých církevních dějin,* 2:153, 167–168.

161. Winter, *Der Josefinismus: Die Geschichte des österreichischen Reformkatholizismus,* 358; Maass, *Der Josephinismus: Quellen,* 3:4–5. Szabo points out that Heinke, unlike Kaunitz, found an inspiration for his reform proposals in the Jansenist Church of Utrecht; see Szabo, *Kaunitz and Enlightened Absolutism,* 229–232, 245, 247, 257.

162. Bedřich Slavík, *Od Dobnera k Dobrovskému* (Prague: Vyšehrad, 1975), 287.

163. Polasky, *Revolution in Brussels.*

164. Jan Lehár, et al., *Česká literatura od počátků k dnešku* (Prague: Lidové noviny, 1998), 162; Bedřich Slavík, *Od Dobnera k Dobrovskému* (Prague: Vyšehrad, 1975), 264.

165. Kutnar and Marek, *Přehledné dějiny českého a slovenského dějepisectví,* 164.

166. Mikuláš Adaukt Voigt expressed his view in *Acta litteraria Bohemiae et Moraviae,* 2 vols. (1775, 1783), cited in Bedřich Slavík, *Od Dobnera k Dobrovskému* (Prague: Vyšehrad, 1975), 115, 208–209, 282. Procházka likewise contributed to the *Acta* concerning Bohemian humanism; Slavík, *Od Dobnera,* 114.

167. Jireček, *Rukověť',* 2:146–147; *Knihopis českých a slovanských tisků,* n. 2359. Sixteenth-century editions appeared in 1563–1564 and 1579; *Knihopsis,* n. 2356–2358.

168. See *Knihopis českých a slovanských tisků,* n. 2354–2355. Sixteenth-century editions appeared from 1519 and 1570; *ibid.,* n. 2351–2352.

169. Vincenc Zahradník, *Filosofické spisy,* ed. František Čáda, 2 vols. (Prague: Česká akademie pro vědy slovesnost a umění, 1907–1908), 1:7–13; J. A. Ginzel, *Bischof Hurdalek: Ein Charakterbild aus der Geschichte der bömischen Kirche* (Prague: Bohemia, 1873). Royko's work provided a link between the two phases of reform Catholicism; Winter, *Der Josefinismus: Die Geschichte des österreichischen Reformkatholizismus,* 199–200, 314.

170. For instance, in "Lieutenant of Bohemia," Karl Mescéry von Tschorn's report to Interior Minister Alexander Bach in February 1851, cited in Magdaléna Pokorná, *Milován a sledován: Český spisovatel Prokop Chocholoušek, 1819–1864* (Prague: Práh, 2001), 41–42.

171. Jan Šimsa, "Respekt k víře jiných—Karel Havlíček Borovský," in *Problém tolerance v dějinách a perpektivě,* ed. Milan Machovec (Prague: Academia, 1995), 132;

Tomáš G. Masaryk, *Česká otázka. Naše nynější krize. Jan Hus,* Spisy T. G. Masaryka, vol. 6 (Prague: Ústav T. G. Masaryka, 2000), 15, 79, 103; Tomáš G. Masaryk, *Karel Havlíček: Snahy a tužby politického probuzení,* Spisy T. G. Masaryka, vol. 7 (Prague: Ústav T. G. Masaryka, 1996), 191–195.

172. Karel Čapek, *Hovory s T. G. Masarykem,* Spisy, 20 (Prague: Československý spisovatel, 1990), 71–72; Karel Mácha, *Glaube und Vernunft: Die Böhmische Philosophie in geschichtlicher Übersicht,* 3 vols. (Munich: Sauer, 1987), 2:150–151; Barry Smith, *Austrian Philosophy: The Legacy of Franz Brentano* (Chicago: Open Court, 1994), 21, 26. E. Husserl credited Masaryk with introducing him to Brentano's philosophy in 1877; Smith, *Austrian Philosophy,* 26.

173. On the liberal Catholicism of Bolzano and Brentano, see Eduard Winter, *Über die Perfektibilität des Katholizismus* (Berlin: Akademie-Verlag, 1971), 87–166.

174. On the ideological connection between Josephinism and Second Vatican Council, see Winter, *Der Josefinismus: die Geschichte des österreichischen Reformkatholizismus,* 345–348.

175. On "great revolutions" and the place of the Hussite Revolution, see Jaroslav Krejčí, *Great Revolutions Compared: The Search for a Theory* (New York: St. Martin's Press, 1983), 22–48; Leslie C. Tihany, *A History of Middle Europe* (New Brunswick, N.J.: Rutgers University Press, 1976), 41.

176. On liberal or reform Catholicism, see David Sorkin, "Reform Catholicism and Religious Enlightenment," with comments by T. C. W. Blanning and R. J. W. Evans, in *Austrian History Yearbook* 30 (1999): 187–235.

177. Alain Dufour, "Humanisme et Reformation," in Dufour, *Histoire politique et psychologie historique* (Geneva: Librairie Droz, 1966), 54. See also Peter Fraenkel, "Utraquism or Co-Existence: Some Notes on the Earliest Negotiations before the Pacification of Nuernberg, 1531–1532," *Studia theologica* 18, no. 2 (1964): 130, 132–134.

178. Howard Kaminsky, "Nicholas of Pelhřimov's Tabor: an Adventure into the Eschaton," in *Eschatologie und Hussitismus,* ed. Alexander Patschovsky and František Šmahel, Internationales Kolloquium, Prague, September 1–4, 1993 (Prague: Historický ústav, 1996), 167.

Epilog

1. Brendan Bradshaw, "The Controversial Sir Thomas More," *Journal of Ecclesiastical History* 36 (1985): 563–564. On canonist ecclesiology, papal monarchism, and noninstitutional ecclesiology, see, for instance, Brian Gogan, *The Common Corps of Christendom: Ecclesiological Themes in the Writings of Sir Thomas More* (Leiden: Brill, 1982), 24–47. The Utraquists' commitment is symbolized by their publication in Czech translation of the two fundamental works on the history of the church in patristic times, namely Flavius Magnus Cassiodorus, *Historia Cýrkevní,* and Pamphilus Eusebius, *Historia Cýrkevní,* both translated by Jan Kocín of Kocinét, and published in Prague by Daniel Adam of Veleslavín in 1594.

2. On the Taborites' primitive church, see Howard Kaminsky, "Nicholas of Pelhřimov's Tabor: An Adventure into the Eschaton," in *Eschatologie und Hussitismus,* ed. Alexander Patschovsky and František Šmahel, Internationales Kolloquium, Prague, September 1–4, 1993 (Prague: Historický ústav, 1996), 162.

3. David R. Holeton, "Sacramental and Liturgical Reform in Late Medieval Bohemia," *Studia Liturgica* 18 (1987): 94. See also Enrico C.S. Molnar, "The Restoration of Holy Communion in Both Kinds," *Anglican Theological Review* 2 (1954): 104–111.

4. Bradshaw, "The Controversial Sir Thomas More," 564.

5. On the concept of "confessionalization," see, for instance, Robert Bireley, *The Refashioning of Catholicism, 1450–1700: A Reassessment of the Counter Reformation* (Washington, D.C.: Catholic University of America Press, 1999), 6–8.

6. See Chapter 8, n. 8.

7. For instance, Ole P. Grell, Jonathan I. Israel, and Nicholas Tyacke, eds., *From Persecution to Toleration: The Glorious Revolution and Religion in England* (Oxford: Clarendon Press, 1991), 1.

Bibliography

Archival Sources

Acta Universitatis Carolinae et praecipuae Facultatis Philosophicae sub variis rectoribus et decanis ab anno MDXCVIII ad an. MDCXXII. Vol. 6, *Memorabilium Universitatis Pragensis* (1768). Manuscript. Prague, University Archive, A 17 VI.

Bydžovský z Florentina, Marek. *Altera pars annalium seu eorum, quae sub Maximiliano rege contigerunt* (c. 1595). Manuscript. Prague, State Central Archive, fond Archív vyšehradské kapituly, inv. č. 796, kniha 358.

―――. *Prima pars annalium seu eorum, quae sub Ferdinando rege contigerunt* (c. 1595). Manuscript. Prague, National Library, XXII A 6.

―――. *Rudolphus rex Bohemiae XXI* (c. 1595). Manuscript. Prague, National Library, XVI G 22.

[Červenka, Matěj]. "Poznamenání a spolu shromáždění některých věcí pamětihodných přítomným i budoucím." Manuscript (entire), dated 1579. (*Děje české 1530–45.*) Prague, National Library, XVII C 3.

Faber, Johann. *O potupení bludu* and *O zpovědi,* arranged by Augustin Schwarzel of Třebenice, 1540. Manuscript. Olomouc, State Research Library, M44.

Illicinus, Peter. *Contra impiam Deoque inimicam haereticorum legem, quod liceat cuique impune ac sine aliquo impedimento de fide sentire et praedicare, ut velit.* Commentarius per Petrum Illicinum, J. U. Doctorem, canonicum ecclesiae Olomucensis. Anno MDLXXVII. (Olomouc, 1577.) Manuscript. Vienna, National Library, 11623.

Staré a stálé vyznání církve Pána Krista, c. 1589. Manuscript. Prague, National Library, XXVI A 14.

Authors, 1517–1648: Bohemian

Note: Rare Czech titles are accompanied by references to entry numbers in *Knihopis českých a slovenských tisků,* vol. 2 (in 9 parts): *Tisky z let 1501–1800* (Prague: Nakladatelství Československé akademie věd, 1939–1967; Dodatky, 1994–), cited as *Knihopis.* Rare Latin titles are accompanied by references to page number in Josef

Hejnic and Jan Martínek, eds., *Rukověť humanistického básnictví v Čechách a na Moravě od konce 15. do začátku 17. století*, 5 vols. (Prague: Academia, 1966–1982), cited as *Rukověť*. Following are abbreviations for location in Prague depositories: NUK (National Library); MK (National Museum); and Strahov (Strahov Monastery).

Arsenius z Radbuzy, Kašpar. *Pobožná knížka o blahoslavené Panně Marii*. Prague: Pavel Sessius, 1629. *Knihopis* 265: NUK (54 E 125).

Bartolomeus, Jiřík. *Kázání krátké ku potěšení a napomenutí pobožným vojákům*. Hradec Králové: Martin Kleinwechter, 1619. *Knihopis* 977: MK (40 G 7).

Bartoš Písař. *Kronika pražská*. Edited by Josef V. Šimák. In *Prameny dějin českých/ Fontes Rerum Bohemicarum* 6, 1–297. Prague: Nadání Františka Palackého, 1907.

Bavorovský, Tomáš. *Kázání o svatém pokání*. Prague: Bartoloměj Netolický, 1552. *Knihopis* 1004: NUK (54 F 19); MK (35 C 11); Strahov (C CH VII 40).

―――. *Postila česká*. Olomouc: Jan Gunther, 1557. *Knihopis* 1005: NUK (54 B 6); MK (35 A 5). Partial edition by Josef Dittrich [Josef Klíč, pseud.], *Kázání na Evangelium, kteréž se čte v Církvi Boží na den Božího Těla*. Prague: Fetterlová, 1822.

―――. *O umučení Pána a Spasitele našeho Ježíše Krista*. Prostějov: Jan Günther, 1552. *Knihopis* 1006: MK (36 G 4 neúpl.).

―――. *Zrcadlo onoho věčného a blahoslaveného života*. Prague: Melantrich, 1561. *Knihopis* 1007: NUK (54 D 203 přív., 54 F 20, 54 E 59 přív.; MK (36 A 2); Strahov (BC VI 97). New edition by Josef Dittrich. Prague: Fetterlová, 1822.

Bechyňka, Jan. "Praga mistica." In *Praga Mystica: Z dějin české. reformace*. Edited by Noemi Rejchrtová, 35–50. Vol. 3, *Acta reformationem bohemicam illustrantia*, edited by Amedeo Molnár. Prague: Kalich, 1984.

Benešovský, Václav. *Ozvání starých Čechů a Moravců před léty osmdesáti, kteréž učinili proti těm, kteříž o nich mluvili, že jsou odřezanci církve svaté*. Prague: Jan Jiřínský, 1588. *Knihopis* 1069

Bidones z Bidenthalu, Konstantin Kristian [pseudonym?]. *Výstraha: Proti v Římsko-Katolické náboženství ubíhání všechněm k Augšpurské neb české Konfesí se přiznávajícím . . .* N.p., 1624. *Knihopis* 1123: MK (31 E 7).

Bílejovský, Bohuslav. *Kronyka Cýrkevní*. Edited by Josef Dittrich [Jozef Skalický, pseud.]. Prague: Fetterl z Vilden, 1816.

Brosius, Václav [Vytolid Poskok, pseud.]. *Koule Danyelova, kterouž podává Draku Pithartskému, jinak Valdenskému*. Litomyšl: [Andreas Graudenc?], n.p., 1589. *Knihopis* 1302: NUK (54 F 28).

Brosius, Václav. *O Přijímání Svátosti Těla a Krve Páně. Rozmlouvání mezi dvěma osobami, prosté, krátké důvěrné a pokojné*. [Litomyšl]: [Andreas Graudenc?], 1598. *Knihopis* 1304: NUK (54 D 43 přív).

―――. *Ohlášení se proti Pithartskému Netopýři*. [Litomyšl]: [Andreas Graudenc?], 1599. *Knihopis* 1303: NUK (54 D 43 přív).

―――. *Šest důvodů pěkných a krátkých*. Litomyšl: Andreas Graudenc, 1591. *Knihopis* 1305: NUK (54 D 43 přív).

―――. *Veystraha všem věrným Čechům . . . : Aby mohli znáti yakey jest rozdíl mezy Učením Mistra Jana Husy a Učením Bratří Boleslavských w Artykuli o Večeři Páně*. Litomyšl: [Andreas Graudenc?], 1589. *Knihopis* 1306: NUK (54 F 28).

Brož, Václav. *See* Brosius, Václav.

Bruncvík, Zacharyáš. *Agonis domini nostri Jesu Christi assertio. To jest. O smrti útrpné a nade všecky smrti pod nebem nejhořčejší prostředníka a vykupitele našeho Krista Pána*. Prague: Matěj Pardubský, 1613. *Knihopis* 1310: NUK (54 E 431 přív.).

_____. *Ascensionis Iesu mediatoris notri aserto.* Kázání o nanebevstoupení prostředníka našeho Pána Ježíše Krista. Prague: Jiří Hanuš Landškrounský, 1612. *Knihopis* 1311: NUK (54 E 431 přív).

_____. *Defensio exulantium notas haereseos, ipsis a papistis inustas, ab alienans.* Obrana Čchů, mezi národy rozptýlených, že oni ne pro rebelii něž relliji, ne pro vrchnosti nepoddanost něž Kristově pravdě, toho nebeského monarchu věrnost, ne pro kacířství, ale v Konfesí české obsažené křesťanství; ne pro vraždu a zločinnost, ale pro krev a svědectví beránka, ven z vlasti bez řádného obvinění, a náležitého vyslyšení, hodného a spravedlivého rozeznání, násilně od Antikrista, proti duchovní i světské spravedlnosti jsou vynutkáni. N.p., 1633. *Knihopis* 1318: MK (31 E 7).

_____. *Ecclesia Catholica Christiani agminis.* Kázání o církvi svaté katolické všeobecné křesťanské, složené a činěné v úterý slavného hodu a výročí seslání Ducha Svatého na Apoštoly. Prague: Oldřich Valda, 1607. *Knihopis* 1319: NUK (54 F 41 přív., 54 B 99).

_____. *Homilia de incarnati verbi massa: To jest, Kázání o vtělení, narození a předivném andělům, lidem pak spasitelném spojení podstatném dvojího přirození Božského a lidského v jednotu osoby Pána našeho Ježíše Krista.* Prague: Typis Schumanianis, 1607. *Knihopis* 1320a: NUK (54 F 41 přív); MK (27 C 63).

_____. *Idolorum pia suplantatio.* Kázání o tom, že obrazové jakož svaté Trojice Boha v podstatě jediného, neviditelného a neobsáhlého, tak i jiných svatých a světic, na něž poklona, vzývání a čest Boží se přenáší, v Církvi Páně trpěni býti nemají. Prague: Matěj Pardubský, 1613. *Knihopis* 1334: MK (35 E 12).

_____. Kázání o Pravém a jediném očistci křesťanském, v němž hříchové naši, samým milosrdenstvím Božím a trvalou zásluhou Krista Pána, zde na světě, kdež čas milosti jest, se očišťují. Prague: Matěj Pardubský, 1613. *Knihopis* 1323: NUK (54 E 431 přív.); MK (35 G 2 neúpl.).

_____. *Mediatoris nostri Jesu Christi assertio.* Kázání o jediném a nejsvětějším mezi Bohem a lidmi prostředníku. Prague: Jiří Hanuš Landškrounský, 1612. *Knihopis* 1313: NUK (54 E 431 přív).

_____. *Michaelis archangeli atque hierarchiae celestis plena assertio.* Kázání o Michaelovi Archangelu Kristu Pánu našem knížeti, monarchovi a obhájci církve jediném. Prague: Jiří Hanuš Landškrounský, 1612. *Knihopis* 1314: NUK (54 E 431 přív, 54 E 149, 54 E 158).

_____. *Pravitatis et impletatis haereticae pia et fida ostensio.* To jest: Zrcadlo Kacířství: Do něhož kdo zdravě nahlídne, Allegata, u Doktorů Církve vykázaná, přeběhne, pozná, že my Katolíci pod obojí nevinně, a bez náležitého vší Svaté Říše vyslyšání od některých se kačeřujeme. Prague: Matěj Pardubický, 1614. *Knihopis* 1329: MK (37 E 29); NUK (54 K 1350 neúpl.).

_____. *Testamenti nostri Iesu Christi pia et fida assertio.* To jest: Kšaftu Večeře Páně svatá Starožitnost, Pobožná posloupnost, dlouhověká až právě do dne soudného trvanlivost: V níž z nařízení Kristového, z učení evangelistského a apoštolského, z doktorů a sněmů osvícených, z kanonu a práv duchovních, z historií církevních, a nejvíce našich českých, etc. Náboženství naše podobojí pravé Katolické, Křesťanské a Starožitné, mocné, patrné a bez falše, od času Krista Pána, až do našeho věku, posloupně se dokazuje a dovodí. Prague: Matěj Pardubický, 1613. *Knihopis* 1316: MK (37 D 19 neúpl., 37 E 1 neúpl.); Strahov (AO XVI 37).

Brykcí z Licska. *Regule, To jest řeholy obecné z latinských učitelův práv vybrané* . . . Prague: Bartoloměj Netolický, 1541. *Knihopis* 1349: MK (32 D 8).

———. *Sentencie philozophice de regimine et iudiciis hominum. Naučení mudrců o spravování a soudech lidských.* Prague: Severýn, 1540. *Knihopis* 1350: MK (27 C 60).

———. *Sentencie philozophicae de regimine et iudiciis hominum. Naučení mudrců o spravování a soudech lidských.* Olomouc: Jan Günther, 1563. *Knihopis* 1351: MK (27 G 20).

———. *Tytulové stavů duchovního a světského.* Prague: Pavel Severyn, 1534. *Knihopis* 1352: NUK (54 B 113).

Budovec of Budov, Václav. *Antialkorán.* Edited by Noemi Rejchrtová. Prague: Odeon, 1989.

———. *Václava Budovce z Budova korrespondence z let 1579–1619.* Edited by Julius Glücklich. Prague: Česká akademie pro vědy, slovesnost a umění, 1908. Historický archiv, no. 30.

Bydžovský, Pavel. *Děťátka a neviňátka hned po přijetí křtu sv. Tělo a Krev Boží, že přijímati mají.* Prague: Bartoloměj Netolický, 1541. *Knihopis,* Dodatky 1388: NUK (54 K 19.480 přív. bez tit. l. a konce).

———. *Historiae aliquot Anglorum martyrum, quibus Deus suam ecclesiam exornare sicut syderibus coelum dignatus est.* Prague: J. Cantor, 1554. MK (45 D 29); NUK (Sd 493 adl. 1).

———. *Knížky o přijímání Těla a Krve Pána našeho Ježíše Krysta pod obojí způsobou.* [Prague]: n.p., 1538–1539. F. 54 [56]. *Knihopis* 1393: NUK (54 E 133); MK (36 C 2). Contains three other items: (1) *Čechové, milí Čechové, jenž žádáte býti věrní,* f. 28v–33 [1537?, cf. *Knihopis* 1387]; (2) *Tyto knížky toto Try v sobě drží,* f. 34r–50v [34r–52v] [1539?, cf. *Knihopis* 1392]; (3) *Spis o Postu,* f. 51r–54v [53r–56v].

———. *Křest'anské Víry upřímné o Těle a Krvi Boží vyznání.* N.p., [after 1546]. *Knihopis* 1397: MK (36 B 9).

———. *Odvolání jednoho Bratra z Roty Pikhartské.* 2d ed. Prague: Jan Jičínský, 1588. *Knihopis,* Dodatky 1395: NUK (f Zc 54, photocopy). First edition, Prague: Jan Kantor, 1559. *Knihopis* 1394: no copy extant.

———. *Tato Knížka toto try ukazuje.* N.p., [after 1541]. *Knihopis* 1391: MK (28 H 28).

———. *Tento spis ukazuje, že Biskupové Biskupa, a Biskup kněží, a kněží od řádných Biskupů svěceni Těla a krve Boží posvěcovati mají.* N.p., 1543. *Knihopis* 1396: NUK (54 I 12498); MK (36 B 10).

Bydžovský z Florentina, Marek. *Svět za tří českých králů: Ferdinand, Maximilán, Rudolf II.* Edited by Jaroslav Kolár. Prague: Svoboda, 1987.

Codicillus, Petr [Petr Kodicillus]. *Orací aneb spis k stavům pod obojí v království českém, aby oni konsistoř dolejší pražskou k své správě zase obrácenou míti se snažili,* February 10, 1582. In *Sněmy české,* 6:165–174.

Collinus of Chotěřina, Matouš. *Dopisy M. Matouše Kollína z Chotěřiny a jeho přátel ke Kašparovi z Nydbrucka, tajnému radovi krále Maximiliána II.* Sbírka pramenů ku poznání literárního života v Čechách, na Moravě a ve Slezsku, Skupina 2, Číslo 20. Edited by Ferdinand Menčík. Prague: Česká akademie pro vědy, slovesnost a umění, 1914.

Comenius, John Amos. See Komenský, Jan Amos.

Crinitus, Zykmund. *Diarium Christianum. Křest'anské dílo denní.* Prague: Matěj Pardubický, 1613. *Knihopis* 1638: NUK (54 D 170 neúpl.); MK (37 E 1 přív.).

———. *Spis kratičký o osobě Pána Krista.* Prague: Oldřich Valda, 1609. *Knihopis* 1644: NUK (54 F 41); MK (37 B 17).

Cykáda, Jan Václav. *Autočiště Křest'ana věrného.* Prague: Impressí Šumanská, [1606]. *Knihopis* 1705: NUK (54 B 91 přív., 54 E 45 přív); MK (35 C 2).

———. *Cesta k životu věčnému.* Prague: Impressí Šumanská, 1607. *Knihopis* 1706: NUK (54 B 91); MK (35 C 2 přív.).

———. *Hody křest'anské na které Bůh Otec skrze Syna svého zuve.* Prague: Impressí Šumanská, 1607. *Knihopis* 1707: NUK (54 B 91 přív.). This book apparently includes 1705, 1706, 1710 with an addition of *Kázání o těle a krvi Páně.*

———. *Bezpečné a pravé křest'anského člověka rozveselení.* Prague: Impressí Šumanská, 1607. *Knihopis* 1710: (54 B 91 přív.), (54 B 110).

———. *Kázání nad mrtvým tělem Anny dcery slovutného Pána Václava Samce ze Stráže.* Prague: Hanuš Landškronský, 1612. *Knihopis* 1708: NUK (54 I 11.371).

———. *Kázání nad mrtvým tělem urozené paní, paní Alžběty Valdštejnské z Valdštejna.* Prague: Matěj Pardubský, 1614. *Knihopis* 1709: NUK (54 B 79, 54 I 11.371).

Dačický z Heslova, Mikuláš. *Paměti.* 2 vols. Edited by Antonín Rezek. Prague: Matice česká, 1878–1880.

Dubravius, Jan. *Ad collegium Pragense de ecclesiae oeconomia epistola* in *Ioanis, Dei gratia episcopi Olomucensis, In psalmum ordine quintum ecclesiae deprecantis typum gerentem, cuius initium est: Verba mea auribus percipe, Domine, enarratio . . .* Prostějov: Ioannes Guntherus, 1549. *Rukovět'* 2:81: NUK (46 C 35, 27 J 32).

Dvorský, František, ed. *Dopisy kněží Šimona z Habru a Jana faráře Německo-Brodského o rozdílech ve víře, 1528–1529.* In *Archiv český* 14 (1895): 324–367.

Dykastus [Miřkovský], Jiřík. *Modlitby pobožných a horlivých rozjímání o milování Boha.* Prague: Daniel Adam z Veleslavína, 1598. *Knihopis* 2169: NUK (54 K 8681 přív., 54 G 256); Strahov (BZ IV 54 neúpl.).

———. *Postylla: nebo Kázání krátká na evangelia svatá,* 2 vols. Prague: Jiřík J. Dačický, 1612. *Knihopis* 2176: MK (35 C 32, 35 C 4).

Felin, Jan. *Rozebrání Obrany Samuela Martinia,* Spisy Jana Amosa Komenského, 6. Edited by Josef T. Müller. Prague: Česká akademie pro vědy, slovesnost, a umění, 1902.

Glücklich, Julius. *O historických dílech Václava Budovce z Budova z let 1608–1610 a jejich poměru k Slavatovi, Skálovi a neznámému dosud diariu Lutheróna Karla Zikmundova.* Rozpravy České akademie pro vědy, slovesnost a umění. Třída I., číslo 42. Prague: Alois Wiesner, 1911.

Hoffman, Jindřich Ondřej. *Ocularia, aneb oči sklenné starého Čecha, které podává Čechu nynějšímu skrze něž by hleděl na předešlou staro-českou nábožnost.* Prague: Jiří Sedlčanský, 1637. *Knihopis* 3099: NUK (54 D 117); MK (38 D 8).

———. *Zrcadlo náboženství.* Prague: Impressí akademická, 1642. *Knihopis* 3100: NUK (54 G 2, 54 F 118); MK (38 D 7 neúpl.).

Jakeš, Vít. *Důvodů 6 dostatečných o nemluvňátkách.* Prague: Jiřík Jakobeus Dačický, [1605?]. *Knihopis,* Dodatky 3425: MK (31 E 7).

———. *Obrana Kalichu svatého.* Perno, Saxony: n.p., [1631?]. *Knihopis* 3433: MK (37 D 23, 37 E 36); Strahov (B U VI 24).

Kapihorský, Symeon Evstachyus. *Dokázání mocné a podstatné, že z potřeby spasení k Přijímání pod obojí způsobou žádný zavázán není.* Prague: Pavel Sessius, 1625. *Knihopis* 3767: MK (38 B 7).

———. *Hystoria kláštera Sedleckého.* Prague: Pavel Sessius, 1630. *Knihopis* 3768: NUK (54 A 39); MK (31 B 3).

Klatovský, Martin. *Rozsuzování upřímné Artykuluov některých*. Prague: Ondřej Kubeš, 1544. *Knihopis* 3937: Stockholm, Sweden, Royal Library

Kocín z Kocinétu, Jan. *Abeceda pobožné manželky a rozšafné hospodyně*. Prague: Daniel Adam z Veleslavína, 1585. *Knihopis* 4159: MK (36 D 6 přív.); NUK (54 C 132, 54 F 1129 neúpl.).

⸻. *Ioannis Bodini Nova distributio iuris universi . . . explicata a Ioanne Cocino*. Prague: J. Negrin, 1581. *Rukověť* 3:53: MK (49 E 33 přív. 2).

Komenský, Jan Amos. *Historia o těžkých protivenstvích církve české hned od počátku jejího na víru Křesťanskou obrácení v létu 894 až do léta 1632 za panování Ferdinanda Druhého. S připojením historie o persekucí valdenských roku tohoto (1655) stálé*. Leszno, Poland: n.p., 1655; Amsterdam: Jan Paskovský, 1663. In Komenský, Jan Amos. Vol. 9, *Opera omnia*, Pt. 1, 53–198. Prague: Academia, 1989.

⸻. *The History of the Bohemian Persecution*. London: By A.A. for Iohn Walker, 1650.

⸻. *Stručná historie církve slovanské*. Edited by Josef Hendrich. Prague: Melantrich, 1941.

[Komenský, Jan Amos]. *Na spis proti jednotě bratrské od Samuele Martinia etc: sepsaný . . . Ohlášení*. Leszno, Poland: n.p., 1635. *Knihopis* 4243: NUK (54 C 177).

Konáč z Hodíškova, Mikuláš. *List pravdy pro řád pokoj lásku a svornost Království českého a Markrabství Moravského sepsaný a Králi Ludvíkovi jeho milosti poslaný*. Prague: Konáč z Hodíškova, 1522. *Knihopis* 4276: MK (32 D 18 přív.).

Konáč z Hodíškova, Mikuláš. See *O Turcích*.

Kožlanský, Bartoloměj. *Dar zlaté ruky*. N.p., 1626. *Knihopis* 4365: NUK (54 F 1130).

⸻. *Monumentum: Památka pohřební o životu a smrti urozeného a statečného rytíře Pana Tomáše z Proseče a na Jirnách*. N.p., 1624. *Knihopis* 4366: MK (40 G 7).

⸻. *Písně na sedm žalmů*. Prague: Pavel Sessius, [1615?]. *Knihopis* 4367: MK (40 G 7).

⸻. *Zlatá některá pravidla*. N.p., 1622. *Knihopis* 4368: MK (40 G 7).

⸻. *Rozjímání utěšené*. Prague: Jan Stříbrský, 1615. *Knihopis* 4369: MK (31 E 7).

Kristián z Koldína, Pavel. *Práva městská království českého*. Prague: Jiří Melantrich z Aventýna and Daniel Adam z Veleslavína, 1579. *Knihopis* 4564: NUK (54 B 31).

Kuttemberger z Kuttembergku, Václav. *Přídavek k dokázání mocnému a podstatnému, že z potřeby spasení k Přijímání pod obojí žádný zavázán není*. Prague: Pavel Sessius, 1625. *Knihopis* 4629: MK (38 B 7).

Linteo z Pilzenburgku, Petr. *Krátká správa o Přijímání velebné svátosti pod jednau a dvojí spůsobau*. Prague: Kargezius, 1613. *Knihopis* 4897: NUK (54 D 87); Strahov (BU IV 37)

⸻. *Jistá a patrná cýrkve svaté znamení*. Litomyšl: n.p., 1593. *Knihopis* 4898: NUK (54 F 58); MK (36 F 7 neúpl.). Second edition, Prague: Wolffkang Wickhart, 1725. *Knihopis* 4899: many locations.

Martinius z Dražova, Samuel. *Hussius et Lutherus, id est: collatio historica duorum fortissimorum Iesu Christi militum*. Prague: Pavel Sessius, 1618. *Rukověť* 3:272: MK (49 E 14, 46 E 34); NUK (51 E 57).

⸻. *Induciae Martinianae: Anebo Správa Skrovná a Potřebná*. Pirna, Saxony: Dědici Jana Ctibora, 1638. *Knihopis* 5369: NUK (54 C 64 přív.); MK (50 C 12 přív.).

⸻. *Obrana M. Samuela Martiniusa z Dražova: Proti ohlášení starších kněží Bratrských*. Pirna, Saxony: Dědici Jana Ctibora, 1636. *Knihopis* 5380: NUK (54 C 64); MK (37 B 13).

_____. *Oratio de concordia ecclesiae his ultimis temporibus plurimum necessaria.*
Prague: Pavel Sessius, 1617. *Rukověť* 3:272: MK (46 D 27, and others); NUK (46 G 441 přív. 1, 51 E 57 přív. 1).

_____. *Pět a třidceti mocných, znamenitých a slušných důvodů a příčin pro které všickni Evangelistští Čechové za jedno býti.* Pirna: Dědici Jana Ctibora, 1635. *Knihopis* 5383: NUK (54 C 177).

Menčík, Ferdinand, ed. *Zápisky kněze Václava Rosy.* Vienna: J. Paška, 1879.

Na spis proti jednotě bratrské od Samuele Martinia etc: sepsaný . . . Ohlášení. See [Komenský, Jan Amos].

Nožička z Votína, Blažej. *Knížka proti bludům některým před tisíci lety odsouzeným.* Prague: Jan Kantor, 1566. *Knihopis* 6491: NUK (54 E 59); MK (36 A 10).

_____. *Vyznání o poctivosti vzývání, přímluvě a o modlitbě za mrtvé.* Prague: Jiří Dačický, 1568. *Knihopis* 6492: MK (36 A 10 přív.).

O Turcích: Odkud a proč Turci slovú. Prague: Mikuláš Konáč z Hodíškova, [1522?]. *Knihopis* 16.343: MK (32 D 18 přív.).

Pačuda, Matauš. *Spis v němž se obsahuje které věci (z stran lidského pokolení) předešly příchod a narození mesiáše pravého Krista.* Prague: Matěj Pardubický, 1616. *Knihopis* 6691: Strahov (BX VI 22 přív. neúpl.).

Paminondas, Pavel. *Písničky křesťanské.* Prague: Anna Šumanova, 1596. *Knihopis* 6828: MK (27 C 1); NUK (65 E 2086).

Phaëton [Žalanský], Havel. *Kázání o velikých modlářských bludích, jimiž v církvi odporné nejsvětější Páně Večeře se zlehčuje a poškvrňuje.* Prague: n.p., [1620?]. *Knihopis* 7123: NUK (54 K 11.048); MK (37 E 9, 37 E 36, 37 E 29).

_____. *O ctných manželkách těhotných a rodičkách křesťanských.* Prague: Danyel Karel z Karlspergka, 1619. *Knihopis* 7153: Strahov (BT VIII 6).

_____. *Spis neb Kázání první o svatých a blahoslavených mučedlnících českých.* Prague: Danyel Karel z Karlspergka, 1619. Contains also *Spisové o mučedlnících českých,* f. D1-K8; *Spis o velikých těžkých a krvavých protivenstvích Církve,* f. Q1-V8. *Knihopis* 7152: MK (37 E 9).

Písecký, Jiří. *Listy a kronika, 1518–1526.* In *Prameny dějin českých/Fontes Rerum Bohemicarum* 6, 346–362. Prague: Nadání Františka Palackého, 1907.

Polon, Valentin. *Pomni na mne: Knižka obsahující v sobě kratičká spasidedlná Naučení a sebrání . . .* Staré Město Pražské: Buryan Valda, 1589. *Knihopis* 14.153: NUK (54 F 226).

Rosacius Hořovský, Jan. *Fama exequialis. Pověst dobrého jména.* Prague: Jiří Hanuš L[anškrounský], 1613. *Knihopis:* 14.885: NUK (54 I 11371 přív. 1).

_____. *O hladu pokutě Boží hrozné kázání.* Prague: Matěj Pardubský, 1616. *Knihopis* 14.887: NUK (54 K 9294).

_____. *Kázání o nejsvětější večeři Pána našeho Ježíše Krista.* Prague: Jan Ctibor, 1620. *Knihopis* 14.888: MK (35 C 4 přív. manuscript copy).

_____. *Koruna neuvadlá mučedlníkův českých.* [Zittau, Saxony]: n.p., 1756. *Knihopis* 14.891: NUK (54 K 6886 přív); MK (50 F 32).

Rvačovský z Rvačov, Vavřinec Leander. *Knížka zlatá.* Olomouc: Fridrich Milichtáler, 1577. *Knihopis* 15.126: MK (36 F 2 neúpl.).

_____. *Masopust.* Prague: Jiří Melantrich, 1580. *Knihopis* 15.127: NUK (54 C 39); MK (36 A 7 neúpl.).

Scribonius z Horšova, Jindřich. *Catechismus: aneb Naučení člověka křesťanského netoliko mládeži ale i lidem dospělejšího věku . . .* Prague: Jan Kantor, 1556. *Knihopis* 15.242: NUK (54 F 222); MK (36 G 5).

Sixt Palma Močidlanský. *Svědectví starých svatých otců, učitelů a mučedníků Božích o důstojném Přijímání Těla a krve Pána Ježíše Krysta pod obojím spůsobem.* Prague: Stříbrský, 1598. *Knihopis* 6808: NUK (54 D 85 neupl.).

Sixt z Ottersdorfu. "Diarium o sněmu 1575, jenž zahájen byl 21. února a zavřín dne 27. září." In *Sněmy české,* 4: 318–392 (n. 88).

──────. *Knihy památné o nepokojných letech 1546 a 1547.* 2 vols. Edited by Josef Teige. Prague: J. Otto, [1920].

──────. *O pokoření stavu městského léta 1547.* Edited by Josef Janáček. Prague: Melantrich, 1950.

Skála ze Zhoře, Pavel. *Historie česká od r. 1602 do r. 1623.* 5 vols. Edited by Karel Tieftrunk. Prague: Kober, 1865–1870.

Škola aneb cvičení křesťanské a věrné duše pobožného člověka. Prague: Daniel Adam z Veleslavína, 1589. *Knihopis* 15.916: NUK (54 F 215); MK (36 F 27).

Slavata, Vilém. *Děje království uherského za panování Ferdinanda I., 1526-1546* Edited by Josef Jireček. Vienna: Slovenské Noviny, 1857.

──────. *Paměti nejvyššího kancléře království českého.* 2 vols. Edited by Josef Jireček. Prague: Kober, 1866–1868.

──────. *Přehled náboženských dějin českých.* Edited by Hanuš Opočenský. Prague: J. Otto, 1912.

──────. *Zápisky z let 1601–1603.* Edited by Antonín Rezek. Prague: Česká společnost nauk, 1887. Rozpravy, řada 7, svazek 2.

Šlechta ze Všehrd, Jan. *Dva listáře humanistické: Dra. Racka Doubravského, II. M. Václava Píseckého, s doplňkem listáře Jana Šlechty ze Všehrd.* Sbírka pramenů ku poznání literárního života v Čechách, na Moravě a ve Slezsku, Skupina 2, Číslo 3. Edited by Josef Truhlář. Prague: Česká akademie pro vědy, slovesnost a umění, 1897.

Slovacius, Václav. *O pokloně ve jménu Jesus, má-li činěna býti.* Prague: Jan Jičinský, [1586]. *Knihopis* 15.509: NUK (54 F53); Prague: Jan Jičinský, 1590. *Knihopis* 15.510: NUK (54 F 183).

Srnec of Varvažov, Jakub. *Apophoreta aliquot in Epiphaniis Domini, amicis dedicata a M. J. R. W.* N.p., 1557. *Rukověť* 5:157–158: NUK (9 K 654).

Štelcar Želetavský z Želetavy, Jan. *Kázání dvoje.* Prague: [Jiří Dačický?], 1586. *Knihopis* 15.982: MK (36 D 9 neúpl.).

──────. *Kniha duchovní o velikých skutcích Pána Boha všemohoucího.* Prague: Jan Jičínský, 1588. *Knihopis* 15.984: MK (36 E 4 neúpl.); NUK (54 F 185 neúpl., 54 G 69 neúpl., 54 K 5673); Strahov (BZ III 4l núpl.).

──────. *Kniha nová o původu kněžství Krista Pána.* Prague: Daniel Sedlčanský, 1592. *Knihopis* 15.985: NUK (54 K 10635 neúpl.); Strahov (DR IV 39 neúpl.).

──────. *Kniha o dobrých a zlých andělích.* Prague: Jiří Dačický, 1585. *Knihopis* 15.987: MK (36 D 9 neúpl.).

──────. *Knížka o pravé a falešné církvi.* Prague: Buryán Valda, 1589. *Knihopis* 15.988: MK (36 E 3 neúpl.).

Straněnský, Jan. *Almanach duchovní z Starého a Nového Zákona k zdraví duše a k navedení života sebraný.* Prague: Jan Had, 1542. *Knihopis* 15.720: MK (36 F 4 přív. 3).

──────. *Zahrádka duchovní k potěšení všem věrným v zármutcích postaveným lidem z Písem svatých sebraná.* Prague: Jiřík Černý, 1576. *Knihopis* 15.733: NUK (54 F 214; 54 C 145); MK (36 F 8).

Stránský, Pavel. *Český stát. Okřik*. Edited by Bohumil Ryba. Prague: Státní nakladatelství krásné literatury, hudby a umění, 1953.
Stříbrský, Matěj. *Cesta k životu věčnému*. Litomyšl: n.p., 1611. *Knihopis* 15.772: MK (37 E 15).
_____. *Knížka spasitedlných naučení*. Prague: Daniel Sedlčanský, 1610. *Knihopis* 15.773: NUK (54 F 214 přív. 2).
Šturm z Greifenberku, Jan. *Křest'anské a pobožné rozjímání na evangelium svatého Jana* . . . Prague: Šebastián Oksa z Kolovsy, 1567. *Knihopis* 16.010: NUK (54 B 132 přív.).
Šturm, Václav. *Krátké ozvání* . . . *proti kratičkému ohlášení Jednoty Valdenské neb Boleslavské*. Prague: Jiřík Dačický, 1584. *Knihopis* 16.006: NUK (54 B 86, 54 B 87 přív., 54 B 83 přív., 54 H 9571); MK (36 A 3).
_____. *Rozsouzení a bedlivé uvážení Velikého kancionálu od Bratří Valdenských, jinak Boleslavských, sepsaného* . . . Prague: Burián Valda, 1588. *Knihopis* 16.007: NUK (54 F 2, 54 B 85, 54 H 9571); MK (36 A 19, 36 A 14 neupl.).
_____. *Srovnání víry a učení Bratří starších*. Litomyšl: Andreas Graudenc, 1582. *Knihopis* 16.009: NUK (54 B 84); MK (36 A 11).
Summa Katechysmu: Přidáni jsou mravové aneb naučení Potřebná. Prague: Dědicové Daniele Adama z Veleslavína, 1600. *Knihopis* 15.793: NUK (54 G 245, 54 G 138 přív.); MK (37 F 23).
Summa religionis verae ex Confessione Bohemica excerpta/Summa náboženství pravého z Konfessí české vybraná. Prague: Pavel Sessius, 1618. MK (37 E 15 přív.).
Taciturnus z Háje [Hájský], Jiří. *Zlatý řetízek pravého katolického náboženství* . . . *k dobrému mládeži školní Aušpurské konfesi*. Prague: Matěj Pardubický, 1616. *Knihopis* 16.050: NUK (54 D 87 přív. 3 neúpl.); MK (37 E 15).
z Valdštejna, Adam the Younger. *Deník rudolfinského dvořana, 1602–1633*. Edited by Marie Koldinská and Petr Mat'a. Prague: Argo, 1997.
z Valdštejna, Jan the Elder. *Modlitby [a řeči] pobožné některé z písem Svatých, jiné pak z naučení Mudrců pohanských vybrané*. N.p., 1576. *Knihopis* 5864 NUK (54 G 294 poškoz.).
Velenský of Mnichov, Oldřich. *See also* Velenus, Ulrichus.
Velenus, Ulrichus. *In hoc libello grauissimis, certissimisque, & in sacra scriptura fundatis rationibus uarijs probatur, Apostolarum Petrum Romae non uenisse, neque illicit passum, proinde satis friuole, & temere Romanus Pontifex se Petri successorem inactat, & nominat*. Basel: n.p., 1520.
_____. *In disem Büchlin wirt in mancherlay tapffern bestendigen und in der Scrifft gegründeten Ursachen klärlich bewert, das der hailig Apostel Petrus gen Rom nicht komen noch alda den Tod gelitten* . . . [Augsburg?]: [S. Otmar?], [1521?]. German translation of previous work.
Walkmberger z Walkmbergku, Jakub Soffian. *Advent a Štědrý den*. Prague: Buryán Walda, 1596. *Knihopis* 16.914: NUK (54 E 125 přív. neúpl.).
_____. *Kořen Jesse*. Prague: Daniel Sedlčanský, 1594. *Knihopis* 16.915: MK (36 E 15 neúpl.).
Zachová, Jana, and Jaroslav Boubín. "Drobné spisky Jana Příbrama na obranu katolické víry." In *Facta probant homines: Sborník příspěvků k životnímu jubileu prof. dr. Zdeňky Hledíkové*. Edited by Ivan Hlaváček, et al., 521–534. Prague: Scriptorium, 1998.

Žatecký, Martin. *Knížka proti ošemetné poctě a pokryté Svatých*. 2d ed. Prague: Jan Štelcar Želetavský z Želetavy, 1593. *Knihopis* 5221: MK (37 D přív.).

Authors, 1517–1648: Other

Adrichomius, Christianus. *Vypsání města Jeruzaléma a předměstí jeho*. Translated by Daniel Adam z Veleslavína. Prague: Daniel Adam z Veleslavína, 1592. *Knihopis* 66: NUK (54 B 14).

Aquinas, Thomas. *Compendium of Theology*. Translated by Cyril Vollert. St. Louis: B. Herder Book Co., 1947.

Barnes, Robert. *Kronyky. A životů sepsání nejvrchnějších Biskupů Římských jináč Papežů*. Translated by Simon Ennius Klatovský. Nuremberg: Woldřich Nejber and Jan Montán, 1565. *Knihopis* 958: NUK (54 C 26, 54 B 111). Second part by Czech author, presumably Klatovský.

Bayly, Lewis. *Praxis pietatis. To jest, O cvičení se v pobožnosti pravé*. Leszno, Poland: n.p., [1630?]. *Knihopis* 1015: NUK (54 C 147); MK (50 G 7).

Calvin, Jean. *Pobožná duše jenž k známosti Boha hoříš*. 3 vols. Kralice: n.p., [1612–1614?]. *Knihopis* 1406: NUK (54 B 44 neupl.); MK (35 B 8, 37 A 8). Parallel edition with Latin introduction by Jean Calvin: *Institutio Christianae religionis, in quatuor libros digesta, Johanne Calvino auctore, in Bohemicam vero Lingvam a Georgio Streyzio versa, et in communem usum omnium latissimae Slavonicae linguae populorum a Johanne Opsimathe edita*. Amberg, Upper Palatinate, 1615. A copy, with printed dedication to James I, is deposited in the Sidney Sussex College, Cambridge; see *Knihopis,* Dodatky 1406.

Campion, Edmund. *Wšech Pikartských, Luteryánských, i jináč zrotilých Prevytkantů, Hostides. To jest: Deset podstatných příčin, kterýchž jistotau, velebný kněz, a zmužilosrdnatý Mučedlník Edmund Kampian, z Tovaryšstva jména Ježíšova pohnut jsa, vše víry Řzímské Odpůrce, k zjevnému před Englickau Královnau, o Víru potýkání, pobídl; Jim se pak z brlochu na světlo vyjíti nechtělo*. Olomouc: Jiř. Handle, 1602. *Knihopis* 1419: NUK (54 F 139 přív., 54 F 154).

―――. *Spis krátký Edmunda Kampiana Societatis Jesu, Theologa a Mučedlníka Božího, ktrý ne tak dávno pro víru S. Katolickau smrt ukrutnau podstaupil: Vznešeným Doktorům a Mistrům učení Oxoniénského a Kantabrigienského podaný*. Prague: Jiřík Nygrin, 1601. *Knihopis* 1420: NUK (54 F 244); MK (38 E 19 neúpl.).

Capello, Carolus. *Epitome apostolicarum constitutionum in Creta insula per Carolum Capellium Venetum repertarum et e Graeco in Latinum translatarum (ad Johannes Cochlaeus)*. Ingolstadt: Alexander Weissenhorn, 1546. Vienna National Library, 19 H 93.

Cassiodorus, Flavius Magnus, Senator. *Historia Cýrkevní*. Translated by Jan Kocín of Kocinét, Prague: Daniel Adam z Veleslavína, 1594. *Knihopis* 1470: NUK (54 B 4, 54 A 65).

Cochlaeus, Johannes. *De Petro et Roma aduersus Velenum Lutheranum . . .* [Cologne]: n.p., 1525.

―――. *Ein heimlich gespraech von der tragedia Johannis Hussen 1538*. Edited by Hugo Holstein. Halle a. Salle: M. Niemeyer, 1900.

―――. *Historiae Hussitarum libri duodecim*. Mainz: Franciscus Behem, 1549. In Folger Library, Washington, D.C., 164–961f.

Cremonensis, Eusebius. *Kšaft sv. Jeronyma.* Translated by Šimon Lomnický of Budeč. Prague: n.p., 1613. *Knihopis* 2391: NUK (54 F 167).

Crespin, Jean. *Histoire des Martyrs persécutez et mis à mort pour la vérité de l'évangile, depuis le temps des apostres iusques à présent (1619).* 3 vols. Edited by Daniel Benoît. Toulouse: Société des livres religieux, 1885–1889.

Dungersheim, Hieronymus. "Dialogus ad Lutherum." In Vol. 2, *Dr. Martin Luthers Briefwechsel,* edited by Ernst Ludwig Enders, 168–170. Calv and Stuttgart: Verlag der Vereinsbuchhandlung, 1887.

Emser, Hieronymus. *De disputatione lipsicensi, quantum ad Boemos obiter deflexa est (1519). A venatione Luteriana Aegocerotis assertio (1519).* Corpus catholicorum. Werke katholischer Schriftsteller im Zeitalter der Glaubensspaltung, 4. Edited by Franz Xaver Thurnhofer. Münster: Aschendorf, 1921.

Erasmus, Desiderius. *The Correspondence.* 11 vols. Toronto: University of Toronto Press, 1974–1992.

————. *Evangelium Ježíše Krista syna Božího podle sepsání Svatého Matouše.* Translated by Jan Vartovský of Varta. Litomyšl: Ondřej Dušík, 1542. *Knihopis* 2348: NUK (54 C 98); MK (35 C 14).

Eusebius of Caesarea [Pamphilus]. *Historia Cýrkevní.* Translated by Jan Kocín of Kocinét. Prague: Daniel Adam z Veleslavína, 1594. *Knihopis* 2390: NUK (54 B 4; 54 A 65, 54 A 155, 54 A 1308); MK (30 A 1).

Eusebius Cremonensis. See Cremonensis, Eusebius.

Faber, Johann. *Confutatio gravissimi erroris asserentis in sacramento altaris post consecrationem nisi corpus tantum et sub specie vini non esse nisi sanguinem tantum.* Leipzig: Nicholas Wolrab, 1537. NUK (35.B.167).

Foxe, John. *Fox's Book of Martyrs: The Acts and Monuments of the Church.* 3 vols. Edited by John Cumming. London: Chatto and Windus, 1875.

Freder, Johann [Johannes Irenaeus]. *Ein Dialogus dem Ehestand zu ehren geschrieben.* Wittemberg: Nickel Schirlentz, 1545.

————. *Čest a nevina pohlaví ženského.* Prague: Daniel Adam z Veleslavína, 1585. *Knihopis* 3389: NUK (54 C 132).

Gwagnin, Aleksander [Alessandro Guagnini]. *Kronika Moskevská. Wypsání předních zemí, krajin, národůw, knížestwí, měst, zámkůw, rzek i jezer, Welikému Knížeti Mozkewskému poddanych . . . Téz o neslýchaném Tyranství Ivana Vasilovice Knížete Moskevského, kteréž on za paměti naší nad poddanými svými provozoval.* Translated by Matouš Hosius z Vysokého Mýta. Prague: Daniel Adam z Veleslavína, 1589. *Knihopis* 2797: NUK (54 F 55, 54 F 11.094); MK (29 E 1 neúpl.).

Hooker, Richard. *The Works of that Learned and Judicious Divine.* 2 vols. Oxford: Clarendon Press, 1865.

————. *The Folger Library Edition of the Works of Richard Hooker.* 6 vols. Edited by W. Speed Hill. Cambridge, Mass.: Belknap Press of Harvard University Press, 1977–1993.

Irenaeus, Johannes. See Freder, Johann.

Jewel, John. *An Apologie, or Answer in Defense of the Church of England.* London: Reginalde Wolfe, 1562. Reprint, New York: De Capo Press, 1972.

————. *Apologia, to jest: Dostatečná Obrana Víry a Náboženství Cýrkví Englických.* Prague: Danyel Karel z Karlspergka, 1619. *Knihopis* 3558: NUK (54 H 994, 54 H 7969, 54 H 7917 přív.).

_____. *An Apology of the Church of England*. Folger Documents of Tudor and Stuart Civilization. Edited by J. E. Booty. Ithaca, N.Y.: Cornell University Press, 1963.

Jordan, Raymond. *Contemplazioni sull'amor divino.*Testi cristiani, Nuova ser., 4. Translated by Emilio Piovesan. [Florence]: Libreria editrice fiorentina, [1954].

Josephus, Flavius. *Historie židovská. Na knihy čtyři rozdělená.* Translated and introduction by Václav Plácel z Elbingu. Prague: Daniel Adam of Veleslavín, 1592. *Knihopis* 3628: NUK (54 C 1988); MK (30 B 2, 30 B 3, 29 B 6); Strahov (AS XI 4, BD IV 42).

Lauterbeck, Georg. *Politica historica: O vrchnostech a správcích světských knihy patery.* Translated by Daniel Adam of Veleslavín. Prague: Daniel Adam of Veleslavín, 1584. LC: Law case: 56–55128. *Knihopis* 4735: NUK (54 B 19); MK (29 B 1); Prague: Dědici Daniele Adama z Veleslavína, 1606. *Knihopis* 4736: NUK (54 B 18); (54 D 7254); MK (29 B 2).

Leunclavius, Johannes. *Kronyka nová o národu tureckém na dva díly rozdělená,* Translated by Jan Kocín of Kocinét and Daniel Adam of Veleslavín. Prague: Daniel Adam z Veleslavína, 1594. *Knihopis* 4823: NUK (54 B 112, 54 C 27, 54 H 5349); MK (30 C 4); Strahov (AO XVI 20).

Luther, Martin. *Dr. Martin Luthers Briefwechsel.* Edited by Ernst Ludwig Enders. Calv and Stuttgart: Verlag der Vereinsbuchhandlung, 1887.

_____. *Werke: Kritische Gesammtausgabe.* 113 vols. in 4 series. Weimar: Böhlau, 1883–1996.

_____. *Kázání velebného a nábožného otce Martina Luthera na desatero přikázání Božích, které lidu obecnému zjevně v městě Witemberce kázal jest.* Translated by Pavel Hlavsa Příbram. Introduction by Anonymous. Prague: Pavel Severýn z Kapí Hory, 1520. *Knihopis* 5110: MK (25 D 12), Strahov (DR IV 12 přív.). Translation of Martin Luther, "Decem praecepta Wittenbergensi praedicata populo. 1518." In Vol. 1, *Werke: Kritische Gesammtausgabe,* 398–521. Weimar: Böhlau, 1883.

_____. *Kázání o novém zákoně aneb o posledním kšaftu Krista pána na své svaté Večeři, to jest o mši svaté.* Prague: [Pavel Severýn z Kapí Hory?], 1521. *Knihopis* 5112: Olomouc, State Research Library (32.113 neúplné? nebo příd. k č. 5103). Translation of Luther. *Ein Sermon von dem neuen Testament, das ist von der heiligen Messe. 1520.* In Vol. 6, *Werke: Kritische Gesammtausgabe,* 349–378. Weimar: Böhlau, 1888.

_____. *O svobodě křest'anské knížka... kterouž Lvovi desátému papeži římskému psal.* [Litomyšl: Alexander Aujezdský], 1521. *Knihopis* 5113: Olomouc State Research Library (32.116, 32.149); MK (70 D 21 přív.). Translation of Luther. *De Libertate Christiana.* In Vol. 7, *Werke: Kritische Gesammtausgabe,* 49–73. Weimar: Böhlau, 1897.

_____. *Před velebností císařskou i přede všemi knížaty říše k napomenutí jich odvolati knihy pod jménem jeho vydané.* [Prague: Pavel Severýn z Kapí Hory], 1521. *Knihopis* 5116: Olomouc, State Research Library (32.111, missing last folio). Translation of Luther. "Doctor Martinus red an Ro. Kay. May't, die Churfursten und Stende des Reichs." In Vol. 7, *Werke: Kritische Gesammtausgabe,* 867–877. Weimar: Böhlau, 1897.

_____. *Pro kterou příčinu papežský a jeho následovníků knihy jest spálil tuto zvíš.* Prague: Pavel Severýn z Kapí Hory, 1521. *Knihopis* 5119: Olomouc, State Research Library (32.112). Translation of Luther. *Warumb des Bapsts und siner Jungernn bucher von Doct. Martino Luther vorbrant seynn.* In Vol. 7, *Werke: Kritische Gesammtausgabe,* 152–182. Weimar: Böhlau, 1897.

———. *O velebné svátosti svatého pravého Těla Kristova a o bratrstvích*, Translated by Oldřich Velenský of Mnichov[?]. N.p., 1520. NUK (54 S 63). Translation of Luther. *Ein Sermon von dem hochwürdigen Sacrament des heiligen waren Leichnams Christi und von den Brüderschaften. 1519.* In Vol. 2, *Werke: Kritische Gesammtausgabe,* 738–758. Weimar: Böhlau, 1884.

———. *O ustanovení služebníků církve slovutné poctivosti Pánèm panu purkmistru a radě starších i všemu lidu slovutného města Prahy hlavy království českého.* Prague: n.p., 1523. *Knihopis* 5125: Olomouc, State Research Library(32.120 neúpl.). Translation of Luther. *De instituendis ministris Ecclesiae, ad clarissimum senatum Pragensem Bohemiae. 1523.* In Vol. 12, *Werke: Kritische Gesammtausgabe,* 160–196. Weimar: Böhlau, 1891.

———. *Výklad o Antikristu na vidění Danielovo: v osmé kapitole proroctví jeho položené.* Translated by Oldřich Velenský of Mnichov. Prague: [Pavel Severýn z Kapí Hory], 1522. *Knihopis* 5127: Olomouc, State Research Library (32.114); MK (25 D 5). Translation of Luther. *Ad librum eximii Magistri Nostri Magistri Ambrosii Catharini, defensoris Silvestri Prieratis accerimi, responsio. Cum exposita Visione Danielis viii. De Antichristo. 1521.* In Vol. 7, *Werke: Kritische Gesammtausgabe,* 698–778. Weimar: Böhlau, 1897.

———. [*Kázání O velebné svátosti svatého pravého Těla Kristova.*] N.p., [after 1520]. *Knihopis* 5122: Olomouc, State Research Library (32.115, missing title page). Translation of Luther. *Von beyder gestallt des Sacraments zu nehmen* 1522, Vol. 10, *Werke: Kritische Gesammtausgabe,* II, 11–41. Weimar: Böhlau, n.d. Czech translation c. 1522, missing title page and end page; hence Czech title unknown, or year, or translator. See Rudolf Říčan, "Tschechische Übersetzungen von Luthers Schriften bis zum Schmalkaldischen Krieg," *Vierhundertfünfzig Jahre lutherische Reformation, 1517–1967 (Festschrift für Franz Lau zum 50. Geburtstag)* (Göttingen: Vanderhoeck and Ruprecht, 1967), 286.

Melanchton, Philipp. "Testimonia sanctorum patrum." In *Defensio coniugii sacerdotum pia & erudita, missa ad regem Angliae . . . Refutatio abusum coenae.* N.p., 1542. Washington, D.C., Folger Library (BR336.D5 1542).

Montagu, Richard. *A Gagg for the New Gospell? No, a New Gagg for an Old Goose.* Amsterdam: Theatrum Orbis Terrarum, 1624. Reprint, Norwood, N.J.: W. J. Johnson, 1975.

More, Thomas. *Complete Works.* 21 vols. New Haven, Conn.: Yale University Press, 1963–1997.

Moryson, Fynes. *An Itinerary Containing His Ten Yeeres Travell.* 4 vols. New York: Macmillan, 1907–1908.

———. *Shakespeare's Europe: A Survey of the Conditions of Europe at the End of the 16th Century. [Being Unpublished Chapters of Fynes Moryson's Itinerary, 1917].* Edited by Charles Hughes. London: Sherratt & Hughes, 1903. Reprint, New York: Benjamin Blom, 1967.

Paprocki z Glogoł, Bartołomiej. *Diadochos id est successio: Jinák posloupnost knížat a králů českých.* Prague: Dědic Jana Šumana, 1602. *Knihopis* 6843: NUK (54 B 20, 54 A 69); MK (31 A 1, 31 A 2).

———. *Zrcadlo slavného markrabství Moravského.* Olomouc: Haeredes Milichtalleri, 1593. Reprint, Ostrava: Genealogická agentura, 1993.

Paulus II, Pope. *Odsudek víry.* Prague: Severýn, 1547. *Knihopis* 6937: MK (36 B 14 přív., 32 D 18 přív.); NUK (54 H 1459 neúpl.).

Paul III, Pope. *Bulle od Papeže Římského Antikrista proti pravým křest'anom vydaná.* [Prostějov?]: n.p., 1546. *Knihopis* 6938: NUK (54 H 1459 přív.); MK (36 B 14 přív.).

Perkins, William. *Anatomia conscientiae. Aneb pobožné rozbírání a vysvětlení svědomí lidského.* Prague: Karel Karlsperk, 1620. *Knihopis* 6994: MK (37 F 4 neúpl.).

———. *O opuštění Božím.* Prague: Daniel Sedlčanský, 1610. *Knihopis* 6995: NUK (54 F 1139 přív.).

———. *Traktát trojí krátký, ku potěšení zarmoucených kajících lidí.* Prague: Matěj Pardubský, 1613. *Knihopis* 6997: NUK (52 F 34 přív.); MK (37 E 9 přív.).

———. *Traktát velmi platný a užitečný.* Prague: Prague: Matěj Pardubský, 1616. *Knihopis* 6998: NUK (54 K 9294 přív.); MK (37 D 31).

Pius II, Pope [Aeneas Sylvius Piccolomini]. *Česká kronika.* Prague: Mikuláš Konáč z Hodíškova, 1510. *Knihopis* 13.884: MK (25 D 27 neúpl.); Strahov (DR IV 10).

———. *Historia Bohemica/Historie česká.* Translated and edited by Dana Martínková, Alena Hadravová, and Jiří Matl. Prague: Koniasch Latin Press, 1998.

Remond, Florimond de. *Husitského v Čechách Kacířství počátku, zrůstu, a pádu vejtah.* Prague: Jan K. Hraba, [1777]. *Knihopis* 14.810: MK (68 G 82, 68 G 43); NUK (54 E 315).

———. *Histoire de la naissance, progrès et décadence de l'herésie de ce siècle.* Paris: C. Chastellain, 1605.

Scultetus, Abraham. *Vysvětlení Žalmu XX v Valdsaxu.* Prague: Daniel Karel z Karlsperkga, 1619. *Knihopis* 15.245; NUK (54 D 46, 54 I 11371); MK (24 D 12).

Tanner, Adam. *Apologia pro Societate Jesu ex Boemiae Regno ab eiusdem regni statibus religionis sub utraque, publico decreto immerito proscripta. Anno M.DC.XVIII. die VIIII Junij.* Vienna: Wolfgang Schump, 1618. MK (42 F 21).

———. *Apologia, oder Schutzschrift der Societet Jesu, so den 9. Tag Junii diss 1618. Jars von den Uncatholischen aus den Landt Staendten des Koenigreichs Boehaimb durch ein angemast offentlich Decret unbillich proscribirt und ausgeschafft worden.* Vienna: Wolfgang Schump, 1618. MK (42 C 444).

Tillemannus, Franciscus. *Krátký výklad aneb vysvětlení sedmi žalmův kajících svatého Davida.* Translated by Jiří Dikast. Prague: Daniel Adam z Veleslavína, 1598. *Knihopis* 16.225: NUK (54 K 8681).

Weller, Hieronymus. *De officio ecclesiastico, politico, et oeconomico, libellus pius et eruditus.* Nuremberg: Montanus and Neuborus, 1552.

Wujek z Wągrowca, Jakób. *Postylla Aneb Kázání evangelitská.* 2 vols. in 4 parts. Translated by Ondřej Modestin. Litomyšl: Andreas Graudenc, 1592. *Knihopis* 17.059: NUK (54 B 90).

Other Primary Sources

Antiqua et constans confessio fidei ecclesiae Christi in regno Boiemiae et Marchianatu Moraviae, quam vulgo partem sub utraque sacramentum venerabile corporis et sanguinis dom. Jesu Christi communicantium appellant. With introduction by Matěj Kolín z Chotěřiny. Prague: n.p., 1574.

Archiv český čili staré písemné památky české i moravské, sebrané z archivů domácích i cizích. Vols. 1-33, 35-37. Edited by František Palacký, Josef Kalousek, and Gustav Friedrich. Prague: for Domestikální fond český published by Bursík and Kohout, 1840–1904.

Artykulowe a snessenij Knězstva pod obogij Spuosobau: Leta Bozijho MDXXXIX. Archived in the National Library in Vienna under the notation, *Articuli Conciliabuli sub utraque specie communicantium.* Bohemice et latine. S.l., 1539. Signatura 24 M 56.

Bejblík, Alois, ed. *Fynes Moryson – John Taylor: Cesta do Čech.* Prague: Mladá fronta, 1977.

Bidlo, Jaroslav, ed. *Akty Jednoty bratrské.* 2 vols. Prameny dějin moravských, vols. 3–4. Brno: Matice moravská, 1915–1923.

Bohemia, Kancelář českých direktorů. *Protokol vyšlé korespondence Kanceláře českých direktorů z let 1618 a 1619.* Sborník archivu ministerstva vnitra, 7. Edited by J. Prokeš. Prague: Státní tiskárna, 1934.

Bohemia, Komisse reformační. *Dopisy Reformační komisse v Čechách z let 1627–1692.* Sbírka pramenů církevních dějin českých stol. 16–18, no. 1. Edited by Antonín Podlaha. Prague: Nákl. vlastní, 1908.

Borový, Klement. *Jednání a dopisy konsistoře katolické a utrakvistické.* 2 vols. Prague: I. L. Kober, 1868.

Castres, Salnar de, ed. *Harmonia confessionum fidei, Orthodoxarum, et Reformatorum Ecclesiarum.* 2 vols. in 1. Geneva: Petrus Santandreanus, 1581. (Bohemian Confession, 143.)

Catholic Church, Corpus Iuris Canonici. *Editio Lipsiensis Secunda post Aemilii Ludovici Richteri curas.* 2 vols. Edited by Emile Friedberg. Leipzig: Bernhard Tauchnitz, 1879–1881.

Compelle intrare. To jest: O násilném lidí k víře mocí tělesnou přidržování . . . N.p., 1625. *Knihopis* 1579: NUK (54 F 1130); MK (37 F 42).

Confessio Bohemica, Vera Augustana in Questiones et Responsiones Resoluta, ac ante quinquennium in lingua vernacula publici iuris cum indultu Venerandi Consistorii Pragensis facta. Konfessí česká pravá Aušpurská na otázky a odpovědi před pěti lety v jazyku českém vůbec s povolením vzácné Konsistoře Pražské vydaná. Prague: Jan Ctibor, 1620. *Knihopis* 1598: NUK (65 F 60).

Druhá Apologie stavův království českého, tělo a krev Pána Ježíše Krista pod obojí přijímajících. Prague: Jonata Bohutský z Hranic, 1618. *Knihopis* 234: NUK (54 E 316); MK (31 C 10; 31 C 7 přív.).

Druhá Apologie stavův království českého, tělo a krev Pána Ježíše Krista pod obojí přijímajících. Prague: Daniel Karel z Karlspergka, 1619. *Knihopis* 235: MK (31 C 11; 31 C 20).

Euangelische Erklerung auff die Böhaimische Apologia. [Vienna?]: n.p., 1618. MK (42 D 17).

Frind, A. "Urkunden über die Bewilligung des Laienkelches in Böhmen unter Kaiser Ferdinand I." *Česká společnost nauk. Abhandlungen* 6, no. 6 (1873): 1–48.

Fučíková, Eliška, ed. *Tři francouzští kavalíři v rudolfínské Praze.* Prague: Panorama, 1989.

Goll, Jaroslav. *Quellen und Untersuchungen zur Geschichte de Böhmischen Brüder.* 2 vols. Prague: J. Otto, 1878–1882.

Jaitner, Klaus, ed. *Die Hauptinstruktionen Clemens' VIII. Für die Nuntien und Legaten an den europäischen Fürstenhöfen, 1592–1605.* 2 vols. Tübingen: Niemeyer, 1984.

―――, ed. *Die Hauptinstruktionen Gregors XV. Für die Nuntien und Gesandten an den europäischen Fürstenhöfen, 1621–1623.* 2 vols. Tübingen: Niemeyer, 1997.

Kameníček, František. *Zemské sněmy a sjezdy moravské, 1526–1628.* 3 vols. Brno: Zemský výbor Markrabství moravského, 1900–1905.

Maass, Ferdinand. *Der Josephinismus: Quellen zu seiner Geschichte in Österreich, 1760–1850.* 5 vols. Fontes rerum Austriacarum, Zweite Abteilung, Band 71–75. Vienna: Verlag Herold, 1951–1961.
Menčík, Ferdinand, ed. *Dopisy Matouše Kollina z Chotěřiny a jeho přátel ke Kašparovi z Nydbrucka, tajnému radovi krále Maximiliána II.* Sbírka pramenů ku poznání literárního života, skupina II, č. 29. Prague: Česká akademie pro vědy, slovesnost a umění, 1914.
Neumann, Augustin. "Francouzská hussitica." *Studie a texty k náboženským dějinám českým* 3, nos. 2–4 (1923): 1–154; 4, nos. 3–4 (1925).
Novotný, Václav, ed. "Bohoslužebná skládání o Husovi z XV a XVI století." In vol. 8, *Prameny dějin českých/Fontes rerum bohemicarum,* 419–472. Prague: Nadání Františka Palackého, 1932.
Nuntiaturberichte aus Deutschland nebst ergänzenden Aktenstücken. Erste Abteilung 1533–1559. 1. Band, Nuntiaturen des Vergerio, 1533–1536, edited by W. Friedensburg. Gotha: F. A. Perthes, 1892; Zweite Abteilung, 1560–1572. 8. Band, Nuntius G. Delfino und Kardinallegat G.F. Commendone, 1571–1572, edited by Johann Rainer. Graz: Boehlaus, 1967; Dritte Abteilung, 1572–1585, 6. Band: Nuntiatur Giovanni Delfinos, 1572–1573, edited by Helmut Goetz. Tübingen: Max Niemayer, 1982; 7. Band: Nuntiatur Giovanni Dolfins, 1573–1574, edited by Almut Bues. Tübingen: Max Niemayer, 1990; 8. Band: Nuntiatur Giovanni Dolfins, 1575–1576, edited by Daniela Neri. Tübingen: Max Niemayer, 1997.
Paměti o bouři pražské r. 1524. In *Prameny dějin českých/Fontes Rerum Bohemicarum* 6, 299–342. Prague: Nadání Františka Palackého, 1907. First published in Antonín Rezek, ed., *Česká společnost nauk. Pojednání třídy pro filosofii, Dějepis a filologii,* ser. 6, 11 (1881–1882).
Pažout, Julius. *Jednání a dopisy konsistoře pod obojí způsobou přijímajících, 1562–1570.* Prague: Historický spolek, 1906.
Polišenský, Josef, ed. *Historie o válce české, 1618–1620: Výbor z historického spisování Ondřeje z Habernfeldu a Pavla Skály ze Zhoře.* Prague: Nakladatelství krásné literatury a umění, 1964.
Reu, Johann M., ed. *The Augsburg Confession: A Collection of Sources with An Historical Introduction.* Chicago: Wartburg Publishing House, 1930.
Rezek, Antonín, and J. V. Simák, eds. *Listář k dějinám náboženských blouznivců českých v století XVIII a XIX.* 2 vols. Prague: Česká akademie věd a umění, 1927–1934. Historický archiv, nos. 46, 49.
Salvart, J. F., ed. *An Harmony of the confessions of the faith of the christian and reformed churches.* Cambridge: Thomas Thomas, Printer to the University of Cambridge, 1586.
Schulz, Václav, ed. *Korrespondence Jesuitské Provincie české, z let 1585–1770.* Prague: Česká akademie pro vědy, slovesnost a umění, 1900. Historický archiv, 17.
―――, ed. *Listář náboženského hnutí poddaného lidu na panství litomyšlském v století XVIII.* Prague: Česká akademie věd a umění, 1915. Historický archiv, 40.
Šimák, J. V. "Z dějin katolické reformace na panství branském." *Časopis Společnosti přátel starožitností českých* 16 (1908): 14–21.
Sněmy české od léta 1526 až po naši dobu. Vols. 1-11, 15. Prague: Zemský výbor, 1877–1941.
Souček, Bohuslav. "Rukopis pražské universitní knihovny XVII C 3." *Reformační sborník* 1 (1921): 45–80.

Šubert, Václav, ed. *Apologie druhá stavův království českého*. Prague: Karel Seyfried, 1862.
Tappert, Theodore G., trans. and ed. *The Book of Concord: The Confessions of the Evangelical Lutheran Church*. Philadelphia: Muhlenberg Press, 1959.
Tento Artykul o Defensí pro obhajování náboženství pod obojí. Prague: Samuel Adam z Veleslavína, 1618. *Knihopis* 377: NUK (54 C 154); MK (31 C 7, 31 C 8, 31 C 13 přív.).
Tischer, František, ed. *Dopisy konsistoře podobojí z let 1610–1619*. Prague: Historický spolek, 1917–1925.
Triska, Josef, ed. *Starší pražská univerzitní literatura a karlovská tradice*. Prague: Univerzita Karlova, 1978.
Trnka, František. "Náboženské poměry při kutnohorské konsistoři r. 1464–1547." *Česká společnost nauk. Věstnik*. Třída filosoficko-historicko-jazykozpytná, 1931–1934.
Truhlář, Josef, ed. *Dva listáře humanistické*. Sbírka pramenů ku poznání literárního života v Čechách, na Moravě a ve Slezsku, Skupina 2, Číslo 3. Prague: Česká akademie pro vědy, slovesnost a umění, 1897.
Uvážení Kurfirstských Saských Theologův v Vitenberce na otázku zdaliby stav Říše Římskému Císaři v této nynější český válce napomáhati chtíc . . . N.p., 1620. *Knihopis* 16.402: NUK (54 H 1568, 54 D 46 přív.); Strahov (FM 4 54).
Veselský, P. M., ed. "Žaloby měst na pány a rytířstvo z některých kusů jim škodných." *Časopis českého musea* 26 (1847): pt. 2, 422–440.
Vysvětlení Nejvyšších a nejpřednejších Zemských Pánův Hrabat, Svobodných Pánův v Engellandu o volení a successi Velikomocného krále Jakuba . . . Prague: Mikuláš Štraus, [1603?]. *Knihopis* 16.806: MK (33 F 8).
Wolf, Ernst. *Die Bekenntnischriften der evangelisch-lutherischen Kirche*. 5th ed. Edited by Hans Lietzmann. Göttingen: Vandenhoeck & Ruprecht, 1963.

Index

Accommodation (*Porovnáni*), 303, 308–9, 310–11, 315; numbers of Utraquists reported, 328; rural population, 322–23
Adalbert (Vojtěch) (St.), 84, 89
Adam of Veleslavín, Daniel, 12, 94, 98; Ivan the Terrible, 460n43; on Prague, 173; urban intellectuals, 196; use of force, 234
Adam of Hradec, 205, 259
Adamites, 26, 133, 289
adoration of Eucharist: Brethren, 69, 117; Bruncvík on, 333; Bydžovský on, 116, 121; Utraquists' continuing practices, 326; *Decretum,* 68; Lutherans, 67–68, 226, 332–33
Agenda (later *Rituales*), 99, 144; infant communion, 125
aggiornamento, 6, 300
Agricola, Johann, 139
Albigensian Crusades, 27, 94, 370
Alchymus, 89, 428n62
Aleandro, Girolamo, anti-Luther-Hus campaign, 138
All Souls' Day upheaval, 25
almsgiving, as a good work, 118, 223
Ambrose (St.), 15, 93, 118, 126, 331
amnesia, religious, 370, 371, 380
Anabaptists, limits of tolerance, 182
Anglo-Bohemian relations, 34–38, 103–110, 153–54, 338–39, 342–46

Antichrist as epithet, 322; Bílejovský, 88; Hooker on, 88; Luther on, 88, 116; pope as, 487n23; Wyclif on, 88, 97. *See also* Man of Sin, Whore of Babylon
anti-Trinitarians. *See* Arians
anti-ultramontane, 140, 260
Apology (Jesuit) (1618), 6; three types of sub utraque, 318; Utraquism assessed, 342; Utraquist rites continued, 325–26
apostolic succession: Eastern Orthodoxy, 38; Luther's teaching, 58. *See also* historical apostolic succession
Archbishop of Prague, restoration: archbishops listed, 385; bizarre arrangement, 147; Brus demands, 159–60; role of, 147; significance of confrontation, 143; Tridentine new order, 279; Utraquist ordinations, 160–66
archbishops: authority over Utraquists, 265–66; checks and balances, 264, 273–76; clerical appointments, 273–76; Consistory subordination, 249–51; ecclesiastical judiciary, 266; ethnic prejudice, 353–54; jurisdiction over clergy, 262–63; listed, 385; Lutheran ministers in German-speaking areas, 276; manorial jurisdiction, 263; non-Czech, 310, 312; power vis-à-vis Consistory, 311–12; role, 250, 251; subordination issue, 310

553

archdiocese, Consistory related, 41, 250, 267–68
Arians: heresy, 482nn 175, 178; limits of tolerance, 182
aristocratic model of Reformation, 202
Aristotle, 331; rationalism, defense of, 1; Luther on, 57
Arnošt of Pardubice, 149
Arsenius, Kašpar, 358
art and decoration, ecclesiastical, 31, 120, 229, 357. *See also* religious images
Assecuration of January 14, 1571 (Lower Austria), 193
assistentes, 252–53
Assumption of Mary, 152
Augsburg Confession, 177, 182; Bohemian Confession compared, 333, 336–37; Bohemian refugees, 367; Bydžovský on, 115, 116–17, 128; Consistory rejecting, 155, 188–89; princely signatories, 116–17; Utraquist rejection, 170–71; Valdštejn objection, 183
Augusta, Jan, 10, 285, 313
Augustine (St.), 15, 118, 121, 125, 131, 331; infant communion, 124; and Luther, 53, 54, 55
Augustine Sancturien, 30, 357, 385
auricular confession, 161; Berka episode, 248–49; Council of Trent, 246; Counter-Reformation, 356, 358; de-emphasis, 203
Austria: class lines, 183; Lower, 193 ; noble threat, 180. *See also* Inner Austria
Austrian Netherlands (Belgium), 371, 375
authoritarianism, papal, 21–22, 106–07, 147–48, 153–54, 300, 301; after White Mountain, 351. *See also* papal authority; papal monarchy
Avignonese papacy, 19

Bacháček, Martin, 16, 17
Balbín, Bohuslav, S.J. 366; as counterpoint to Bílejovský, 371
Barnes, Robert , 35, 152–55
baroque spirit, of Council of Trent, 287–88; Counter-Reformation art, 357

St. Bartholomew's Night, 180, 181, 191
Bartoš Písař. *See* Písař, Bartoš
Bartolomeus, Jiřík, 337, 347
Battle of White Mountain: emigration, 349, 350; Marian shrine, 357; significance, 349; Virgin's patronage, 357–58
Bavorovský, Tomáš, 140–41
Bayly, Lewis, 367
Bechyňka, Jan, use of force, 234
Belarus, lay communion of both kinds, 100
Bellarmine, Robert, 504n142
Benedikt, Jan, 261, 268
Benešovský, Václav, 244, 252, 256
Bergeron, Pierre, 216
Berka of Dubá, Zbyněk: background, 507n44; on "Catholic" religion, 248, 270; censured on auricular confession, 246, 254; clerical appointments protested, 273; Consistory jurisdiction, 251; Dačický relations, 258; English nonconformists, 345; error described, 248–49; jurisdictional issues, 264; Lutheranization threat, 276; monastics expelled, 328; prayers for victory over Turks, 266; resistance to, 310; Rezek affair, 257; role, 266
Bernard of Clairvaux (St.), 15, 19, 331; Hus, 119
Bessarion, infant communion, 123
Bible, access to, Anglicans compared, 105, 434–35n167; Utraquists on, 65,105
Bílejovský, Bohuslav: background, 424n1; on "Catholic" church, 269; erudition, 15; general significance, 80, 110; monasteries' destruction, 411n119; task compared, 81; use of force, 234; writings, 80–81
bishops: absence of governing, 149; administrative, rejected, 224; aristocracy, 174; listed, 385; prerogatives, 245; restrictions, 224. *See also* episcopate
Biskupec of Pelhřimov, Mikuláš, 25
Blahoslav, Jan, 10, 313
blood of Christ, significance, 162–63

bodily presence of Christ in the Eucharist, 135; Hus on, 36. *See also* adoration of Eucharist
Bohemia: as fountainhead of Protestant Reformation, 5; Jewish cultural life, 33
Bohemian Confession (1575): Augsburg Confession compared, 333, 336–37; Brethren's Confession confused, 194; Consistory evaluation, 188; Cykáda, 316; full legalization, 302, 305, 310–11; guarantees to towns, 180–81; joint Consistory sub utraque, 321; king not approving, 190–91; liturgical practices, 315–16; as Neo-Utraquist document, 481n169; noble layman role, 177; objections of Consistory, 303; opposition to, 184–86; party sub una, 191; political acceptance, 321; political strategy, 327, 348; as protective umbrella, 309; published, 194; religious acceptance, 303–4; significance, 168, 182, 196–97; support, significance of, 303–4; text, history of, 193–94, 465n153; translations, 4; Unity of Brethren, 168, 169, 481n169; Valdštejn and associates, 184–86
Bohemian Reformation: adherents, 25; Bohemian Brethren link, 24, 402–3n46; communion in both kinds, 24; Enlightenment, 374; foreign theologians on Hus, 280–82; Hus on theological openness, 21–22; influence, 91; interpreting, 3; Josephinism, 374; leadership, 18, 20; Luther's doctrines compared, 61–64; main features, 18; nobility, 27; progenitors, 18; as religious or nationalist, 92; rewriting history of, 364–65; role of violence, 94, 430n96; royal authority, 109; stature assessed, 7; Tridentine conformity, 279; wars of, 27–28
Bohemian uprising (1618–1620), 346–48; Lutheran theologians, 334; noble role, 346–48, 355; reluctance of towns, 346, 351
Bohemian Utraquist Church: accession of Roman priests, 146, 165, 272; basic beliefs, 30; Bydžovský and Bílejovský contributions, 130; centrism, 30; champions of renewal, 293; defectors, 77; demise, 326, 351–53, 372; ecumenical significance, 80; as High Church, 389–90n2; jurisdictional independence, 30; loyalty to, 77; Luther's impact, 133–37; as plebian, 329–31; renewal and revitalization, 46; universal mission, 291–92; *via media*, 182; as voice of conscience, 292
Bolzano, Bernard, 375, 376
Bonomi, Giovanni, 252, 271, 305–6
book burning, 78, 235–36, 365
Book of Common Prayer, 105, 432n129; Prayer Book Calendar, 345; prayer book men, 317–18
Bossuet, Jacques B., 402–3n46
Brethren of the Free Spirit (Berghards, Picards or Pitharts), 26, 443n125. *See also* Picards
Brethren's Confession of 1535, Faber, 113
Brezhnevite normalization, 529n133
Bridget of Sweden (St.), corruption of church, 19; Utraquists' denunciations, 88, 428n53
Brikcí of Licko, 71
Brož, Václav, 283, 285
Bruncvík, Zachariáš: adoration of host, 333; ecumenism, 320; English influence, 338; English radicalism, 137, 343; good works, 334; on Hus, 336; infant communion, 332; veneration of images, 333–34
Brus, Antonín: appointment, 150; Campion ordination, 281; Nožička on, 159; ordination of priests, 160–66, 164, 271; strategy outlined, 157
Buda (Hungary) negotiations, 75; on "Catholic" church, 269; significance, 77; status quo, 138
Budovec of Budov, Václav: coexistence of three groups, 313–14; Letter of Majesty, 304–5, 308; nonexistence of Utraquism, 329; religious diversity, 319–20
Bydžovský, Matěj, 178

Bydžovský, Pavel, 15–16; on Brethren, 95; courteous language, 63; on Eastern Orthodoxy, 39; Greek patristic literature, 102; infant communion, 227; Luther in his theological works, 114–28; Luther's critique of the Brethren, 113; mildness toward Luther, 236; More compared, 154; More's admiration, 148; on papal errors, 89; on Pius II, 163; praises of Luther and Melanchthon, 154; renewal of church, 296; respect for bishop of Rome, 244; significance, 130; training theology students, 130; Witzel endorsed, 132; Wyclif on Eucharist, 97

Byzantine Church. *See* Eastern Orthodox Church

Cahera, Havel: banished, 72–73; Buda negotiations, 75; Candlemas Day Articles, 64–65; historical censure, 111, 436–37n1; invective against, 76–77; Luther, 47; Lutheran advocacy, 64; Luther's doctrines, 62; perfidy analyzed, 71–72; vacillation alleged, 134

Calcagnini, Celio, Luther censured, 53

Calvin, John, 131; Hooker on, 135, 472n34; on Pikarts, 430n87

Calvinism: Bohemian uprising, 347–48, 520n229; Brethren related, 69; clergy expatriated, 349; Czech translation, 344; Dutch resistance, 471n25; emigration, 367; English nonconformists, 343; English resistance, 203; joint Consistory sub utraque, 314; limits of tolerance, 1575, 182; Lutherans influenced, 338–39; Poland, 307

Campeggio, Lorenzo, 74, 75, 297

Campion, Edmund, S.J. 38, 280–82, 343, 345, 497n15; *Rationes decem,* 281

candidates for ordination: Counter-Reformation, 359; discipline by Consistory, 212; oath of submission, 341

Candlemas Day Articles (1524), 45, 64–69; access to Bible, 105; Bohemian Diet on ministry, 72; consensus mode, 473n65; crisis assessed, 72; as Lutheran or near-Lutheran, 65–69; Lutheran upsurge alleged, 77; open-mindedness, 78; retrenchment of Utraquism, 69–73; views summarized, 65

canon law, 144; Anglicans, 442n109; Bydžovský's use, 126; Erasmus, 442n109; infant communion, 124; Lutheran, 176; Luther on, 442n109; papal power, 148; Utraquists, 176

Cappello, Carlo, 127

capital punishment, 369–70

Caraffa, Carlo, 356, 360, 363

Catholic church: after White Mountain, 350, 521n7; use of term, 258–70, 292, 493n190, 500n84; Utraquist sense of belonging, 40, 43

Catholic religion: clergy in Utraquist parishes, 267–70; use of term, 248, 267

celibacy issue, 68, 212, 224–25, 326. *See also* clerical marriage

censorship, 215, 279, 349, 486n16; homosexuality, 236. *See also* Index of Prohibited Books

ceremonialism. *See* ritual

Černá růže (Black Rose), house of, 24

certificates of confession, 358, 363, 366

chalice, depictions of, 229. *See also* lay chalice

Charles of Münsterberg, 64

Charles University. *See* University of Prague

Charles V (Emperor), Utraquist model, 297–98

Chelčický, Petr, 24

child, concern and respect, 227, 332, 479–80nn149, 151. *See also* infant communion

Church of the Bohemian Brethren. *See* Unity of Brethren

Church of England: attempts to Lutheranize, 114; bishops, view of, 435n169; class lines, 178; comparative perspective, 1; compared, specifics, 103–10; concept of monarch, 109; concrete links, 34–38; doctrinal dissent compared, 80; Eastern Orthodoxy, 38, 101, 433n136; as fossil, 224; internationalism, 345–46; Interregnum compared, 317–18; knowledge of Utraquism, 518n207; liturgical vernacular, 478n140; Lutheran borrowings under Cranmer, 507n53; moderate language, 63; national isolation, 291; occasional nonconformity, 184–85; Prayer Book Calendar, 345; Puritan criticisms, 11; on Roman Church, 82; Roman orders, 488n48; Roman threat, 307; Scylla and Charybdis simile, 103, 433n149; separation from Rome foreshadowed, 30; state dependence, 108; *via media* denied, 200–201, 469n13

Church of Our Lady before the Týn (Prague), 172, 321, 363; Counter-Reformation, 357; decor retained, 321–22; shared, 335

church-state relationship, 108, 210, 231, 250

civic liberalism, religious conservatism, xii, 78–79

civil disobedience, 250

Clement VII (Pope), liberal ecclesiology, 298

Clement VIII (Pope), Hooker praised, 104, 434n157

clergy: Accommodation, 309; active participation in combat, 28; anti-Donatist stance, 163; "Catholic" in Utraquist parishes, 267–70; charges against, 10–11, 14; Consistory discipline, 212; control over appointments, 262–67; transfers from Roman Church, 11, 146, 165, 272; Counter-Reformation, 359–60, 362, 364, 365–66; double apostasy, 10, 14, 398n90; earthly affairs, admonitions, 140; erudition, 15–16; exalted view of calling, 13–14; good works, 224; heresy charges, 213, 474n78; ignorance alleged, 15; incomes, 209; joint Consistory sub utraque, 314; Lutheran leanings, treatment, 72; Luther's view, 58; Nicodemism, 365–66; parsimonious use of clergy, 146; questionable behavior, 9; rural areas, 209; separate jurisdictions, 264–65; sins chastised by Hus, 87; Unity of Brethren, 314; Utraquist poverty vs. Roman Church, 176

clergy sub una, separate jurisdictions, 264–65

clergy sub utraque, separate jurisdictions, 264–65

clerical immunity from secular courts, 149

clerical marriage, 212; Candlemas Day Articles, 68, 154nn154, 155; Counter-Reformation, 355–56; history, 225; tolerance of, 224–25

Cochlaeus, Johannes, 5, 50; anti-Lutheran campaign, 74; anti-Luther campaign, 138; expert on Utraquism, 437n10; history censored, 279; on Hus, 112, 446–47n185; index of prohibited books, 139, 279; Luther on Bohemians, 53; Luther-Hus differences, 138–39

Codicillus, Petr, 228

collective memory, 370, 380

Collingwood, Robin G. 373

Comenius. *See* Komenský, Jan A.

commoners: after White Mountain, 350; praised, 330–31; respectability as theme, 204; urban, 174; Utraquism's popularity, 327. *See also* plebeian strata

common priesthood of the faithful, Evangelical faction, 136

communicants sub una, Brož on, 285–86; university requirements, 41

communion: beliefs about frequency of, 20–21; centrality of, 18; frequency dispute, 20–21

communion of both kinds: Bílejovský on, 82–84, 91; Candlemas Day Articles, 66; Compactata, 29; Counter-Reformation, 356; criticized, 339–40; Linteo on, 289; Locika, 361; Luther on, 53; Orthodox practice, 38; proscribed, 362

communion sub una: after Compactata, 32; Bílejovský on, 82–84; as "Catholics," 270; Counter-Reformation imposition, 355; documentary bias, 86; Linteo on, 340–41; origins, 425n16;

communion sub una *(continued):* Roman formula, 85; Roman laxness to biblical injunctions, 86; vernacular languages, 89–90

communion sub utraque: Bílejovský on continuity, 86; Bílejovský on, 98–99; Brož on, 285–86; Byzantine-rite Roman prelates, 100, 432n132; cooperation, 140; Counter-Reformation, 355; hiatus in Bohemia, 85–86; Hus allegations, 340; Jesuits, 290; New Testament, 65; Orthodox vs. Roman, 98–99; popes distributing, 83, 425n18; reaction to papal decrees, 162; restrictions enforced, 84–85; theological underpinnings, 162–63; university requirements, 41; Valdštejn proposal, 184–85. *See also* infant communion

"community of the predestined," 36

Compactata (1436), 29; abrogated, 157; abrogation, 40, 247; authority, 141; communion sub una, 32; cooperation, 141; Curial representatives, 162; images and veneration of saints, 31; Linteo on, 340; monarchs and papacy, 108; monasteries, 32; papal recognition, 75; primitive church, 242–43; religious tolerance, 234; removal, 170; Roman Church tactics, 156; sub una party, 304; tolerance, 139; two "Catholic" churches, 269; university relations, 32; veneration of images, 120

"Compactata Utraquism," 29

compromise of 1575. *See* settlement of 1575

conciliarism, Hus vs. 22

concubinage, 224, 274–75, 355–56

Conference of Czech Catholic Bishops' Hus Commission (1993), 6

confession, auricular. *See* auricular confession

confessionalization: avoidance of travails, 234–36; progress, 278; tolerance related, 379

confessional statements, Utraquist, 188–89, 303, 314

Confession of the Unity of Brethren, 178, 182, 188–89, 194

Confutatio gravissimi erroris (Faber), 112–13, 437n14

consensus mode, 211, 214, 301, 473n65

Consensus Sandomiriensis. *See* Sandomierz union

Cosistory sub una, 32, 42, 75, 141; administrators listed, 384–85

Consistory, Utraquist, 147, 200; administrative authority, 108–9; administrative and court records, 10; administrators listed, 383–84–; alleged Luther influences, 136; allies included, 311; appointments, 109; archdiocese related, 267–68; Articles of 1539, 452n61; Augsburg Confession, 187–88; Bohemian Confession, 169, 187–90; booklet of 1572, 189; campaign of repression, 179; candidates for priesthood, 14; Candlemas Day Articles, 64, 67; "Catholic" religion, 268–69; chancellery and archbishop, 249–51; class origins, 174; clerical appointments, 263–65, 491n144; continuing negotiations, 250; convergence with Roman Church, 240; Diet influence, 41, 260–62, 302; discipline for priests, 212; ecclesiastical authority, 249–64; ecclesiastical judiciary, 266; ecumenical ea, 311–18; efforts to co-opt, 252; enforcement apparatus, 210; fasts and feast days, 118, 119; governance, 106; grievances, 208–11; guardian of orthodoxy, 187–90, 211; historical apostolic succession, 221; historical background, 311–13; Hus feast day, 119; identity, 250; independence, 15, 43; influence of Diet, 260; insubordination to Rome, 161; jurisdictional issues, 210; landowners, 205; legitimacy, 247; as lesser evil for Rome, 248; liberal ecclesiology, 43; Lutheran clergy disputes, 313; Lutheran errors noted, 134,155; Lutheran exclusion, 201; Lutheran priesthood, 221; Lutheran takeover frustrated, 73, 112, 113–14; Maximilian II on, 190–91; nobles' rudeness, 175–76; ordination of priests, 164, 272; petition for restoration (1617), 323–24; petitions to Rudolf II, 209–11; pleading missives, 209–10, 211; reaction to Brus initiatives, 161–62; recognition of pope, 244; renewal and maintenance, 260–62; resistance to royal requests, 156; restoring election, 183–84; Rezek affair, 253–58; royal appointments, 250–51; rural priests appointed, 206, 274, 276; settlement of 1575, 198, 211; status shifts, 312; structural vulnerability, 311; sub una cooperation, 141; towns, 211–15; transfers of priests, 212; transformed into joint Consistory sub utraque (1609), 311–12; Unity of Brethren on, 169; Valdštejn relations, 189–90

Consistory, joint. *See* joint Consistory sub utraque

Consistory, "Lower" and "Upper," 491n150.

Constantinople, fall of, Utraquist reconciliation, 101

Contarini, Gasparo, 294–95, 296, 503n120

Convention of Passau (1552), 193

Corpus Christi, 68, 121, 208, 209, 216, 226–27, 332; glamour, 478n141; Letter of Majesty, 321, 322

corruption, Bílejovský on, 80, 83

costs of Utraquist establishment, 203

Council of Basel, origins of communion sub una, 83; Utraquist ordinations, 14. *See also* Compactata

Council of Constance: anti-Jewish, 34, 408n117; Campion on, 282; critique, 22–23; Dubravius on, 142; Hus challenge, 22; Luther censured, 53; primitive church, 242

Council of Trent: agreements and definitions, 160; archbishop for Prague, 146; authoritarianism, 287; baroque spirit, 287–88; Consistory on, 161; Dubravius on, 141; ecclesiology, 242; implementing, 265; infant communion, 227, 246; innovations, 279; liberal ecclesiology defeat, 298–99; liberal line, 295; liturgical reform, 245; model rejected, 293; opposition, 132; ordination issue, 165; recognition of pope, 244; rejection, 245–46; resistance on four issues, 245–46; Roman theology after, 278–79; Tridentine Catholicism irrelevant, 371–72; Utraquist differences with, 299; Utraquist model rejected, 300; Western opposition, 246

Counter-Reformation: assessing effects, 368; authoritarian and triumphalist resurgence, 287; aversion to, 327; Bohemian victory, 6; capital punishment, 369–370; compulsion justified, 369; as de-Catholicization, 371; distortion of past, 364–65; Dobrovský on, 375; documents destroyed, 215; Ferdinand II, 352–53; intimidation, 369–70; intolerance compared, 317; methods of obliteration, 354–61; nobles, 350; as "Re-Catholicization," 368, 371; religious amnesia, 351; resistance and collaboration, 361–66; spiteful character, 353, 357; threat posed, 307; Utraquism's continued existence, 366; victory questioned, 368–70; Zdeněk of Lobkovice, 259

Cranmer, Thomas, 105, 344, 345, 432n129; and Hermann von Wied, 293; and Lutheranization, 114, 137, 236; and papacy, 148; on primitive church, 243

Crato of Krafftheim, Johann, 178

Crespin, Jean, 5

critical Catholics, 246, 295

Crypto-Lutheranism, alleged, 152

Cykáda, Jan Václav, 204, 225; Bohemian Confession, 316; images of children, 332; joint Consistory sub utraque, 316, 317; tolerance, 236–37; Tridentine oath, 341; Týn Church, 321

Cyprian (St.), 331; infant communion, 99, 124

Cyril (St.): Bílejovský on, 98; liturgy of St. Peter, 99

Czech historiography: abuse and derision, 2–3; anti-Lutheran, 12; Bohemian Confession, 169; Bohemian Counter-Reformation, 354, 368–72;

Czech historiography *(continued):*
Bydžovský, 111–14; Cahera, 71–72, 76–77; Candlemas Day Articles, 65; canonical priesthood issue, 291; class bias, 329; common folk as conservative, 78; conceptual adherence to Roman Church, 291, 500n81; convergence between Utraquism and Roman Church, 240–41; counterfeit image of largely Protestant Bohemia, 365; fixed ideas of sixteenth-century, 325, 327; fusion with Roman Church, 339; Letter of Majesty, 302–3; Lutheran takeover failing, 78; near-transformation into Lutheranism, 45–46; Prague anti-Lutheran campaign, 70–71; settlement of 1575, 198–99, 200; stature of Bohemian Reformation, 6–7; superiority of West, 8; systemic ineffectiveness of Utraquism, 204–7; teleological interpretations, 78; *via media* disappearance, 200. *See also* historiography; history of the Utraquist Church

Dačický, Václav: appointment, 257; Berka relations, 258; Consistory authority, 265; Consistory jurisdiction, 251; disrespect, 312; ordination of priests, 272; replacing Rezek, 213, 214; uncivil treatment by chancellor, 175–76, 260
deaneries, creation of, 41, 272, 495n226
Decree of Kutná Hora (1409), 401n22
Decretum of Gratian: communion sub utraque, 83; infant communion, 124; status of bishops and priests, 126; use of, 144
defensores: Bohemian uprising, 346; Brethren clergy in Utraquist parishes, 323; joint Consistory sub utraque, 312; named, 192, 193; Utraquist liturgical practices, 315–16, 322
Denis, Ernst, views and influence, 12
Diet of 1444, Bílejovský on, 95
Diet of Bohemia: absolutism of Counter-Reformation, 354; archbishop appointments, protested, 258; Bohemian Confession, 168, 185; Consistory appointments, 255; Consistory control, 191, 260, 302; Consistory renewed, 41; disclipinary and liturgical rules, 109; episcopal elections, 30; on Faber, 113; infant communion, 125; infiltration of Lutheranism, 72; political alliances, interdenominational, 232; protection of Utraquism, 261–62; Rezek affair, 255; town support of Consistory, 214; Utraquist independence, 257
Dionysius the Areopagite. *See* Pseudo-Dionysius
Dionysius de Franciscis, 145
diplomacy, equivocacies and exigencies, 14–15. *See also* papal diplomats
Directorium, 346–47
dissidents, post-White Mountain, suppression legalized, 350
Dobrovský, Josef, 375
doctrinal incompatibility: Utraquist-Lutheran, 55, 57–59, 226–31
Dolfin, Giovanni, 11, 15
Dominic a Jesu Maria, 358, 523n49
Dominis, Marco Antonio de, 295
Dubravius (Skála z Doubravky), Jan, 141–42; ordination issue, 145–46
Dudić (Dudith), Andreas, 132, 295, 502n105
Dungersheim, Hieronymus, anti-Luther campaign, 138
Dvorský of Helfenburk, Jindřich, 16, 134, 151, 160, 454n107; appointed, 165; Consistory's formulations, 256; fusion with Rome, 252
Dykastus (Miřkovský), Jiří: appointment, 335; exile, 356; good works, 334; invocation of saints, 333; on sovereigns, 334; Týn Church, 321

Eastern Orthodox Church: Constantine Anglikos, 37; contacts with, 38–39. *See also* Russia, Orthodox Church
Eastern Orthodoxy: Bílejovský on, 81, 97–103; Church of England, 101, 433n136; criticisms of *via media,* 8; equality with Rome, 102; Gregorios Scholarios, 307, 506n24; kinship, 8; Roman union, 490n100

Easter processions, 326, 332
ecclesiastical jurisdiction, Candlemas Day Articles, 67. *See also* secular power
ecclesiastical manors, 140, 274–75
ecclesiastical organization (deaneries), 41, 272, 495n226
ecclesiology: Anglicans compared, 105; authoritarian, 290; concession to liberalism fading, 287; earlier model, 242; later differences, 287; liberal, 287, 291–301; Roman, 242–45; theological contribution, 1; universalism and, 299–301
Eck, Johann, 49; anti-Luther-Hus campaign, 138; Luther on Bohemians, 53; Luther on Hus's articles, 54, 55
ecumenicism: early councils, 222, 477n120; joint Consistory sub utraque, 311–18; Letter of Majesty, 320; Prague, 335; Utraquism, 150
Edict of Nantes, 193, 353
elites: plebeian bias, 175; religious division, 168–69; settlement of 1575, 205; Utraquist support, 109–10
Elizabeth I, 158
emigration: Battle of White Mountain, 349, 350; ethnic origins, 360; Lutherans, 366; Saxony, 350; Unity of Brethren, 367
Emmaus Monastery, 32, 209, 275, 311, 495–96n253
Emser, Hieronymus, 50; anti-Lutheran campaign, 74; anti-Luther campaign, 138; Hus denounced, 446n184; Lutheran divergences, 139; Luther on Bohemians, 53; Luther on, 51
England, influences. *See* Anglo-Bohemian relations
English Blasphemy Act (1650), 304
English Reformation: church of apostolic times, 243; messianism, 91; misperceptions of Bohemia, 4, 344–45; positions of mainstream Utraquism, 35; preaching freely, 105; radicalism misperceived, 345; Utraquist view, 345
Enlightenment, 372–73, 529n148; Bohemian Reformation, 374

Ennius. *See* Klatovský, Šimon Ennius
epiclesis, 99
episcopate, Anglicans compared, 105–6, 435n169; Utraquist view, 150, 224, 243
Erasmus, Desiderius: on Bohemian culture, 196; Brethren critique, 60; canon law, 442n109; criticisms of Roman Church, 77, 423n210; halfway settlements, 160; as heretic, 504n142; on Hus and Jerome, 297; iconographic linkage with Luther, 55–56, 417n82; influence in Bohemia, 295–96; linkage to Luther, 299; Luther on Bohemians, 53; Luther censured, 63; moderation in religious discussions, 62,131, 444n142; More and Fisher, 294; papacy, 148, 163; praises and accusations, 4, 391n14; rapprochement between Rome and Lutherans, 74, 296–97; St. John Chrysostom's liturgy, 133; Utraquism compared, 294; Utraquist Bohemia, 16; on Utraquist church, 297
Erasmus, re-publication, 375
ethical perfectionism: opposed to *via media,* 7–8
ethnic prejudice, 49–51, 90, 353–54
Eucharist: adoration issues, 67–68; Bílejovský on Payne, 95; blood of Christ, significance, 162–63; Brož on, 285; exhibited, stories of, 121; Lutheran belief lauded, 115, 116; Lutheran differences, 222, 226–27; Lutheran idolatry, 67, 421n152; occasional conformity, 184–85; Orthodox and Roman compared, 98–99; Unity of Brethren, 115–16, 117; Utraquist practices criticized, 326. *See also* real presence issue; remanence; transubstantiation
Eusebius of Caesarea, 102, 243
Evangelical faction, 113, 136. *See also* Lutherans
Evans, Robert J. W., views and influence, 2
excommunications and anathemas, 49; criticized, 149; freedom from threat, 203; Luther, 48, 135

Faber, Johann, 6; anti-Reformation campaign, 138; Bydžovský collaboration, 111, 113; controversy, 112–13; Witzel's sponsor, 132
Fabri, Johann. *See* Faber, Johann
fasting, as a good work: Bydžovský on, 118–19, 439–40n50; Luther on, 57; St. James Day Synod of 1434, 118; stipulations, 267
feast days: Candlemas Day Articles, 66; Luther on, 57; of saints, 144
Ferdinand I, 73; clerical marriages, 225; liberal ecclesiology, 298; Nožička praise, 158; ordination issue, 145, 146; Roman Church initiatives, 156; Rudolf II respecting mandates, 263; towns' grievances, 174; Utraquist ordinations, 146–47; Utraquist stance, 293; Witzel, 132
Ferdinand II: Counter-Reformation, 352–53; suppression of lay chalice, 356; issue of Utraquism, 351–53; reign restored, 349; repression of dissent, 352. *See also* Styrian model
Ferreri, Giovanni Stefano, 260–61
Fifteen Articles (1539), 136
Fisher, John: on Bohemian Reformation, 133; Bydžovský on, 132; on Hus, 133; Luther censured, 53; on Luther and Hus, 138; Utraquism celebrating, 345; on Velenský (Velenus), 64, 344
force, use of: aversion to, 234, 238; Counter-Reformation, 352–53; Czech military reputation, 483n186. *See also* just war
foreign priests and monks, 362, 525n82
foreign theologians, 279–82
Formula of Concord (1577), 201, 337, 470n16
Four Articles of Prague: described, 25; free discussion, 61; Luther on, 79; Payne defense, 38; Prague Party, 26; preaching freely, 105; procedural nature, 314; religious tolerance, 234; Rome's reaction, 40; town estates, 172
Foxe, John, 5, 37, 367
France, 24, 91, 121, 131, 237; St. Bartholomew's Night, 180, 181, 191; Council of Trent, 246; diplomatic reports, 216, 318; Edict of Nantes compared, 193, 200, 280; Guises vs. Bodin, 186; instability, 232; Lutheran interest, 338; sources of Josephinism, 529n148. *See also* critical Catholics, University of Paris
Franciscans, 327, 328, 354
Frederick of Palatinate (King of Bohemia), 338–39, 344, 347
free discussion: Hus on, 61; Linteo denouncing, 340; Luther's stance, 47–48; university circles, 61. *See also* Judge of Cheb
free teaching of the word of God, Lutheranism, discussions, 152
frequent communion: bond with Rome, 106; communion in both kinds related, 24; Eucharist for young children, 25; Wyclifism, 36
Frith, John, 5

Gaugnini, Alessandro. *See* Gwagnin
Gelastus Vodňanský, Havel, 151, 452n56
George of Poděbrady (King of Bohemia), 39–40, 41; crowned, 172; excommunication, 88–89; papal relations, 108; promises to Holy See, 158; statue removed, 357
German Reformation: disappointment with, 45, 137; intolerant self-righteousness, 78; Rome's accommodation, 296; significance for Czechs, 135
Germans: Bílejovský's attitude, 90; in Bohemia, 92, 429n84; Czech delight with Luther, 49–51
Germany: Czech Lutherans, 337–39; detachment from, 337; exiles from Bohemia, 360–61, 366; ethical perfectionism, 8; reform, 293, 501n90
Gerson, Jean, 22, 29
Gifford, William, 343
Gnesio-Lutherans, 337
good works: askance at Luther, 13; Bydžovský on, 118–19; categories of, 224; Lutheran opposition, 334, 367, 477n126; Luther on, 57, 58; priests as models, 224; salvation, 223–24;

scholastic derivation, 61–62; solafideism vs. 223; source of income, 203. *See also* almsgiving; fasting; prayer
Great Schism. *See* papal schism
Greek Church: Bílejovský on, 98; contributions, 102. *See also* Eastern Orthodox Church; Eastern Orthodoxy
Greek patristic literature, 93,102, 127, 242, 294, 296, 298
Gregorios Scholarios (Gennadius), 39, 307, 506n24
Gregory I (Pope) the Great, 222, 331
Gregory VII (Pope), 153
Gregory XIII (Pope), 279
Grosseteste, Robert, 37, 409n135
Gunpowder Plot (1605), 344
Gwagnin (Guagnini), Aleksander, 98, 432n121

Habsburg rule: Austrian Enlightenment, 380–81; Battle of White Mountain, 349; charges against, 324–25; Counter-Reformation's success, 369; intimidation of towns, 180; Josephin reforms, 372; interdenominational alliances against, 232; religious repression, 179; retribution for Bohemian uprising, 355; Spanish influence, 352, 370; Treaty of Westphalia, 350
Hádání u Zmrzlíků synod, 26
Hájek of Libočany, Václav, 76–77, 141, 450n31
Hájek, Vojtěch, 362
Hanžburský of Kopeček, Vavřinec, 351, 363
Harant of Polžice and Bezdružice, Kryštof, 467n165
Harrach, Ernst Adalbart von, 353
Harvard College, 367
Havlíček Borovský, Karel, 375–76
Hegelianism, 7–8, 291–92, 200
Heinke, Franz Joseph von, 374
Henry of Beaufort, 38
Henry VIII: Barnes, 154; break with papacy, 153, 345; on Luther and Bohemians, 50; Luther's insults, 63; papal primacy, 294

heresy, 5; cases during Counter-Reformation, 369; Compactata, 29; Council of Constance, 23, 401n36; Faber on, 112; Hus on heretical books, 21–22; stigma lifted, 29; use of term, 249; Utraquist injunction on derisive labeling, 62; vernacular languages, 90
heretic, as code word, 364
historical apostolic succession: Anglicans compared, 105–6; Bydžovský on, 126–27; complications of Utraquist position, 107; Consistory, 221; as distinction from Lutheranism, 230; Lutheranism, 127, 221; Utraquist stance, 143–45. *See also* apostolic succession
historiography: nationalism, 329; postmodern evaluation, 17; radicalism, 6–8; Utraquist histories of patristic church, 532n1. *See also* Czech historiography
history of the Utraquist Church: Eastern Orthodoxy, 38–39; English influences, 34–38; gestation, 18–24; Jewish role, 32–34; mature era, 39–42; Reformation and Taborite challenge, 24–32; summarized, 42–44
Hlavsa of Liboslav, Jan, 64, 69
Hoë von Hoënegg, Matthias, 317, 339
Hoffman, Jindrich, 364–65
holy oils, 165, 272
homiliary of 1540: communion for little children, 84; communion sub una, 84; good works, 118–19; justification, 118; Luther on, 118; ministry, ordination of, 127; vacillation toward Luther, 134; vernacular languages, 90; wealth of Church, 87; Wyclif on priests in sin, 97; Žižka, 91
Homines intelligencie, 26
Hooker, Richard, 79; Bílejovský compared, 81; on Calvin, 63, 131, 135; view of Bohemians, 4; disagreement with other Protestants, 103–4, 130–31; gentleness in polemics, 63, 131, 135; on Roman Church, 82, 104; scholasticism, 104; sola scriptura, 96–97; universalism muted, 91–92, 104

Horák, Jan, 147
Hortensius Zahrádka, Jan, 16
human inventions, 298
humanist theologians: Erasmus, Fisher, More, 242; Pole, 294
human rights, Hus, 18
Humphrey, Laurence, 343, 517n191
Hurdálek, Josef, 375
Hus, Jan: Bílejovský on, 95; Bohemian Reformation, 18–19; Bruncvík on, 336; Campion on, 280–82, 497n15; Candlemas Day Articles, 66; on clerical vices, 89; Cochlaeus on, 139, 446–47n185; Counter-Reformation, 369; Counter-Reformation polemics, 288; doctrinal relationship to Wyclif, 36–37; on Eastern Orthodoxy, 39; Emperor Joseph II as second Hus, 374; Emser on, 445n184; equivocation, 14; Erasmus on, 297; execution, 24; Faber on, 112; Fisher on, 133; foreign theologians on, 280–82; Foxe's view, 5; frequent communion, 23; heresy charge, 290; human rights, 18; "Hussitism," 4; impact on Utraquist theology, 504n140; intellectual openness, 61, 233; invocation of saints, 119; Jews and Czechs compared, 34, 91; as lesser evil, 282–86; Linteo on, 288–89, 340; liturgical books, 217–19; as liturgical reformer, 23; Luther, basic distinction, 55; Lutheran view, 336; Luther as counterpoint, 54–56; Luther on, 46, 48, 52–53; Martinius on, 336–37; metaphysical realism, 28–29, 405n81; miracles, 288; More on, 5, 133; Oddo of Colonna, 88; ordination of priests, 126–27; predicament, 293; priestly sins, 87; as propaganda vehicle, 54, 55–56; as proto-Lutheran, 4; as proto-Protestant, 344; reevaluated, 6; religious tolerance, 233–34; repudiated, 365; revolt against, 364; rights of individual, 21–23; Roman Church on, 4, 5; stature at Trent, 299; Stokes debate, 37–38; Šturm on, 284; veneration of, 217–18; vindication, 6; Wyclif related, 35, 36, 95

Húska, Martin, 128
Hus's *De ecclesia,* as model at Second Vatican Council, 6
Hussites: post-White Mountain, 359; use of term, 86, 270, 359, 364

idolatry: Easter procession, 326; Lutherans on, 219–20, 475n105; Taborite iconoclasm, 93
Illicino, Petr, 279–80, 496–97n7
Index of Prohibited Books: Cochaleus, 139, 279; Erasmus, 504n142; introduced, 287; liberal ecclesiology censored, 299
individual rights, Hus, 21–23
indulgences: Hus on, 36; Hus opposition, 22
infant communion: anathemas, 246; Aquinas on, 124; Bílejovský on, 84, 99; Brethren, 480n156; Bruncvík on, 332; Brus on, 159–60, 161; Bydžovský on, 121–26; Candlemas Day Articles, 66; Compactata, 29; Council of Trent, 227, 246; Cyprian (St.), 99; deflecting royal pressure, 156; denounced, 227; described, 420n145; foreign narratives, 217, 475n94; instructions for parents, 125–26; instructions for priests, 479n148; Koranda on, 99; Lutheran opposition, 121–22,136, 226–27, 332; Roman Church, 480n156; Taciturnus on, 288, 499n62; three parables, 122; trivialized, 227
Inner Austria, 183, 306, 337, 352. *See also* Styrian model
Innocent III (Pope), 88; communion sub una, 83; infant communion, 84, 124
Inquisition, 23, 26, 287insularity compared, 345, 518n207
intercession of saints, 218, 228
Interim of Augsburg (1548), 74, 160
Interim of Regensburg (1541), 160
International Symposium on Master Jan Hus (1999), 6
Interregnum (British, 1649–60): status of "prayer-book men" and Utraquists compared, 317–18

invocation of saints: Bydžovský on, 119; denounced, 228; differences with Lutherans, 228, 333; maintained, 217; Matěj Lounský on, 151
Ireland, 178, 353, 354
irenic or mediating theologians, 138
Islamization, 232, 482n175; resisting, 308, 506n29
Ivan the Terrible, 174, 460n43

Jakoubek of Stříbro, 27; as devil's instrument, 339–40; divine violence, 27–28; Eucharist for young children, 25, 403n51; ordination of priests, 126–27; purgatory and prayers for dead, 96; religious art, 31; on Wyclif, 95
Jakub the Organist, 52
James I, 320, 494n206
James II: Hooker praised, 104
St. James Day Mandate (1508), 42
St. James Day Synod of 1434, fasting, 118
Jan of Dražice, 149
Jan of Německý Brod, 63; controversy over Luther, 134
Janov, Matěj of: church reform, 19, 400n6; communion sub una, 85, 86, 426n33; frequent communion, 21; human inventions, 298; influence, 27; on Jews, 33; on monasteries, 32; ordination of priests, 126–27; role, 18; veneration of saints, 120; views of women, 225; Wyclif's influence, 36
Jan of Příbram, 27; affection for Catholic Church, 269; Emmaus monastery, 32; Eucharist for young children, 25; Faber on, 112; ordination of priests, 126–27; veneration of saints, 31; on Wyclif, 131, 431n102
Jansenism, 163–64, 366, 530n150
Jenštejn, Jan of: frequent communion, 21; tension with academics, 20
Jerome of Prague: Campion on, 282; Erasmus on, 297; erudition, 22–23; execution, 24; Orthodox churches, 38–39; as proto-Protestant, 344; regard for, 297, 503n125

Jerome (St.), 15, 31, 93, 118, 126; Bílejovský on, 98; Slavic script and liturgy, 432n119
Jesuits: *Apology* (1618), 318, 325–26; attack rumors, 328; communion sub utraque, 290; dislike of, 328; Hus and Utraquists praised, 6; implanting in Bohemia, 153; influence on nobles, 260; mediation with Consistory, 164; Modestin, 288; Mystopol link alleged, 158; Pole, 295; political alliances decried, 335–36; post-White Mountain, 350; Puritan propaganda against, 345; on religious laissez-faire, 318; Rezek affair, 254; "salami tactics," 305; Šturm, 283–85; taxonomic frustration, 309; Tridentine new order, 279; University of Prague, 362; on Utraquist Eucharist, 247; Utraquist ordination, 164
Jewel, John, 131, 154, 516n191; compared to Bílejovský, 81, 82, 92, 103, 110; on patristic literature, 104, Czech translation, 342
Jews: Bavaria, 34; economic development, 33; language preservation, 34; role, 32–34; Vienna, 34
Johann Georg, 352
Johann Sigismund: from Lutheranism to Calvinism, 353
John Chrysostom (St.), 331; infant communion, 123; liturgy translated, 133; priestly issue, 126–27
John Paul II (Pope), on Hus, 6
John XXIII (Pope), indulgences, 22, 89
joint Consistory sub utraque: abolished, 356; administrators, 316–17, 384; advantage, 311; antecedents, 312–13; Bohemian Confession, 321; Brethren, 314; as ecumenical council, 313–14; friendly ambiance, 315; Lutheran clergy, 316; official name, 506n38; Utraquist need for protection, 312; Utraquist purpose, 311; *via media*, 317
Josephinism: Bohemian Reformation, 374, 379; sources, 374, 530nn148, 149; Utraquism compared, 373–74

Judge (or Test) of Cheb (1432), 29–30; free discussion, 61; Nožička on, 159; religious tolerance, 234
jurisdiction of Roman Curia: clerical independence, 262–67; Consistory independence, 249–262; repudiated, 29, 162, 147
justification sola fide: Bydžovský on, 117–118; Contarini on, 503n120; Hooker on, 104; Luther's rejection, 60–61; Utraquist tradition, 118. *See also* solafideism
just war, Bartolomeus, 347; Taborites, 33

Kadaň, 207–8, 265, 268, 473n49
Kapihorský, Symeon, 364, 365
Kara, Avigdor, 33
Kaunitz, Wenzel. *See* Kounic Václav
Keltes, Konrad, 49
Kilian, Henrick, 216
kings of Bohemia, listed, 383. *See also names of individual kings*
Klatovský, Martin: civility, 236; infant communion, 125
Klatovský, Šimon Ennius, 132; Barnes, translation of, 152, 154–55; More's admiration, 148; papal powers, 296; praises of Luther and Melanchton, 154; Utraquist grievances, 153–55; *via media,* 154
Klesl, Melchior, 254, 261, 341
Kocín of Kocinet, Jan, 243–44
Komenský, Jan A.: Eastern Orthodox connection, 100–101; Foxe's martyrology, 367; Harvard College, 367
Konáč of Hodiškov, Mikuláš, 60
Koniáš, Antonín, S.J. 365
Konrad of Vechta, 27, 144–45, 147
Koranda the Younger, Václav, 40, 82, 411n58; on Aquinas, 104; archbishop role, 147; Bethlehem Chapel, 41; Brethren attacked, 40; communion sub utraque, 85–86, 99; infant communion, 99, 125; successors, 41; veneration of images, 120; vernacular languages, 90
Kornelius of Všehrdy, Viktorin, 102

Kotva, Ctibor, 357
Kounic, Václav, 374
Kravař, Pavel, 37
Křišt'an of Prachatice, 27, 28
Kristián of Koldín, Pavel, 171
Kronyka česká (Bohemian Chronicle) (1537), 80–81; significance, 81
Kuen, Marek, 146, 161
Kutná Hora: attempted desecration of host, 121; mural paintings, 229; *See also* Peace of Kutná Hora
Kutná Hora Synod (1441): fasting, 118; veneration of saints, 31, 119

Lamberg, Karl, 258, 271–72
Lamormaini, William, 369
language, temperate use of, 62, 131
language issues: Czech speakers' religion, 216–17; German, 217, 475n93; golden age, 196; Latin resurgence, 225–26; Latinization, 89–90; liturgical Czech, 225, 478n137; translations for Germans in Bohemia, 129. *See also* vernacular languages
Last Supper, communion issues, 83–84
Law of God: Candlemas Day Articles, 65–66; as leitmotif, 13; opposed to sola fide, 223, 230–31
lay chalice: abrogation, 356, 357; adoption, 403n48; Linteo on, 289, 340; Locika, 361; Luther on, 53; Modestin on, 288; Roman Church, 75; temporary toleration, 287. *See also* communion sub utraque
legalism, mindless: Council of Constance, 23
legal status of Utraquism, 29, 201–4, 308–09
Leipzig disputation of 1519, 46, 49; Luther on Hus's articles, 52–53
Lenin, Vladimir I., elitist view of the masses, 329, 512n132
Letter of Majesty (1609): abrogation, 349; Accommodation (*Porovnáni*), 303, 308–9; joint Consistory, 302; guarantees to Utraquists, 308; interdenominational political alliances,

304–7; as provisorium, 320; settlement of 1575 compared, 220; significance, 198, 311, 348; Utraquist strength and vitality, 321–29
Lev of Rožmitál, 75
liberal Catholicism, 374, 375–76, 379. *See also* critical Catholics; humanist theologians; Jansenism; Josephinism; *spirituali* (Italian)Lichenstein, Karl, 352, 356
Linteo, Petr, 288–90; frigid relations, 339–41; monastery riots, 342
literary heritage, 196
litigation: as sign of Utraquist vitality, 214
liturgical books, 144; Anglicans compared, 105; commoners, 204; Counter-Reformation, 365; Czech Lutherans, 219; importance, 334, 514n152; Lutheran opposition, 334; Luther's missal compared, 217; pre-Tridentine, 41–42; prevalence of Utraquist worship, 217–20; "sanitized," 365; Tridentine reforms, 245–46
liturgical calendar: temporal and sanctoral cycles, 144
liturgical languages, 144; Counter-Reformation, 356; Czech as, 89; Latin use, 89
liturgical practices: Bílejovský on, 96; Bohemian Confession, 315–16; joint Consistory, 314, 315–16; Lutheran compared, 217; restoration, 80; *Second Apology,* 310; veneration of saints, 228
liturgical vestments: Bílejovský on, 97; Hus lauded, 284
liturgy: as evidence of faith, 218; of St. James, 101; of St. Peter, Western origins, 99
Lobkovice, Bohuslav Felix Hasištejnský of: Bohemian Confession, 180–81, 336; petition, 170
Lobkovice, Jiří the Elder of, 209
Lobkovice, Zdeněk Vojtěch Popel of: appointment, 259; behavior criticized, 466n163; Counter-Reformation, 259; Dačický insulted, 260; insolence, 312; Roman lobbying, 261
Locika of Domažlice, Jan, 280, 332–33; communion in both kinds, 361; critical of Roman Church, 341; martyrdom, 351, 361; numbers of communicants, 360; persecution, 348
Lohelius, Johann, 258, 280, 323, 354, 355, 356
Lollards: and Czech religious movement, 35–36; influence, 36, 37; literature, 23–24
longue durée, 371, 529nn133, 135
Louis Jagellon (King of Bohemia), 42, 64, 71, 73
Lounský, Matěj: accused of Lutheran innovations, 151–52
Loyola, Ignatius, S.J. 283, 295
Lukáš of Prague, 69, 115
Lupáč, Martin, 40; Compactata abrogated, 163; infant communion, 25, 123, 125; venerable priest, 129
Luther, Martin: Bohemian open-mindedness, 62; breach of Utraquist etiquette, 60; Bydžovský on, 114, 115, 131; in Bydžovský's published works, 114–28; Cahera's perfidy, 71–72; Cochlaeus on, 138–39; on Council of Constance, 23; Erasmus on, 294; excommunication, 135; Greek card, 101; harsh stance, 235; on Hus, 79; Hus, basic distinction, 55; Hus as heretic, 55; Hus as precursor, 336, 515n172; Hus's fate, 49, 405n73; ideas of Bohemian Reformation, 49; immunity to his appeal, 59–61; impact of, 133–37; Jewel on, 131; legacy of first encounter, 76–79; Linteo on, 289–90; magisterial authority of Rome, 56; missal compared, 217; plea to Bohemian estates, 51; radicalism, per Bydžovský, 129; revolt against Rome, 47; significance for Czechs, 79; teachings in Bohemia, 46–47; use of Hus, 353; Utraquism vindicated, 51–53; Utraquist areas of agreement, 48; Utraquist response summarized, 79;

Luther, Martin *(continued):* Utraquists on his role, 55; view of Utraquism, 3–4, 391n11; at Worms, 47, 48
Lutheranism: adherents characterized, 226; alleged turn to, 151–52; Bílejovský defense of papacy, 107; Bohemian Confession, 168; Bydžovský on, 111, 112, 117, 128–33; Calvinist influences, 338–39; cardinal issue, 152; clergy expatriated, 349; compromise of 1575, 192; converts, 77; Czech historians on, 12; English religious thought, 342–43; entente genesis, 178–83; estates of landowners, 205, 206, 207, 472n40; as foreign entity, 171; foreign narratives, 215–16; Germans in Bohemia, 129, 276; Hus exclusion, 338, 516n172; idolatry, 219; image of upsurge, 76–77; impact exaggerated, 327; influences summarized, 166; intolerance of Utraquist liturgy, 219; legalizing, 170; literary campaign against, 60; martyrs, 153; nobles, 174, 176; nobles prevented from imposing, 202; open-mindedness about, 135; Pacification of Nuremberg, 297–98; political alliances, 232, 307; on popes, 222; post-White Mountain, 5; Prague, 173, 207; priests accused of innovations, 151–52; Prussia, 490n100; repression, 179; royal towns, 207; rules under joint Consistory, 316; sacramental priesthood, 221, 476–77n113; on saints, 524n62; secular powers, 176–77, 461n63; sentimental ties to Utraquism, 229; solafideism, 223; Utraquism equated, 12; Utraquist confrontation, 199–200; Utraquist entente, 190–94; Utraquist orthodoxy, 319; veneration of saints, 229–30; *via media* abandonment, 151–52, 452n61
Lutheran Reformation, 7; Bydžovský's prescription, 128–29; Candlemas Day Articles, 64–69; déjà vu quality, 60; significance for Bohemia, 49–51, 414n27; significance for Utraquism, 45
Lutherans: Brethren on, 170; Brethren polemics, 367; Bydžovký on innovators, 121; Czech and German compared, 237–38; differences persisting, 332–35; differences summarized, 335; exiles to Saxony, 360–61; Germany, 337–39; religious tolerance, 238, 335; sentimental ties to Utraquism, 229; settlement of 1575, 201; Slovene, 337; succor among Germans, 307; threat of Rome, 300; Transrhenish influences, 338–39; Utraquist alliances, 76; Valdštejn quarrel, 185–86; veneration of images, 219–20

Magni, Valerian, 353
Man of Sin as epithet, 59, 88
manorial captains: as defenders of Utraquism, 263, 323
manors, private: Accommodation *(Porovnáni)*, 322–23; Brethren on estates, 209; incomes of Utraquist clergy, 209; Letter of Majesty, 322; negotiating about pastors, 323; non-Utraquist clergy, 209; principle of non-interference, 322; Roman Church, 205; settlement of 1575, 205; royal protection of Utraquists, 193, 205–6; Unity of Brethren, 205–6; Utraquist clergy, 275. *See also* ecclesiastical manors; noble estate/nobles; royal manors
Marian Column, 357, 523n48
Marian veneration, 357–58; Assumption, 150; Príbram and Rokycana, 229; sodality of the Virgin Mary, 280–81
marriage cases: Consistory jurisdiction, 209, 266; Prague, 213; town-Consistory clashes, 212–13
marriage for clergy. *See* clerical marriage
Marsilio of Padua, papal power, 148
Martinius of Dražov, Samuel, 317, 335, 336–37, 337–38, 367, 527n110
Martin V (Pope), 87–88, 90
Martinice, Jaroslav Borita of, 270
martyrdom: Campion, 281, 497n22; Hanžburský of Kopecek, 351, 363; Locika of Domažlice, 332–33, 351; major martyrs listed, 385–86; More and Fisher, 345; veneration of saints, 119, 440n61

Marxian critique, 2–3
Masaryk, Thomas: Eastern Orthodox influence, 410n150; Franz Brentano, 376; primitive church, 485n11; on Utraquist decay, 12, 397n76; view of *via media,* 8
mass: Candlemas Day Articles, 66; Council of Trent, 245; for dead, 144, 326; elements preserved, 144; Luther on, 57; order of, 66; as sacrifice maintained, 217, 326, 336
matrimonial cases. *See* marriage cases
Matthias Corvinus, 40, 108
Matthias (King of Bohemia), 322, 323
Maximilian II: Bohemian Confession, 168, 178; Brethren on Consistory, 169; on Consistory, 190–91; Consistory letter, 188; countervailing reassurances, 190; defensores, 192, 193; Lutheran exercise of religion, 170, 171; nobles' rudeness, 175; religious tolerance, 181, 197; role in settlement of 1575, 231–32; shielding Utraquism, 181, 189, 190,192; son's coronation, 186; Valdštejn and associates, 184; on *via media,* 192; Witzel, 132
Medek, Martin: clerical appointments, 263; Consistory relations, 251; convergence alleged, 240–41; Gregorian calendar, 265; Lutheranization threat, 276; ordination of priests, 271
Melanchton, Philipp: Bydžovský on, 117, 131; Bydžovský praise, 114, 115; dangers of tolerance, 235; Dvorský, 16; Utraquist correspondents, 134
Mělnický, Martin, 10,151, 175, 313, 488n65
messianism:Bílejovský on, 91; Puritans and Anglicans, 91; Utraquist, 28, 214
Methodius (St.), Bílejovský on, 98; liturgy of St. Peter, 99
Mezoun, Jan, 279
Michna of Vacínov, Pavel, 324, 355, 356, 361
middle classes, 195. *See also* towns
Mikulášenci (Nicolaitans), 286
Mikuláš Biskupec of Pelhřimov, 25, 31, 119, 532n178

Milíč of Kroměříž, Jan: communion sub una, 85; Four Articles foreshadowed, 25; frequent communion, 21; influences, 19; role, 18
ministerial service, Luther's definition, 58
Minority Party (Unity of Brethren), 40
miracles, Hus, 288
Mitmánek, Václav, 11, 136
Modestin, Ondřej, S.J. 288
monarchs: Bohemia, 108–10; listed, 383; papal authority vs. 108; protection for Utraquist Church, 108–10
monasteries: attacks on, 327–28, 511n119; Bílejovský on, 94, 511n119; hostility to Roman Church, 341–42; mendicants, 88; runaway monastics, 146; three-dimensional images, 481n165; Utraquist attitude, 32
Monluc, Jean de, 295
Montagu, Richard, 270, 345, 482–83n183
moral activism, Luther's rejection, 60–61. *See also* Law of God
morality, 12; Lutheran Church, 9; priests, 10–12; Roman Church, 9; solafideist charges, 13; Utraquism questioned, 9, 12–13; Utraquism's inherent immorality, 13
Moravia: priestly conflicts, 395n56; religious tolerance, 484–85n209
Moravian Church (Unitas Fratrum), 387n7, 411n163, 450–51n36. *See also* Unity of Brethren
More, Thomas, 50; Bohemian open-mindedness, 62; Bydžovský on, 132–33; on Hus, 133; liberal ecclesiology, 294; Luther on Bohemians, 56; Luther censured, 53; papal power, 148, 296; Utraquism celebrating, 345
Morton, Thomas, 343, 517n197
Moryson, Fynes, 215, 227–28
Mozarabic rite, 99, 432n129
Müntzer, Thomas, 62
Murner, Thomas, 51
Mystopol, Jan: accused of Lutheran innovations, 151, 152; attribution of Roman beliefs, 158; commitment to Lutheranism, 136; Evangelical faction,

Mystopol, Jan *(continued):* 113; historical censure, 111, 436–37n1; vacillation alleged, 133–34, 136

Na Slovanech. *See* Emmaus Monastery
national church: Hooker on, 104; model of, 1
nationalism: historiography of, 329; Utraquist self-image, 92
national revival (awakening), 372–73, 375, 380
Nausea, Friedrich, 138; Erasmus, 297; ordinations, 146; *via media,* 154
Neoplatonic radical realism. *See* realism, radical metaphysical
Neo-Utraquism, 166, 167; Bohemian Confession as, 481n169; concept of, 7, 107, 230–31; dissident population, 359; evidence lacking, 332; fabrication of, 499n53; as historiographical issue, 7; opposition to a syncretic religion, 220, 226
New Believers: Bydžovský on, 117
Nicholas of Dresden, 62, 96
Nicholas of Lyra: communion for little children, 84; communion sub utraque, 83; infant communion, 122, 124
Nicodemism, 365–66
noble estate/nobles, 171–72; alienation, 197; aristocratic model of Reformation, 202; Battle of White Mountain, 350; Bohemian uprising, 346–48, 355; class bias to Utraquism, 174–76; confiscated lands issue, 260, 490n117; Consistory distrust, 255; Counter-Reformation, 259–60, 350; as dysfunctional, parasitic, 194–95, 347, 466n157; historical bias, 329; joint Consistory, 316; legal status of Utraquism, 202; Lutheranism, 174, 176; manual labor, 331; origins vis-à-vis towns, 173; perfidy, 173–74; political weight, 202; political alliances with Utraquists, 261–62, 305; population, 199, 469n6, 512n132; pride castigated, 330; private chapels, 206–7, 262; religious tolerance, 193; settlement of 1575, 205; social distance, 175–76, 461n55; sub una, 259–60; towns vs. 173, 175; ultra-Utraquists as spoilers, 183–86; urban Utraquist support, 313; Utraquism underrepresented, 328–29; Utraquist priests vs. 204; would-be defensores, 193. *See also* manors, private
nonconformists, English, 342–45; occasional conformity, 184–85
Nova Villa, Philip de. *See* Philip of Novavilla
Nožička of Votín, Blažej, 94, 158–59, 234
nunciature established, 252; Tridentine new order, 279

Oddo of Colonna, 88
Oldcastle, John, 37
Old Catholics, 101, 366
Old Utraquism, 107; fabrication of, 278; fictitious images, 303; as historiographical construct, 165–66, 167; illusion of, 286–90; imaginary or phantom, 150, 452n56; as red herring, 290; unreal character, 257
openmindedness: criticized, 340; Luther's impact, 133–35
ordination of ministers: Brethren, 69; Candlemas Day Articles, 67; Lutheran, 67
ordination of priests, 143–50, 221; Accommodation, 309; *Apology* (1618) on, 310; Bílejovský on, 106; Brus instructions to candidates, 161, 162; Bydžovský on, 126–27; by Roman bishops, 14, 100, 106–07; Consistory arguments, 164–65; distinctiveness from Lutheranism, 220; Dubravius on, 141–42; Ferdinand I urging for bishop, 150; Roman fusion alleged, 271–73; Roman promises, 157; as servility to Rome, 144; solid position under Rudolf II, 214–15; submission to Tridentine oath, 271, 272–73; theological training, 272, 494n223; traditions maintained, 272; Venice, 145, 146, 450n26

ordinations by archbishop of Prague, 160–66; Accommodation statements, 315; by Berka, 271; pressure on Medek, 251; profession of faith, 245; recognition of pope, 244; Rezek affair, 256; submission to Tridentine oath, 271, 272–73; Utraquist wariness, 179
Orebites, 27, 94, 234
orthodoxy: Bohemian Confession, 187–90; confessionalization avoided, 235; Consistory as watchdog, 211; joint Consistory, 318–20; towns and Consistory, 208, 211; Utraquist leadership, 214; of *via media,* 380
Ottersdorf. *See* Sixt of Ottersdorf
Ottoman Empire, 163, 191, 229, 265–66, 307
Oxford University, Prague links, 35

Pacification of Nuremberg (1531–32), 297–98
Pacifism. *See* force, use of
Pačuda, Matauš, 16, 330–31, 365; presumed administrator of restored Utraquist Consistory, 324
Palacký, František, views and influence, 3, 65, 78, 391n9
Palma Močidlanský, Sixt, 285, 499n47
Palomar, Juan de, 156
Paminondas, Pavel, 135
papacy: Luther's teaching, 58–59; pope as Antichrist, 59, 153, 154; Utraquist acceptance of system, 59, 244; Utraquist grievances, 153; views of, Anglicans compared, 106–9
papal authority: abuses listed, 147; Barnes on, 153; compared to Anglicans, 35; Consistory, 244; early church, 243–44; first millennium, 222, 223; Kocín on, 244; More on, 294; Nožička on, 159; popes as untrustworthy, 153; positive view, 222; resisted, 161–63; teaching authority, 40; transmission of sacerdotal power, 222; three components, 148, 503n117; Utraquist view of, 107, 147
papal diplomats, 11–12; "Catholic" church, 269–70; Rezek affair, 252

papal monarchy: attacks on pope, 47, 53, 223 ; Council of Trent, 245; critique, 19–20; English critics, 345; Erasmus, 294; Hus on improper authority, 22; Luther on, 48; objectionable characteristics, 153, 242; reformers, 294–95; universalism, 301; *via media,* 1
papal schism, 22, 35, 82
Parker, Matthew, 516n191
Pašek of Vrat, Jan, 64, 69; anti-Lutheranism, 70; anti-Lutheran persecutions, 76; banished, 72–73; Buda negotiations, 75; Candlemas Day Articles, 68; election analyzed, 72
Passauers: invasion by (1611), 327
patristic ecclesiological tradition, 378. *See also* Greek Patristic literature
Paul II (Pope), 89; denouncing Utraquism, 147; George of Podebrady excommunicated, 40
Paul (St.), 308, 319–20; and Luther, 53–55
Pavel of Olešná, 25
Pavel of Žatec, 149
Payne, Peter, 32; arrest, 38; Bílejovský on, 95, 96, 97, 431n102; Utraquist indulgence, 62; Wyclif influence, 37; Wyclif interpreted, 95–96
Peace of Augsburg (1555), 42, 193
Peace of Kutná Hora (1485, 139; expanded, 202; Linteo violation, 290, 500n77; peasant religious freedom, 205; reconfirmed, 75; religious tolerance, 420n149; Roman theology after, 278; spirit of forbearance, 181–82; sub una, 32, 42
Peasant Rebellion of 1381 (England), 35
peasants: bargaining powers, 205; ceremonial appeal, 203; Peace of Kutná Hora, 205; resistance, 363, 525n86
Perkins, William, 137, 343–44
Pernštejn, Vojtěch of, lay bishops, 176–77
Peter of Dresden, 62, 339
Phaëton Žalanský, Havel: continuation of Utraquist rites, 326; processions criticized, 322; prominence, 314
Philibbert, bishop of Coutances, 30

Philip of Novavilla, 30, 149, 224, 406n89
Philippists, 337
Picards: Beghardi, 430n86; Bílejovský on, 92–93, 94–95, 430n86; errors per Bílejovský, 93; flameout, 43; as folkish sectarians, 24, 402n42; Luther associating with, 74; origins of Brethren, 128, 443n125; Rudolf II's edicts, 283, 305, 498n28; use of term and translations, 430n86; view of papacy, 59. *See also* Unity of Brethren
Piccolomini, Aeneas Sylvius (Pope Pius II), 11, 26; Bydžovský on, 163; censored, 279, 496n5; Compactata, 40, 157, 163; influence on Englishmen, 37, 133
Pikarts. *See* Picards
Pilgrimage of Grace (1536), 5
Písař, Bartoš, 49; biased narrative, 76; Cahera letters, 71; and Luther, 50, 63; negotiations at Buda, 75
Písecký, Jiří, 61
Pius II (Pope). *See* Piccolomini, Aeneas Sylvius (Pope Pius II)
Plácel, Václav, 237; on clergy in politics, 243
Platejs, Johann Ernst, 354, 356, 357, 359, 363
Plato. *See* realism, radical metaphysical
plebeian strata: ceremonialism, 203; historical bias, 329; manual labor, 330–31; nature of Utraquism, 329–31; satire about, 458n21; Utraquist concern, 204; Wyclif, 175, 460n46. *See also* commoners
pluralism, religious. *See* religious tolerance
Plzeň, 42
Poduška, Jan, 47
Poland: 352 Brethren refugees, 367; Calvinism, 307; class lines, 461n67; English attention, 518n207; Sandomierz union, 183
Pole, Reginald, 294
political alliances, interdenominational, 304–7; Bohemian Confession support, 303–4; early analogies, 307; Jesuits on, 335–36; Letter of Majesty, 304–7;

Lutheranism, 232, 307, 335; noble tolerance, 255, 313; reasons, 306–7; religious tolerance, 232, 255; Roman Curia, 241; Taborites, 307; Utraquist orthodoxy, 319; wars of Bohemian Reformation, 307
political culture, liberal, 196, 232, 375–76
Polon, Valentin, 13–14; "Catholic Church," 269; disapproval of sects, 233, 482n176; priesthood, 221; mass as sacrifice, 222; good works, 224; mildness, 236, 484n198
Pontificals, 99, 144; infant communion, 125
Popes. *See* papacy, papal: population: dissidents, 359, 360; nobles, 513n132; post-White Mountain, 359, 360; rural, 470n22; towns, 470n22; Utraquist majority, 238
Porovnáni (Accommodation to Letter of Majesty). *See* Accommodation
power, secular. *See* secular power
Prague, 26; anti-Lutheran campaign, 69–70; attacks on monasteries, 327–28; Candlemas Day Articles, 64, 69; defending Utraquism, 172–73, 208; Jewish cultural life, 33; Lutheran ministers, 321; marriage cases, 213; pogroms, 34; Unity of Brethren, 211–12
Prague Manifesto, 62
Prague Party, 26–27
Prague Synod of 1388, frequency of communion, 21
prayers: as a good work, 118; for the dead, 96, 217; litanies, 228–29; Lutherans on, 480n157
predestination, dread of, 388n13, 471n28; Hus's use of term, 36
presbyterialism, 106, 435n172. *See also* episcopate
Příbram, Pavel, 46
Příbram. *See* Jan of Příbram
priesthood, Bydžovský on, 126; church order of 1610, 315–16; Luther's concept compared, 48, 126; Polon on, 221; two orders, 222

priestly marriage. *See* clerical marriage
priests. *See* clergy
primitive church: as church of the first millennium, 242–44, 298, 378; councils of Constance and Basel, 242–43; infant communion, 123; Masaryk on, 485n11; as model, 242, 243, 378; theology on, 222–23
private chapels, 206–7, 262
Procopius (St.), 89
progressivism 78, 391n9; Whig interpretation of history, 7;
Protectorate of World War II, 529n133
Protestant Reformation: aristocratic model, 202; assessing impact, 370–71; Bílejovský and, 81; as irresistible historical force, 199, 202–3; princely model, 202; Roman Church neutralized, 73–74; urban model, 202; Utraquism compared, 292; Utraquist refusal, 248; Wyclif anticipating, 36
Pseudo-Dionysius, infant communion, 122, 123
purgatory: Bílejovský on, 96; Taborites, 25; Wyclif, 96
Puritans: Anglican ceremony, 219; *Book of Common Prayer,* 105; Brethren, 330, 367; on Calvin, 131; Hooker opposed, 104; Hus appropriation, 344; influence on Czech Lutherans, 343; preaching freely, 105; reputation of opponents, 11

Questenberg, Casper von, 354, 356
quodlibet disputations, 20, 400n9

Raňkův, Vojtěch, 18
real presence issue, 285, 286, 314; remanence, 36, 112, 431n103
realism, radical metaphysical: 28–29, 405n81
Reform Catholicism. *See* liberal Catholicism
Reformation models: aristocratic, 202; princely, 202; urban, 202
Regensburg Diet of 1541, 503n120
Regius, Jan, 344
relics of saints, 31; Rokycana on, 120

religious art. *See* art and decoration, ecclesiastical
religious conservatism, civic liberalism, xii, 78–79
religious images: continuing practices, 326–27; Counter-Reformation, 357; Jesuits, 328; Lutheran opposition, 333–34; Taborite iconoclasm, 93, 120; *via media,* 31. *See also* art and decoration, ecclesiastical; veneration of images
religious tolerance, 236; adherents to Roman Curia, 42; after White Mountain, 351–61; arguments against, 279–82; basis of, 231–38; Bohemian uprising, 348; Candlemas Day Articles, 66–67; communion sub una, 238, 484–85n209; compromise of 1575, 192; discussion not edicts, 482–83n183; Erasmus, 131, 444n142; exceptionality of pattern, 323; foreign theologians, 282; freedom of religion noted, 318; Hus, 233–34; Josephin reforms, 373–74; laxness related, 318–20; legal system, 142; Lutherans, 238; Maximilian II, 181, 197, 231; Moravia, 484–85n209; nobles, 193; parable, 237, 320; Peace of Kutná Hora (1436), 420n149; political culture, 232; Roman Church, 83; royal absolutism, 349; Rudolf II, 193; settlement of 1575, 239; spurious images of strife, 481n172; towns, 187; Utraquist role, 200; Venice, 145. *See also* political alliance, interdenominational
remanence, 36, 103, 112, 284, 431n103
Remigius of Rouen, 124, 126, 441–42n94
Renewed Land Ordinance (1627), 349–50
republican government. *See* Directorium
Rezek, Fabian apostasy, 213, 214, 252, 253–58,474n83; Consistory-archbishop relationship, 310; Consistory's vulnerability, 312; frigid relations, 339; penance, 489n76; significance, 241; Utraquist errors, 249
Richard II, 35

ritual, 144; appeal, 203; Bydžovský on, 118; Counter-Reformation, 362; Czech commoners, 203; joint Consistory sub utraque, 314, 322; stipulations, 267

Rokycana, Jan: Brethren attacked, 40; "Catholics," 269; communion sub utraque, 82, 85–86; duplicity of Council of Basel, 157; election, 30; Faber on, 112; on Roman Church, 160, 269; saints' relics, 120; tombstone removed, 357; on Wyclif, 95, 431n102

Roman Church: attempts at rapprochement, 277; benefits of liberal stance, 299–300; Bílejovský on, 82, 107, 110; bolstering status of Utraquism, 249; Bydžovský, 138; charges of co-optation, 155–60; clash of ideas, 292; clergy in Utraquist parishes, 267–70; convergence alleged, 240–41; Counter-Reformation, 353–54; on Czech role, 5–6; disparaging songs, 520n231; dissimulation, 157; divergence with Utraquism, 277; early critique, 19; ecclesiology, 242; elite appeal, 174; failed rapprochement, 73–76; foreign priests and monks, 362, 525n82; formal links, 80, 247–49; fusion charged, 158–60, 339, 341; greater threat to Utraquist integrity, 241; on Hus, 5; Hus and Luther, 4; false image of Lutheran upsurge, 76–77, 365; infant communion, 124; Luther-Hus propaganda, 74; Luther on, 48; on Luther's Bohemian sympathies, 53; militant tone, 339–42; modus vivendi with, 73–76; monasteries attacked, 327–28; "nation of heretics" charge, 5; number of adherents, 268; obstacles to full unity, 157; passive resentment, 372; patience with Utraquists, 249; priestly transfers to Utraquism, 146, 165, 272; reconciliation prospects, 300–301; relations after Rezek affair, 258; religious amnesia, 370; religious tolerance, 238, 484–85n209; restrictions after Bohemian uprising, 348; reuniting, 366, 368, 371; royal manors, 323; seigneurs, 205; separation from, 107, 166; strategy for Utraquists, 157; "submission" issue, 160; temporal wealth, 87; threat posed, 306–7; Utraquist liberal ecclesiology, 291–99; on Utraquist priests, 11–12; vestigial ties, 247–49

Roman Curia: adherents, 42; anti-Luther-Hus campaign, 138; *assistentes,* 252–53; Bohemian cast to Luther, 49, 50; Byzantine-rite ordinations, 100; Consistory subordination, 249–51; differences characterized, 241; Hus and Utraquism as lesser evils, 282–86; independence of Consistory, 241; intransigence, 262; Letter of Majesty estrangement, 262; liberal Catholicism haunting, 376; Luther-Bohemian divergence, 75; as main threat, 300; *nomenklatura,* 149; polemics summarized, 290; political alliances, 241; recognition of pope, 244; salutary critique, 43; sporadic negotiations, 247; Utraquist model rejected, 300; Utraquist negotiations, 74–76

Roman ecclesiology, Utraquist critique, 242–45. *See also* papal monarchy

Roman party in Bohemia. *See* sub una party

Royal Chancellery, 250–51, 259

royal manors: Consistory jurisdiction, 274, 276; managers, 273, 274, 276; Roman Church, 262, 323

Royko, Kaspar, 374

Rožďalovský, Václav, 54

Rudolf II: ambiguous attitude, 312, 407n45; Bohemian Confession published, 194; "Catholic", use of, 267, 270; "Catholic" councillors, 268, 493n185; clerical appointments, 262–63; joint Consistory sub utraque, 302; Consistory apprehensions, 255, 489n84; Consistory petitions, 209–11; Consistory transactions, 259; fasts and ceremonies, 266, 267–68; Letter of Majesty, 303, 304; married clergy, 225; ordination of priests, 214–15; protection for Consistory, 205–6, 207, 251; religious tolerance, 193; "salami tactics," 306; separate clerical jurisdic-

tions, 265; settlement of 1575, 201, 210
rural areas: Accommodation (*Porovnáni*), 322–23; archbishop jurisdiction, 263; Counter-Reformation, 360; legal status of Utraquism, 201–2, 205–7; secret Utraquism, 363; towns versus, 202, 470n22. *See also* manors, private; royal manors
Russia: Orthodox Church, 102–3, 244; Slavophiles on Bohemian Reformation, 38, 410n147. *See also* Eastern Orthodoxy; Ivan the Terrible
Rvačovský of Rvačov, Vavřinec Leander, 13; commoners, 204; erudition, 16

sacramental confession. *See* auricular confession
sacramental priesthood. *See* clergy; priesthood
sacraments: 231, 325; Eastern Orthodoxy, 38; Roman affirmed, 144
Sadoleto, Jacopo, 296
saints' intercessions, 218; efficacy of, Bílejovský on, 96. *See also* veneration of saints
"salami tactics," 282, 305, 497–98n27; after White Mountain, 352, 354–55; practice of, 305–6; Rudolf II, 306; Utraquist view, 324
salvation: good works, 118–19, 223–24; Roman apology, 340. *See also* solafideism
Sandomierz union (1570), 183, 314–15
Saxony, 47; Calvinism as alien religion, 171; Lutheran intolerance, 318, 339; Martinius, 337–38; occupation of Prague, 363; refugees from Bohemia, 350, 360–61, 366–67
Sázava Monastery, 89
schismatics: as code word, 364; Eastern Church on, 101; Jansenists, 164; Orthodox as inferior, 101–2; post-White Mountain, 359; seen by Rome, 292; Utraquists compared, 107
Schmalkaldic League, 451n39
Schmalkaldic War, 180

Scholasticism, Hooker on, 104; Sadoleto on, 296; Utraquists on, 104–5
scholastic philosophy: Bílejovský on, 93, 105; criticized, 296; Luther on, 57–58, 61–62, 418n108; rehabilitated at Trent, 298–99. *See also* Nicholas of Lyra; Thomas Aquinas
Scultetus, Abraham, 137, 317
Second Apology (Druhá Apologie stavův království českého) (1618) charges against Habsburgs, 324–25; interpretations, 309–10; liturgical practices, 310; oath of submission, 341; principle of seigneurial noninterference, 322–23; Utraquist ordinations, 271, 273; Utraquist priests' withdrawal, 324; Utraquists supported, 315
secular learning, Brethren, 237, 484n204
secular power, 87; exercise by clergy condemned, 19, 87, 287; Lutherans, 334, 514n155; per Lutherans, 176–77, 231, 334, 461n63, 514n155; priestly interference, 243. *See also* papal powers
Sega, Filip, 252, 488–89n71
seigneurs. *See* manors, private settlement of 1575: characterized, 241–42; Consistory, 198, 209, 211; Czech historiography, 198–99, 200; different perspectives, 210; drawbacks, 201; Letter of Majesty compared, 220; religious tolerance, 239; royal towns and rural areas, 192–93, 205–7; Rudolf II, 210; significance, 197, 220–21; stability provided, 231. *See also* Bohemian Confession
sexual licentiousness. *See* Adamites
Sigismund (King of Bohemia), 27, 404n71; charter of ecclesiastical liberties, 30; replacement, 172; town estates, 172
Silesia, 158
Šimon of Habry, 63; controversy over Luther, 134
Sixt of Ottersdorf, 171, 173–74, 178; Augsburg Confession, 186; Bohemian Confession, 181; defensor, 192; nobles' anger, 180, 462n81

Skribonius, Jindřich, 141
Slavic aspects: Bílejovský on, 98; Russian Slavophiles on Bohemian Reformation, 38, 410n147
Šlechta, Jan, 60
Slovacius, Václav, 231, 233
Sobek, Burián, 47, 58; exile, 70; Luther's teachings, 63
social class: alienation of nobility, 197; divisions compared, 178, 461n67; intellectual leadership, 195; middle classes, 195; nobles' behavior, 194–95; religious division, 168, 174–76; social cleavage, 194–97
Society of Jesus. *See* Jesuits
solafideism, 13; Anglicans, 103; Bydžovský on, 117; Candlemas Day Articles, 65–66; good works vs. 223, 231; Linteo on, 289–90; Luther's teaching, 57, 63; Unity of Brethren on, 170
sola scriptura: Anglicans, 103; Bílejovský on, 96; Bydžovský on, 118, 129; Candlemas Day Articles, 66; Hooker on, 96–97; Luther's teachings, 57
Španovský, Michal, 181
Speciano, Cesare: auricular confession, 246, 248–49; Berka consecration, 248–49; Bohemian Chancellery, 259; Rezek affair, 253–55, 257–58
Spinelli, Filippo, 268
spirituali (Italian), 294
Srnec, Jakob, 130
state authority, Utraquist dependence, 43, 108, 250–51; qualified, 109, 176, 231
Štelcar Želetavský, Jan, 204, 472n35 231, 332; on Brethren, 233; against communion for infants, 227; on Hus and Luther, 229–230; on Šturm, 233; against Utraquist rites, 219–18; against veneration of saints and images, 228
Štěpán of Kolín, influence on Hus, 37
Stokes, John, 37–38
Straněnský, Jan, 140–41, 223–24
Stránský, Pavel, Eastern Orthodox connection, 100–101
Stříbrský, Matěj, 317

Šturm, Václav, S.J.: Brethren's theology, 283–85; Lutherans citing, 367; narrative on Utraquists, 216–17, 475n94; sowing discord, 306; Štelcar on, 233
Styrian model, 180, 462n79
"submission", meaning of, 160
sub una party: Bohemian Confession, 186, 191; religious tolerance, 139–40, 238, 484–85n209; as Utraquist opponent, 197. *See also* Consistory sub una
sub utraque party: defined, 308; federation of three types, 313–18; as self designation, 309. *See also* joint Consistory sub utraque
Šud, Eliáš, 272
Sutcliffe, Matthew, 343
Sweden, 19, 59, 350, 430n95, 483n185
Switzerland, 338; clerical transgressions, 10, 395n10
Synod of 1420, Taborite errors, 93
Szalkán, Ladislaus, 75

Taborites: aversion to, 521n20; basic beliefs, 25; Bílejovský and Bydžovský compared, 128; Bílejovský on, 93; Brethren pedigree, 69; commentary on Diet of 1444, 95; ecclesiastical edifices, 120; era of glory, 27; Eucharist, 115–16; German victims, 353; influences, 430n86; Jewish influence, 33; military defeat, 29; polemics before Luther, 60; political alliances, 307; radicalism's folk roots, 24; role and legacy, 376–77; suppression, 31; use of force, 234, 238; on violent destruction, 28
Taciturnus Hájský, Jiří, 499n62
taxation, nobles shirking, 177, 195, 204, 347
Theodoret of Cyr, 243
theological training, 130, 145, 272, 362, 494n223, 524n80
Theophylactus of Ochryda, 126–27
Thermidorian role, 7
Thirty Years' War, 350
Thomas Aquinas, 15, 31, 50, 104;

baptism, confirmation, and communion, 122; communion sub utraque, 83; infant communion, 122,124, 125; Luther on, 57
Thomistic realism, 35
tolerance, centrist position, 8. *See also* religious tolerance
Toleration Patent of Joseph II (1781), 3, 371
Tomáš of Soběslav: Consistory leadership, 257; Consistory records, 313, 314; objections to Lutheran and Brethren confessions, 303
Tomáš of Štítné: frequent communion, 21; role, 18
towns: allegiance to Utraquism, 213–14; ascendancy, 173; Augsburg Confession, 171–72; Bohemian Confession, 178–80, 181, 191; Bohemian uprising, 346–48; clerical appointments protested, 273–74; Consistory, 211–15; defensores, 192; guarantees under Letter of Majesty, 308; intellectual leadership, 195–96; legal basis, 173; Letter of Majesty, 321; nobles on, 173, 175; patronage over churches, 212; pragmatic politics, 179, 182; of Prague, 172; Prague municipalities, 458n22; religious tolerance, 187; royal protection of Utraquists, 192, 207–8; separate Utraquist Consistory, 324; tax burden vis-à-vis nobles, 195; Utraquist political alliances, 305; transubstantiation, 35, 36, 215, 284, 325. *See also* remanence
Treaty of Westphalia, 350
Trent. *See* Council of Trent
tribunals, ecclesiastical: consanguinity cases, 266; exemption, 30; Utraquist, 175, 212–13, 266. *See also* marriage cases
Turks, 5, 39, 112, 288, 337; fall of Constantinople, 60, 101; history in Czech, 232. *See also* Islamization; Ottoman Empire
Twelve Articles (1420), 25
Týn Church. *See* Church of Our Lady before the Týn (Prague)

Ukrainians (Ruthenians), lay communion of both kinds, 100
ultramontane, 260, 530n150
Uniates: Greek bishops, 100, 145–46; "Unia" formula inappropriate, 100, 300; Union of Brest (1596), 100, 300
Unity of Brethren: alliance with Lutherans, 182–83, 187; as anomaly, 166; Bílejovský on, 92–95, 128; Bohemian Confession, 168, 169, 481n169; Brož on, 285; Bydžovský on, 114, 127, 128; on Bydžovský role, 113–14; Candlemas Day Articles, 68–69; child communion, 121–22; clergy, 314; clergy expatriated, 349; coexistence with others, 238; confessional statements, 4; Confession of the Unity, 178, 182; contacts with Eastern Orthodoxy, 39; contacts with Luther, 73; controlling, 41; critique of Utraquist establishment, 11; doctrines rejected, 60; emigration, 367; English perceptions, 344; English religious thought, 342–43; Eucharistic position, 115–16, 117; Evangelical faction, 113, 114; Foxe's martyrology, 5; good works, 439n44; humor in narratives, 457–58n8; Hus allegations, 284; as Hus's followers, 290; indulgent critique, 237; influences, 43; joint Consistory sub utraque, 314; lay bishops, 176, 177; legal recognition, 171, 458n16; Luther on Eucharist, 67; Luther's teachings, 63–64; mainline Utraquism, 69; moral rigorism, 8; ordination, 449n14; origins debated, 128; polemics before Luther, 60; political alliances, 232; Prague, 207, 211–12; Puritans compared, 330; records, 10; repression, 179; reputation of opponents, 11; Roman attacks, 282–83; secret membership alleged, 12–13; seigneurs, 205–6; separation from Utraquists, 40; snobbery, 330; solafideism, 117, 439n44; Štelcar on, 233; Šturm on, 283–85; Taborite affinity, 40, 41; threat of Rome, 300; unacceptable to Luther, 69; Utraquist moral laxity, 14, 235; Utraquist

Unity of Brethren *(continued):* orthodoxy, 319; Utraquists compared, 14; on Valdštejn, 184, 463n101; veneration of saints, 119–20. *See also* Moravian Church
universalism and liberalism, 299–301
universal mission, 80, 91, 291–92, 345–46
universities, 16–17; Utraquist attitude, 31–32. *See also* Oxford University
University of Paris, role, 35
University of Prague: Bohemian Reformation, 27; classical languages, 226; disparaged, 16; Jesuit control, 362; Müntzer at, 62; Oxford links, 35; quodlibet disputations, 20, 400n9; repression, 179; role, 31; tension with archbishop, 20; theological training, 145; urban intellectuals, 196; Utraquist control, 40–41
urban model of Reformation, 202
utopian Christianity, Müntzer, 62
Utraquism: demise, 372; evolution, 234–36; insights summarized, 378–81; Josephinism compared, 373–74; as lesser evil, 282–86; mainline, 24; modern critique, 2; non-Protestant model of Catholic reform, 292; "Utraquistization," 297; women's rights, 225, 331. *See also via media*
Utraquist Church. *See* Bohemian Utraquist Church
Utraquists: use of term, 86

Valdštejn the Elder, Jan of, 134, 162–63; Augsburg Confession rejected, 170, 171; Consistory relations, 189–90; Maximilian's assurances, 181; shielding Utraquism, 192; spoiler role, 183–86; warning to nobles, 177
Valla, Lorenzo, 147–48, 154
Vaníčkovic, Ziga, 70
Vartenberk, Čeněk of, 172
Vartenberk, Zdeněk of: Bohemian Confession, 185
Velenský, Oldrich, 46, 48, 344, 446n185; Luther's teachings, 63–64
Velenus, Ulrichus. *See* Velenský, Oldrich

Veleslavín. *See* Adam of Veleslavín, Daniel
veneration of images, 229; Bruncvík on, 333–34; Bydžovský on, 119, 120; continuing practices, 326; Counter-Reformation, 288, 357; flamboyance of baroque, 357; Lutheran opposition, 33–34; Luther on Brethren, 119; restraint reaffirmed, 328; as spiritual adultery, 220, 334
veneration of saints: affront to Lutheranism, 218–19; call for moderation, 120; continuing practices, 326; Counter-Reformation, 288, 357; liturgical books, 217–19, 228; Lutheranism, 229–30, 333; Luther on, 50; publications, 42; restraint reaffirmed, 328; Unity of Brethren, 119–20, 367; *via media,* 31
vernacular languages: Bílejovský on, 89–90; Candlemas Day Articles, 66; Church of England, 478n140; Counter-Reformation, 356; Jews compared, 91; resurgence of Czech, 225; Roman Curia, 246; rural appeals, 363; sub una priests, 274. *See also* language issues
via media: Anglicans on left, 107; appeal to elites, 176–77; approach summarized, 166; basic beliefs compared, 1–2; Bohemian Confession, 182; Brethren vs. 92; Bydžovský as representative, 130; comparison, 379; confrontation with Lutheranism, 199–200; criticisms of, 8; deconstruction, 364; encounter with Lutheranism, 77; as exemplified by Bílejovský, 81; images and veneration of saints, 31; intellectual tolerance, 234; joint Consistory sub utraque, 317; Josephinism, 374; Locika as symbol, 361–62; Maximilian II on, 192; mutual knowledge, 342; negative views, 1; pre-Protestant theology, 220–26; reaffirmed, 77; reform from within, 291; Utraquists on right, 107; veneration of saints, 119
via moderna: ontological nominalism, opposed to metaphysical realism, 35

violence: aversion to, 234, 237; Bílejovský on, 94; Counter-Reformation, 369–70; Nožička on, 234; of elect (Müntzer), 62; opposed, 237; papal weapon, 27; Sweden, 430n95, 483n185; Taborite radicalism, 93–94; Taborites on, 28. *See also* force, use of
Virgin Mary, Hus veneration, 119; symbol of repression, 357. *See also* Marian veneration
St. Vitus Cathedral, 172, 347–48
Vladislav II Jagellon (King of Bohemia), 41; Compactata recognition, 75

Waldensians, 23–24, 55, 112, 344; Bílejovský on, 94, 430n86, 430–31n97; Bydžovský on, 128; flameout, 43; influence on Taborites, 25; origins, 94–95; and Unity of Brethren, 40, 283
Waldhauser, Konrad, 19
Walkmberger of Walkmbergk, Jakub Sofian, 222
warrior-priests, 28
Wars of the Bohemian Reformation ("Hussite Wars") (1420–1431): 27–28, 404n78; Bílejovský on Martin V, 87–88; Bílejovský on, 90–91; Germans' antagonism, 49; German victims, 353; Jewish role, 33–34; Luther's influence on memory of, 51; nonviolent extension, 293; openmindedness as result, 233; political alliances, 307; radical elements, 43; Russians on, 38
wealth, ecclesiastical: primitive church, 243; of Roman Church, Bílejovský on, 87–92; Utraquists as an inexpensive church, 203; Wyclif on, 87
Wenceslaus IV: authority and role, 109; restoration of communicants *sub una,* 25; suppression of Utraquism, 85
Whig interpretation of history, 7
Whitaker, William, 343

White Mountain. *See* Battle of White Mountain
Whitgift, John, 81, 92, 103
Whore of Babylon as epithet, 88
Wied, Hermann von, 293
Wilde, Jan, 32
William of Ockham, 22, 148
Williams, Roger, 320
Witzel, Georg, 132, 138, 149, 293
women: communion sub una refused, 364; subordination criticized, 331; theology, 331, 513n138; views of, 225. *See also* clerical marriages
word of God, preaching freely, 135; Four Articles of Prague and Compactata, 25, 67, 152; views compared, 105
World Council of Churches, 227
Worms, Diet of, (1521), Luther on Bohemians, 53; Luther charged, 54
Wyche, Richard, 37
Wyclif, John: Bílejovský on, 95–97; book burning, 61; Campion on, 281; contacts with Orthodox Church, 38; denunciation of priestly wealth and governing power, 87; Hus as disciple, 5; indulgences, 36; influence, 19, 35; Jan of Příbram on, 131; Judaizing elements, 33; philosophical appeal, 35; plebian bias, 175, 204, 460n46; pope as Antichrist, 88; theological reception, 35–36. *See also* remanence

Žák, Jan, 75
Zajíc of Hasenberk, Zbyněk: Bílejovský on, 95; tension with academics, 20
Želinský of Zebuzín, Kryštof, 259
Želivský, Jan, 26, 404n60
Žerotín, Karel the Elder of, 195, 466n164
Zittau (Žitava), 32
Zitte, Augustin, 374
Žižka, Jan, 91
Zofian, Jakub, 254–55
Zwingli, Huldrych, Jewel on, 131